ROWAN UNIVERSITY
CAMPBELL LIBRARY
201 MULLICA HILL RD.
GLASSBORO, NJ 08028-1701

Rural by Design:
Maintaining Small Town Character

Rural by Design:

Maintaining Small Town Character

by

Randall Arendt, MRTPI

Contributing Authors

Elizabeth A. Brabec
Harry L. Dodson
Christine Reid
Robert D. Yaro

Cosponsored by
Lincoln Institute of Land Policy
Environmental Law Foundation
Center for Rural Massachusetts

Planners Press
AMERICAN PLANNING ASSOCIATION
Chicago, Illinois   Washington, D.C.

HT
167
A834
1994

Copyright 1994 by the American Planning Association
122 S. Michigan Avenue, Suite 1600 Chicago, IL 60603
Paperback edition ISBN 0-918286-85-9
Hardbound edition ISBN 0-918286-86-7
Library of Congress Catalog Card Number 93-71517

Printed in the United States of America
All rights reserved

3 3001 00858 9102

Contents

Acknowledgments

It is not possible to adequately thank all those friends and colleagues who gave me help, suggestions, insights, and encouragement during the long preparation of this book. Needless to say, without the understanding and support of my wife, Linda, and our children, Greig and Johanna, this undertaking would not have succeeded. And without agreement to underwrite this project, from Hugh Davis, director of the Center for Rural Massachusetts and John Mullin, chairman of the Department of Landscape Architecture and Regional Planning, University of Massachusetts, who allowed me time away from my regular duties at the Center, this book could not have been written.

Several people deserve special thanks. My former colleague, Christine Reid, associate director of the Center for Rural Massachusetts, proofread every page of manuscript and provided literally hundreds of very useful comments and recommendations. Others to whom I am deeply grateful for reviewing sections of my manuscript are: Hugh Davis and John Mullin, University of Massachusetts; Frederick Steiner, University of Arizona; Mark Lapping, Rutgers University; Robert Coughlin, University of Pennsylvania; Bryon Hanke, Chevy Chase, Maryland; Jeff Lacy, Center for Rural Massachusetts; Patrick Hare, Maryland National Capital Parks and Planning Commission; Lane Kendig, Lane Kendig Inc., Mundelein, Illinois; Nancy Schroeder, Amherst (Massachusetts) Housing Authority; Peter Coughlan, Maine Local Roads Program; Chester (Rick) Chellman, White Mountain Survey; Joseph Molinaro, National Association of Home Builders; John Mori, National Small Flows Clearinghouse; James Kreissl, Municipal Environmental Research Laboratory, U.S. Environmental Protection Agency; David Rigby, Clean Water Engineers, Sterling, Virginia; Donald Hoxie, Maine Division of Health Engineering; William Moeller, University of Lowell; John Sheaffer, Sheaffer & Roland, Wheaton, Illinois; Robert Scarfo, University of Maryland; Tom Daniels, Lancaster County Agricultural Preservation Board; Deborah Bowers, Farmland Preservation Report; Bob Wagner, American Farmland Trust; William Flournoy, North Carolina Department of Environment, Health, and Natural Resources; Charles E. Little, consultant to The Conservation Fund; Grant Dehart, Maryland Department of Natural Resources; Steve Elkinton, National Park Service; Donald Belk, Greenville Greenways; Tim Brown, Cary (North Carolina) Planning Department; Ed McMahon, Conservation Fund; Michael Clarke, Natural Lands Trust; William Sellers, John Snook and John Gaadt, Brandywine Conservancy; Donna Mennitto, Howard County (Maryland) Division of Comprehensive Planning; Suzanne Sutro, Montgomery County (Pennsylvania) Planning Commission; Marlia Jenkins, Livingston County (Michigan) Planning Department; Gail Owings, Kent County (Maryland) Planning Department; and Randi Vogt, Calvert County (Maryland) Planning Department.

Except where noted, the line drawings in this book were prepared by Elizabeth Thompson, a recent graduate of the landscape architecture program at the University of Massachusetts. The aerial perspective "bird's-eye" sketches in Chapters 5, 6, and 7 were drawn by Kevin Wilson of Haydenville, Massachusetts, who teaches in the architectural studio at Smith College in Northampton and is an architectural designer and illustrator at Juster, Pope, Frazier in Shelburne Falls, Massachusetts. I also wish to acknowledge the following agencies, institutions, or firms for the artwork in Part II and Appendix D: Chapter 5, the Center for Rural Massachusetts; Chapter 6, the Blackstone River National Heritage Corridor Commission; Chapter 7, the New Yorker and Alfred A. Knopf, Inc.; Chapter 8, Dodson Associates; and Appendix D, Do Chung Architects.

Finally, I want to acknowledge the Design Arts Program of the National Endowment for the Arts, an independent federal agency, which awarded a grant to the Center for Rural Massachusetts to cover a major part of the cost involved in researching and writing this book.

Contributors

Randall Arendt is vice president, conservation planning, with the Natural Lands Trust at Hildacy Farm in Media, Pennsylvania. Previously director of planning and research at the Center for Rural Massachusetts in the Department of Landscape Architecture and Regional Planning at the University of Massachusetts in Amherst, he is an elected member of the Royal Town Planning Institute. A member of Phi Beta Kappa, he holds a B.A. degree, magna cum laude, from Wesleyan University and a M.Phil. degree in Urban Design and Regional Planning from the University of Edinburgh, Scotland, where he was a St. Andrew's Scholar. He has lectured in thirty-three states and five Canadian provinces, and has designed open space subdivisions in ten states.

Elizabeth Brabec is cofounder and principal of Land Ethics, a land-use consulting firm located in Washington, D.C. She is a registered landscape architect and holds degrees in landscape architecture and law from the University of Guelph and the University of Maryland respectively, and is a frequent collaborator on projects with Dodson Associates.

Harry L. Dodson is founder and principal of Dodson Associates, an award-winning land planning and landscape architecture firm in Ashfield, Massachusetts, specializing in rural land use issues and the visualization of change in the countryside. A registered landscape architect, he holds undergraduate and graduate degrees from Harvard University, and is a trustee of the Conway School of Landscape Design in Conway, Massachusetts.

Christine Reid is associate director of the Center for Rural Massachusetts in the Department of Landscape Architecture and Regional Planning, University of Massachusetts at Amherst. A graduate of Williams College and the University of California at Berkeley, she was formerly editor of the *Journal of the New England Landscape*.

Robert D. Yaro is the executive director of the Regional Plan Association in New York City, a private nonprofit organization promoting regional solutions to land-use problems in the New York metropolitan area. Formerly associate professor in the Department of Urban Design and Regional Planning at the University of Massachusetts and director of the Center for Rural Massachusetts, he holds degrees from Wesleyan University and the Graduate School of Design at Harvard.

Cosponsors

The American Planning Association—the publisher of this book—is a national nonprofit membership organization serving 28,000 planners, elected and appointed officials, and concerned citizens involved with urban and rural planning issues. APA provides professional assistance and current information to all who work for better planned communities—through books, research and technical reports, conferences and workshops, special interest technical divisions, and seven periodical publications. It has offices in Washington, D.C., and Chicago.

APA's three cosponsors in the publication of this book are the Lincoln Institute of Land Policy, the Environmental Law Foundation, and the Center for Rural Massachusetts.

The Lincoln Institute of Land Policy is a nonprofit educational institution located in Cambridge, Massachusetts. Its leaders explore the complex linkages between public policies and land policy, and the impact of these linkages on major issues of our society. The institute seeks to understand land as a resource, the choices for its use and improvement, the regulatory and tax policies that will result in better uses of land, and effective techniques by which land policies can be implemented.

The Environmental Law Foundation—in New Paltz, New York—is a nonprofit education and research organization dedicated to helping people participate in the creation, implementation, and enforcement of sound environmental laws and policies. Through a network of legal and technical professionals, the foundation provides information and assistance to organizations, businesses, individuals, and government to help them understand and address local environmental issues.

The Center for Rural Massachusetts conducts applied research into special problems faced by small communities. As a branch of the University of Massachusetts at Amherst, the center seeks to teach practical skills to help town officials prepare and implement new programs for the effective management of change.

Preface

The inspiration for this book comes from the "grass roots": those people who are involved in land-use decisions at the local level in small towns and rural counties where growth is changing the character of established communities and the surrounding countryside.

In my travels around the United States, delivering slide lectures on creative rural planning techniques, I have been asked countless times for further details and more specific information regarding implementation.

There has been a consistent pattern to these questions. The primary questions are extremely practical and focus on the disposal of household sewage, minimizing conflicts with farmers, and convincing local road superintendents that highway standards are not appropriate for residential subdivisions.

Nearly as frequently posed are questions relating to affordable housing, creating town-wide and regional strategies for land conservation (including linkages), and halting the commercialization of rural highways. These and other queries have formed the basis for the chapter topics in Part III, "Implementation Techniques."

This volume goes beyond the first book that our research team produced, *Dealing With Change in the Connecticut River Valley*, in several important ways. First, it supplies the reader with a great deal of substantive material on a broad range of subjects selected for their relevance to residents and local officials in rural and suburbanizing areas. However, in writing these chapters, the aim has not been to produce a definitive text, for each chapter's subject could have become a book in its own right. Instead, the objective has been to present information most pertinent and useful from the perspective of people working in small town and rural area planning, with an emphasis on design issues and the type of material that is not readily available from existing nontechnical publications.

Another goal has been to present this information in a very readable manner so as to increase its accessibility to a broad audience, including generalist town planners, their volunteer board or commission members, landowners, developers, land trusts, and local residents concerned about the way that current growth patterns are reshaping and changing their communities.

In addition to providing answers to commonly asked questions, this book supplies readers with examples of a wide range of residential and commercial projects that have utilized creative design techniques. These are described in Part IV, "Case Examples," through photographs and schematic site plans, accompanied by brief expository text, showing that viable alternatives to conventional design approaches really do exist and work well.

Because so many people have expressed frustration and sadness at witnessing the gradual transformation of their once-distinctive communities into bland, formless, suburban agglomerations of subdivisions and shopping centers, this book contains an extensive section devoted to the "traditional town." It is my belief that these communities will be able to conserve much of their remaining character and "sense of place" only if residents and local officials gain a fuller understanding of some of the basic principles underlying the form and functioning of traditional towns. The challenge is to encourage (or require) new development to complement, enhance, and build upon historic town patterns.

Most of the chapters in this book stand alone. In other words, this book is intended to be primarily a reference work to which planners, developers, conservationists, local officials, and concerned residents may turn for detailed information about specific topics, or for examples of well-designed projects to show to landowners and/or intending developers. Anyone reading the book straight through, from cover to cover, will note a certain degree of overlap among some of the chapters. This is partly unavoidable, because planning is essentially an integrated and interdisciplinary endeavor, with many connections and linkages among its various topical areas.

A final goal has been to write the chapters so that much of their content will be relevant and useful to people living in a broad range of small communities in various regions of the country. That the Connecticut River Valley "design manual" (now in its fifth printing) has struck such a responsive chord among people from New England and the southern states, to the Rockies and the Pacific Northwest, is evidence that there is a great demand in small towns across the nation for practical information and examples relating to the problems posed by conventional development patterns, which threaten to overwhelm and transform the rural communities lying in their path.

Throughout my career I have tried to follow Aldo Leopold's advice that, in order to be useful and creative, one must "think at right angles to one's profession." I have never had much trouble, constitutionally, in questioning the "standard" way of doing things, and in challenging the type of authority that justifies status quo approaches on the basis that "this is the way that things are done." My attitudes toward conventional suburban zoning and subdivision practices have no doubt been influenced by growing up in a traditional neighborhood characterized by compact houselots, shady tree-lined streets, and homes within walking distance of shops, schools, and the public library. My later childhood years were in turn influenced by living in a well-planned rural community containing huge expanses of open space, interlaced with trails, brooks, ponds, and a large lake where shorefront development was specifically prohibited. Impressions casually created in my mind by those experiences were further shaped by spending five years in Great Britain, intellectually challenging years as a post-graduate student at Edinburgh University and as a young planner with the Norfolk County Planning Department. After several decades of first-hand experience with traditional neighborhoods, rural open space developments, and whole countrysides protected from suburban sprawl by sensible land-use policies requiring more compact development patterns, by age thirty I had little affinity for the conventional "tools of the trade" employed by fellow professionals in my native country.

In the long process of trying to reinvent land-use planning techniques so they would produce better results than had been achieved with conventional zoning and subdivision regulations, I have been exceedingly fortunate to have met numerous kindred spirits, who had similarly become deeply disillusioned with the present system of land planning and development. Much of their work has been cited in this book to inform readers of relevant and useful material that might possibly help them deal with the specific problems they face in their own communities.

This volume represents an effort to write the kind of book I wish had been available for me to consult fifteen years ago, as a young planner facing the special challenges of working in those outlying parts of metropolitan regions that one seasoned observer calls "penturbia" (Lessinger, 1991). In this age of personal computers, modems, and faxes, those rural hinterlands, with their small towns and surrounding open spaces, will very possibly be the destination of the "fifth migration" during the coming decades—the first four described by Lewis Mumford as the early expansion westward from the coastal colonies, the movement into the first industrial towns during the 1830s and 1840s, the growth of major industrial cities after the Civil War, and the exodus to the suburbs (Sussman, 1976).

It is the authors' hope that this book will become a handy reference tool for the residents, local officials, and planning staffs of many transitional suburban and penturban communities around the country, where the ineffectiveness of conventional zoning is visibly becoming more apparent with each new development, and it is to them that this volume is dedicated.

Randall Arendt
Malvern, Pennsylvania

The Character of Towns

1

Common Qualities of Traditional Towns

PLANNED ORIGINS

Until the present century, the United States had a very long history of founding new settlements—of nearly every size—according to a set of central organizing principles. That conscious planning was the norm is evidenced not only by the large number of surviving original drawings (many of which are reproduced in John Reps's seminal volume *The Making of Urban America*), but also by countless examples of formal rectilinear street patterns for small towns and boroughs that one may find depicted in the plates of practically any good nineteenth century county atlas. (See also Easterling, Keller, 1993: *American Town Plans—A Comparative Timeline.*)

Even in New England, famed for its irregular street layouts, many villages are arranged around a central common area or green, a feature that was not at all accidental, even in cases where it occupies only a widened segment of the main street.

After their founding and first period of growth, those settlements that had been laid out according to a regular grid tended to follow that same pattern in succeeding decades, probably because it was practical, economical, and within established custom. In many areas, this tendency continued until the advent of the commuter car suburb, when zoning became a convenient substitute for physical planning in most communities.

DIVERSE USES WITHIN A COMMON BUILDING VOCABULARY

With the demise of conscious planning of streets and neighborhoods came a new emphasis on separating unlike land uses. The goal of creating separate and internally homogeneous "zoning districts" was seen by many as being more important than continuing the established traditions of town development that had produced such interesting and livable communities. Practically no one was critically examining the future implications of the physical form taken by the new style of development: subdivisions, shopping centers, and office parks, typically disconnected from each other and totally dependent upon cars to provide linkage.

Although towns were more orderly from a physical viewpoint during the nineteenth century, with regular street patterns and more harmonious buildings (due to a limited architectural vocabulary, simpler technologies, and fewer choices of building material), they also tended to be more diverse, with a wider variety and richer mixture of land uses, more fully integrated into the fabric of the community than is typically the case in areas developed within the last several decades.

Without the benefit of codes and regulations, changes evolved more or less spontaneously over years. Changes occurred in response to specific and varying stimuli—such as local job growth, and public sanitation improvements.

The parts of these towns that predate zoning are far from perfect, but for the most part they function reasonably well, especially considering the fact that they grew up on their own, without a great deal of parental oversight or control from professional regulators.

DISTINGUISHING FEATURES

The principal characteristics of traditional small towns include the following features:

- compactness and tighter form
- medium density (somewhere in-between that of cities and sprawling postwar suburbs)
- "downtown" centers with street-edge buildings, mixed uses, gathering places, public buildings, parks, and other open spaces
- commercial premises meeting everyday needs (grocery, newsagent, drugstore, hardware, etc.)
- residential neighborhoods close to the town center, sometimes with house lots abutting commercial premises
- civic open spaces within, and rural open space at edges
- pedestrian-friendly but also auto-accessible
- streets scaled for typical uses (rather than being oversized and overengineered to accommodate "worst-case scenarios")
- incremental growth outward from core

Traditional towns are not without problems, of course. Residential sections may experience varying degrees of annoyance because their houselots back up to other kinds of land uses, such as a filling station where the operator stores used tires behind the building. Or, there may be a pizzeria or convenience store down the street that attracts late-night traffic. The house lots often tend to be fairly modest, sometimes with minimal front or side yards, and the streets are frequently narrow, so that vehicles must slow down in order to pass each other when they meet where there is also a parked car.

SENSE OF COMMUNITY

Nonetheless, most residents also live within walking distance of typical town amenities, such as schools, shops, churches, and playgrounds. They often feel a real attachment to their neighborhood and a definite sense of place about their street, where they know many of their neighbors. When queried about what they like about living in a traditional town, the same items surface time and again: they enjoy the variety, convenience, and neighborliness that comes with living in such places.

After numerous forays and conversations with small-town residents, I am convinced that these people like the mixture that results from having smaller houses next to large ones; families and individuals of all ages, from young couples to elderly widows; houselots of varying widths and sizes; and streets that link together, connecting homes with other neighborhoods, shops, and public facilities. One resident's characterization of Cranbury, New Jersey, summed it up: "It is [this] pleasant and useful mix . . . that fosters a pedestrian lifestyle which, in turn, gives residents a strong sense of community" (Houstoun, 1988).

Three advantages of small-town living have been expressed by James Rouse, the innovative developer of Columbia, Maryland (Breckenfeld, 1971):

- the greater liklihood for a broader range of relationships and friendships
- an increased sense of mutual responsibility and support among neighbors
- a closer relationship to nature through informal outdoor recreation opportunities

The results of Rutgers University's research into people's preferred community types is therefore not very surprising: "small towns" ranked the highest on the list of five different types of living places, at 50 percent, compared with a rating of 22 percent for "new suburbs" (Eagleton Institute, 1987).

From this research and volumes of anecdotal evidence, it is clear that a great number of Americans yearn for the attributes offered by traditional towns, and for the open space that has typically surrounded them. Although people generally do not yearn to live in a seamless web of sprawling subdivisions, shopping centers, and office parks, that is the ultimate future being provided for them and their children by the current planning system in almost every jurisdiction in the country (with assistance from engineers, developers, land-use lawyers, and realtors, most of whom uncritically accept the standard suburban approach to community growth).

OPPORTUNITIES FOR CASUAL SOCIALIZING

In his book, *The Great Good Place*, Ray Oldenburg underscores the importance of typical small-town gathering places (such as coffee shops, general stores, post offices, bars, and other hangouts) in helping people "get through the day." A critical missing element in American suburbs is what Oldenburg terms "the third place," by which he means locations other than one's home or workplace, where informal public life may be experienced. "Third places" can rarely be found in suburbia, where people build family rooms "so that their children may have a decent place to spend time with their friends" within subdivisions "that offer them nothing" (Oldenburg, 1989). Gathering places, from soda fountains to taverns, from neighborhood parks to cafes, are noticeably absent from most modern suburbs. Some of these uses have been zoned out, and some (such as local parks or open spaces) are no longer being created by either developers or municipalities.

OPEN SPACE WITHIN AND AROUND

Another favored aspect of traditional small towns, especially those located in rural areas, is the open space that often exists around the edges, and occasionally occurs also as scattered pieces of undeveloped land throughout the community. Although most people take these spaces for granted, hardly noticing them in any conscious way as they go about their daily business, they are strongly affected when such land begins to sprout buildings and parking lots. Few things change the character of small towns and rural communities more than the conversion of these natural areas to development. Whether appreciated for their aesthetic, recreational, or sporting benefits, such areas often hold deep meaning for long-term residents.

Perhaps not surprisingly, these places often produce rather profound effects upon the people who played in them as children. When asked to write "environmental autobiographies" describing a favorite childhood place, 80 to 90 percent of Clare Cooper-Marcus' students at the University of California at Berkeley cited "wild or leftover places . . . that were never specifically designed. . . . If they grew up in a developing suburb they remember the one lot at the end of the street that wasn't yet built on, where they constructed camps and dug tunnels and lit fires" (Cooper-Marcus, 1986). Criticizing planners for lacking any real understanding of the importance of such natural areas, Cooper-Marcus notes that "it is just those wild leftover or unassigned spaces that we tend to plan out of existence".

COMPACT FORM AND INCREMENTAL GROWTH

Towns have been growing and evolving since the first days of colonial settlement, but up until the middle of the twentieth century the changes have not only tended to be more gradual, they have also generally reflected customary patterns of town layout and structure. Extensions to existing neighborhoods usually involved no significant departures from established principles of town design in terms of lot sizes or street geometry. Any differences were found chiefly in newer building styles. In other words, the town's preexisting grain was respected (perhaps unconsciously) by subsequent development designers.

An almost pristine example of such a town is Essex, New York, located on the western shore of Lake Champlain. Once an active port and regional trading center, Essex began to stagnate after 1850, as many small subsistence farming families moved westward. Because of its relatively remote northern location and the decline in its local economy, few changes occurred in the town fabric, and the place remains something of a time capsule for students of nineteenth century townscape. A plan of the town as it exists today is shown in Figure 1–1, where the scale and pattern of the house lots, the relation between commercial and residential

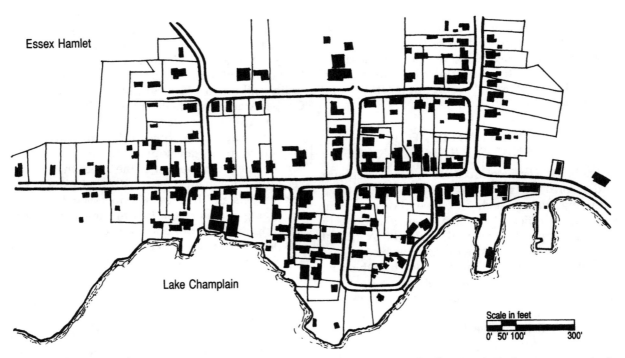

Figure 1–1. Plan of the small nineteenth-century village of Essex, New York, showing typical arrangements of buildings, setbacks, lot size variety, and interconnected rectilinear streets. Such places appeal to a great number of people in this country, yet very few new developments are designed to look, feel, and function like traditional towns. Ironically, it is illegal in most rural jurisdictions to create new subdivisions having these physical characteristics, even though they would utilize land more efficiently, allow significant parts of the site to remain as open space, and provide the opportunity for more social interaction among members.

uses, and the interconnectedness of the street layout are clearly visible. This is just one of thousands of places where traditional town-building values have created an environment that is very livable and walkable. (A photograph of an Essex streetscape appears in Figure 4–14, in Chapter 4.)

Figure 1–2 offers a magnified view of a typical compact neighborhood from another such town (Brunswick, Maine), dating from a slightly later period (1870–1910). This sketch was drawn by local architect Steven Moore, who notes that "The street has a very pleasant ambience and a delightful scale. The houses are generally two- and three-story wood frame buildings, in which about half

the homes have been divided into multiple rental units or accessory apartments, yielding a density of approximately 20–25 persons per acre."

Although this density is greater than might feel comfortable in many smaller towns, the ability of such neighborhoods to absorb so many people without undue strain is worth noting. However, it also needs to be said that an essential ingredient in the livability of compactly built neighborhoods is the provision of open spaces, both formal and informal, within easy walking distance. Without parks, squares, greens, commons, or protected natural areas nearby, these neighborhoods would not meet some very basic "quality of life" criteria.

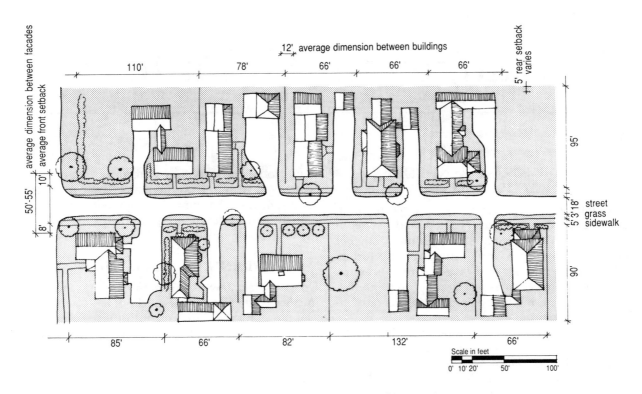

Figure 1–2. Plan view of a late nineteenth-century neighborhood of homes on modest lots in Brunswick, Maine, illustrating densities of 20 to 25 persons per acre achieved in a traditional manner. *Source:* Adapted from an original drawing by architect Steven Moore.

2

Changes in the Pattern

ZONING UNCONNECTED TO PLANNING

During the decades following World War II, an increasing number of towns enacted land-use regulations to control growth. Although many smaller rural communities have yet to adopt any formal rules, a huge number of local governments across the country have turned to zoning and subdivision codes as a method of preventing incompatible development.

As understood by most zoning practitioners, the "incompatibility" issue has referred to uses whose external characteristics would conflict, such as industrial odors wafting into nearby residential areas. Unfortunately, the use of this narrow definition has resulted in a different type of incompatability: conventional zoning and the livable, walkable community. Ironically, the uncritical adoption of conventional suburban zoning and subdivision regulations has created a virtual sea of standardized, sprawling development incompatible with other equally important aspects of traditional towns: their ambience, character, and vitality. These characteristics are inextricably related to the layout, design, structure, use mix, and densities now outlawed under most modern land-use regulations.

Unfortunately, relatively few communities have recognized the critical importance of *planning* in this process, and have failed to connect their regulations with any overall document describing a vision of what they would like to become after their zoning is fully implemented. Even in those towns where a comprehensive plan (or master plan or general plan) has been adopted, it is often regarded as purely advisory, is infrequently updated, and—most unfortunately—fails to address one of the most critical questions facing these towns today: how to grow gracefully, in a manner consistent with the traditional character of the community, so that new development fits harmoniously into the town fabric and helps to reinforce the local sense of place.

PLANNING EDUCATION

Unfortunately, few planners' training has included much detailed study of traditional towns, and planning students are generally not required to analyze how the scale and arrangement of such towns' component parts contributes to their functioning as livable, workable places. By and large, collegiate schools of planning have focused, instead, upon subjects such as demographic trend analysis, sociology, engineering basics, land-use law, public policy formulation, quantitative methods, environmental systems, and cartography. All of these areas are important, of course, but it is curious that one of the central subjects of the town planning profession (i.e., towns) is typically studied so little. It is somewhat analogous to training physicians exclusively through courses in chemistry and biology, without ever requiring medical students to spend time examining and studying the human body itself (or attempting to cover this topic in a solitary lecture or as part of a single course).

Until the committees that determine accreditation standards for planning schools begin to include people who are more interested in the physical aspects of town design, it is unlikely that planning curricula will change much in this direction, so numerous are the nondesign subjects presently required to be offered for professional accreditation.

In this context is it not surprising that planners have, for several decades, operated in a system that knows how to produce all the component parts of a town (shops, offices, homes, roads, public facilities, etc.), but that has demonstrated time and again that it does not understand how they should be scaled, mixed, arranged, and connected to produce anything resembling a normal town of the type this country produced by the thousands during its first three centuries. It is as if carmakers did a good job of manufacturing engines, steering wheels, brakes, transmissions, and auto bodies, but somehow had not mastered the technique of assembling them into vehicles that ran safely and comfortably.

REDISCOVERING TRADITIONAL TOWNSCAPE ELEMENTS

To address this situation, interested professionals, local officials, and residents could conduct their own survey and analysis to obtain greater insight into town structure and design. For example, the following exercises might be conducted in a small but diverse section of an older, more traditional part of town:

1. Listing all the different land uses in a three-block area (including nonconforming uses), with particular reference to those that create convenience and/or annoyance to immediate neighbors.

2. Describing the various sizes and types of residential buildings, checking the number of electric meters to determine the number of dwellings, where applicable.

3. Measuring the distance relationships between housefronts (or porchfronts) and the sidewalk and the street, the width of the street pavement, the distance between opposing house/porchfronts, and the distance between houses on the

same side of the street. (The same should be done for the "Main Street" shopping area, too.)

Residents concerned about the inappropriate suburban layout and design of a new subdivision proposed on the outskirts of the Village of Honeoye Falls, New York (in the Finger Lakes region), performed exercise three above. They tallied their figures to determine the greatest, shortest, and average distances for the variables listed. The results showed that the new development would be completely out of character with the scale and pattern of their nineteenth century village context (See Table 2–1).

When these figures were compared with the minimum standards for lots, building setbacks, and street construction contained in their official subdivision and zoning regulations, it became clear why recent residential subdivision development in their village looked as if it had been airlifted in from Long Island: the standards that their consultant had prepared were grounded firmly in the principles of suburban sprawl.

The immediate result of this volunteer effort was a temporary moratorium and adoption of new village-scaled design criteria for new subdivisions. The developer of the contentious subdivision (who had strenuously opposed any zoning changes) promptly brought in completely revised drawings complying with the full spirit of the updated regulations, including narrower streets, a diversity of lot and building sizes with many smaller lots, formal recreation areas, and open space easements along the major road. Village officials, greatly assisted by an extremely well organized and dedicated citizens committee, updated both the old comprehensive plan and the zoning ordinance to reflect the tradition-based

Table 2–1. Character-defining dimensions found in the Village of Honeoye Falls, NY, compared with its zoning requirements

	Existing Village			Required by Code
	Min.	Max.	Avg.	
House-to-sidewalk (ROW)	20'	33'	24.8'	70'
Housefront-to-housefront	86'	132'	101.2'	180'

vision overwhelmingly supported by local residents. The leaders of this effort have also been asked to conduct workshops in surrounding communities and at statewide planning conferences, to share their experiences and methodology with other lay planners in small rural towns.

A QUESTION OF SCALE

In his book *Spaces: Dimensions of the Human Landscape*, Barrie Greenbie illuminates some of the physical relationships that subtly affect our perception of streetscapes. After comparing the "feel" experienced by walking along residential streets in older and newer neighborhoods, Greenbie suggests that one of the more critical elements is the

ratio between the "width" of the street corridor (as measured between opposing house facades) and the height of the "walls" of that corridor (the foundation-to-eaves dimension). His research indicates that "the most satisfactory ratio is generally a width that is two to three times the height of the defining wall or edges. If the width exceeds the height more than four times we begin to lose any sense of enclosure" (Greenbie, 1981). When streets are viewed as "outdoor rooms" this conceptual approach makes even greater sense, and the rationale for establishing parameters, such as "maximum setbacks" for buildings, becomes clearer. Figure 2–1 (patterned after Greenbie's drawings), and the accompanying photos (Figures 2–2 and

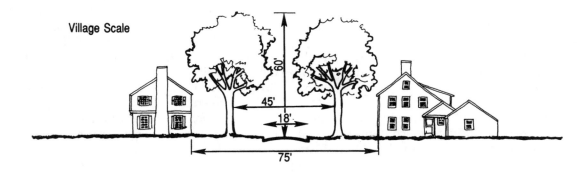

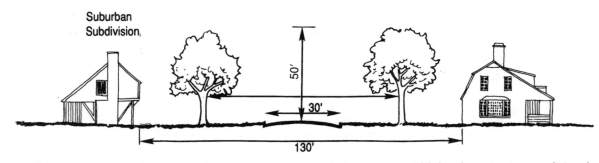

Figure 2–1. Cross-sectional sketches of two streets, showing differences in width:height ratios in a traditional village or small town, contrasted with those in a modern subdivision. Modern subdivision standards have created a building form completely out of scale with historic development patterns in older settlements, with distances between opposing housefronts literally double that typically found in traditional neighborhoods. *Source:* Greenbie, 1981.

Figure 2–2. Typical rural subdivision of conventional design with wide streets and deep front setbacks in Middlebury, Vermont. People living on opposite sides of the street often hardly know their neighbors, whom they would need a megaphone to greet in the morning because of the vast distances between their front doors.

Figure 2–3. Traditional streetscape with appropriately scaled road pavement, sidewalks, street trees, and modest front yards or "dooryard gardens" (Cummington, Massachusetts).

2–3) of street corridors (contrasting traditional neighborhoods with typical modern subdivisions) illustrate these relationships.

For many years various architects, planners, and landscape architects have espoused the view that the social relationships between families living on the same block are partly determined by the location of their homes relative to each other and to the street. Although the jury is still out with

regard to this question, it seems likely that the social dynamics of a neighborhood are influenced to some degree by the distance between homes, their setback from the sidewalk, and the length of time it takes to walk to the nearest park (if indeed there are any footpaths or common areas).

A cross section of the proposed Lyons Farm project in Easton, Maryland, designed by Redman-Johnston Associates, illustrates how an understanding of traditional scale can inform designs for new building ventures (see Figure 2–4). As

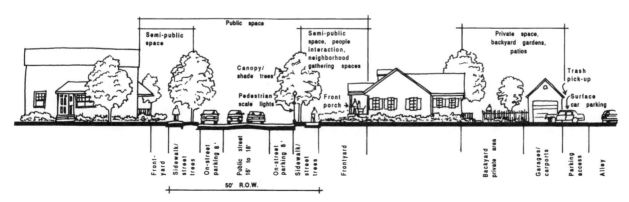

Figure 2–4. Cross-section of new development designed according to traditional neighborhood principles with a pedestrian-friendly ambience, including compact lots, front porches, dooryard gardens, sidewalks, street trees, curbside parking, and rear garages. Lyons Farm, Easton, Maryland (Redman Johnston Associates).

noted by New York architects Albert Moore and John Sullivan, "the right combination of site design and building orientation can mean the difference between a 'development' where people exist and a 'neighborhood' where families thrive" (Moore and Sullivan, 1991). They conclude that "in healthy neighborhoods there repeatedly exists a clear definition between private and public spaces," and that "the public space is arranged in such a way that it fosters natural social interaction among neighbors while allowing residents to maintain 'visual control' over their surroundings." Because too much emphasis on the provision of private spaces can create isolation, disconnectedness, and defensive attitudes, Moore and Sullivan advocate balancing the picture with "well planned public spaces which allow healthy social exchanges."

In a typical cross sectional view of Lyons Farm, this public space consists of the lawns, sidewalks, and the street itself. Design principles for such a streetscape could include the following:

1. Sidewalks where people may walk leisurely around their neighborhood, and from which they may converse with people sitting on front porches, without having to raise their voices to be heard. Sidewalks are an essential ingredient and constitute an important link tying all the homes together, like a common thread.

2. Front yards not greater than 20 feet in depth, to facilitate conversation with passersby, and to enable rear yards to become correspondingly larger (which is desirable to facilitate activities such as cookouts, badminton, etc.).

3. Picket fences or hedges at the edge of the sidewalk to demarcate the fully public space from the semipublic space of the front yards.

4. A row of deciduous shade trees between the street and the sidewalk to enclose the street, separate pedestrians from parked cars, and form the "walls" of a leafy corridor. Spaced about 40 to 45 feet apart on opposite sides of the street, they frame the view, provide visual cohesion on a street that may contain varied building styles, and influence drivers' peripheral vision so that they will tend to proceed more slowly, even though the paved street itself may seem quite wide (especially during the

working day when few cars tend to be parked there).

5. On-street car parking spaces (where residential densities are four dwellings per acre or greater) because lot sizes are too small to accommodate all parking needs comfortably. When cars are parked in front of homes they provide another opportunity for social interaction as residents cross their front lawns and the sidewalk on their way to and from the vehicles.

6. Front porches where folks may sit and pass a quiet afternoon or evening, punctuated by casual conversations with passing neighbors.

Most of these features were normally provided well into the automobile age, as shown in Figure 2–5, an illustration from a design manual for affordable housing published in 1919 by the U.S. Housing Corporation. Originally prepared by this

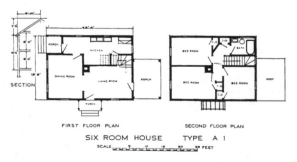

Figure 2–5. Perspective sketch of traditional neighborhood housing built by the U.S. Housing Corporation for shipbuilders' families during World War I (showing that federal housing officials clearly understood neighborhood design principles in the beginning).

short-lived agency during World War I to help meet the family housing needs of men employed at naval shipyards (which were under tremendous pressure to increase production), this report—and a companion volume by the Emergency Fleet Corporation—are veritable treasuries of neo-traditional elevations and floor plans for modestly sized and priced housing, from single family and semidetached to multifamily. Excellent examples of this program survive today in dozens of locations around the country, perhaps most notably in Fairview at Camden, New Jersey, in Bridgeport, Connecticut, and at Mare Island in Vallejo, California. That Congress decided to discontinue this excellent program—because the designs were "too ambitious and expensive for practical dwellings for the general run of workmen"—is a national disgrace (Emergency Fleet Corp., 1920).

Perhaps one of the best known of the neo-traditional developments to have incorporated these design principles is Seaside, Florida, designed by Duany/Plater-Zyberk Associates, of Miami. Variations on this theme might or might not involve garage space, which could be located toward the back of each houselot. Access might be by a driveway skirting alongside the house from the street in front, or they might face onto a rear lane (or alley), typically designed at a 10 to 12 foot width for one-way traffic.

Consistent with Greenbie's observations regarding the scale of buildings and the streets onto which they face, the width:height ratio in the Lyons Farm project is roughly 3:1 (75 feet between opposing housefronts, and about 24 to 32 feet to the peak of the roof gables). Interestingly, these are also the same dimensions and ratios found in the back yard spaces bordering a "greenway footpath" running along the rear lot lines in the 1939 New Orleans subdivision known as "Lake Vista," and those yards and the footpath operate as a very social space for informal neighborhood interaction. Because of the rear yard footpath, Lake Vista did not feature back lanes, and its garages were located alongside the homes, facing the streets.

Similar width:height relationships can also be found in "Main Street" locations in many different parts of the country, such as Newtown, Pennsyl-

vania, and Mt. Dora, Florida, where the ratios do not exceed the maximum 1:4 relationship mentioned earlier. (See Figure 2–6.)

In many towns where no such analysis has been done, there is an understandable lack of comprehension about the direct linkage between the adoption of conventional suburban land-use regulations (with their reliance on "minimum" dimensions) and the steady erosion of a town's unique identity. Many towns that now regulate their growth through zoning do not consciously plan the future pattern of development, except in an exceedingly broad way, through the establishment of large, internally homogeneous use districts, for residential, commercial, or industrial activities.

However, even when districts are zoned for multiple uses, the result is not necessarily a pleasing or functional one. Consider the case of Tyson's Corner, a country crossroads 20 years ago that is now a beltway exurb of 60,000 people in northern Virginia. It is a placeless development lacking any connectedness or relationship to its region. As Ellen Dunham-Jones, professor at the University of Virginia, writes in her essay "Of Time and Place," "It has no sidewalks; it is a place through which one is meant to drive. Not only is there no

Figure 2–6. The proportions of main streets in many older downtowns create a pleasing, humanly scaled "outdoor room" with sidewalks, street trees, parallel curbside parking, and often about 60 feet between opposing storefronts (Newtown, Pennsylvania).

provision made for the pedestrian, there is no public realm (other than the parking lots), no sense of community or sense of place, other than the two internalized shopping malls. But are they adequate substitutes for public space? Compare them to any downtown. . . . Tyson's Corner is anywhere, it is owned by nobody, and no one feels it belongs to them or they to it. It was never designed to bond place, community, and individual. It was not built for the citizen but for the consumer. When it grows old and begins to decay, who will care for it?" (Dunham-Jones, 1990).

MENTAL CONNECTIONS AND CONSCIOUS CHOICES

The belief that having conventional zoning regulations will protect a town from unwanted growth and change remains a widespread misconception. Probably few members of the general public have ever made the mental connection between their diminishing sense of place and the land-use regulations that govern growth in their communities. Still fewer realize that the disfigurement of their approach roads by strip commercial development, and the wholesale conversion of farmland and woods to an unrelenting blanket of houselots and streets, is not inevitable.

One of the greatest challenges now facing small-town planners is to inform their local boards, commissions, and the general public that the future of their communities is not preordained by conventional zoning: it is really a matter of choice.

Town officials are not required by state or federal law to implement sprawling patterns of development, driven by suburban-oriented design criteria. To the extent that there is any guidance at the state level, the trend is clearly in the opposite direction. In Oregon, Florida, New Jersey, and Maine, for example, the bulk of new development is being guided to designated urban-growth areas, keeping sprawling subdivisions from marching across the landscape.

Mark Twain was right on target when he observed that "in a democracy, people usually get what they deserve." That judgment is perhaps a little severe, given that the information provided the voters (or town councillors) has usually been very incomplete. It should be the planners' professional responsibility to fill that information gap, and to educate residents of the long-term consequences of following particular land-use policies.

Planners who may feel reluctant to criticize established norms of suburban-sprawl development would be helped by new state laws requiring that zoning amendments be preceded by the preparation of a general "impact statement" outlining the probable social and visual effects of the proposed regulatory changes. Since many major new development proposals are currently subject to specific impact statements, it is only logical to extend a similar requirement to the ultimate development document (the zoning ordinance), so that the cumulative effect of its long-term implementation may be evaluated in at least a general way. In fact, it might be even more helpful if all current zoning were required to be reviewed and voted upon again, say within five years, in the light of the fuller disclosures resulting from such an impact-statement requirement. It is interesting to speculate on how much of our current zoning might survive this kind of scrutiny and analysis.

VISUAL TECHNIQUES TO INCREASE AWARENESS

Because many planning concepts can be presented more effectively through graphics than they can be described verbally, the value of graphics can hardly be understated. Computer imaging does an excellent job of presenting this kind of material in various formats (videotapes, laser prints, 35 mm color slides), especially with respect to particular building sites. However, recent improvements in image-processing technology have expanded the scope of this valuable tool so that entire neighborhoods can now be looked at easily and comprehensively.

An excellent example of the application of this technique is the Davie Settlement in Broward County, Florida. Computer imaging was employed to illustrate how traditional neighborhood and town-center design principles could reclaim an existing area of highway "commercial strip" and underutilized backland in this small community (see Chapter 9, "Development in Town Centers and Along Highways"). For further information on this technique, readers are referred to the American Planning Association's Planning Advisory Service Memo *Image Processing in Planning and Design* (Gerdom, 1988).

The impact of zoning policies on large parcels can also be accomplished with hand-drawn "birds-eye" sketches, such as those included in this volume and in *Dealing With Change in the CT River Valley* (Yaro, Arendt, et al., 1988). Although laborious and costly, this older technique has its own distinct advantages, because people sometimes react more positively to highly realistic sketches (which are obviously hypothetical) than they do to the "high-tech" photographic imagery possible on today's sophisticated equipment (which is occasionally perceived to be "slick" and manipulative). Another concern is that when imaging is visually perfect, people may tend to focus too much on the site itself rather than on the concepts.

Other practitioners use cardboard and wooden models to demonstrate the visual and physical impacts of alternative development proposals. At the Visual Laboratory in the University of Vermont's Historic Preservation Program in Burlington, for example, Chester Liebs has used accurately scaled simulations of natural landscapes and existing townscapes to help communities preview the results of proposed new construction, road widening, or redevelopment. In order to increase accuracy and a lifelike atmosphere, Liebs glues perspective-corrected color photographs of actual building facades to his models of existing buildings, and then locates the models precisely on a "groundboard" showing streets, sidewalks, lawns, ponds, and other such features (Liebs, 1989).

At the Vermont Design Institute, a two-day workshop sponsored by the Vermont Council on the Arts, lay planners from small towns in the Green Mountain State participate in a hands-on exercise in which they are asked to arrange Liebs' models of houses, shops, a school, a factory, and a gas station on a 40-acre parcel containing an existing village. Without any prior orientation to the principles of traditional towns, planning board members predictably arrange models in the manner in which they expect new development to occur: businesses lining the highway and houses widely spaced on farm fields, in general accordance with the regulations they are used to applying. When they stand back and take a real look at what they have created, they tend to be highly critical of the results (unattractive examples of suburban sprawl), but the exercise succeeds in heightening everyone's awareness of the difficulty most people have in envisioning what their community will look like when typical zoning codes are fully implemented (Humstone, 1992). The rest of the workshop involves analyzing the model as arranged, to determine what is displeasing about it and how it could be improved. During the course of the institute participants listen to illustrated lectures by design professionals, and visit selected villages to identify those features that add or detract from their ambience.

In New Jersey, Anton Nelessen has won wide acclaim (and an APA chapter award) for his work in constructing entire new hamlets and villages with similar wooden models shaped and scaled to reflect traditional buildings in his area. The value of such tools in helping town officials, residents, and even developers visualize the effects of development proposals can hardly be overstated. In some of his workshops, Nelessen involves townspeople and members of local government in participatory exercises to construct new hamlets of up to 40 structures, using a variety of model buildings (scaled at 1 inch = 20 feet) representing homes, garages, shops, churches, civic halls, and so forth. (See Figure 2–7.)

After conducting a visual preference survey to help participants understand the particular characteristics of traditional towns that they like (and the aspects of most contemporary development they dislike), Nelessen presents a slide lecture explaining his principles for creating "communities of place" (further discussed in Chapter 3). A final step in the workshop process involves participants arranging the scale models in a manner reflecting Nelessen's design principles. With this preparation, most groups tend to create relatively short streets, often ending with "terminal vistas"

Figure 2–7. Example of one of the new village-scaled developments designed by local residents attending one of Anton Nelessen's seminars. When sensitized to the issues, nontechnical people are often perfectly capable of arranging different types of development in a manner that reflects how they would rather see their community grow, as opposed to the way that development typically occurs when guided by nothing more than conventional zoning and subdivision regulations. *Source:* Photo by Nelessen Associates.

of some of the larger structures. Homes are closely spaced, recreating the grain or texture of traditional villages, with modest front yards, rear garages, and narrow roads lined with trees and sidewalks. Participants then trace the building "footprints" and locate trees and additional streets on large sheets of vellum, to create a two-dimensional plan.

This sequence of preference survey, slide lecture, and hands-on exercise is perhaps the best way professional planners can help volunteer board members to understand the variables and relationships that drive the design process. Such participatory workshops also help prepare board members for the type of critical thinking and analysis necessary to administer design-review regulations for new subdivisions, commercial complexes, and mixed-use projects. After observing many such exercises in different parts of the country, Nelessen notes that he has never seen any workshop group produce a design with cul-de-sacs, or without some kind of central open space. Developers

should take note (and many of them have, as Nelessen's growing client list demonstrates).

For an appreciation of the longer range, town-wide implications of implementing existing or proposed zoning, few tools are more effective and inexpensive than the "build-out maps" devised by the Center for Rural Massachusetts (CRM). These maps, which are further described and illustrated in Chapter 15, show typical street and building patterns over large areas of presently vacant but buildable land, all drawn according to present zoning and subdivision regulations.

Spurred by the work of CRM, planners in Delaware have applied the "build-out mapping" concept to a multitown area in the eastern half of Sussex County. In proposing this project, state officials noted that "It is often the case that the physical consequences and infrastructure needs of additional development are not fully contemplated in the development patterns outlined in comprehensive plans. This is particularly true as it applies to the carrying capacity of the coastal region, the preservation of open space for local recreational needs, and the present or planned infrastructure required to serve allowable densities" (Chura, 1990). This mapping technique is being used to heighten awareness among county officials and residents that the cumulative impact of further development around the inland bays, in accordance with present zoning, will result in very little open space and will further deteriorate wildlife habitat, water quality, recreational opportunities, and the area's aesthetic appeal.

CONVENTIONAL ZONING AS "PLANNED SPRAWL"

The actual long-term results of conscientiously applying conventional suburban zoning and subdivision standards in rural areas is illustrated in Figure 2–8 and Figure 2–9. Figure 2–8 shows the changes that have occurred in Upper Dublin Township, Montgomery County, Pennsylvania, since 1937. By the late 1980s it had essentially become blanketed by "wall-to-wall subdivisions."

Suburbanization has proceeded in much the same way in countless other jurisdictions around

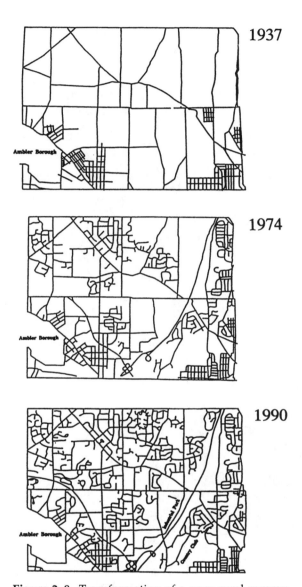

1937

1974

1990

Figure 2–8. Transformation of a once-rural community to a conventional suburb with little open space and relatively few new connecting streets, over the period from 1937 to 1990: the promise of conventional zoning, fulfilled after decades of methodically applying conventional regulations (Upper Dublin Township, Montgomery County, Pennsylvania).

the country. The result of applying conventional zoning regulations in the recently rural Red Oaks Mill section of Dutchess County, New York (near Poughkeepsie), over a 30-year period is that the only remaining open spaces are the playing fields behind the middle school and the wetlands along the creek, which is rather sad news unless one is a 10-year old or a frog.

A third example shows a similar pattern created by implementing larger lot zoning standards, essentially over a 20-year period, in one Connecticut town. Although the two-acre minimum lot size was originally adopted to help preserve rural character and open space, it actually worked to produce the opposite effect. After several decades of carefully following these rules, townspeople were amazed to discover that the only open space that had not been platted and sold was land in the country club and the hunt club. (See Figure 2–10.)

Those unable to afford the substantial membership fees—and those who are forced to become part of a long waiting list—must be content with strolling about their two-acre houselots, or walking around the block; a rather difficult task since few of the new roads connect with one another. This situation is one manifestation of the triumph of zoning over planning, where there is no overall, town-wide design for future residential patterns, traffic circulation, open space, wildlife corridors, or pedestrian linkages. The inconvenience thus created, for school buses, mail delivery, rubbish collection, and recycling vehicles, could have been avoided if the town had simply insisted, through its regulations, that every new street shall connect with another street. Exceptions would of course be granted when the land is too steep or wet, or when such a connection would create a major shortcut likely to attract significant through traffic down the new street (unless such a collector relief road were part of the town's overall traffic management program). When such exceptions are granted, however, foot trails and bike paths should be provided at a minimum. A fuller discussion of street and road design criteria appears in Part III, "Implementation Techniques."

These three very typical examples demonstrate why I describe conventional zoning as "planned

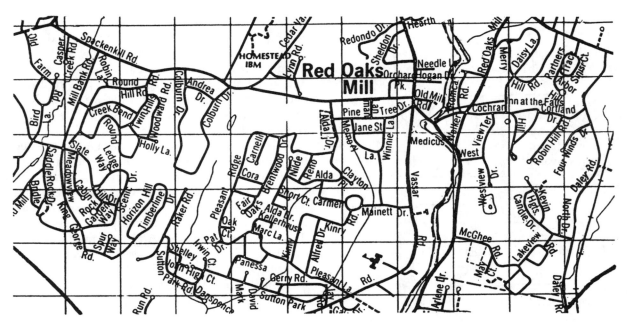

Figure 2–9. "Wall-to-wall subdivisions" in Dutchess County, New York, in an area that was predominantly farmland and woods just thirty years earlier, illustrating "the triumph of zoning over planning."

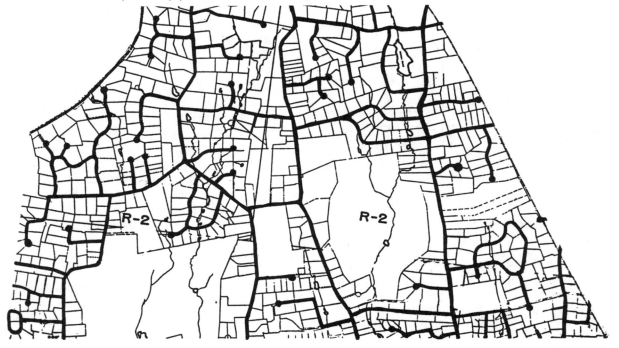

Figure 2–10. The long-term result of implementing large-lot (two acre) zoning in Darien, Connecticut, over a twenty-year period (1960–1980) was to blanket the community with contiguous subdivisions, foreclosing open space opportunities in the northern half of the town to all except those who belonged to the hunt club or the country club.

sprawl." The legacy of decades of reliance upon conventional suburban zoning techniques has been documented in various parts of the country. In Florida, statewide figures from the Governor's Task Force on Urban Growth Patterns show that developed land area grew twice as fast (by 80 percent) as did total population (38 percent) between 1974 and 1984 (Probst, 1989). The experience was even worse in four metropolitanizing counties around Puget Sound, where the Washington State Institute for Public Policy has calculated that, between 1970 and 1990, total acreage of developed land grew two and one-half times faster than population growth (87 percent versus 36 percent) (Pivo et al., 1990). (See Figure 2–11.)

In its own study of land-use changes in western Massachusetts, the Center for Rural Massachusetts examined the three largely rural counties bordering the Connecticut River. While the average per capita land consumption in the three Massachusetts counties had been 0.51 acres per new resident during the period 1950–70, the same figure jumped to 1.83 acres during the period 1970–85. The lesson is obvious: the more land

there is available to use for development, the more we, as a society, tend to squander it. We have clearly institutionalized the art of low-density suburban sprawl. If American policymakers had deliberately set out to construct the most wasteful, inefficient and land-consumptive pattern of development possible, they could hardly have been more successful.

Another form of sprawl, more insidious because its lower density masks its long-term impacts, is occurring in many presently rural areas at the far edges of metropolitan regions. The causes vary from ultralarge-lot municipal zoning regulations to state laws exempting large lots from certain types of review procedures. In New York State, for example, developers are given a very strong incentive to create sprawling subdivisions of 5.1 acre lots by Section 1115 of the Public Health Law, which requires Health Department approval only for subdivisions containing five or more lots under five acres in size (Miner and Steelman, 1987). The wasteful practice of platting subdivisions with such large lots effectively forecloses any future options for using the majority of unbuilt

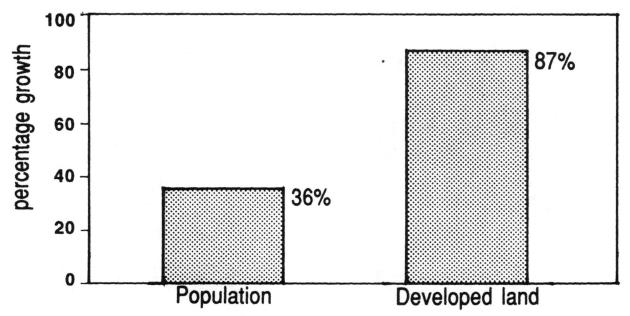

Figure 2–11. Land Consumption per Capita in the Puget Sound Area, 1970–1990 (after Pivo and Russell, 1990). This bar graph shows how conventional zoning policies of suburban sprawl can consume developable land two and one-half times faster than the rate of population growth.

woods or pastures for forestry or agriculture, or even for informal recreation (such as trails for hiking and cross-country skiing). Studies of a random sample of such unregulated subdivisions in the Catskills reveal that two-thirds of such developments contain one or more unbuildable lots; on average, 11 percent of the lots were found to be unbuildable in mock reviews undertaken by county planning staffs (Lamb, 1989). (See Figure 2–12.) Situations such as this are typically dealt with not by redesigning the subdivision in a more sensible and sensitive manner, but rather by combining unbuildable lots with adjacent ones where "perc tests" succeed. Thus, these "meat cleaver" layouts become reality, slicing up rural resources with no regard for natural features or cultural landmarks, such as stone walls, hedgerows, or old woods roads.

In Maine, where similar environmental laws exempt most five-acre lots from state review, developers were in reality being discouraged from employing any variation of the "cluster" principle to locate their houselots on the most buildable (or least sensitive) portions of their properties, because the resulting smaller lots would have triggered state review. From the viewpoint of most subdividers, the problems with state review were not substantive but procedural: a 12 to 18 month delay was typical, during which time only relatively minor changes were usually required.

Fortunately, for the cause of open space preservation, recent amendments to these rules by the Maine Department of Environmental Protection extend review exemption to low-density rural subdivisions where the overall average density remains five or more acres per dwelling, provided that at least 50 percent of the developable (nonwetland) area is placed under a permanent conservation easement prohibiting future development. (See Figure 2–13.) The resulting lots are still subject to septic system soil testing, but not until the time of sale to prospective buyers.

Similar amendments to regulations in other states, such as New York, could help to improve

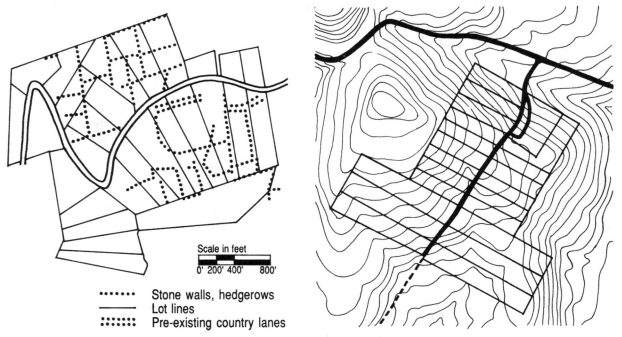

Scale in feet

0' 200' 400'   800'

••••••• Stone walls, hedgerows
——— Lot lines
:::::::: Pre-existing country lanes

Figure 2–12. Rural subdivision patterns are typically unrelated to natural or cultural features in the landscape, as dramatically illustrated by these plats from the Catskill region of New York. *Source:* Lamb, 1989.

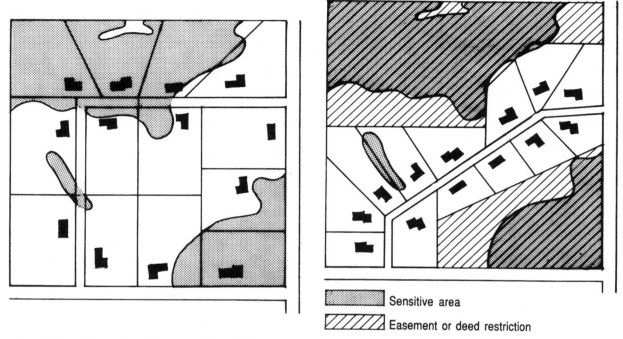

Sensitive area

Easement or deed restriction

Figure 2–13. Conventional two-acre lot subdivision with homes located on sensitive but buildable land, compared with improved layouts protecting those resource areas, as encouraged by new regulations adopted by the Maine Department of Environmental Protection.

the quality of low-density rural subdivision design, and even to increase the level of environmental protection ultimately afforded, by locating lots on the most suitable soils and slopes, and away from critical natural areas such as streams, wetlands, deer wintering "yards," and so forth.

PERFORMANCE ZONING FOR OPEN SPACE

Fortunately, there are some practical—and proven—alternatives to standard large-lot subdivision design. Twenty years ago the Bucks County (Pennsylvania) Planning Commission suggested that rigid prescriptive regulations be replaced by a performance-based approach. The essence of this planning method is fully described in one of the classic books of the profession, *Performance Zoning* (Kendig, 1980). Back in the 1970s, Bucks County planners were discovering what architects had known for years: there was no logical reason to

prohibit new materials and methods, so long as they would perform at least as well as the "old way" of doing things. This thinking has for long been reflected in the "BOCA" Building Code (Building Officials and Code Administrators), though only a small fraction of the thousands of towns that have adopted BOCA in their Building Department have also adopted any type of performance zoning in their planning department.

In the rural examples just cited in Maine and upstate New York, the response of performance zoning would be to establish a large "open space ratio", say 0.8, which means that 80 percent of the parcel must remain as an undivided block of land permanently restricted to farming, forestry, watershed management, wildlife habitat, informal recreation, or some combination of the above. The developer would be entitled to the same number of lots as he or she would ordinarily receive; however, he or she would not be allowed to spread them out across the entire parcel. Additional design standards regarding the quality, quantity, and configuration of the resultant open space, which go beyond the basic approach to performance zoning, are discussed in Chapter 15, "Requiring Open Space Design."

The lesson to be learned is that creative rural land-use planning can offer practical and constitutionally sound methods of ensuring that significant usable open space is preserved every time a major parcel of land is subdivided. The need to supplement costly government "buy-back" programs (such as full-fee acquisition, or the purchase of development rights) has never been greater, nor public funds more scarce. The point is well illustrated in Massachusetts, where a 100-year-old private conservation organization and a state agency have worked individually and together to protect dwindling land resources. Despite their efforts, the total acreage each has been able to preserve over their entire history approximates the average amount of land developed in the Bay State *every year* over the past three decades: 18,000 acres.

It is clear by now that we are steadily losing ground, despite the notable successes of various "buy-back" programs and efforts to encourage land donations for conservation purposes. What needs to be said, repeatedly, is that there are certainly much smarter ways to grow. While the need for continued open space acquisition and farmland easement programs is unquestioned, the need to overhaul the present system of sprawl zoning is no less urgent.

PIGEONHOLE ZONING OR TRADITIONAL MIX?

Standard Euclidean zoning, which pigeonholes uses into certain districts on the basis of their activity type (rather than on the basis of their actual attributes), is relatively easy to administer, as it is essentially a clerical exercise, involving far less evaluation and judgment than applications seeking approval under performance-based standards. As time has shown, however, the results of such simplistic land-use controls are sterile single-use districts. It might puzzle a visitor to see vacant

second and third floors above the busy shops on Main Street in Uxbridge, Massachusetts, unless he or she guesses (correctly) that the town's zoning prohibits all but commercial uses in the downtown business district. As this upper-story space is unattractive to most retailers, most of it remains empty. This is in spite of the fact that the building owners, shopkeepers, and local people looking for reasonably priced apartments would all benefit if this strictly Euclidean regulation were replaced by a performance-based approach that would allow flats to be created, as long as adequate tenant parking were provided within easy walking distance.

Standing in sharp contrast to the example in Uxbridge—not atypical in small-town New England—is the philosophy of the Chestnut Hill Realty Trust, a private nonprofit group formed in the late 1950s in this community of 18,000 people in northwest Philadelphia. This organization has purchased and rehabilitated several buildings, leasing ground-floor space to small family-owned neighborhood businesses it wanted to encourage, and reserving upper stories strictly for residential use. Community leaders there recognize the value of having people live in their "town center," enlivening the area in the evenings and providing "eyes and ears" to reduce crime and vandalism at night.

Many drafters of contemporary zoning ordinances are probably unaware that one of this country's most successful planned communities consciously integrates apartments above shops. In Mariemont, Ohio, residential and retail uses have been successfully combined in the Dale Park Center, which faces onto the village green, around which a church and school were also located. (See Figure 2–14.) (It was also originally just one block away from the trolley to downtown Cincinnati, ten miles to the west.) Designed by landscape architect and pioneer town planner John Nolen in the early 1920s, Mariemont was conceived as "a national exemplar," embodying the highest principles of progressive town planning (The Mariemont Company, 1925). Students and practitioners alike could learn much by visiting communities such as these (several dozen of which are described in thumbnail fashion in Stern and Massengale,

Ripley & Le Boutillier Cottages   Apartments   Shops and Apartments   Apartments   Shops and Apartments   Apartments

ARTIST'S SKETCH OF DALE PARK CENTER GROUP
Corner of Oak & Chestnut Sts.
RIPLEY APARTMENTS AND SHOPS

RIPLEY & LE BOUTILLIER, Boston, Mass.
Architects

Figure 2–14. Shops and apartments designed together in a group of buildings in the Dale Park section of Mariemont, Ohio, a new town near Cincinnati planned by John Nolen in the early 1920s, where mixed uses continue to flourish in this village subcenter.

1981). Built of brick in the neo-Tudor style popular in the 1920s, this development resembled many other shop/flat combination buildings constructed during that era, such as the one in the center of Flossmoor, Illinois (an early twentieth century railway suburb of Chicago). (See Figure 2–15.)

Another example of deliberately combining housing, shops and offices to produce a traditional town center mix can be seen at Mashpee Commons, in Mashpee, Massachusetts, on Cape Cod (illustrated in Part IV, "Case Examples"). Built to replace a marginally successful 1960s style shopping center, this development incorporated the rather revolutionary idea of building several intersecting streets across the old oversized parking lot and lining them with sidewalks and shops, above which were offices and flats. Several sites were also set aside for public buildings and a church.

Although the architectural styles are not historic replicas by any means, the resulting development appears as if the designers had just stepped out of the nineteenth century, without a clue about the

Figure 2–15. Village center shops with apartments above in Flossmoor, Illinois, typical of those built in small towns around the country during the early decades of the twentieth century, before zoning prohibited mixed uses in many communities.

modern way of arranging buildings and asphalt. However, they recognized the aesthetic and functional advantages of scaling their streetscapes traditionally, and appreciated the social and economic benefits created by providing such use mixtures. Most new shopping centers are single story and single use, and they miss some important opportunities. Since the ground-floor use in these developments essentially pays for the land, it stands to reason that any upper-story uses could be created at a near-zero ground-rent cost. They could therefore become a significant opportunity for the provision of affordable housing in a community.

This principle of using high ground-floor rents to help pay for the rest of a building is historically well established, and can be traced back to medieval Europe. In this country, an outstanding example is the old city hall in Lowell, Massachusetts. Built in 1836, it was specifically designed to house the municipal offices on the upper two stories, the first floor being reserved for retail space, whose rent payments were applied against the building debt. (See Figure 2–16.) There are lessons here for enterprising communities looking for innovative ways to make new public-facility construction economically more feasible.

Readers wishing to familiarize themselves with the principles of traditional town planning, including compact neighborhoods, mixed uses, and interconnected street networks, should consult the work of Andres Duany and Elizabeth Plater-Zyberk (two examples of which are briefly described in Chapter 3). Their philosophy is articulately expressed in a 1992 article in *Land Development*, which also contains a two-page summary (in tabular form) of their now famous "Traditional Neighborhood Development (TND) Ordinance." Their pedestrian-friendly approach contains many "maximum dimensions" to prevent low-density suburban forms from reappearing in projects designed according to their principles. Other hallmarks are their extensive use of alleys (to avoid garages dominating streetscapes), a wide variety of house types (including dwellings above ground-floor shops), substantial public open space (often formal in nature, such as squares and plazas), and prominently located par-

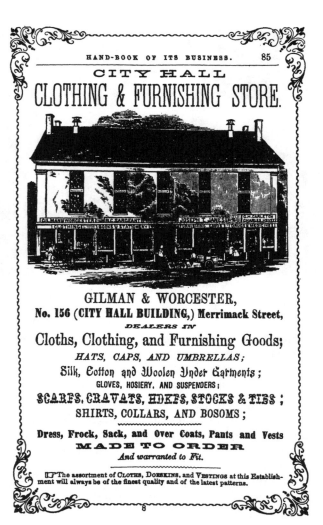

Figure 2–16. Nineteenth-century engraving of Old City Hall, Lowell, Massachusetts, which was designed with shops at ground level, rental income from which helped defray the costs of this multiuse municipal office building (in which city offices were located on the upper floors).

cels donated for civic and institutional uses (municipal buildings, libraries, churches, etc.) (Duany and Plater-Zyberk, 1992).

3

Future Prospects: Choosing among Alternative Patterns

There is, of course, no single planning or design solution to ensure that new developments in small towns will fit in comfortably with their physical surroundings. Towns vary too much in their layout, topography, history, economy, culture, and functions to allow for any standard answer. However, the design approach followed in most communities—which has given free rein to suburban subdivisions and shopping strips—can be validly criticized for imposing standardized patterns on towns regardless of their particular features or unique character.

PUBLIC DISSATISFACTION WITH CONVENTIONAL ZONING

Professional planners throughout much of the country are beginning to feel the effects of citizens' initiatives based on a growing public awareness that the special qualities of their small towns are being needlessly eroded by conventional sprawl development. The slowly rising tide of public dissatisfaction with typical suburban approaches to new development in small towns can be distinguished in many cases from purely antigrowth attitudes and certain valid, but more specific, environmental concerns.

William H. ("Holly") Whyte put his finger on a large part of the problem in the late 1960s with his wry observation that developers seem always to name their subdivisions after precisely those attractive features they have destroyed (e.g., "Orchard Valley Estates" and "Hickory Grove Manor"). This approach of subdivision names memorializing that which has been lost is actu-

ally much older, and probably even predates the 1920s, when Sinclair Lewis sarcastically described the normal approach of realtors in his day: "When George Babbitt laid out Glen Oriole acreage development, when he ironed woodland and dipping meadow into a glenless, orioleless sunburnt flat . . . he righteously put in a complete sewerage system."

CITIZEN PLANNING

Initially spurred by the prospect of a large, "cookie-cutter" subdivision on farmland at one gateway to their town, residents in the Village of Honeoye Falls, New York, gathered over 500 petition signatures to protest the proposal and soon organized themselves into a more formal "Citizens Advisory Committee" to study wide-ranging issues that planning board members were too busy to examine, from housing and public services to business, commerce, and open space. The committee's recommendations, which are being incorporated into new zoning and subdivision regulations, include the following highlights:

Commercial Areas

• zero front setback, rear parking

• pedestrian access via a continuous sidewalk system

• building scale and design to harmonize with village context

• new "Traditional Mixed Use District" for downtown business expansion and transition to residential areas

• new "Gateway Business District" with traditional scale and grouping of buildings, interior courtyards, and rear parking

Residential Areas

• diversity of housing types encouraged by allowing accessory apartments to be built into large homes and onto smaller ones

• development designs required to include a variety of lot and house sizes in the same developments

• residential design standards for critical features such as roof shape and pitch, gable orientation, and front setbacks

• rectilinear streets that connect with each other

Open Space/Trails

• village-wide trails and sidewalk system to link neighborhoods with one another, and with schools, shops, natural areas, and other open spaces

• significant open space setasides in new development by requiring more compact building clusters on parts of each parcel

One of the most remarkable aspects of this citizens' effort was that is was almost 100 percent voluntary, with extremely little advice from outside consultants that the town could not have afforded to hire. Perhaps that is why committee members relied so heavily upon simple observation and plain common sense. Led by an able local organizer, John McNall, residents began to take "the critical second look" at everything in their village, and articulated what they liked and did not like. They then examined their ordinances to determine the connection between the rule books and the nontraditional development of recent decades. Naturally, they found a strong causal relationship: zoning really was a type of genetic code shaping all new growth. The trouble was that the current "gene pool," as expressed in the regulations, lacked many of the traits necessary for new growth to retain any "family resemblance" to the village core districts and neighborhoods. In other words, the place was on its way to losing its identity because its regulations had much more in common with generic suburbia than with the village itself.

In the small coastal town of Lewes, in Sussex County, Delaware, a citizens committee was appointed by the mayor in 1988 to prepare a long-range plan to guide growth in this attractive community of nineteenth-century neighborhoods and traditional downtown buildings. Having witnessed several parcels developed into characterless subdivisions during the preceding 25 years, residents were concerned about continued erosion of Lewes' identity. Recognizing that their challenge had many different facets, the committee listed five "core values," representing those "irreplaceable qualities of Lewes that make it an uniquely desirable place to live, work, and visit" (Lewes Long Range Planning Committee, 1988). These core values reflected those positive aspects of the community that citizens felt were essential to retain. Among them were the following:

1. The town's special and historic relationship with the sea, characterized by open views to the ocean and the Lewes & Rehoboth Canal, was the first core value to be identified. Development along two roads had historically been on the landward side only, maintaining unobstructed views to the water across a long linear open space. This tradition has not been respected by new developments, which crowd the water and prevent visual access from the public way.

2. A second value felt to be essential was the town's diverse character as a year-round working community with a mixture of ages, incomes, building styles, shops, jobs, and environments (from the natural to the human-made). As more vacationers and affluent retirees discover Lewes, however, this diversity could disappear. Changes in the local housing patterns and the commercial base reflect this trend, with homes being occupied only seasonally and with tourist business replacing typical "Main Street" stores.

3. The town's human scale and "sense of face-to-face intimacy," its third core value, are the result of many factors, including compact neighborhood design with easy walking distances to the downtown area, schools, and parks, along a sidewalk system where many homes have front porches that are still used. Shallow setbacks, colorful gardens, and mature street trees give the streetscape interest, texture, and variety.

4. The town's life-style as a busy daytime tourist destination and as a community of quiet, slow-paced evenings distinguishes it from many other coastal resorts. The absence of night-clubs, discos, and other commercial amusements greatly enhances Lewes' livability.

5. The town's professional and social communities are also very important assets. Without the hospital staffs, college faculty, churches, and fraternal and service organizations, town life would not be as deeply enriched.

STANDING UP FOR DESIGN ISSUES

In another rural village in upstate New York (Geneseo), local officials came under heavy pressure from county political leaders and economic development staff to endorse a large (160,000 sq. ft.) new retail shopping plaza including a Wal-Mart, a major grocery, and about ten small shops. The proposed design consisted of 12 acres of asphalt parking in front of a straight 1,200-foot-long building, set back 500 feet from a two-lane highway that functioned as the main entrance to the historic village.

Throughout the discussions the developers emphasized their flexibility, but it soon became apparent that the site plan was absolutely fixed, and that their "flexibility" related only to very minor items, such as paint color and landscaping materials. The developers ridiculed the village's site plan review standards, which called for "parking at the side or rear and screened from the public roadway," as being contrary to all accepted principles of retail site design. Nonetheless, the thought of constructing such a building nearly one-quarter-mile long at the far edge of a huge, blacktopped field deeply disturbed many residents, who prided themselves on Geneseo's traditional small-town character.

Because the site lay just outside the village's official boundaries, in the Town of Geneseo, it was not served by the village's water or sewer system, necessitating a small land annexation and infrastructure extension, actions controlled by the village board. Aside from concerns about the impacts that such a large development would predictably have upon businesses in the Village center and in other nearby retail areas, the developer's inflexible attitudes regarding site design issues catalyzed

Village officials. Village board members pointed out that Wal-Mart had shown much greater sensitivity to local preferences in Steamboat Springs, Colorado, where a similar mix of retail uses was then being constructed. The building layout at that site effectively internalized the parking and screened most of the asphalt from direct view from adjacent roads. The contrast between Wal-Mart's proposal in Geneseo and the site plan they agreed to in Steamboat Springs is shown in Figure 3–1.

After the village board flatly rejected Wal-Mart's request for public water and sewer extensions to their site, Wal-Mart's agents began a strenuous public advertising campaign, touting the tax-base expansion their facility would create, according to local officials. Many citizens felt their community was under siege by the corporate giant, whose well-funded advertising effort paid off when two pro-Wal-Mart candidates were later elected to the village board. At the first board meeting after the election, the newly constituted majority passed an open-ended resolution to extend water and sewer to the construction site, without any caveats or conditions relating to traffic studies, impacts upon the existing village business center, environmental factors, or aesthetic issues. Wal-Mart did, however, keep its word about being flexible as to paint color: their mammoth edifice is now painted in two shades of brown, instead of two shades of grey.

The primary lesson to be learned from the Geneseo example is that community politics can be influenced by concerted advertising efforts mounted by large corporate interests. The campaign in Geneseo was extraordinary in the annals of small rural towns. The more common situation is that when developers are faced with rejection by local officials they return to their drawing boards and consider their "fallback" positions. Towns need to be prepared to confront applicants who initially insist that more creative ways of arranging buildings and parking are simply not viable. They can often be pressed into following local site design standards (provided, of course, that the standards themselves are not unreasonable). Those developers who remain inflexible risk plan disapproval and losing their market to competi-

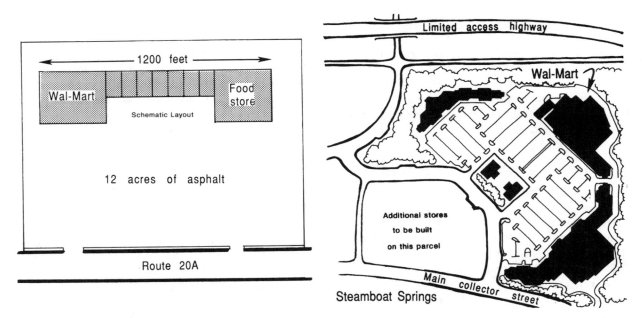

Figure 3–1. Schematic version of site plan submitted by agents of Wal-Mart at the entrance to the historic Village of Geneseo, New York, compared with a more creative building arrangement Wal-Mart agreed to accept in Steamboat Springs, Colorado, disproving the corporation's claim that it never varies from its standard plans.

tors who are willing to accommodate themselves to community standards. Occasionally, however, when irresistible forces meet unmovable objects, those with the most money and the greatest staying power ultimately win out.

In all fairness, the entire burden cannot be shouldered by busy officials alone; they need the support of their constituents, who must organize themselves to help define a *positive vision for growth* in their community. It is they who must determine what the character of their community is and what it should be, so that their fragile "sense of place" will not be overwhelmed by succeeding waves of conventional highway strips and cookie-cutter subdivisions.

The problem has been nicely stated by Dunham-Jones at the University of Virginia: "Unaffected by place, the new developments are interchangeable. Despite superficial stylistic or marketing differences, a new shopping mall in Vermont differs little from one in Alabama, either in terms of physical design (they both only really look like parking lots), air temperature or products for sale.

While a developer will conduct a market survey to determine the particular habits of local consumers, he/she is still likely to bulldoze a site flat, effacing its particular nature, so as to more easily impose the standard plan. In the continual search for new markets, trusted formulae are reproduced such that the new market bears an uncanny resemblance to all other markets and any sense of place is eradicated" (Dunham-Jones, 1990).

Several examples of commercial developments where a very considerable effort has been made to blend in with the local or regional vernacular are presented in Part IV, "Case Examples," particularly the sites in Waitsfield, Vermont, and Belchertown, Massachusetts.

COMMUNITY IMAGE PREFERENCE SURVEYS

Planners have for decades relied upon surveys to better understand what types of change local residents would prefer to see in their towns, given the fact that some magnitude of change is inevitable. This has often taken the form of a written survey mailed to registered voters; in other instances an "open community forum" or "sounding board" technique has been used, where residents are encouraged to share their hopes and fears about the future of their town. Both of these are healthy and often productive exercises, with the best results usually achieved when the atmosphere is casual and the responses candid and interactive.

Although survey techniques can provide valuable information unobtainable in any other manner, they provide no solid basis for evaluating the one element of new development of concern to all: its physical appearance, and the way it relates to the existing town and surrounding landscape.

To address this imbalance in survey information, Professor Anton Nelessen of Rutgers University employs a visual preference survey "as a technique to facilitate citizen participation in the process of determining the desired spatial and visual features of both current and future development within a community" (Nelessen, 1989). Similar approaches had previously been used to document how people perceive and value various types of natural landscapes, most notably by Ricki McKenzie in a report for the National Park Service on the New Jersey Pinelands (McKenzie, 1980), but Nelessen has elaborated upon this technique and has sharpened its applicability to townscape issues. In a demonstration study conducted in the rural but suburbanizing township of Chesterfield, New Jersey, 240 color slides were projected onto a large screen in the local middle school during two sessions attended by 264 adult participants. Respondents were asked to record their reaction to each of the images on a computer form, rating each on a scale ranging from +10 to −10.

The results were tabulated, analyzed, and published in a format useful to township officials looking for guidance in proposing future land-use regulations. Under consideration was the adoption of a municipal "transfer of development rights" (TDR) program, with designated "sending zones" (which would remain undeveloped) and "receiving zones" (where the new development would be transferred and constructed). Ancillary issues involved the potential for mixed uses, compact single-family homes and lots, attached dwellings, and design standards for buildings and development layouts.

Among the *lowest* preference ratings found were those for classic "cookie-cutter" subdivisions, apartment or condo complexes, and highway strip development and shopping plazas with large front parking lots. Not surprisingly, the most *highly* rated images were those of the existing local countryside: farm fields, narrow rural roads, woodlots, ponds, and streams. Together, these parts of the results indicated a clear preference for preserving open space and avoiding conventional suburban sprawl. However, the third and perhaps most revealing result was the clear preference for a built environment consisting of pedestrian-orientated "downtown" areas designed at a human scale, and for village-style housing located on narrow lots with modest street setbacks, front porches, and traditional roof pitches. (See Figure 3–2.)

The Chesterfield survey also included written questions to supplement the visual preference results. Among the strongest responses were rejection of a town policy encouraging highway strip commercial development (by 87 percent) and agreement with the idea of compact construction in new hamlets and villages to preserve open farmland (78 percent). The final component of the consultant's project was the creation of two devel-

Figure 3–2. Streetscapes such as this one, in Crosswicks Village, Chesterfield Township, New Jersey, are consistently ranked very highly by participants in Anton Nelessen's visual preference surveys.

opment prototype models, and a list of community design principles for incorporation into future zoning regulations. These principles are discussed later in this chapter. The use of visual preference surveys as a planning technique is becoming more widespread. In rural Georgia, for example, the Oconee River Resource Conservation and Development Council has published a "Development Primer" with color photographs of local land uses ranked according to scores from 354 visual preference surveys conducted in small towns in rural Madison County (Krohn, 1992) to assist local planners as they seek to revise local zoning ordinances to more accurately reflect community preferences.

Since his work in Chesterfield, Nelessen has produced possibly the most extensively illustrated set of residential development regulations in the country, for Manheim Township in Lancaster County, Pennsylvania. The premise is a sound one: since the results of zoning are so visually evident, decision makers and applicants alike really need to understand the sort of future such regulations will produce. By including a large number of line drawings in the code, its intent will become clearer to all parties involved, not least the public. The Manheim ordinance, therefore, represents a significant step forward in the evolution of zoning, and provides a helpful example for other localities to emulate (based upon their own vernacular design traditions and townscape patterns, of course). It is discussed again later in this chapter, with sample illustrations from the code.

A less sophisticated but very transferable technique to determine community preferences has been employed by the Livingston County (Michigan) Planning Department, which prepared short questionnaires containing simple line drawings illustrating basic alternative development types. The questionnaires were filled out by volunteer members of township planning boards, who were asked to indicate which of the alternatives looked more rural to them, and which they liked best.

The use of the simple graphics (see Figure 3–3) to augment written questions proved invaluable. This not only let participants visualize often abstract design concepts, but also helped the county planning staff to discover—and document—the consensus opinion of their constituents with regard to critical land-use issues facing many of the townships. Having respondents react to clearly drawn graphic representations was far more useful than simply talking about the issues or circulating standard written questionnaires.

The results of this illustrated questionnaire gave the county planning office the support it needed to devise new zoning and subdivision regulations requiring developers to preserve open space through more compact subdivision design, and to strengthen the appearance of new commercial projects by setting design standards based on "downtown" principles of building location, parking arrangement, and so forth. By presenting alternative approaches to designing new development in a simple and readily understandable manner, with inexpensive sketches accompanying a brief questionnaire, county planning staff was able to determine what local board members really wanted to see in their communities after the next generation of new development. In short, there is no substitute for visual aids when dealing with the types of impacts that new developments usually create when they become reality in small communities. (The commercial area sketches used by the Livingston County Planning Department are included in Chapter 9, "Development in Town Centers and along Highways.")

IDENTIFYING "PLACES OF THE HEART"

Despite the best of intentions, conventional planning studies frequently overlook some of the most important aspects of a community that make it a special place. This concern was the driving force for local officials and residents in the small town of Wendell, Massachusetts, to devise a more creative means of identifying the features most needy and worthy of extra protection. Basic to their approach was the recognition that many times these important elements are either too obvious or too subtle to be noticed until they are gone. Advising citizens that "change will continue to take place with or without our guidance," Wendell's Rural Design Assistance Committee worked with consultants Walt Cudnohufsky and Molly Babize to

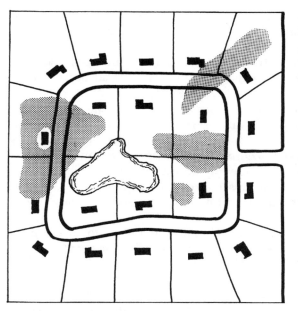

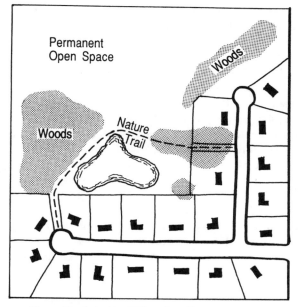

Figure A   (rated by 25% as "rural")

44 acre parcel
20 lots (2 acres each)
No open space
No pond access except from four lots

Figure B   (rated by 75% as "rural")

44 acre parcel
20 lots (3/4 acre each)
25 acres of open space
Pond access for all residents

Figure 3–3. Schematic illustrations from the preference survey conducted by the Livingston County (Michigan) Planning Department to identify the kind of rural subdivision layout most desired by local residents and officials.

create a participatory process to determine what aspects of the town were most valued or cherished by residents.

The first part of this process involved a survey asking respondents to locate "places of the heart" on a town map, and to list "landmarks, frequently visited or memorable places, aspects of the town that represent 'home,' qualities and feelings that represent the community, and perceived threats or opportunities" (Babize and Cudnohufsky, 1990).

Survey participation was encouraged by volunteers who hand-delivered questionnaires to each household, and by telling everyone that by returning a completed form they would automatically be entered in a raffle. A "vision workshop" was conducted two weeks after the survey forms were handed in, at which time residents gathered into small groups to describe—in words and sketches—

what they wanted their town to look like and be like in 10 to 30 years. Children were also encouraged to participate in specifically prepared exercises and drawings, which yielded some different ideas and added important perspectives.

Excluding sites mentioned fewer than five times, 39 locations were identified by the 134 respondents, and included a variety of natural and human-made features visible from public roads (ponds, peaks, fields, farm complexes, civic buildings, etc.).

"Buildings rather than natural settings were most frequently mentioned as places 'used,' and of the range of buildings mentioned—rather than their frequency of use—town buildings dominated. . . . [However] much of a community's daily and weekly life centers around personal business and commercial exchange. . . . Whether public or private, attention must be paid to design, convenience, safety and attractive image of frequently used buildings and places" (Cudnohufsky and Babize, 1990).

Of the 39 special places identified in the survey, 21 were unprotected in terms of their character preservation (i.e., they were privately owned with no restrictions on future changes). These included rural landscapes along back roads and edges of several ponds, brooks, and wetlands.

Concluding that "much of Wendell's sacred structure remains vulnerable to undesired and compromising change," the organizing committee identified twelve "areas for controlled growth." Recommendations included a mix of regulatory and nonregulatory approaches. Two key suggestions were to contact owners of large parcels where special character-defining features would be threatened by conventional development, to encourage either land conservation measures or "open space development design."

In addition, compact traditional development (including locally affordable housing on smaller lots) was recommended in a new "village center district", where septic systems could be located "off-lot," sharing nearby areas of better soils on one portion of the development property (see Chapter 13 for a fuller discussion of the possibilities for septic system location in rural subdivisions). Among the regulatory approaches mentioned were techniques to protect the visual quality of rural roadsides, such as deep buffered setbacks, vegetative clearing restrictions, and encouragement of small housing clusters sharing common driveways. The product of a Rural Design Assistance Grant from the Massachusetts Council on the Arts and Humanities, this creative approach received an award for "outstanding comprehensive planning in a rural area" from the New England chapter of the American Planning Association in 1990.

CONTEXTUAL STANDARDS FOR NEW DEVELOPMENT

In response to growing public interest in how new development can fit more comfortably into existing downtowns, neighborhoods, and the surrounding landscape, researchers at the Center for Rural Massachusetts have begun to develop a practical "how-to" manual to help people rediscover the components, configurations, and relationships that make the traditional parts of their towns special and pleasing. *This Place, Our Place: A Workbook for Town Character Assessment and Planning* combines line drawings and photographs into a format that can be written in directly by users, leading them along a step-by-step procedure for identifying the spatial and dimensional relationships that operate in a subtle manner to produce their town's unique sense of place (Fabel, 1992).

Fabel's workbook grew out of town character analyses he made of three Massachusetts towns: Wellfleet, Harwich, and Leverett. Inspired by the work of Christopher Alexander and his colleagues, these three town character evaluations are based upon the concept of "patterns within patterns," an approach that relates elements up and down the spatial scale, from regions to towns to neighborhoods to buildings to architectural features (see Alexander et al., 1977). "For example, it is important to consider not only how houses relate to other houses and the road, but how the cluster of houses becomes a landscape element itself when the view is broadened to include the patterns of the larger landscape. In the opposite direction, when we narrow our view to include only the house, we find that it too is a composition of diverse elements such as doors and windows" (Fabel, 1989). (See Figure 3–4.)

Some of the elements Fabel examined in his three towns are listed below (at various scales) to provide at least a general idea of the type of features one might choose to look at if a similar approach were to be taken in your town:

Regional Scale
• distance between freestanding towns or villages
• nature and clarity of town "edges"

Village Scale
• road network (principal thoroughfares, connecting streets, narrow lanes, footpaths)
• land-use diversity (residential, commercial, services, institutional)

Figure 3–4. This organic cluster of homes along a winding street in the shadow of an old church in Wellfleet, Massachusetts, contains many of the character-defining elements and patterns identified by Fabel in his study *This Place, Our Place.*

• "hierarchy of formality" [buildings become increasingly larger and more formal as one approaches the village center (churches, town halls, schools, etc.)]
• pedestrian scale
Site Scale
• orientation of facades ("public" side-facing street)
• front setbacks (modest dimensions, fairly consistent)
• facade widths (minimum, maximum, most common)
• spacing between buildings (rhythmic element)
• street proportion and closure (width between "walls" of this "outdoor room")
Lot Size and Proportion
• area dimensions of village lots for shops, homes
• typical range of lot widths and depths
• normal locations of buildings on their lots
Relationship among Public, Semipublic, and Private Spaces
• boundary markers (height and location of fences, hedges, tree lines)
• sidewalks (widths, continuity, frequency, location vis-à-vis the street curbing)

• porches (location on building, open/enclosed, width)
Building Scale
• building types (materials, roof shape)
Bulk, Proportion, and Scale
• height to ridge line
• facade proportions (height:width ranges found)
• scale and bulk of traditional structures
Massing
• basic building form with "simple massing"
• additive massing ("connected architecture")
Roofs
• shape, pitch, overhangs, dormers, chimneys
Windows
• type, dimensions, proportions, pane size/number, spacing on facade, shutters
Other Details
• doors, porches, trim elements
Surface Materials
• cladding, roofing, colors, textures

The value of the work described above lies not in the specific results obtained from the detailed study of any particular town, but in the understanding that a common vocabulary and set of general principles may emerge that can be used to inform new development. Just as the original building of these older towns was not dictated by rigid rules and regulations, it is vital that the form of new neighborhoods and business areas be expressed through the town's common "pattern language," which would allow elements to be assembled in a variety of ways, but always within understood limits that fit in with the existing traditional context.

The language analogy is apposite, as words may be arranged in various manners to express the same thought but, to remain intelligible, some norms of order and relationship must be respected. Alexander was right on target when he described the creation of towns as "fundamentally a genetic process . . . and this process can be in good order only when the language which controls it is widely used and widely shared" (Alexander et al., 1977). A simple workbook-like tool that can be understood and used by large numbers of local people offers one opportunity to help towns regain their bearings and original direction, assuming that is what their citizens wish.

Highly recommended reading in this regard is *A Design Guideline Manual for Sustainable Development on Cape Cod*, a heavily illustrated publication offering 61 guidelines with two overall objectives: preservation of rural landscape and land-use patterns, and preservation of existing village centers. The 61 recommendations address specific issues relating to development site selection, site development, open space planning, streetscapes and roadways, architecture, adaptive reuse, infill construction, landscaping, pedestrian and bicycle networks, accessibility, parking, infrastructure, signage, and community involvement. Also included are four case studies with site plans and aerial perspective sketches focusing on village centers, commercial strip redevelopment, compact residential development, and large-scale commercial development (Community Vision, 1992).

COMMUNITY DESIGN FORUMS

Citizen involvement in the planning process was harnessed by planners in Lancaster County, Pennsylvania, who launched a major public participation effort in October 1990 with an extremely well-publicized "Liveable Communities Forum" to discuss future planning options for this solidly agricultural, but growing, county. In addition to hosting a half-dozen national experts on development design, the two-day conference included some highly productive work sessions in which local residents actively participated in village and townscape analyses of five different actual development sites around the county. These sites were carefully selected by county staff to epitomize the problems and opportunities for urban infill, urban extension, new suburban communities, rural village extensions, and rural clusters outside villages.

Workshop participants were led by local professionals and had the benefit of a draft set of "Community Design Guidelines" prepared by the county planning commission's Innovative Design Task Force. These guidelines dealt with four basic issues: community character (design, scale), community diversity (mixed uses), accessibility/affordability, and "decisive protection" (special features and functional ecosystems). Detailed objectives were listed under each of the four issue headings mentioned above (character, diversity, accessibility/affordability, protection), for each of the five site-types (urban infill, etc.).

Not surprisingly, there was some repetition of guideline objectives because many were common to more than one site-type (e.g., "avoid excessive street widths and setbacks," or "establish interconnecting greenways between urban/suburban areas and the rural countryside"). However, each site-type also contained objectives unique to its character, and because the guidelines were intended to establish general directions for thinking, workshop participants were encouraged to suggest compatible new objectives of their own.

Four months later, county planners reconvened the forum to discuss the development plan recommendations created by the citizen participants for each of the five site-types. The results were not only imaginative and useful on the individual site level, but they also had broader applicability for similar situations around the county. The exercise also helped stimulate interest in creative land development possibilities (including the potential for open space conservation as a side benefit) among a wide cross-section of the public (including lay persons, developers, engineers, and attorneys). Results of the forums and the attendant citizen input were incorporated into the county's new comprehensive plan, whose creation process emphasized public participation during all its phases.

Overall, the new county plan seeks to "provide for growth in appropriate areas" (which are defined as contiguous extensions to existing settlements), for the establishment of new villages, and for rural clusters. Major new development in the countryside would, however, be further constrained and directed by exclusive agricultural zoning in areas of prime farmland.

To assist implementation of these policies a county-wide Growth Management Plan (GMP) is being prepared, which will classify all land into "growth areas" and "limited growth areas," based upon criteria contained in the goals of the comprehensive plan. Briefly stated, the GMP takes a performance-based approach to land-use recommendations, provided the use is proposed to be located "within a growth area where the proper infrastructure exists" (Lancaster County, 1988). In addition to linking progressive performance criteria with locational mandates and an infrastructure concurrency requirement, the GMP also includes a "cross-acceptance" process, similar to the one recently adopted in the New Jersey State Plan. In this process, local plans are reviewed to identify points that are either consistent or inconsistent with county policies. Negotiations to bring about a greater degree of consistency are then conducted, with some compromise expected on both sides. This is, however, a voluntary process because county government in Pennsylvania is not legally empowered to enforce its views.

VILLAGE AND HAMLET PLANNING

Another very notable effort commenced in 1988 in northern Virginia, when the Loudoun County Board of Supervisors announced their Rural Vision Initiative. Sparked by deepening public concern about the highly negative visual impacts of large-lot (three-acre) zoning upon Loudoun's fragile and extremely scenic open landscapes, the county supervisors commissioned a six-month study by its planning staff and sequestered themselves on a two-week retreat to contemplate the most practical and effective solutions to the problem. Reluctant to further down-zone (equity arguments had been strongly voiced by many landowners), and aware that the continued fragmentation of the countryside into three- to five-acre parcels threatened groundwater quality, compromised long-term agricultural viability, and generated higher public service delivery costs, the county supervisors considered five preferred alternative growth patterns. Two were eventually rejected (major expansion of existing towns, and the creation of five new towns) and two others were ultimately endorsed (creation of 20 new rural villages and an unspecified number of new rural hamlets).

The heart of Loudoun's "Vision" is neatly summarized by its board of supervisors in the following excerpt:

"The Board envisions a continuation of Loudoun's traditional land use pattern of rural villages and low density development. To achieve this Vision the Board will encourage the development of new mixed-use villages, each consisting of a few hundred houses grouped together in a comfortable human scale and surrounded by significant amounts of permanent open space. Each village would be served by its own water supply and sewer facility. Beyond the village boundaries the Board's policy will be to encourage low density development.

It is envisioned that the rural landscape will consist primarily of new and traditional agricultural uses, low intensity recreation uses, and the preservation of natural and historic features. . . . The Board is convinced that of all possible alternatives exhaustively examined for preserving the essential character of rural Loudoun, a combination of the traditional concepts of villages surrounded by open space and low density development is the most compelling, because it has remained the foundation of Loudoun's development for over 200 years" (Loudoun County, 1988).

After a great number of heavily attended public meetings, Loudoun County adopted rural hamlet and village zoning ordinance amendments specifically to encourage the "compact grouping of homes located so as to blend with the existing

Figure 3–5. Aerial view of the sprawling development pattern of houselots and streets that ultimately consumes every unprotected acre of buildable ground in residential zoning districts in suburbanizing rural areas.

Figure 3–6. Waterford, Virginia, is a frequently cited example of the kind of traditional streetscape that Loudoun County's rural hamlet and village zoning design standards are intended to create. *Source:* Photo by Richard Calderon.

landscape—such as the rise and fall of the topography, hedgerows and wooded areas—and to preserve to a greater extent the agricultural, forestal and visual character of the landscape" (Calderon, 1990).

With a mandate to draft new zoning regulations based upon the county's traditional pattern of settlements, the planning staff undertook specific studies of building and street configurations in historic villages. Based upon these investigations, new rural hamlet forms were generated consisting of four different types of lots or parcels: compact houselots (with designated "building envelopes"), peripheral common open spaces, interior greens or squares, and large conservancy lots. A similar classification of land exists for the new villages (village proper, buffer, and conservancy). These categories, and the design regulations applicable to each, are described in considerable detail in the Appendix.

Planning for new small-scale settlements in the countryside involves different approaches than those that are applicable and appropriate for larger developments, such as the "new towns" currently being proposed in many places around the country. However, plans for new villages and for new towns should both derive from an under-

standing of the patterns found in existing examples of these settlement forms within the immediate region. Older towns typically exhibit grid-like street patterns, occasionally terminating in planned vistas, such as of a church at the end of a street, and usually contain less but more formal open space (often civic or public). On the other hand, village road systems tend to be more irregular, following natural topographical features, and most of the open space often consists of private undeveloped land (frequently in the form of meadows, orchards, backyard vegetable gardens, etc.), in addition to any small green, common, or pond that is sometimes also present.

In Loudoun County, plans for the proposed new town of Belmont were based upon a careful and detailed study of the scale and pattern of streets, houselots, civic buildings and public spaces found in the Town of Leesburg, the county seat, by the architectural and town planning firm of Duany/ Plater-Zyberk (DPZ) of Miami, and others. The proposal, resulting from a planning charrette held in September 1988, was suitably formal and urbane, with approximately 25 percent of the land designated for open space and civic uses, as shown in Figure 3–7.

When it later turned its hand to the challenge of designing a smaller development in a rural part of Montgomery County, Maryland, in January 1990, DPZ shifted gears accordingly, to design two traditional concepts for a 300-acre site adjacent to the existing Village of Sandy Spring. Both plans designate approximately three-quarter of the property as open space, suitable for continued farming, scenic enjoyment, and outdoor recreation (but, notably, no golf courses). With compact houselots laid out along streets, roads, and lanes, emphasis has been placed on human scale, pedestrian mobility, and the aesthetic integration of village functions and the open countryside.

The two traditional concepts proposed for the site differ in form and feeling. The "Hamlet" concept involves a smaller number of residences, located on lots ranging from about 10,000 sq. ft. to 80,000 sq. ft., with most being in the ¼ acre to one-acre category. Five small neighborhoods having from 25 to 40 homes, each with modest areas

Belmont Street Pattern

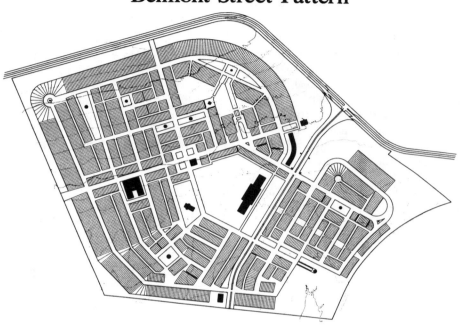

Civic Buildings and Spaces

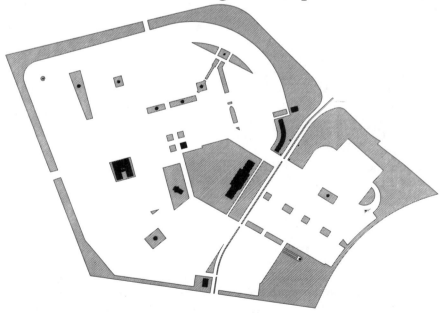

Figure 3–7. Proposed plan for Town of Belmont, Maryland, and the location of civic buildings and public spaces within that plan. *Source:* Duany/Plater-Zyberk Architects and Town Planners.

for active or passive recreation, are all situated within a 10-minute walk of the center, where sites for commercial and civic buildings have been reserved. In the alternative "Heath" concept, a greater number of houselots are offered at both ends of the spectrum (small 7,000 to 9,000 sq. ft. lots, and larger two- and three-acre lots). Its street system is also more formal and geometric, with a shorter network due to narrower frontages on many of the lots. To demonstrate the differences between these two traditional design approaches and the results that would normally be produced by following the county's existing R-2 zoning, a third plan consisting of checkerboard coverage by two-acre lots was also drawn. All three designs are reproduced in Figure 3–8.

A number of smaller design firms around the country have begun to do similar work, in response to increased interest by developers and professional planners. A dramatic example of the contrast between typical "cookie-cutter" subdivision layout and neo-traditional possibilities has been illustrated by architect Richard Bono of York, Pennsylvania, on a 195-acre site near Littlestown in Union Township, Adams County, Pennsylvania. In 1989, "Kosmos Estates" was proposed under the township's existing zoning, containing 192 one-acre houselots covering the entire tract, with no public open space, sidewalks, or amenities.

Two years later, the developer submitted an alternative plan for a new village ("Alba"), holding the total number of units constant but offering a wider variety of housing choice: 54 townhouses on lots averaging 2,330 sq. ft., 99 neighborhood houses on lots ranging from 4,800 to 11,000 sq. ft., 20 perimeter homes on one-acre lots, and 19 estate lots of at about four acres each. Front setbacks on all but the estate lots would be from 6 to 18 feet (compared with 50 feet under the current ordinance). Amenities would include sidewalks on tree-lined streets, 76 acres of open space and parks, and a village center with four to six shops plus a convenience store and 90 off-street parking spaces, as well as two sites donated for a day-care center and a meetinghouse or church.

Another notable difference between the two plans is that Alba contains a network of intercon-

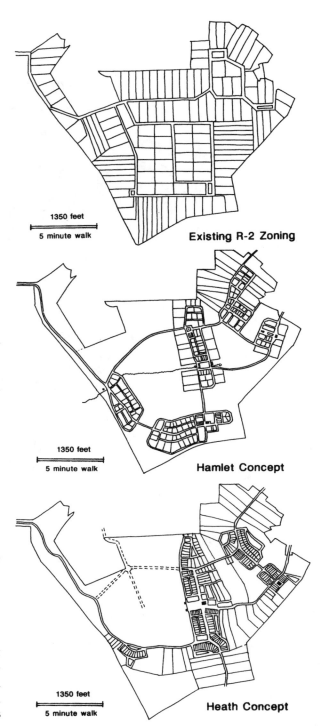

Figure 3–8. The development pattern allowed under existing zoning in Sandy Spring, Maryland, contrasted with two alternative concepts for the same site with agricultural greenbelt areas, designed by Duany/Plater-Zyberk Architects and Town Planners.

nected streets that are "knotted together" from several directions from the village center. In the words of designer Bono, "At no point can one simply make a high-speed entry and exit from this community. One must stop, turn, slow down, or perform some other appropriate act of vehicular respect before leaving." Although the proposal is in substantial noncompliance with the township's existing regulations, a new ordinance amendment proposed by the site designers has been endorsed, with suggestions, by the county. (See Figure 3–9.)

Communities interested in exercising greater influence over the appearance of new development, and desiring to ensure that developers and their designers "get the picture," should consider following the lead of Manheim Township, in Pennsylvania's Lancaster County. Drafted by Anton Nelessen Associates, the new standards for Planned Residential Developments (PRD) in Manheim's zoning ordinance are very probably the most heavily illustrated set of land-use regulations in the country, with 84 images in 101 pages of text. Their purpose is, quite simply, to more effectively convey to developers the intent of the ordinance, so that the proposals they submit for review will be as close as possible to what the community actually wants.

This approach should significantly reduce the time required for development reviews, and help to produce results that are more in line with the township's objectives. Of the 84 illustrations 27 were photographs, many of which were highly rated images from the visual preference survey conducted by Nelessen soon after the project commenced. Among the other types of illustrations were aerial perspective sketches (16), building elevations (13), streetscape views (13), schematic site plans (8), and street cross-sections. (See Figure 3–10.)

OPPOSITION TO PLANNED COMMUNITIES

Many of the neo-traditional villages and towns proposed in recent years have been controversial because of their location and their scale, often involving hundreds or even thousands of new

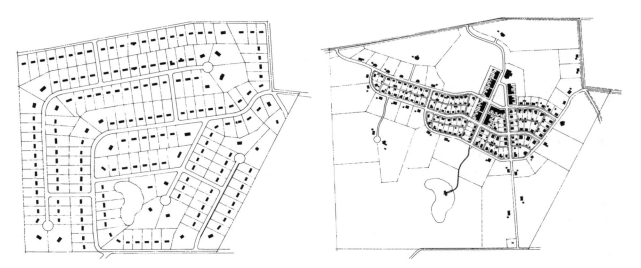

Figure 3-9. "Kosmos Estates" in Adams County, Pennsylvania, as laid out according to current zoning, and the Village of "Alba," as designed by Richard Bono and Richard Calderon to yield the same number of dwellings (with greater variety) plus a small commercial core and significant greenbelt open space.

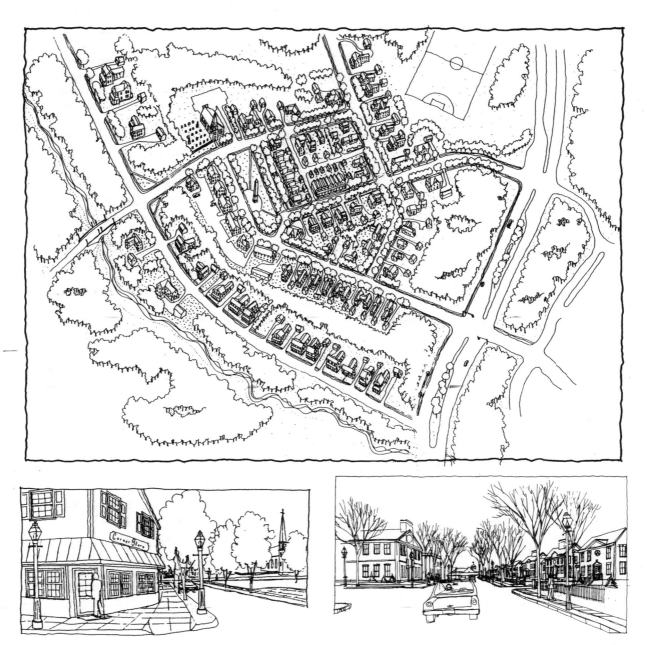

Figure 3–10. A few of the 84 illustrations contained in the 101-page Planned Residential Development amendment to the zoning ordinance of Manheim Township, Pennsylvania, intended to help developers better understand the type of results the community wishes to achieve as it grows. These graphics represent a quantum leap forward in the art of planning regulation, and demonstrate the potential contribution of "architect/planners" in helping towns shape their future development. *Source:* Nelessen Associates.

homes. In most rural counties, low-density single-use zoning necessitates amending the existing zoning and comprehensive plans, typically a highly charged political process. Such was the case in 1992 when the Caroline County (Virginia) Board of Supervisors was asked by a developer to revise the current land-use policy and regulations to allow the large, mixed-use Haymount project to be approved. Because of its scale and the substantial density increases requested, this DPZ-designed new town of 4,000 homes and 750,000 sq. ft. of retail, office, and warehouse space sharply divided residents in this rural county, located at the terminus of a new commuter rail line to Washington, DC.

Without discussing the specific merits of the case (and they were numerous), it is important to note that rural and suburbanizing counties are generally unprepared for any large-scale proposals, as their planning and zoning documents are geared for a conventional "suburban sprawl" pattern of low-density, disconnected single-use subdivisions, shopping centers, office parks, and so forth. Any proposal to follow more historic patterns of compact neighborhoods surrounding mixed-use centers is bound to trigger a major re-evaluation of existing plans and ordinances, especially when coupled with a density increase.

Local governments should anticipate such proposals, prepare for them in a rational manner, and perhaps even encourage them as a desirable alternative (within reasonable density limits, based upon carrying capacities and service thresholds). Appropriate locations should be designated in official planning and regulatory documents to guide progressive developers to areas that make sense from the standpoint of infrastructure provision, service delivery, and natural resource management. Such documents should also be updated as frequently as necessary to account for changes in infrastructure, such as new road or rail links, increased or declining capacity in water and sewerage, technological alternatives to public water and sewer, and so forth.

However, land-use planning often involves many political considerations and, regardless how thorough or rational a policy, major development decisions are usually very controversial. Ironically, the Haymount project was ultimately approved for the wrong reasons: the councillor who cast the deciding vote stated that his support of the controversial project was based upon the construction jobs it would generate, a criterion that a poorly designed proposal could have as easily met.

Even in the United Kingdom, where the land-use regulatory process is highly professional and structured, one county's recent experience with encouraging planned villages has been disheartening. In its official long-range plan, Cambridgeshire formally acknowledged the need for and desirability of accommodating about 2,500 new residents in a planned village. Locational criteria were established and ten proposals were submitted over the course of the last decade. All ten met the locational criteria and were also well-designed internally. However, abuttors and neighbors objected so vociferously to each one that all ten proposals were reviewed and ultimately rejected by the relevant cabinet minister in London. (Under the British system, large-scale developments are subject to examination by the central government, not unlike the state-level review processes for similar kinds of projects in Maine and Vermont, for example.) This experience prompted observers such as Martin Shaw, director of planning and transportation in the neighboring county of Norfolk, to describe such extreme opposition with a new acronym for local protests that exceed normal NIMBYism: "BANANA," standing for "Build Absolutely Nothing Anywhere Near Anybody".

It is sadly true that large-scale proposals offer, on the one hand, the best possibility for good site design (featuring compact neighborhoods, traditional mixed-use centers, and significant open space setasides) and, on the other hand, the greatest potential for organized opposition. Planners at all levels (including citizens serving on local boards or commissions) should become vocal advocates of planned growth coupled with planned conservation. The alternative is too easy, and it is too dismal to contemplate: sitting back and letting developments take the course of least resistance, through a framework of conventional codes that will ultimately produce endless acres of low-density, single-use subdivisions, shopping centers, and office parks, each proposed and approved independently of the others, eventually spreading over square mile after square mile of countryside that today offers the potential for more imaginative ways to accommodate inevitable growth.

Having said this, it is important to advise readers that sometimes self-styled "neo-traditional planned developments" contain serious flaws. Such was the case recently in Orange County, North Carolina, where a real-estate promoter requested a 67 percent increase in density for a suburban golf course development that contained a high-density core with a rectilinear street layout. Apart from relatively insignificant slivers of lawn and woods between development areas, the much-touted "60 percent open space" was found, upon deeper examination, to consist of extensive wetlands, numerous detention basins, steep slopes, a major high-tension line right-of-way, eighteen holes of golf course, and parking for the clubhouse (in addition to a comparatively remote corner of the property set aside to meet statutory 5 percent parkland dedication requirements in the local regulations). Scores of local citizens turned out to criticize the requested density increase, reminding officials that such bonuses are normally offered as an incentive to encourage developers to preserve natural areas that would ordinarily be built upon. (Practical techniques enabling local governments to require more compact development patterns, with significant open space in addition to unbuildable areas, are discussed in Chapter 15.)

INITIATING BETTER DESIGN SOLUTIONS

The Appendix item by Richard Calderon contains an excellent example of a traditionally designed development alternative, generated by the Loudoun County planning staff to help a developer produce an improved arrangement of buildings and streets, conforming with newly adopted village and hamlet design standards. Thoughtfully conceived, it eliminates cul-de-sacs, extends the modified grid pattern with new slightly curving streets aligned to take advantage of good views (toward historic buildings or outward to the mountains), and creates a nicely proportioned and handsomely sited "green" or "common."

Although it is unfortunately quite rare that members of county or township planning staffs are encouraged—or even allowed—to suggest specific design solutions, such involvement should be promoted if the present "low common denominator" standard of development that confronts many small communities is to be substantially improved within the foreseeable future. The view is often expressed that the proper function of the public sector should be limited to reviewing proposals drawn up by developers. However, some developers would welcome specific guidance early in the process, such as at a preapplication conceptual sketch plan stage. That would be an appropriate moment for the public-sector representatives to state clearly what they would like to see regarding street connections, open space provision, and other key elements.

Municipal officials with conservative instincts concerning the appropriate role of local governments in this process would do well to ponder the historic precedents in countless locations around the country, where the town fathers exercised considerably greater influence over the resultant development pattern than most officials would ever dream of attempting today. Bozeman, Montana, is a fairly typical example of a nineteenth-century municipality that had a far clearer idea of what it wanted to become than many towns now have regarding their own future. The most striking features of the 1898 bird's-eye lithograph of Bozeman (see Figure 3–11) are the laying out of the street pattern decades before it was filled in, and the advance provision of a fairly major park to serve a then-unbuilt section of town. Until about 60 years ago, it was not uncommon for town plans to include an "official map" showing the locations of at least the major new connecting streets. This sort of forward thinking should be resumed, and be supplemented by another overlay map showing all the natural areas to be protected as permanent open space preserves, linked together with trails and green corridors. Such open spaces could be easily and inexpensively designated by requiring new development to follow traditional princi-

Figure 3–11. 1898 bird's-eye perspective of Bozeman, Montana, showing future streets and park locations as envisioned by the city fathers, and as built by their successors. This early lithograph contains an implicit challenge to planners and municipal leaders in similar small towns around the country today: to match their foresight and their will to provide open space in traditionally scaled neighborhoods.

ples of compact design, with the land thus saved placed under conservation easements to create a network of natural areas and parklands for both formal and informal recreation. These concepts are treated more fully in the chapters in Part III dealing with street standards, open space development design, and greenways.

At the village level, much could be done to encourage (or require) more traditionally scaled streets and lot layouts, together with formal and informal open spaces. Figure 3–12 compares two alternative conceptual plans for extending a nineteenth-century mill village in Sutton, Massachusetts, prepared by the Center for Rural Massachusetts for the Blackstone River Valley National Heritage Corridor Commission, a branch of the National Park Service that is promoting development design standards appropriate to the local historic pattern. On the left is a conventional suburban layout, contrasted with a more imaginative design on the right, where nearly all the lots

either face onto a common or back up to a playing field.

Designs recently completed for a proposed extension to the Annandale Village in New Jersey's Clinton Township illustrate the possibilities for integrating new development with historic neighborhood patterns. Rather than creating separate suburban development "pods" for conventional subdivisions, shopping centers, and office parks, the plan integrates all these uses with an interconnected, asymmetrical grid street network, locating many homes within easy walking distance of town center shops and civic functions (including a new community center), a formal green, a small public park in the Olmsted style, and the railway station. Grafted onto the edge of Annandale, the new street system was carefully laid out to align with the historic pattern of blocks, also mirroring the village's scale and development densities. Residential densities vary in intensity, with 40 townhouses and 141 single-family homes on

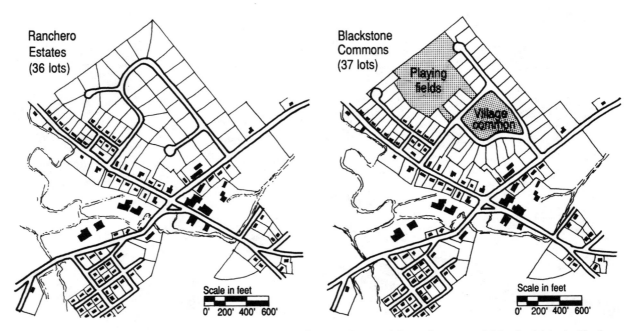

Figure 3–12. Two alternatives for expanding a mill village in Sutton, Massachusetts, within the historic Blackstone River Valley. Note that one offers both a green and a ballfield, a bonus lot for the developer, and lot dimensions more in keeping with those of the original, adjoining neighborhood. *Source:* Designed by the author for the National Park Service.

smaller lots close to the center, 63 suburban dwellings on somewhat larger lots, and six "country estates" at the far edge (buffering adjacent subdivisions). Together with 35,000 sq. ft. of retail and office space in the new town center, "Annandale North Village," covers 161 acres, and was designed by John Madden of Flemington, New Jersey (who is also preparing architectural drawings to provide consistency of approach within the neo-traditional building style adopted by the developer). (See Figure 3–13.)

Readers who are particularly interested in village design issues are referred to the *Village Planning Handbook* (Bucks County, Pennsylvania, Planning Commission, 1989) and to the American Planning Association's PAS Report No. 430, *Re-Inventing the Village* (Sutro, 1991). Additionally, the thoughtful "Village Design Standards" adopted by Kent County, Maryland, are reproduced in the Appendix.

GETTING STARTED

If you feel that some of the changes that have occurred in your town over the last 10 or 15 years could have been handled better (with the benefit of hindsight), you are not alone. In many cases local land-use regulations were adopted without any clear picture of their ultimate consequences when implemented.

In order to help concerned residents and officials get a better sense of how well existing zoning and subdivision ordinances address community character enhancement, the National Trust for Historic Preservation has issued a small guidebook entitled *Saving Place*. This concise publication provides a list of simple but penetrating questions about local planning and development control practices, which users are encouraged to answer as a means of evaluating the effectiveness of those approaches and mechanisms (Herr, 1991). Longer lists tailored to each of the six New En-

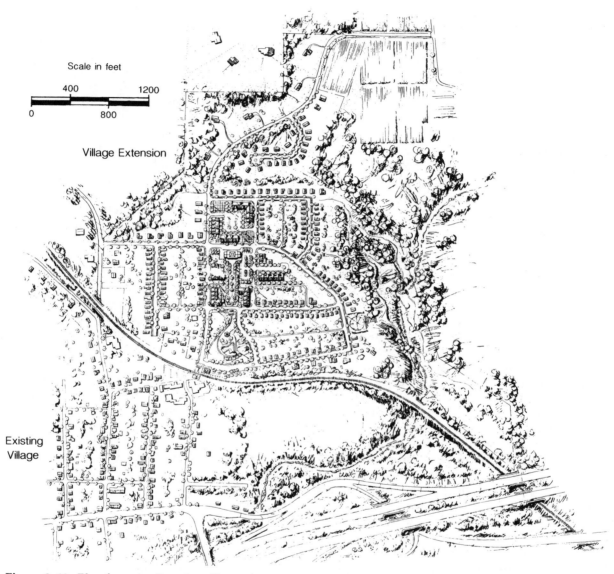

Figure 3–13. Plan for extending the village of Annandale in Clinton Township, New Jersey, in a manner respectful of the locality's traditional form and established pattern of neighborhood lots, streets, and open spaces. *Source:* Madden/Kummer Associates, Flemington, New Jersey.

gland states and New York have also been published by the Trust.

This self-diagnostic exercise, designed by planning consultant Philip Herr, begins with three tasks each resident or official is asked to perform, itemizing:

1. ten things that are most important to the quality of life in their town;
2. the ways that new development could damage each of those ten attributes; and
3. the ways that new development could potentially improve those ten attributes.

One of the strengths of this exercise is how it challenges participants to think both positively and negatively about potential impacts of growth. All too often discussions in small communities are polarized between groups or individuals who tend to view new development as either beneficial or detrimental. Development, if designed sensitively and located appropriately, can certainly complement and enhance the character of small towns, in the same way that much turn-of-the-century development improved the quality of life in many small nineteenth-century villages. The common perception of growth as a generally negative force is understandable in view of the serious damage inflicted upon traditional town character by much of the development that has occurred over the past several decades. But, in most situations, the problem is not with development per se, but rather with its pattern, scale, location, and design, all functions of duly adopted local codes and regulations.

The usual case is that the type and location of development allowed under most local regulations bear absolutely no relationship to the qualities that have made the older parts of the community relatively pleasant places in which to live, work, and shop. This is because local governments in rural areas often operate on shoestring budgets, typically creating their own regulations with volunteers photocopying ordinances from other places without investing sufficient time or resources to find out whether those regulations have produced the type of long-term results that are locally desired. It is probably not an unreasonable guess that most zoning documents in small rural communities are not closely based upon any thoughtfully conceived vision statement of what the people wish their locality to be like in 15 or 20 years. The reality is that most local governments have adopted very conventional regulations (or slight variations thereof) with standards set so low that sprawling subdivisions and roadside strip development have become perfectly legal. (In some cases, however, development standards have been set inappropriately "high," as with requirements for excessively wide, flat streets through new residential areas. More on this in Chapter 11.)

Herr's "Socratic" approach to focusing attention on issues, by posing incisive questions intended to stimulate the thought processes of respondents, is likely to be very effective in motivating residents and officials to get started on improving the ways in which their town conducts "the development business." A dozen of these questions follow.

1. Do controls in village centers allow real compactness by permitting lots and setbacks as small, densities as high, and roads as compact, winding, and steep as those already existing in well-liked areas?

2. Do the combination of public parking provisions and zoning parking requirements allow compact business development by waiving on-site parking in village centers, perhaps using impact fees to help create new municipal parking areas nearby?

3. Do subdivision regulations avoid mandating uniform development in all contexts by having standards that vary for different locations, such as villages, farmlands, and woodlands?

4. Does the town lead the way through centrally locating such public development as town offices, elderly housing, post offices, and recreational facilities, and removing from central areas inappropriate uses, such as public works yards?

5. In outlying areas, does the town strictly limit the extent of business zoning along highways, and impose strict egress and landscaping controls?

6. Do town regulations effectively encourage or require affordable housing support as part of new town development, resulting in such housing in more than a single location?

7. Are there architectural design controls in historic districts, or appearance codes elsewhere?

8. Has the town established site-plan review procedures with approval based upon specific site design and development criteria?

9. Are there scenic road controls protecting trees and stone walls, strict billboard controls, and on-premises sign controls that go beyond numerical rules to deal with design quality?

10. Has the town adopted cluster regulations or similar controls allowing preservation of open space by compact siting of housing, and made it possible for the town to decide where and when cluster development must be used?

11. Has the town more than once appropriated funds for property or property rights acquisition to protect natural or cultural resources?

12. Has the town created mechanisms (such as a community development corporation) to encourage economic development that is compatible with protecting community character?

4

The Aesthetics of Form
in Town Planning:
Learning from the Past

The issue of aesthetics is not as freely discussed in the profession today as it was at the turn of the century, during the "beaux arts" period when the "City Beautiful" movement began to gather momentum.

In the fourth edition of *The Improvement of Towns and Cities, or the Practical Basis of Civic Aesthetics*, published in 1901, Charles Mulford Robinson charged that "We are plodding along. . . , marring with improvements that disfigure, ignoring all teachings of the past, unconscious of all the possibilities of the future." Although many parts of this book are now dated, the above statement is almost timeless: it still rings true with respect to much that is occurring in our small towns today.

If one wishes to be guided by the best of the past, while still incorporating useful—or inevitable—features from the present, it makes sense to begin by analyzing the various components of traditional towns in one's region to determine what makes them especially characteristic of that place. Early in the town planning movement, architects and landscape architects began turning their attention to the question of building form and layout. Although this subject is no longer addressed in most codes or in the standard planning curricula today, the literature in this field offers some choice lessons.

THE UNWINIAN SCHOOL

Perhaps the most famous, if least widely read, volume on this subject is Raymond Unwin's 1909 classic *Town Planning in Practice: An Introduction to the Art of Designing Cities and Suburbs*. The title is well chosen because Unwin clearly approached his subject from an artistic point of view, a perspective that is nearly absent from the profession as it is practiced today. Unwin construed the term "art" in a much broader sense than is usually applied: "the well-doing of what needs doing" (Unwin, 1909). And he set his sights high: "Does the town need a market-place, our rule would teach us to build the best, most convenient, and comely market-place we can design; not to erect a corrugated iron shed. . . . " (which would have wounded rather than heightened civic pride). Robinson reminds us again: "We shall not attain to towns and villages that are beautiful until we learn artistically to plan them."

How many examples of cheap and tacky construction, from fire stations and libraries to shops and roadside eateries, could people enumerate in their towns today? If they haven't actually lost their pride of place, many small towns seem to overlook the importance of good design when reviewing plans for new construction in highly visible locations, such as within central areas and alongside approach roads. To help remedy this situation, county and state planning offices should place greater emphasis on the value of design review in the educational and training materials they make available to local planning officials. An excellent source in this regard is *Appearance Codes for Small Communities* by Peggy Glassford (APA PAS Report No. 379), although its focus is limited to building facades, signage, and landscaping standards.

Unlike most planners today, Unwin and others of his generation stressed the significance of building locations and road arrangements that are also of great importance to the creation of visually interesting town designs. (See Figure 4–1.) While Unwin's work has been criticized by modern traffic engineers for its irregularity and the resultant confusion of traffic movement, it is possible to adapt many of his model intersections to accommodate such concerns. Figure 4–2 includes updated versions of Unwin's original drawings, showing how roadway junctions could be regularized while still retaining the essential visual objective of "closing the view" (arrows indicate view lines).

UNWIN'S RELEVANCE TODAY

Although Unwin's work is dated, and decidedly European and British, his approach has potential value and relevance for American planners and development designers. Much of the highly acclaimed work of Andres Duany and Elizabeth Plater-Zyberk, for example, has its roots in the Unwinian school. Their neo-traditional designs for Seaside, Florida, Kentlands (in Gaithersburg, Maryland, Mashpee, Massachusetts, and Avalon, Florida owe much of their initial inspiration to Unwin, who stressed the importance of town edges and approaches, town centers and enclosed places, the arrangement of roads and intersections, the spacing and placing of buildings and fences, and the harmonious design of buildings (to paraphrase from his chapter headings).

These ideas were much more commonly practiced in the United States 80 years ago than they are today. Perhaps the best sourcebook documenting and illustrating examples of this early plan-

Illus. 182.—Sketch of a road junction similar to 181 D.

Figure 4–1. Townscape sketches by Raymond Unwin, illustrating the importance of curving streets and architectural focal points in terminating vistas. *Source:* Unwin, 1909.

ning movement is *The Anglo-American Suburb* (Stern and Massengale, 1981). Nearly 50 different planned suburbs, most built between 1850 and 1940, are described and illustrated with original drawings and contemporaneous and current photographs. The range encompasses industrial villages, railway, streetcar, subway, and automobile suburbs, as well as resort developments. In his introduction, Stern extols the virtues of pedestrian-scaled, compact development and suggests that, because of their enduring popularity, railway suburbs should become a model for both the redevelopment of blighted and decaying urban areas and also for the development of new "greenfield" sites.

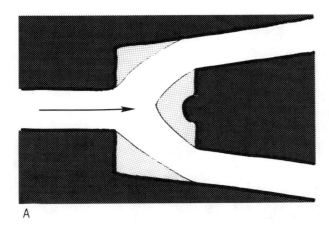

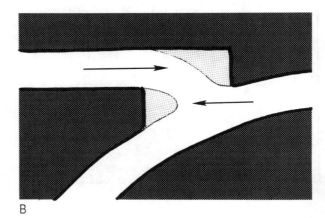

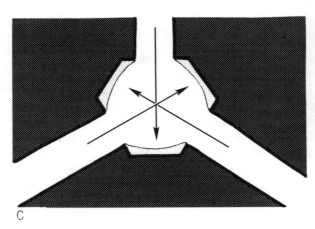

Figure 4–2. Updated version of three street intersection designs by Unwin, showing public open space in front of buildings that "close the view" of approaching traffic.

In this regard, it is encouraging to note that some of the participants in Lancaster County's "Livable Communities Forum" (described in Chapter 3) chose to visit and study the planned community of Wyomissing, Pennsylvania (adjacent to Reading), in order to study the basic principles of good, classic town planning. Built largely between 1896 and 1928, Wyomissing features a full range of land uses, from industrial and commercial to residential and institutional. In addition, its compactly designed residential areas include housing for executives, middle management, and blue-collar workers. Multifamily housing is designed to harmonize with surrounding architecture, and many of the homes (of all price levels) are accessed through rear lanes, with garages in the back garden. The fact that Wyomissing is a highly desirable address in the Reading area speaks well for its ability to compete with newer low-density suburban developments. (See Figure 4–3.)

VILLAGE FORM AND TOWNSCAPE

Another book influencing neo-traditional rural planners is Anthony Sharp's *Anatomy of a Village*.

Figure 4–3. Wyomissing, Pennsylvania, and other planned towns of its era, provide an outdoor laboratory for designers and developers interested in exploring the potential of traditional townscapes. Training courses for professional and lay planners should include field trips to such planning landmarks, which could not be built in most jurisdictions today because they do not conform with current zoning ordinances (whose standards everyone should question).

What Sharp had to say in 1946 still holds true for designers of small developments in the countryside. Unlike the more urban street layouts, Sharp notes that village streets are usually not very straight. The careful use of both gentle curves and sharp turns serve to create enclosed space: "a way in and a way out, and not merely an incident on the roadside," as so many of our newer residential and commercial "centers" seem to be.

Also important to Sharp was the use of terminal vista points, wherein buildings or groups of buildings "may be so situated as to give an emphasis, a 'punctuation' to one or more points." (Robinson made the point more prosaically back in 1901, when he said that "Unless there be plainly visible an eminence, or and architectural or sculptural mass, at the end of a street, distance becomes only wearisome.")

Sharp commended the judicious use of squares, greens, and commons (even broad, paved "places") where incoming roads are staggered to prevent clear views straight through these central areas, which "thereby attain the stature of being something of a local climax." Likewise, views out are limited, or at least framed by buildings or trees, "instead of trailing out down the long vanishing perspective of a straight road." He warned against making the greens so large that they reduce the surrounding buildings to insignificance, and emphasized that these areas not simply be "spaces," but "enclosed spaces." He also cautioned against the tendency to beautify and formalize such areas, stressing their essential quality of "unconscious and unsophisticated simplicity." In order to retain these qualities he discouraged the installation of curbing around the edges of central greens and advocated informal plantings rather than "flowerbeds and rockeries." Were he alive today it is likely he would endorse the use of native species of shade trees, woody plants, and perennial wildflowers, provided they were not too formally laid out. In his view, larger settlements (i.e., towns and cities) were the appropriate locations for more regular and formal treatment of public spaces.

A different perspective can be gained from Gordon Cullen's *Townscape*. It is impossible in this brief sketch to do justice to this comprehensive and extensively illustrated treatise. What fol-lows, however, are highlights of Cullen's work, accompanied by photos from traditional towns in this country (which may be more useful to readers than his British and European examples).

Central to Cullen's work is the notion that "there is an *art of relationship* just as there is an art of architecture. Its purpose is to take all the elements that go to create the environment: buildings, trees, nature, water, traffic, advertisements and so on, and to weave them together in such a way that drama is released" (Cullen, 1961). This is the interface between the professions of town planning and architecture as they are typically practiced today, and clearly neither profession has shown much inclination to transcend its normal bounds and engage the critical issues that lie exactly between them. Architects are paid to design buildings or, at most, "complexes"; planners typically concern themselves with land uses and regulations pertaining to drainage, traffic, parking, and similar but rather mundane issues. Landscape architects sometimes play a role in between.

Cullen articulates three broad ways of experiencing traditional towns: serial vision, human position in relation to its surroundings, and content/fabric. The concept of serial vision refers to "a series of revelations" as one walks or drives slowly through the streets of a town. Key here are notions of the "existing view" and the "emerging view." Long, straight streets produce little of visual interest: "the initial view is soon digested and becomes monotonous." People respond to contrasting elements, which help towns "come alive through the drama of juxtaposition." The concept of serial vision is illustrated by Figure 4–4, streetscape photographs taken in Jim Thorpe, Pennsylvania.

Cullen's second concept, concerning "place," or the position of the body in its environment, refers to one's feeling that he or she is outside, entering, or inside a space that is enclosed, or a space that lies above or below the surrounding land. The idea of a "hereness" and a "thereness" is fundamental to this experience. Said succinctly, "the typical town is not a pattern of streets but a sequence of spaces created by buildings." (See the case example of The Village Commons in South Hadley, Massachusetts, illustrated in Chapter 21, for an example of this point.)

Figure 4–4. These photographs show part of the visual sequence regularly experienced by drivers and pedestrians as they move through the curving streetscape of Jim Thorpe, Pennsylvania, illustrating Gordon Cullen's principle of "serial vision." This main street is laid out in an essentially east-west manner and its gentle curves, caused by topographic constraints, are just enough to close the view at a half dozen points along its 2,500-foot length. It is not accidental that large public and institutional buildings, such as churches and the county courthouse, were built at locations where they would be visually prominent and form terminal vistas.

Cullen's third concept, concerning the fabric of townscapes, is perhaps the most obvious: the visual importance of colors, textures, scale, and detail elements (such as fences, railings, trees, steps, etc.). These elements have long been the domain of architects and landscape architects, and to a lesser extent of professional planners. Hopefully this situation will change, with more planners and their constituents insisting that greater attention be paid to such issues and features, because the ultimate success or failure of many projects (in terms of how the average townsperson feels about them) is definitely affected by details such as these. A simple railing and a line of shade trees, a serpentine brick wall, or even a thick hedge, for example, between a sidewalk and a parking lot, can make a world of difference. The extra cost involved in doing a project properly, especially when viewed over the longer term, is insignificant compared with the improvement in its final appearance, which is exactly what towns have to live with for decades thereafter.

Inscribed above the entrance to every town hall in the country should be the words of Justice Douglas in the landmark 1954 U.S. Supreme Court decision *Berman* v. *Parker:* "It is within the power of the legislature to determine that the community should be beautiful as well as healthy" (348 U.S. 26). This majority opinion also held that "the concept of the public welfare is broad and inclusive. . . . The values it represents are spiritual as well as physical, aesthetic as well as monetary." This ruling has never been overturned, or even substantially altered, by subsequent decisions. Significantly, this case did not involve a designated historic district or other such "special place"; rather, it concerned a rather average and run-down part of Washington, DC, which had been slated for comprehensive urban redevelopment. Although case law in some states might impose greater restrictions on the use of aesthetic considerations as a principal justification for codes governing the siting and exterior appearance of buildings, the legitimacy of such approaches is gaining widespread acceptance. Their potential role in future town planning efforts should not be discounted or underestimated. (See Figure 4–5.)

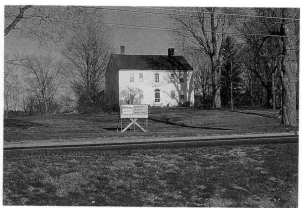

Figure 4–5. Civic pride and civic beauty go hand-in-hand in Woodstock, Vermont, where there is broad agreement about the benefits of protecting the common townscape heritage.

Figure 4–6. This archival photograph from Belchertown, Massachusetts, illustrates the fragility of the common townscape that many local residents simply take for granted . . . until the appearance of signs like this one ("Coming Soon—Mini-Mall"). Efforts to persuade the developer to expand and reuse the historic building to meet contemporary business needs failed, in spite of numerous local examples where that kind of sensitive approach had been successfully implemented. This house and all the tall maples have been replaced by a standard McDonald's restaurant.

If Cullen's approach can be summed up in a single phrase it might be *"interplay within a commonly accepted framework."* He acknowledged the need for overall agreement upon basics, but stressed that it is also essential to "manipulate the nuances of scale and style, of texture and color and of character and individuality, juxtaposing them in order to create collective benefits." Of course, there is danger at both ends of the spectrum: rigidity produces conformity and anarchy leads to chaos. However, the almost complete absence of appearance codes at the local level place the vast majority of municipalities in a position of "design anarchy." In their unwillingness to accept collective responsibility for the public appearance of new development, local officials in many small towns have contributed to the visually chaotic intrusions that have disfigured these communities and stripped them of much of their traditional character. (See Figure 4–6.)

Nothing would be more effective in correcting this current imbalance than a ground swell of public support to show local officials that their constituents are indeed concerned about the way new development fits into their towns. (See Figures 4–7 and 4–8.) As the saying goes, "When the people lead, the leaders will follow."

TIMELESS PRINCIPLES

The final book highlighted here was inspired by a profound dissatisfaction with the impact produced by typical modern infill buildings located in traditional towns and cities. In 1984, when he described the proposed extension of the National Gallery in London as "a monstrous carbuncle on the face of a much-loved and elegant friend," Prince Charles predictably drew heavy fire from the architectural establishment. However, he was greatly heartened by a spontaneous outpouring of public sentiment applauding his outspokenness. Over the next few years, Charles collected more material and produced a TV film and a book, *A Vision of Britain*, to document the problem, to publicize recent examples of good development design, and to offer a set of principles to help future projects fit more harmoniously into their surroundings. Sensing the public mood, a growing number of local officials and property devel-

Figure 4–7. When local residents of Honeoye Falls, New York, let their bank know how upset they were about the proposal to build a boxy modern branch "worthy of a second-rate shopping center" in the heart of their historic village, a different architect was commissioned to produce a design based on the Greek Revival style prevalent in the area.

Figure 4–8. Even large corporations have "fall back" positions for accommodating aesthetic controls contained in local appearance codes. This 7-11 convenience store in Sanibel, Florida, was designed in the "Florida cracker" tradition, with standing-seam roofing and a long veranda. In addition, all landscaping was required to be selected from the lengthy list of native species contained in the Sanibel ordinance.

opers have responded positively to the points raised in these works.

Although Charles' focus was on architecture and architects, much of his thinking is applicable to town planning. Quoted below is a selective condensation of his remarks of relevance to both lay and professional planners.

On "Place": "We must respect the land. . . . The landscape is the setting. . . . New buildings can be intrusive or they can be designed and sited so that they fit in. . . . It is seldom enough to disguise them by planting. . . . Often large buildings can be separated into elements which will humanize the scale. . . . If new buildings avoid sprawl and are grouped together more of the landscape can be preserved."

On "Scale": "Buildings must relate first of all to human proportions and then respect the scale of the buildings around them. . . . Almost all our towns have been spoiled by casually placed over-sized buildings of little distinction, carrying no civic meaning."

On "Harmony": "Harmony is the playing together of the parts. . . . All the participants need to understand the basic rules and traditions."

On "Enclosure": Enclosure "is an elementary idea with a thousand variants, and can be appreciated at every level of building. . . . Cohesion, continuity and enclosure produce a kind of magic . . . . The application of these ideas makes a place unique. . . . A community spirit is born far more easily in a well-formed square or courtyard than in a random scattering of developers' plots."

On "Community": "People are not there to be planned for; they are to be worked with. . . . Planning and architecture are much too important to be left to the professionals."

Three final quotations from the book round out this section:
• "Discriminating observation of the past must be the inspiration for the future."
• "Attention to detail and to human scale creates that elusive quality of character."
• "Use a familiar language to create an expression of harmony and proportion."

DESIGN AWARENESS INITIATIVES

Although no one in this country has raised design issues to such a prominent level of discussion, encouraging new initiatives from professional groups are beginning to focus more attention on townscape concerns. In Massachusetts, the state chapter of the AIA (known as the Boston Society of Architects) has created a traveling slide show that blends neo-traditionalism with the open space development concepts portrayed in *Dealing with Change in the Connecticut River Valley*, published in 1988 by the Center for Rural Massachusetts (Yaro, Arendt, Dodson, and Brabec, 1988). This effort continues in the tradition of the Governor's Design Awards Program in the Bay State, which gave 57 awards in five regions during the 1980s, plus 14 additional awards for projects deemed worthy of statewide recognition.

Until state budget cuts forced its elimination, the Massachusetts Council for the Arts and Humanities had administered a "Rural Design Assistance Program," which awarded grants to small towns (under 15,000 population) to engage in town planning or project implementation efforts specifically concerned with design issues. Projects included revising existing codes dealing with street width and building setbacks, designs for the creation of new mixed-use "centers," as well as support for the "Places of the Heart" project described in Chapter 3. The council also funded the production of a *Primer on Design*, and a similar handbook tailored to the needs of Maine communities was recently issued by the Design Arts Project at the University of Southern Maine's New England Studies Program, funded by a grant from the state humanities council (Craighead, 1991).

THE COMMON TOWNSCAPE

One of the more comprehensive studies of traditional towns is *Vermont Townscape* (Williams, Kellogg, and Lavigne, 1987). In their survey work of 30 towns, the authors looked for recurring elements that by their frequency and repetition defined the essence of community character. Focusing upon town centers, which provide both a sense of identity and a central point for interaction, the authors identified ten typical amenity characteristics commonly shared by the majority of study towns. These ten characteristics, recounted briefly below, demonstrate once again the often-subtle features that, in unison, are essential to a town's identity and sense of place.

1. *Institutional Buildings Around a Town Common.* Of the 23 towns with central commons, nearly all the greens were surrounded by homes and churches, half had an inn or minor business establishment, and lesser numbers supported a school, library, post office, or town hall. This mixture of uses is generally quite harmonious, and makes these centers actively used. The commons in the study towns ranged from a fraction of an acre up to 7.5 acres, but by far the most typical area was one to two acres. Figure 4–9 shows the various sizes and shapes of greens in 14 towns and provides a useful frame of reference for new projects, residential, offices, or shops.

2. *Human Scale.* Most buildings (other than the large institutional ones, which properly dominate) are 1½ to 2½ stories in height, and not wider than a large house.

3. *High Quality of Architecture.* Although the buildings represent a very wide range of nineteenth-century styles, they tend to be well-crafted, traditional, and appealing to the average person. Most are described as having lots of "personality."

4. *No Heavy Traffic.* Remote locations, bypasses, or other vehicular routing arrangements shelter most of the centers from heavy through traffic.

5. *Limited Commercial Facilities.* These rural towns tend to be small, with few retail stores. Incompatibility is a typical problem only with gas stations, which are exceptionally intrusive. Other businesses tend not to be set so far back with front parking; their customers park along the curb or to the side or rear.

6. *Landscaping.* The presence of mature deciduous shade trees is a *major* amenity in these town centers, although they are often overlooked or taken for granted. Systematic planting of a variety of younger specimen trees is absolutely essential for long-term character preservation, so that the younger trees may grow larger as the older trees gradually die off.

7. *No Incompatible Architecture.* Buildings of different historic styles manage to harmonize due to their similar scale, roof shapes, gable orientation, and texture (typically wooden clapboards or red brick).

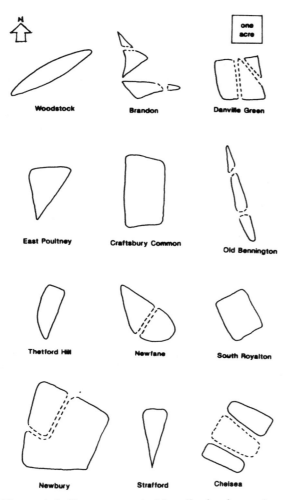

Figure 4–9. Town greens in New England vary in both shape and scale, although their average size is about two acres, with irregular configurations—facts that should be borne in mind by development designers today. *Source:* Williams et al., 1987.

8. *A Sense of Enclosure.* Space is well-defined in most of the study towns, with buildings and shade trees lining the streets and the commons.
9. *A Lack of Clutter.* Apart from overhead wires and numerous traffic signs, these towns have escaped the detritus found in most larger settlements, where tall business signs tower over juniper plantings in nearly treeless townscapes.

10. *Special Features.* In this category are barns, carriage houses, front porches, recessed balconies, monuments, bandstands, gazebos, park benches, and occasionally a small pond or a fountain.

A final amenity feature of the traditional Vermont town is its clearly defined outer edge, a fragile element whose importance is generally underestimated, and whose future is threatened by most conventional zoning ordinances that designate such areas for increasingly long strips of roadside businesses (see Chapter 9 for details on handling retail development pressures).

HAMLET DESIGN CRITERIA

Several sets of "preferred characteristics" for new development have been suggested by Anton Nelessen, based upon the results he obtained from the visual preference surveys he has conducted in small rural towns in New Jersey (described in Chapter 2). These results formed the basis of several hypothetical three-dimensional hamlet and village development models. They also proved useful in generating alternative design solutions for an infill project where the developer and township officials had stalemated in court over a conventional layout that was unacceptable to the municipality.

The development redesign mentioned above occurred in Dover Township, New Jersey, on a small 5.7 acre site that also included steep slopes and wetlands. Although it was located in a traditional neighborhood of single-family homes, the parcel was zoned for multifamily units, and the developer submitted a plan that was consistent with zoning but entirely inconsistent with what the neighborhood wanted to see on the property. When the municipality decided to rezone the tract the developer sued, and Nelessen was eventually consulted for help. As the Figure 4–10 illustrates, the contrast could hardly be greater between the conventional and the neo-traditional approach. Yet the latter provided an overall gross density acceptable to the developer, while meeting the public's demand that this infill project fit into the grain and texture of the surrounding neighborhood, with smaller structures and a proper streetscape, instead of mammoth buildings facing onto large expanses of asphalt.

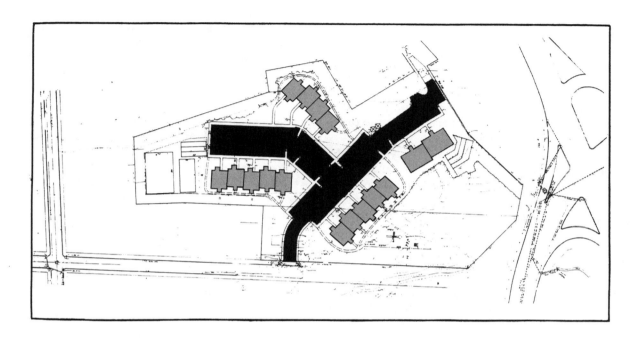

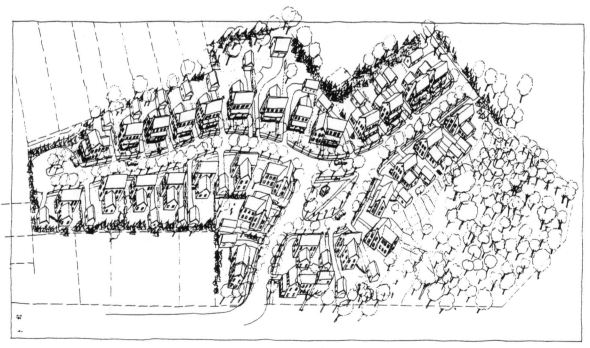

Figure 4–10. Conventional plan for moderate-density residential development in Dover, New Jersey, with attached units arranged around a large asphalt parking lot, contrasted with a more traditional alternative providing the same number of dwelling units in a housing pattern and density similar to the nineteenth-century neighborhood illustrated in Figure 1–2. *Source:* Nelessen Associates.

The developer in this case was convinced to accept Nelessen's plan, in part because he was anxious to cut his legal costs and proceed with the project. But local officials who are serious about ensuring that new development will harmonize with the character of their towns should consider enacting design *requirements* based upon the principles of traditional town design.

The issue is not whether one may mandate certain standards; municipalities do that already. Unfortunately, the model that is incorporated into their design standards for subdivisions, apartment complexes, shopping areas, and new streets tends to be thoroughly suburban. The real issue, then, is whether the standards ought to be in line with what towns are all about in the first place.

In an interesting and instructive postscript to the above example, the Nelessen plan to which the developer agreed was rejected by the municipal engineer, who demanded certain "improvements" before he could sign off on it. Some of the very features that differentiated the neo-traditional alternative plan from the standard suburban subdivision design were ones that the engineer found objectionable because they did not meet the letter of his code. As a result of his intervention, the central green in the main intersection was eliminated, the small treed island in the cul-de-sac was removed, and the street curve radii were lengthened to make the curve more gradual.

All of these changes were ordered to make the plan fit the engineering manual. It did not matter to this official that the engineering criteria in his manual were really only applicable to major streets with larger traffic volumes and higher design speeds. It is usually useless to argue logic in such cases. Nelessen's staff have observed that, in their experience, township engineers in the older suburban communities are generally more accommodating and reasonable than those in the newer developing townships. This is perhaps because engineers in the older communities may realize that many current street design standards are excessive and unnecessary, based upon their first-hand experience in dealing with narrower streets, smaller curve radii, and more modest cul-de-sacs. In the Dover Township example, the standards

themselves were clearly inappropriate to the situation at hand, and their revision is what was really needed. (The issue of inappropriate street design standards is addressed in Chapter 11, where a reappraisal of conventional criteria by the American Society of Civil Engineers is cited.)

Nelessen's survey-based standards for village streets, residential areas, retail commercial districts, and hamlets are summarized below:

Village Streets
• two travel lanes, each 10-feet wide
• indirect travel routes to slow speeds
• curbside parallel parking for visitors
• street trees spaced at 20-foot intervals
• relatively short and narrow streets to define "spaces and places"
• low traffic volume (250–500 ADT)
• low speed limit (25 mph)

Residential Areas
• modest front yard setbacks (15–20 feet)
• fences or hedges 2.5 to 3.5 feet high to define front yard from sidewalk
• tree-planting strips between sidewalk and curbing
• minimum roof pitch 8:12, dormers preferred
• porches on 10 to 50 percent of front facades
• traditional cladding colors and materials
• window proportions tall and narrow
• garage or parking located at rear of lot
• housefronts facing the street
• main floor at or above grade

Retail Areas
• modest-sized stores
• spacious sidewalks 10 to 14-feet wide, with texture or pattern (brick, slate, etc.)
• mixed uses with one or two floors of offices or flats above the shops
• storefront awnings
• streetlamps of interesting design and in scale with pedestrian area standards
• discreet signage, maximum 8 percent of facade area
• shade trees on both sides of street
• curbside parallel and rear parking
• exteriors of brick, stone, or clapboard
• building massing to produce a fine grain of visually smaller, discrete units

For his design purposes, Nelessen defines a hamlet as having up to 40 building units, arranged in a traditional manner. His proposed *hamlet design principles* are as follows:

• gross residential density of two dwelling units per acre

• open space totaling 50 percent, including a small common and an encircling greenbelt onto which 80 percent of homes abut

• commons fronted by a limited number of buildings devoted to commercial, institutional, or mixed uses

• housing mix predominantly single-family with some semidetached units

• modest 10 to 20 foot front setbacks for homes

• nonuniform lot widths, areas, shapes for variety

• rear garages or parking

• common building design language governing massing, shapes, forms, materials, window arrangements, "creating continuity within each grouping of units"

THE "LAND-USE FORUM" PROCESS IN NEW JERSEY

Similar design results are being achieved by another New Jersey planner, Karl Kehde, who is working under the sponsorship of the Association of New Jersey Environmental Commissions (ANJEC) to organize a series of "Land-Use Forums." Kehde places heavy emphasis on citizen involvement: his forums are as important for the educational experience of participants as they are for the finished product. In other words, the discussion and conflict-resolution process is a very significant part of this process. The forums bring together residents, local officials, and the developer to creatively design a layout of streets, buildings, and open space that meets both the developer's and the community's needs, typically applied to site-specific development proposals. Kehde is also beginning to apply this approach on a town-wide basis. Like Nelessen, he uses small models that are arranged by forum participants on top of a large-scale aerial photograph. A manual describing how to initiate a forum process, as well as an ordinance

authorizing the forum process and "flexibility in the configuration of open space, recreational facilities, housing types and other land uses" is available from ANJEC (Smith and Kehde, 1991).

SUBDIVISIONS OF THE FUTURE

The term "subdivision" is so ensconced in our language we rarely stop to think how appropriate it is: subdivision emphasizes the fragmentation of land, rather than the creation of a proper neighborhood of homes and relationships. What people yearn for these days is not another wave of "real estate developments," but rather the chance to live in a real human settlement with a sense of place and a sense of belonging. Development based upon the principles of traditional streets, informal outdoor recreational amenities, open space preservation, and the pedestrian scale of the classic American small town is often criticized by conventional developers as having nostalgic value but very little market appeal.

Underlying this criticism is the biased assumption that people will not be willing to pay as much for a home located on a more compact lot. (Similar thinking in the 1970s caused Detroit to ignore the emerging demand for smaller cars, which they mistakenly equated with reduced prices and lower profit margins.) Unfortunately, this conventional thinking misses the essential point: higher quality design and greater amenity provision can counterbalance—or outweigh—the effects of lesser quantity. Furthermore, the quantity (lot size) argument is really a red herring because it discounts the value and benefits of the preserved open space provided by the land not consumed for houselots and streets. The results of a comprehensive study documenting the faster appreciation rates of clustered single-family homes in an "open space development," compared with a standard-lot development of the same era and overall average density in Amherst, Massachusetts, is described in Chapter 14, "Encouraging Open Space Design." Just as consumers will seek out and sometimes pay more for smaller cars that are well-engineered and carefully assembled, so too will they favorably respond to real estate marketing strategies that emphasize the tangible and intangible benefits of living in a well-designed subdivision where significant open space has been preserved and where certain basic recreational amenities have been provided.

Despite conventional thinking, a growing number of neo-traditional developments are being planned and built, and these are based upon "two clear and related premises: 1) the layout of the land is as important as the layout of the houses; and 2) the social dimensions of life are as important as the physical ones" (Williams, 1991). After all, a neighborhood should consist of more than merely houselots and streets, but, unfortunately, that is the legacy of most postwar suburban development—interspersed with isolated shopping centers and office parks. For far too long, planners have been content with approving subdivisions where the only formal considerations have been for such mundane (but admittedly important) items as drainage, soil suitability, traffic, and emergency vehicle access. Consider the standards typically employed by the overwhelming number of small-town planning boards, and it is difficult to escape the conclusion that the present system treats new development as essentially "isolated structures connected by roads, pipes, and wires" (Williams, ibid). We have attended reasonably well to a large number of objective physical needs, but where is there anything to nourish the spirit, any recognition that human beings need more than buildings, streets, and drains? One wonders if town planning as a profession has lost its soul, and forgotten the values and high aspirations that characterized many of its early proponents.

Noticeably absent from codes—or even the orientation—of most local planning boards are any standards for pedestrian-scaled design, significant open space setasides, linkages, critical minimum densities, public amenity provision (or site dedication), and even a modest mixture of housing types or related land uses. Ironically, the lasting legacy of four decades of building undifferentiated suburban sprawl can make it easier in some ways to effect more creative solutions, for the innovative developers will be offering something unique, special, and in tune with the deeply felt (but not always clearly articulated) desires of a growing number of home buyers. Insofar as their needs are not being met in the conventional marketplace, more visionary entrepreneurs will reap the coming harvest.

Harold Williams of the Rensselaerville Institute has articulated nine organizing principles for "those who envision settlements as more than subdivisions." Presented below with some further elaboration, these could become a credo for professional planners, volunteer board members, site designers, and developers.

"Define public space clearly and with a purpose." Public spaces, whether highly developed (squares, playing fields) or primarily natural (trail systems) should be treated as both visual and physical focal points around which streets and building lots are arranged. Instead of being the leftover bits of land (if any is provided at all), they could be consciously and deliberately planned from the very beginning, as the critically important value-adding elements they really are. The opportunity to protect scenic views and link such areas with neighborhoods, formal centers, and with each other is greatest at this formative stage. (See Figure 4–11.)

Figure 4–11. The provision of public open space, like this common in Rochester, Vermont, was one of the central organizing principles followed by those who laid out many of this country's older settlements, a beneficial precedent that could continue to influence the design of subdivisions and shopping centers if today's codes were revised to require such basic concepts of townscape.

"Focus on the core rather than on the boundary." The importance of core areas serving as centers of gravity to draw people together, such as parkland, bodies of water, and neighborhood businesses, cannot be overstated. Without them, convenient opportunities for residents to interact casually are severely reduced. (See Figure 4–12.)

"Use order rather than repetition." The neat ordering of townscape elements creates a sense of cohesion even when the individual elements themselves are far from identical. Rectilinear streets lined with shade trees and front yards bordered by white picket fences are some typical elements. (See Figure 4–13.)

"Use human proportion." Whether it be sidewalk-to-porch distances that allow casual conversation without raised voices, or pedestrian courtyards and passageways within shopping areas, it is important to design at a scale comfortable for people to be in and to use. (See Figure 4–14.)

"Encourage walking rather than riding." Footpaths and connecting streets allow people to get around more easily on foot, whether in their own neighborhood or in a central mixed-use district. (See Figure 4–15.)

"Encourage a range of residents rather than only one type." A variety of house and lot dimensions al-

Figure 4–13. The trees that line the older streets of Honeoye Falls, New York, provide an orderly edge to these long "outdoor rooms," and also buffer pedestrians and homes from vehicular traffic.

Figure 4–12. Basic open space with simple, low-maintenance elements such as grass and trees provide the common ground on which neighbors meet casually, recreate, and sometimes congregate for special events, such as the annual community picnic and foot races on the green in South Amherst, Massachusetts.

lows people to remain in their neighborhood as their housing needs change with family sizes. "Echo" housing and accessory apartments (discussed in Chapter 10) offer opportunities for young couples and the elderly to have independent living quarters, and provide extra income for the owners of the main house. (See Figure 4–16.)

"Use housing shapes and styles that connote small towns and not spreading suburb." Homes should generally face their narrow (gable) end toward the street or be squarish in plan with hipped roofs. Narrower lot frontages (50 to 60 feet) make it easier to get to know and visit neighbors 10 to 15 houses away. Long roof ridgelines parallel to the roadway are expansive and land-consumptive,

Figure 4–14. This quiet street in Essex, New York, is lined with homes set back modestly from the pavement, with well-tended dooryard gardens and an occasional picket fence. The atmosphere is low-key and the scale is friendly, with dimensions just about perfect for striking up casual conversations with passing pedestrians or neighbors.

Figure 4–15. This footpath links two subdivisions in Tredyffrin Township, Pennsylvania, crossing a small creek via a footbridge built by Eagle Scouts. Without such open space and the informal connections it makes possible, there would probably be less neighborhood spirit and fewer community projects. (In this case, much of the land was donated by the subdivider to the Open Land Conservancy, a local land trust in Paoli, Pennsylvania.)

requiring wider lots. Garages can often be located at the rear of the lot. (See Figure 4–17.)

"Encourage a mix of activities rather than a purely residential land-use." Control techniques, such as "good neighbor performance standards," can reduce potential disturbances from nearby small businesses. Small day-care centers, home occupations, churches, and recreational facilities are usually appropriate complements to residential uses. (See Figure 4–18.)

"Fit within the environment rather than on top of it." New development can be designed to nestle into rather than to intrude upon its natural setting. Scenic views both into and out from the property can be protected if this criterion is one that site designers are required to use. (See Figure 4–19.)

By way of closing this section on the future form of subdivisions designed as settlements for living and interacting, a final observation on the scale, arrangement, and patterns found in traditional towns is appropriate: "It is the proportion of the buildings in their relationship to each other, to nature, and to human activity which is impressive" (Williams, ibid.). Fortunately what we as planners, developers, and local officials have over-

Figure 4–16. Although the volume of this house in Deerfield, Massachusetts, is large enough to accommodate three dwelling units, its massing would allow it to do so without intruding on the streetscape, or appearing out of character with its village surroundings.

looked or forgotten over the years is easily rediscoverable, and is in fact almost literally under our feet.

Figure 4–17. These new gable-end homes in a rural subdivision outside Chapel Hill, North Carolina, fit comfortably on lots that are narrower than was typical in the area 20 years ago.

Figure 4–19. Tucked down behind a stone wall and a line of trees, these new homes allow the roadside meadow to dominate the view, as experienced by townspeople driving along this rural road in North Berwick, Maine.

Figure 4–18. Located at one corner of the well-known Radburn development in Fairlawn, New Jersey, is this attractive mixed-used building, close to a fairly central street running through the borough. Directly behind lies a group of multifamily apartments, with a neighborhood of detached and semidetached homes also within convenient walking distance.

Alternative Scenarios for Conservation and Development

CHAPTER

5

Residential Development Patterns Along the Connecticut River

HARRY DODSON

EXISTING SITUATION

The Bye River, a tributary of the Connecticut, runs through a quiet agricultural valley in western Massachusetts. Famous for its rich farming soils, historic villages, and unspoiled natural scenery, the Bye River Valley has seen only modest amounts of development since the last building boom following the construction of the railroad in the 1880s. But a new interstate highway exit is being planned that should change things rather dramatically.

The Bye River Bridge connects the town of Helmsford in the foreground with the town of Chemsfield on the opposite bank. The bridge, built in the early twentieth century, is well-known in the region for its use of stone containing geologically unique "armored mudballs" dating from the Pleistocene era. Chemsfield's village center and church are shown in the middle distance of the scene, located along a state highway that parallels the river from Connecticut to Vermont. (See Figure 5–1.)

Both towns have conventional zoning regulations mandating two-acre lots with 200 feet of road frontage, and subdivision regulations requiring the construction of heavily engineered roads and utilities. These regulations, originally drafted 20 years ago by an engineering firm from a nearby city, have been only infrequently used and have never been seriously questioned by local residents. Even after experiencing a series of spectacular floods, the town still lacks floodplain zoning, groundwater protection, or minimum setbacks from bodies of water, owing to deep concern among certain officials about possibly infringing "property rights."

The land in the scene is owned primarily by three major property owners. In the foreground, Mildred Bye, the widow of a farmer and member of one of the town's distinguished founding families, owns the fields on the north side of the road. Across the road to the south, her son Larry, a local merchant, owns forty riverfront acres. On the far side of the river most of the undeveloped land is owned by the Checkerboard Realty Trust, and is leased to Henry Barnard, a local farmer.

CONVENTIONAL DEVELOPMENT SCENARIO

Feeling pinched for cash, Mildred sold the land bordering the river to a local developer and, without thinking about it too deeply, gave each of her four children a houselot alongside the road in the immediate foreground. The children built attractive homes, but each was located exactly in the middle of their two-acre lots in the open field. Rows of landscaping shrubs and mounds of bark mulch define the property lines. Meanwhile, the

Figure 5–1. Aerial view of existing situation.

developer subdivided Mildred's riverfront acreage, putting in as many houselots as possible to offset the high costs of building the wide paved roads, sidewalks, curbs, and catchbasins required by the town's subdivision regulations. The developer's protestations that the required pavement width was nearly twice as wide as the well-traveled town collector road that bordered his property were dismissed by the planning board as self-serving and irrelevant. (See Figure 5–2.)

Across the road to the south, Mildred's son decided to develop a marina with a large parking lot, boat storage area, and buildings lining the waterfront. Since the town has never adopted any site plan review standards, the parking lots and buildings were placed in the most convenient locations, which also happened to be the most visually and environmentally damaging ones.

Across the river in Chemsfield, Checkerboard Realty has lived up to its name by subdividing its entire waterfront property into a grid of uniform rectangular houselots, with absolutely no open space, not even a path along the water. Faithfully following the town's subdivision regulations, Checkerboard built a 35-foot wide subdivision road through the middle of the field. They cleared wide expanses of riverbank woodland to open up broad views for the new homes, damaging the river's ecology in the process. Runoff and erosion resulting from the construction of the homes, and continuous nutrient pollution from fertilized lawns extending down to the water's edge, have begun degrading the water quality of the river, which had only recently been improved through the expenditure of millions of dollars of federal funds. The development has also permanently marred the scenic quality of the historic village center, reducing the quality of life of its inhabitants and hurting the area's formerly thriving tourist and second-home industries.

CREATIVE DEVELOPMENT SCENARIO

Instead of allowing her children to lay out frontage lots in the middle of some of her late husband's most fertile fields (rated "prime" by the county soils conservationist), Mildred Bye instructed her surveyor to arrange the lots so that the houses would be tucked up against the tree line, providing the new homes with expansive views out over the undeveloped fields. Mildred worked with the planning board and the town's new site plan review ordinance, which encourages careful siting of new homes to avoid needlessly impacting sensitive resources. Her children enjoyed the new locations, which actually added to the value of their homes. (See Figure 5–3.)

The developer who bought her waterfront land was prevented from lining the banks with new homes and lawns by the town's new "open space zoning" (i.e., rural cluster) and floodplain ordinances. This did not reduce the number of allowed lots, but required homes to be located away from the floodplain and grouped back from the water, to provide long views across the riparian meadows sloping down toward the river. (See Chapter 15 for details on requiring "open space design".) The developer arranged his homes close to the quiet country road that had accessed his property, in the traditional fashion of a small rural hamlet. This allowed preservation of the fields and the riverbank, which was made accessible to the residents of the new homes through a "greenway" trail system and a shared dock.

To the south of the bridge, Larry Bye hired a landscape architect to revise the marina drawings originally prepared by the local surveyor, based upon findings by the planning board that his original sketch did not meet all requirements of the town's recently adopted site plan review ordinance. In conducting its review, the planning board had hired a consultant to conduct an environmental impact analysis of the property. He found the original marina location to be sensitive due to its ecology, scenic quality, and the presence of an historic bridge abutment. The consultant also suggested ways to more effectively and attractively lay out the marina development to avoid environmental and visual impacts.

Among the board's findings was that feasible alternative locations definitely existed that would be visually less intrusive and environmentally sounder. The town paid for this consulting with the review fees it had received from the applicant. Under the provisions of its ordinance, it could also

Figure 5–2. Aerial view after conventional development.

Figure 5–3. Aerial view after creative development.

have billed Larry directly for the technical assistance it required to conduct its review of his proposal, if the review fees were not sufficient.

Across the river, Checkerboard Realty Trust's initial subdivision plan was rejected by the Chemsfield Planning Board due to excessively large impacts on farmland, the riverfront environment, and the town's historic and scenic quality. However, officials actively encouraged Checkerboard to make use of the town's "open space subdivision" regulations, which offered an alternative to the standard, heavily engineered regulations used previously. Open space subdivision regulations allowed Checkerboard to downsize roads and utilities and eliminate curbs and catchbasins in exchange for using a traditional village layout to preserve over 80 percent of the site, including all environmentally sensitive lands. The savings in site development costs allowed Checkerboard to provide special amenities to its subdivision lot purchasers, including a riverbank trail system and a cleared area suitable for informal or organized games (sandlot baseball, touch football, etc.). Instead of a 35-foot-wide road with curbs and catch basins, they built a 20-foot-wide road

similar to the majority of rural roads crisscrossing the town, with a paved footpath on the far side of a gentle drainage swale. Even the chief of the volunteer fire department agreed to the proposal, after it was pointed out to him that the new access streets would be slightly wider than the town's traditional rural collector roads, and that they would carry only a fraction of the traffic. He also admitted that his vehicles and equipment had never failed to reach a burning house promptly, even when it was located on any of the town's narrower streets or back roads. And the public works director reminded the planning board that the wide residential streets normally required in new subdivisions cost nearly twice as much for the town to repave every seven to ten years, in addition to shedding much more storm water after every rainfall. He also mentioned that 20-foot-wide roads would be easier to plow in the winter, and would require considerably less shoulder room for snow storage than the wider standards, which he said looked to him as if they had been copied from a state highway design manual by mistake. (See Chapter 11 for further details on appropriate street design standards.)

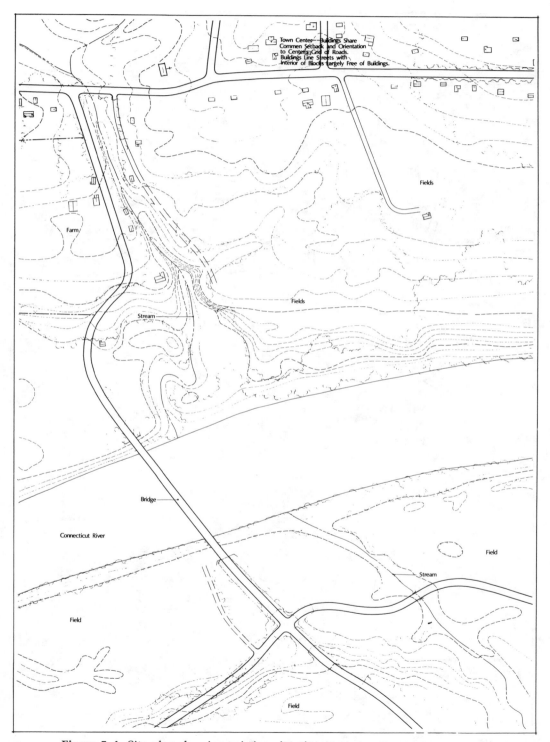

Figure 5–4. Site plan showing existing situation.

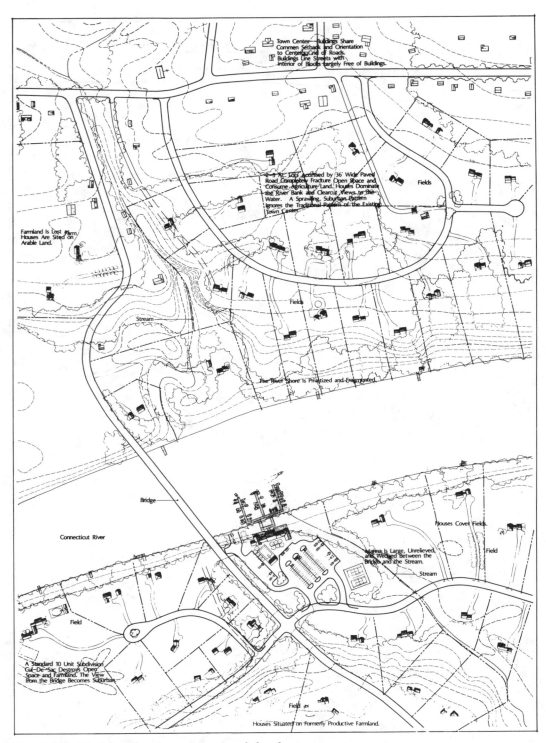

Town Center Buildings Share Common Setback and Orientation to Centerline/Grid of Roads. Buildings Line Streets with Interior of Blocks Largely Free of Buildings.

2–3 Ac. Lots Accessed by 36' Wide Paved Road Completely Fracture Open Space and Consume Agriculture Land. Houses Dominate the River Bank and Clearcut Views to the Water. A Sprawling, Suburban Pattern Ignores the Traditional Pattern of the Existing Town Center.

Fields

Farmland Is Lost. Farm Houses Are Sited on Arable Land.

Fields

Stream

The River Shore Is Privatized and Fragmented.

Bridge

Connecticut River

Houses Cover Fields.

Field

Marina Is Large, Unrelieved, and Wedged Between the Bridge and the Stream.

Stream

Field

A Standard 10 Unit Subdivision Cul-De-Sac Destroys Open Space and Farmland. The View from the Bridge Becomes Suburban.

Field

Houses Situated on Formerly Productive Farmland.

Figure 5–5. Site plan showing conventional development.

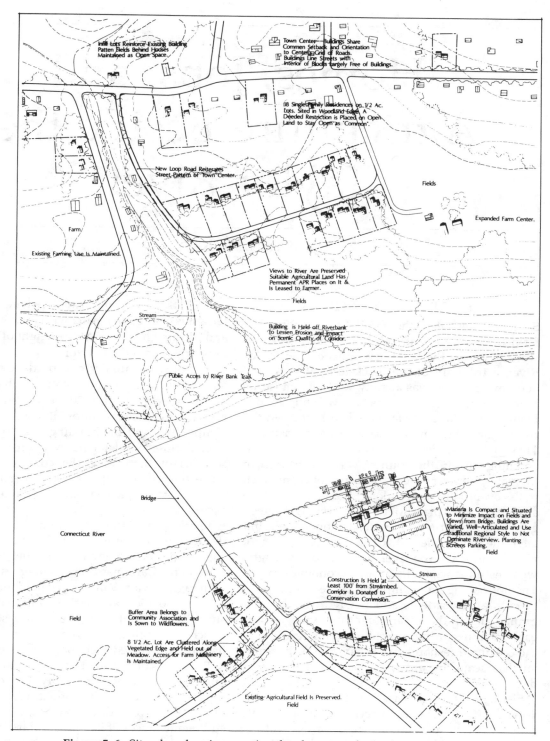

Figure 5–6. Site plan showing creative development alternatives.

6

Homes, Jobs, and Agriculture Beside the Taylor River

CHRISTINE REID

EXISTING SITUATION

Samuel Phelps left the family's struggling hill farm on his fourteenth birthday and headed to work in one of the large new mills on the Taylor River, a tributary of the Blackstone. It was 1808 and Taylor Valley was already well-known for its inventive use of water to power weaving looms. Even in colonial days, farmers had harnessed the river's current to run their sawmills and gristmills. Then, in 1794, the first water-powered cotton-spinning mill in the country was constructed in the valley's lower reaches, the first of many such mills eventually built along the river to take advantage of its plentiful flow and relatively steep gradient. Construction of the Union Canal, and later the Johnsville—Shattuck Railroad, both of which paralleled the river for most of its length, were instrumental in the valley's economic growth. The flourishing mill complexes served as magnets to both area residents and newly arrived immigrants, fueling the expansion of mill villages near each manufacturing operation. The result was the continual reshaping of the once mostly agrarian landscape by growing pockets of industrial development.

Situated at the northern end of Taylor Valley, the Town of Crafton never experienced a large-scale transformation to manufacturing. Its agricultural roots remain evident today, particularly north and east of the river and canal, where the rolling terrain is clothed in a patchwork of open farmland and wooded hillsides. At the height of the valley's industrial period, Crafton was an important source of wool, lumber, and produce for the mills and mill villages. The one cotton mill constructed in town operated for 20 years, but when the railroad bypassed Crafton it could not remain competitive, and the building burned eight years after it closed. But for many towns in the lower sections of the valley, the communication and trade generated by the canal soon enabled manufacturing to surpass farming as the leading local occupation.

Textile production remained a cornerstone of the region's economy until the mid-1920s, when changes in technology and cheaper unorganized labor in the Carolinas drew companies southward. Although Taylor Valley was hard hit, Crafton's relative isolation and lack of rail access had resulted in much of its agricultural base remaining intact, providing an economic buffer not shared by its more urbanized neighbors downstream.

To visitors of Crafton today, its dual character as an old agricultural community and as an emerging industrial center is evident. (See Figure 6–1.) Flowing east-west through town, the Taylor River still retains traces of its industrial heritage, including an overgrown dam and large stretch of wet-

Figure 6–1. Aerial view of existing situation.

lands upstream. Also evident is a dry, although relatively intact, section of the former Union Canal. The river and canal divide the town into two halves, both literally and figuratively. To the south lies a large gravel operation and a scattered mix of low-end industrial buildings, while the northern half of town fulfills the quintessential image of rural New England, with its rolling fields, white farmhouses, and miles of stone walls. In the far northeastern corner rises Lazy Hill, the highest point in Crafton and a cherished landmark still used by the town for its annual July 4th hike and picnic. Although mostly wooded, the summit of this drumlin affords a 360-degree view of Taylor Valley and the diverse mix of uses now common throughout much of the area.

The Simpson Extraction Company opened its Crafton plant in the late 1950s. It has since grown from a small operation supplying local road and construction projects to a regional enterprise providing sand, gravel, and fill for many area towns as well as for the new highway extension in neighboring Sutford and for the airport expansion near metropolitan Shattuck. Simpson's was not only a major business in town, but a local point of reference. As new extraction sites were opened and older ones abandoned, there evolved a characteristic, if somewhat characterless, topography of undulating mounds accented by deep "pit" lakes.

Every so often, town officials would discuss the need to plan ahead for the day when the land's mineral reserves were depleted and Simpson's closed. But they didn't want to demand too much from the business, afraid of losing the immediate benefits of needed tax revenues and local jobs. In fact, town leaders hoped to sell Hank Simpson its abutting parcel of land, a remnant piece of the original surface grade now 50 to 60 feet above the current floor of the pit. At one point the town thought of turning this piece into a small park, but an accident several years ago in which a child slipped down the steep, unstable bank led the town to approach Simpson's about buying that parcel to expand its operations.

In recent years, environmentalists also entered the picture. Although most of the land south of the river is zoned industrial, the gravel operation overlies a major aquifer possessing excellent and abundant water. In addition, the only well for the Crafton-Sutford Water District is located between two of the largest pits. The water district serves all of central Crafton as well as neighboring Sutford, which has started to experience tremendous pressure from new residential and commercial development. To environmentalists, this mining is overshadowed by the town's inadequate industrial zoning regulations, which are so broad and permissive as to allow many uses incompatible with maintaining a quality water supply.

Tucked in and around the gravel pits are several one-story utilitarian buildings. One was built to expand a home-based candle-making operation and is now used primarily as a warehouse, except on weekends when its expansive parking lot is transformed into a "flea market" bazaar. Simpson's also erected several prefab structures for truck and equipment maintenance in connection with its mining operation. Under the town's basic zoning regulations, none of these buildings were subject to any design standards or screening requirements, and to visitors they often seem in sharp contrast to the old orchards next door or to the agricultural fields across the river.

The landscape north of the river offers a glimpse of the agrarian economy that once existed throughout the Taylor Valley. In the early 1960s, when zoning was first adopted by the town, all this land was designated residential: one-acre minimum lots with 200 feet of street frontage, identical to the standard suburban pattern adopted by most other towns in the area. But with few houses being built, and most of them located along existing roads, the future impact of these requirements was hardly recognized. Residents knew they had zoning and felt "protected" from the ugly sprawl they saw around metropolitan Shattuck, 25 miles to the east. The Whitten farm, covering more than 500 acres just north of the dam impoundment, formed the heart of rural Crafton. A community-oriented family with long ties to the area, they open their lower hayfields each year to host the town's Fall Harvest Festival and May Day celebration. Bernie Whitten's death last winter, mourned by old and young alike, also generated concern about the possibility of Crafton losing this town treasure because the family could not afford to pay its inheritance taxes—based upon the land's development potential—without selling off most of the property. As they saw it, the only constraints to new houses sprawled over the landscape were the family's desire—or financial ability—to stay in farming and the suitability of the soil.

One didn't have to look far to see the potential result of such a conversion. Despite its distant location, Crafton had already seen several older orchards leveled and reborn as characterless subdivisions, their open, flat landscapes making them both easy and appealing to develop. And one had only to travel to neighboring Sutford to see the real potential for low-density checkerboard subdivisions: in a mere five years, over 300 new units of tract housing had all but destroyed the rolling hills and open countryside that once rivaled those in Crafton. In Sutford, officials' concern over the potential for multifamily housing, which they mistakenly thought was synonymous with "clustering," caused them to prohibit this useful design technique, thereby inadvertently setting the town on a course leading to blanket coverage by cookie-cutter developments with no open space preservation areas except unbuildable wetlands. Crafton still felt immune from the sprawling growth being experienced by "those suburban towns," but plans for a new highway extension to Sutford would soon produce a "can-opener" effect, literally paving the way for hundreds of commuters to live in this previously isolated rural area.

CONVENTIONAL DEVELOPMENT SCENARIO

Simpson's announcement that it planned to close its gravel operation in Crafton came as no surprise. Over the past several years it had been cutting back, and recently it had declined the town's offer to buy some of its unmined land. Although town officials had over the years discussed the impact Simpson's closing would have on the town and its tax base, there had been no coordinated action to encourage or require Simpson's to undertake any reclamation efforts, or to

plan for what type of business venture the town would like to see in its place. Few even paid much attention when the entire Simpson parcel was deeded over to Hank's nephew, Cy. Cy Simpson owned Simpson Realty Trust, the development arm of a local real-estate firm, and was well aware of the commercial and industrial potential of the land, given the soon-to-be completed highway extension to neighboring Sutford. With little regard to the landscape or to protection of the underlying aquifer, crews set to work leveling the site, filling in the smaller gravel pit ponds and erasing all traces of the former mine mounds. Although encouraged by two local conservation groups to seek the advice of the U.S. Army Corps of Engineers in developing a restoration program for the former extraction site, Cy shunned what he envisioned as massive bureaucratic hassles.

Cy recognized the need for low-end manufacturing and warehousing space in the northern end of Taylor Valley and had no difficulty finding several firms interested in building on the newly created site. Its flat, treeless topography allowed ample room for large trucks and, given the wide latitude of the town's basic zoning ordinance, the firms were relatively free to develop as they pleased. The availability of public water and sewer was also touted, although the town's antiquated system was already overloaded. Economy and function were the two words Cy used to sell the site, and the area soon hosted a patchwork of boxy, one-story prefab structures surrounded by large parking lots or, sometimes, small lawns dotted with an occasional tree or obligatory juniper. With no restrictions on signs, color, or screening, the disorganized mix of buildings and uses bore little resemblance to what most Crafton residents had envisioned for the site. (See Figure 6–2.) Eventually the tenants and a few of the closer neighbors became more than a little upset by one of the new businesses: a wholesale seafood dealer whose operation produced unpleasant fishy aromas, especially during the hot summer period. Particularly jarring to many older residents were the tall sodium vapor lights installed as an economy measure and the brighter mercury vapor security lights. The pervasive orange glow of the

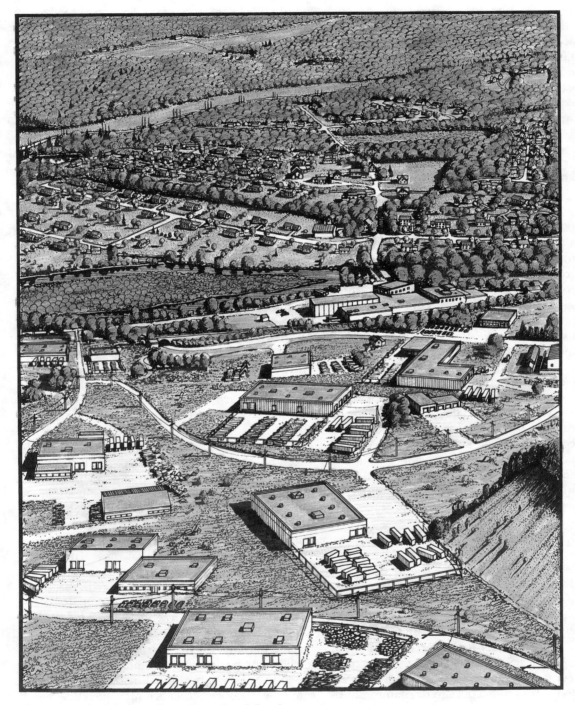

Figure 6–2. Aerial view after conventional development.

sodium lamps cast an unnatural aura over the whole neighborhood, and the brilliant mercury security lighting spilled into yards and bedrooms of nearby homes.

The first half-dozen tenants in the "business park," as Cy was partial to calling it, covered the spectrum from a truck-repair garage to a plastics recycling facility. This hodgepodge led one old-timer to kid Cy, remarking that his place more resembled a zoo or a circus than it did any park he had ever seen. Unfortunately, the lack of any regulations over the types of firms building on the site produced more than visual consequences: it also opened up the possibility for serious contamination of the underlying aquifer. The reality and magnitude of this problem was realized only several years later when the owners of the truck-repair garage discovered leaks in one of their underground tanks that were possibly contaminating the aquifer, a discovery that prompted them to file for bankruptcy to avoid cleanup costs.

Although the businesses provided welcome tax income that helped Crafton fund its schools and roads, other problems began to surface as more companies moved into the business park. Because the site had been graded and filled without any effort toward reclamation or stabilization, severe dust and erosion problems arose, resulting in never-ending battles among the business owners, their banks, and the Simpson Realty Trust. The fact that this area lay over a major aquifer serving the town's main well continued to be ignored; extensive parking lots and paved storage areas increased runoff dramatically, with measurable impacts on the quality of the aquifer.

Interested in diversifying its operations south of the river, Simpson Realty sold a large parcel, adjacent to the town's inholding, for office construction. Once a profitable apple orchard, the site was cleared for a multistory office complex organized around a large parking area, all in full view of the main road through Crafton. Unfortunately, the developer had little prior experience with this type of venture and soon found himself burdened with thousands of square feet of half-empty floor space—with neither the interest nor the money to provide the landscaping and other visual ameni-

ties promised when the development was first approved.

Across the river, unplanned residential growth was taking its own toll. Despite protests of the state historical commission and last-minute negotiations by its lawyers, local developers filled the old canal bed, cut down a huge number of trees, and regraded the site. This was soon followed by large "Execu-Track" homes built on spec, sited just shy of the state-mandated 50-foot setback from the river. Because there were no standards to prevent clearing or to provide screening along the riverbank, most owners extended their lawns down to the water's edge, disrupting important wildlife habitat, eliminating the natural storm water filtering once provided by the native vegetation, and destroying the scenic views canoeists had enjoyed from the water.

Inland from the river, the Whitten's farm was developed into a sprawling subdivision of uniform two-acre lots, served by excessively wide, curbed streets (30 feet in width), erasing all traces of the former historic landscape. The local Board of Health insisted on two acres of ground around each house, even when it meant some lots contained two acres of mediocre soil just barely passing the minimum requirements. Board members felt that two-acre lots are always better than one-acre lots, even when it was pointed out to them that flexible site design could give everyone access to better soils with smaller acreages. When concerned residents learned that this ugly and land-consumptive pattern of growth was actually mandated by the town's zoning and septic system regulations, a small grass-roots movement began advocating for more compact growth. There soon surfaced, however, a counter-fear among other homeowners that cluster zoning meant multifamily housing, and as one resident stated at a Town Meeting, "That is just not in tune with Crafton's values or character." Although the town did eventually adopt more flexible standards allowing for smaller lots balanced with significant open space provision, they were photocopied from an old ordinance in neighboring Sutford, which was limited to new subdivisions on public sewer and water, thereby denying use of more creative development patterns in the large areas of Crafton where public utilities did not exist.

Fueled by a booming economy and a growing desire among urbanites for country living, requests for new building permits overwhelmed the Crafton Planning Board. Eager to maximize their profit, developers tried to fill every possible building lot; backyards encroached on wetlands, disrupted wildlife corridors, and wiped out informal stream-bank paths visited for generations by Crafton's avid fly-fishing enthusiasts. Closer to Lazy Hill, mini-estates on three- to five-acre lots were carved into once-productive forest land, served by long winding driveways that further fragmented the land and greatly reduced the area usable by local hunters. But it was not until Lazy Hill itself was developed into a wealthy retiree's enclave that many finally acknowledged that Crafton had changed. The chained gate and 'No Trespassing' signs posted at the entrance to former hiking trails were stark indicators of what had really been lost—the heart and soul of the community.

CREATIVE DEVELOPMENT SCENARIO

When he first took over the gravel operation from his father, Hank Simpson assumed that someday one of his sons would follow in his footsteps. But in the ensuing years, they had both pursued other interests, and when Hank's wife died he decided it was time for him to sell the business and fulfill his dream of moving to Florida. He knew there was not much left to be extracted, but that the land was in a good location given the recent completion of the new turnpike extension to neighboring Sutford. Talking with a local landscaper one afternoon, he mentioned his dilemma of how best to market his parcel and was surprised at the landscaper's immediate interest in the site. Several days later, Hank Simpson met with Bruce Wilson, owner of Wilson Landscaping Service, and Jay Brown, a building contractor and developer. Wilson and Brown told him that they had been looking for a large parcel of land on which to site a high-quality office and research park, and that his land met many of their requirements. Prior to their meeting, Jay had contacted the U.S. Army Corps of Engineers to determine what services it could offer in terms of a reclamation plan for the former gravel operation.

At Bruce's suggestion, Hank met with the Taylor Valley Land Trust to explore the possibility of donating part of his land for conservation purposes. Land trust staff walked the parcel and drew up a package that proposed placing the undisturbed portion of the site under a permanent conservation easement. Realizing that the potential tax deductions available to developers for giving up buildable land were not enough to compensate them for the loss in value, the land trust modestly proposed "easing" only the wetlands and floodplain portions of the site—which were precisely those areas it really wanted for habitat protection and to help it extend its greenway trails network. After considering the trust's proposal and discussing it with the planning board, Wilson and Brown signed on, recognizing they had given up no development potential but had gained local goodwill and a new marketing advantage. Renaming their project the "Taylor Greenway Office Park," they became enthusiastic about enhancing the park-like features of the site, designing a pedestrian and jogging path system to link up with the town's new greenway trails network. (See Chapter 16 for further discussion of greenways and trails.)

While first formulating their concept for the site, Bruce and Jay met informally with town officials and members of the planning board to discuss options for reclaiming the gravel mines and to identify precautionary measures needed to protect the aquifer. Of immediate concern was whether the town's industrial zoning was compatible with long-term protection of its water supply. Given that a high-end office/research facility might attract firms that required pure, high-quality water, protecting the aquifer was of utmost interest to the business partners. Once it was clear that Bruce and Jay recognized the benefits of sensible environmental requirements, the town adopted stricter performance standards within its industrially zoned areas. These governed the raw materials, processes, and by-products of manufacturing operations, and also prohibited certain high-risk industrial uses. In seeking support for these changes, town officials promoted the idea that a well-planned and environmentally safe industrial park could have positive financial benefits without negatively impacting groundwater quality. In a complementary move, the town voted to rezone one section of the parcel as Office Park/Light Industrial, allowing for increased building densities in exchange for restricting development to one small part of the aquifer.

As plans for the former Simpson land began to take shape, the town joined forces with the land trust to develop recreational facilities on the land donated by Mr. Simpson. Using funds willed to the town by a former resident, other private donations, and state open space monies, the town constructed tennis courts, a soccer field, and a baseball diamond on the flat, dry floodplain. Bruce donated his services to help site the facilities, ensuring their distance from the town well, and he designed a border of native trees, shrubs, and wildflowers to screen the parking lot from the road. This project soon became a symbol of town unity, with residents of all ages volunteering time to erect a playground, plant flowers and trees, and raise funds through bake sales, fairs, and raffles. The land trust tapped into this community enthusiasm and invited residents to help it plan a town-wide system of trails connecting existing and potential open space parcels. With funding from the state's new greenway program, the land trust coordinated completion of the first two-mile section of trail linking the new recreation fields with the river and canal.

At the other end of the former gravel operation, a plan conceived years earlier was also beginning to take shape. Before signing over his land, Hank walked the site with Bruce and Jay, and shared with them one of his early dreams. Pointing to one of the lakes, he explained he had let gravel be extracted to a level well below the water table with the idea that someday he would create a small pond and nature sanctuary for the town. Jason and Bruce incorporated the idea into their own plans to revegetate the area with native species and special plantings to attract wildlife. Simpson's Pond, as it was officially dedicated, was soon incorporated into a larger restoration effort

of bank regrading, slope stabilization, and soil amendment, followed by successional plantings of native species using many seedlings made available by the county office of the U.S. Soil Conservation Service. As the town's greenway system unfolded, the preserve was incorporated into that network.

With their market research underway and a detailed site analysis complete, Wilson and Brown Associates drew up plans for their office and research park. Inspired by the region's industrial heritage, the developers proposed two- and three-story office buildings that mirrored the vernacular design of former mills and historic mill villages. The buildings were sited in a compact, energy-efficient, campus-like arrangement, with an emphasis on pedestrian access and amenities. (See Figure 6–3.) Parking was located to the rear of the buildings and screened by plantings that wrapped around them to form a continuous landscaped garden of ornamental and native species. As required under the town's new Office Park/Light Industrial designation, development was focused onto one part of the parcel, affording protection to the aquifer, reducing dependence on the automobile, and protecting open space. Bruce and Jay contributed a portion of the money they saved from reduced infrastructure and development costs to upgrading the town's sewer treatment facilities. They also provided seed money for a "challenge fund" to create a comprehensive vegetation restoration program designed to restore several glacial kettle ponds for wildlife habitat and passive recreational use, as well as to stabilize steep slopes with soil-enhancing plantings. Under this program, the business partners agreed to match, dollar for dollar, all private contributions and proceeds from fund-raising efforts.

Crafton's open-minded approach to development and willingness to consider innovative land-use regulations paid off in attracting the interest of a high-quality retail developer. The Blythe Company had been closely following the work of Wilson and Brown Associates and had targeted the need for a small shopping center convenient to local employees and residents. Working with Bruce and Jay, they proposed a small commercial

Figure 6–3. Aerial view after creative development.

complex adjacent to the office park to include a grocery, druggist, video rental, hair salon, and hardware store. Their plans incorporated many of the same architectural and design features highlighted in the office park, and included a central pedestrian area connected by landscaped walkways leading to screened parking at the side and rear of the complex. The commercial center design also helped to preserve some open space by incorporating professional offices and a few affordable housing units above the shops, thereby consuming less land and reducing construction costs because the same foundations and roofs served all three uses.

Despite a sense of well-being brought on by its new business ventures, Crafton was not immune to the growing need for more affordable housing in the area. Not quite sure how to address this issue, the town hired a group of graduate students from the state university's regional planning program to do a housing affordability study and master plan for the town. Based on projected population growth and housing needs over the next 30 years, the report suggested Crafton would experience a severe housing crisis in the future if it did not take action to address this issue head-on. The town formed a Housing Committee and in response to its recommendations rezoned a parcel of land west of Simpson's Pond to accommodate 24 duplex and 34 single-family units in traditionally designed buildings on one-quarter acre lots in a compact village pattern. To create a land subsidy to make the units affordable, town officials worked closely with the land trust, which agreed to purchase an option on the 20-acre development site based on its current zoning potential for 15 house-lots. The trust agreed to resell the land, at its original purchase price, after the town rezoned it for 58 units of affordable housing. The increased land value, which would normally have accrued to a real-estate speculator, was passed on to a community development corporation that used the "windfall" to commission first-rate architectural designs, high-quality construction, enclosed garage parking, extensive landscaping, and site amenities, including neighborhood recreation facilities. All the units were within the financial reach of young families and older residents on fixed incomes. This well-designed open space subdivision was also connected to the office park and town recreation fields via Crafton's expanding network of greenway pedestrian trails. (See Chapter 10 for further details regarding affordable housing and open space preservation.)

Affording protection to the river and enhancing its scenic and recreational values was another item addressed by the planning board. One of its members, who had a summer home in Maine, brought back a copy of that state's riverbank zoning regulations as a model of what kind of action might be taken. After reviewing their options, the board advocated designation of a riverbank overlay district with setback requirements of 100 to 150 feet for new buildings and additions and limitations on the clearing of natural vegetation, including a total prohibition against clearing 75 feet from the water's edge. Members of the Conservation Commission joined forces with the local garden club to work with riverbank landowners on a program to plant buffers of native species aimed at promoting wildlife habitat, improving water quality, and enhancing the scenic character of the river. The Taylor Valley Historical Society and the local chapter of Trout Unlimited lent their support to this effort as a way to restore the historic pattern of the natural riverbanks, which were originally cleared only at the sites of the mills and mill villages. They also sponsored several interpretive programs, including a combined hiking and canoe trip along the river to build a local network of support for continued protection of the river and canal resources. (See Chapter 16 for further discussion of greenways and buffers alongside rivers, etc.)

North of the river, the Taylor Valley Land Trust identified the Whitten parcel and Lazy Hill as top priorities for protection. The trust worked with the Whittens on a comprehensive preservation package that allowed the family continued use of their house and nearby fields, while permitting "limited development" on a portion of the site and placing the majority (including the summit) under conservation easements. Under this approach, the number of building lots was reduced, but each was able to be sold for a premium price due to the outstanding views afforded by this location. This arrangement benefited the town in protecting a historic and scenic landscape in perpetuity. It also provided the family with desired protection from excessive inheritance taxes; by not trying to maximize the property's legal development potential, the family was entitled to a charitable deduction from the estate's taxable value. Key to successful completion of this package was use of the state's agricultural protection program, which purchased the development rights on the farmland to keep it in productive use.

However, despite these efforts, the town's underlying zoning for this area still called for sprawling, one-acre houselots. Concerned about the cookie-cutter subdivisions being built in neighboring towns, the planning board organized a growth management forum on open space development design, which led to the adoption of an open space zoning amendment by the town several months later. Under this approach, the planning board is authorized to require developers to submit two conceptual sketch plans, one illustrating the maximum number of allowable houselots given site constraints (e.g., wetlands, steep slopes, etc.), and the other showing the same number of houses on smaller lots located according to design guidelines aimed at minimizing the loss of farmland, wildlife habitat, and other open space. Under the new ordinance, the planning board is authorized to select either plan, depending on which it feels best advances the purposes of the town's zoning regulations, which for Crafton includes the maintenance of rural character.

Crafton's adoption of the zoning amendment requiring open space development design came at an opportune time: more and more builders were eyeing the community, hoping to cash in on its high-quality image. The first developer to test the new ordinance was Harris Brothers, a local contracting firm that had built a number of standard subdivisions in other parts of the valley. At first annoyed at having to submit two plans to the planning board, their skepticism began to fade when pro forma calculations showed the potential for significant savings from shorter roads and reduced utility costs. More importantly, they also

began to recognize the marketing potential offered by this design approach, which allowed them to advertize "permanently protected rural views" and access to the burgeoning greenway trail network. Their proposal for the Whitten farm grouped all the homes on the half of the farm most suitable for development, where houses could be tucked back at the forest edge. Drawing on the expertise of a landscape architect and planner, their open space design combined a total of 96 single-family units on downsized lots, some of which were arranged around a common green and connected to surrounding open space by a community trail system and protected wildlife corridor. Although many lots were less than the standard two-acre size normally required by the local board of health, the board's new chairman, who had recently attended a seminar on creative subdivision layouts that provide every houselot with part of the best septic-system soils available on the parcel, saw the advantages offered by more flexible arrangements (e.g., where a few of the individually owned leach fields were even located in the common open space). (See Chapter 13 for further discussion on this point.) Designated road setbacks, vegetation buffers, and screening requirements contributed to a quality development proposal that won the quick approval of the planning board. Fifteen months later town officials and the chair of the planning board were honored to receive a Municipal Planning Award from the State Office of Communities, which cited the town's adoption of this innovative ordinance as a positive example of how a community can take charge of its future, shaping growth patterns for both development and for conservation. The success of this approach was further acknowledged by other developers who proposed similar designs on their own, after seeing how well Harris Brothers' homes were selling.

One of the last areas of town to be developed was the woodland on Lazy Hill's gentle northeast slopes. Although the summit was protected under the plan drawn up by the land trust, the foothills to the east were considered prime houselots. When the owner made public his intent to sell his land, the town decided it had to act to protect this resource. The planning board promoted designation of the road skirting the base of Lazy Hill as a scenic byway, requiring deep setbacks for new construction, with one-half to two-thirds of the setback distance designated as a no-cut buffer to screen new homes from the street. They also added a provision permitting flaglots and shared driveways off designated scenic routes to reduce the number of new road cuts. These safeguards were instrumental in keeping the roadside and woodlands mostly intact while allowing the owner to construct twelve new units of housing. (See Chapter 12 for further details on scenic road protection techniques.)

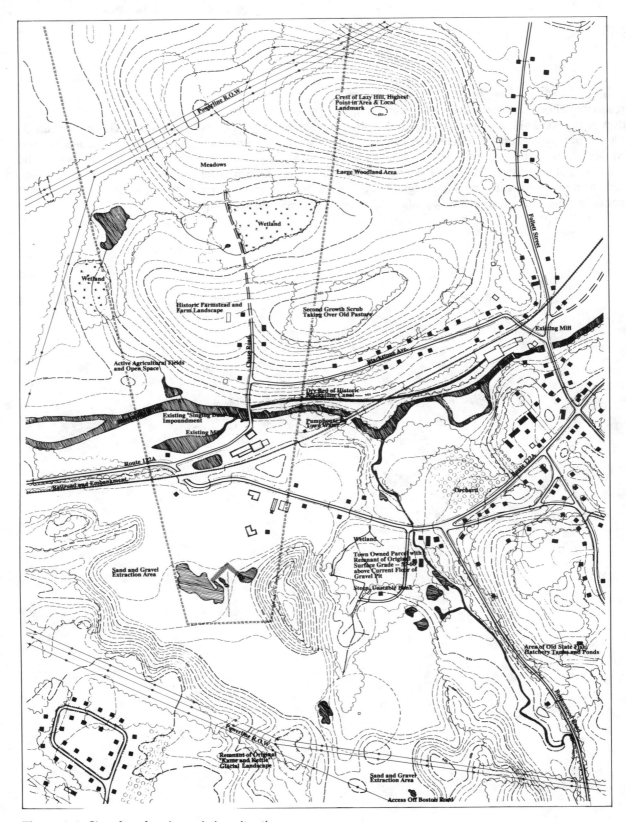

Figure 6–4. Site plan showing existing situation.

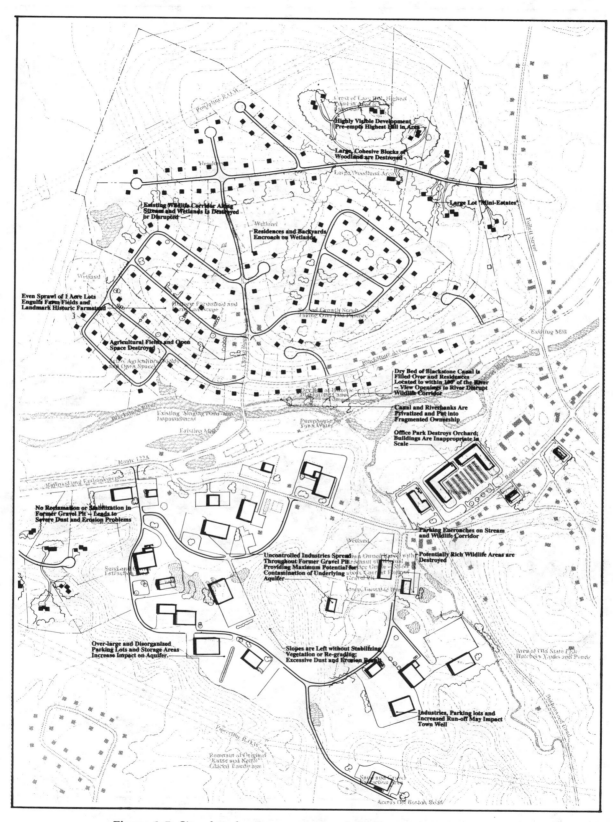

Figure 6–5. Site plan showing conventional development.

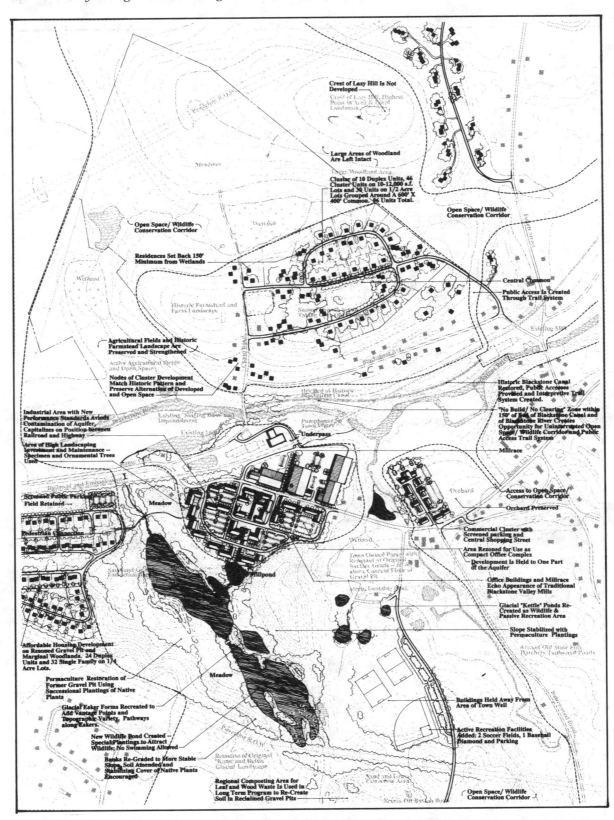

Figure 6–6. Site plan showing creative development alternatives.

7

Evolution from Village to Town in a Typical Inland Site

Christine Reid

EXISTING SITUATION

"A little piece of Switzerland" is the way Katherine Harris describes the rolling patchwork of open fields and wooded hillsides in her town. A direct descendant of one of the area's oldest families, Mrs. Harris's natural feeling for the landscape is apparent. (See Figure 7–1.)

The Huntington Plateau was first settled in the 1750s by Elijah and Sarah Harris. For the early settlers the thin rocky soils and harsh winters proved a constant test of endurance, but plentiful supplies of timber and large game helped them survive the long cold seasons. As more families joined the Harrises, the hills surrounding Mt. Jessup, as the community came to be known, were stripped of their forest cover and much of the land was converted to fields and pastures.

Farming survived in the hill towns while land was cheap and trade limited. But with improved transportation and wider access to markets a number of the more marginal operations failed, resulting in a major exodus of farm families to the more fertile lands farther west. Mt. Jessup lost over half its population by 1820, partially rebounding when sheep farming became popular in the mid-1800s. The burgeoning wool industry influenced the character of the rural landscape,

which became increasingly pastoral, but it also set in motion a much larger set of changes.

Never ones to shy away from risk, the Harrises early on increased their landholdings and converted it to pasture, supplying high-quality wool to local mills. But within decades local wool production began to wane; the large-herd owners resettled in the fertile Midwest, following the pattern of the small farmers two generations before them. As the agricultural base moved westward, much of the less productive farmland surrounding the Harris property reverted into second-growth forest, but the patchwork of open fields and wooded hillsides that emerged with the decline in sheep farming remains evident today.

The Harris Farm continues to rely on a diversified base to survive. The family operates a sizable timber and firewood business, keeps a herd of dairy cattle, and runs a small petting farm and U-pick berry operation. Several forested parcels are managed as large sugar bush stands, from which they operate a well-known maple sugar operation and seasonal restaurant. Katherine also runs a bed and breakfast operation in the old family farmhouse, targeted at summer travelers and fall foliage watchers ("leaf-peepers"). The open acreage that remains is kept in pasture and

Figure 7–1. Aerial view of existing situation.

hay. The forests, in addition to being an economic resource, provide ample recreational opportunities; only the abundant stone walls—and occasional lilac bush—are reminders of the land's former use.

CONVENTIONAL DEVELOPMENT SCENARIO

Although located 20 miles south of town, the state university's decision to upgrade its small satellite campus into a major research center had a tremendous effect on Mt. Jessup and its environs. At first, new residential and commercial growth was seen primarily in communities adjacent to the university campus; Mt. Jessup remained largely unchanged, insulated by distance and the condition of the rural roads. But the state's new rural highway improvement program and a growing desire among university employees for "country living," were catalysts for rapid growth. This road widening acted like a "can opener," spurring development of widely scattered homes. Pressure by many newcomers to preserve some open space contrasted with locals' desire for more employment and a larger tax base. No one knew this better than Katherine Harris, recently widowed and, for the first time in her life, uncertain how to proceed.

Lemuel Harris had been the heart and soul of the farm and his sudden death left the family with an unexpected dilemma: sell the farm or continue to pour money into an operation that was no longer economically viable. The Harris's oldest son had recently decided that the farming base in the area was too sparse to support his veterinary practice and moved to more secure farm country in the south. Their daughter had married a former university student and moved to the city. Their youngest son was stationed overseas with the army.

After a year of trying to keep the operation going, Mrs. Harris decided it was too big a job for her to manage alone. Word of her interest in selling spread quickly and she was soon recontacted by a local real-estate agent who had sent her flowers and a business card when Lem had passed away. Now representing an out-of-state

developer, the agent assured her that the township's new zoning regulations, which had been drawn up by her friends and neighbors, would "protect the town's resources and rural character." He even discussed the possibility of clustering some homes to save Katherine's favorite pasture. Impressed by the agent's knowledge of the township and his expressed concern for its well-being, Mrs. Harris agreed to sell everything except the original house and building lots for each of her children along the main road.

Feeling the need to put distance between herself and the farm, Mrs. Harris left for six months to visit her daughter. When she returned she was shocked and dismayed: What had happened to the fields and forests that had been her home? She was astonished to learn that the sprawling subdivision that had been carved out of her land followed the township's zoning to the last detail. Houses, each on a one-acre lot, with 200 feet of street frontage, were spread all over the fields. Connected by new excessively wide (30-foot paved width) subdivision roads modeled on county highway standards, the densities and setbacks of the new housing bore little relation to traditional hamlet and village settlement patterns in the area. Although the real-estate agent correctly stated that the township had zoning, its regulations, adopted nearly verbatim from a suburban community miles away, were a blueprint for land-consumptive sprawl. Although they separated incompatible uses and established maximum densities, they did nothing to protect open space or the township's rural character. (See Figure 7–2.) The agent also underestimated the resistance to building even a small modified cluster development to preserve Mrs. Harris's favorite pasture. The inflexibility of the planning board and the township's regulations forced the developer to design the entire parcel as a conventional subdivision. Hedgerows, stone walls, and the apple orchard were all removed.

The Harris Farm development was not an isolated incident. The planning board was soon overwhelmed by applications for new subdivisions, as well as by requests to widen and pave former woods roads and country lanes that were still

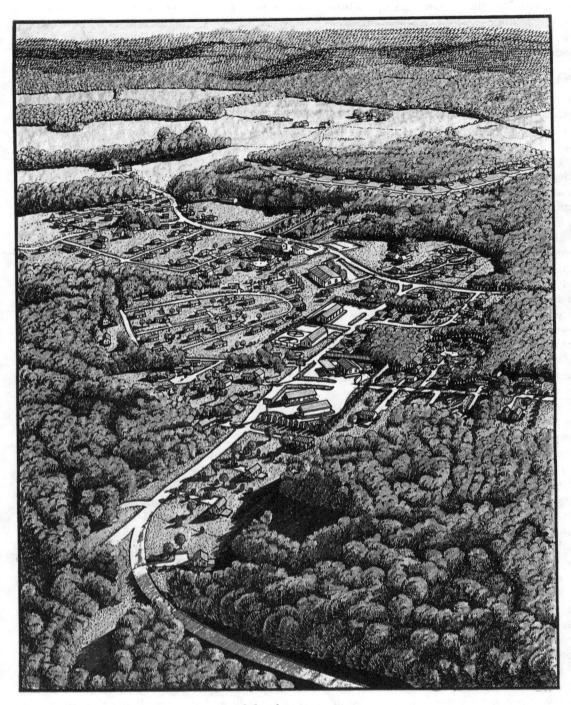

Figure 7–2. Aerial view after conventional development.

officially listed as township roads. The cul-de-sac, a popular road design in many suburban communities, was liberally incorporated into many new housing layouts. Concerned about issues of safety and access, the planning board required the end circles be 130 feet in diameter, resembling flying saucer landing pads. The sprawling nature of the new development in Mt. Jessup not only erased all of its former hamlet-and-farmstead character, it also consumed most of the more productive soils for crops and timber production. The few farmers who did try to keep working their land grew discouraged by the lack of understanding and appreciation of agriculture by many of the new suburbanites, and moved their operations to other states.

Once the most easily developed fields and pastures had been subdivided, developers looked to the wooded hillsides. The west end of the township, considered excellent wildlife habitat, and which for years had been managed as a sustained-yield woodlot, was developed into large ten- and fifteen-acre houselots, effectively removing all the land from any productive resource use. Serviced by long drives, many of these homes were set high on the ridge, clearly visible from the main road, reminding everyone of poor planning represented by their new zoning. To many longtime residents, the large "No Trespassing" and "No Hunting" signs were an affront to what had long been considered a semipublic resource.

Commercial services to meet the demands of new residents soon followed. A large development firm proposed a medium-sized shopping plaza including a supermarket, department store, and fast-food restaurant. Township officials shunned the idea, claiming they would never allow their community to be overrun by such "commercial slosh." But in failing to address the issue head-on, they opened the door to what eventually emerged: an endless series of smaller retail complexes, lining much of the central "artery" through town. Each had its own separate entrance and exit from the highway, with no interconnections between the parking lots even being considered or required, thereby magnifying traffic congestion severalfold. At what had once been an attractive

country intersection with an old farmhouse surrounded by huge maples, a superette/video store and gas station complex emerged. The regional chain that owned and operated these two franchises was fixated on the need for conspicuous signs and highly visible parking spaces. Facing few regulations with regard to building siting and design, it constructed a boxy, unimaginative structure surrounded by asphalt, accentuated by a tall, internally illuminated plastic sign. Landscaping consisted of a bark mulch island dotted with small junipers. Other new commercial buildings followed a similar pattern, with deep setbacks and large front yard parking lots preventing any sense of cohesion, completely missing the opportunity to create any feeling of a traditional small town "Main Street" retail core.

CREATIVE DEVELOPMENT SCENARIO

When the state university decided to upgrade its small satellite campus near Mt. Jessup, a group of concerned citizens formed a long-range planning committee to look at how the town could encourage growth compatible with its rural character. In reviewing the township's resource base and the need for local jobs, the committee proposed that officials concentrate on attracting an educational center or research park, using proximity to the university and its natural amenities as major drawing cards. Several of the township's newer residents had ties with preparatory schools and helped compile a strong prospectus on the town and its resources, opening the way for local officials to meet with school administrators. In addition to location and rural character, the township emphasized the availability of several large contiguous tracts of land (including space for future expansion), its commitment to developing zoning and subdivision regulations that would ensure the township's resource base remained intact, its willingness to seek funding to upgrade and expand its infrastructure network, and its interest in providing housing for all income levels. The township's forward-looking view and progressive strategy paid off: within one year, Dennison Preparatory Academy chose Mt. Jessup as the site for its new school. Dennison's decision was met with enthusiasm by most residents. Many had already witnessed the visual and physical impacts of haphazard development that followed in the wake of the university's expansion. Securing Dennison's commitment to their community gave many a new sense of pride—and urgency—to protect their town.

As a first step, the long-range planning committee regrouped into several task forces. One subcommittee created a set of resource maps for the town showing current land uses and various constraints to development (steep slopes, wetlands, etc.). These maps formed the basis for a "Township-wide Map of Conservation and Development," a regulatory map that identifies areas that would best remain open and those where growth should be encouraged. This exercise helped the town to identify the best location for the new academy and also created a formal structure for requiring new residential subdivisions to be clustered away from proposed open space and into the areas best suited for development. Working with school officials, the town delineated areas for classroom buildings and living quarters, all within walking distance of the emerging town center.

A second task force reviewed the township's zoning regulations and requested help from the university's Rural Studies Center in identifying options for future growth. Through this assistance, the township prepared a master plan that laid out a long-term vision for its future. This helped local residents determine the type of development it wanted to encourage. Important considerations resulting from this study included the desire to avoid highway strip malls; the need for incentives and regulations encouraging infill development; the desire to create tighter neighborhoods rather than sprawling subdivisions; the importance of keeping large tracts of land in agricultural or forest use; the aesthetic importance of the gateways into town and the scenic ridges; and the desire to create a mixture of housing types so that elderly and younger residents could afford to remain in town.

Armed with these guidelines, the town approached the county planning department for help in developing appropriate zoning and subdivision regulations to address these goals. A key provision was a compulsory "open space development" amendment to the zoning ordinance. This required that in all new subdivisions, lots and roads should not cover more than 50 percent of the parcel and that at least half of this open space be designed as usable for active recreation or agriculture. (See Chapter 15 for further details on this zoning technique.) The open space concept was first tried near the west gateway to town on a 50-acre parcel bordered by the main road. Drawing on expertise from the Rural Studies Center, the developer built a new road at the woodland edge with tightly clustered houses, reflecting the area's existing settlement pattern and vernacular architecture and providing views out onto the preserved hayfield. When this development was later expanded back into the woods, it resulted in the creation of a small village setting, an aura enhanced by zoning modification that allowed for lot sizes and setbacks similar to those found in the existing village.

During the planning process, the township was also introduced to the notion of a Transfer of Development Rights (TDR) program by a seasonal resident who also lived in Sumner, where a TDR system had been implemented several years earlier. The concept is simple: areas of town most suitable for development are declared receiving zones with increased use densities, leaving intact open farm and forestlands as the sending zones from which the development rights are "sold." The key is the increased densities allowed for infill development and for clustering new building at the edge of town or within other designated growth centers. The county planning department saw the TDR approach as an excellent avenue for the township to implement some of its long-range goals. The zoning subcommittee used the township's new resource maps to identify areas that would best remain open and where compact growth could best be accommodated. The result was to encourage a more compact mix of uses—commercial and residential—surrounding the new academy. (See Figure 7–3.) Through promoting infill development in this area, the township was able to link the school with the municipal offices, two churches, and several retail and pro-

Figure 7–3. Aerial view after creative development.

fessional enterprises to create a more cohesive center. This new growth was promoted along a tree-lined, pedestrian-friendly road within easy walking distance of the new open space development and the academy. The use of the density bonuses had the immediate advantage of helping a young farmer in one of the outlying sending zones whose cousin owned land within the receiving district in town and who bought the farmer's development rights. The cash infusion enabled the farmer to finance the silo and tractor he needed to stay in operation.

Having seen the beneficial results of the concrete benefits from its open space zoning and TDR programs, Mrs. Harris was receptive when approached by a local land trust interested in combining land preservation with the provision of permanently affordable housing for local families. Since her husband's death, Mrs. Harris had been searching for a way to keep her family's legacy alive through preservation of at least part of the farm. The project set forth to her combined a number of objectives, including placing restrictions on use of the farm's prime soils. Under the arrangement worked out with the land trust, about 90 acres were acquired by the Audubon Society as a natural area, with plans to open a self-guided nature trail or agricultural education center in the future. The farmhouse and 50 acres were sold at below-market rates to a young farmer who had all but given up hope of being able to start her own operation in her hometown. Tucked back in the woods were ten houselots (ranging in size from two to fifty acres). To ensure that these homes would blend in with their surroundings, deed restrictions accompanied each site indicating required setbacks, driveway widths, treed roadway buffers, and the like. Of these units, one was sold to Mrs. Harris for construction of a new house; two others were sold to the county Community Development Corporation for use as permanently affordable housing, with preference given to local residents.

In the two decades following the construction of Dennison Academy, the township found itself the focus of different ventures hoping to capitalize on the school's reputation. Fearful that the town was living on borrowed time, Roger Phelps began voicing his concerns. A former professor at the university's School of Landscape Architecture, he had been an avid believer in controlled growth and ecological planning ever since taking a course from Ian McHarg while a graduate student at Penn. When he got wind of plans for a major four-season resort in the area, he joined forces with his son Kent to pioneer the concept of a "landowner compact" or real-estate syndicate. (See Chapter 14 for further details.) The effort started slowly with Roger and his son meeting with several other large landowners from Mt. Jessup and surrounding townships. Using some simple perspective sketches, Roger was able to show them that the 900 acres they collectively held could be developed a better way if they worked in unison as developers—and conservators—of the landscape. The landowner compact works much like a "cluster development" that covers a wide geographic area and includes multiple owners: internal property lines are erased, directing development density to appropriate locations, especially those serviced by public infrastructure. He also likened the compact to a large-scale TDR program that puts together a number of parcels of land under multiple ownership to manage growth and compensate landowners proportionately for their participation. The compact gives townships, landowners, developers, and conservationists a vehicle to cooperate in protecting important farmland or open space by directing development density to appropriate locations.

The idea did not take off until two landowners proposed major subdivisions on agricultural parcels long considered key to the rural heart of the region. Neither of the townships in which these developments were proposed had compulsory open space zoning ordinances, and the site plans circulated among abutters showed sprawling subdivisions of two- to five-acre lots in a pattern synonymous with suburbia. Calling on the services of friends with experience in marketing and real estate, the Phelps's used these proposed developments to show how a landowner compact would prevent such unplanned growth *without* eliminating the owners' financial investment in their properties. With each such case, the Phelps's found a more educated and receptive audience, including more farmers and large landowners whose holdings were not ideally suited for development.

Throughout this time, Roger and Kent had been in contact with a regional land trust and had convinced them to use the Mt. Jessup area as a model case of this land management technique. The trust transformed talk into action. Twelve years after his father first introduced the concept, Kent Phelps helped orchestrate the first compact arrangement covering 3,000 acres and involving three townships and eight landowners. The trust provided the necessary skills in real estate, marketing, law, and finance to serve as an effective intermediary among all parties—developer, landowner, township— and to serve as interim property-holder while deed restrictions and covenants were structured for some parcels, allowing more intensive development on others.

While skeptical of this new form of regional cooperation, each participating township saw the advantage of the landowner compact as a way for the township to gain more control in implementing a growth center concept and in protecting its vital farm and forestland resources. The concept also gained support from those who saw it as a way to control physical design standards in developable areas through deed restrictions on the land. This attention to preserving a township's "sense of place" and architectural features went a long way toward calming some residents' fears of "townhouse grottos." Developers saw the financial benefit of avoiding unnecessary permit or legal hassles, and of cutting back on capital expenses by concentrating development where infrastructure such as roads and sewer already existed or could be easily extended. These savings allowed the developer to contribute to upgrading the local sewage treatment plant. The landowners who cooperated on the project benefited from a shared sense of vision and from knowing that important township resources would be permanently protected. It was especially important for residents whose land—due to physical constraints or lack of access—was not ideal for development, because they could enroll in the program and receive benefits prior to the time when their property would become feasible to develop.

To follow up on the town's new zoning regulations, Mt. Jessup residents hired a group of regional planning students from the university to do a roadside build-out analysis for several routes through the township that were experiencing a steady increase in commuter traffic and commercial development interest. On the group's recommendation, the township applied for state scenic highway designation for two roads that skirted one of the area's last dairy farms. Although this property was not part of the landowner compact, the new road designation nicely complemented the larger growth management effort. It also reinforced the township's goal of confining any new commercial expansion to specific "nodal" points determined by existing development (or the site's location within a development area). The university group also suggested the town consider enacting site design standards such as maximum front setbacks for new commercial buildings and siting of parking and loading facilities at the rear of a building. (See Chapter 9 for further details on these regulatory approaches.)

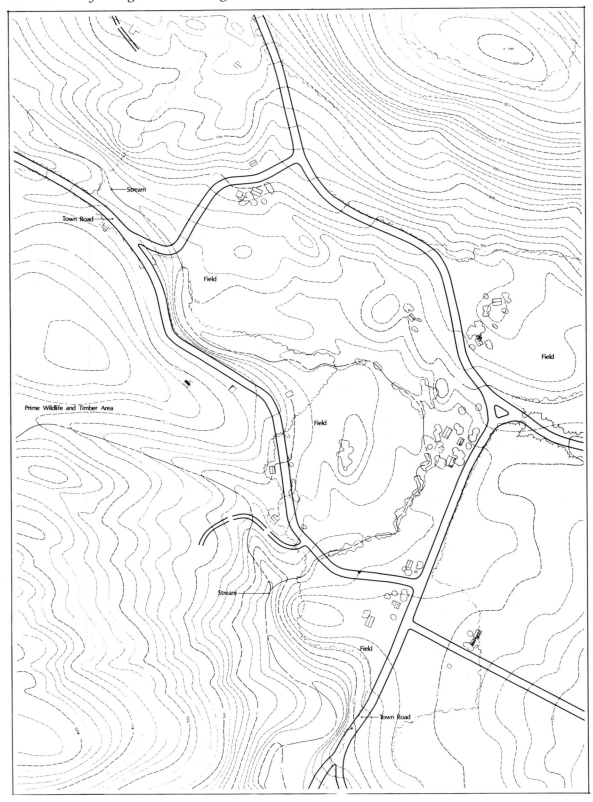

Figure 7–4. Site plan showing existing situation.

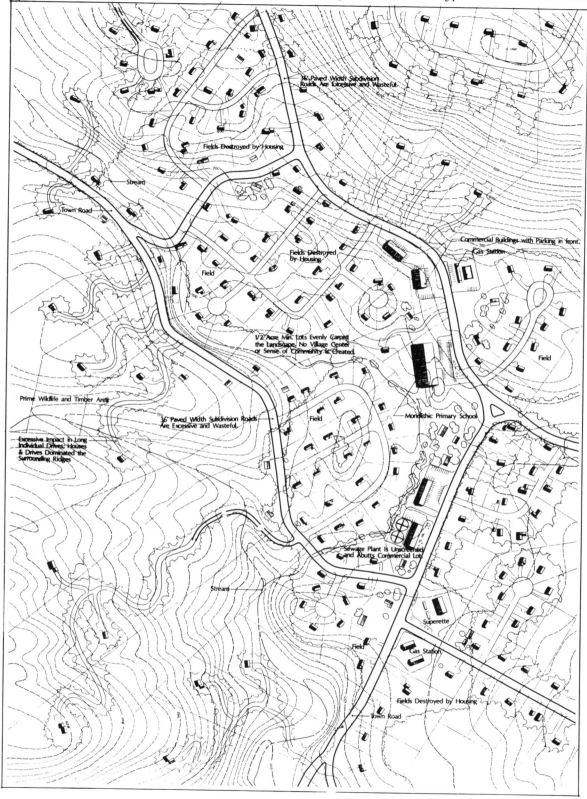

Figure 7–5. Site plan showing conventional development.

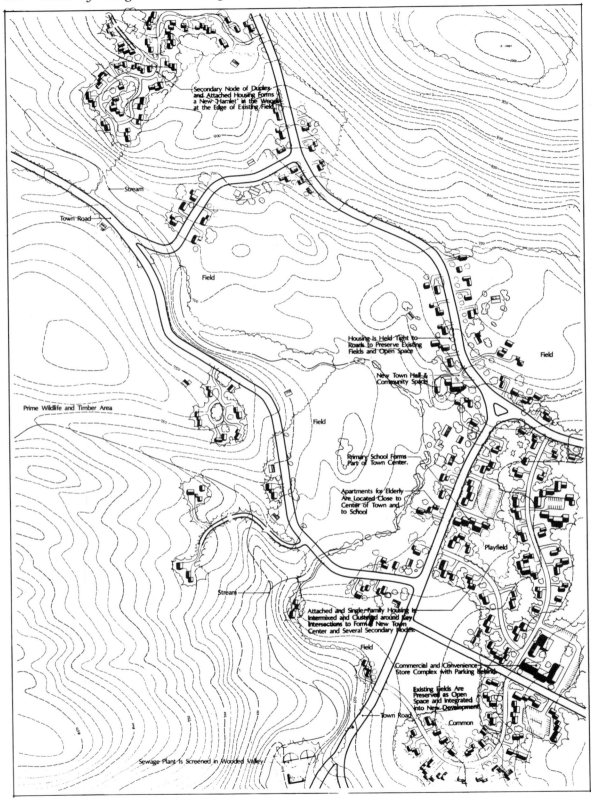

Secondary Node of Duplex and Attached Housing Forms a New "Hamlet" in the Woods at the Edge of Existing Field

Stream

Town Road

Field

Housing Is Held Tight to Roads to Preserve Existing Fields and Open Space

New Town Hall & Community Space

Field

Prime Wildlife and Timber Area

Field

Primary School Forms Part of Town Center.

Apartments for Elderly Are Located Close to Center of Town and to School

Playfield

Stream

Attached and Single-family Housing Is Intermixed and Clustered around Key Intersections to Form a New Town Center and Several Secondary Nodes.

Field

Commercial and Convenience Store Complex with Parking

Existing Fields Are Preserved as Open Space and Integrated into New Development.

Town Road

Common

Sewage Plant Is Screened in Wooded Valley.

Figure 7–6. Site plan showing creative development alternatives.

8

Commercial Infill Development Along a Major Street

HARRY DODSON

Unlike the first three chapters in Part II, this chapter describes an actual chain of events that occurred in a small town on the island of Martha's Vineyard, located off the coast of Cape Cod. The drawings depicting alternative future situations were created as part of the town's master planning process, and proved very useful in illuminating the broad choices facing town voters.

INTRODUCTION

In the spring of 1988, the Edgartown (Massachusetts) Planning Board, with the support of the Martha's Vineyard Commission, received a grant from the Massachusetts Council on the Arts and Humanities to develop a plan for Edgartown's B-2 commercial district, along Upper Main Street. The board hired the landscape architectural firm of Dodson Associates to help Edgartown develop a vision for the future of the district and to formulate a process by which this vision could be practically implemented. The law firm of Mark Bobrowski and Associates assisted in translating the site planning and design recommendations into specific legal terms, to be incorporated into the town's zoning regulations. These recommendations were presented to the voters at a town meeting in the spring of 1989 and were approved by a large majority.

Development in the Upper Main Street corridor over the previous five years had been intensive, and Edgartown's residents and officials were very concerned about preventing the district from degenerating into a typical commercial strip. Although the quality of recent construction was generally superior to that normally found in other commercial strips, the growth had nevertheless caused serious visual, traffic management, and environmental impacts in the area. While individual new buildings were often nicely designed, development in the district was taking the typical form of a dispersed, auto-related roadside sprawl, similar to that which has disfigured many other traditional towns across the country. With its rich design tradition, Edgartown felt that the site planning and design of future development should be required to meet new standards for harmony and functionalism, based upon those informal "timeless ways of building" that had successfully shaped the town in the past.

BRIEF HISTORY AND EXISTING CONDITIONS

Edgartown's B-2 District is located along both sides of Upper Main Street, on the western outskirts of the historic town. The eastern section of the district includes numerous residences dating from the turn of the century, many of which have been converted to commercial or office use. The western end of the district, formerly an area of farm and forestland, has experienced rapid commercial development during the last 15 years.

Upper Main Street has rapidly evolved from a rural fringe to the new commercial corridor it is becoming today. (See Figure 8–1.) In the nineteenth century, Upper Main Street was a country lane winding through open farmland. A few of the farmhouses from this era remain and, along with the last of the district's open spaces, should be preserved as historic links with the area's agricultural past. Standing on Upper Main Street, one can imagine how it probably appeared 100 years ago: occasional farmsteads along a tree-lined road with open fields beyond, extending over the nearby hills.

This era ended as farming declined around 1900, when commercial activities began creeping westward along this thoroughfare. With improved road conditions and increased traffic, Upper Main gained importance and began to attract new homes and small businesses. The houses at the eastern end of the district date from this era of residential expansion and constitute one of the island's earliest suburbs. Several roadside businesses, mainly filling stations and small shops, developed during this time as well, but the district consisted primarily of homes, pastures, and woodland until the early 1960s. These relatively recent changes provide a striking example of how quickly the character of a street can be transformed from rural fringe to highway business under conventional zoning regulations.

What does the district's past portend for its future? First, change has always occurred in the district, and it has not always been a negative process. Second, this change has been oriented, over the past 50 years, toward the automobile, and

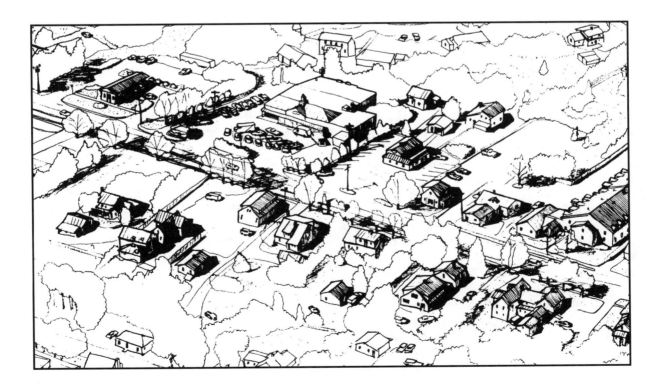

Figure 8–1 Aerial view of existing situation.

will continue in this manner unless strong action is taken to moderate that trend. Third, change sometimes happens very quickly and, if left to evolve on its own, it generally follows the path of least resistance: namely, in the direction of becoming a typical roadside strip. (See Figure 8–2.) Fourth, recent trends show the corridor is emerging as the town's predominant shopping area, providing many basic goods and services formerly available only in the historic center. This trend may be disappointing, but it is a fact of life that must be reckoned with.

The town should build upon the positive aspects of this trend by ensuring that the district becomes a vibrant, pedestrian-oriented business area, rather than just another line of shops along a congested thoroughfare. Edgartown greatly values its history and its historic resources. These features are not as prominent along Upper Main as they are in the old center, but salvageable aspects of the district's past, including several open fields, some woodland, and the remaining older homes should be preserved, both to connect with the area's heritage and to create a smoother transition between Upper Main and the historic core.

THE MASTER PLAN AND ITS RECOMMENDATIONS

The plan and the proposed zoning regulations are founded on the assumption that careful site planning and design based on townscape principles will allow the district to grow in a manner that better reflects the community's special character. Instead of rigid dimensional requirements, basic performance standards have generally been drafted to guide the design and the review of future proposals. A wide range of design and planning tools are available to help landowners meet the goals outlined in the master plan. The follow-

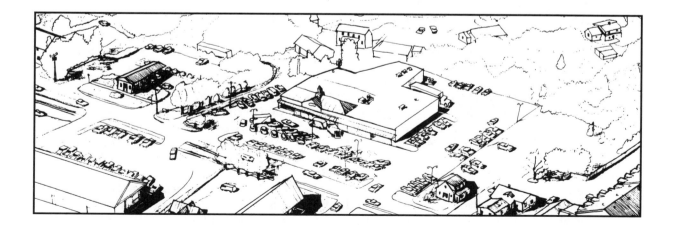

Figure 8–2. Aerial view after conventional development and redevelopment.

ing is a summary of the major recommendations contained in the master plan and the proposed regulations.

General

• Use carefully planned and designed growth as a means of transforming the district from an incipient highway strip into a more pedestrian-oriented commercial area.

• Emphasize creative site planning and design as an approach to resolving development/conservation conflicts and managing growth along Upper Main Street. Base all new planning and design solutions on the master plan drawings and the proposed regulatory improvements, with these documents forming the foundations of a problem-solving process involving all concerned parties.

Landscape Architecture/Site Planning

• Locate new buildings or additions close to Upper Main Street, with parking and service areas screened to the rear. This will create a traditional "street line" of facades, with buildings forming an attractive edge to the roadway, instead of allowing the thoroughfare to become visually dominated by large areas of parking.

• Encourage variety, irregularity, and uniqueness in building location and design, reflecting the context of traditional Edgartown patterns.

• Use fences, hedges, and other traditional devices to define a property's "formal but friendly" relationship to the street.

• Create large, meaningful, pedestrian-oriented open spaces by grouping buildings together in clusters along Upper Main Street and consolidating the resulting preserved open space along other sections of the street and behind rows of buildings.

• Preserve some of the last remaining open spaces in the district by implementing a transfer of commercial development rights program to compensate landowners (see Chapter 9).

• Encourage the planting of large deciduous "street trees" along the roadside to help shade and enclose the street, creating the atmosphere of an "outdoor room."

• Arrange buildings in varied, clustered masses, relating closely to the street.

• Encourage attractive pedestrian-oriented environments along Upper Main Street and around the shopping areas. Allow the district to become a destination rather than simply a collection of parking lots.

Architecture

• New building design in the district should not slavishly copy traditional Edgartown buildings, but should be sympathetic to the historic architecture in the older parts of town in terms of scale, massing, roof shape, gable orientation, window size, shape, and spacing, and exterior materials.

• Creative adaptation of traditional Edgartown building forms and styles is encouraged, with special attention paid to older adjacent buildings.

• Owners should reuse and add-onto older buildings, rather than tearing them down.

• New buildings should not create large, bulky masses, but should be scaled down into groupings of smaller attached structures.

Parking and Traffic

• Require parking behind commercial buildings to screen it, to create a strong building edge along Upper Main Street, and to reduce traffic congestion.

• Encourage efficient and attractive design of parking lots. Require ample landscaping to provide shade and to buffer cars from neighboring properties. Reduce large expanses of asphalt into smaller visual units, without sacrificing parking spaces.

• Encourage the consolidation and sharing of parking lots, rationalizing the current haphazard distribution of unconnected parking areas serving adjacent premises.

• Create new roads and interconnected parking lots behind existing commercial buildings to reduce traffic congestion.

• Consolidate the many scattered, disorganized "curb-cuts" into a smaller number of clearly defined entrances and four-way intersections which can be controlled at peak hours by police.

• Create a new shuttle parking lot with capacity for 450 cars in a wooded area north of Upper

Main Street. Expand and encourage maximum use of the shuttle system to reduce traffic loads on Edgartown's streets.

Utilities

• The sewer extension offers a unique opportunity to bury overhead utility wires, which detract from the character of Upper Main Street.

Zoning

The proposed zoning modifications translate master plan recommendations into specific legal terms, stressing the use of design and performance standards to achieve master plan goals. They were written to be used in tandem with the master plan policies and drawings, and are meant to encourage creative adaptation of development proposals to the requirements of that plan. The zoning modifications include:

• Improving enforcement capabilities by making most commercial uses in the district subject to a revocable special permit, with required conditions of approval.

• Requiring, as special permit conditions, that proposed projects follow master plan criteria concerning setbacks and massing, location of driveways and parking lots, landscaping and buffers, building size, and percentage coverage of the lot.

• Requiring, through the special permit process, that new development be consistent in character and scale with traditional structures in Edgartown, that it promote pedestrian and traffic safety, that it consolidate existing curb-cuts, that it prevent the intrusion of incompatible commercial uses into established residential areas, and that it conserve scenic views from publicly accessible locations.

• Encouraging mixed uses by allowing residential units above most types of shops and offices, to reflect traditional town center functions, to provide a variety of housing types, and to increase pedestrian activity levels.

DESIGN GUIDELINES

The following guidelines supplement the master plan drawings and general recommendations. They are not legally binding but are intended to advise anyone with plans to build, expand, or renovate. In the future, the town may wish to formalize these recommendations into an official design review process.

Building Massing

Traditionally in Edgartown, buildings have been located close to the street, forming a strong architectural edge. Although their front setbacks are not uniform, they have generally been consistent. Variety in building types and massing, small variations in setbacks, areas of lawn or open space, and site features such as fences create diversity within the overall consistency of the groups of buildings lining the streets.

The character of the town center should be broadly emulated by applying the principles of massing seen there. For example, buildings should be located along the edge of the street with minimum and maximum setbacks of 15 to 30 feet. This siting allows new buildings or additions to fill gaps and to screen rear parking lots and vacant spaces, creating a unified edge of harmonious structures. Furthermore, new buildings should be scaled down into smaller masses of more residential proportions, of various sizes and orientations, in groups creating smaller enclosed pedestrian spaces and enclosing entrances and driveways. (Two good examples of this type of approach can be seen in Part IV, Chapter 21, in the illustrated descriptions of "Village Commons" and "Kent Town Center.") The rambling additions so typical of old Edgartown could be adapted for commercial structures in the district, allowing a larger building volume to appear as a group of smaller connected masses.

Building Height

Buildings of two to two and one-half stories should be encouraged along Upper Main Street. One-story buildings typical of newer commercial development are too low to create a strong sense of enclosure along a main street (a point that is further discussed in Chapter 9). Single-story shops also preclude the diverse upper floor uses that create variety and interest. In taller structures, ground floors are generally devoted to retailing, while upper stories can house offices, residential units, or specialty services not requiring ground floor locations (copy centers, hairdressers, dentists, travel agencies, etc.).

Rooflines

Pitches ranging from 8-over-12 to 12-over-12 are standard for Edgartown. Flat or low-pitched roofs, as well as very steep roofs, should be avoided. A diversity of roof heights, gable orientations, and volumes in new buildings could help reinforce the town's traditional but varied character.

Architectural Design

Architectural designs should reflect but not slavishly imitate the massing, proportions, and street relationship of traditional buildings. The key is to achieve a measure of variety and individuality without designing buildings that are idiosyncratic or out of scale with their surroundings, or which disrupt the traditional front setback pattern and historic "street edge" of building facades. Front facades should be tall enough to relate properly to the traditional scale of the Upper Main streetscape. A restrained postmodern style utilizing traditional elements in a relevant, balanced way, and avoiding historical parodies could work very well in the district. Creating village-like clusters of buildings, rather than erecting individual structures isolated by asphalt parking or grassy lawns, is also critically important.

Architectural elements, such as dormers, should be in proportion with the overall building and should also be in keeping with the surrounding neighborhood context. Exaggerated or excessively large (or tiny) architectural elements should be avoided. Used properly, traditional and contemporary architectural detailing can create variety, interest, and texture on new buildings.

Materials

Traditional materials, such as weathered shingles, white wood trim, and clapboards, can help blend new buildings in with the old. But these elements should not be relied upon by themselves to create a sense of character. Historic materials are not effective when used on buildings that are otherwise inconsistent with basic principles of traditional scale, proportion, and siting.

Fenestration

Careful proportioning and placement of windows on all major facades is essential for blending in new construction. Typical Edgartown windows are rectangular with a strong vertical orientation, accented and set off by mullions and white trim boards. New fenestration can draw its inspiration from a variety of traditional windows. Excessive regularity or irregularity should be avoided, however, as should large picture windows and glass curtain walls. Circular, octagonal, and bay windows should be used with great restraint, if at all. Window location should reflect traditional "rhythms" on the facade, and provide architectural balance. Overall balance is important, though Edgartown facades sometimes contain window eccentricities. Designers of new buildings should study and adapt from local window patterns.

Signage

Appropriate signage can facilitate the transition between driving and walking in the district. The new shuttle parking lot, reorganized traffic flows, and the use of common driveways will require a well-coordinated signage system to guide drivers to their destinations and to encourage use of the shuttle. To accomplish this, some signs may have to be larger than the 12 square feet maximum area currently allowed. A 16- to 22-square feet size range may be generally more appropriate in the B-2 zone, where traffic speeds are higher and distances greater than in the center of town. Carefully designed wood or metal signs with external illumination would blend in well at these sizes. A well-designed signage system could help to unify the district and provide it with a more positive image.

Lighting

The character of the district at night is important because it is used frequently in the evening, especially during winter. Typical commercial strips are often marred by glaring high-intensity sodium vapor lights casting an eerie orange glow over the streets and parking lots. To avoid this situation, outdoor lighting in the district should be color-corrected and should be screened by shields or hoods to prevent glare onto adjacent premises. Intensity levels of individual fixtures should be reduced by utilizing a larger number of smaller light poles, in the 12- to 18-foot range. Incandescent lights should be used in smaller pedestrian spaces where quality of light is especially important.

IMPLEMENTATION PROCESS

To facilitate implementation in the everyday world of conflicting interests, divergent interpretations, and fuzzy recall, master plans must be sufficiently specific to describe a real, tangible future, while also being flexible enough to deal with unique circumstances as they develop. By describing a clear and specific *vision*, a well-prepared master plan can assure landowners that their rights will be respected and that they will be able to develop (or redevelop) their properties, while protecting the concerns of the town and of abutters about uncontrolled growth. Implementation typically involves several steps.

Communication

When landowners and developers understand what is expected of them, they are more likely to submit plans that are consistent with town goals and standards. For this reason, the master plan for Upper Main Street includes bird's-eye perspective sketches and other drawings clearly showing the desired form and design of the district, without dictating too many specific elements. (See Figure 8–3.) Since this master plan was adopted in 1989, landowners and developers have started presenting proposals that are very compatible with the master plan policies and drawings, because they know what the town wants. Clear and well-defined public objectives can help improve the quality of development proposals, because applicants want to avoid delays in the review process. In addition, the bird's-eye perspective illustrating the district's probable future under a continuation

of conventional "highway business" strip zoning informs applicants about the type of development that Edgartown has specifically rejected (large blocky buildings set back from the street beyond expansive asphalt parking lots, etc.).

Negotiation

Once initial plans are submitted, a process of dialogue and negotiation should take place to allow all parties to solve their problems creatively, within the framework of the master plan and applicable regulations. Local officials, proponents, abutters, and other concerned individuals with standing should approach the review process less as antagonists and more as problem-solvers. All parties to a potential conflict should be encouraged to sit down together to work out their difficulties using the site planning and design recommendations of the master plan. Early review of initial concepts is highly desirable to avoid later confrontation and to allow discussion of proposals before plans have proceeded too far.

CONCLUSIONS

Upper Main Street is becoming Edgartown's busiest commercial area, providing many of the essential goods and services formerly located in the historic town center, as shops in the old core area become increasingly tourist-oriented. Even though the district has already developed a linear, highway pattern, some steps can be taken to reverse this trend as the area continues to grow. This future development, if carefully planned and designed, can become a positive force for reshaping the district along more traditional lines.

The master plan outlines a vision for this process, blending the need to manage growth with the rights of landowners. The plan describes this vision with enough specific physical and procedural detail to provide a clearly defined course for the district, without creating a rigid document that cannot respond to changing circumstances.

In this sense, the plan is a hybrid between the old physical master plans popular during the first half of this century, and the much looser policy/procedure-oriented plans and land-use regula-

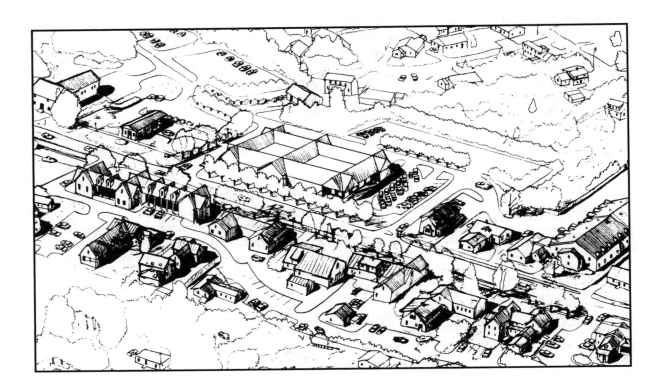

Figure 8–3. Aerial view after creative development and redevelopment.

tions widely used over the past 40 years. Purely physical master plans often became unworkable because they were too inflexible to respond to changing events. Being so far-reaching and detailed, they were often impossible to implement by local officials constrained by legal, financial, and regulatory limitations. On the other hand, plans based solely upon written policies, data, and land-use regulations have often ignored important physical planning and design issues that determine how the resulting development looks and feels to the public.

The Upper Main Street master plan allows for give and take, based upon a clear and specific physical plan. Development simply needs to occur in a careful manner that respects the town's char-

acter. In exchange for developing sensitively, in accordance with the master plan, landowners and developers are given a more reasonable chance of seeing their projects approved expeditiously. Conservationists and historic preservation advocates can be assured that this future growth will occur in a manner that in some cases improves the recent character and environment of the district.

Design based upon an area's historic traditions can translate the best elements of the past into new approaches for shaping future growth. The outstanding design sensitivity evidenced in Edgartown's first three centuries should be continued into its fourth, even though this means dealing with parking lots and utility lines instead of carriageways and wharfs.

Implementation Techniques

Development in Town Centers and Along Highways

The title of this chapter deliberately avoids the term "commercial development" because it is important to encourage—if not require—mixed uses in both town centers and in appropriate locations along certain types of highway. Sadly, the legacy of several decades of conventional zoning in many small communities has been to segregate residential, office, and commercial activities into their own "districts." The result of these well-intentioned but poorly conceived regulations is often that owners of nineteenth century commercial blocks in town centers, as well as entrepreneurs proposing central area infill construction or new development at town edges or highway intersections, are discouraged or prevented from combining these types of activities on their properties. This chapter examines issues of development (and redevelopment) first as they pertain to town centers and then as they apply to outlying lands alongside the primary road network. As will become clear, many lessons from the former also have relevance to the latter.

TOWN CENTERS: MAINTAINING THEIR VITAL FUNCTIONS

Because the central areas of small towns have traditionally accommodated their principal shopping facilities, it is understandable that the idea of a town center has become almost synonymous with retail functions. Frequently, this limited per-ception has led to one-dimensional zoning regulations restricting such uses to commercial activities.

Although both civic and institutional uses are also commonly allowed in central areas, their *critical* importance to the continued life and vitality of town centers is often not fully appreciated until the loss is a fait accompli and its consequences are keenly felt. In fact, it is probably true that, in order to be successful, town centers must possess both a strong *civus* (town hall, commons, post office, churches, etc.) and a healthy retail base. When one is weakened, so is the other.

With powerful centrifugal forces (such as the attractive power of large parking lots adjacent to high-volume highways) operating like magnets to both shoppers and shopkeepers, maintaining the vitality of town centers can be a continual challenge for conscientious public officials. They increasingly find themselves fighting reactive battles simply to retain key facilities (such as post offices) or to locate new or expanded public buildings in central areas.

With strong competition from an extensive commercial strip along a highway in an adjacent municipality, the town center of Amherst, Massachusetts, appears to be slowly and gradually losing the struggle to maintain its key businesses, despite a series of very conscious efforts by local officials to reinforce the center. For example, town center zoning not only permits mixed uses, it also

113

encourages them by allowing shared parking, wherein some of the required off-street parking spaces serve multiple purposes—daytime shoppers, nighttime residents, Sunday churchgoers—when complementary periods of usage can be demonstrated.

In addition, a large off-street parking area was created behind a major row of shops, pieces of which are owned by the town and two private shop owners. Public-private agreements have allowed the parking stalls and circulation lanes to be arranged without strict adherence to individual property lines. Town officials and the Chamber of Commerce pressed the U.S. Postal Service into keeping its old main post office open as a branch facility after a huge post office was built outside the center, concluding a 12-year struggle with the Postal Service.

A similar view of appropriate central area land uses underlies an earlier public decision to support construction of the town's major elderly housing complex in a location convenient to both the post office and to the principal shopping street. When a new police station was needed, a site was chosen just a stone's throw from the Town Hall and the Common, despite difficulties involved in acquiring such nearby land, including relocating the large and somewhat historic building that had previously occupied that parcel. And, when selecting architects for that police station and for a major expansion of the public library (also located in the center), town officials placed heavy emphasis on demonstrated ability to harmonize new designs with the surrounding historic context.

A map of Amherst's center appears as Figure 9–1, showing a traditional arrangement of small to medium-sized structures lining both sides of the main streets, with a considerable amount of off-street parking tucked in behind various commercial and mixed-use buildings.

The point is not to spotlight Amherst in particular, but rather to show how many different decisions and actions, both large and small, have been necessary to enable one New England town to avoid the depletion of its center. In addition, in many of these situations officials have been proactive rather than reactive. This has been extremely important, since some of these accomplishments would probably not have been achieved without municipal forethought and initiative.

Despite all these efforts, certain changes have occurred in situations beyond municipal control or influence. The most notable was the relocation, several years ago, of the center's only food store to a larger site a half-mile away. More recently the town's leading women's clothier, whose customer base was much the same as the grocery's (according to its manager), announced plans to vacate its downtown premises and reopen in a large mall in a neighboring town. Other defectors in recent years have included the center's only independent pharmacy and both of its hardware stores.

Another difficult challenge to this town center's ability to survive functionally was created by Mobil Oil, which in 1991 announced plans to close the only auto repair garage downtown, converting this popular service station into a 24-hour gasoline and convenience store with no mechanics. Community outrage was expressed in a long series of letters to the editor of the local weekly, arguing that the proposed conversion would profoundly affect the center's viability by eliminating an extremely useful and convenient facility. This was the only gas station offering repair services within walking distance of the University of Massachusetts campus, and was easily accessible to faculty, staff, and students, as well as town center shoppers and merchants.

Like ordinances in most other small towns, Amherst's zoning laws did not anticipate the issue of replacing gasoline station service bays with a prepackaged gum, soda, and snack shop, and the considerable difference such a change would produce in the makeup and mixture of vital downtown functions. An outpouring of community support for retaining the station in its current state strengthened the bargaining position of the Zoning Board of Appeals and the Design Review Board (whose authority to prevent the conversion was debatable). Not wishing to engage in a lengthy struggle that might have included litigation (not to mention the poor public relations), Mobil eventually scaled back its proposal to include only new pumps and larger underground

Amherst, Massachusetts

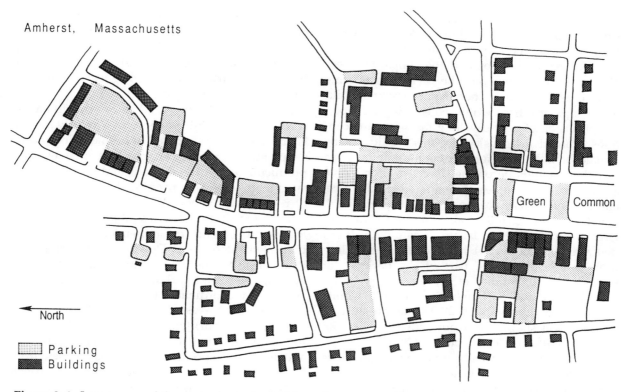

Green Common

North

Parking
Buildings

Figure 9–1. Large areas of the center in Amherst, Massachusetts, provide convenient parking for patrons of local shops and services, while the locations of these parking facilities behind buildings do not intrude on the traditional, shop-lined townscape. A considerable amount of customer parking exists in many communities like Amherst, and it functions well despite the fact that it is largely out of view from the streets (disproving the pervasive myth that businesses will not be viable unless drivers can see parking lots in front of them).

storage tanks (Lehrer, 1991). To the end, Mobil representatives maintained their decision was not influenced by public opinion. However, to the extent that public opinion emboldened public officials to take a firmer stand against the proposal (in the absence of clear standards in the ordinances), the strategy succeeded.

Of all the threats to the centers of small towns, as illustrated in Amherst's example, Mobil's proposed conversion is perhaps the most worrying, insofar as it represented the conscious policy of a large corporation to pursue a narrow course defined by its own self-interest, irrespective of the negative impacts that policy may produce upon the general good, as perceived by the local citizenry and their official representatives.

In pondering how the town might in the future exert more influence upon the mix of shops in its center, to help bring back a hardware store and a grocery, for example, the chair of the planning board wrote a guest editorial for the local weekly, advocating public purchase of one of the large commercial buildings so that specific types of retailers could be attracted through subsidized rents. The idea of the town becoming a commercial landlord was not well received, although historic precedent for that type of involvement certainly exists in New England (e.g., the Old City Hall in Lowell, Massachusetts, built with ground-floor shops in 1836, is discussed at the end of Chapter 2).

With regard to ensuring a healthy residential component in town centers, zoning regulations could be amended to include provisions requiring—not simply allowing—new and expanded commercial floor space to be supplemented with housing units, above and/or behind the shops. Business district designations could be revised to become "mixed use districts," wherein permission to build new shops or offices would be conditioned upon the provision of new dwelling units (with exceptions granted for sites where this would not be practicable). Without such strong measures, towns risk their centers becoming deserted after 5 or 6 PM. Two good examples of integrated retail, office, and residential uses are the new "Village Galleria" development in La Jolla, California, and "Winslow Green" on Bainbridge Island, Washington (both described in Chapter 21). In La Jolla, five dwelling units were built above part of the parking lot behind a small complex of six retail shops and a branch bank, and on Bainbridge Island, 34 units occupy two floors above 20,000 square feet of ground-level shops (on a downtown corner site behind a half-acre "common").

Such mixtures routinely occurred in the days before zoning instilled in local officials the doctrine of use segregation. But it is not too late to reincorporate some good ideas from the past into our future planning. Although the need to provide handicap access to commercial and office uses on upper floors can add extra costs to new or extensively remodeled buildings, these requirements generally do not apply to upper-level residential units in new buildings, and are not a valid excuse for avoiding expansion of upper-story apartments.

Where true incompatibility among land uses can be reasonably expected, however, a mixture requirement should be relaxed. In situations where certain types of ground-floor businesses (such as discotheques or fried fish or chicken outlets) would ordinarily disturb or annoy residents upstairs, those business types should either be excluded entirely or become subject to strict "good neighbor" performance standards (such as through adequate soundproofing or proper venting of kitchen aromas via tall stacks).

Wholesale separation of all residential uses from all commercial uses is as harmful as it is simplistic.

The real world is a little untidy at times, but with proper safeguards the most vexing problems can be intelligently avoided. (Examples of performance standards are contained in the model site plan review ordinance in *Dealing with Change . . .* , Yaro, Arendt, et al., 1988.)

Efforts should also be taken to strengthen the town center's retail function. In Westerly, Rhode Island, steps were initiated to promote downtown shops and to attract certain types of new ones, producing a mixture of goods and services calculated to draw a wider range and a greater number of regular customers. Westerly's emphasis is beginning to shift from the desirable but costly physical improvements recommended in its largely unimplemented 1985 Downtown Development Plan (historic building renovation, new street lighting, increased parking, and better traffic circulation) to coordinated marketing.

In 1991, the Westerly (Rhode Island)/Pawcatuck (Connecticut) Joint Development Task Force hired a consultant to develop a marketing strategy and to recruit specific kinds of businesses, from large chain stores to small shops in other coastal New England towns whose owners might be persuaded to open a branch in Westerly (Liberman, 1991). At the heart of this approach was a recognition that, in order to compete with well-organized mall marketers, town centers need to adopt similar techniques, such as hiring a single manager to develop an appropriate retail plan and to bring targeted businesses into the shopping district.

To deal with the problems arising from having multiple landlords and sometimes irksome municipal regulations, Westerly is also addressing the need to form an association of retailers, landlords, and local officials, to pursue customers (both patrons and shopkeepers) cooperatively. It is counterproductive for one downtown landlord to attract tenants by deliberately luring retailers from neighboring buildings (as has already happened). In short, to survive, downtowns in many communities are going to have to become much better organized and adept at beating the malls at their own game. Many of the approaches suggested in Westerly are similar to ones promoted by the Main

Street Program of the National Trust for Historic Preservation, to which readers are referred for further information.

A truly remarkable degree of cooperation among town center property owners and merchants exists in Chestnut Hill, a nineteenth-century Philadelphia suburb of 18,000 people, where the local business association coordinates special sale days and promotions every month, and advertises participating businesses as a "horizontal department store." More unusual are Chestnut Hill's achievements in providing convenient customer parking. Over the last 40 years a private nonprofit parking foundation has created eight new parking lots (with 379 spaces) on land held by multiple owners behind rows of long-established shops. The foundation leases individual parcels for $1 per year and receives substantial cash contributions (to pay for paving, striping, snow removal, litter pickup, etc.) from landlords and merchants who recognize the common benefit of joining together to offer well-planned parking facilities adjacent to their premises. Parking fees of $1 per half hour (standard in this area) are collected from users, who receive stickers for 30 minutes of free parking with every purchase they make from participating businesses. All eight lots are completely self-financing, with no monetary contributions from local government.

TOWN CENTERS: MAINTAINING THEIR TRADITIONAL FORM

It is inevitable that town centers will change over time, but it is not preordained that such changes must rob a community of its special character. While it is easier to imagine the potential for change where properties are presently vacant or underutilized, two important forces place even mature town centers at risk: fire and redevelopment. One can never predict when a building may burn down, and the gradual rise in property values that usually precedes demolition and rebuilding similarly takes most residents and local officials by surprise. The most prudent policy is to take nothing for granted, and assume that virtually all buildings and land uses are subject to change.

The conventional development scenario illustrated in Figure 8–2, Chapter 8, "Commercial Infill Development Along a Major Street," is not an exaggeration but rather a careful analysis of the scale and pattern that new buildings and parking lots could easily create in Edgartown, Massachusetts, under its current zoning regulations. Unfortunately, the scale, pattern, design, and location of new buildings and parking areas are scarcely addressed in most land-use regulations, in spite of the fact that these are the variables that really determine whether new development fits comfortably into a community, or whether it upsets the traditional rhythm of the townscape.

These are not matters of mere detail with only minor consequences. When a two-story gable-end wooden building with a shallow front yard is replaced by a single-story masonry structure set far back on its lot to accommodate an eight-car parking area in front, this is a fundamental change that profoundly affects the character of a street.

The laissez-faire stance of most municipal land-use regulations with respect to the scale, pattern, design, and actual setback location of new development along a town's principal streets might suggest that residents and local officials do not really care about how future changes would affect the visual character of their community. Some, it might be said, subscribe to the notion of "disposable streetscapes in a throwaway society."

It is much more likely, however, that they have never been encouraged to think through the possibilities for significant negative change that are permitted under their current zoning. In Livingston County, Michigan, county planners circulated an illustrated questionnaire among their local commission members to determine their preferences with regard to the physical form of commercial development. The simple line diagrams reproduced in Figure 9–2 are from these questionnaires, with the question "Which figure looks more rural/small town to you?" Of the 89 respondents, 73 percent answered "A" and 24 percent chose "B." As a result of this survey and numerous workshops and discussions, county planners in Livingston have begun helping local com-

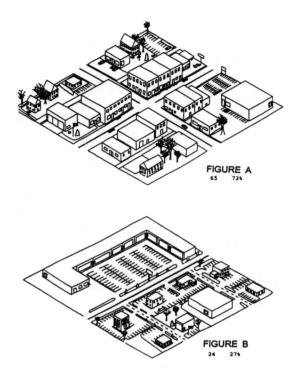

Figure 9–2. Illustrations from a visual preference survey conducted by the Livingston County (Michigan) Planning Department to determine the type of building and parking arrangements most pleasing to local residents and officials. Three-quarters preferred the one at the top, a pattern that does not conform with most ordinances in the area. To achieve traditional streetscape patterns, it is usually not sufficient merely to eliminate zoning impediments: adoption of maximum front setbacks and rear parking requirements are also necessary.

missioners reevaluate their local zoning regulations, with a view toward introducing changes designed to encourage more traditional "A" type development.

To the extent that rural residents and officials have considered the potential for their existing town centers and other commercially zoned areas to lose their special character and gradually become formless and unattractive, many presume that the types of controls needed to protect their townscape would conflict with property owners' basic constitutional rights. But zoning techniques

such as establishing *"maximum* front setbacks" and requiring off-street parking to be located behind buildings are perfectly permissible regulations.

Further restrictions on building height (or number of stories) are similarly legal, while restrictions on building design typically require special ordinances. Municipal authority to regulate building design (outside designated historic districts) varies from state to state, but an approach that may enjoy potentially wide applicability ties design variables to permitted land-use intensities. Using this technique, communities may designate certain low-intensity commercial uses (such as haircutters, gift shops, bookstores, florists, antique shops, etc.) as "by right" uses, subject only to standard requirements (minimum setbacks, minimum parking area, etc.).

All other uses could be subject to design review criteria, perhaps under "conditional use" or "special exception" procedures. Establishing or expanding such uses would be a privilege, not an absolute right. In return for permission to create or enlarge higher-intensity uses (which typically generate more traffic congestion on public streets, and presumably greater profits benefiting landowners), developers of higher-intensity uses would be required to conform to certain principles of infill construction design to harmonize with the town's traditional character.

In a publication with a geographically broad audience it would be inappropriate to attempt a definition of "traditional character." It varies too much from region to region, and often more frequently than that. For this reason, the composite qualities that comprise "traditional character" should be defined locally, through an examination of building materials, architectural styles, front setbacks, street cross-sections, landscaping elements (including fences, hedges, and walls), and formal and informal open spaces, both among buildings and between buildings and streets.

Reproduced in the Appendix is a list of architectural design standards for new infill construction in areas with traditional streetscapes. Although they relate to small nineteenth-century mill towns in New England, the standards can easily be adapted to suit other contexts, where roof shapes or exterior materials may be different. Among the key sections are those balancing the need for "continuity" and "contemporary approaches." In the former, buildings are discouraged from being designed as freestanding objects, unrelated to their immediate surroundings. In the latter, contemporary design is encouraged, as long as it respects and reflects the traditional scale, proportions, rhythms, and mood of neighboring historic structures. "These traditional architectural values should be interpreted into contemporary building design, but the use of imitation historic building details and ornaments is discouraged. Building design must also be internally consistent, and amalgamations of historically unrelated stylistic elements shall generally be prohibited."

Good examples of contemporary buildings that have fit easily into their surroundings are discussed and illustrated in Part IV. An excellent example of a well-defined infill development is "Heritage Square" in Belchertown, Massachusetts, in which a modern bank and professional office building were shaped and scaled to blend with the nineteenth-century building tradition of their immediate neighbors (a church and a residence). Just as important, they were located in line with those adjacent structures, holding the established streetscape pattern intact. Parking was provided in the rear, along with a new post office.

Unfortunately such sensitive design is a hit-or-miss situation in this town, as it is in most other communities: several years later a second group of office buildings was constructed a little farther down the same side of the main street, but they were located in the middle of the lot with a substantial parking area between them and the roadway. The visual effect of this out-of-step arrangement is very disruptive to the continuity of the town's traditional "Main Street" appearance, despite the buildings' sensitive architectural styling. Furthermore, a good opportunity to ameliorate this situation was missed when a landscaping plan consisting of junipers, flowering ornamentals, and bark mulch was approved. Instead, local officials should have insisted upon a grassy verge planted with a row of proper shade trees, as is traditional along this street. Such a planting scheme would

have helped to create a "street line" to strengthen the front edge of this weakly designed building group. This point is illustrated in Figure 9–3.

Principles of traditional downtown design should be articulated in master plans and zoning regulations of every town that wishes to retain the best aspects of its central areas, and that also wants new development to follow the older patterns as much as possible. A notable example of such articulation appears in the "Community Design and Appearance" section of the *Sterling Forest Comprehensive Plan*, which describes townscape design objectives for Sterling Crossing, the proposed mixed-use center for a planned community in Orange County, New York (Sterling Forest Corp., 1991). (See Figure 9–4.) These guidelines include requirements such as the following:

• building facades must maintain a consistent street edge, except to provide pedestrian passageways to rear parking areas;

• ground-floor space shall be reserved for pedestrian-oriented retailing and services, with offices and housing above;

Building set back too far from street

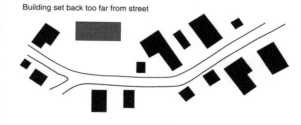

Buildings maintain close relationship to street

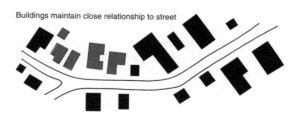

Figure 9–3. Simple graphics such as these can be used to illustrate the point (in a zoning ordinance, e.g.) that a greater number of smaller buildings (with perhaps more rentable floorspace) located closer to the street will harmonize better in many town centers than larger structures set back in a way that disrupts the traditional scale and rhythm. *Source:* Dodson Associates.

Figure 9–4. Multistory buildings holding a traditional "street line," with shade trees, rear parking, and a small "green" (in the lower left corner) illustrate the principles of sensitive downtown design in this aerial perspective sketch of Sterling Crossing, a pedestrian-friendly center for a new town proposed to be built in Sterling Forest, New York. *Source:* Sedway Cooke Associates.

- building height shall be limited to a minimum of two stories, a maximum of five, with the third to fifth floors set back to allow sunlight onto the streets during autumn, winter, and early spring;
- building designs shall be encouraged to utilize contemporary interpretations of earlier styles, utilizing native stone and pitched roofs with dormers and gables; and
- three major public spaces with major community buildings will include a central square (sized to accommodate fairs and concerts), a grassy tree-lined plaza modeled after a New England town green (with a hotel and a multipurpose hall housing a library, day-care center, senior center, and clinics), and a community park (adjacent to a congregate-care facility).

Different factors would apply, however, at the level of a very small village or a rural hamlet, where the sheer size of a new building may simply be out of scale with the surrounding context. This was the case in Sherman, Connecticut, where a new IGA grocery store was built about ten years ago. The creative design solution in this case was to tuck the grocery behind a strip of natural woodland, with a clearly marked sign at the driveway entrance. Both the IGA and its parking lot are visually inconspicuous, but that has not affected sales, as everyone in the area knows exactly where the store is located, because it is their only major local grocery. Also sharing this site is a small bank. As shown in Figure 9–5, these buildings are well integrated with the village pattern, which includes a firehouse, town hall, old school and church, and a number of homes.

INFILL DEVELOPMENT AS PATTERN ENHANCER

Infill techniques can be used to create strength and order in situations that today may be rather formless, particularly in areas where growth has been haphazard and essentially unplanned. Many communities possess examples of such situations, where additional development could, if carefully conceived, help create form, cohesion, and order, the same attributes that subtly operate in traditional towns (oftentimes so subtly that many people are not consciously aware of their significance until it is pointed out to them). Some of these elements are discussed in Chapter 4, but an outstanding reference on this subject is *Making Infill Projects Work* (Smart, 1985). Although written with a strongly urban cast, it contains many fine examples illustrating the principles of harmonious design.

A redevelopment plan recently prepared for Davie Settlement in Broward County, Florida, provides a dramatic example of design principles used to create a well-ordered traditional town form in a location that had, over the last several decades, grown into a hodgepodge of sprawling low-density suburban uses. On a 42-acre site, where Davie Road and Orange Drive intersect, the Davie Redevelopment Agency commissioned a visionary plan to introduce a modified grid of new streets to access an orderly arrangement of interior building lots. The layout, prepared by the Miami urban design firm of Dover, Correa, Kohl, Cockshutt and Valle, is reproduced in Figure 9–6, show-

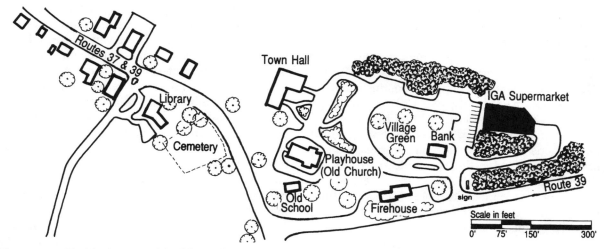

Figure 9–5. Highly functional buildings that are very large or otherwise incompatible in the context of a small rural village can sometimes be made less intrusive by positioning them behind a group of trees, as was done with this grocery in Sherman, Connecticut. (In unwooded areas, or in larger settlements, another effective approach could involve lining the street-edge of the building site with a number of small shops, locating the parking and the food store behind them.)

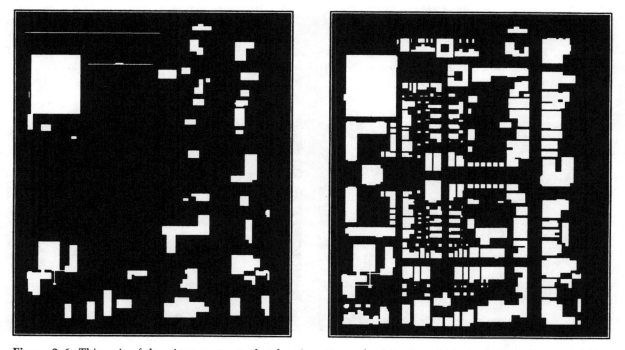

Figure 9–6. This pair of drawings contrasts the chaotic pattern of existing roadside "strip" development in Davie Settlement, Broward County, Florida, with a more orderly and traditional arrangement of buildings, side-streets, alleys, and rear parking areas now possible through the recently adopted comprehensive physical master plan, which calls for sensitive infilling and redevelopment along just these lines. *Source:* Dover et al., 1990.

ing building locations, street patterns, curbside and rear parking areas, and public open spaces.

In addition to serving vehicular traffic, the streets were designed to become "significant public spaces," as important as parks and plazas (Dunlop, 1991). Spaces between existing buildings will be filled in gradually over a 20-year period, so the streets will eventually be lined by a combination of building types designed according to certain dimensional and locational parameters, based upon an understanding of building form and street/building relationships in older Florida towns such as Winter Park and Mt. Dora. Buildings will also be subject to certain use criteria, with a finely grained mixture of residential, commercial, and civic uses existing together in close proximity, if not in the same structure.

Readers are invited to compare the Davie "infill" plan with the map of downtown Amherst, Massachusetts, at the beginning of this chapter, and to note the similarity in the scale and arrangement of both buildings and parking areas. Towns that wish to retain their character should insist that their consultants, and intending developers, familiarize themselves with the important matters of pattern, scale, and context. Otherwise, suburban intrusions are very likely to occur.

Interestingly, the proposed redevelopment plan became a hotly contested issue in local elections. As things turned out, all the candidates who opposed the plan lost, while those who had supported it were elected. When time came for the local council to endorse or reject the plan, it was approved unanimously. The decision-making process was made easier by the consensus generated by the consultants' graphics, which included crisp aerial perspectives illustrating what the main thoroughfare and the area immediately behind it would eventually look like if the proposed neo-traditional design standards and mixed-use zoning regulations were implemented.

Figures 9–7, 9–8, and 9–9 show existing and future views of the redevelopment site, with the main road becoming a landscaped shopping boulevard, behind which will be compact residential neighborhoods punctuated by civic/institutional buildings and small parks. Local officials found widespread community support for a redevelopment strategy designed to produce a familiar "Main Street" form, with mixed uses and residential areas based on patterns found in most American towns before 1940. Parking will be handled both on the street and in interior parking lots located behind commercial buildings; garages in

Figure 9–7. Aerial photograph of existing conditions, compared with a computer-generated image of potential redevelopment creating a traditional pattern of vernacular buildings containing shops and residences (Davie Settlement, Broward County, Florida). *Source:* Dover et al., 1990.

Figure 9–8. Proposed elevations of shops and residences, Davie Settlement, Broward County, Florida. *Source:* Dover et al., 1990.

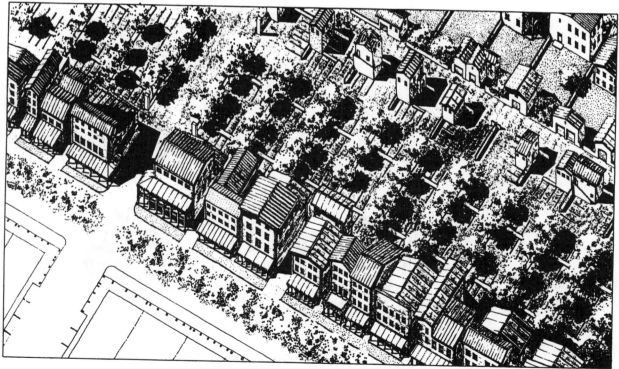

Figure 9–9. Aerial perspective sketch showing new "street edge" and rear parking areas, Davie Settlement, Broward County, Florida. *Source:* Dover et al., 1990.

residential areas will be accessed via rear lanes or alleys.

One of the more creative aspects of this plan lies in its use of shared parking facilities for the commercial buildings along the principal streets. (See Figure 9–10.) Using formulae developed by the Urban Land Institute, parking calculations were performed for every hour of the day from 8 AM to 10 PM, on both weekdays and weekends. Due to the mixture of uses on the site (shops, offices, apartments, civic buildings, a cinema, and a rodeo) it was possible for many of the parking spaces to be used at different times by different types of people. In the plan adopted by the redevelopment agency, calculations show a substantial parking surplus most of the time, with only a 10 percent deficit on weekend afternoons when the rodeo opens. However, this problem will not arise until 91 percent of the buildings are constructed and occupied, and would never occur if one out of every seven rodeo fans carpooled with a friend, or if 9 percent of the projected demand for spaces were eliminated by people riding public transport.

Although it is very ambitious, the Davie Plan is based upon principles applicable to smaller towns and more modest sites. The need for a coherent street and access plan can be just as critical on parcels of only a few acres in size, situated in key locations. Such street layouts should be part of the community's master plan (or town center plan). To quote from the Davie Settlement designers: "Today it should no longer be acceptable to approve 'master plans' which are composed only of aggregate figures and bubble diagrams. . . . City and county governments must insist on master plans that illustrate real streets, building positions and uses. Otherwise it is impossible to verify that a project uses an integrated approach. . . . Abstract

Figure 9–10. Alternative locations for buildings, parking, and access, Davie Settlement, Broward County, Florida. *Source:* Dover et al., 1990.

land use maps alone do not constitute a community vision" (Dover et al., 1991).

SHOPPING STREETS AS "OUTDOOR ROOMS"

For shopping streets in newly developed areas to feel traditional they must exhibit the characteristics of "outdoor rooms." As mentioned in Chapter 2 with regard to residential streets, it is critical that designers be aware of the importance of the ratio between street width and building height. Width/height ratios (as measured horizontally between opposing shop fronts and vertically from the sidewalk to the eaves line) have been found to be the most pleasing when they lie within the range of 2:1 and 3:1.

The 3:1 ratio is quite common in older towns where the streets are about 60 to 80 feet wide and the building facades are 24 to 36 feet tall (two to three stories high). In some small coastal towns in New England, even higher ratios occur (1.5:1 on Water Street in Stonington, Connecticut, and 1.2:1 on Commercial Street in Provincetown, Massachusetts (Nigrelli, 1990). In addition to being aesthetically pleasing, however, the 3:1 ratio (as found on the Main Streets of Warrenton, Virginia, and Wellfleet, Massachusetts) allows more opportunity for parallel curbside parking on both sides of the shopping street, a feature that commercial developers would probably favor. Indeed, when a new streetscape was created in a former shopping plaza in Mashpee, Massachusetts, the designers employed width/height ratios varying from 2.3:1 to 2.9:1, as shown in the cross-sectional sketches in Figure 9–11 (Nigrelli, 1990).

It is perhaps no simple coincidence that the width/height ratios of the spaces inside many malls conform to these same pleasing proportions. For example, in the Hampshire Mall in Hadley, Massachusetts, where interior shop fronts (and the ceiling over the space between them) are about 15 feet high, the pedestrian circulation "street" tends to be about 35 feet wide. Where these "streets" intersect in a Disneyesque imitation of a "town square," the shop fronts become several stories high and the space between them widens out into a sort of plaza, filled with benches, planters, and a fountain. The same understanding of proportions should (but rarely does) inform the designers of outdoor spaces in shopping facilities. This is an area where sensitive guidance and design criteria from local government are much needed.

THE VALUE OF PUBLIC OPEN SPACE IN TOWN CENTERS

Whether designing new mixed-use areas or retrofitting an existing town center, the opportunity for creating comfortable public spaces should be carefully considered. That they may possess economic significance as well as offering aesthetic benefits gives an additional reason for their provision.

A study of 21 rural towns in Georgia enrolled in the "Main Street Program" of the National Trust for Historic Preservation found the vitality of the centers (as expressed by their peak pedestrian volumes) was related, in part, to the physical form of the central business district. Of the four broad physical forms (courthouse square, multiblock, cruciform, and stem), pedestrian activity was by far the strongest in the towns with courthouse squares. (See Figure 9–12.)

In explaining these differences in pedestrian activity, researchers at the University of Georgia cited the courthouse square's "superior form in terms of human activity" (Kenyon, 1989). In these towns "the business district is built around, or partly around, a central block of non-business uses. . . . The courthouse town is thus compact, yet not heavily concentrated at one intersection, and therefore perhaps most conducive to enhancement as a social center."

In other words, the economic success of central business districts can be linked to their ability to serve also as "central social districts," characterized by a "pleasant human scale," small amenity parks in which pedestrians may relax comfortably, and establishments for eating, drinking, socializing, and entertainment. The layout and form of courthouse squares, which often provide inviting oases of quiet open space in the midst of the downtown bustle, are apparently very conducive to many different types of business activity.

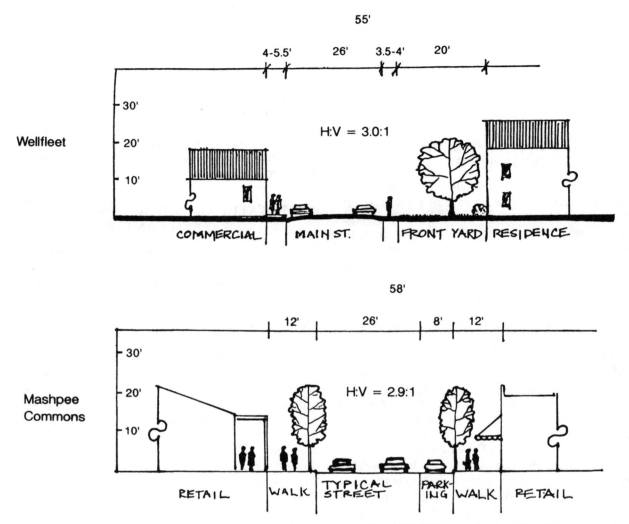

Figure 9–11. Streetscape cross-section comparisons showing similar width:height ratios in a historic town center and in a neo-traditional mixed-use development, both on Cape Cod. The proportions of the "outdoor rooms" created in new developments are basic elements of the type of character these places will possess, yet they are among the least regulated aspects of commercial or mixed-use development design. *Source:* Nigrelli, 1990.

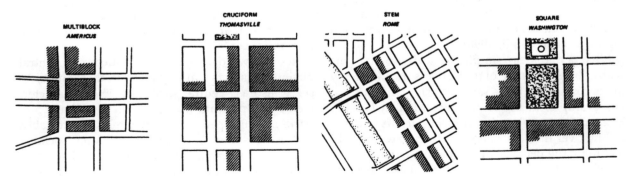

Figure 9–12. Four basic patterns of public open space in small towns in rural Georgia, where sidewalk pedestrian counts have shown that towns with central open spaces typically enjoy the highest level of pedestrian activity. *Source:* Kenyon, 1989.

OFFICIAL MAPPING TO SET THE PROPER PATTERN

"Official mapping" is a planning technique to reserve land for future streets, parking lots, and open spaces. It enables some of the features of places such as Davie Settlement and Georgia's "courthouse square" towns to become incorporated as design elements in other municipalities. The 1896 bird's-eye drawing of Bozeman, Montana (reproduced in Chapter 3), showing future streets and park locations in a frontier community, is a graphic reminder that the task of laying out patterns of streets and public open spaces was not beyond the ability of our great-grandfathers, who certainly had fewer techniques and resources at their disposal than we do today. In current parlance, such an approach is known as "official mapping." The definition of an "official map" is one that is adopted by the local governing body to inform landowners, prospective developers, and the general public of the location of streets and public spaces that the municipality or the county has committed itself to acquire (Brower et al., 1984).

Ownership patterns remain unchanged until the land is purchased or conveyed. Sale of the land to other parties is not prohibited, but unauthorized improvements on land identified as future streets are not subject to compensation. Such regulations have generally been upheld in the courts, except when existing parcels are rendered undevelopable by the official map. Such occurrences may happen when existing parcels are small and the map is not drawn carefully to respect current property lines. However, in most cases, official mapping improves the developability of land because it shows an official commitment by the local government to see that street access is provided to the land alongside mapped streets, with the express purpose of facilitating its conversion to more intensive uses. Compensation could become an issue if land were earmarked to become public open space, but this could probably be avoided by allowing the developer a residential density bonus (or business use-intensity bonus) so that he or she could still build as many units or as much floor space on the remaining land.

RURAL HIGHWAYS: MAINTAINING THEIR FUNCTION

The practice of land-use planning along rural highways often seems more closely related to the goals of maximizing local property-tax revenues and adjacent land values than it is to any commitment to ensure the proper functioning of the existing arterial road network. However counterproductive this approach may be to the future integrity of the transportation system, this orientation is completely understandable, considering that these land-use decisions are typically made by local governments that are essentially acting in their own short-term interests.

Insofar as such governments depend heavily upon local property-tax revenues, it makes good economic sense to designate generous lengths of highway frontage for business uses, which can be taxed at higher rates than homes, and which typically place the smallest burden on public services. Small wonder that, in a recent study of zoning in the predominantly rural Connecticut River Valley of western Massachusetts, 57 percent of the state highway frontage in Hampden, Hampshire, and Franklin Counties was found to be zoned for commercial uses (Valley Futures, 1988). As only a small fraction of this land is already developed, and because rural highway business zoning is normally quite unrestrictive, this situation offers commercial developers virtually a carte blanche invitation to set up shop almost anywhere, anytime, along most of the region's arterial network.

The long-term consequences of following such an "open road policy" are illustrated by the experience of one Cape Cod town, which has for three decades consistently rejected all major recommendations for controlling highway land-use contained in local and regional plans and studies. The situation at present in Eastham, Massachusetts, is graphically depicted by the diagrams in Figures 9–13 and 9–14. Together they show the close correlation between high-intensity roadside land-uses—fast-food restaurants, gasoline stations, souvenir shops, and other tourist attractions—and the location and incidence of traffic accidents. Studies such as this should become a standard part of

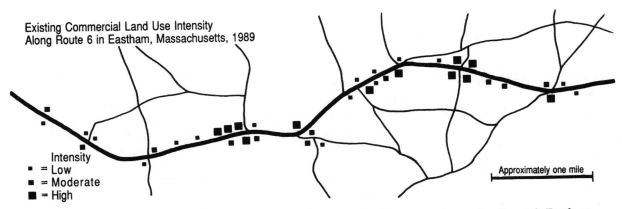

Figure 9–13. Commercial land-use intensity along Route 6, the major spine road running through Eastham, Massachusetts, on Cape Cod, where strip commercial development is very extensive along this busy highway. *Source:* Schaefer et al., 1989.

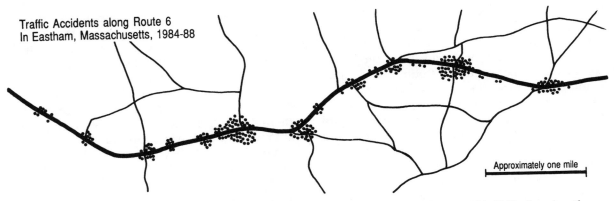

Figure 9–14. Location of traffic accidents along Route 6 in Eastham, Massachusetts, 1984–1988, showing the high correlation between accidents and intensive land uses depicted in the accompanying diagram, demonstrating the disastrous results of zoning major traffic corridors for such commercial activities. *Source:* Schaefer et al., 1989.

training courses for local planning board (or commission) members in every state. Today, Eastham's Route 6 enjoys the dubious distinction of having the highest highway fatality rate in the entire Commonwealth, higher even than the notorious "Suicide Alley" in nearby Orleans, Massachusetts (Schaefer, 1989).

The congested, dangerous, and often ugly mess created by inappropriate land-use policies is well documented. For example, a 1930s survey of 47 miles of highway between Trenton and Newark,

New Jersey, revealed no fewer than 300 filling stations, 472 billboards, and 440 other commercial uses (Tunnard and Pusahkarev, 1963). "The continued, almost miraculous expansion of roadside commercial strips right through the lean years of the Great Depression so impressed tax-hungry local officials that they referred to these strips as 'miracle miles,' a name by which they are still known today, in some quarters" (Arendt, 1989). Rural areas were by no means immune to this phenomenon. In a 1928 monograph entitled *The Les-*

sons of the Mohawk Trail (Massachusetts State Route 2 from Boston to the Berkshires), noted planner and essayist Benton MacKaye had this to say:

> We want the tourist. He in turn is attracted by natural scenery; he wants to visit our historic shrines and to enjoy our delightful summer climate. Who then would think of removing or marring Bunker Hill Monument or Plymouth Rock? Yet, in the midst of the grandest scenery the state possesses, a few individuals for personal gain are permitted to erect notoriously ugly shacks of flimsy construction and plaster them over with barking hot dog signs. . . . Scarcely were (the tourist's) eyes focussed upon a distant peak, a canyon or other feature of scenic interest, when suddenly it was blotted out with a broadside of paint and an appeal to buy something. He was spending good money to escape from the howls of commercialism, and here it was hounding him on his vacation.

Around the same time, MacKaye wrote an article for the *Boston Transcript* describing the transformation of the New England roadside as a "metropolitan invasion which has suddenly come upon us: this bedlam of filling stations, hot dog stands, road houses, souvenir stores, billboards, and amusement parks. This is not the architecture of the well-ordered town; it is the architecture of the slum: not the slum of poverty but the slum of commerce" (MacKaye, 1928).

Master of the colorful phrase, MacKaye termed these businesses "malignant growths" and "wayside funguses." The problem then, as now, was how best to deal with a clearly deteriorating situation. In 1930, MacKaye supplied a visionary answer: a system of "townless highways." In an article printed in *The New Republic*, MacKaye argued for "a highway built for the motorist and kept free from every encroachment except the filling stations and restaurants needed for his convenience," and even these would be located at designated "wayside stations." In an unpublished draft of this article, MacKaye explained the logic of his proposal in simple analogies:

> This is the story of a divorce—not of man and wife but of town and highway. The cause is incompatibility—the clash between the home and the road, between the domestic cozy spirit of the one and the wild dashing spirit of the other. The home is a place for us to stay, to work and play and rest; the road is a place for us to go, and to see as we go. Home and highway are mutual blessings, but when too close they are mutual nuisances. Each should have its own way, and since their ways are profoundly different the answer is simple: separation.

> Home and highway did not clash in the calm old days of the horse and carriage. And when the railway came along we kept away from the snorting locomotive and did not build our homes along the track. We now have a new kind of "locomotive" and a new kind of "track," one made of cement instead of iron. The dirt road has turned into a cement track. But we persist in building our homes along this new kind of track (except here and there, as in Radburn, New Jersey). And we persist in building the track right through the town, so the track clutters up the town, as any resident will tell you. And the town clutters up the track, as any motorist will tell you. Each invades the other. (MacKaye, 1930).

MacKaye's solution was simple. "Town" functions (homes, shops, offices, factories) would be physically segregated from the "highway" users (freight haulers, commuters, tourists) by building bypasses around existing towns and insulating through-routes from frontage development. In short, the motor-roads would be designed along the principles of railroads (see Figure 9–15).

The resulting urban form would not be radically new. It would, in fact, reinforce traditional historic settlement patterns, with compact towns surrounded by rural land uses.

In MacKaye's words, "A town is worthy of a personality and our New England towns have their personalities. To have a personality, however, a town must first of all be a separate geographic unit. It must have open space around it." This was in sharp contrast to commercial strips where "the effect . . . is to create 'roadtowns' instead of centers—to make a row of buildings . . . with no beginning and no ending, instead of a group of buildings around a common center or purpose. Such development does not meet the conception of a true town or unit of society; it is not a town,

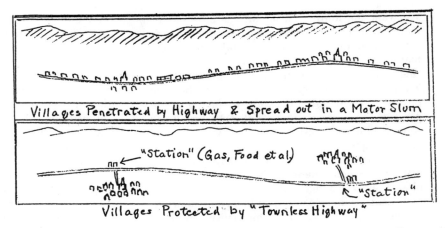

Figure 9–15. Benton MacKaye's 1929 sketch of the "Townless Highway" and the "Highwayless Town," two of the earliest planning diagrams making the case for keeping major traffic corridors uncluttered with roadside commercial uses. *Source:* Dartmouth College Archives.

it is merely a linear spreading of humanity" (MacKaye, 1930).

RURAL HIGHWAYS: AN APPROPRIATE FORM

Six decades later, it is still difficult to argue with MacKaye's basic proposition: business districts and traffic corridors should be physically separated. In modern highway planning this takes the form of new limited-access arterials (including the Interstate System). Another approach involves "parallel access roads" (or "frontage roads") built to accommodate commercial enterprises desiring clear visibility from, and intermittent access to, the major highways they follow. However, at a cost of $4 million per mile to build even a new two-lane highway, this is clearly not a viable option (Valley Futures, 1988).

Assuming that it is too costly and too extravagant to construct a new parallel highway network, the obvious question arises: Is it politically feasible to protect the existing route structure? In other words, is there sufficient political will to "just say no" to the continued degradation of this nearly

irreplaceable public asset? It is a rare municipality that refuses to alter its zoning to allow commercial uses along its section of state highway. Route 9 in Loudonville, New York, Route 5 in Longmeadow, Massachusetts, and Route 114 in Newport, Rhode Island, are three unusual examples where pressures to rezone the highway corridor from its established residential usage to "roadside commercial" have been successfully resisted for decades.

It is even more difficult to "down-zone" vacant land, currently zoned for retail expansion, to more appropriate and less intensive uses, but this is exactly what happened in York, Maine (along Route 1) and in Kent, Connecticut (along Route 7) during the 1980s. In both cases zoning was revised to conform with the local comprehensive plans, which were far more forward-thinking than the land-use regulations then on the books. In York, the highway corridor was rezoned from "general purpose" (where nearly every type of business or industrial use could be established, without any special review or standards) to a series of districts allowing various intensities of usage, subject to a long list of specific performance and landscaping standards. Strongly resisted by certain business-men and landowners, the town not only voted in the new restrictions, but also upheld that action in a subsequent referendum repeal challenge.

In Kent, the Planning and Zoning Commission amended the town's zoning by placing strict new limitations on business expansion along its "gate-way corridor," Route 7, restricting most such activity to the village center. Commercial development along this highway is now limited to professional offices, roadside farm stands, campgrounds, golf courses, private clubs, stables, kennels, veterinary clinics, hospitals, nursing homes, funeral homes, hotels, nursery schools, and indoor restaurants. Of course, in order to avoid opening the door to a string of fast-food franchises in years to come, some specific wording (as York adopted) prohibiting such high-intensity eateries will be needed.

Because these arterials are owned and maintained by state governments, it would be logical for state legislators to amend their respective zoning enabling acts to take back some of the zoning authority they granted to localities many years ago. This was essentially the proposal floated by the Maine State Planning Office in 1987, when then Director Richard Barringer suggested that land adjacent to state highways be subject to minimum zoning requirements set by the state, to control access and regulate use intensities. The proposal was conceptually similar to Maine's 1973 Shore-land Zoning Act, which has successfully implemented setbacks, tree clearing, and use intensities along the state's rivers, lakes, and oceanfront. The 1987 proposal recommended a similar hierarchy of linear zoning districts, each with different permitted uses and use intensities, together with a set of development performance standards.

Although never officially debated by the legislature, this concept could be adopted and applied by individual local governments in Maine, as well as in other states. Approached properly, this technique could produce a pattern in which development is grouped at nodes around major intersections, leaving the vast majority of highway road frontage free of linear commercial development. The future of that land could be for "open space residential uses" (see Chapters 14 and 15),

with part of the required open space forming a greenway buffer alongside the highway, and houses or apartments set deep within the parcel's interior.

An example showing how this policy could be applied in a rural context is reproduced in Figure 9–16, from the 1989 Comprehensive Plan of Ston-ington, Maine, prepared by Dodson Associates. The five commercial buildings are shown in alternative patterns: evenly spread out along the main road, and tightly clustered in traditional village form at the intersection. Also of great importance is the difference in building setbacks and parking locations: deep setbacks with asphalt parking areas out front, or shallow setbacks with ample parking tucked unobtrusively behind the buildings.

Another way of implementing the principles embodied in Maine's short-lived highway zoning policy proposal is through TDR ("transfer of development rights") planning: certain highway nodes could become "receiving districts" to accommodate development rights exported from "sending districts" located along other sections of the highway. This technique has been used in some states to protect farmland and other natural resources, but is possesses great potential to protect our highway network as well.

The idea of creating two compact receiving districts to which commercial development rights from the majority of state highway frontage could be transferred under a voluntary TDR system has also been proposed in Wellfleet, Massachusetts. To be considered for such designation, sites had to contain at least 20 acres of vacant or underutilized land, be close to existing commercial development, have no serious environmental constraints and little scenic or aesthetic value, and possess the highway capacity to accommodate new turning movements. The parcels identified as meeting these criteria included a drive-in theatre and a private campground (Schaefer, 1989). For such proposals to be feasible, however, the receiving areas must first be zoned for only relatively low-intensity uses, so that sufficient opportunity will exist for intensifying future usage with the addition of extra development transferred in from the sending districts.

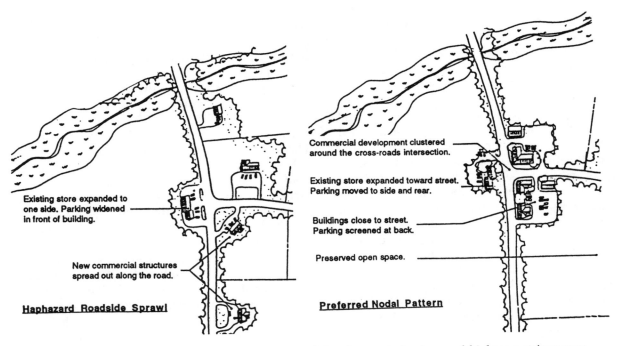

Figure 9–16. Two alternatives for arranging commercial development along a rural highway: strip versus nodes. Within the node, stores are located toward the front of their lots, with interconnected rear parking provision. *Source:* Dodson Associates.

New England's first example of TDR usage to counterbalance the land devaluation caused by highway frontage down-zoning was enacted in Acton, Massachusetts, in April 1990. In order to avoid the undue traffic congestion and costly infrastructure extensions that would have resulted from implementing the town's existing zoning (which had designated the Great Road corridor as a "general business" district), Acton voters approved scaling back the number and intensity of commercial activities allowed there, in new "limited business" and residential districts (Bobrowski, 1990).

This ordinance authorizes the municipal officers (selectmen) to increase the residential density and/or allowable commercial floor space in certain "receiving zones" when such development would support the stated goals of creating "a sense of community, through a concentration of a variety of uses," and facilitating "the development of a viable village center providing convenient and attractive commercial and personal services." Des-

ignated as receiving zones were the nineteenth-century villages of East Acton and North Acton, where essential infrastructure was already in place.

As an incentive to use this technique, the TDR ordinance sets a relatively stringent limit on the amount of new parking that will be allowed to be created along the Great Road corridor (one parking space per 3,000 square feet of site area), which is much less than is required to be provided under zoning regulations for most intensive uses. In other words, these two regulations, taken together, encourage either lower intensities of land use in this corridor, or the transfer of higher-intensity uses from this corridor to the designated villages.

To help entrepreneurs envision the type of structured, higher-intensity development intended for the receiving zones in Wellfleet, the nearby example of Mashpee Commons in Mashpee, Massachusetts, was recommended for comparison. Featured as one of the case examples in Part IV, this development created a sense of traditional townscape on the site of a previously unsuccessful conventional suburban shopping plaza. This site was "reclaimed" by the introduction of a matrix of new streets running across the old parking lot, streets that are now lined with shops built alongside the new sidewalks. Other notable features of Mashpee Commons include its mix of retail, office, and residential uses; the dedication of several prominent sites for civic and institutional buildings; and a combination of parallel curbside parking and larger rear parking lots.

The idea of a traditional form for new nodal developments has been taken several steps further by the Miami design firm of Dover, Correa, Kohn, Cockshutt and Valle, in the alternative concept plan it prepared for a land parcel slated to become a regional mall. Although it is true that a conventional mall could satisfy many criteria for nodal development (and could receive additional use-intensity via a TDR system), this solution would not normally produce anything resembling a proper town or village. However, the results might be improved if such a node were made subject to design standards governing certain attributes characteristic of traditional settlements: street patterns, width/height ratios of streets and building facades, building size, public spaces, parking distribution among a large number of relatively small parking lots nestled behind "Main Street" buildings, and so forth. (See Figure 9–17.)

The amount of land paved over for parking in this proposal would be smaller than that needed in a conventional design because the mixture of uses allows many parking spaces to be shared by different functions occurring at different hours. For example, the cinema, which requires 338 spaces on weekend evenings, needs only 189 spaces on weekday afternoons, meaning that nearly 150 cinema spaces would be free for office workers, for example. Similarly, of the 139 spaces needed by project residents at night, only 101 would be

 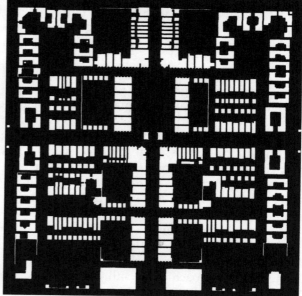

Figure 9–17. Figure-ground diagrams of a proposed shopping mall and apartment complex containing massive buildings and expansive parking lots, contrasted with a counterproposal laid out according to traditional town center design principles, with smaller elements varying in size, type, and character, and with housing distributed throughout the project. *Source:* Dover et al., 1990.

needed for daytime parking during the week, allowing 38 spaces for shoppers (Dover et al., 1990). These calculations were based upon the methodology recommended by the Urban Land Institute in its 1985 publication *Shared Parking Method*.

Whenever major new development at highway nodes is being designed, it would be a great loss if the opportunity were not taken to create a useful mixture of shops, offices, and homes (including "affordable" units), connected by a recognizable internal street system and punctuated with civic buildings and public spaces. Indeed, planners, concerned residents, and local officials should initiate discussion on this topic in their communities by posing the question: Why should society settle for less? The essential steps are to lay down a ground pattern, establish a reasonable use mix, and generate a set of building and parking standards based upon the common experience of what has worked well in the past. Like the real towns on which these nodes would be modeled, there is no necessity to build everything at once or to have the entire area under single ownership and control. In fact, there are advantages in doing it "the old fashioned way," with various entrepreneurs entering the project and completing their sections independently (within the preestablished design standards).

One of these advantages is that the commercial base would grow gradually with the local population, instead of taking a quantum leap that instantly creates a surplus of retail space. This often leaves many downtown merchants with the choice of suffering sales losses in their old locations or moving into the new malls with their higher rents and sales potential. Another advantage of incremental growth is that it is likely that more variety in building design will emerge if different developers are involved over a period of time. With overall design criteria within which all construction must occur, some level of harmony and consistency of approach could still emerge.

The "official map" procedures described above, which are allowed in the zoning enabling legislation of many states, provide an ideal vehicle for creating an interconnected network of streets serving a combination of retail, office, and residential uses on land located at strategic nodal points along state highways. Some of the new streets, perhaps those lying perpendicular to the highway, might be designated for clusters of auto-related uses, which do not generally mix well together with other types of uses (gas stations, muffler replacement centers, car washes, lubrication services, tire companies, parts shops, etc.).

Other perpendicular streets could be set aside for "by right" location of other heavy traffic generators that also mix poorly with other land uses, such as fast-food franchises. Permitting them in selected other locations would be by "special permit," with attendant site planning and architectural requirements to ensure they harmonize well with the town's character. The process envisioned here is one of incremental growth by a variety of individual entrepreneurs. What is so urgently needed is an appropriate framework of convenient side-streets and internal roads, into which such uses may be safely and appropriately inserted.

One rural area that has successfully applied the concept of "official streets" is Carroll County, Maryland (northwest of Baltimore). The county planning department there has designated, in advance of development, the preferred locations of planned streets, major roads, and bypasses so that these alignments will be preserved. Developers of major projects lying in the path of such proposed roadways are generally required to build that part of the road that lies within their parcel. In some cases, the county purchases and "land banks" property where major streets are planned (Carroll County Master Plan, 1987). Although Carroll County planners have not yet used this procedure in the specific manner recommended above (for commercial subdivision loop roads adjacent to highways), they have demonstrated that this general technique, rarely used in rural communities anywhere in the country, is indeed a workable concept. They have been applying it with considerable success not only in the county seat of Westminster, but also in a number of the smaller surrounding towns, where planned streets are officially mapped in local comprehensive planning documents.

Another example of official mapping is given at the end of this chapter, where a proposal for reshaping a haphazard collection of buildings at an undistinguished highway intersection in Warren Township, New Jersey, is described, involving incentives offered to developers helping to create a proper town center with a rationalized street pattern and a traditional streetscape designed according to locally adopted architectural standards.

Once the idea of nodes with traditional street patterns and a mixture of compatible uses is firmly established as appropriate places for new businesses, offices, and townhouse or upper-story apartments to be created, one significant problem remains to be addressed: how to deal with the prospect of "super-nodes" whose sheer size and or noncentral location may pose a grave threat to the continued functioning of existing downtown hubs.

COPING WITH MALLS: DOCUMENTING THEIR IMPACTS

Perhaps the greatest threat to retaining town center functions is posed by large corporations, which create attractive, convenient alternative shopping locations.

Whenever a mall is proposed, developers can be counted upon to emphasize its positive aspects. Seeing through all the data to obtain a fuller perspective can be very difficult for local officials and generalist planners working in small towns. The information that is submitted is usually prepared by the developer's own handpicked team of consultants, who are hired to present the project in the best possible light, typically emphasizing new property-tax revenues and jobs. In the resulting review process most small communities, lacking experience in sophisticated impact analysis techniques, operate at a marked disadvantage. Based upon experiences in the Bay State, researchers at the University of Massachusetts prepared a short paper on the probable negative impacts of mall development on small towns, the findings of which are summarized below (Mullin et al., 1990).

First, the downtown will almost certainly decline. Particularly vulnerable are the downtown "anchors," such as large department stores (especially the independent, family-owned variety) that

tend to fold or to relocate (sometimes to the new mall). This typically generates a downward spiral of declining customer traffic and further closures, particularly by smaller retailers. As tenants leave, building owners have trouble meeting their fixed overhead costs (heating, taxes, electricity, mortgage payments, etc.).

The combination of vacant storefronts and the implied statements by departing shopkeepers that they have found a better place to sell merchandise produces a profoundly negative impression on customers, one that is extremely difficult to reverse. This negative perception affects the remaining merchants as well, who are susceptible to a group psychology in which the tendency to "follow the herd" is widely felt. "Mall operators know this and will attempt to attract local merchants to their facility. When they do attract such businesses they win in three ways: a) they rent space, b) they weaken the strength of an alternative market area, and c) they are able to demonstrate that they are part of the community by attracting local merchants to the facility" (Mullin et al., 1990).

To the extent that some communities have succeeded in avoiding massive downtown vacancies, their business district functions almost always change dramatically. Downtown Leominster, Massachusetts, for example, was transformed from a regional shopping provider to an administrative office and service center, with many former retail premises converted into government offices. Large-scale vacancies were avoided only through continued support by local and state governments, but the attractive mix of users that had characterized the center 30 years earlier no longer exists.

The example of Pyramid's Holyoke (MA) Mall provides a first-rate case study of what a mall does to a New England region. With more than 600,000 sq. ft. of retail space, it was built in a region that had virtually no growth, with struggling but active shopping districts in Holyoke, Springfield, and Westfield where the city governments were providing public funds to improve the aesthetic qualities of their downtowns. Ten years later, downtown Holyoke is the home of the derelict, downtown Westfield's commercial base has eroded by 60 percent and downtown Springfield is in doldrums (Mullin et al, 1990).

Perhaps the most dramatic example of "stripping and malling" is offered by Huntsville, Alabama. Shortly after World War II, German rocket scientists hired by the U.S. government to boost the national aeronautics program settled in Huntsville, which was then becoming the country's "space center." Frustrated by traffic congestion in downtown Huntsville, the scientists proposed building autobahns, those superhighways begun in Germany during the 1930s and the precursor to America's interstate system. Forty years later, *every last one* of Huntsville's downtown retail stores has been launched into the outer space of those numerous suburban strips and malls that now line the widened highways on the city's edge. This outward migration was also abetted by Huntsville's vigorous urban renewal program (sometimes referred to as "urban removal"), which wiped away many blocks of residential neighborhoods—and the local customers they housed—close to the former central business district. Today, downtown Huntsville exhibits a depressing collection of abandoned, boarded-up storefronts and several burned-out buildings, punctuated by empty lots on sites of former shops pulled down to provide off-street parking for customers who have long since been siphoned off by the surrounding highway retail strips.

On a smaller but no less disturbing scale is tiny Walpole, New Hampshire (population 3,100), where the once-lively commercial center has been sucked dry by a new mall three miles out of town, on Route 12. Gone is the "anchor," the IGA grocery that reluctantly moved out of the center in fear that it would not survive competition from a new food store located on the highway. It is only a matter of time, in the eyes of many residents, before the local pharmacy, which has remained in its premises beside the vacant IGA, succumbs to the new drugstore chain outlet in the mall.

"It used to be Walpole residents would make a daily visit to the village. They'd walk beneath the veranda from one end of the white clapboard building to the other. Along the way they picked up their mail, shopped for their groceries, filled their prescriptions and maintained their friendships. But now the anchor store for this way of life is gone" (Rourke, 1991). Other vacancies include a former gas station, a former dress shop, and a fire station. The central parking lot, where spaces used to be difficult to find, is nearly empty most of the time. The real culprit in this sad scenario was not the developer, who simply took advantage of an economic opportunity in a legally permissible manner, but the conventional zoning ordinance that designated extensive highway frontage for high-intensity commercial development.

As Pogo once observed, "We have met the enemy and he is us." (See Figure 9–18.) In this case (as in so many others), the town's land-use regulations encouraged the chain of events described above by "strip zoning" the highway, which encouraged it to become a linear retail corridor whose easy accessibility and available parking have created an unfair match for existing town centers, which require much nurturing and help (as described above in Amherst, Massachusetts).

Land-use trends along rural highways such as those detailed above are, unfortunately, often encouraged by municipal actions and inactions. Among the actions are suburban-based zoning provisions (extensive off-street parking requirements, deep building setbacks, single-use districts), which make it much easier for entrepreneurs to develop new retail sites on open land along highways than to expand or redevelop properties in or adjacent to small town centers. Other actions include zoning very large acreages of highway frontage for retail and office uses, as noted above. Among the inactions are a lack of proactive planning to make it easier for businessmen to enlarge or rebuild existing downtown buildings and to utilize upper floors for income-producing apartments.

It is possible to expand historic structures without destroying significant storefronts and facades or damaging the overall character of such buildings. Local governments in many states are authorized to form redevelopment authorities, which can adopt architectural design standards for new or expanded buildings, while facilitating conver-

Figure 9–18. Views looking westward along Route 9 in Hadley, Massachusetts, in 1964 and in 1989, proving "Pogo's Rule": "We have met the enemy, and he is us" (we who zone our arterial highways as if they were disposable, to be bypassed whenever they become too congested to serve their original purpose of conducting large volumes of traffic safely and efficiently).

sions, use changes, and selective demolition (or building relocation) to create better parking opportunities (preferably behind a row of shops).

Local governments that do not actively work to keep their downtowns attractive to current and potential new retailers are failing to perform one of their most important functions; as the old adage has it, "Failing to plan is planning to fail." All too often local officials are reactive, not proactive.

Frequently their greatest involvement in retail business promotion consists of zoning nearby highway frontage for commercial uses, and this is actually the type of move that is counterproductive to protecting the existing downtown shopping district.

What is needed is a more restrictive policy toward "highway strips" and a more positive, proactive agenda to improve the attractiveness and competitiveness of central business areas. Some more progressive communities are beginning to commission studies to determine what types of uses are either missing or would have to be retained for their downtowns to offer a sufficiently wide mix of retail functions to remain viable. Some are also hiring specialists (as do mall developers and industrial park promoters) to recruit new businesses to their centers.

In addition to allowing potential developers the steady rental-income opportunities that second-story office or apartments offer, they are relaxing their outmoded parking requirements to permit shared parking, and are sometimes even taking the initiative by creating new municipal parking spaces in convenient but unobtrusive locations. In short, to compete effectively with mall developers, local officials must start thinking and acting like their rivals, giving their downtown centers as many advantages as possible.

In college towns and affluent suburbs where malls have altered the commercial landscape of the older centers, the shift in downtown functions has generally been toward more restaurants, bookstores, record shops, copy centers, bars, specialty shops, and expensive boutiques. In both cases it is not uncommon to be unable to buy a loaf of bread, a container of aspirin, or a packet of nails, as groceries, pharmacies, and hardware stores have departed from the centers and have set up shop either in a new mall or (more likely) in one of the small highway "strip centers" that frequently follow mall construction.

These relocations are normally accompanied by a host of other uses, such as fast-food franchises, muffler and lubrication services, gas stations, and factory outlets; a motley mix of high-intensity businesses that towns must expect and prepare for, hopefully in more appropriate configurations than typically emerge without proper planning. In this context, one is reminded of "Mullin's Law" (named after University of Massachusetts planning professor John Mullin): "It is the nature of malls to 'breed and dribble.'" The "linear carnival" of garish uses that malls usually spawn is almost unstoppable if nearby land is zoned (or rezoned) to allow such activities, and therein lies the crucial lesson: conventional zoning is the critical element in the degradation of these areas and of the highways running through them.

Impacts projected by mall developers are based upon their initial proposals and typically do not address the issue of later expansion. Such expansion is often predictable, given the fact that zoning in many communities frequently permits greater intensities of use than most mall applicants include on their plans. Where land is relatively inexpensive (before the first mall is built), smart developers often buy much more property than they initially need, to facilitate enlargement of retail space and parking areas.

The ultimate impacts of malls remain unseen and unsuspected by local residents and officials who are experiencing mall proposals for the first time. "Even when there are deed restrictions that deny or curtail further expansion, mall owners will, at some future time, approach the legal signers of the agreement and go to court to seek its abrogation. For these reasons it is important to base all planning assessments on the maximum buildout" (Mullin et al., 1990). In the same way that many local planning authorities require residential subdivision applicants to show, at least conceptually, the full extent of potential development on their property, including future phases not presently proposed, shopping center developers could be required to do the same.

Malls attract additional traffic to local highways, which must often be widened to accommodate the larger volume of cars and to provide turning lanes. Frequently signalization also occurs, further slowing through traffic (i.e., the vehicles for which the arterial roads were originally built to accommodate). Mall developers can often be pressed into contributing toward the monetary costs of such "improvements," but other costs occur as well. The character of the community's "gateway" changes rapidly in appearance, function, and feel. Two-lane rural highways that formerly handled pre-mall traffic reasonably well often become inadequate and congested with left-turning vehicles and stop lights only five or ten years after such roads are widened. If water and/or sewer lines are extended outward to serve a mall site, adjacent lands along the highway will be reassessed for their increased potential development value, thereby adding to the strip development pressure. In the end, the highway degenerates from an arterial route to a local shopping street. Regardless of whether there are strict landscaping, signage, and architectural controls—resulting in what can be called a "designer strip"—or whether asphalt and plastic emerge as the dominant aesthetic, the "level of service" (a measure of driving ease) on these gateway roads typically declines, while traffic accident rates can rise dramatically (as documented in the graphics showing accidents and high-intensity land uses along Route 6 in Eastham, Massachusetts, in Figures 9–13 and 9–14).

Although malls like to portray themselves as friendly members of the local business community, their records indicate otherwise. As private corporations, their primary objective is to maximize financial returns for their investors. To accomplish this, they are fiercely competitive, and they typically use every advantage they possess to drain as much business as possible away from every competitor in their shopping catchment area. It matters little whether those competitors are downtown merchants or other retailers along the highway.

One commentator has described a mall's principal function as "distributing goods which are often easily available elsewhere. A shopping mall is not usually built because it is needed, or even because it will be profitable to the enterprises that occupy it, but because it means a quick buck for the developer who, when it is complete, moves onto the next socially superfluous project" (Barnard, 1988). To illustrate this point, Barnard recounted the saga of three large shopping developments along Route 9, in Hadley, Massachusetts:

The first to be built, near the Amherst-Hadley town line, may have met a local need, providing competition for business in the center of Amherst and relieving traffic congestion there. But soon a second developer built a second mall, much larger than the first; and though it was obviously aimed at attracting customers from outside the local area, several enterprises in the first soon went out of business. And hardly had the new center become established when a third developer put up an even huger one beside it, and the third mall has dealt a devastating blow to the second, which is now nearly empty. This is the result of unregulated free enterprise. [In this particular case, the negative consequences were compounded by the fact that these three developments were located on exceptionally prime farmland, where rich loamy soils averaged over 10 feet deep.]

Given the above, what positive benefits do malls offer? Most frequently cited by developers is the employment opportunities that the shops provide. However, although job creation is often cited as a positive result of mall construction, the vast majority of these positions pay low wages and many are part-time. While annual full-time mall wages in the Northeast average $13,000, the mean figure for industrial jobs is $18,000 (Mullin et al., 1990).

COPING WITH MALLS: STRATEGIES

Most rural communities are poorly equipped to deal with proposals to construct alternative retail floor space. The first step, which is obvious to intending developers but not always evident to others, is to conduct a market study to determine whether one's community is a likely prospect for mall development. Among the factors that mall developers typically examine, and which are equally relevant for local officials to study in advance, are the amount of market leakage already occurring from the community (purchases elsewhere by local residents), the current or potential catchment area for shoppers (considering existing and planned highways), recent increases in affluence or purchasing power, and the degree to which existing shopping facilities are unattractive in terms of access, retail mix, appearance, and

parking. It is difficult to overestimate the value of such "community market surveys." Professional retail developers appreciate their importance, and municipalities choosing not to commission them operate at a marked disadvantage.

The safest course is to make sure that developable land zoned for such uses is too small and/or lacks the locational attributes sought by mall developers. When potential mall sites lie outside one's local political jurisdiction and are controlled by a neighboring town, a regional approach is essential. This goal may be achievable when county government is involved, unless officials are so totally "pro-business" that they cannot see or acknowledge any negative consequences of highway business expansion. The opportunity for regional cooperation is much more limited when the land in question is under the control of another jurisdiction that stands to gain in property-tax collections.

To the extent that the approval process also includes state-level review, there may be an opportunity to raise environmental or traffic-related issues. But many of the statutes requiring state review for projects over a certain size fail to include two factors that some people think are the most relevant of all: the demonstrated *need* for additional commercial floor space of the proposed quantity, and its *impact* upon the business centers of surrounding communities.

Vermont is one of the few states where such considerations are part of the state's official project review processes. But, even there, applicants have been willing to offer to purchase any building whose owners can demonstrate that the new mall has made it impossible for him or her to rent it to shopkeepers. If a developer were prevailed upon to keep such a pledge, the law contains no restrictions requiring that traditional retail functions be maintained, and he or she would be at liberty to rent the premises for offices or apartments, a move that would not boost or even maintain the center's commercial viability.

The criterion of "need" is more difficult to define, and the Vermont legislation is not very explicit. If it allowed mall applications to be denied when it could be shown that a large majority of the potential tenants already existed within the shopping catchment area, oversized malls that are bound to drain existing centers of their lifeblood could be rejected. In fact, such a case was heard during a recent proposal to build a large mall outside of Burlington, Vermont. Although an estimated 70 percent of the shops typically found in such malls were already established in the county catchment area (and although many of them would probably relocate to such a mall, depleting centers of their vitality), this evidence was considered insufficient grounds for denial under the state law. Until such laws are refined, the struggle to prevent overdevelopment of retail space will continue to be an uphill one.

In refining those laws, care must be taken to avoid an illegal limitation on competition, and to justify restrictive policies on the grounds that

there is a legitimate public interest in protecting the enormous public investment in central area infrastructure (streets, sidewalks, parking lots, utilities, etc.), which would be threatened by haphazard retail development in unserviced fringe areas. The rationale is that such peripheral development will negatively impact established downtowns, causing underutilization of the existing infrastructure, while necessitating service extensions to outlying shopping strips as they expand and draw further customers away from central business districts. (See Figure 9–19.)

Another approach to dealing with the impact of malls and other strip commercial development is to levy an impact fee on such uses. In Collierville, Tennessee (population 18,000), which is feeling growth pressures from Memphis, a 1992 city ordi-

Figure 9–19. Photo montage of Route 9, Westborough, Massachusetts. Existing buildings contrasted with future development allowed under current zoning; a comparison commissioned by a local land trust to arouse public awareness of the kind of results that would eventually be produced by implementing existing ordinances. *Source:* Dodson Associates.

nance places a tax of 25 cents per square foot on new office and commercial development outside the town center. The large amount of projected development on the city's fringe is expected to generate about $500,000 in revenue. These proceeds are dedicated toward an ambitious $1.2 million improvement project in the town square, which is listed in the National Register of Historic Places. The law on impact fees varies from state to state and, where they are allowed, they are generally required to be proportional to the anticipated impacts, and dedicated to programs that are specifically designed to ameliorate those problems that will be created or aggravated by the new development subject to the tax.

PLANNING HIGHWAY USES IN GUILFORD, CONNECTICUT

One example of a small town that is planning ahead to control the location, scale, and character of new businesses along its principal highway corridor is Guilford, Connecticut. Four decades of relatively uncoordinated highway development along Route 1 produced a variety of retail and office uses, but all were built with a very conventional, suburban car-oriented character. At the core of Guilford's present planning approach is the philosophy that many economic development opportunities should be provided without significantly altering the town's essentially rural character (Kendig et al., 1990). Significantly, the town fathers hired a consulting team including both planning and economic development specialists to evaluate the economic development potential of land lying along Route 1, and to recommend zoning controls to ensure that new construction would be consistent with existing community character.

Among the major recommendations were that two road segments be rezoned (one "upward" to generate more intensive development, the other "downward" to conform with surrounding residential uses); that mixed uses (including affordable housing) be encouraged in certain locations; that sewerage be extended to serve particular sites; and that new regulations pertaining to building scale, architectural style, signage, site planning, parking location, and landscaping be adopted.

Just as important, the study recommended expanding staff capability to help market land in the designated growth areas and that this individual be the sort of person who would understand the importance of maintaining Guilford's special character, while promoting new nonresidential development to increase local employment and the property-tax base (Kendig et al., 1990).

At the heart of the report is an analysis of the Route 1 corridor, in which land was classified into "opportunity categories" based on current land-use patterns, size, accessibility, and natural features. Among the categories identified were three "major opportunity areas" (totaling 545 acres), seven "minor opportunity areas" (5 to 25 acres each), "small lot areas," and "infill areas." There were also two environmentally sensitive areas (with steep wooded hillsides and extensive ledge outcroppings) where development is to be limited to low-density residential uses.

All these opportunity areas were mapped. On three major sites selected for detailed examination, two conceptual plans were prepared: the first illustrated development guidelines, while the second offered possible site planning layouts. All three locations were designed with preservation of the town's rural character in mind. While the strategy on one site was merely to screen otherwise conventional commercial development behind a thickly wooded buffer, clustering smaller-scale buildings around central open spaces was recommended on the other two parcels. These sites varied in size from 140 acres to 220 acres. The purpose of preparing these layouts was not only to offer ideas for three specific sites, but also to establish a direction for regulatory standards applicable in other parts of the highway corridor.

Although the preparation of guidelines or standards was beyond the scope of this particular planning study, it did describe two approaches for evaluating the physical scale of a potential development proposal. One approach relates the volume of new structures to their building sites and to the volume of landscaping material on the property. The underlying premise is that the impact of buildings that are intrinsically out of step with a community, because of their sheer size or their architectural style (or both), can be mitigated by heavy plantings of trees and shrubs.

The other approach, which does not rely upon greenery to mask inharmonious buildings and building arrangements, utilizes a "scale unit" by which structures may be measured and compared with the human scale. Such a method is particularly appropriate in towns such as Guilford, where most buildings have been built at the residential scale. "Many of the buildings are of a size and scale similar to dwellings. Even in the commercial areas of the Green, the buildings are of a scale that relates easily to the pedestrian. The largest buildings are the churches which are important to the community and, thus, were designed to stand out. The commercial buildings are not much different in scale than the residential buildings except that sometimes there are no yards between them. The introduction of modern shopping centers, offices and industrial buildings brings with them a new scale. The conflicts raised at zoning hearings are often a reaction to buildings that are out of character with the rest of the community" (Kendig et al., 1990).

The "bird's-eye" drawings in Chapter 8, "Commercial Infill Development Along a Major Street," illustrate these issues clearly. Design review regulations must be carefully worded to avoid both monotony and discord. Dramatic contrasts should occasionally be allowed, but should be limited to buildings with significantly different functions, such as town halls, churches, post offices, and schools.

RECLAIMING EXISTING "COMMERCIAL STRIPS"

Although the linear pattern of roadside business usage is virtually impossible to eradicate once it is firmly established (hence the term "commercial kudzu"), with sufficient political will its continued spread can be halted, its outward appearances can be much improved, and its functions can be broadened. All of this requires much time, patience, and political support. The last situation will be easier to create if the local business community is engaged as an active player in all policy discussions about the proper role of the highway and its adjacent lands.

The most effective techniques for halting the continued spread of "strip development" have already been mentioned. The most direct method is simple "down-zoning" and "up-zoning" in areas appropriate to less intensive and more intensive development, respectively. Such a course is likely to be unpopular politically, although it was successful ten years ago in York, Maine (even surviving a subsequent referendum challenge).

In order to avoid "wipeout/windfall" results for the various landowners, TDR can be employed, as described in the Wellfleet and Acton examples. However, for this technique to be used it must contain either very strong economic incentives (such as significant use-intensity bonuses) or else be compulsory. To accomplish the latter, zoning would be amended to require developers of land in high-intensity zones to purchase development rights from landowners in other highway districts. The land from which the development rights are sold would either be permanently restricted from future development, or allowed to be developed at very low intensities, depending on how the ordinance language was worded. Once the issue of "form" or "linear spread" is dealt with (and, in some cases, maximum sprawl may already be a fait accompli), the next issue to address is function. As was mentioned with regard to the two Florida examples of creative development, mixing uses enables a certain proportion of parking spaces to be shared, reducing asphalt coverage and increasing the number of potential local customers and employees (some of whom may live within walking distance of shops and offices in their new neighborhood). It is easy to exaggerate the degree to which traditional use-mixes will reduce the number of vehicle trips likely to be made, and such claims should be closely examined if they are pushed strongly as a reason for approving a specific development (or redevelopment) proposal. But it is logical to expect that some lessened car usage is probable when homes, shops, and jobs lie within a 10-minute walk of each other.

Simply eliminating zoning restrictions against mixed uses is a step in the right direction, but certain types of use mixes could become a *require-*

ment for approval if real change is desired. If this approach is taken, it would be advisable to introduce some flexibility so that every parcel would not have to provide for all uses. Residential development rights could be traded or sold for commercial development rights among adjacent properties, for example. (Allowing district-wide exchanges might be counterproductive, as they could lead to retail "pods" being created in one area, completely separated from housing "pods" at the other end of the district.) Less elaborate approaches would require new development to be of two- or three-story construction, with upper floors designated for residential uses. By utilizing the same foundation and roof to obtain an additional rental income, developers would benefit while also providing much-needed housing, affordable to young couples and elderly people, in a location convenient to shops and services.

The physical appearance of existing strips can also be vastly improved. One of the most significant (and difficult) steps involves the amortization of tall plastic signs and their gradual replacement with heavy plantings of proper shade trees along each side of the roadway. Such trees are not incompatible with business uses, as demonstrated by the photograph of a tree-lined commercial corridor along Route 900 (NE Sunset Boulevard), connecting the Seattle suburbs of Renton and Issaquah (see Figure 9–20). It is noteworthy that this was a rather typical commercial highway 20 years ago, not filled with upscale stores or any particularly attractive buildings. Yet, its appearance has been transformed in a mere 15 years through a simple tree-planting program initiated and implemented by a farsighted local government.

The branching pattern of most shade trees is such that they will not block sight-lines between drivers and shop fronts or signs of modest height (up to six feet tall). However, their spreading canopies will help to establish the feeling of a "street-line" or formal edge to the highway corridor.

Sign amortization is not commonly used, although it is legal in many states, because of the ferocious opposition typically mounted by owners of highway businesses. However, their efforts can be blunted to some extent by the local government

Figure 9–20. Route 900, a tree-lined commercial corridor between Renton and Issaquah, Washington, showing that continuous plantings of shade trees are not incompatible with business uses, and that they can completely transform the appearance of areas that would otherwise remain characterless. Such vast improvements do not require expensive consultants, cutting-edge technology, or local geniuses—just a few well-placed community officials who care enough to commit a tiny fraction of the municipal budget to planting rows of trees along the principal "gateways" to their town. *Source:* Photo by Don Erickson, AICP.

offering to share the costs of sign replacement, with the state department of transportation (DOT) providing the trees for free. Such planting schemes must be closely coordinated with DOT landscape architects, so that inappropriate species (such as flowering ornamentals) are not substituted for proper shade trees (oaks, maples, lindens, sycamores, hickories, etc.). The former tend to be relatively short and short-lived, and will never produce a stately line of full-canopied trees 50–70 feet tall upon maturity.

Although improved signage and shade tree planting are critically important to the visual rehabilitation of a commercial strip, it may be advisable to begin visual improvements on a note that is likely to be more positively received by the local business community. Such an approach would involve inviting owners of shopping centers with large front parking lots to submit plans for adding rentable floor space in a number of small buildings located along the front edge of their parking areas. Most such parking lots were oversized from the beginning, and are never full. The huge expanses of asphalt in front of these buildings prevent the highway corridor from achieving any semblance of townscape, but this situation is easily mitigated by introducing new structures along this front edge. They can sometimes be located just a few feet back from the right-of-way line, but if future road widening is a distinct possibility, they should be built at a distance that would allow the right-of-way to be increased. (DOT engineers can provide information on appropriate right-of-way widths for highways with different numbers of lanes, and they can give you their best guess about the likelihood of such projects, based upon traffic trends.)

Aerial perspective drawings showing how existing conventional shopping strips can be "reclaimed" by infill construction of new shops in small traditional buildings along the roadside edge of large parking lots can be found in Chapter 8, and also in *A Design Guideline Manual for Sustainable Development on Cape Cod* (Community Vision, 1992).

It should be emphasized that it is not necessary to erect a continuous line of shops along this front edge to achieve the desired visual effect. Indeed, shopping center owners (and tenants) will probably be concerned about the visibility of both the parking and the older shops behind them. A reasonable compromise would be to allow a filtered view of the parking and the other shops through the gaps between the new buildings out front. (See Figure 9–21.) One may have to grant shopkeepers the right to display the name of their business on a "ladder" type of directory sign at the entrance, but most of them probably advertise themselves already as being located within a certain shopping center.

Being able to see each and every shop front from the highway is really not very important at all, as

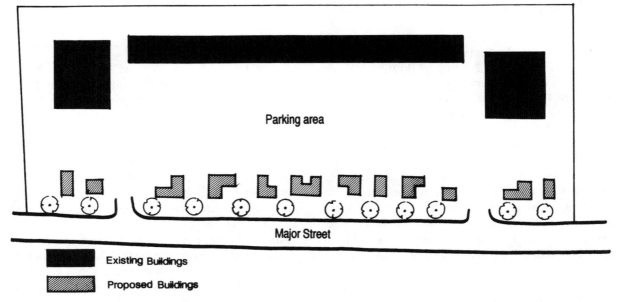

Figure 9–21. Oversized parking lots in front of older shopping centers offer a unique opportunity for local officials to invite developers to submit plans for additional rentable space in a row of small-scale, traditionally designed buildings, buffering views of the large asphalt lots and helping to reinforce streetscapes in a more townlike manner. Gaps between the new buildings could be filled with shade trees and low railings or picket fences (about the height of car hoods), with frequent openings for pedestrians.

has been proven in numerous instances where shops have been built around "internalized" parking areas (as illustrated in Part IV, "Case Examples"). However, proposals to screen parking with buildings or other visual barriers remain controversial, and discussions on this point in the town of Constantia, New York, on the north shore of Lake Oneida, typify the range of reactions. Although most residents felt that front parking was unattractive, comments by small business owners revealed that merchants often see parked cars as an expression of the popularity of a store, a kind of subtle "advertisement," and therefore consider visible parking lots to be positive elements. Following further discussion with planners from the Tug Hill Commission, however, "most people seemed in agreement that businesses on the North Shore received their primary support from local residents, and that decisions to use a particular business were influenced more by reputation and service than by the number of cars visible in a parking lot" (Doble et al., 1992). This is to say that what really counts in retailing is convenient location, free parking, the range of goods, competitive pricing, helpful sales assistants, and courteous service.

In other instances not involving shopping centers, existing businesses with front parking can be required, when rebuilding or expanding, to move the shop front forward on the lot, and to relocate parking to the side and/or the rear. The drawing in Figure 9–23 shows both the "before" and "after" situation, as just described.

Also of note on the improved scenario drawing is the interconnection of rear parking areas, a practice that could eventually reduce the amount of traffic entering and exiting the highway as vehicles move along the corridor making multiple stops at different shops. The schematic diagram in Figure 9–22 illustrates how this principle could connect a large number of adjacent businesses already existing along a section of highway frontage. By making it possible for shoppers to visit numerous stores without having to frequently reenter (and disrupt) highway traffic, accident potential could be reduced and shopping experiences could become easier and less stressful.

Merchants ultimately benefit from these results and from the improved accessibility they bring. Such an undertaking could be approached in several phases, the first one being to create interconnecting access lanes and parking areas behind existing retail and office buildings. Over a period of years front parking could be phased out or greatly reduced in size, with any future building expansion being required to locate in that direction. Alternatively, new commercial rental space could be constructed in a line of smaller buildings arranged along the highway frontage, as shown in Figure 9–21.

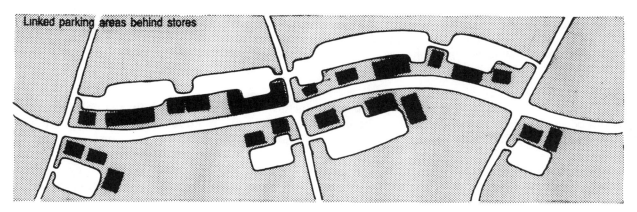

Figure 9–22. Connecting rear parking lots allows customers to drive to many other shops in the corridor without re-entering the highway and interrupting traffic flow. Such arrangements can be required for new development, expansion of existing buildings, and redevelopment.

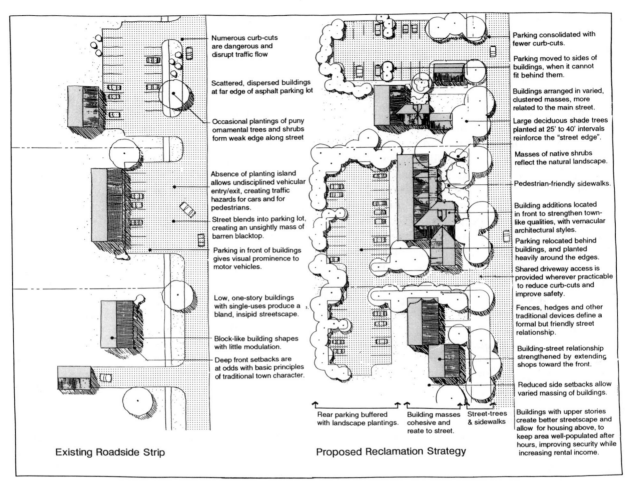

Numerous curb-cuts are dangerous and disrupt traffic flow

Scattered, dispersed buildings at far edge of asphalt parking lot

Occasional plantings of puny ornamental trees and shrubs form weak edge along street

Absence of planting island allows undisciplined vehicular entry/exit, creating traffic hazards for cars and for pedestrians.

Street blends into parking lot, creating an unsightly mass of barren blacktop.

Parking in front of buildings gives visual prominence to motor vehicles.

Low, one-story buildings with single-uses produce a bland, insipid streetscape.

Block-like building shapes with little modulation.

Deep front setbacks are at odds with basic principles of traditional town character.

Parking consolidated with fewer curb-cuts.

Parking moved to sides of buildings, when it cannot fit behind them.

Buildings arranged in varied, clustered masses, more related to the main street.

Large deciduous shade trees planted at 25' to 40' intervals reinforce the "street edge".

Masses of native shrubs reflect the natural landscape.

Pedestrian-friendly sidewalks.

Building additions located in front to strengthen town-like qualities, with vernacular architectural styles.

Parking relocated behind buildings, and planted heavily around the edges.

Shared driveway access is provided wherever practicable to reduce curb-cuts and improve safety.

Fences, hedges and other traditional devices define a formal but friendly street relationship.

Building-street relationship strengthened by extending shops toward the front.

Reduced side setbacks allow varied massing of buildings.

Buildings with upper stories create better streetscape and allow for housing above, to keep area well-populated after hours, improving security while increasing rental income.

Rear parking buffered with landscape plantings.

Building masses cohesive and reate to street.

Street-trees & sidewalks

Existing Roadside Strip

Proposed Reclamation Strategy

Figure 9–23. Proposals to expand existing businesses along a commercial street or highway offer a good opportunity to require that parking be relocated to the rear, with building extensions brought forward closer to the roadway, creating a more traditional "street edge." Over the long term, design approaches such as this, coupled with street-tree planting and sign replacement, can help a community reclaim ugly "gateway" corridors into their centers. *Source:* Dodson Associates.

In the second or third phase, highway curb-cuts could be substantially reduced in number or eliminated altogether, with customers approaching the premises by way of side streets (controlled by traffic signals) accessing the rear parking areas. In time, as customers become fully accustomed to the changes, they will come to think of the facade facing the rear parking as the real "front" of the store. This process can be accelerated by simple superficial architectural treatments to that wall,

including the creation of a formal entrance door. An even more ambitious proposal, showing how a standard "strip mall" can be transformed into a town center with small plazas, outdoor cafes, well-treed "parking orchards," dwellings and offices above shops, and a farmers' market, appears in *A Better Place to Live* (Corbett, 1981), a book that deserves to be more widely known.

Many similar ideas (and others) are included and illustrated in *Design Objectives Plan for Entry-*

way Corridors, adopted by the City Commission of Bozeman, Montana. Prepared by Mark Hinshaw, this plan received broad acceptance from local officials, businesspeople, and residents because of its clarity, its basic good sense, and an extensive public involvement process. Seven general design objectives and 15 design guidelines were articulated as applicable to all the "gateway" corridors leading into this historic county seat. Each of the city's six entryways, and Interstate 90 as well, were then evaluated, followed by more specific objectives and guidelines relating to each of the thoroughfares.

Intended to be implemented with a degree of flexibility to avoid stifling creativity, while maintaining an agreed direction for achieving the overall vision of the corridor plan, these guidelines place repeated emphasis on building design (encouraging varied massing, pitched roofs, and strong entrances), site design (reducing the visual impact of parking areas with landscaping and building arrangement), signage (lower and smaller freestanding signs), and pedestrian access and amenities.

Quoting the plan, "Very few developments have recognized that once people park their cars, they are immediately pedestrians with completely different needs. . . . Site development must include a number of features such as landscape accents with seasonal color, seating, separated pathways, and windows facing walking areas. . . . Public open spaces can be located near the main entrance points to buildings so that they can take advantage of the presence of shops and cafes" (Hinshaw, 1992).

Regulations applicable to the entryway corridors have been amended to incorporate a number of these ideas. For example, front parking lots must be landscaped so that "they appear from any entry roadway as an extension of the natural Gallatin Valley landscape," using berms, depressed parking, native species plantings, and so forth. Minimum depth for such areas are 50 feet parallel to the interstate and the two numbered state highways, and 25 feet parallel to arterial roads. Applications for development or redevelopment must receive a Certificate of Appropriateness from the

city's design review board, a body that previously had jurisdiction only in Bozeman's historic areas. For logical reasons, review standards in the entryway corridors are not as strict as those in the city's architecturally significant districts.

A final example of "reclaiming the strip" will serve to close this chapter. The location is Warren Township, New Jersey, a suburbanizing rural community of some 11,000 people located 30 miles west of Manhattan. What passes for a "town center" has been more accurately described as "an uninspired collection of parking lots and strip commercial developments scattered around the intersection of two regional arterials" (Rodrigues, 1992). The challenge was to adopt an overall growth strategy that would include both the design standards necessary to create a proper "center," and the economic incentives needed to encourage developers to undertake some rather special work.

In a nutshell, the solution lay in adopting a "town center urban design plan" containing a commercial core, three adjoining mixed-use zones, and a rational network of interconnected streets. To accomplish this a number of significant incentives were offered to developers: the commercial "floor area ratio" (FAR) was boosted by 60 percent, building height was raised to three and one-half stories, parking requirements were lowered (to realistic levels), and multiuse zoning was adopted, permitting considerably greater flexibility in allocating or combining uses on individual properties. In addition, residential lot sizes were reduced to 10,000 square feet, and some two-family homes were also allowed.

In return, the township is requiring developers to dedicate land for a number of new roads (including a new Main Street), provide substantial townscape improvements (sidewalks, lighting, landscaping, street furniture, etc.), build a certain percentage of affordable homes, and comply with strict standards relating to architecture and site plans. New buildings, especially those in visually prominent locations, will be required to relate to the township's historic traditions, according to standards that also encourage a variety of building masses, roof shapes, and "footprints" (varying from 2,000 to 15,000 square feet), a range deliberately selected to produce a medium-size "grain." And streets and building sites are to be laid out "to create a pedestrian realm, offering a continuous, safe and pleasant network of paths, sidewalks, bridges, and crosswalks, enhanced by places to rest (e.g., benches and seating areas) and socialize (plazas, squares, courtyards)" (Rodrigues, 1992).

The adopted plan includes both an illustrative site plan (showing preferred locations for new streets and buildings) and an aerial perspective sketch (see Figure 9–24). One shortcoming, however, is the need for numerous variances from the township's preexisting zoning ordinance, which should have been more extensively amended to allow most of the new construction without so many waivers and public hearings.

Figure 9–24. This diagram shows the location of proposed connecting streets and new buildings whose siting and scale were designed to help create a proper "town center" at a highway intersection in Warren Township, New Jersey, where only a scattered and random assortment of buildings now exists. *Source:* Anton Nelessen Associates.

Affordable Housing

OVERVIEW

Because the topic of affordable housing is so broad, no attempt is made in this chapter to cover it comprehensively. Instead, a more selective approach has been adopted, focusing upon topics chosen for their relevance to small towns where standard "affordable housing projects" may not be popular. Fortunately, there are many other methods available to local residents and officials to encourage the creation of residential opportunities for the increasing number of young householders who are not financially able to purchase their own homes.

One could begin thinking about this issue by asking two questions. First, how many graduates attending their tenth high-school reunion could afford to purchase a house in town today? Second, how many couples do you know whose grown children are returning home for lack of housing? Middle-class people have rarely considered their family members as needing "affordable housing," but all beliefs about housing today are rapidly changing. It is no longer a question of "them versus us" but rather "them and us," or more properly, simply "us."

When altruistic arguments fail to move people, one may appeal to their "enlightened self-interest." The future of their community will be profoundly influenced by the availability (or lack) of housing for local schoolteachers, firemen, police officers, and the general wage-earning work force. Put simply, jobs and ultimately commercial property-tax revenues are at stake. Several years ago a successful publishing firm in rural Deerfield, Massachusetts, opened a second plant, but chose to do so in the Midwest because its wage scales could not keep pace with the rapidly accelerating housing prices around their New England headquarters.

The grim reality is that housing is not affordable to many people unless they already own a home, which they can trade for another. Without home equity, a family trust fund, or two very good salaries, most people these days are not able to qualify for home mortgages. In many parts of the country, house price inflation has clearly outpaced salary increases, widening the affordability gap with every year that passes.

The growing gap in affordability has been documented in the Connecticut River Valley in western Massachusetts, where the required mortgage payment for an average-priced home remained in balance with incomes throughout the 1960–80 period (Valley Futures, 1988). By 1987, however, 30 percent of average household income ($550) could meet only half of the required mortgage payment for an average-priced home ($1,000). In Hampshire County, where an annual household income of $44,000 was required to purchase the average home, the average income level was only $27,645. In typical rural communities such as Ashfield, the median-priced house could be afforded by just 13 percent of existing residents (ibid.). In other words, most current homeowners could not afford to buy their own homes at present-day prices. Nationwide, only 9 percent of renters can afford home ownership, according to a 1991 survey by the U.S. Census Bureau (Downey, 1991).

Although selling prices have softened during the recession of the early 1990s, a substantial gap still exists in many areas, across which creative bridges must be built. This chapter discusses some of these "bridges"—compact neighborhood layouts, two-family house design, multifamily dwellings, community involvement, accessory dwellings, preserving affordability, "affordable limited development" (including a land conservation component), mixed uses, and mobile home design.

COMPACT NEIGHBORHOOD LAYOUTS

It does not seem obvious until it is said: "The reason our housing problem doesn't go away is because we keep raising our standards" (Peter Salins, quoted in Knack, 1988). The standards to which this Hunter College professor was referring are not those that are essential to public health, safety, and welfare, but rather those that have crept in quietly as communities grew in size and wealth. There was, and still is, nothing wrong with the type of (affordable) housing produced in vast quantity for returning GIs and others after World War II. For the most part, these modest homes (typically 1,000 square feet, on 9,000 square foot lots) were well constructed and had all the necessary infrastructure: properly paved streets, public water and sewer, sidewalks, and, occasionally, even small neighborhood parks.

This is probably the type of housing that was bought by the parents of many readers of this book. But pity the builder who tries to provide a similar product today: in most suburban and rural communities zoning is geared to the current standard of an 1,800 square foot house (or larger) with an attached two-car garage. Minimum legal lot sizes have typically doubled for fully serviced lots (from 9,000 square feet to about one-half acre), and have risen from one-half acre to two acres (or more) for lots with wells and septic systems. While some of the size increase for unserviced lots is based upon sensible environmental considerations, similar necessities have generally not governed lot-size inflation in areas served by central water and sewerage. In both cases there is often considerable potential to reduce lot areas and expensive street frontages. When lot widths are reduced from 125 feet to 75 feet, for example, hefty costs associated with road construction and utilities installation are cut by about 40 percent. These differences are illustrated in the set of three alternative subdivision designs shown in Figure 10–3

(see page 152). Each of these layouts contain 39 houselots, but road and utility runs range from 2,500 feet down to 1,650 feet.

Builders' magazines are beginning to feature some attractive new models for "starter housing," incorporating traditional architectural lines. The illustration in Figure 10–1 is of an 1,100 square foot house with three bedrooms, designed for a narrow 50-foot lot. There is adequate room for a driveway

Figure 10–1. Design for a small neo-Victorian house, containing 1,100 square feet, that fits comfortably onto a 50-foot lot. In neighborhoods built before 1940, lots 50 to 70 feet wide were the norm, with garages in a back corner of the lot, accessed either by long driveways to the street, or facing alleys in the rear. *Source: Affordable Plans* (Cahners, 1991).

at one side, with a garage located in the rear of the lot, a common practice during the 1920s. The photograph in Figure 10–2 shows a more contemporary residence designed to fit on a 60-foot wide lot, even with an attached garage.

A number of architectural drawings of very compact but expandable single-family homes, proposed for a new "open space subdivision" in Pawling, New York, showing variations on a basic six-room house (featuring an optional family room, bay window, front porch, and garage), are reproduced in the Appendix.

To increase the amount of usable yard space in small-lot developments, creative site designers are beginning to locate houses off center, toward one of the front lot corners. The greatest efficiencies are achieved when homes are built at the minimum front setback and directly against one of the side lot-lines ("zero lot-line"). In this way, both side yards are effectively combined on one side of the house, forming a reasonably proportioned outdoor space. To conserve privacy, such homes are typically constructed with a blank or nearly windowless wall built against one of the side lot-lines, facing onto the neighbor's yard immediately next door.

As lots become narrower, the proportion of the house facade consumed by garage doors grows larger. For example, on a 45-foot wide lot with a

Figure 10–2. A modest single-family house in Northampton, Massachusetts, designed in a more contemporary manner, with a garage attached to one side.

home measuring 35 feet across, more than half the facade would be garage, presenting a boring and lifeless aspect to the street. One solution favored by an increasing number of development designers is to move parking and garage spaces to the rear of these lots, accessing them through alleys or lanes (typically 12 feet wide, with one-way traffic flow). Many of the older suburbs around Baltimore and Philadelphia were built along similar lines during the first several decades of this century, and their "curbside appeal" stems partly from the fact that the view from the street is "all house."

According to one Seattle architect with experience building homes on very compact neo-traditional houselots, the primary target audience for such housing includes people "who would rather enjoy life than maintain a yard, empty-nesters tired of mowing lawns, other childless households, and singles with or without children whose priorities do not include a large yard" (Kreager, 1992). The key to success when following this type of approach is to pay close attention to architectural and site design, to create the most pleasing product for the customer's money.

It should also be noted that providing adequate yard space becomes even more important when lot dimensions are reduced. Although some extra backyard area can usually be created by moving the house closer to the front lot line (creating "dooryard gardens" 15 feet deep, measured from the sidewalk), that is no substitute for designing special areas for walking the dog, having a game of catch, playing informal games, or participating in more organized sporting activities. The green spaces shown in the "open space subdivision" (Figure 10–3) were created by shaving 20 percent to 40 percent off each standard houselot in the conventional layout. Lot sizes were reduced from 17,600 square feet (110' × 165') to 12,000 square feet (80' × 150').

Reductions from slightly larger lots could also be used to produce similar open space areas. For example, if development built at these dimensions does not fit comfortably into the scale, pattern, and context of the community, then a reduction in lot size from 25,000 square feet (125' × 200') to 15,000 square feet (100' × 150') might be more acceptable.

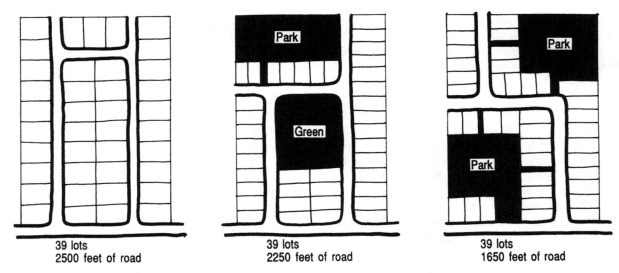

39 lots
2500 feet of road

39 lots
2250 feet of road

39 lots
1650 feet of road

Figure 10–3. Three alternative layouts producing 39 houselots, showing how neighborhood parks can be created while also lowering construction costs by reducing the length of new streets, water mains, and sewer lines.

Note that there is nothing special about these particular numbers. The point is that in many cases lot dimensions can be easily reduced without loss of livability, and the degree to which this can be done is related to whatever is appropriate in the traditional townscape context of the reader's community. (Evaluating townscape elements is discussed at length in Part I).

To the extent that the neighborhood open space is located in central areas without directly abutting any roads, for example, at the back of the more compact houselots, street and utility runs can be substantially reduced. This is clearly illustrated in Figure 10–3, which shows three ways to arrange 39 houselots of the sizes and proportions discussed in the first example above (110′ × 165′ versus 80′ × 150′).

The first layout requires 2,500 feet of street and utility lines and provides no neighborhood open space. The second plan reduces infrastructure costs by 10 percent and provides a handsome "common" or "green" as a central focal point, plus a playing field or park behind one row of houses. However, the most significant savings occur with the third alternative, which requires only 1,650 feet of roads and utilities, while offering two neighborhood parks. The trade-off between the

second and third plans lies in the choice between open space that is more visually prominent and the cost reductions arising from a more efficient circulation pattern.

Three village greens provide the basic organizing concept at the Outer Commons development in Amherst, Massachusetts, which combines 25 modest single-family homes with five larger houses, each containing two dwelling units. The design of the homes is based upon traditional houses in the surrounding neighborhood. Because of its careful attention to its context, and its preservation of half the site as open space (including a trail system through some seasonally wet woodlands), the project was endorsed by local planning officials, neighbors, affordable housing advocates, and land conservationists. (See Figures 10–4 and 10–5.)

Dollar figures for the cost savings achievable through more compact residential development designs have been documented in a well-illustrated study by the National Association of Home Builders, *Cost Effective Site Planning: Single Family Development* (NAHB, 1986). For example, on a 166-acre parcel near Canton, Ohio, site development costs per dwelling were one-third less for the more compact layout ($8,512 versus $12,856),

Figure 10–4. This aerial sketch shows homes grouped around one of the three greens at the Outer Commons, a 35-unit infill development on 18 acres in Amherst, Massachusetts, including ten affordable dwellings in five two-family homes designed to look like large, traditional single-family residences, which serve as visual anchors at the head of each green. The site also contains an extensive trail network through eight acres of wooded wetlands. *Source:* Dodson Associates.

which also left 20 percent of the property as open space, compared with 6 percent open space for the conventional layout involving the same number of homes (472).

Subdivision layouts, floor plans, and ordinance standards for San Antonio's "Small Lot Home District" are detailed in *Affordable Single Family Housing* (Sanders et al., 1984), although the site plans are deficient in neighborhood open space provision.

The need for privacy fences or hedges to provide screening for backyard activities would be about the same in each of the alternatives illustrated in Figure 10–3. Also, a similar degree of neighborly consideration would be necessary in

Figure 10–5. Children playing catch on one of the three greens on the Outer Commons development also depicted in Figure 10–4.

all three layouts, with respect to noise levels, as sound does not diminish rapidly over any of the distances involved here. Unless the site is heavily wooded, there is no substitute for landscape screens to create pleasant and inviting conditions for the enjoyment of one's own private backyard. The sketch in Figure 10–6 and the photo in Figure 10–7 show how this was done on a 11,000 square foot lot in Cranford, New Jersey, located in a 1920s compact neighborhood, built (unfortunately) without a local park or natural open space nearby.

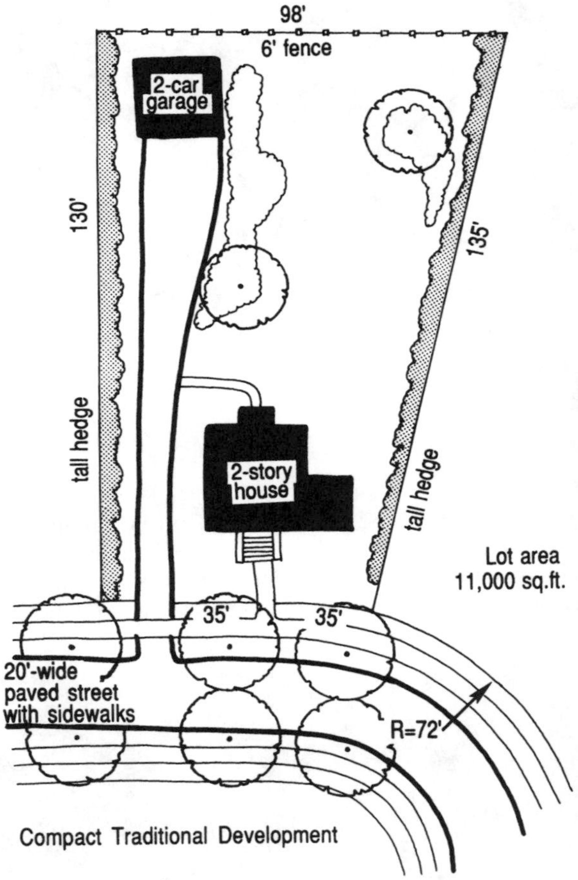

Figure 10–7. Photograph of the house illustrated in the site plan in Figure 10–6. *Source:* Photo by H. C. Arendt.

Figure 10–6. Site plan showing how backyard space and privacy has been achieved on a small lot dating from the 1920s in Cranford, New Jersey, by positioning the house closer to the street and planting hedges along side lot lines. Also notable are the presence of sidewalks and shade-trees, and the 72-foot radius curve in the street (which slows down traffic to 15 mph), all of which makes this neighborhood pedestrian friendly.

Figure 10–8. Attractive but modestly scaled homes built on relatively compact lots during the 1920s and 1930s can be found in every part of the country, providing numerous examples of how pleasant yet affordable neighborhoods could be created again to meet the needs of individuals and families entering the housing market for the first time. The importance of requiring developers to provide sidewalks and to plant deciduous street-trees capable of growing at least 50 feet tall, at 40-foot intervals, cannot be overstated, for these new neighborhoods to become as nice as the one shown here.

TWO-FAMILY HOUSES:
NOT ALWAYS "UGLY DUCKLINGS"

It is difficult to imagine a less inviting term for homes shared by two families than "duplex." Historically they were often known as "double-houses" or "twins," and in Britian they are referred to as "semidetached." Today's nomenclature for this building form is as unappealing to the ear as most current designs for it are unappealing to the eye. To be honest, the exterior appearance of many of our twentieth-century duplexes has been second-rate, at best. Until the architectural design of this residential type is generally improved, many people will undoubtedly continue to think of it as "second-class"—rather than "second family" housing.

The importance of building design can hardly be overstated. In small towns across the Northeast and mid-Atlantic states, double-houses built in the classic Greek Revival style are an accepted part of the townscape. But introduce a raised ranch duplex or a stark and boxy contemporary duplex sided with "T-111" plywood sheeting into the neighborhood and the uproar will begin.

The section on "Community-Assisted Design" found later in this chapter discusses the value of involving neighborhood residents in design decisions for new infill housing. From the author's experiences and observations about how people typically react to new housing proposals, physical appearance from the street is a key element in local acceptance of new two-family homes in the neighborhood. (See the discussion of Anton Nelessen's role in redesigning an infill project in Dover, New Jersey, in Chapter 4).

Well-designed two-family homes can be a significant part of a community's affordable housing strategy. Their size lends them easily to single-lot infill situations, where they can be assimilated into a neighborhood. For obvious reasons of scale, this is not as true for multifamily structures, unless the individual units are modestly proportioned and the surrounding homes are large.

Two-family homes help owner-occupiers to defray their mortgage payments and property taxes. Buying a two-family home, and treating half as an income-producing property, is a time-honored method for young couples to gain a toehold in the housing market and to build their equity. Many people have gained their financial ability to buy a fully detached house by first purchasing a duplex as their starter home.

Two-family homes also enable renters to live in traditional neighborhoods as part of the community mainstream. Many would prefer this situation to the isolation inherent in huge apartment complexes surrounded by acres of asphalt parking, and often located on the outskirts of town or adjacent to a railway line or industrial facility.

The trick in making two-family housing blend in with single-family neighborhoods is to design the buildings to look like large single residences. Perhaps the most visible indication of duplex status is the pair of front doors facing the street. Although the door pair can be concealed by locating it inside a recessed opening, or by placing the doors on the left- and right-hand sides of the building, perhaps the best arrangement is to create a large central entrance on the front facade, together with a secondary entrance on one side. This is the approach taken by Bill Thompson, an architect from Wiscasset, Maine, who designed the "Georgian double-house" shown in Figure 10–9 (for which construction plans are available). This two-family home, disguised as a house of the Georgian period, contains a two-bedroom unit with 1,164 square feet on the left half and a three-bedroom unit with 1,356 square feet on the right, in a compact upstairs-downstairs arrangement with 1½ baths for each family.

Other lessons can be drawn from the numerous examples of historic two-family homes throughout small town America. In New England, many were built in the local nineteenth-century vernacular style, although some are strongly Greek, Gothic, or Italianate in derivation. Often the missing link lies in getting word out to local contractors, designers, and developers. Persons interested in promoting a small revival of nicely designed double-houses could photograph a whole range of these buildings in their area, mount copies in an album and/or on special posters for display in libraries and other public buildings. One of the more effective spots for such displays would prob-

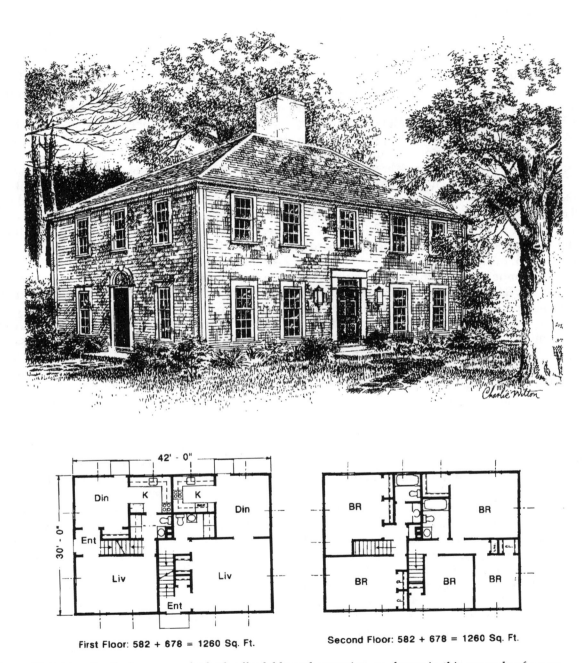

First Floor: 582 + 678 = 1260 Sq. Ft.

Second Floor: 582 + 678 = 1260 Sq. Ft.

Figure 10–9. Two-family homes can be both affordable and attractive, as shown in this example of a neo-Georgian duplex (designed by William Thompson, AIA, Wiscasset, Maine). Scaled to resemble a large, 2,500-square foot single-family residence, the building unobtrusively accommodates its second front door as a side entrance (an arrangement that is not uncommon on older homes in New England).

ably be in the local building inspector's office, visited daily by contractors and developers. Short, illustrated talks before local service groups and realtors' associations could also help to generate support for the idea, and might also elicit some press coverage as well.

In addition to the special treatment regarding main entrances (i.e., to avoid "door pairs"), architectural design guidelines should address basic issues such as roof shape, roof pitch, building massing/width/height, window size/proportion/spacing, exterior materials, and inobtrusive parking. If retention of traditional character is desired, the content of such standards should be related to photographs of historic double-houses in the area.

Several subdivisions where single-family and two-family homes have been successfully combined are illustrated in Part IV ("Radburn" in Fairlawn, New Jersey, and "Merriam's Close" in Concord, Massachusetts, representing different income groups).

Zoning regulations often need to be refined to permit double-houses on reasonably sized lots (some communities have adopted inappropriate standards—some requiring no lot area increase, others requiring twice the lot area). The most reasonable course lies between those two paths. To prevent investors from becoming absentee landlords, ordinances could stipulate that new duplex approvals in predominantly single-family areas be conditioned to require that half the unit be owner-occupied. When landlords live on the same premises with their tenants, building maintenance and landscaping tend to be handled much more responsibly.

In most states it is probably not possible to regulate the aesthetics of building design outside historic districts. However, local land-use laws could be amended to offer attractive density bonuses to applicants who agree to design their two-family homes according to special zoning guidelines and performance standards. Developers would be free to apply or not to apply, and as the standards would be tied to the bonus, mutual benefits would accrue from this voluntary action.

Actually, there is no reason why all two-family approvals could not be handled in this way, so that such buildings could not be constructed un-

less certain design standards were met. However, applicants must also have the legal right to build single-family homes without design restrictions, albeit at the standard density without any "duplex bonus." In other words, an individual with enough land to build four single-family homes might be allowed to build three double-houses (with six units altogether). In this case, each duplex lot would be 1.3 times as large and just as wide as a single-family lot, to accommodate the extra parking and yard space needed for the two families.

The scale of density bonuses needed to encourage compatible architectural design and sensitive site planning will vary among different localities. Although in many small towns a density of 6,000 square feet per unit may seem extraordinary, it certainly can be accomplished in a manner that is a credit to many neighborhoods. In Winslow, Washington, on Bainbridge Island, three semi-detached dwellings have been constructed on a 35,000 square foot houselot without disrupting the streetscape in this predominantly single-family area. (See Figures 10–10 and 10–11.) Although they were built within existing zoning parameters and not as "affordable" units, in areas where such a project would require a density increase that bonus could be tied to standards of affordability, building design, and site layout.

To assure affordability beyond the first buyer (who could otherwise realize a windfall profit when he or she sells the unit), some states (e.g., California) are requiring developers to grant deed restrictions of 30 years or longer, limiting resale prices. In New England, both Maine and Rhode Island have laws enabling town governments and nonprofit housing groups to control resale prices, typically through covenants (White, 1993). Similar strategies are further discussed in the section on community land trusts, later in this chapter.

MULTIFAMILY DWELLINGS

Much of the preceding text regarding two-family homes is equally applicable to multifamily dwellings. The principal difference, of course, is scale. Due to their larger size, multifamily dwellings harmonize best when located in areas where the existing homes are above average in bulk, or are

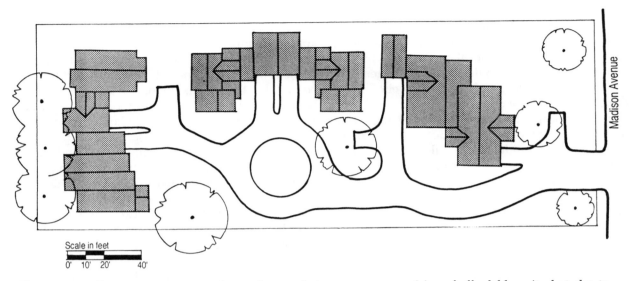

Figure 10–10. Density incentives can be used not only to encourage provision of affordable units, but also to encourage voluntary compliance with special architectural guidelines to ensure compatibility with the surrounding neighborhood. On this site in Winslow, Washington, three semidetached residences (containing six units) occupy a 35,000-square foot site, but they have been sensitively designed and sited to blend in with the single-family context, as seen from the street. In many places where developers would be permitted to construct only two units, doubling or trebling the allowable density effectively slashes per-unit land costs, enabling the units to be let at affordable rents while still providing an attractive return on investment. While density is of utmost importance to developers, design compatibility is often the greatest concern of local residents and officials. Fortunately, these goals are not mutually exclusive. (Design by Thomas Johnston, AIA.)

Figure 10–11. Photograph of two-family dwelling shown in Figure 10–10, as seen from the street.

located on a separate site where immediate comparisons are not possible.

One clever approach to disguising multiunit housing as large traditional homes was the brain-child of William Rawn, an award-winning Boston architect who recognized the potential of the classic New England "connected farmhouse" to accommodate several dwelling units. These long, rambling structures, which gradually evolved during the mid-nineteenth century, represent successive additions to the basic homestead and are recalled in the children's chant "big house, little house, backhouse, barn" (Hubka, 1984).

Determined to avoid the image of apartment buildings or townhouses in his "Battle Road Farm" project in Lincoln, Massachusetts, Rawn faithfully followed the lines of traditional rural New England architecture, with long porches gracing the fronts of many of his structures. (See Figure 10–12.) Although the subject of much debate during its proposal stages, the final design was approved by a 10-to-1 margin at town meeting. According to Rawn, "The plan neutralized the opposition because no longer could they say "This is ugly" (quoted in Leccese, 1990). Perhaps most

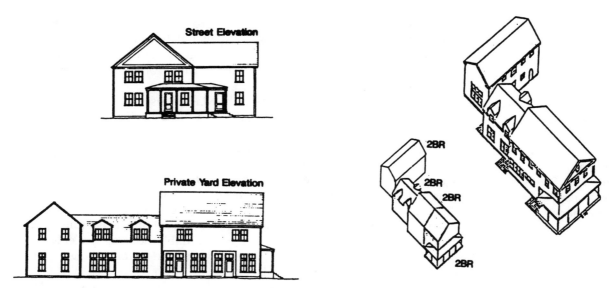

Figure 10–12. Elevations and axonometric views of one of the four-unit buildings designed to resemble large New England farmhouses with connected outbuildings, at the Battle Road Farm development in Lincoln, Massachusetts. *Source:* William Rawn Associates, Boston.

amazing, Rawn achieved this construction for just $54 per square foot, in the Boston suburbs in the late 1980s.

One of the most commendable features of this project was the initiative demonstrated by local officials, who felt that the town should play an active role in the promotion of affordable housing. By taking the first step itself, Lincoln was able to select the most appropriate site for this type of development and to influence its design, rather than waiting for other developers to come in with an ill-conceived site plan in a less suitable location. (The layout of this project is shown in Chapter 20, "Residential Cases.")

After purchasing the Battle Road Farm parcel for $2 million, town officials published an RFP ("Request for Proposals") in the *Boston Globe*, inviting qualified professionals to submit conceptual plans for competitive review. Site information and a short list of development principles (e.g., that the project be designed to harmonize with the town's traditional rural character) were made available by the town.

Of the 120 units at Battle Road (in a combination of quadruplexes and duplexes), 72 were priced at roughly 50 percent below market rates. Subsidies

from the Home Ownership Opportunity Program, administered by the Massachusetts Housing Partnership, enabled these units to be virtually indistinguishable from the other 48 full-priced ones, erasing the image of publicly assisted housing as "cheap and undesirable." In addition, a Community Development Action Grant helped to defray infrastructure construction costs (Massachusetts Housing Partnership, 1989).

Another interesting feature of this project is the protection of seven acres of the 31-acre site as permanent open space, including a network of walking trails planned to loop through the woodlands and connecting with the townwide trail system.

Two examples of subdivisions that have successfully combined multifamily homes with single-family residences are illustrated as "case examples" in Chapter 20: "Martin Meadow" in Plainfield, Vermont and "Long Hill Farm" in Guilford, Connecticut. Coincidentally, in both cases the multifamily units were accommodated in old barn buildings or barn-like structures.

Other towns that wish to exercise more control over the location and design of new affordable housing projects would do well to study Lincoln's example. When advocating affordable housing, local officials will be assisted by the knowledge that producing sensitive designs and mixing market-rate units together with subsidized ones can soften the opposition. However, it may be even more useful to cite the conclusions of property value impact analyses, such as the statewide survey in Maine and the national study conducted by the state of California. In both cases, researchers "found that there are no significant negative effects from locating affordable housing near market-rate developments" (Peterson and Sternberg, 1990).

In Kalispell, Montana, mixing market-rate and below-market units has not affected the rentability of the former, and has generated profits used for subsidizing the latter. At Samaritan House, a church remodeled into 23 market-rate studio and one-bedroom apartments in 1985, half the units have been converted to subsidized housing since 1990. Remarkably, the facility is economically self-supporting, and provides not only some desperately needed sheltered housing in this economically depressed county, but also furnishes an example for other rural communities across the country to emulate.

In Falmouth, Massachusetts, a Strategic Planning Grant through the Executive Office of Communities and Development was used to evaluate 150 sites and to select the four most appropriate for affordable housing. After site selection, the local landscape architecture and planning firm of Bunker, Stimson and Solien prepared conceptual development plans for each of the four sites. These were used to generate a set of site planning guidelines usable in affordable housing projects there and elsewhere around the Commonwealth (Bunker et al., 1988).

The conceptual plans for one of the sites, "Martha's Bottom," is reproduced in Figure 10–13,

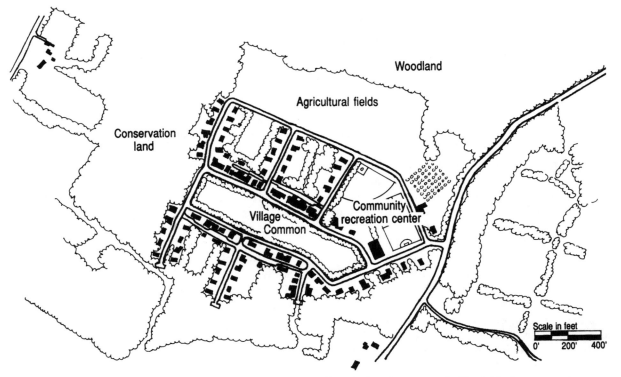

Figure 10–13. Proposed layout for "Martha's Bottom," a 90-unit development of affordable homes on town-owned land in Falmouth, Massachusetts, containing a village common and a greenbelt of farmland, orchards, and woodland in addition to wetland open space. *Source:* Bunker, Stimson & Solien.

showing 90 units in a combination of single-family and multifamily structures, and Figure 10–14 provides sketches. Of the 90 acres on the property, about 40 percent are either too wet or inaccessible for development. As a result, the construction area is limited to roughly 30 of the remaining 54 acres, both to save on development costs and to preserve a significant area of flat, dry land for a variety of conservation and recreation purposes (e.g., village common, community recreation area, wildlife habitat, or community gardens). Because the town already owns the property, it could be offered to a developer at below-market rates in return for his or her agreeing to conform to the spirit of the conceptual plan, including provision for well-

designed affordable units and permanent protection of designated open space areas.

Dealing with parking is a perennial challenge to designers of multifamily sites. On sloping sites it is possible to incorporate garages into lower building levels, as was done successfully at Chatham Village in Mount Washington, near Pittsburgh (see Chapter 20, "Residential Cases"). On flat sites the choices lie between individual garages (usually projecting in an ungainly way from the front facade), group garages, on-street parking, and separate parking lots. The most usual method is to mass the parking either in a central courtyard location or to surround the perimeter with parking lots. Either way, the extensive asphalt is visually unattractive.

Figure 10–14. Perspective sketch and a cross-sectional view of the village green surrounded by modest homes proposed at "Martha's Bottom" in Falmouth, Massachusetts. *Source:* Bunker, Stimson & Solien.

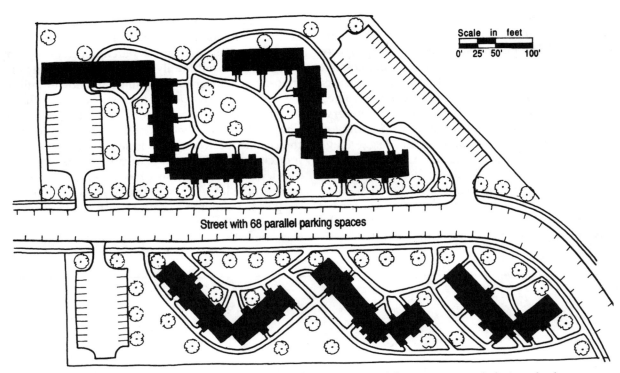

Street with 68 parallel parking spaces

Figure 10–15. Site plan of modestly-priced condominiums (converted from apartments) designed where a "parking street" with parallel spaces substantially reduces the need for large off-street parking lots. The streetscape in this neighborhood is very traditional, with sidewalks, street trees, and some very modest front setbacks. Unlike 99 percent of more recent multifamily developments, this 1942 example from Cranford, New Jersey does not arrange the units around a large central parking lot, nor does it place all the parking around the perimeter.

More pleasing results can be achieved by reviving the old tradition of town streets with parallel parking on each side, and modest front yard setbacks for buildings. In the schematic diagram in Figure 10–15, this straightforward approach is exemplified in the layout of an apartment complex built in 1942 in Cranford, New Jersey. Nearly half (70) of the total 153 parking spaces are accommodated in convenient curbside spaces in front of the units. Shade trees, sidewalks, and small lawns create a traditionally scaled streetscape, and the residents enjoy grassy, secluded interior courtyards behind their homes, as shown in Figure 10–16. The density figures on this four-acre site are surprisingly high for two-story construction (20 dwellings per acre), but the units themselves are

Figure 10–16. Photograph of traditional streetscape in the garden apartment development illustrated in Figure 10–15.

compact and affordable (48 one-bedroom units, 507 to 560 square feet in size, and 32 two-bedroom units, 630 to 690 square feet). Greater consistency of design could have been achieved by repeating the "S"-shaped units on both sides of the street, but the fact that off-street parking lots could be substantially reduced in area by building a "parking street" through the center of the site is a planning technique that should be considered more often. (Although 90-degree angle parking spaces along the curb would have further reduced off-street parking lot sizes, this temptation should be resisted because it produces a very suburban and untraditional pattern, and increases total street width to an unfortunate extent.)

"COMMUNITY-ASSISTED DESIGN"

During this era when design issues appear to be dominated by professionals, it is refreshing to be reminded that ordinary people working together can deal successfully with architectural and site planning problems, when there is agreement on basic fundamental objectives. An initially controversial proposal to locate six units of "affordable" infill housing in the center of Cushman Village in North Amherst, Massachusetts, is a case in point. Responding negatively to conceptual proposals to introduce three "Prairie style" duplexes into their nineteenth-century New England mill village, local residents articulated an alternative design solution that they felt was more in keeping with the hamlet's character, and presented their case directly to the elected members of the local housing authority that was administering the project.

The problem arose, as it usually does, through insufficient consultation with local residents by housing authority staff and their architect, who was selected more on the basis of his experience with public housing than on his record of designing buildings to harmonize with their historic contexts. Although staff members encouraged public participation from the outset, the response was modest, possibly because in the beginning there were few specifics to which to respond. However, as soon as the architect showed his conceptual drawings to the appointed citizens' advisory board, local interest levels increased markedly, for the sketches indicated no serious attempt to relate the new buildings to the traditional rural vernacular homes predominating in this area.

The trouble began when the architect denied that the unusual shape of his buildings' "footprints" was anything more than a hypothetical concept, but then appeared at the next meeting with elaborate elevation drawings based on the very same configurations. At that point it became clear to many of the citizen advisors that the architect was pursuing his own design agenda for the building: this led to a frank discussion of what they wanted the new housing to look like. The citizens asked him to reduce the wide, overhanging "Prairie style" eaves, increase the roof pitch, lengthen the windows and separate window pairs, and provided him with basic sketches of their proposed changes.

At the next meeting, the architect returned with a three-dimensional model of his original building that incorporated none of the requested changes. The frustration felt by many of the citizen advisors prompted one of them to produce his own scale models that embodied the sentiments of his fellow board members. During this period, housing agency staff were caught in the cross fire. These staffers had no preset ideas about design; their primary mission was to expedite the project and to speed its approval and implementation. One of the complicating difficulties was that the housing design also had to fit into two other neighborhoods with a rather different, and much less historic, architectural tradition (where other infill projects were being planned).

Eventually the elected members of the housing authority voted to instruct the architect to pay close attention to the citizen advisors, which he was thus obligated to do. Therefore the resulting plans ultimately reflected community preferences, which was critical to obtaining local acceptance of the project. It is important to note that the designs advocated by the citizens were basically modifications of exterior architectural features (roof pitch and overhang, window proportions and spacing). These suggestions did not interfere with the arrangement and size of rooms, or the cost of most materials. Shown in Figure 10–17 are sketches of

Architect's Contemporary Proposal

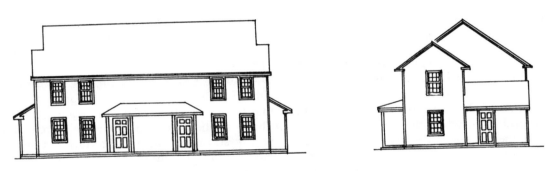

Citizens' Traditional Alternative

Figure 10–17. Contemporary design for two-family infill housing in Cushman Village, Amherst, Massachusetts, compared with a more traditional exterior redesign drawn up by a community resident responding to criticism that the original submission was insensitive to the predominantly nineteenth-century homes in the immediate neighborhood. The project gained broad local support after the architect (very reluctantly) agreed to a more contextual design.

the design originally proposed by the architect, and the final result after citizen involvement.

At the same time that the housing designs were being debated, the architect's proposed building arrangement was also questioned. The original site plan called for the creation of a short curvilinear cul-de-sac with three duplexes. This was considered by some citizen advisors to be an inappropriate suburban approach. The traditional pattern in Cushman Village has been for homes to be situated reasonably close to the old, fairly straight "grid" of through roads and connecting streets.

Another facet complicating the project involved citizen interest in saving a large, dilapidated, but highly visible and historic house on the housing

authority's property (it had originally been built by the local mill owner and village founder). Town officials were prevailed upon to consider its rehabilitation, to cancel demolition plans, and to offer it publicly for one dollar to anyone willing to restore it faithfully. After several months, a good proposal was submitted and accepted.

Because the original cul-de-sac layout had assumed the historic home's removal, the housing site plan had to be revised, and citizen advisory board members pressed for a more traditional arrangement of buildings vis-à-vis the existing road network. The three sketches in Figure 10–18 illustrate the historic village pattern (black squares) along with two approaches to locating the new

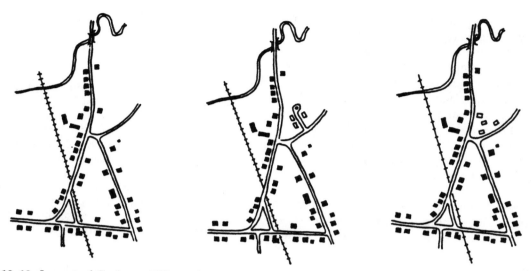

Figure 10–18. Layout of Cushman Village showing the historic relationship of buildings to each other and to the streets, compared with two infill alternatives involving three new two-family residences, one with a cul-de-sac, the other with separate driveways.

development (white squares). The two diagrams in Figure 10–19 are enlargements showing the original cul-de-sac proposal and the alternative arrangement that was finally approved.

The entire experience was stressful for everyone involved. In addition to satisfying local objectives, agency staff also had to meet the state's official requirements (chiefly pertaining to interior layout

Cul-de-sac Design   Street Design

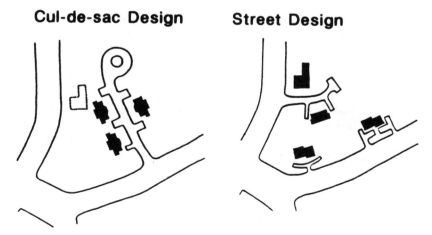

Figure 10–19. These more detailed sketches of the two infill alternatives at Cushman Village illustrate their basic differences. One isolates the new affordable homes from their historic village context, arranging them along a suburban cul-de-sac. In the other plan, two of the three new buildings face an existing street in the traditional way, while the third shares a driveway with a fourth building (with four units) reconstructed to resemble the original Greek Revival house the first plan would have eliminated. The extra units represented a density bonus that enabled the developer to afford the added expense of rebuilding that house authentically.

and cost per square foot). Those requirements certainly complicated many of the choices and often limited the available alternatives. In retrospect, the most important lesson learned was that architect selection is an absolutely critical element in any building design project. If the architect had been interviewed and if his past work had been examined, it would probably have been evident that this particular individual was professionally committed to contemporary design, and that he would therefore not be the most appropriate person to perform this work.

It is useful to recognize that the often berated approach of "designing by committee" does not always produce uncomely results, especially when there is agreement on a common approach (such as matching the vernacular surroundings). In projects such as this, the choice may be between "community-assisted design" and "community-resisted design." Local officials should consider helping neighbors gain a sense of ownership in the development of such projects by encouraging them to invest their constructive thoughts and positive feelings in the design process. When that happens, and when they are listened to, these people can become strong advocates and supporters.

On a more positive note, the inclusion of the historic rehab added four more "affordable" rental units to the site, an increase that was accepted by the village residents because of the project's sensitive design.

ACCESSORY DWELLING UNITS: A HIDDEN RESOURCE

One of the potentially best—but typically overlooked—opportunities for small towns to accommodate new growth is the accessory dwelling unit. This traditional housing type requires no additional conversion of open land, and normally involves little or no alteration to the existing townscape. The steady decrease in average household size over the past several decades has made such housing easier than ever to provide, for two reasons: many homeowners have more rooms than they need, and the number of people looking for small apartment space has risen markedly.

The multiple benefits of accessory units have been clearly articulated by Patrick Hare, a national advocate for this sensible approach to new housing provision:

> Accessory dwellings are complete and separate housing units typically created in the surplus space in single-family homes or on their lots. They may take the form of internal apartment units in under-utilized space within existing houses, or they may be located in small cottages on the same houselot, often toward the rear. Their principal benefit to homeowners is rental income, but there are other benefits, including a way to provide for relatives, added security, companionship, and the possibility of getting services in return for rent reductions.
>
> These benefits can help older homeowners age in place in comfort, single parents hang onto a home in the wake of a divorce, and young homebuyers buy a home they might otherwise be unable to afford. It should also be noted that accessory dwellings typically create affordable rental housing, integrated into the community, without any public subsidy.... Surveys show that homeowners with accessory dwellings are generally pleased with them (Hare, 1991).

If this sounds too good to be true, that's because it is in fact a dream that is rarely realized in most municipalities. The problem is not cost, technology, or administrative complexity. It lies largely in our codes (typically, zoning and building regulations) that either prohibit or make it exceedingly difficult for homeowners to create accessory apartments or "echo units" in their houses or on their properties. (The term "echo housing" refers to small cottage-like outbuildings modeled after the principal residence.) Towns interested in encouraging the use of accessory units should first take a critical look at their local codes. It may also be necessary to provide information about the advantages of such conversions to existing homeowners, remodeling contractors, and realtors, who may have little experience in creating new units of this type.

Hare documents the growing demand for accessory apartments, especially as the national population continues to age. The "boom" of postwar babies was followed 30 years later by an upsurge in "empty nesters," parents of those children. Most empty nesters and many elderly people live in homes that are larger than they actually need. Accessory apartments offer them a way to trade surplus space for extra income, money that many retirees need to offset rising property taxes and for help with building upkeep (routine maintenance, yard work, roofing, painting, etc.).

The implications of tapping this great stock of underutilized housing are tremendous. In 1987, the American Housing Survey estimated there were 48 million owner-occupied single-family dwellings, and that one-third of these homes with five or more rooms were occupied by only one to two people. If just 7 percent of these homes were to be converted, Hare estimates that 1 million new accessory dwellings could be created *without* adding to suburban sprawl or building new apartment complexes.

According to one observer, young couples who would not be able to purchase a house without creating an income-producing apartment could be the largest single group implementing this concept (Gellen, 1985). However, Hare advises that housing advocates and realtors interested in promoting accessory units should offer help by providing a coordinating service to assist applicants as they deal with permits, contractor selection, tenant screening, and so forth (Kennedy, 1992).

Because the cost of creating accessory apartments ($16,500 to $25,000) is roughly one-third that of building a conventional rental unit ($50,000 to $75,000), they can be rented for less. Assuming 12 percent interest over 15 years, the full cost could be recaptured with monthly rents of $200 to $300 (Hare, 1991). Rents at these levels could enable families to help young married children save money to buy a home for themselves, or to help elderly relatives live independently, yet conveniently close, at bargain rates. Even when they are let to non-family members, accessory apartment rents are often below-market rate because it is in the homeowner's interest to retain good tenants, whose presence may also deter burglaries when the main unit is unoccupied. The different names for accessory apartments in various parts of the country illustrate these functions: "ohana" (extended family) units in Hawaii, and "caretaker units" in the Rockies.

One practical difficulty associated with accessory apartments involves parking, but this is a significant obstacle only in areas where houselots are already very small and/or in neighborhoods where there is no spare capacity for curbside parking. However, most postwar subdivisions in small towns or rural areas were laid out in a relatively spacious manner, often with broad local access streets far wider than needed for existing traffic volumes and parking loads. In such instances, and in a great many other situations, there is fairly substantial potential to accommodate these new units, as Figures 10–20 and 10–21 illustrate.

Two of the principal impediments to creating accessory apartments involve overcoming the fears of local officials and residents that amending zoning to allow this type of housing would detract from their neighborhoods, and overcoming the

Figure 10–20. The far end of this early nineteenth-century house was extended in 1990 to include a connected apartment and garage, in a manner that does not detract from the home's historic appearance. Income from the accessory dwelling will pay the entire 15-year loan that financed this addition. Accessory units make more efficient use of land that is already developed, and provide rental accommodation in an inobtrusive fashion for students, young adults, single parents, widows, and widowers who prefer to live in a real neighborhood setting in their own community.

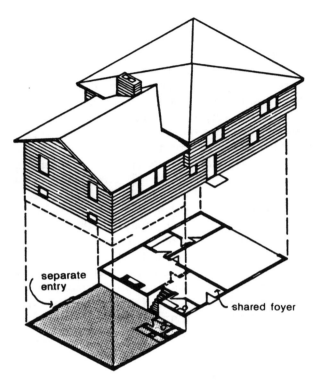

Figure 10–21. Cutaway view showing how a split-level house can be converted to include an accessory dwelling unit. Lower levels of such homes lend themselves to such adaptation because they are easily separated from the main house and are often already served by their own bathroom. *Source:* Patrick Hare, 1991.

reluctance of individual homeowners to file an application in a system they perceive to be bureaucratic and sometimes unfriendly. Hare offers a six-point strategy for addressing these concerns:

Public Input

Providing ample opportunity for the public to be heard is critically important. Requiring full-blown public hearings in all cases could, however, add delays and discourage elderly applicants who are often reluctant to appear under a municipal spotlight. Streamlining the process is desirable and may be accomplished by delegating such decisions to staff for action within two weeks from receipt of a complete application, unless a hearing is specifically requested by neighbors (who would be notified by postcard of their right to ask for one).

Renewable and Revokable Permits

Permits should be renewable and revokable, and issued to the property owner, not to the property itself. The owner should also be required to live on the premises. A revocation clause would provide strong incentives for zoning standards and permit approval conditions to be faithfully observed. By the same token, the owner should be assured of renewal if these requirements have been met.

Exterior Appearance

Permitted alterations to the home's exterior appearance should be minimal, and should never be allowed to detract from the visual character of the single-family neighborhood. (This is particularly true with respect to doorways and parking.)

Conversion Ceiling

A ceiling should be set on the percentage of homes in a given area that may be converted. Public acceptance of such units is likely to grow as more people become familiar with real examples in their own town. Initial limits on additional conversions (say, 10 percent of properties within 300 feet of an existing accessory unit) could, for example, be gradually relaxed after a 10-year trial period.

Zoning Review

The zoning amendment authorizing accessory dwellings should be structured so that this provision must be renewed or, preferably, officially reviewed after a certain period of years. If the amendment is repealed, units legally created under its authority should be "grandfathered" and remain subject to the original requirements and permit conditions.

Neighborhood Evaluation

Neighbors must be reassured that valid complaints will be heard, by soliciting evaluations from them (via comment cards mailed to their homes) prior to permit renewal.

Because of the time and energy typically required to address the fears of homeowners concerned about their property values potentially declining if accessory dwelling units are allowed in their neighborhoods, Hare suggests that advocates of revised zoning focus their efforts on more receptive towns, where programs can be more easily implemented, to document an actual track record with such housing. Where nearby communities already permit accessory dwellings, their experience should be cited. In this regard, Hare stresses the critical importance of short application processing times, otherwise few units are likely to be created (since applicants are just ordinary citizens, inexperienced in zoning and real-estate matters). In Fairfax County, Virginia, for example, only two applications for accessory unit creation were filed during the first 18 months of the ordinance amendment (despite the percentage of renters in its 600,000 inhabitants). "Once there are some communities with real success, it will be much easier to get other communities to change their zoning. This has been the case in southwestern CT, where the successful experience of Weston and Westport have provided an example that has led the way for almost every other town in the area to amend its zoning" (Hare, 1991).

PRESERVING AFFORDABILITY THROUGH "COMMUNITY LAND TRUSTS"

"Community Land Trusts" (CLTs) are a special type of land trust whose primary focus is to create affordable housing and to maintain its affordability over the long term. They typically achieve this goal by removing (or reducing) land costs as an element of housing rental and sale prices. This is normally done by purchasing land with their own private funds (sometimes supplemented by public monies) and making it available at reduced or zero cost to qualified buyers. It can also be accomplished by negotiating with local governments for zoning density increases, which would typically be tied to a restriction on the use of the land for a specific number of subsidized housing units.

This approach is also being used by some local and state housing authorities, which subsidize the land costs of full-market housing prices to bring units within the economic reach of more people. For example, if the land component comprises 25 percent of the total house value, and if this piece is fully subsidized, qualified purchasers could buy the unit for 75 percent of its normal market price. However, to ensure the unit's continued affordability for future purchasers, the original buyer would receive the same 75 percent of the market value when he or she eventually sells it.

While this is an excellent mechanism for preventing the first buyer from pocketing the subsidy and converting the unit into a market-rate dwelling, this approach is not without its drawbacks. The most obvious one is that participants in the program may face the same "affordability gap" when they sell their units and move to another community without similarly subsidized housing. In other words, this approach does not allow people to rise up into full middle-class status. This might not be a problem for people who remain in their homes until they become "empty nesters," when they can trade down to smaller dwellings. Nor would it be a problem for people whose household income increases during their time in the subsidized unit. However, for those who do not fall into these groups, finding another home in a different town or state would probably be very difficult.

Clearly, it is impossible to have it both ways: either the units remain affordable with the sellers receiving only the same proportion of value they originally contributed (which is fair), or the units' sale prices (and their owners' equity) rise with the market, denying other potential owners the opportunity to purchase the property at a reduced rate.

Recognizing this dilemma, some programs have begun to modify their approach. The simplest method allows the owner/seller to receive full value after 10 or 20 years, with adjustments figured proportionally for people who sell before the end of the stipulated period. A more complex but possibly fairer approach may be to relate the owner/seller's proportional share of the market-rate sales price to his or her income level at the time of sale.

A good example of a project that preserves affordability is "Misty Meadows" in Amherst, Massachusetts, shown in Figure 10–22. This neighborhood contains a combination of housing types (12 two-family and 17 single-family homes) and a mixture of subsidized and market-rate units (in a 40 percent to 60 percent ratio, respectively). The fact that the subsidized units were sold to owner-occupiers and were not rentals helped to reduce the social stigma normally associated with projects such as this (Massachusetts Housing Partnership, 1989). The site design utilized Amherst's cluster option to locate the units on half the land normally required for this number of units, creating a jointly owned central open space seven acres in size, which most of the homes abut. In addition, the project involved town participation in purchasing an extra 97 acres of the original farm as open space, including 15 acres of arable farmland, 40 acres of wetlands, 12 acres for passive recreation, and a 15-acre future school site. For this acreage the town paid $325,000 (80 percent of which was reimbursed by state open space funds).

Figure 10–22. These two-family homes at "Misty Meadows" in Amherst, Massachusetts, are modular units, with four sections per duplex. Grouped around a large common open space, these units were sold at 75 percent of their market value under an arrangement whereby homeowners will receive 75 percent of the future sales price when they move out. This allows the current owners' equity to grow, while providing the same level of affordability to succeeding owners.

PRESERVING LAND WITH AFFORDABLE HOUSING THROUGH LAND CONSERVATION TRUSTS

Another branch of the land trust movement involves "land conservation trusts" (usually called simply "land trusts"), whose principal objective is to protect natural lands and working landscapes from development. Over the last decade a growing number of land trusts have discovered the advantages of broadening their range of activities to include affordable housing provision. One of the most common ways that land trusts protect land is by designing so-called "limited developments," wherein a reduced number of high-priced houselots are sold (typically) to affluent commuters or second-home buyers, with the majority of land remaining open and permanently protected through perpetual conservation easements.

The most obvious way for land trusts to help lessen the growing housing crisis is to create several affordably priced houselots each time they prepare a subdivision plan for "limited development" (Rubenstein, 1989). Because this type of development is normally designed well below legally permissible maximum density, there is no problem with adding several extra units onto the plan. However, because the principal goal of such subdivisions is to limit the amount of land that is developed, the extra units would normally be carefully sited on smaller lots (Dodson, 1989).

Employing the principles of "open space development design," creative planners and landscape architects should find it relatively easy to accommodate some additional affordable homesites. Instead of designing seven very high-priced building parcels (where perhaps 24 would normally be allowed), a land trust could create five at the high end of the scale and three or four toward the lower end. Done skillfully, no more land would be taken out of natural or agricultural use, and the net proceeds to the trust would remain the same.

Benefits would flow both ways. New housing within the reach of local people would become available, and land trusts would be seen as caring as much about the human resources of their area as they do about the natural resources. Because conservation of buildable land in areas with tight housing markets reduces the total acreage available for construction, critics argue that land preservation only pushes up new houselot prices. To the extent that this is true, it probably most affects local people at the lower end of the economic spectrum. When land trust supporters are sensitized to this situation, and when they are shown a relatively easy way for their organization to help counteract this effect, chances are that they will respond positively. Again, enlightened self-interest can be the source for lasting improvements in a community's quality of life.

One early example of this technique occurred in Ashfield, Massachusetts, at the initiative of the Franklin Land Trust. Although done at a very modest scale, the Loomis Farm project illustrates the principles of combining land preservation with housing objectives. Under local zoning regulations, the 410-acre site could have been subdivided into 43 market-rate houselots. Instead, 180 acres of pastureland were permanently protected and were sold to two young farmers at below market-rate, 46 acres of natural habitat remains for public use and enjoyment, and 9 houselots were created, two of which sold at 67 percent below market-rate to local moderate-income first-time homebuyers (Zenick, 1988).

This project was difficult because the town's zoning did not permit either "cluster development" or "flag lots," so none of the houselots could be smaller than two acres or have less than 200 feet of road frontage. Obviously, these rigid standards stymied the creative development design process. Although the total parcel size was quite large, it was not possible to create a greater number of smaller or flag-shaped houselots and still preserve the dairy farm, too.

With more flexible zoning, the number of affordable houselots could have been increased without compromising the other project goal of farmland preservation. Also, because so few houselots could be created on the buildable woodlands, the viability of this project depended upon the infusion of state funds to pay for the farmland development rights. With extremely limited funds for such programs in the future, projects like this

one will simply not be possible *unless* local governments allow more flexibility in the subdivision design process (see also Chapters 14 and 15 on "open space development design").

Vermont now leads the nation in its programs combining land conservation and affordable housing. In just four years, the Vermont Housing and Conservation Board (VHCB) has maintained or created more than 2,000 units of perpetually affordable housing, while protecting over 40,000 acres. Unfortunately, these two objectives have been combined relatively infrequently on the same property. The agency is especially proud when housing and conservation goals are achieved together, as has happened in Marshfield and Norwich. In Marshfield, the 470-acre Walter Smith farm has been preserved, with four new houselots, a cottage, and the original farmhouse, which the retiring farmer occupies and also rents to elderly individuals interested in living in a rural "extended family" setting. This project involved VHCB, the Vermont Land Trust, the Central Valley Community Land Trust, and Shared Housing for Rural Elders. In Norwich, the Upper Valley Land Trust has combined forces with the Twin Pines Housing Trust to build 14 affordable single-family homes on 15 acres of the 150-acre Farrell Farm (see Figure 10–23). In both these cases, VHCB applied public funding to purchase the farmland development rights, in a typical "PDR" transaction (see Chapter 18 for details on the "purchase of development rights" as a land preservation tool). Similar examples exist in the towns of Monkton and Newbury, where four affordable lots and 15 units of elderly housing are being provided respectively (Vermont Housing and Conservation Board, 1990).

In other cases, it makes more sense to locate new housing in other parts of the community, closer to central facilities and services. Planning techniques such as the "transfer of development rights" (TDR) are available in a growing number of states to facilitate land preservation in areas with important rural resources, and to make possible the utilization of development rights from the protected land elsewhere in the community. As public monies decline for the outright purchase of such rights, using more creative techniques,

Figure 10–23. This perspective sketch and site plan of the Farrell Farm in Norwich, Vermont, illustrates some of the possibilities that exist for blending affordable housing with both traditional design and open space preservation. *Source:* Jeremiah Eck, AIA, Boston.

such as TDR and "open space development design," will become imperative. Whether land conservation and affordable housing provision occur on the same property or on different sides of town as a result of a program such as offered by VHCB, it is clear that there is considerable scope for traditional land trusts to broaden their activities to ameliorate the housing affordability crisis existing today.

Efforts similar to those in Vermont are becoming more common in other states, but are typically occurring at the county or township level. In southern Rhode Island, for example, a regional group known as South County Community Action has recently created a new organization (the Action Community Land Trust) to hold title to the land to a wooded site adjacent to Route 138 in the Town of Richmond.

To help keep home purchase prices low, the land will be owned by the land trust and leased to future owners of the 10 one- to three-bedroom units (four of which will be reserved for seniors and handicapped applicants). The other 16 units will be sold to other members of the community, who live in an area where housing prices are so high that even people earning 115 percent of the median income cannot afford to purchase their own homes at market rates. This project will be targeted to help those earning from 40 to 80 percent of that median figure (Parsekian, 1992).

Site planning costs were minimized by enlisting technical help from the Conway School of Landscape Architecture in Conway, Massachusetts, which conducted a design competition among students and faculty to help the fledgling land trust. Development costs will be reduced by constructing the units in a semidetached ("twin") style, clustered in a manner that will minimize road construction and also preserve much of the site as permanent open space.

Other projects of this land trust include restoring a Second Empire home in Westerly, Rhode Island, as a multifamily dwelling (observing state guidelines for historically correct rehabilitation), and moving an attractive 1930s-era two-family home (donated by a local developer) to a new site in Westerly. The trust also negotiated a below market-rate mortgage for that property with a local savings bank.

MIXED USES, OR LIVING OVER THE SHOP

Allowing (or even requiring) certain types of new commercial structures to be combined with housing is an idea that should not be overlooked. Key to understanding this approach is the fact that the most inflationary element in housing costs tends to be its underlying land value. It therefore makes sense that one could provide housing at close to zero land cost if it were built as additional stories above nonresidential uses, where such uses would be economically self-sustaining without any extra rental income from the proposed housing.

Since much of the retail and office space currently being built in small towns is being designed in one- or two-story structures, it would not be difficult to add another floor to accommodate new apartments or condominiums. And, to the extent that new federal regulations under the Disabilities Act now require elevators to shops and offices not at ground level—but do not mandate similar accessibility to residential units—local officials may find developers more willing to consider providing "flats above shops" to maximize their land, foundation, and roof costs, which remain relatively constant for single and multistory buildings.

Although the mixed-use approach is not appropriate for every site, it should be strongly encouraged in town centers and other nodal areas where a variety of goods, services, and jobs would be available within convenient walking distance. (For further information, see Chapter 9 and several "case examples" in Part IV, describing new mixed-

use infill developments in La Jolla, California, Winslow, Washington, and South Hadley, Massachusetts, and a shopping center with apartment units in Waitsfield, Vermont.)

Besides offering the opportunity to create profitable housing at below-market rents, the central location of such units in downtown areas could enable some tenants to save significant expenditures on the costs of owning and maintaining a second car. These second-car ownership costs were conservatively estimated to be $3,000 per year in a 1984 report by the Federal Highway Administration (quoted in Hare and Honig, 1989). People who live and work in a central location, and who are able to walk or ride a bike to their jobs, can boost their home purchasing power by more than $24,000 by applying their transportation savings to their monthly mortgage payments.

If a central living location does not enable them to walk or ride a bike to work, but at least gives them access to public transit, their net savings would be in the range of $1,750 per year. This extra income would increase the amount of mortgage they could qualify for by $14,000, which still represents a significant increase for people who are close to (but below) the economic level for home ownership (Hare and Honig, 1989). It should be remembered that these dollar figures are low by today's prices, and should be adjusted upward to reflect current conditions. Also, the same upward boost would apply to renters, who would have more disposable income if they could live in a centrally located apartment at below-market rates, and walk, ride a bike, or take a bus to work.

Relatively few examples exist of recent development featuring residential units above ground-floor shops and offices in small towns. However, two excellent examples can be found in Winslow, Washington, on Bainbridge Island. In addition to "Winslow Green" (described in Chapter 21), a second project in that same town illustrates another way that these uses can be successfully integrated. Known locally as the "Hobble & Hayes Building," this 1987 development incorporates three dwelling units over several shops and offices, in a traditionally styled corner building with rear parking. Each of the three dwellings adjoins

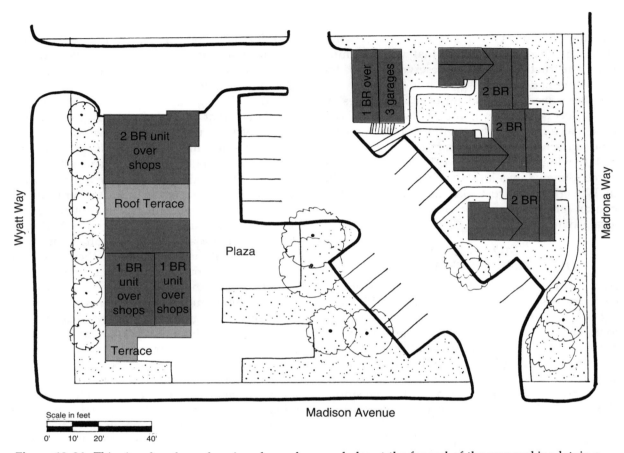

Figure 10–24. This site plan shows housing above shops and also at the far end of the rear parking lot, in a new development on Bainbridge Island, Washington. The practicability of combining residential, retail, and office uses is being rediscovered by a growing number of developers, although such projects are unfortunately uncommon in small towns (where such examples are typically confined to nineteenth-century "Main Street" situations, because of habit, inertia, ignorance, building codes, and single-use zoning). Planners should take the lead in making the viability of well-designed multiple-use buildings better known among developers and bankers in their communities. *Source:* Robert Hobble, AIA.

an elevated terrace providing accessory outdoor patio space. Four small additional dwellings occupy another corner of this ¾ acre site, designed in a manner that allows them to be perceived as detached units. (See Figures 10–24 and 10–25.)

COMPATIBLE MOBILE HOME DESIGN

Because mobile homes constitute such a significant percentage of new housing in many rural states, the location of these units has become an increasingly controversial topic. Due to the pas-

sage of excessively restrictive ordinances in many municipalities, legislatures in some states (such as Vermont) have enacted equally extreme laws to counteract local policies, effectively preventing municipalities from regulating mobile homes in any special way (except in historic districts, where they may be prohibited).

Because their appearance is often so different from that of standard "stick-built" housing, an argument can be made for their special treatment. The basic premise is that "if it looks like a house, it should be treated like a house, and if it looks like

Figure 10–25. Photograph of a mixed-use project on Bainbridge Island, Washington, whose site plan is shown in Figure 10–24.

These variables might include roof pitch, siding material, and foundation type. Units with flat tops, two-tone metal siding, or concrete block supports could be required to be located either in a mobile home park or deep within a heavily wooded site (with larger minimum setbacks and no-cut buffers). At the other end of the spectrum might be the newer type of mobile homes with pitched roofs and with asphalt shingles, vinyl clapboard siding, and concrete frost-walls or foundations. These units could be allowed in every zone, except in official historic districts and perhaps in village areas with small houselots and traditional homes.

In village areas, mobile homes built along more conventional residential lines might still appear out of place, especially if narrow lot widths required them to be arranged perpendicular to the street. This orientation could become visually acceptable, however, if the unit were also connected to a breezeway and garage, as shown in Figure 10–26. The front facade would then be about 40 feet wide, consistent with most "stick-built" homes, without becoming too broad to fit comfort-

a trailer, it should be treated accordingly." It is not difficult to draw up a short list of visual characteristics of mobile homes and to regulate the various types of units according to their compatibility with surrounding conventional homes.

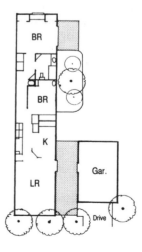

Figure 10–26. Manufactured housing represents one of the most popular housing alternatives in many rural areas, yet few developers have recognized the possibilities this offers for traditional neighborhood design. The units shown here, in a demonstration project in Elkhart, Indiana, are arranged with their narrow end facing the street, but with a breezeway and attached garage so that their building width resembles that of site-built homes.

ably onto a cost-efficient lot only 75 feet wide. In fact, during the early 1980s, a whole neighborhood of new mobile homes, arranged in this manner with attached garages, was built in Elkhart, Indiana, as a demonstration project sponsored by the U.S. Department of Housing and Urban Development. Located on lots measuring 75' × 100', this subdivision created a very attractive living environment. (Homes were located off-center on the lots, about five feet from one of the side boundaries, so that backyards could still be 50 feet wide, as illustrated in Figure 10–27.)

Figure 10–28 contains visual evaluation standards for manufactured housing (including "single-wide" modular homes), which were prepared by a working group consisting of the author, a leading mobile home manufacturer, and representatives from the Maine State Planning Office and the Maine Manufactured Housing Board (a regulatory body). It was devised to help small rural communities in that state deal with a legislative mandate requiring each town's zoning to accommodate mobile homes "in a variety of locations" (Arendt, 1982). Depending upon statutory and case laws, similar approaches might be viable in other states, where people are looking for a balanced and defensible method of dealing with this large component of rural affordable housing.

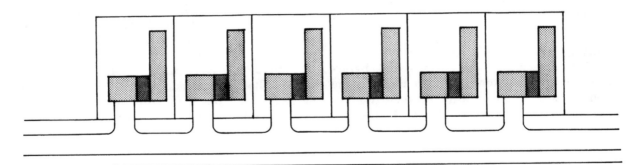

Figure 10–27. This plan-view sketch shows how mobile homes are sited in a manufactured housing subdivision in Elkhart, Indiana. Garages provide screening from the street, while the long, narrow units located near one of the side lot lines provide private backyard space.

Possible Standards for Siting Various Types of Manufactured Housing, According to Visual Character

	Village Residential	Suburban or Developing Residential	Multi-family Residential	Historical Areas	Rural - Restrictive	Rural - Non-Restrictive	Mobile Home Parks*	Mobile Home Subdivisions	Shoreland: Limited Residential
Proportions									
Minimum horizontal dimension 20'	P	P	P	P	P	P	P	P	P
Minimum horizontal dimension 14'	–	C	P	–	C	P	P	P	C
Minimum horizontal dimension 12'	–	–	P	–	C	P	P	P	–
Minimum horizontal dimension under 12'	–	–	–	–	–	–	–	–	–
Single Section unit designed, by manufacturer, to accept T or L addition	P	P	P	P	P	P	P	P	P
Appearance and Materials									
Minimum roof pitch of 6/12 or steeper (about 28°)	P	P	P	P	P	P	P	P	P
Minimum roof pitch of 3/12 (about 14°)	–	P	P	–	P	P	P	P	P
Rounded or flat roof	–	–	–	–	–	–	P	–	–
Roofing shingle or shingle-like*	P	P	P	P	P	P	P	P	P
Roofing smooth or corrugated surface	–	–	–	–	–	–	P	–	–
Exterior walls of traditional site-built appearance	P	P	P	P	P	P	P	P	P
Exterior walls not of traditional site-built appearance	–	–	–	–	–	–	P	–	–
Treatment Below Unit									
Frost Wall	P	P	P	P	P	P	P	P	P
Grade Beam or Floating Slab (with masonry-type skirting)	–	P	P	–	P	P	P	P	P
Gravel pad only	–	–	–	–	–	–	P	–	–
Construction Standards									
Not certified as meeting HUD or State standards	–	–	–	–	–	–	P	–	–

P = Permitted

– = Not Permitted

C = Conditional upon the narrow sections being attached in T or L shapes

* Traditional "standing seam" metal roofs are permissible

Criteria for Rural Restrictive Zone: moderately densely settled areas, or areas where smaller lots (1 acre or less) predominate, or areas with concentrations of traditional or significant architecture.

Criteria for Rural Non-Restrictive Zone: fairly thinly settled areas with lots having larger dimensions (including longer frontages and greater setbacks), and areas with mixed housing types with no significant architecture.

DEFINITIONS

Frost Wall: A masonry foundation wall extending below the ground surface, supported by footings located below the frost-line, to protect structures from frost heaves.

Grade Beam: That part of a foundation system (usually in a building without a basement) which supports the exterior wall of the superstructure; commonly designed as a beam which bears directly on the column footings, or may be self-supporting. The grade beam is located at the ground surface and is well-drained below.

Floating Slab: A reinforced concrete slab which is designed to withstand pressures both from below and above.

Exterior Walls of Traditional Site-Built Appearance: Siding materials such as clapboards, shingles, and shakes, including synthetic or metal siding manufactured to closely resemble clapboards, shingles and shakes. This term shall also include masonry, wood board-and-batten, and "Texture III" exterior plywood, but shall not include artificial masonry, or fake board-and-batten made from metal.

Masonry-type Skirting: This refers to concrete blocks which are arranged to resemble a foundation, but which are not necessarily mortared.

Mobile Home Subdivision: A subdivision designed and intended to accommodate mobile homes, either exclusively or primarily. Lots in such a subdivision would normally be sold to individuals wishing to live there.

Any such approach must be adopted to local needs and problems. This should NOT be cut out and put into your zoning ordinance.

Figure 10–28. Visual evaluation standards for manufactured housing in Maine. *Source:* Arendt, 1982.

Street Design for Rural Subdivisions

OVERVIEW

A great many of the subdivision street design standards currently used in rural communities were generated decades ago to accommodate large traffic volumes in huge tract-housing developments built in many metropolitan and suburbanizing areas. Rarely have these standards been updated, or adapted specifically for use in more rural locations. In setting local standards for new subdivision streets, small communities have tended to copy the most readily available technical provisions already adopted by their more urban counterparts, without realizing the inappropriateness of those regulations to their rural situation.

The result has been the construction of local access streets that are typically 50 percent wider than the existing rural collector roads that serve them. Other problems have involved inflexible and inappropriate standards for curve designs, gradients, storm-water management, and pedestrian circulation. In fact, the typical subdivision road required by many municipalities today is overdesigned, needlessly expensive to build and maintain, dangerous to neighborhood residents, problematic for storm-water management, and decidedly nonrural in appearance.

A FRESH LOOK

To their enormous credit, the American Society of Civil Engineers, in cooperation with the National Association of Home Builders and the Urban Land Institute, recently issued an extensively revised "second edition" of its classic handbook,

Residential Streets. Based upon the logical premise that "the design of a residential street should be appropriate to its functions," the book begins with a harsh critique of current practices, which it attributes to early standard-setting based upon readily available state highway department manuals (ASCE, NAHB, ULI, 1990). (In fact, in some states, such as Connecticut, Virginia, and Montana, local subdivision street design standards are still provided by the state Department of Transportation.) Simply put, the major problem has been that "public officials and professional associations have often promulgated standards that, while reasonable for major, high-speed thoroughfares, are inappropriate for local residential streets" (ibid.).

THE WIDTH FACTOR

One of the most obvious differences between new subdivision streets and the rural collector roads that typically serve them is their respective widths. In the Northeastern states, rural collector roads that easily handle traffic loads of several thousand vehicles per day tend to be between 18 and 20 feet in pavement width. This is true for a number of rural county highways as well. Unfortunately, many of these roads lack shoulders, bike lanes, or proper footpaths, serious deficiencies that are gradually being corrected as traffic volumes continue to rise. However, their two travel lanes between 9 and 10 feet wide are very adequate for the amount of traffic and its average speed (30 to 40 mph). After all, the average car or pickup is only about 5½ to 6½ feet wide, and even dump trucks and school buses rarely exceed seven feet in width. But as traffic becomes heavier—vehicles, bicycles, pedestrians—the rationale for widening such collector roads to 24 feet of pavement, with gravel shoulders and a separate footpath, becomes compelling.

Most subdivision streets, on the other hand, provide only local access for residential purposes, yet they are required to have paved surfaces wider than the rural collectors that serve them. Local codes often mandate paved widths ranging from 24 to 30 feet, and occasionally up to 36 feet for streets serving more than a few dozen homes. Such excessive widths are not justified by the traffic routinely using these streets. If each home were to generate an average of 10 trips per day, three dozen residences would create only 360 vehicle trips. If spread out over the course of a 16-hour period, this would amount to only one car every three minutes. Even if two vehicles were on the same stretch of road at the same time, there would clearly be no problem with 18 to 20 feet of paved width. (See Figure 11–1.)

The rationale for wider residential access streets is based on the notion that such streets should provide for a continuous line of parked vehicles, leaving sufficient room for ordinary traffic and emergency vehicles to move around them. This is not an unreasonable idea when residential densities are fairly high, that is, in neighborhoods where there are four or more dwelling units per acre. When homes are built at such densities, there is less room for two-car garages and driveways, and many residents and their visitors regularly use the streets for parking. However, as densities decline so does the need to provide on-street parking. Most residents prefer driveways or garages for parking convenience and safety. (See Figure 11–2.) Many visitors follow suit, but traffic problems are not created when, instead, they park along the edge of an 18–20 foot wide street (they can even pull part way off the pavement when shoulders are provided instead of curbs).

With the relatively low volume of traffic using most subdivision streets, it is not likely that very many cars will pass by while the visitor is parked. But even if two vehicles were to approach a parked car from opposite directions, the solution

Figure 11–1. In most contemporary subdivisions, people usually park in driveways and garages. In residential areas with low traffic, the occasional car parked along an 18- to 20-foot-wide street will, at worst, cause one of two approaching vehicles to slow down, allowing the other to pass, as shown in this example from Malvern, Pennsylvania. Cars and trucks should travel slowly through residential neighborhoods, where there tends to be many children and pets, but this occurs infrequently when roads are lightly traveled and pavements are four to six times as wide as most vehicles (which typically measure less than six feet across).

Figure 11–2. Streets as wide as this one in Cranbury, New Jersey, are not only needless, expensive, and ugly, they are also dangerous because they encourage speeding and other antisocial activities (note tire marks in the foreground). Few people park in the street because these houses all have adequate driveways and garages, which are more convenient. Ironically, this street is about 50 percent wider than those in Cranbury's highly acclaimed historic neighborhoods, which function very well despite their smaller lots and shorter driveways.

is obvious: one of those approaching vehicles would slow down a bit to let the other one pass, as the street is clearly not wide enough to accommodate all three vehicles simultaneously (Chellman, 1990). In fact, if maximum driving speeds of 20 mph are desired in residential neighborhoods, the occasional parked car is a real advantage, because it forces vehicles to slow down as they briefly enter the opposite lane.

"Slowing down" is not a bad thing to encourage in residential areas, where children and pets tend to abound. But that is precisely what does not happen (because it does not need to happen) when streets are built 26 to 30 feet wide to accommodate parking lanes in areas where off-street parking is provided in driveways and garages. People do tend to drive more quickly on wide, empty pavements than they do on more traditionally scaled rural lanes. Our peripheral vision informs us that 25 to 30 mph is the maximum comfortable speed on residential streets that are about 20 feet wide (especially when planted with rows of shade trees on each side), whereas we can reach speeds of 35 to 40 mph on wider streets before we sense we are traveling too fast for the road conditions (Greenbie, 1981). The importance of encouraging slower traffic speeds on residential streets can be appreciated from the statistics that stopping distances on wet pavements rise from 107 feet at 20 mph to 196 feet at 30 mph, a 66 percent increase (Chellman, 1990).

The illustrations in Figure 11–3, adapted from two nationally recognized publications, show that not more than 20 feet of pavement width is necessary to accommodate two vehicles. In *Performance Streets*, paved widths of 18 feet are recommended in subdivisions where the average daily traffic (ADT) is 200 or less (i.e., up to 20 homes), and just two more feet of width are recommended for curbless collector streets handling up to 2,000 ADT (Bucks County Planning Commission, 1980). In *Performance Zoning*, paved widths of just 19 feet are considered adequate on local streets serving up to 160 homes (Kendig, 1982). Loop roads with up to 40 homes are also included in this category, because traffic will usually tend to distribute itself evenly over each half of the loop. In very low-density

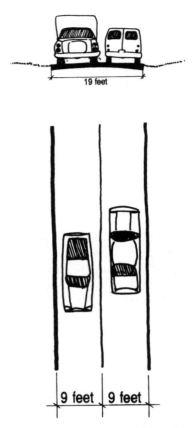

Figure 11–3. The adequacy of two lanes for residential access streets, where houselots contain sufficient off-street parking in driveways and garages, is almost self-evident. Yet many subdivision ordinances require paved widths broad enough for one or two parking lanes (27 to 34 feet wide), regardless of lot size, a vestigial carryover from regulations written long ago when lots were generally so small and narrow that streets had to accommodate large numbers of parked cars. *Source:* Sketches adapted from *Performance Streets,* Bucks County Planning Commission, 1980 and *Performance Zoning* (Kendig, 1982).

developments with multiacreage lots, road widths of 16 feet would be reasonable. As the authors note, "Most rural townships in the county have several miles of existing 16-foot wide roads which are comfortably serving low traffic volume conditions" (Bucks County Planning Commission, 1980).

In Albemarle County, Virginia, the planning staff has proposed amending current policies to allow private subdivision roads in areas of rolling terrain to be designed to the state's less stringent "mountainous terrain standards." By reducing right-of-way and pavement widths, allowing for shorter curve radii, and permitting slightly steeper gradients, earthmoving, disturbance to landforms, and tree removal will be considerably lessened, improving aesthetics and reducing environmental impacts.

If one must strike a compromise with local engineers or public safety personnel on this issue, one approach would be to concede a 24-foot width for the sand-and-gravel road base, with the 18-foot paved driving surface lined by shoulders three-feet wide on each side. In the more humid and temperate Northeastern and mid-Atlantic states, these shoulders could be topped with 3 inches of loam and seeded with a hardy, low-growing ground cover such as white clover. In that way, the effective width for parking is increased, while the rural ambience is maintained (including slower traffic speeds). In hotter and/or more arid regions, attractive design solutions might involve specially graded gravel (or even clamshells, in coastal areas).

At the other end of the scale, where subdivisions are intensively developed with small narrow lots and a clear need for on-street parking (such as might be built as an extension of a nineteenth-century village or small town), local access streets should be about 26 to 28-feet wide for one-side parking, or about 32 to 36-feet wide where the road must accommodate two parking lanes and two travel lanes. To the extent that there is a real need for these parking lanes, they will tend to be filled at any given time, and the greater street width will not induce higher travel speeds (nor will it be so visually unappealing).

Related to pavement width is the issue of cleared width, where new subdivision streets are created in wooded areas. Occasionally one encounters local public works directors who insist on clearing the entire right-of-way (typically 50 feet wide). Unfortunately, such officials frequently wield enormous influence and control. As with pavement width, often the best approach is to document existing conditions along older roads that give the town its rural character. Those by-ways typically manage to accommodate 18-foot pavements, nominal shoulders, drainage swales, and utility poles without being clear-cut across the entire right-of-way.

By studying the arrangement of these features, and showing their location on a cross-sectional sketch drawn to scale, one can present the best case for continuing the town's traditional approach (as contrasted with an overengineered solution that is out of step with the existing norm). In areas receiving heavy snowfall, adequate provision must be made for snow storage, but this rarely requires more than an eight-foot wide "snow shoulder" on each side of the 18 to 20-foot wide access street, even where winter conditions are particularly severe. And because some of the snow can be pushed onto lightly wooded margins, totally clearing the "snow shoulder" is usually unnecessary.

THE FORGOTTEN PEDESTRIAN

Apart from wider pavements, which encourage higher vehicle speeds, another dangerous condition often unintentionally created by inappropriate design standards is lack of provision for pedestrians in new subdivisions. If an excessively broad street were reduced in width by five feet, and if this paving material were used to create a sidewalk on the far side of an 8 to 10-foot wide planting strip (for shade trees), there would be a safe place for children to pull their wagons, wheel their tricycles about, draw hopscotch boxes, and walk to the homes of their friends. There would also be a safe place for parents to push baby carriages, to go for evening strolls around the block, and to engage in casual conversation with their neighbors.

The social importance of sidewalks has been all but forgotten in suburbia, where they have been built only infrequently in recent decades. As one observer from Louisville has noted: "Families get to know one another better when there are sidewalks. Without them, it is awkward to take a walk. You feel you're intruding. A man walking along a sidewalk appears to have a purpose; a man walking in the street or across your front yard looks suspicious . . . . Without sidewalks, houses are just houses. When sidewalks tie them together with a neat ribbon of concrete, they become part of something more: a neighborhood" (Pearce, 1980).

KINDER BUT NOT GENTLER CURVES

One of the sadder results of applying highway design criteria to residential streets is not only that vehicles tend to speed more often, but also that they are given no reason to slow down appreciably when rounding the curves. When curves are very gentle, there is little need to touch the brake pedal more than very lightly, as all bends have been eliminated by the subdivision street design criteria. It is not uncommon to encounter "minimum centerline curve radii" (the measurement used to draw road curves accurately) of 350 feet or 450 feet. Occasionally (as in Newtown, Connecticut) the minimum distance is 600 feet!

Since a centerline radius of 140 feet is considered adequate for traffic speeds of 25 mph (Chellman, 1991), a good argument can be made, on

public safety grounds, for not requiring much more than this distance when designing road curves in subdivisions, where a principal objective is to discourage traffic from exceeding that speed. If we wish vehicles to slow down to 20 mph when rounding curves, a centerline radius of 90 feet would be an appropriate choice, based upon tables relating centerline radius to design speed, published by the American Association of State Highway and Transportation Officials. In the 1920s subdivision in which I grew up, a 72-foot radius road curve in front of our house slowed cars to about 15 to 18 mph, which was ideal for safety. (See Figures 11–4 and 11–5.)

A gentler road curve is not kinder to the residents who live alongside it, because it enables vehicles to cruise by more quickly. *Residential Streets* suggests design speeds of just 20 mph for both access streets and subcollectors in subdivisions. Centerline radii of 100 to 125 feet would be

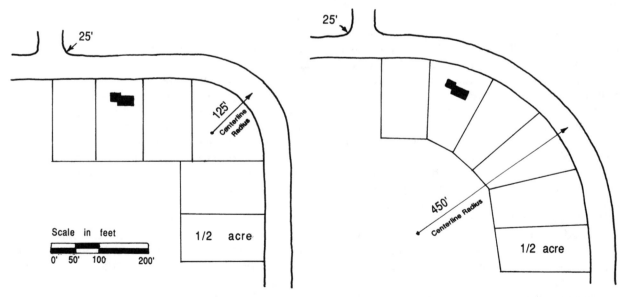

Figure 11–4. Many subdivision ordinances require street curves with centerline radii of 350 to 450 feet, making them so gradual that drivers can round them easily at 30 to 35 mph. A more sensible approach would be to set a maximum radius of 150 feet, with the norm being more in the range of 90 to 120 feet, to force drivers to operate their vehicles more safely as they travel through our neighborhoods. This would be considerably more gentle than corners at typical residential street intersections, where the centerline radius is usually 25 feet (with a curbline radius of perhaps five feet).

Figure 11–5. Photograph of a street curve built to a 72-foot centerline radius, designed to prevent traffic speeding through this residential neighborhood.

appropriate for access streets; for subcollectors this figure could rise to 150 or 175 feet. Beyond that, one is inviting faster traffic. With smaller curvatures drivers will have to slow down when they round the bend, or else they will tend to slide sideways on their seats. When one realizes that the longer radii were originally introduced into the standards to prevent highway users from experiencing this uncomfortable sliding sensation as they steered into the curves, one can begin to appreciate how out of place such standards are when applied to residential subdivision streets.

The above recommendations apply, of course, to situations where streets take typical right-angle turns. The exception to this "rule" (of setting maximum centerline radii) occurs when roads must curve gradually because they parallel a curving stream, when they follow the contours along the base of a large hill, or when for aesthetic reasons site designers wish to introduce a deliberate meander as the road traverses a meadow or field. (A good example of this can be seen in the site plan for "Dragon Hill," a residential case illustrated in Chapter 20.)

In such instances it is often desirable to employ "reverse curves," a technique commonly prohibited by conventional subdivision standards, in which road curves change their direction (from right to left, or vice versa) without an intervening

straight segment. Although this prohibition is sensible for roads where vehicles travel 40 or 50 mph, when applied to residential developments it is just another inappropriate carryover from state highway manuals. The visual appeal of deliberately meandering lanes through small rural subdivisions is destroyed by such engineering standards, which instantly transform them into graceless, mechanical streets.

TO CURB OR NOT TO CURB

In many rural communities it is likely that one of the principal reasons for requiring curbing and underdrainage systems is to elevate construction costs to the point where developers will decide not to subdivide, or will build only expensive houses from which they can more easily recoup their extra costs (larger houses, which will also contribute more tax dollars to the municipality). Several texts on subdivision street design strongly discourage the use of curbing. The authors of *The Subdivision and Site Plan Handbook* state emphatically that "Since curbing intensifies runoff, every opportunity for a natural drainage system should be encouraged" (Listokin and Walker, 1989). Similarly, the Bucks County (Pennsylvania) Planning Commission, in *Performance Streets*, advises that "Curbs should not be provided unless they are found to be essential for stormwater management," citing the example of high density development of four or more units per acre. The only other areas where curbing appears to make sense is along steep roads, for example, those with gradients of 8 percent or more. However, in the case of steep roads in rural areas it is still preferable simply to line the drainage ditches with 4 to 6-inch diameter stone, to prevent erosion and sedimentation.

The Connecticut Department of Environmental Protection has begun to actively discourage towns from requiring curbing and underdrains in many new rural subdivisions. One of their concerns is that pollutants from the roadways (including dissolved salts and waterborne oils) should not be channelized into receiving streams, but should be allowed to drain evenly off the road along its entire length, thereby seeping into the ground in a much less concentrated manner.

When curbing is required, concrete is normally the most suitable material. Asphalt curbing is very easily damaged—sometimes whole sections are deeply gouged or relocated by snow plows—and should generally be prohibited. Granite is exceedingly expensive, and Belgian block is both costly and visually inappropriate for curbing rural roads (being essentially an urban street paving material).

Curb shapes vary as well. Vertical curbs (including ones with a slight angle from the perpendicular) are generally best suited for subdivisions in more central areas where there is an established tradition of such curbing. In outlying areas where curbs are considered essential, the most appropriate shapes are those that incline back away from the road at a low angle. Several types exist, including "mountable curbs" and "Cape Cod berms." (See Figure 11–6.) Both appear less urban than the more vertical variety. They also enable vehicles to pull out of the travel lane onto the grassy verge (tree planting strip) for short-term parking. Where continuous underdrains are needed but where curbing itself is not essential, precast concrete gutters with a slightly concave cross-section are another option. They also serve to stabilize the edge of the asphalt roadway, and allow vehicles to park on the grassy shoulder that typically abuts them on the far side.

The necessity for curbing is often overstated. When one considers that storm-water drainage is generally not a problem along the many miles of uncurbed country roads that serve most rural communities (including many roads that are now lined with homes built at different times over the last century or so), it is obvious that there are more natural ways to handle storm runoff. Broad grassy swales have been used to great advantage in many subdivisions, where narrower, deeper ditches are less appealing. Low spots on one side of the road, where water would otherwise be trapped, may be provided with a drainage grate leading to a culvert, conducting the excess water under the road to lower land on the other side. In many cases the storm water will tend to seep into the ground along the roadside, unless the soil is heavy and impermeable, or frozen.

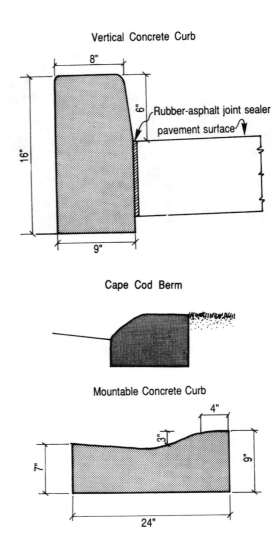

Figure 11–6. Where curbing is required to control storm water flow, designs with gently sloping profiles are often adequate. Besides being less urban, less intrusive visually, less prone to damage, and sometimes less expensive, they are also more easily mounted by emergency vehicles. On Bainbridge Island, Washington, engineers have been specifying "thickened edges," a more modest variation of the "Cape Cod berm" where there is just enough upward lift to the pavement edge to direct storm water into catch basins.

Curbing actually increases the amount of storm water that must be handled because it does not allow any natural absorption into the soil, and because it channelizes the water into specific discharge points. To prevent this concentrated flow from overwhelming a receiving stream or any culverts downstream, a second engineering solution is often required to mitigate the problems caused by the first one (i.e., the curbing). The second "solution" typically takes the form of a detention basin or a retention pond, features that are generally regarded as undesirable by abutting residents because they tend to become collecting areas for windblown rubbish and breeding grounds for mosquitoes. Although drainage ponds are sometimes inevitable, it is best to avoid their construction whenever possible. When their provision is essential, the least objectionable approach is to design them as self-draining detention basins (see Figure 11–7). Several well-used neighborhood recreation areas in subdivisions in Flossmoor, Illinois, for example, also serve as large, flat detention basins where storm water is held back for several hours after heavy rains. The grass is mowed regularly, and a perimeter berm contains the excess water, which is allowed to drain out continuously through a small "choker" pipe at the low end of the playing field (which remains flooded only for a matter of hours after major cloudbursts).

CUL-DE-SACS AND THEIR ALTERNATIVES

Because they interrupt the pattern of connecting streets, thereby decreasing accessibility between adjacent neighborhoods (for residents, mail vehicles, rubbish trucks, school buses, etc.), cul-de-sacs should be strongly discouraged. In fact, it would help stem the further erosion of interneighborhood accessibility if all future residential streets were simply *required* to connect with other streets, either existing or planned.

Exceptions would of course be granted if such connections were possible only by filling wetlands, felling a particularly handsome stand of mature trees, or leveling a knoll, or if such a connection would create a shortcut attracting a significant volume of through traffic through the subdivision. In areas lacking any existing or planned streets with which to connect, the cul-de-sac should include stubs extending to adjoining parcels in locations where future connections appear to be feasible. Where no vehicular connection is feasible, provision should definitely be made for at least a bikeway and footpath connection.

It should be noted that the tendency toward cul-de-sacs originally arose because excessive street design standards had created virtual raceways through residential neighborhoods. These potential raceways can be easily avoided by designing shorter street lengths with numerous three-way "T" intersections to discourage through traffic, as is deliberately done in Australia and the United Kingdom (Chellman, 1991). Traffic speed can also be controlled very effectively by posting "all-way" stop signs, not only at four-way intersections but also at three-way ones as well, as is done in many new subdivisions in Chester County, Pennsylvania.

Figure 11–7. When it is necessary to collect and detain storm water within a subdivision, these "basins" should generally be designed as very broad, nearly flat lawns, with a low berm along the lower edges, through which runoff is allowed to flow at a slow rate via small outlet pipes. These self-draining areas provide excellent places for neighborhood children to play catch, throw a Frisbee, or kick around a football or soccer ball. Mowed weekly during the warmer months, and dry on all but a small number of days each year, these facilities can help developers meet local recreational needs generated by their subdivisions, and to manage runoff in a far more attractive and useful manner than is usually the case.

Adopting the design recommendations in this chapter will bring the desired level of safety and quiet back to all new subdivision streets, rendering the cul-de-sac form unnecessary in the majority of instances. The developer's frequent desire to set his or her housing group apart, for marketing reasons, on a separate cul-de-sac or nonconnecting loop, is essentially an antisocial technique and should not be condoned. There is already more than enough stratification in society today, without unnecessarily reinforcing it through structural strategems such as exclusive neighborhood road systems.

Standards for maximum cul-de-sac length in rural communities are often based on an urban rationale. For example, the ubiquitous 600-foot rule, which is pervasive among subdivision regulations in many communities lacking central water distribution systems, was originally based on the fact that, historically, fire trucks carried 600 feet of hose line to connect to hydrants typically located at cul-de-sac entrances. This standard makes little sense in most rural settings. A more sensible rule would be based upon the number of families that would be at risk if their only access road were to become blocked during an emergency. In Maine the state model subdivision regulation requires a second entrance after the fifteenth dwelling unit, but a fairer standard is suggested in *Residential Streets*, based upon a maximum traffic load of 200 vehicles per day (or "average daily traffic": ADT)—25 dwellings, with a maximum cul-de-sac length of 1,000 feet.

Turning areas at the end of cul-de-sacs may take many forms. The most common one should probably be allowed only as a last resort: the huge paved circle of asphalt, typically measuring well over 100 feet in diameter. For streets with up to a dozen homes, a simple "hammerhead" or "turning-T" is sufficient (as illustrated in Figure 11–8). When a larger number of homes and vehicles are involved, turning loops are highly recommended. For visual interest, these loops should be almost any shape except perfectly circular (unless the effect of a flying-saucer landing pad is desired). They should contain, where possible, a

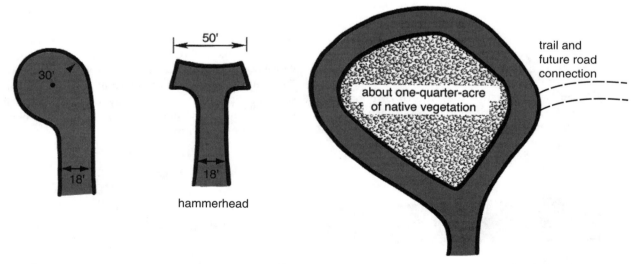

Figure 11–8. When cul-de-sacs are unavoidable because it is not feasible to connect them with other streets, developers should be required at least to provide footpath or bikeway links with adjoining neighborhoods (existing or future). A variety of design approaches can satisfy vehicular turning needs while also reducing asphalt coverage. "Hammerheads" are appropriate for up to 10 or 12 homes, and substantial islands thickly landscaped with native trees and shrubs offer a greener, low-maintenance alternative to completely paved circles (or boring grassy ones that need weekly mowing).

quarter-acre island of undisturbed native vegetation. In village settings, more formal arrangements, such as grassy tree-lined commons, would be more appropriate. In New England, the average size of central town commons is about two acres; but as a focal point in outlying subdivisions, a half-acre green would be adequate. Where land is at a premium, the next-to-last resort should be a circular cul-de-sac, totally paved, with a radius of 30 feet. This size is sufficient for large cars and pickup trucks. Other trucks and fire engines would need to execute a three-point turn, but that would not create undue hardships, as most fire fighters in small towns do not need to dash away to other fires immediately after extinguishing the first one.

STREET CONNECTIONS AND OFFICIAL STREET MAPS

As noted above, local governments could, through a simple amendment to their subdivision regulations, prohibit further isolation of new neighborhoods by *requiring* that new streets connect with the existing street network (or be paved to the edge of the property where the parcel abuts a future development site). Taking this approach one step farther, official maps could be prepared showing the approximate location of streets, trails, and open space reserves the community would like to see created as each land tract is subdivided. Although some of these possibilities are also discussed in Chapters 15 and 16, it is important to illustrate the desirability of proactively planning future street links.

Despite that fact that most states provide for the adoption of "Official Maps" through their zoning enabling legislation, very few local governments take advantage of this authority. The result is either the absence of good road connections to help spread the increased traffic that inevitably accompanies continued growth, or prolonged arguments with uncooperative developers who see themselves as having been "singled out" to provide land for these special road links.

Although "Official Maps" can be very detailed (in the manner of typical nineteenth-century "town plans" that showed every street and alley envi-

sioned by the town fathers), the relatively small number of jurisdictions utilizing this approach employ it to reserve rights-of-way for strategic links in the arterial road network. Such is the case around Westminster, Maryland, where the city council and the Carroll County Commissioners have been reserving such rights-of-way since 1968. Based upon a local "Traffic Operations Study to Increase Capacity and Safety" ("TOPICS"), about 20 miles of right-of-way have been reserved for connecting roads in the comprehensive plan for Westminster and environs. Some of these links involve major highway construction (such as bypasses), but other segments represent principal streets connecting county roads radiating out from the old town center.

Construction responsibility varies according to the type of roadway specified on the Official Map. In the case of subdivision streets that are required to connect with adjoining public thoroughfares, costs are typically borne by the developer. When the road is to be a major arterial (and certainly when access is to be limited), construction costs are normally shared among various levels of government.

Figure 11–9 shows how a small village could begin to unravel with new cul-de-sac developments isolating themselves from the surrounding neighborhood, and how the same growth could be redirected to conform with the traditional interconnected rectilinear street pattern, based upon the community's "Official Map." In order to be most effective, such maps should be designed not only to work around natural site constraints (topography, wetlands, stone walls, tree lines, etc.), but should also be based upon a tax-parcel map showing tract boundaries. (See also the Appendix concerning village planning in Loudoun County, Virginia.)

STREET TREE PLANTING

One of the most significant, and often least emphasized, aspects of neighborhood street design is the planting of shade trees along each side of new roads. Many arborists recommend planting intervals of 50 feet on-center, but closer spacing (25 to 30 feet apart) creates an even more salubrious effect. To improve survival, a mixture of several

Figure 11–9. These three sketches show an existing village compared with two approaches to accommodating new development: a typical pattern of unrelated suburban-style cul-de-sac growth around the edges, laid out in a way that begins to unravel the traditional fabric, compared with the logical alternative of simply extending the established pattern of interconnected streets in a manner that reinforces village character. *Source:* Adapted from Doble et al., 1992.

hardy native deciduous species is preferable, not less than 2½ to 3 inches in diameter at chest height. They should be maintained by the developer for 18 months (1½ growing seasons) after planting, and ensured with an effective performance guarantee. Species that attain an ultimate height of at least 50 feet will create a very stately atmosphere in the fullness of time, and provide cool shade on front lawns and sidewalks during hot summer months.

One of the sadder details of municipal affairs is the large number of small communities that have allowed their once active shade tree planting programs to lapse, victims of budget constraints, bureaucratic indifference, and short-term thinking. Many such programs, which had been initiated after World War II in response to federal housing standards for new subdivisions, were quietly dropped when federal involvement began to fade in the 1970s.

It is ironic to drive through some of these towns today and see the maples and oaks growing into maturity in these postwar subdivisions where the houses are relatively modest, and then to pass into more recent developments where more expensive homes sit on larger lots facing streets without any street trees whatsoever. Landscaping there tends to be haphazard and often inappropriate, with only low shrubs or flowering ornamental and coniferous trees in scattered locations on front lawns.

In the absence of public funds for coordinated street-tree planting, the very least that local governments could do is to require developers to plant such shade trees as part of their street improvements. Rather than adding to their costs, such provisions should be tied to reductions in excessive street pavement widths, curb requirements, and so forth.

One of the best sources for further information is *Street Tree Factsheets* (Gerhold, 1989), published by the Pennsylvania State University School of Forest Resources (generally applicable only in the northern and eastern parts of the country, however).

One of the most inspiring examples of street-tree planting in medium-sized towns comes from Pottstown, Pennsylvania (pop. 25,000), where slightly more than half of the borough's 2,925 trees have been planted by a local nonprofit group formed in 1983. Headed by a former borough manager, Trees, Inc. raised about $470,000 during its first five years, attracting numerous large contributions from local businesses (in the $10,000 to $45,000 range), plus $100,000 from Philadelphia Electric. In addition to planting 1,500 trees, the group regularly trims them to remove dying or low-growing branches, and has donated a $13,000 leaf sweeper to the borough as a goodwill gesture.

The energy, commitment, and accomplishments of Trees, Inc. helped persuade local councillors to reinvigorate the dormant Pottstown Shade Tree Commission. With fresh blood, the commission has created a computerized spreadsheet inventorying each of the borough's shade trees (address, species, diameter, condition, well size, growing room within the well, sidewalk condition, utility wire location, and specific maintenance needs). As a result of its survey, the commission has quantified the need for larger tree wells, and has put into proper perspective the common complaint that street trees damage sidewalks (only 2 percent were cracked, 2 percent were slightly lifted, and 2 percent were lifted and cracked). Sidewalk maintenance costs pale into insignificance when compared with the tremendously large offsetting values created by street trees (as outlined by the Pottstown Shade Tree Commission):

• softening the urban environment with their green foliage;

• reducing pollution by removing airborne dust and particulate matter;

• reducing the greenhouse effect by removing carbon dioxide;

• cooling air temperatures in the summer by shading people, buildings, streets, and sidewalks;

• soothing people's spirits with their natural beauty;

• elevating property values by enhancing neighborhood aesthetics;

• providing places for birds and wildlife, bringing nature into town; and

• increasing neighborhood pride, as people plant flowers in tree wells and spruce up their properties.

In addition, as pointed out by a recent editorial in the Pottstown *Mercury* by Tom Hylton, such beautification efforts in cities, towns, and villages offer an additional benefit: they can help to halt suburban sprawl. "Town dwelling is a most environmentally friendly and sensible way of life. It can also be pleasant and enjoyable—if we soften asphalt and concrete with lots of trees and greenery" (Hylton, 1991).

Positive examples that are more easy to emulate than Pottstown's are those of Honeoye Falls, New York, and Kent, Ohio. In Honeoye Falls, a local service club shares costs of planting street trees with the village government and with the property owner, each party paying one-third, which helps everyone's dollars go farther. And a new rebate program in Kent allows property owners to receive a maximum of $50 per tree for up to two trees (at least one-inch caliper) that they plant. Funding in the municipal budget covers approximately 300 trees each year.

To heighten public awareness of the beauty of trees, local citizens in Greensburg, Indiana, have published *A Self-Guided Tree Tour of Distinctive Trees*. An annotated street map identifies the locations of 30 noteworthy specimens of different species that can be found in the community. What makes that effort all the more special is the fact that it was sponsored by the Hardee's fast-food chain, which went out of its way to save several large trees on the site of its new restaurant in Greensburg. Such efforts might help to build public support for tree planting programs. The need is great: according to a recent survey by the American Forestry Association of 20 cities around the country, only one tree was planted for every four that were removed (Arnold, 1992).

The value of street trees is being promoted by a relatively new program cosponsored by the National Association of Home Builders and the American Forestry Association. Called Global Re-Leaf for New Communities, the program presents a coveted award—particularly useful in marketing homes to environmentally conscious buyers—only to those developments that have met stringent review criteria. At Northridge, developer Mike Rose obtained the cooperation of the city of Bowie, Maryland, and Prince George's County to vary their normal requirements to help him save more trees in two significant ways: 1) reducing road width from 30 feet to 22 feet, thereby eliminating eight feet of tree clearing throughout the subdivision; and 2) allowing slopes to be graded at 2:1 instead of 3:1 (further reducing the land area that would need to be denuded and bulldozed). Other environmental features include grassy drainage swales (no curbs and gutters), vegetated traffic islands, and an interlocking network of greenways and wildlife corridors (Davis, 1991).

To avoid future disfigurement of street trees by pruning contractors hired by utility companies, new subdivisions should be provided with underground electric, telephone, and cable TV lines. Where it is not feasible (such as in shallow bedrock areas, where trenches would have to be blasted), poles should be installed along easements running between adjoining backyards. (This is the location used in many subdivisions developed in Pennsylvania during the period between the demise of the rear alley and the late 1970s, when the state subdivision law was amended to require undergrounded utilities in new developments.) Such easements could, if desired, also be designed to serve as greenway paths through these subdivisions. (Footpath networks in such locations are a deliberate, and highly successful, feature of the planned open space communities of Radburn in Fairlawn, New Jersey, Lake Vista in New Orleans, and Hilton Head Island in South Carolina.)

Another alternative is to take this thinking one step further and provide rear access lanes (or "alleys") serving each houselot from the back. This is how scores of traditional neighborhoods were designed in all parts of the country until the 1930s, as witnessed by examples as distant as Winter Park, Florida, Wyomissing, Pennsylvania, and Bozeman, Montana, where driveways and garages generally face in the opposite direction from the homes. These lanes are typically designed for one-way traffic and, because they do not attract through traffic, they are fairly safe for children playing catch, riding bikes, and so forth.

STREET NAMES

To the extent that municipalities have set any standards or guidelines for naming new streets, they usually do not go beyond a prohibition against duplicative or similar-sounding names, which could be confusing to public safety personnel when responding to emergencies. In addition, communities should consider encouraging developers to name new rural subdivision streets after natural features in the immediate area (such as

hills, ridges, meadows, brooks, native plant or animal species) or to local historic family names, buildings, or events. Terms such as "road," "lane," "street," or "way" should be used, rather than suburban words such as "drive," "circle," "place," "court," "view," "vista," "manor," or "terrace." New streets adjacent to older, village neighborhoods should relate to that context, and use traditional names such as "High Street," "Chestnut Street," "Grove Street," "Prospect Street," "Church Street," "School Street," and so forth, (presuming that there is a church or school in the vicinity). Personal first names should be strongly discouraged ("Barbara Road," "Robert Circle," e.g.), unless they are also readable as surnames ("Douglas," "Leslie," "Tracy," "Thomas," etc.).

COUNTRY LANES AND COMMON DRIVES

The notion of "country lanes"—meaning narrower roads serving up to a dozen homes, often deliberately finished with a good gravel surface—deserves to be reconsidered. All but banished from the rural scene by well-meaning but suburban-based street regulations, such lanes occupy an important place in the hierarchy of roads in the countryside. Especially in areas where existing public roads are gravel surfaced, it makes good sense to continue the established tradition.

Hardly anything could be more bizarre than requiring a 30-foot wide asphalt street to serve twelve homes on a pair of cul-de-sacs stemming off an existing public road that is barely 16-feet wide with pronounced ruts in its dirt surface. However, this was exactly what a developer was told he must do to receive subdivision approval in one Connecticut town several years ago. His proposal was to construct an 18-foot wide access road with a 15-inch layer of sand and gravel topped with 3 inches of trap rock stone mixed with quarry fines to enhance compactibility. It was initially rejected because it did not meet the town's official standards. After bringing in his lawyer to argue monthly with the planning commission over a one-year period, the applicant hired a well-known rural planner to show slides of various road widths, explaining their functions and capabilities. After seeing the slides and discussing the issue extensively, the commission approved the applicant's proposal, which it agreed was both adequate and appropriately designed to fit in with the neighborhood's rural context.

It is not uncommon for New England towns to require that any new gravel access roads be privately maintained. This is an unfair practice, because such roads are actually less expensive to maintain than asphalted ones (see Chapter 12, "Scenic Roads," for details). If gravel roads are properly constructed in the first place (which "performance guarantees" can ensure), and if they are appropriate for the scale and location of a particular rural subdivision, they should be publicly maintained.

When a smaller number of homes is involved (up to five or six), a slightly different approach should be considered: the common drive. For traffic at such low levels the width could be adjusted to 15 or 16 feet, maintaining the same depth and type of construction materials. Common drives require the establishment of a homeowners' association (HOA) to ensure regular maintenance (further details on HOAs are provided in Chapters 14 and 15). Most people will readily contribute their share of expenses, for few wish to become known as deadbeats to their neighbors, but the HOA mechanism establishes methods for ensuring a steady cash flow to pay for regraveling, grading, snowplowing, and so forth. Common drives are a particularly useful device in avoiding duplicative access driveways to adjacent lots, including back lots (sometimes referred to as "flag lots", "pipestem lots," or "porkchop lots"). They can be located on easements when necessary to provide more direct access to interior lots, or they can be restricted to a dedicated right-of-way.

12

Scenic Roads

OVERVIEW

Public perception of community character is based largely on what can be seen from an automobile. A line of tall shade trees or a stone wall alongside a road may have as much—or more—significance to the appearance of a rural town as might a small woodland or field somewhat farther away from the traveler's eye. This is not to suggest that the wood or the field are insignificant, but rather to point out that a number of fairly common or typical roadside features often taken for granted do indeed play a critical role in shaping the mental images of the places in which we live and work. "The view from the road" is more than a phrase— for most of us it comprises virtually everything we know about the natural and human-made features of our towns.

Because roadside land is so easy and relatively inexpensive to develop, it is often the first to be converted to residential or commercial uses. Once this is understood, the truth underlying "Appleton's Principle" becomes clear: "the first 10 percent of development usually destroys 50 percent of the countryside" (quoted in Hiss, 1989).

The importance of scenic roads was highlighted in the Report of the President's Commission on Americans Outdoors, which found that:

• 77 percent of the population enjoys driving for pleasure and sightseeing;

• pleasure driving accounts for 15 percent of all vehicle miles driven; and

• pleasure driving is the second most popular recreational pastime, after walking.

Action programs to protect the scenic qualities of relatively "unspoiled" roads must be supported by documentation of their value. This is especially true if regulatory controls are to be used, because most courts require a factual and rational basis for land-use restrictions. It is no less necessary, however, if implementation is through advice and persuasion, or if federal tax benefits are being sought for donations of scenic lands or easements.

In a growing number of states, such as New York, Vermont, Colorado, and California, state government actively encourages local designation of scenic roads. While funding is minimal, both New York and Vermont have published "field guides" or handbooks explaining the steps involved in evaluating and designating roads as scenic. In addition to providing a common method for evaluating roadside landscapes, thereby promoting greater consistency among towns and counties, New York's Department of Environmental Conservation reviews all requests for scenic road designation. Only those road segments that exhibit "exceptional compositional merit," provide travelers with substantial opportunities to view the distinctive features of the region (historic, natural, cultural), and enjoy significant local support are approved by the commissioner (NYS Dept. of Environmental Conservation, 1988).

One graphic approach to engendering public support for scenic road designation involves the use of computer-assisted design (CAD) techniques to produce photographable/printable video images showing a series of visual alternatives (Libby and Wear, 1988). Such tools can produce variable sizes and shapes of potential new buildings, and different parking arrangements. The CAD approach can easily illustrate the ultimate effect of allowing merchants to string their business out along the roadside with front yard parking, as opposed to having them clustered at intersections or around nodes, surrounding interior "court-yard" parking areas.

The visual results of such imaging can be shown at public forums. "As the participants in the forums view the alternatives, a voting system would determine which patterns have greater acceptance. With sufficient public participation a set of desired design patterns would emerge. From these patterns a series of 'community standards' would be defined for the local Design Review procedure. . . . Development proposals submitted would be required to include a Visual Impact Statement showing how they would positively or negatively affect the standards developed during the public forum process" (ibid.).

The following sections provide an overview of two fairly comprehensive scenic road studies in Delaware and Kentucky, plus a description of methods used to designate and maintain scenic roads in Connecticut and Vermont. Although these are certainly not the only approaches that could be taken (and other strategies may be more appropriate in different situations), they are included to provide information that might be useful to readers as they try to adapt those experiences to their own communities. The chapter closes with some thoughts about controlling the pattern of roadside development through various zoning techniques. Although different categories of roads may be designated as scenic routes, from local byways to state highways, the emphasis here is on the former, where municipal and county residents or officials have the greatest opportunity to be effective. Strategies for dealing with development along arterial highways are discussed in Chapter 9.

DELAWARE'S RED CLAY VALLEY

One well-documented example is the Red Clay Valley Scenic River and Highway Study, prepared by the New Castle County (Delaware) Department of Planning, in conjunction with the Brandywine Conservancy of Chadds Ford, Pennsylvania, and Gaia Design Consultants of Kennett Square, Pennsylvania. Its principal goals were to inventory and evaluate the historic, natural, and scenic attributes of the valley, to suggest a variety of means to protect these resources, and "to propose

a scenic road network to minimize traffic and land-use impacts within the watershed" (Gaadt, 1989). Since adoption and implementation of its recommendations are clearly dependent upon public support, an additional objective was to familiarize or reacquaint area residents with the special features of the valley. The study's three main components were:

- inventory/analysis (of natural, historic, and scenic resources);
- priority targeting (evaluating, refining, and prioritizing the resource elements); and
- recommendations (of specific techniques to protect the resource base).

For those interested in following a similar approach, the main components of this study are described in some detail below.

Inventory/Analysis

Natural Resources Features were selected on the basis of their environmental sensitivity or connection with public health, safety, and welfare—watercourses, floodplains, wetlands, slopes over 15 percent and 25 percent, geologic formations (Cockeysville marble), and "significant natural areas" and "state big trees" as identified by state and forestry staff.

Historic Resources In addition to the existing "historic zones" designated under current zoning and properties already included on the National Register of Historic Places, buildings in two other National Register categories were also included—"confirmed eligibility for listing" and "deemed eligibility" (in other words, resources having sufficient attributes to be added to this federal roll).

Scenic Resources The visual landscape analysis identified natural landforms and cultural (human-made) elements, both positive ("accents") and negative ("intrusions"), visible from public roads. Scenic resources were classified into six categories of landforms and elements: watercourse, wetland, floodplain, terrace, ridge, and village. Specific land areas were then rated according to whether they:

- illustrated natural or historic processes;
- comprised a system or grouping containing two or more visually important resources; or

• possessed outstanding features of unusually high quality.

In addition, a melding of scenic roadway criteria listed in the Federal Highway Administration's *Scenic Byways* book and the visual landscape analysis criteria contained in the study were applied to roadways in the study area through field investigations. This resulted in both a preliminary list of scenic roads and a refined set of criteria (based on the unique conditions of the Red Clay Valley) by which roads in the study area were judged. Roads that had been preliminarily identified were then subjected to further analysis by using the refined criteria to analyze each road according to the natural, scenic, and historic resource inventories. Through this rating process, 25 roads in the study area were identified as meriting official status as "scenic."

Priority Targeting

A composite map was then created, synthesizing the above findings. This map revealed areas where particular attributes "co-occur," that is, areas possessing multiple reasons for protection. Further refinements were made by eliminating lands already committed to specific development projects, and those under public ownership, held by institutions, or used actively for private recreation. Also highlighted were lands felt to be particularly vulnerable to development pressures due to their location, building suitability, or other attributes. First priority protection areas were identified in this way.

Recommendations

Recommendations for protecting the scenic resources fell into six categories: regulation, communication of site planning objectives, private land stewardship actions, historic structures, highway planning, and interagency coordination. Although all these suggestions involved challenging tasks, the study identified the most critical one as coordinating the various public and private organizations playing separate but complementary roles. Implementation will succeed or fail depending on "the County's willingness and desire to act as the catalyst for action" (New Castle County Planning Dept., 1989). The study recommendations are described below, by category.

Regulation Beyond the existing zoning (basic low-density residential uses, with flexible layout standards), cluster or "open space design" was recommended to become mandatory within the highest priority resource areas, to ensure that these significant locales would not eventually become platted in a typical pattern of houselots and streets (for further details about requiring open space development design, see Chapter 15). Conservation easements were strongly urged, not only to protect the open spaces designated in such subdivisions, but also to limit the range of permissible activities allowed on lands identified as priority resource areas, when these lands lie within proposed houselots in any type of new development. The easements would be held by either the county or an independent conservation group, such as a land trust or conservancy. Scenic road corridors would be further protected by deeper front setbacks, stronger rules to prevent removal of existing vegetative screening, and enhanced buffer planting standards around new construction. Also recommended were density transfers ("TDRs") between parcels owned by different people and density exchanges between parcels owned by the same party. A final set of regulatory recommendations would provide further protection to selected historic structures by extending the current six-month demolition delay into a permanent prohibition against their destruction, increasing fines for violations, providing density incentives to encourage adaptive re-use and rehabilitation, and broadening the definition of historic districts to include large estates and contiguous properties.

Communication of Site Planning Objectives Greater success can be achieved under these flexible site planning regulations if landowners are familiarized with the county's planning and conservation objectives *before* they begin to contemplate development scenarios for their property. The county's philosophy can be conveyed by staff, elected officials, like-minded private organizations, and other landowners, so that the attractive open space development design opportunities offered by site-layout flexibility may be widely appreciated from the start. The importance of both formal and informal communications with landowners, before they commission inappropriate conventional layouts, cannot be overstated. This is a point that has also been strongly emphasized by Robert Lemire, one of the country's leading experts in gaining private landowner acceptance of creative land planning principles (see Lemire, 1988). To further this understanding, the study also recommends that subdivision sketch plans be required to include an inventory of natural and historic features (including typical elements of the common landscape, such as stone fences), around which the development would be designed. At this stage it is also suggested that the parcel's context be considered, so that the protected open space and buffers may be required to linkup and connect with similar resource areas on adjoining properties. This would ensure continuity of resource protection, thereby maximizing the potential for conserving larger blocks or longer corridors.

Private Land Stewardship Actions Individual landowners should be encouraged to take conservation actions on their properties, particularly on those lands that are less easy to regulate. An example is an area that is not designated as having high priority because it scored highly on only one variable (e.g., high scenic value but low environmental significance, or vice versa). Landowners may receive tax benefits for donating property (which they may continue to occupy during their lifetimes), donating conservation easements, or selling land to a conservation organization at a reduced (bargain) price. Public access, although often desirable, is not essential under IRS rules if the easement property possesses certain features (visibility from public roads, parks, rivers, or waterbodies; or ecological, agricultural, or historic significance). Such significance is recognized by the IRS when an official level of government designates an area or a corridor as scenic, on the basis of a comprehensive scenic analysis (which also provides the legal underpinning to defend related land-use regulations in court).

Another stewardship tool, in addition to donations of land or easements, is "limited development," in which fewer lots of higher value are created. These lots may be very large, or they may be more modestly proportioned and clustered to permit joint usage of the open space thus conserved. Whichever of these two design approaches is followed, "limited development" typically allows more land to remain undisturbed, with the smaller number of buildings located in the least sensitive or visible parts of the property. Because it depends on buyers at the higher end of the market, this technique is most applicable in areas attractive to affluent commuters or second-home owners looking for "mini-estates". Cash-producing "limited development" is often combined with easement donations on the balance of the property because few landowners can afford to give up future development rights (i.e., potential income) on their entire holdings.

Historic Structures Besides the regulatory mechanisms outlined above, historic structures and sites could be better protected by updating the statewide listing of cultural resources, nominating additional properties to the National Register of Historic Places, enacting local tax incentives to encourage facade preservation easement donations and building restoration within designated historic districts, and initiating a public education program to broaden awareness of these tools and techniques. Part of this program should include personal contact with owners of historic resources to secure their support for building listing and district designation.

Highway Planning A joint approach between the county planning department and Delaware's state highway authority (DelDOT) was deemed essential. Both parties must work together to determine which roads should be widened to accommodate expected traffic increases, and which roads should be protected. Both parties should press the legislature to authorize a statewide system of scenic roads, and convince federal highway officials to revise existing road improvement standards to allow federal funds to be spent on scenic road repairs and sensitive modifications (i.e., without alterations such as wide paved shoulders, long gradual curves, large-scale tree removal, and metal guardrails installed along every bend).

Interagency Coordination Key to the success of such a scenic road program is the extent to which the county acts as a catalyst and coordinator among the various governmental bodies that regulate different aspects of the corridor: the state environmental agency (surface water quality), state highway department (road widening, etc.), U.S. Army Corps of Engineers (wetlands), county department of public works (floodplains), and the county planning department (land use).

The resource data and the policy recommendations in the Red Clay Valley scenic roads study must be made known to all the above authorities, which must then make their views known to each other so that draft policy suggestions may be modified as necessary to gain broad governmental support. The county planning department occupies the pivotal role in providing impetus and coordination; its efforts could be assisted by the formation of an interagency advisory group to help keep the various interests speaking with each other and working together.

KENTUCKY'S OLD FRANKFORT PIKE

In the Bluegrass area of Kentucky, the special quality of the Old Frankfort Pike has been officially recognized by the Lexington–Fayette Urban County Government, which has designated the pike as a scenic corridor "having unique historic and aesthetic significance worthy of enhancement, preservation, and protection." In creating this corridor, officials recognized two basic rules of the land. One is that attractive locales tend to attract more and more development, which if not carefully controlled will inevitably decrease the area's appeal and quality of life. The other is that where protective standards are adopted and implemented, property values benefit.

Consultants were engaged to study not only the landscapes visible from the Old Frankfort Pike but also a much broader swath of rural lands, several miles wide, comprising "a rich mosaic of field and pasture, woodlot, farm complex and rural settlement, stitched together by historic roadways and strands of treelines, fencelines, and stone walls" (Lexington–Frankfort Scenic Corridor, Inc., 1990). Their study began with an analysis of the environ-mental processes and historic building patterns that have shaped the natural features and human settlements that give the corridor its distinctive character. It then identified the visually significant elements of both a positive nature (pastures, trees, hedgerows, walls, fences, farmhouses, barns, churches, bridges, waterfalls, wetlands, rock outcrops, etc.) and of a negative nature (certain types of businesses, power lines, auto graveyards, mining operations, degraded landscapes, and inharmonious buildings).

Instead of constructing an elaborate numerical scale for evaluating landscapes, a simpler approach was followed, in which areas exhibiting typical visual elements characteristic of the broad corridor area were deemed to possess visual significance. Thus, instead of quantifying, the selection process resembled editing. Areas were included or excluded on the basis of features they contained. Since the corridor possessed several different types of special landscapes, lands were further classified into four categories, two based on broad views and two with more confined boundaries (called "outdoor rooms"). "Broad views," where wide landscapes were mostly unbounded by fences, walls, hedgerows, or tree lines, could be either expansive and virtually treeless, or "parklike" with scattered trees or tree groups. Less frequent but visually significant were the "outdoor rooms" where pastures or fields were clearly bordered by tree lines on three or four sides. Like the broad landscapes, these smaller "rooms" could be either "open" or "parklike." Villages constituted a fifth type of visually significant landscape.

Maps were prepared showing the location and extent of the five categories of visually significant landscapes, plus particular "visual accents" (e.g., noteworthy trees, tree groups, structures, or land formations) and "vista points" along public roads. Also mapped were nonvisible or nonscenic areas, together with any specific visual intrusions.

In addition to recommending the creation of a "Scenic and Historic Corridor Overlay District" wherein TDR would be encouraged and open space subdivision design would be either allowed or mandated (with special landscape buffers), the consultants supported conservation easement donations and purchases, compatible village infill development, and the creation of a landscape design handbook "to show how development might be skillfully fitted in, encouraging traditional approaches to the siting and form/character of buildings and planting material, and demonstrating different approaches to siting within landscape 'rooms' versus 'broad' views." This handbook would be tailored to the specific region and would help landowners, developers, residents, and local officials to visualize the types of approaches that would be most appropriate in different types of places.

HISTORIC CORRIDORS IN SPOTSYLVANIA COUNTY, VIRGINIA

Running southwest from Fredericksburg to the village of Spotsylvania Courthouse, Virginia Route 208 connects two historic centers with Civil War battlefields. Because of its strategic location, this thoroughfare could become the major through route to the southern parts of Spotsylvania County. Concerned that Virginia Department of Transportation (VDOT) plans to widen Route 208 into a four-lane highway would simply transfer traffic congestion from the corridor to Spotsylvania Courthouse, the county commissioned UDA Architects from Pittsburgh to study alternatives. Their 46-page report is notable for its emphasis on graphics, presenting its findings, analysis, and recommendations essentially as detailed captions to page-sized illustrations.

Based upon natural features and topography, the corridor was divided into four segments. The first is a commercial district where landscaped areas 30-feet deep are recommended along both sides of the road for intensive boulevard landscaping to create a "parklike setting." In the second segment, existing woodland retention reinforced by new landscaping is recommended to provide roadside buffers 100-feet deep between new residential development and the highway, which is intended to give the road a parkway character (UDA Architects, 1991).

Because the third segment constitutes the final gateway approach to the Spotsylvania Courthouse historic district, the study recommends the preservation of adjoining farm fields and roadside woodlands where they exist, essentially by extending the county's Conservation Zone to envelop the village. Within the Courthouse village itself, Route 208 becomes a traditional main street, from which traffic could be diverted through either a four-lane bypass or with several new streets designed to distribute traffic to several rural highways leading out of the village.

Among the study's graphics are three bird's-eye aerial perspective sketches, reproduced in Figure 12–2, illustrating the benefits of the recommended strategy, contrasted with the likely future of the corridor if current zoning continues to be implemented. Visual materials such as these sketches enable the public and their elected representatives to understand the implications of various policy alternatives as they would ultimately manifest themselves on the ground.

So well received was the Route 208 corridor study that the county engaged UDA again to prepare recommendations for protecting the integrity of the 12-mile long Route 3 corridor leading west from Fredericksburg, crossing through two Civil War battlefields (Chancellorsville and the Wilderness). Of the road length not traversing National Park Service land (about six miles), half is open field and half is wooded. The first task was to identify the Route 3 viewshed, as determined by vegetative cover and topography, and to locate the most visible areas on a tax-parcel map to show how various potentially developable properties would be involved.

All properties within the viewshed were recommended for inclusion in a new zoning overlay district, which would contain three different types of standards. For parcels with woodlands along the highway, a 200-foot deep wooded buffer was recommended, with further provisions allowing no more than 30 percent of the trees beyond the buffer to be removed in the course of development. For parcels where some of the land is highly visible from Route 3 but also containing other areas that are screened by trees or topographic features, "the permitted density on the site should be concentrated on those portions of the property

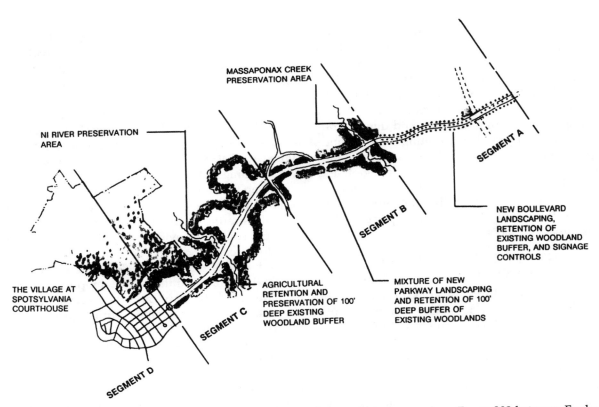

Figure 12–1. The recommended strategy for dealing with growth pressures along Route 208 between Fredericksburg and the historic village of Spotsylvania Courthouse, Virginia, is to divide the highway into several segments, based upon the terrain and natural features. Key recommendations include intensive landscaping in 30-foot planting strips in front of businesses in the commercial district, retaining 100-foot wooded buffers between new subdivisions and the highway, and protecting open landscapes through low-density conservation zoning in the "gateway" area. *Source:* UDA Architects, 1991.

outside the viewshed," with supplemental planting, where necessary, to screen the rooflines of new development (UDA Architects, 1992).

In the third kind of situation, where most of a parcel is visible from the highway corridor, three alternative design approaches were recommended, involving 18, 24, and 100 dwelling units. The smallest version, containing up to 18 dwellings, was based upon a typical farm complex set well back from the roadway, comprising the main house, tenant cottages, barns, and working buildings, in which no more than 8 percent of the parcel is covered by buildings, paving, and lawns.

In the second prototype, 24 dwellings are accommodated in a larger grouping of buildings and trees based upon historic plantations such as Mount Vernon, with stables, barns, and other large structures designed to function as multifamily condominiums (as was done at Long Hill Farm in Guilford, Connecticut, described as a "Residential Case" in Chapter 20). Critical to the success of the plantation option is compact site design, generous tree planting, and surrounding open space.

The third design option involves a neo-traditional village of approximately 100 dwellings surrounded by a greenbelt that buffers it from the highway (and vice versa). The majority of homes could be single-family detached, facing onto a rectilinear street pattern with garages accessed from back lanes or alleys. Formal open space within

Figure 12–2. These aerial perspective "bird's-eye" sketches contrast existing conditions with two alternative future choices for the Route 208 corridor in a way that graphically illustrates the disadvantages of continuing with existing zoning "controls." *Source:* UDA Architects, 1991.

central greens or squares is also recommended, with open "greenbelt" land leased for field-crop production.

The final part of this very impressive study applies the above design principles to three contiguous parcels totaling 324 acres, on which the consultants estimated that 172 dwellings could be built under conventional zoning. Maintaining that same "yield," two creative alternative scenarios were illustrated. The first accommodated 65 dwellings in four traditional farm complexes and 110 homes on wooded half-acre lots outside the viewshed. The second comprised a 105-unit village, a 23-unit farm cluster, and 43 one-acre wooded lots not visible from the highway. Both of these alternatives were contrasted with the conventional "checkerboard" layout in site plan format and with aerial perspective sketches.

To ensure implementation, the study recommended that a new corridor zoning district require these or similar approaches to be used in the design of new development visible from Route 3.

Alternatively, the study recommended "downzoning" to reduce current building densities, with provisions to allow landowners or developers to "recapture" the original density only when these design approaches are utilized. (Further information on encouraging or requiring more compact designs with greater open space may be found in Chapters 14 and 15.)

LOCAL SCENIC ROADS: DESIGNATION

Enabling legislation exists in many states, allowing local governments to designate certain rural roads as "scenic." In Connecticut and Massachusetts, for example, the local legislative body ("town meeting") may, by a majority vote, designate scenic roads on which alterations such as widening, paving, straightening, or removal of trees or stone walls within the right-of-way is subject to certain specified proceedings. This usually takes the form of a hearing to determine if the full extent of the proposed actions are really necessary to accomplish safety objectives, and

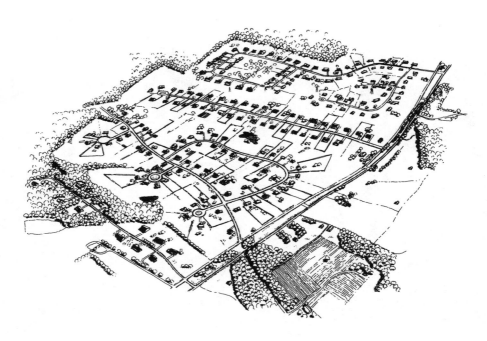

CURRENT DEVELOPMENT POLICY

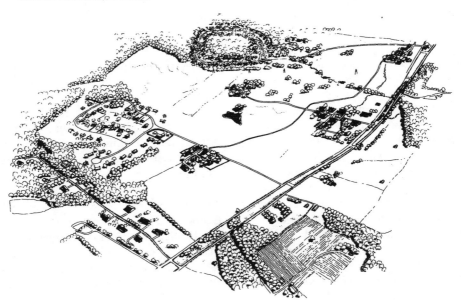

PROPOSED DEVELOPMENT POLICY AND DESIGN GUIDELINES   FARMHOUSE CLUSTER PROTOTYPE

Figure 12–3. In the Route 3 corridor west of Fredericksburg, Virginia, more detailed aerial perspective sketches were prepared for Spotsylvania County by UDA, to show how conventional suburban zoning would eventually destroy the cultural landscape along this rural highway linking two major Civil War battlefields, and to demonstrate how prototypical farm clusters and compact villages could be employed to preserve the essential character of this historically significant area. The adoption of these design approaches was recommended as a

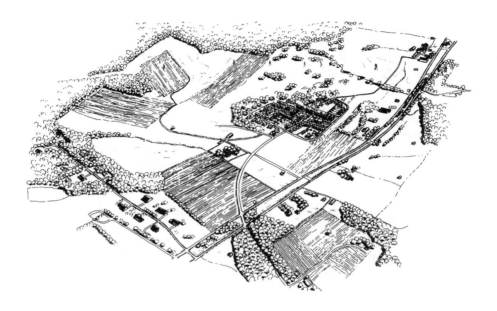

VILLAGE CLUSTER PROTOTYPE

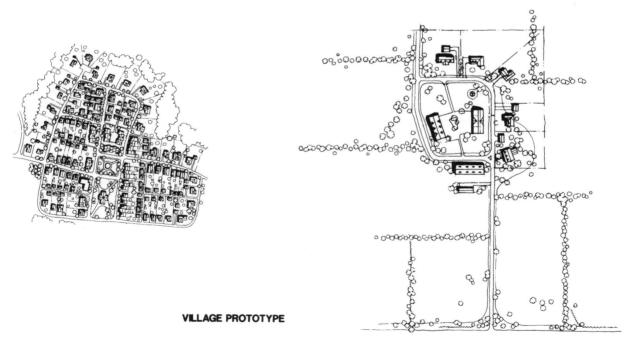

VILLAGE PROTOTYPE

TYPICAL FARM HOUSING PROTOTYPES

requirement in areas visible from the roadway, within a new corridor overlay zone. (An alternative recommendation was to reduce permitted densities within the corridor, allowing original densities to be achieved only if subdivision designs followed the principles contained in the study.) Larger scale site plans of a farm complex and a rural village were also produced, to illustrate to developers how these forms could be designed.

whether any modifications to lessen the impact of the "improvements" would be feasible.

To be considered scenic under Connecticut law, a local road must possess at least two of the following characteristics:

1. Unpaved gravel surface
2. Borders of stone walls or mature trees
3. Narrow traveled way (not more than 20-feet wide)
4. Scenic views
5. Natural integration into surrounding terrain
6. Alignment parallel to brooks, streams, ponds, or lakes (or bridges crossing streams, etc.).

Such designation does not prohibit routine maintenance. This is clearly defined and includes such activities as removing dead trees or limbs, trimming limbs that encroach over the roadway below a set height, trimming to protect utility lines or to enhance scenic views, and correcting drainage problems. Designation also does not prohibit removal of trees or wall sections to allow driveway entrances to newly developed lots.

In Vermont, towns have had the authority to designate local roads as scenic since 1977, when the state's Scenic Highway Law was established. (This contrasts sharply with the New York program, in which only the state Commissioner of Environmental Conservation is authorized to grant such designation.) In order to create some uniformity of approach among different towns, the State Scenery Preservation Council (part of the State Planning Office) published a "field guide" containing guidelines for selecting scenic roads and suggested standards for their maintenance.

The field guide recommends that a survey be undertaken (typically by volunteers) to evaluate all roads within the municipality, according to scenic value, in order to document their different characteristics. The survey results would "allow officials to fairly compare their scenic character in determining which should be officially designated as scenic" (Vermont Scenery Preservation Council, 1979).

Whether or not such an extensive survey is conducted, roads recommended for designation must be quite intensively examined. The model survey form was designed for use by volunteers, and contains 26 examples of positive features and 14 examples of negative features. Some of the features are described with special terms (such as "leaf tunnel effects" and "forest patterns"), which are defined in a glossary at the back of the field guide with accompanying photographs. Among the positive features that should be considered are roadside trees and plants, stone walls and traditional fences, topography (outcrops, summits, steep grades, sharp curves, drainage factors), outward views (of fields, ponds, waterfalls, barns, distant hills, etc.), and wildlife areas (habitats that could be disrupted, such as trout streams, waterfowl nesting areas, deer yards and beaver ponds) (Longfield, 1974).

During the first step of the survey process, it is suggested that volunteer teams drive each potential scenic road twice (once in each direction) to record their findings. Generally speaking, only those roads (or road segments) containing a net total of at least 10 positive features (after subtracting negative features) should be considered for step two. However, if team members feel a certain road merits designation despite a low numerical rating, the model survey form includes space for them to explain their reasons.

Step two involves retraveling the roads, even more slowly, and recording all positive and negative features at one-tenth of a mile intervals. (The box grid on the survey form contains ten boxes for each listed feature: one box for each one-tenth of a mile segment.) Again, the team travels the road in both directions, to be sure it has not missed anything worth noting. It should be understood that this process is not merely an exercise in counting, because each feature might or might not produce truly positive or negative effects. For example, a farmhouse might not be stated as a positive feature if it no longer possesses any architectural integrity as a result of too many inappropriate remodeling efforts. A junkyard might not be rated as a negative feature if it is effectively screened from view. There is also room on the form to note "other factors," such as a distant view that is visible only when there are no leaves, or a view whose potential could be realized through some judicious thinning or clearing of roadside vegetation.

After the forms have been completed, the teams should organize their material and display their findings on large-scale maps for use at public hearings. The final decision to designate roads as scenic (or to discontinue a previous designation) lies with the elected Board of Selectmen. In taking their decision, the selectmen are encouraged to consider other factors as well, such as the road's existing and anticipated function (strictly local, versus collector/cross-connector, etc.), traffic volume and type, and projected changes in land use.

After designation, such roads are subject to maintenance guidelines. The basic rule, as stipulated in the regulations adopted by the Vermont Transportation Board, is that "scenic roads will be maintained as nearly as possible in the condition which existed at the time of designation; that is, the essential components such as width, alignment, and grade of surface will not be changed materially; elevations and locations of ditch lines shall remain constant except for minimal adjustments required by normal cleaning operations. The roadway surface shall not be changed except for gravelling or re-treatment." The official guide for scenic road maintenance is *The Vermont Backroad*, described in the next section. Essentially the same evaluation procedures are used for designating state highways as scenic. However, the law authorizes only the Vermont Scenery Preservation Council to conduct such analyses, with designation power lying with the State Transportation Board (the governing body of the Vermont Agency of Transportation).

LOCAL SCENIC ROADS: MAINTENANCE

One of the most useful guides to maintaining the scenic quality of rural roads is a modest volume not widely known outside New England. *The Vermont Backroad* (Longfield, 1974) provides excellent guidance not only in the physical design of "improvements," but also in the planning steps that should precede designation (weighing operational requirements, social factors, and scenic features). Because of its clear diagrams and wealth of information, it has been officially adopted as Vermont's maintenance manual for designated scenic roads,

but this distinction does not limit its relevance to situations in many other states.

When roads must be altered to handle more traffic, it is very important that the new alignment follow the lay of the land as much as possible. This guide suggests designing the roadway to avoid long, straight lines (except on level terrain where there are also some visual features to line up with, such as a row of trees or a distant farmhouse), and curving the alignment as the road approaches a hillcrest, crossing the contours and reducing its steepness.

Beyond the protection of such features, rural residents and officials should work toward road plans that actively incorporate them as focal points. This could be done, for example, by introducing gentle curves bending the roadway toward a particular scenic element (such as a pond, farmland tree group, woodland clearing, or opening in the woods) (Longfield, 1974).

One of the first "improvements" generally proposed for narrow rural roads is widening. For low-volume access roads serving a small number of homes (five or less), a 15-foot wide traveled way is not unreasonable. For most other situations, an 18-foot surface (with two-foot shoulders) should be adequate in most cases. In fact, those are the dimensions for about 90 percent of the local country roads in New England, and many of the older county highways in upstate New York and rural Pennsylvania as well. Many of these handle thousands of vehicles daily with no apparent problems.

Apart from widening, one of the most common questions concerning scenic roads in rural areas involves the issue of whether to pave existing gravel surfaces. Although many local officials see paving as an improvement, well maintained gravel roads are often an effective alternative (except on very steep gradients, which should usually be paved to prevent erosion). According to authorities in Vermont:

Gravel roads have the advantage of lower construction and often lower maintenance costs. They are easier to maintain, requiring less equipment and less skilled operators. Potholes can be patched more effectively. Gravel roads generate lower speeds and thus may be safer roadways than paved surfaces. Another advantage of the unpaved road is its forgiveness of external forces. For example, it is common today for vehicles with gross weights of 80,000 pounds to operate on Vermont local roads. Such vehicles could damage a lightly paved road so as to require resealing. The damage on a gravel road would be much easier and less expensive to correct (Vermont Local Roads Program, 1987).

However, there eventually comes a time when the volume of traffic rises to levels where paving begins to make practical sense. The rule of thumb among rural road commissioners in Vermont is that asphalt paving should begin to be considered after traffic volumes start to exceed 500 vehicles per day, although higher volumes can be sustained on such roads with frequent grading and graveling. The consequences of applying smooth paving material are generally an increase in average traffic speeds (usually by 10 to 15 mph) and some flattening and straightening (to accommodate the faster vehicles).

A 1987 study by the Vermont Local Roads Program showed that gravel roads were actually less expensive to maintain over a six-year period than were asphalt surfaces. Although per-mile annual maintenance costs were certainly higher for gravel ($4,674, compared with $716 for patching, striping, and sealing asphalt surfaces), over the longer term the cumulative costs of graveling and grading turned out to be less than the expensive repaving periodically required of asphalt roads. For example, over a 12-year period, the maintenance cost of one mile of gravel roadway was estimated to be $56,090, compared with $75,036 for a three-inch bituminous concrete surface (which has a 12-year life, at best). In fairness to these comparisons, it must be said that gravel roads do involve higher user costs (in terms of lower gas mileage and greater tire wear), but these are not significant if the lengths of gravel roadway normally traveled by residents constitute only a tiny fraction of their total annual driving mileage.

If roads are to be paved, it is strongly recommended that their shoulders be loamed and seeded with white clover and/or a hardy fescue, to create a greener and more rural appearance. Such varieties are salt-tolerant and survive occasional traffic. In areas with light rainfall and long summers, graded gravel could provide an alternative landscape accent.

THE DEVELOPMENT PATTERN ALONG SCENIC ROADSIDES

In addition to protecting the road and its right-of-way from inappropriate changes, amending existing zoning and subdivision regulations should be considered to prevent certain types of development patterns from occurring. As noted above, the recommended approach is to require open space development design (described in detail in Chapter 15). Such an approach would establish reasonable design standards for siting new construction. Broadly speaking, several alternatives might be incorporated into such a zoning amendment, as shown in Figure 12–4. These include screening the

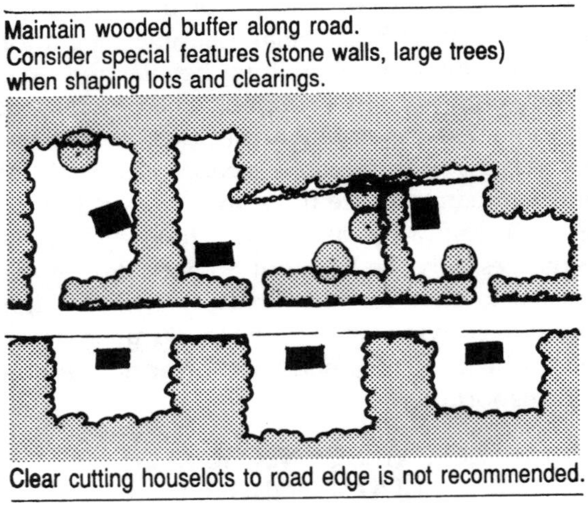

Maintain wooded buffer along road.
Consider special features (stone walls, large trees) when shaping lots and clearings.

Clear cutting houselots to road edge is not recommended.

Figure 12–4. Simple site planning techniques for protecting the scenic character of rural roads include maintaining (or establishing) a wooded no-cut buffer along the front lot line and angling driveways so that lawns, houses, and garages are not directly visible from the road. Combined with deep front setbacks for construction, such approaches could become design requirements in a scenic roads overlay zone. Where such principles remain guidelines rather than enforceable standards, conventional clearing and siting patterns can be expected to continue, as illustrated in the bottom half of this sketch.

new development behind a "no-cut buffer" at least 50-feet deep (preferably 75 to 100-feet deep) along the road right-of-way, except for a 20-foot wide driveway entrance.

On unwooded sites, where there are no topographical features to help conceal the development, it may be designed in small clusters resembling groupings of farmhouses, barns, and outbuildings, employing a traditional, vernacular architectural "vocabulary," in terms of scale, massing, roof pitch, relationship of buildings to each other and to the road, and protection of adjacent open space, preferably visible from the public roadway.

Figure 12–5 shows how a seven-lot cluster (involving two shared driveways) could be offered as an incentive to rural landowners who would ordinarily divide their land into six "frontage lots."

By allowing the shared driveway access to be gravel surfaced, (perhaps 12-feet wide for one pair of homes, and 16-feet wide for the group of five), instead of requiring the rural landowner to construct expensive subdivision streets, local officials can eliminate one of the greatest obstacles deterring such owners from subdividing the property in a creative, nonstrip fashion. (Additional commentary on shared driveways and appropriate standards for "country lanes" can be found in Chapter 11.) In this example, half of the farm parcel has been protected, and the new homes have been related to existing hedgerows or buffered behind new roadside tree plantings.

In situations involving very simple splits of existing parcels into two halves, there are practical alternatives to creating additional "frontage lots," which suburbanize rural roadsides and block views to the open land behind them. As illustrated in the *Rural Siting Guidelines* prepared for Hillsdale, Columbia County, New York, a second dwelling can often be tucked into a group of trees toward the far end of the property, with a long driveway providing access to the town road (Tate, et al., 1992). Such an approach typically involves the use of "flag lots" (or, alternatively, interior lots without road frontage, but having guaranteed access via a permanent right-of-way across an adjoining parcel, which is the preferred method in Albemarle County, Virginia). In Figure 12–6, the speckled

area has also been protected from further change through a conservation easement over the entire property, except for two "building envelopes" within which all construction must occur.

Strategies for controlling new development along arterial roads and state highways, where pressure for "strip commercial" zoning is great, are described in Chapter 9. In California, which has one of the strongest scenic roads programs in the country, eligibility depends not only on the presence of outstanding visual features (both natural and human-made), but also on the existence of land-use controls capable of maintaining that beauty. Prerequisite for designation as a scenic byway is the adoption of a roadside management plan developed by the local government and the state DOT. Controls are usually handled through overlay zoning standards that regulate construction, land use, signage, grading, and native vegetation removal within a 2,000-foot-wide corridor (Mastran, 1992).

In Ventura County, a Scenic Highway Protection Overlay Zone along Route 33 requires special permits for grading more than 1,000 square feet of land, stockpiling more than 10 cubic yards of material, removing protected trees and long-established native vegetation, erecting new structures, rebuilding destroyed structures, and enlarging existing structures by more than 10 percent of their floor area. In addition, trenching, excavating, or applying poison within the drip line of a protected tree, or within 15 feet of its trunk, is also prohibited.

Regulations such as these (or the others described in this chapter) are urgently needed in hundreds of jurisdictions around the country, where rural highways have been designated "scenic" but where local zoning routinely permits the kind of roadside clutter described as "commercial kudzu" in Chapter 9. Nowhere are the conflicts between conservation and development more acute than along the rural highways around our National Parks. The situation at the Gettysburg National Military Park in Adams County, Pennsylvania, is typical in that the role of park service staff there is essentially advisory, with only limited means available to encourage local officials,

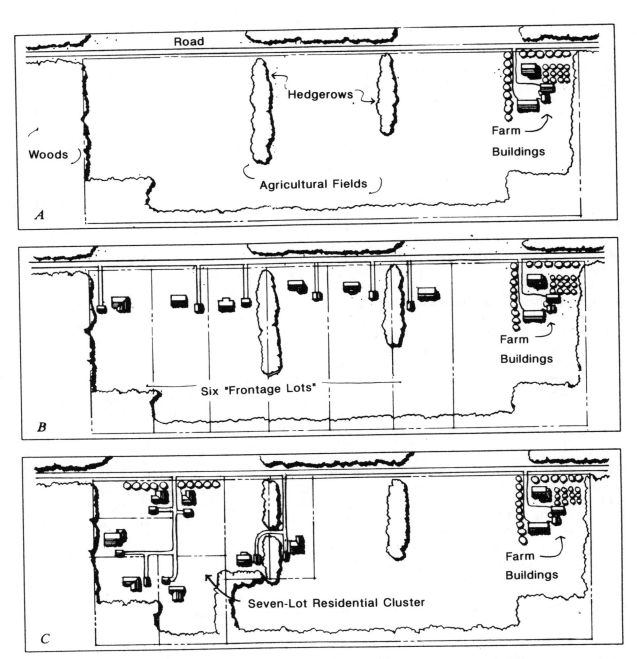

Figure 12–5. On unwooded sites, such as open fields or pastures, it is even more important to encourage (or require) clustering of new development. Even on relatively shallow sites, where there is little opportunity to locate homes far from the road, such as against a distant treeline, clustering principles can help reduce roadside clutter and preserve some open vistas. These three sketches, from *Managing Change: A Pilot Study in Rural Design and Planning* (Doble et al., 1992) show techniques being advocated by the Tug Hill Commission in upstate New York, where the cost of constructing paved subdivision streets operates as a strong disincentive for rural landowners to subdivide their property in any way other than through "strip lots" along existing public roads. This example shows several gravel-surfaced shared driveways, built to standards appropriate for the amount of traffic they must accommodate.

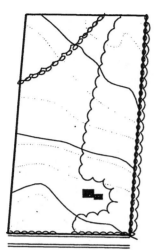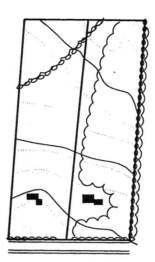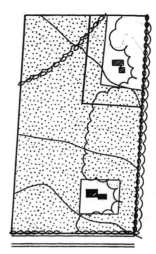

Figure 12–6. It is very difficult to control the creation of single lots and the construction of individual homes without overlay district standards regulating all changes within a scenic corridor. But graphics such as these could help with a less formal approach involving "landowner outreach" efforts by local planners, conservation commission members, or a land trust. When approached properly and presented with low-cost alternatives to "road stripping," many rural landowners respond positively. This set of three sketches illustrates a reasonable alternative to creating another "frontage lot" with a new house that would interrupt the rural vista, as seen by drivers along this country road. In order to locate a second house at the back end of a property, however, local regulations must allow "flag lots," or interior lots linked to the public road through deeded rights-of-way. *Source:* Tate et al., 1992.

landowners, and developers to employ more creative techniques when dealing with land-use changes on properties visible from "gateway" approach roads.

Figures 12–7 and 12–8 depict a common problem and one partial solution that was generated to show a better way of dealing with land already zoned for fairly intensive commercial and residential development. Although it is difficult to fashion a silk purse from a sow's ear, it is usually possible to improve upon the standard layouts typically submitted by intending developers. Where funds are not available for purchasing development rights, and where the local political climate is not favorable to adopting stricter minimum standards for limiting, transferring, or buffering new roadside development, preparation of practical alternative development plans—including significant conservation features—probably offers the most reasonable strategy for rural planners and preservationists to follow.

EFFORTS OF LOCAL LAND TRUSTS

In areas where there is not sufficient public support or political will to enact strict regulations to protect scenic roadsides, some land trusts have been actively working to secure voluntary conservation easements from owners of land bordering such routes. In the Charleston, South Carolina, area, the Lowcountry Open Land Trust has begun helping local landowners place roadside "buffer easements" along roads of historic and scenic significance. Such easements normally prohibit clearing or thinning of vegetation (except for future access roads), in addition to excluding commercial signage. Varying between 100 and 500-feet deep, these eased areas can typically be counted toward acreage requirements in a cluster development. For example, on Wadmalaw Island, the Longcreek Plantation subdivision recently donated a 200-foot deep buffer easement along the Maybank Highway. And along Route 162 on Yonges Island, the

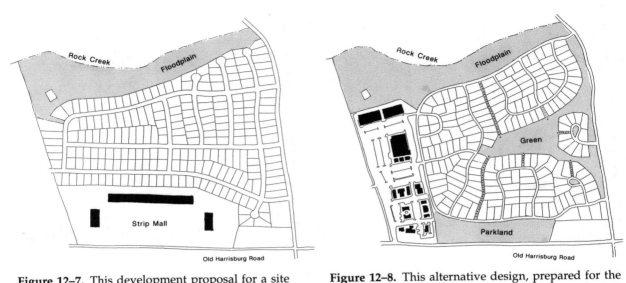

Figure 12–7. This development proposal for a site along one of the rural arterial roads leading toward the Gettysburg National Military Park, consisting of a "strip mall" parallel to the highway and a checkerboard of one-quarter-acre houselots covering the balance of the parcel (except for flood-prone areas), is typical of the kind of land use that routinely degrades the scenic qualities of these "gateways" to our National Parks.

Figure 12–8. This alternative design, prepared for the National Park Service (which has neither the funds nor the authority to acquire many key parcels near the battlefield), demonstrates a "density-neutral" approach that would create a long natural buffer alongside the approach road, with significant internal open space for the new neighborhood. (The residential area was modeled on Radburn and Echo Hill, while Market Square and Sycamore Square formed the basis for the shopping center design. All four of these developments are described and illustrated in Part IV, "Case Examples.")

Dixie Plantation donated a mile-long vegetated buffer in 1989.

In order to deal more effectively with multiple landowners along the canopied Ashley River Road near Drayton Hall, easement donations have been placed into an escrow account until a substantial number of roadside landowners have agreed to donate easements on their properties— at which time those agreements will become legally binding. This is a technique used by many land trusts around the country to help secure easements from a larger number of people, many of whom would ordinarily be reluctant to participate in such efforts if their neighbors did not join in as well (Mastran, 1992).

As noteworthy as voluntary approaches may be, they are rarely effective without the cooperation of local officials, who must also agree to limit water and sewer extensions, lower residential densities, deny commercial rezoning requests, and require undisturbed buffers paralleling the public right-of-way. Five years after such recommendations were made to Charleston County, Dorchester County, and the city of Charleston, implementation has yet to occur, and suburban development pressures have begun to seriously degrade the scenic quality of the Ashley River Road.

13

Sewage Disposal

The issue that most frequently dominates discussions of creatively designed development proposals in unsewered rural areas concerns the treatment and disposal of human wastes. Recognizing the importance of this subject, the scarcity of factual information readily available to local decision-makers, and the incomplete understanding among municipal and county officials about reliable alternatives to standard individual septic systems, this chapter has been included to provide insight regarding many lesser known but viable approaches to dealing with sewage disposal. Further details about many of the systems described below are readily available through the National Small Flows Clearinghouse at West Virginia University in Morgantown, West Virginia (1-800-624-8301).

Nationwide, nearly one-quarter of all homes depend on individual septic disposal systems, and the number is growing by about 500,000 per annum. When they fail the reasons most often cited are inappropriate soil conditions, inadequate site evaluation, poor design and/or installation, disposal of improper items or substances by system users, and insufficient maintenance. Indeed, preventive maintenance is necessary for the longevity of even well-designed systems that have been properly installed. Operational life can be substantially lengthened by periodically pumping septic tanks (every three to five years for a "typical" family of four using a 1,000 gallon tank, for example). Such pumping removes the accumulated solids and greases from the septic tank where they settle when first entering the system. When these solids are not pumped they can eventually fill the tank and begin to overflow into

the subsurface drainage field, biologically overloading and clogging the pores in the soil.

Although this procedure is relatively simple and inexpensive, it is rarely performed until problems manifest themselves, and irreparable harm has been done. Local health authorities and management districts in some parts of the country have begun to mandate periodic pumping for systems located in particularly sensitive areas, such as along lakefronts or riverbanks, near wetlands, or over aquifers. Preventive maintenance is worth the political effort and individual cost for public authorities to require it, and the reluctance of local governments to take such action is an expensive choice in the long run, considering the very large costs involved in correcting situations of widespread system failure.

OPEN SPACE DESIGN AND SEPTIC DISPOSAL

When addressing themselves to potential sewage disposal problems that may be created by new development, municipal and county officials typically express deep concern about "clustering" homes closer together to preserve open space. However, unless soils are uniformly poor across the entire parcel (shallow bedrock or restrictive layer, seasonal high water table, steep slopes, or excessively fine or coarse soil texture), the variations in soil conditions that typically occur within a parcel offer an opportunity for clustering to produce *better* systems than would be possible following a conventional approach with standardized lot sizes in a checkerboard layout.

The reason is that a truly *flexible* approach to the location of houselots allows one to "design with nature," drawing the lot lines carefully to include the best available soils on the site for septic system locations (and their reserve areas as well). As shown in Figure 13–1, a conventional approach produces larger lots but in many cases these are located on soil that is only marginally suited for subsurface disposal areas. When the choice is between unsewered lots of 60,000 to 80,000 square feet with soil conditions that are at the lower end of legally acceptable limits, and lots that are 30,000 to 60,000 square feet where the systems can all be installed in the best available soils on the site that are deeper and better drained, it is difficult to justify the former.

In fact, progressive regulations could begin to *require* such layouts, coupled with an added level of protection calling for wells and septic systems to be located 150 feet apart (or farther, if practica-

ble). The nearly universal *minimum* separation distance (100 feet) between these installations has in fact become a regular design *standard* that is rarely exceeded, even when doing so would be easy and sensible. Failing to see the logic of having a "one size fits all" approach to these separation distances when their soil conditions varied so greatly within individual subdivision parcels, several communities in coastal Maine have instituted a sliding scale approach for houselots within 250 feet of the shoreline or major watercourses. In York, for example, the separation requirement varies from 100 feet on the best soils, to 175 feet on those soils that barely manage to qualify for septic system approval. Even on unsewered 30,000 square foot lots, separation distances of up to 200 feet are achievable, assuming 100 foot × 300 foot dimensions. When water is supplied through a

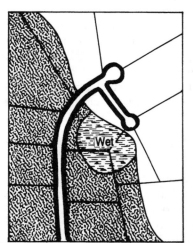
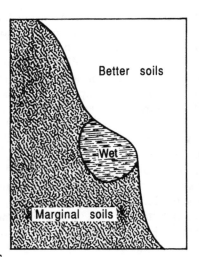
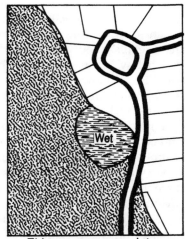

Thirteen two-and-one-half acre lots
Six on marginal soil

Thirteen one-acre lots
All on better soil

Figure 13–1. Reducing lot size can sometimes help subdivision designers locate all homes on the better soils contained within a development site. On the left, six of the thirteen 2.5-acre lots would have septic systems on marginal soils, barely meeting minimum legal requirements, because these lots contain nothing better. By decreasing lots to one acre in size, all thirteen can be laid out to contain deeper, drier soils (with all wetlands in the open space preservation area, a treed island at the end of the street, and a future street and/or trail connection to adjoining properties). Sometimes such arrangements require a few "flag lots" with a relatively narrow strip of land providing driveway access, a very useful design approach that should generally be allowed, subject to certain safeguards to prevent abuses (such as the infamous "rat-tail" subdivisions with numerous lots having long, snake-like appendages connecting the lots to a distant public road—all to avoid the cost of providing internal streets).

central system (public or private), the lots may be much smaller—in the range of 12,000 to 15,000 square feet—provided that the soils are above average for septic disposal.

COMMON SEPTIC SYSTEMS

A more cost-effective, and potentially superior, approach can be achieved by combining individual septic leaching areas into larger absorption areas that are jointly owned and maintained. Because there is growing evidence that large rectangular disposal "beds" do not allow for sufficient exchange of carbon dioxide and atmospheric oxygen in their centers (causing anaerobic conditions that prevent proper sewage treatment), researchers in this field recommend that large disposal areas be laid out in a series of parallel subsurface "trenches" (an unfortunate term, as it wrongly implies open ditches). These covered "trenches" must be far enough apart to allow CO_2 gases to escape from the soil, and for oxygen to penetrate into disposal areas to promote aerobic treatment of the waste. Trench systems also provide some additional absorption capacity, per cubic foot of gravel, as the lower parts of side walls also absorb effluent. For example, in deeper soils, a two-foot wide trench with 18 inches of gravel has an effective absorption area of 3.5 square feet per linear foot.

The other main component of these systems—the septic tank—may be handled either through individual tanks owned and maintained by each homeowner, or through larger jointly owned tanks. Such systems have been operated successfully for decades by a variety of users, including apartment complexes, shopping centers, laundromats, hospitals, schools, and restaurants. The technology for designing and constructing what the U.S. Environmental Protection Agency calls *large soil absorption systems* (referred to hereinafter as simply *LSA systems*, for brevity), has existed literally for generations. To avoid problems, some jurisdictions require that each dwelling have its own individual septic tank (as a primary collection point for inappropriate items and substances, such as disposable diapers and cooking grease). When such tanks are pumped regularly (once every three to five years) by a homeowners' association or by the municipality, system life is greatly extended.

The reluctance of many county and state health authorities to allow LSA systems in subdivisions stems from their concern about the long-term maintenance responsibilities where ownership is divided among a number of individual homeowners. This very real concern can be addressed quite easily, however (please see item 5 under "Maintenance of Common Systems," below). It is, therefore, puzzling that more jurisdictions have not adopted this approach, unless part of their reasoning is based upon growth limitation considerations. Such prohibitions are ill-conceived because they necessitate a multiplicity of individual systems, which may not be installed as carefully, pumped as regularly, or monitored as often. In addition, as separate systems, not every one could occupy the best sites in the subdivision for septic disposal.

There are a number of essential steps to assuring that LSA systems will perform at least as well as—if not better than—a larger number of smaller systems. Conditions of approval should include the following items, recommended by the USEPA, for systems designed to handle up to 30,000 gallons per day (approximately 100 dwelling units).

Design of Common Systems

1. In addition to meeting minimum statutory criteria for acceptability, soil types under proposed LSA systems should be shown to be the best available on the site, and their septic suitability should also be above average among soils on which septic systems are legally permitted. A professional soil scientist or hydrogeologist (experienced in such facilities) should evaluate the soils down to at least six feet below the infiltrative surface, with special attention to both the horizontal flow potential of the site and the vertical permeability characteristics.

2. Sites should preferably have convex ground contours and should not be in locations that receive substantial runoff from the surrounding terrain. The base of the filter bed should be at least three feet above the seasonal high water table (some states require four feet); this will sometimes require that carefully graded fill material be placed on the site prior to disposal area construction to elevate the system. Curtain drains may also be used upslope to divert the flow of surface water and groundwater away from the disposal area.

3. Septic tank effluent should be pumped, under pressure, into the filter fields two to four times per day, to create alternating cycles of system operation and "rest." At least three field systems should be built, with each capable of treating 50 percent of the average daily flow.

Maintenance of Common Systems

1. Septic tanks should be pumped at regular intervals, at a frequency determined by the design engineer based upon the size of the tank and the contributing population. Pumping operators should be required to send confirmation notices to the local health authority, which could monitor their receipt and contact the LSA system ownership if such notices are not received on schedule. Pumping reminder notices could also be mailed to system owners by local health officials, along with regular municipal mailings (such as property tax bills).

2. Absorption units should be inspected monthly to detect surface ponding problems or "breakouts"; if they occur the unit should be rested and expanded (if there is a capacity problem) or replaced. Another option would be to provide some pretreatment of wastes, such as with a sand filter, to improve the quality of wastewater going into the absorption field. In all cases, the volume of effluent pumped into the absorption field should be carefully recorded.

3. During its first year of operation the LSA system should be monitored quarterly for BOD (biochemical oxygen demand), TSS (total suspended solids), TKN (total Kjedhal nitrogen), NO_3N (nitrate nitrogen), and pH (a measure of acidity/alkalinity). These reports should be sent to the local health authority and/or to the state environmental agency that licenses these systems. Thereafter these parameters should be examined annually (with groundwater monitoring being done semiannually).

4. The LSA system should be owned by a homeowners' association (HOA), in which membership should be mandatory for owners of all dwelling units connected to it. The HOA should be vested with the authority to place liens (with interest penalties) on the properties of owners who fail to pay their annual dues or special assessments. Annual dues should be divided into two subaccounts: one for year-to-year operational costs (pumping, monitoring, etc.), the other for long-term capital repairs/replacement. Dues shall be structured so that system replacement can be financed every ten years (a conservative estimate), accounting for inflation. In the event that the cost of repairs exceeds the amount of dues collected, the HOA may borrow the difference from a lending institution, or may levy a special assessment on its members, or do both. According to the National Small Flows Clearinghouse, properly maintained absorption fields, designed with 50 percent reserve capacity for biannual resting, could last as long as 50 years. Absorption area size might also be reduced if systems were designed to include sand filters to provide pretreatment, so that effluent reaching the fields would be of a higher than normal quality to begin with.

5. In the unlikely event that a HOA cannot act quickly enough to undertake needed repairs, the local health authority may hire a private contractor to perform such essential work and then bill the individual homeowners accordingly, also placing a lien against their homes until payment is received. This is essentially the same procedure followed in cases of individual systems that are not fixed promptly.

As is evident in these rules, the number of safeguards provided for LSA systems far exceeds those a community normally enjoys with smaller, individually owned systems. They are usually required to be installed more carefully (typically with engineering review), are monitored more thoroughly, are provided with sensible and straightforward institutional arrangements to ensure their regular maintenance and eventual repair, and they are located on the best soils available on the development parcel (among those meeting state criteria for septic systems). Regular monitoring should prevent any wholesale system failure by providing early warning signals. Even in a "worst-case" scenario, the municipality would still be able to correct any malfunction by authorizing a private contractor to perform all the necessary repairs and passing the costs directly along to the system owners (as is normally done when individual septic systems fail and are not promptly fixed). An excellent summary description of this approach is available in a free government leaflet entitled "Large Scale Absorption Systems: Design Suggestions for Success" (U.S. E.P.A., June 1986).

"CONTOUR SYSTEMS"

An innovative variation on the theme of the LSA systems described above has recently been developed and tested in the Canadian maritime provinces. It was devised in response to the widespread failure of individual systems built in outlying rural villages before the importance of soil suitability was generally appreciated. Although this approach was developed to correct existing problems, it is certainly applicable to system design for new developments as well.

Put simply, "contour systems" are elongated versions of LSAs, designed to follow ground contours in a linear formation (Pask, 1988). The principle underlying this design is based upon field research findings that rectangularly shaped absorption areas located on sloping terrain were not distributing the effluent very evenly. Filter beds that were 40 feet × 50 feet in area tended to concentrate the effluent in the ground across a 50-foot wide band of ground, downhill from the system. In other words, the filtered effluent was tending to travel laterally in the direction of the ground slope, rather than vertically. Better treatment could be achieved by redesigning the bed into a trench system measuring 10 feet × 200 feet, which would spread the underground infiltration out along 200 feet of hillside. The length of the system would be directly proportional to the number of dwellings served; 50 to 220 feet of trench length per dwelling unit would be a preferred range, according to the Nova Scotia Department of Health and Fitness. Dimensions would be smaller or larger depending on the suitability of the soils for septic disposal. To ensure even distribution of the effluent throughout the entire length of the system, pressurized "dosing," in which waste-

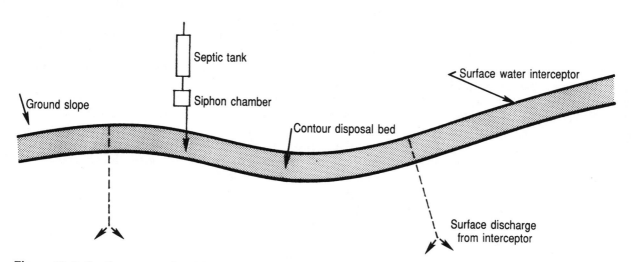

Figure 13–2. Septic systems that follow the contours of a sloping site provide better treatment than standard rectangular filtration beds, and cause considerably less site disturbance. They have been used very successfully for retrofitting rural villages in the hills of Nova Scotia where previous systems on individual lots have failed.

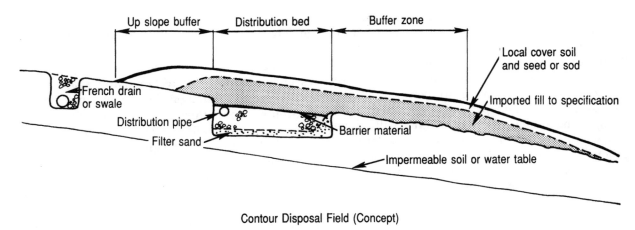

Contour Disposal Field (Concept)

Figure 13–3. This cross-sectional view of a "contour system" shows the upslope diversion for surface drainage, the narrow distribution bed, and the downslope fill. *Source:* Adapted from Pask, 1989.

water is pumped into the perforated pipes, is recommended.

This approach was developed for sloping terrain in the comparatively harsh Canadian climate, making it particularly applicable for steeper terrain typical of our northeastern states. It could also be applied in warmer and/or flatter areas, however, where greater dilution is a goal.

INTERMITTENT SAND FILTERS

Another variation on the LSA system is the *intermittent sand filter* (ISF), which consists of a septic tank, a large filter bed composed of graded sand two to three feet deep, and an underdrainage collection system that carries the filtered effluent to a final chamber for disinfection via chlorination or ultraviolet irradiation (Anderson et al., 1984). After settling occurs in the septic tank, the effluent is applied intermittently to the filter bed surface, where it percolates down through the sand and drains into the disinfection chamber. The highly treated waters are then discharged to infiltration basins, absorption fields, or watercourses. The disinfection stage may be omitted, provided that the effluent is conducted to subsurface absorption trenches or fields.

There are many variations of ISFs, which may be described as exposed, buried, recirculating, or

nitrifying. The type focused on in this section is one of the most basic and reliable, and has a very good track record of performance when properly designed and maintained. It is recommended that ISFs for neighborhoods or small communities be designed with sand filters that are either open or fitted with removable covers. This will ensure easy access for periodic visual inspection. Routine maintenance, such as surface raking, to prevent an impermeable layer of organic matter from forming on top of the sand, is also facilitated. For the natural treatment processes to work properly, it is essential that the sand remain unclogged, so that the effluent may drain through it easily, pulling oxygen down into the filter behind it. When an even higher level of treatment is desired, the effluent can be recirculated for a second pass (or more) through the sand filter. (Some recirculating filters use coarser media, such as pea gravel.)

The final disinfection stage with chlorine or UV treatment is designed to allow these systems to be installed in locations where in-ground discharge of partially treated wastewater would not be legal, due to adverse soil conditions (shallow bedrock, high seasonal water table, etc.). Different arrangements of ISF components can also be created to reduce potential nitrate pollution. For over a century, intermittent sand filters have been a favored technology in riparian or coastal locations where the fully treated effluent can then be discharged into rivers or the open ocean.

This approach was, in fact, frequently used by small communities at the turn of the century (Anderson et al., 1984). However, as these communities grew their wastewater volumes increased, while new land available for disposal areas became scarcer and more expensive. Most of these early systems were gradually replaced by mechanical sewage treatment plants, but the escalating costs of the newer mechanical systems (which require continual monitoring by skilled staff) are focusing attention back onto the simpler and time-tested ISF, especially in small rural communities where land is still relatively cheap and abundant. Reduction of federal cost-sharing programs for conventional treatment plants has provided an additional stimulus to reexamine this older approach, which holds considerable promise for new rural development projects. The simplicity and reliability of this technology also meets the needs of many small communities, according to the National Small Flows Clearinghouse.

According to the EPA, these filters "are ideally suited to rural communities and small clusters of homes. They can achieve advanced secondary or even tertiary levels of treatment consistently, with a minimum of attention. . . . Concentrations of BOD and TSS equal to 10 mg/l or less, and nitrification of 80 percent or more of the applied ammonia, are typically achieved They are also relatively inexpensive to construct and have low energy requirements." (Anderson et al., 1984). Being almost automatic in their operation, their greatest advantage is that they do not require continual monitoring by trained technicians. Another reason many engineers favor ISFs is that they can be repaired relatively easily. By contrast, once conventional drain fields fail, replacement is necessary.

The U.S. EPA has published performance data on a dozen ISFs serving entire villages or small towns, ranging in size from 49 in Glover, Vermont to 1,500 in Hanover, Illinois (Anderson et al., 1984). Most of these systems appear to be municipally owned and operated. However, with monitoring requirements, and institutional arrangements for ensuring regular maintenance similar to those described for LSA systems, there is now no reason this technology could not be applied to new rural developments where ISFs would be jointly owned and managed by homeowners' associations (or by special sanitary districts or small utility districts). These systems are fairly simple and run virtually on their own, with only periodic management/operation personnel.

ISFs for individual homes in coastal Maine have been approved by the state for several decades. Towns such as York have, since the late 1970s, required homeowners to contract with local engineering firms to change the chlorine tablets monthly, analyze effluent samples for BOD counts quarterly, and inspect the sand filter triennially, with reports sent to the town offices confirming the work performed and the results obtained. Septic tank pumping is also required on a triennial basis. Other communities that have not established such reporting procedures have found that individual homeowners cannot always be counted on to maintain their own systems properly. The lesson is clear: the technology works well when sensible arrangements for monitoring, periodic pumping, and so forth, are institutionalized.

LAND TREATMENT

While different "land treatment" processes have been designed, this approach has been broadly defined by the U.S. Environmental Protection Agency (USEPA) as "the controlled application of wastewater onto the land surface, to achieve a designed degree of treatment through natural physical, chemical and biological processes within the plant-soil-water matrix" (USEPA et al., 1981) .

It is important to emphasize that, before it is applied to the land, this wastewater has typically experienced a "secondary" level of treatment already, usually in aerated lagoons. This is the level that is commonly provided by conventional sewage treatment plants prior to discharging into a water body.

Because of this, the track record of land treatment systems is extremely impressive. Studies cited by the EPA have shown no increase in harmful contaminants, no increased health risks, and there have been no reported disease outbreaks from any of these facilities. Nevertheless, many nontechnical people respond negatively to the idea of applying treated wastewater to the land surface. Recognizing the multiple advantages offered by this approach, which has operated very successfully in other parts of the state, the New Castle County (Delaware) Public Works Department has published a 15-page booklet written in a user-friendly manner to provide objective facts and to answer common concerns about land treatment systems (Tatman and Lee, 1992).

Land treatment systems differ from conventional plants in one very significant way: instead of discharging their treated wastewater into a river, lake, or ocean, they apply it to a designated area of land. While conventional systems pass large quantities of nutrients, such as nitrogen and phosphorus, into water bodies or watercourses, where they act as fertilizer or pollutants, many land treatment systems recognize these substances as "resources out of place" and utilize them for plant production (Chester County Planning Commission, 1990). Consider the fact that the daily effluent from a conventional sewage treatment facility serving a community of 10,000 persons with a wastewater flow of 1.0 mgd dumps the equivalent nutrient load of 375 fifty-pound bags of fertilizer each day into its receiving waters (Sheaffer and Sellers, 1994). This is not unlike dumping more than 15,000 such bags into the local river every year. One might ask whether there is a practical way to turn this negative into a positive? Besides using these nutrients as fertilizers for various crops (from turf to trees), the land treatment method returns renovated water to the local aquifer, rather than exporting it many miles downstream. Over the long-term, this can have profoundly beneficial effects upon local water supplies.

Land treatment sites range from woodlands (which can be selectively harvested every ten years) to turf farms, agricultural fields, golf courses, and even residential yards. The ability to consume nutrients productively is the basis for the nickname "living filter," used by researchers at Pennsylvania State University to describe land treatment. Because of the nature of their opera-

tion, they require that rather extensive land areas be set aside for their use, certainly more than many in-ground disposal systems require. For this reason, traditional wastewater planners consider them to be most appropriate where land is abundant and available at a reasonable cost, although they have been successfully incorporated into large suburban developments containing parks and natural open space.

Land treatment processes fall into three broad categories: *slow rate, rapid infiltration,* and *overland flow.* To absorb both moisture and nitrogen, the slow rate approach utilizes vegetation, such as perennial grasses, trees, or food crops. This process is also particularly effective in removing BOD, TSS, phosphorus, pathogens, metals, and trace organics (USEPA, 1981). The top inch of soil removes bacteria and reduces organics substantially through filtration, adsorption, and biological oxidation. Most viruses are removed in the first four inches, and phosphorus reduction is achieved through fixation processes in the soil, for example, adsorption and chemical precipitation. However, because soils differ in their ability to treat wastewater, as measured by cation exchange capacity, the importance of expert soil evaluations cannot be overstated.

The expected quality of wastewater treated with the "slow rate" approach is very high: 2–5 mg/l BOD, 1–5 mg/l suspended solids, 3–8 mg/l total nitrogen (depending on crop), 0.1–0.05 total phosphorus, and 0–10 fecal coliform bacteria per 100 ml, as it enters the groundwater. In slow rate systems the treated effluent can be used to irrigate and fertilize crops in both arid regions (where the moisture value is critical) and in more humid areas (where the benefit is primarily nutritional). Application rates should vary between one and three inches per week. In Muskegon, Michigan, where 5,000 acres of cornfields are irrigated with such treated waters, crop yields are reported to be 25 percent higher, compared with non-wastewater farming in the same locale (USEPA, 1981). However, when sprayed on parks or golf courses, additional polishing or treatment is required. This is usually achieved through natural processes in treatment or storage ponds, maintaining a chlorine residual for further pathogen reduction when the water is going to be irrigated in these heavily visited public places.

Natural woodlands provide another opportunity for land treatment, and can in fact offer some advantages because of their typically lower land cost, higher winter soil temperatures, and superior filtration as compared with farmland. However, farmland benefits more from the nutrients that this process provides. Steeper slopes (up to 20 percent, with "spray irrigation") can also be used when they are forested. Among the states where slow rate systems are operating are Pennsylvania, Illinois, Delaware, Colorado, Texas, New Hampshire, Vermont, Maryland, Michigan, Washington, Oregon, North Carolina, Florida, Georgia, and California. This approach to wastewater treatment must be balanced with the characteristics of the crops, soils, geology, and climate. When forested areas are irrigated, installation of stationary sprinklers are required, which increases the cost of irrigation. Because young trees take up more nitrogen than mature ones, some selective harvesting is often advisable.

Spraying has taken place in some forested areas during periods of subfreezing temperatures. For example, the very large system at Pennsylvania State University operates year-round, with ice at ground level gradually melting and infiltrating into the soil. However, because biological activity in the soil is nil when ground temperatures fall below 40° F, nitrogen problems can build up over the colder months.

A reference publication available to the nontechnical reader, *Utilization of Spray Irrigation in Wastewater Treatment,* prepared by a county planning agency outside Philadelphia, documents experience with 14 spray irrigation systems in its service area, and four other sites in neighboring locations (Chester County Planning Commission, 1990). It describes a wide range of such facilities, which are often located only several hundred feet away from residential uses. The schematic diagram in Figure 13–4, from the above-mentioned report, illustrates the basic components of a spray irrigation wastewater treatment system.

Because these systems require relatively large areas for their operation (typically one acre of land application area for every 10 to 30 equivalent dwelling units, depending upon soil type), they are usually appropriate only in rural or outlying suburban locations where land costs are not nearly as high as they are in more urbanized places. In addition to cropland, suitable receiving areas can include golf courses, parks, school playing fields, and residential yards.

Where drinking water supplies are very limited, as in arid regions or built-up areas where growth is seriously depleting groundwater reserves, recycled wastewater is even being used to water residential lawns (several Florida cities have dual water distribution systems for this purpose).

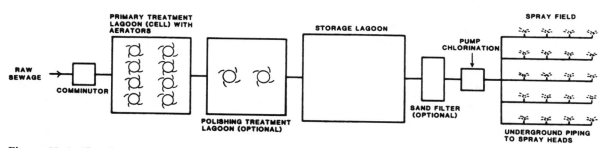

Figure 13–4. "Land treatment" or "spray irrigation" relies on simple, proven technology, consisting of multiple steps basically involving heavy aeration, lagoon storage, and carefully controlled distribution to farm fields or woodlands. Sand filtration and/or chlorination are optional features not normally required except when used on lawns, golf courses, and public parks. This approach has been used extensively in Pennsylvania, Delaware, Florida, Illinois, and California. *Source:* Chester County Planning Commission, 1990.

In some townships in Bucks County, (Pennsylvania), spray irrigation is the preferred method of treatment partly because the land it utilizes for spraying is designated as permanently protected open space (Chester County Planning Commission, 1990), and also because it helps to recharge local groundwater supplies. Studies funded by the EPA have found that homes located next to spray sites do not experience lower property values. In fact, the opposite is frequently true, as these sites constitute permanently protected open space, typically farm fields, woodlands, or golf courses (Tatman and Lee, 1992). Numerous examples exist in southeast Pennsylvania and southern Delaware where people reside contentedly in expensive homes adjoining spray sites serving their development. (See also the "Residential Case" of The Fields at Long Grove in Chapter 20.)

Because subfreezing temperatures hamper the spraying of treated wastewater, larger holding lagoons are typically required in northern states (capable of holding effluent for 150 days in Muskegon, Michigan, for example, compared with as little as 15 days in Sussex County, Delaware). Being heavily aerated, these lagoons do not create odor problems, and they do not have to be located at any great distance from dwelling units.

A second approach to land treatment, known as *rapid infiltration*, typically utilizes highly permeable soils (such as sands and loamy sands), and can provide excellent levels of treatment. In contrast to slow rate applications measured in inches per week, rapid infiltration systems often handle a foot of effluent per day, over a three-day application period, typically followed by 9 to 12 days of drying (depending on soil hydraulic capacity). Very little effluent is taken up by crops or other vegetation in this approach. Fecal coliforms, suspended solids, and BOD are almost completely removed; nitrogen and phosphorus removal averages 50 percent and 70 to 90 percent, respectively, through proper dosing and resting patterns (USEPA, 1981). The residual nitrogen, phosphorus, and potassium are relocated into the groundwater. In some areas, such systems are often used to recharge aquifers. (In Phoenix, Arizona, for example, renovated water is pumped back up for crop irrigation).

Overland flow (OF) is the term used to describe the third land treatment process, wherein filtration, sedimentation, and biological oxidation are used to cleanse the sprayed wastewater as it trickles down carefully graded, sloping terraces planted with water-tolerant turf grasses (such as reed canary grass and fescue) planted on relatively impermeable soils. The treated runoff is collected in drainage channels or ditches at the toe of the slope, from which it is usually piped to subsurface disposal areas. As with all land treatment systems, pretreatment is necessary, and could range from primary clarification to one day of aeration in a containment cell.

OF typically removes 50 to 70 percent of phosphorus through soil adsorption and precipitation, and 75 to 90 percent of nitrogen through crop uptake and denitrification (USEPA, 1981). Over 20 municipal OF systems are operational around the country. They can be designed to work successfully in cold-winter climates, as has been demonstrated in Hanover, New Hampshire.

The three types of systems can also be designed to operate in combination. For example, overland flow can be followed by rapid infiltration or, alternatively, the effluent treated through rapid infiltration can be pumped via recovery wells and applied to the land through the slow rate (USEPA, 1981).

WASTEWATER RECLAMATION AND REUSE

A much refined variation of the "land application" method is called "wastewater reclamation and reuse." Unlike "land application," it does not depend on soils or plant vegetation to provide necessary additional treatment. It is distinguished by significantly higher levels of treatment of the wastewater before it is recycled. This treatment is achieved in deep aerated "cells" with a residence time of 14 to 40 days. Aeration rates vary with climatic conditions, but typically far exceed those occurring in conventional secondary sewage treatment plants.

As in typical "land treatment" processes, wastes are macerated or pulped before being introduced near the bottom of the first cell, and they do not come into contact with the atmosphere until after rising up through 10 to 20 feet of heavily aerated wastewater. By that time, odors have been virtually eliminated. In the classic three-cell system the effluent stays in the first cell one day, the second cell four days, and remains in the third cell for nine more days. The macerated solids accumulate at the bottom of these cells. Over time, the organic matter (up to 90 percent of the solids) breaks down into carbon dioxide, methane, and water. Space is provided at the bottom of the cells to accommodate solids that do not decompose in the superaerated wastewater. Due to this minimal sludge accumulation rate, cells can typically accommodate this material for 10 or more years before removal is necessary (Sheaffer and Sellers, 1994).

A distinguishing feature of such systems, which they share with "land treatment," is their much larger storage capacity, which is designed to hold the reclaimed wastewater during cold or rainy periods when crops cannot make effective use of the nutrients (up to 150 days of storage in northern locations such as Michigan, but just 1/10 that in southern Delaware). In some states, no further treatment is required when the effluent is used for crop watering. In Northglenn, Colorado, this type of system (14 days of aeration in deep lagoons, followed by storage) is used to turn household sewage into nutrient-rich irrigation water. In annual city reports from Northglenn, BOD and TSS levels are listed as having averaged 7.9 mg/l and 5.3 mg/l, and fecal coliform counts as having averaged 15.2 per 100 ml between 1983 and 1989 (Sheaffer and Sellers, 1994). These results are surprisingly low for systems without slow sand filters, and without any form of disinfection.

Additional "polishing" by sand filtration is recommended by some leading officials at the USEPA. When wastewater is filtered, particulate matter is removed. These particulates are actually tiny bits of organic matter that cling to, surround, and would otherwise protect viruses from biological processes and chlorination. Table 13-1 shows the water quality levels reported by the Wheaton, Illinois, engineering firm of Sheaffer and Roland for various stages of their system design for wastewater reclamation and reuse at Hamilton Lakes, in Itasca, Illinois, involving a closed loop of storm water, wastewater, water facilities, and reuse for irrigation purposes (Sheaffer and Sellers, 1994). Treatment is provided by a two-cell deep aerated lagoon, storage, and intermittent sand filtration. Chlorination is available if needed to destroy fecal coliforms. The performance data were recorded at the Hamilton Lakes system. The figures are considered to be unusually low by other water quality engineers.

The irrigation water contains essentially no fecal coliforms per 100 ml. When the reclaimed water is to be used to irrigate and fertilize golf courses, public parks, or landscaped areas around buildings, filtration and disinfection should be included in the system design. In St. Petersburg, Florida, the city has installed a secondary water supply system to pipe reclaimed wastewater to public parks, golf courses and other open spaces, and to private properties for lawn watering purposes.

Living proof that this technology performs very well can be seen at many of the 50 such systems in the greater Chicago area designed by the Wheaton, Illinois, firm of Sheaffer and Roland. Perhaps one of the most convincing is the one now in operation

Table 13–1. Hamilton Lakes System Water Quality: February 1983 to May 1989

Location	BOD	SS	NH_3-N	NO_3-N	TKN	TOTAL N
Influent	236.0	215.8	23.5	0.5	34.2	34.7
Aeration Cells	23.9	44.9	8.0	4.8	11.3	16.1
Storage Lagoons	8.6	25.6	4.1	1.4	6.6	8.0
Sprinkler Head	3.7	9.5	3.1	3.8	3.5	7.3

Note: All values in milligrams per liter.

at an upscale residential development known as The Fields of Long Grove, which received the 1988 "Best in American Living Award" from the National Association of Home Builders, Better Homes and Gardens, and Professional Builders. This project is further described in Chapter 20, "Residential Cases."

Another region where this approach is currently being applied by many institutions and municipalities is southeastern Pennsylvania, where the Brandywine Conservancy, the Brandywine Valley Association, and the Red Clay Valley Association have been enthusiastic advocates for many years. One of the long-term goals of these groups is for all sewage treatment facilities in the Delaware River watershed to employ this technology, so that most of the wastewater produced in the region will be renovated and recycled on lands permanently dedicated to agricultural, recreational, or other open space uses. The objective is to make this watershed the first area in the country to attain the national goal of eliminating pollutant discharge into navigable waters.

When applied to cropland, sprinklers in a wastewater renovation, reclamation, and reuse system administer the recycled water typically at a rate of $\frac{1}{10}$ to $\frac{1}{4}$ inch per hour, for 8 to 20 hours a week, but only when the soil temperature an inch below ground level is above 40° F, when soils are not wet, when it is not raining, and when wind speeds are low. Spray rates are typically adjusted by system operators, who monitor site conditions. In areas where the natural groundwater is high, horizontal site drainage must be designed to avoid surfacing of partially treated wastewater. Another more costly alternative is to install underdrains to keep the upper soil layers from becoming saturated from below. Well-engineered systems will also include monitoring wells both upslope and downslope from the irrigation areas.

Land treatment systems of these types have been installed in Itasca, Illinois; Northglenn, Colorado; Pot Nets, Delaware (inland bays); and The Fields of Long Grove, Long Grove, Illinois. In Muskegon, Michigan, public officials rejected plans for a costly conventional treatment plant when the engineers admitted that it would only prevent further degradation of the quality of the water in Muskegon Lake, which was then almost as murky as pea soup. Since the installation of the innovative wastewater reclamation and reuse system (which contains underdrains because of high groundwater conditions), lake water has become clear again, with visibility down to 15 feet. Formerly unusable for recreation, the lake is now the second most popular location for the sale of three-day out-of-state fishing licences (Sheaffer and Sellers, 1994). Although less expensive to build than conventional treatment plants, the Muskegon system is still more costly to create than many small rural communities could easily afford, unless the irrigation value of its treated effluent (about $150 per acre, per year) can be realized. When its relatively low annual operating costs are taken into consideration, this system is less expensive than package treatment plants offering comparable performance.

This approach, and similar "land treatment" systems, are conceptually different from the others described in this chapter as they reuse, rather than dispose of, the wastewater generated by new development. The environmental engineers who design these systems view pollutants essentially as "usable resources out of place." As in "land application," this approach provides nutrient-rich irrigation water, recharges groundwater, and enables development to be designed in a more compact manner to preserve farmland, scenic landscapes, and the rural settings of historic properties.

IMPLICATIONS OF PRIVATE SEWAGE FACILITIES

Rising concern about the negative effects of low-density rural sprawl caused by large-lot zoning requirements (which are themselves a crude attempt to achieve "pollution dilution"), and the presumed impacts on housing affordability, led nine Massachusetts state agencies to evaluate the environmental impact of allowing much wider use of small, privately owned sewage treatment facilities (PSTFs) in the Commonwealth. The prospect of the state significantly liberalizing its hitherto very conservative position regarding new PSTFs literally struck fear in the hearts of many municipal officials who envisioned the new technology acting as a "can opener," allowing developers to subdivide large tracts of land that were otherwise legally unbuildable under existing requirements for individual septic systems.

The nine agency sponsors hired engineering and planning consultants to collect and interpret the best available hard data and verbal information from a wide range of experienced practitioners and officials in Massachusetts and 11 other states. After a long series of public meetings, a preliminary and a final "generic environmental impact report" (or "GEIR") were printed and distributed, in which all voiced concerns were addressed.

Acknowledging that some problems have been occasionally experienced in other states, the sponsors pointed out that actual results logged by the several dozen PSTFs operating in Massachusetts were very respectable in terms of BOD_5 and TSS. This success was attributed to the higher standards set in Massachusetts for several measurable criteria of water quality and the introduction of an additional standard for total nitrogen reduction.

After reviewing all the data and listening to numerous public comments, the sponsors concluded that "there is no reasonable environmental public health basis for prohibiting PSTFs outright everywhere in a community" (Final GEIR, Nov. 1990). However, two classes of areas were identified as warranting restrictions on PSTFs. "Off-limits" areas would include floodways, rare and endangered species habitats, restricted wetlands, and "Zone I" of public drinking water supplies. Other environmentally sensitive areas require "special care" in permit review: 100-year floodplains, and land within one-half mile of public water supplies or adjacent to rare/endangered species habitats. Rather than continuing to rely upon archaic regulations on septic tank installation as a crutch to compensate for inadequate zoning, the sponsors felt that towns should be encouraged to link PSTF use with progressive land-use planning. PSTFs can be viewed as a tremendously positive opportunity to implement real growth management, enabling village centers to become development nodes even if they have only relatively small areas of good soils. Development rights transfers

(TDRs) could also be implemented to protect rural farmland, scenic vistas, and outlying habitat from low-density sprawl development on septic systems, by deflecting that growth to revitalized village centers outfitted with PSTFs.

In comments submitted to the sponsors, the Center for Rural Massachusetts strongly urged that permits for PSTFs be tied to a requirement that the resulting development be designed in such a way that significant open space would be preserved as a consequence. In addition to TDRs, the use of compulsory open space subdivision design techniques was also urged to accomplish this goal. It was widely felt that PSTFs should not be allowed to become a technological solution enabling developers to subdivide otherwise mostly unbuildable land in the conventional checkerboard fashion, with little or no open space provision (other than wetlands or steep slopes).

The only remaining issue is not a technical but an administrative or legal one: Massachusetts laws will need to be amended to ensure long-term enforceability of state health regulations against multiple-ownership entities, such as homeowners' associations. The Massachusetts Department of Environmental Protection has identified six conditions it feels are necessary to guarantee accountability for jointly owned PSTFs. Because this issue frequently arises in many other states, and because it is so fundamentally important, these conditions are listed below.

1. To ensure that a single entity, fundamentally identical to the users of the facility, is responsible for the operation, maintenance, repair and replacement of the facility

2. To ensure that all the users share the financial and operational responsibilities the above obligations entail, that record notice of the responsibilities is given to all prospective purchasers, and that no user can avoid these responsibilities

3. To ensure that the entity has the authority to institute a user-charge system capable of generating adequate revenues

4. To ensure that the entity maintains a "ready fund" to finance emergency repairs and a "capital fund" adequate to replace the system and key components at the end of their useful lives

5. To ensure that the entity could not alter these arrangements without prior written approval of the Massachusetts Department of Environmental Protection

6. To ensure that the entity owns or has a legal easement to the land on which the PSTF is situated

In North Carolina, the state Department of Environment, Health, and Natural Resources comprehensively addressed issues of operation and maintenance relating to large septic systems in 1991 amendments to its *Laws and Rules for Sanitary Sewage Collection, Treatment, and Disposal* (15A NCAC 18A .1900). For example, septic systems handling more than 3,000 GPD (about 12 dwellings) are classified by the state as "Type V," and are required to obtain an operating permit from the state, which is reviewed annually. All system owners must also contract with "certified management entities," which are required to inspect the facilities regularly and to report their findings regarding certain variables to the local health department at specific frequency intervals. Required inspection frequencies vary from monthly for systems handling between 3,000 and 10,000 GPD, to weekly for larger systems. Reports must be filed every six months.

In Pennsylvania, state officials require municipal governments to be co-permittees of all new community septic systems, as a way of ensuring that there will always be a responsible authority to perform repairs promptly in the event of a system failure. In Delaware, "trust indentures" assign system responsibility to a chain of governmental bodies, from municipalities to counties to state agencies.

SEPTIC SYSTEM DESIGN INNOVATION

In Maine, a fresh approach to subsurface septic disposal system design has relevance to other rural areas where the majority of soils are rated poor to very poor for this purpose. In that northern state, 81 percent of the mapped land acreage is classified into these two categories on the basis of slow permeability, shallow bedrock or restrictive hardpan, or seasonally high water tables.

After extensive field checking in the early 1970s, that state's health engineering officials found per-

colation testing to be unreliable under the above-described conditions. Many unsuitable areas had been (in effect) illegally developed with conventional systems that were not designed to compensate for the difficult soil conditions, and these ultimately experienced high failure rates. As a result, Maine's site evaluation methods and system design criteria were extensively revised in 1974.

After the new rules had been in effect for a decade, state officials reviewed the track records of the 64,000 new systems and found that failure rates had decreased dramatically, to 0.1 percent, 1.0 percent, and 5.0 percent for systems in place for one, five, and ten years respectively (Hoxie and Trick, 1984). Newer design techniques, using concrete chambers over disposal beds, posted the same success rate even though their bed areas covered only half the land area required for conventional systems.

Another significant finding was that decreasing the required vertical separation distance between the bottom of the disposal bed and the bedrock, hardpan, or seasonal high water table from 48 inches to 24 inches may not adversely affect system performance. It has long been documented in the engineering field that nearly all the bacterial treatment of septic wastes occurs in the first 12 inches of soil around and under disposal beds, by soil adsorption, so that the bacterial population that is found more than a foot below the bottom of the bed is "about the level of the population in the control soil" (USEPA, Sept. 1978).

In addition to using concrete chambers to reduce bed area and the minimum required vertical separation distances, Maine authorities also abandoned percolation testing in favor of pits dug 48-inches deep (or until bedrock is encountered), into which "licensed site evaluators" enter to determine the depth of the seasonal high water table. These evaluators are trained, examined, and licensed to make such determinations based upon visual and tactile inspections of factors such as soil texture, color, and rooting depth. Soil is then classified according to three categories of depth to bedrock, four categories of depth to seasonal high water, and eleven soil profiles based on textural differences at various depths. Although more complex than pouring water into a hole and timing its seepage into the earth, Maine's test pit evaluations have proven to be a very effective way of determining a soil's ability to filter and treat septic effluent. Such testing has the additional advantage of being able to be performed at any time of the year when the land is accessible (while many jurisdictions limit "perc" testing to a 6 to 8-week period in the spring).

CONSTRUCTED WETLANDS

The use of artificial wetlands for domestic wastewater treatment is gaining wider acceptance as experimental systems around the country are being refined. No fewer than 120 such systems were installed at individual homesites in Kentucky during 1991. Other states where this technique is being applied, at least on a trial basis, include Virginia, West Virginia, Arkansas, Louisiana, Alabama, and Colorado. Seen as a supplement rather than as a substitute, constructed wetlands are being designed as intermediate components providing further treatment of septic tank effluent before it is conducted to drainage fields.

Based on standards developed by the Tennessee Valley Authority (TVA), these systems typically outperform conventional designs in the reduction of solids and biological oxygen demand (Schutz, 1992). Depending on their design, all or some of the effluent they produce is still disposed of in filtration fields, but its finer quality reduces the risk of soil clogging (and also makes artificial wetlands very suitable as replacements for failed conventional systems located on marginal soils).

The newer designs for constructed wetlands for individual homes are typically shaped like volleyball courts 300 square feet in area, with plastic membrane liners and 12 or more inches of gravel on which cattails and bullrushes are planted. In the dense mat formed by their roots, biological, physical, and chemical processes occur, purifying the wastewater. In the new TVA model, a second cell contains gravel topped with layers of loam and mulch, in which ornamental wetland species such as iris, arrowhead, and elephant ear are planted.

In addition to their use in residential applications, such wetlands are beginning to play a role in treating agricultural animal wastes, such as milk-house wastes and effluent from animal waste treatment lagoons and aquaculture ponds. Cost sharing in this experimental program is available to farmers from the Agricultural Stabilization and Conservation Service of the United States Department of Agriculture.

ALTERNATIVE SEWER SYSTEMS

A novel idea for simplifying sewer design could achieve significant cost savings for private centralized and municipal sewage systems. Called "septic tank effluent drains," this approach has been widely used in South Australia since 1961.

Briefly stated, effluent drains are small-diameter gravity lines that can potentially be installed inexpensively with simple trenching machines. As their name implies, they conduct liquid effluent from septic tanks, which collect the settleable solid wastes (that must be pumped out periodically). The fact that effluent drains carry no solids, grease, or grit allows them to be designed with smaller bores and to be installed without a continuously downward-sloping gradient, as minimum flow velocity normally needed for self-cleansing is not necessary. According to the USEPA, "Excavation costs could be reduced substantially since these drains could follow the natural topography more closely than conventional sewers and avoid most obstructions within their intended path" (Otis, 1983). Five other advantages also characterize these innovative systems, as described by Otis:

1. Material costs are lower because septic tanks absorbing surges from peak flow periods allow pipes to be downsized (to 2 inches), and manholes may be replaced by less expensive cleanouts or flushing points.

2. Operation and maintenance costs are lower because unskilled labor can perform the few necessary tasks of septic tank pumping and drain flushing.

3. Compared with conventional sewers, groundwater infiltration is lessened because the drains are smaller in diameter and can be installed at shallower depths.

4. With no solid wastes to push along, minimum flows are not required, and much less wastewater is therefore needed, reducing loads on the treatment facility and avoiding concerns that wide use of water-saving devices or fixtures could create blockages in the lines.

5. Treatment plants can be built more simply as it is not necessary to provide screening, grit removal or, sometimes, even primary sedimentation, as settleable solids are collected in septic tanks at each dwelling.

Construction costs of effluent drains can range up to 50 percent lower than conventional sewers. However, despite three decades of very successful use in South Australia, officials in the United States have generally not permitted effluent drains to vary substantially from the design of conventional sewers, citing "uncertainty in their long-term performance" [!] (Otis, 1983). The USEPA reports, however, that an effluent drain system installed in Westboro, Wisconsin, in 1977, serving 200 people with 85 connections, "has had an excellent record of operation, only requiring pumping of septic tanks every three years" (Kreissl, 1984).

When these innovative systems are allowed to be designed less elaborately, more in line with the actual character of the liquid effluent they convey, significant savings will become possible. This is because drainage pipes typically absorb 60 percent to 80 percent of the total construction budgets for new sewage collection and treatment facilities. Because of their lower residential density, the average length of sewer pipe per user in small rural communities can be up to five times greater than the national average (15 feet), meaning that savings in piping could dramatically reduce total project costs in such places (Otis, 1983).

The potential for retrofitting existing villages experiencing widespread septic system failure, and encouraging compactly designed village extensions (based on historic settlement patterns), offers new opportunities to creative planners, enterprising developers, and alert officials. When combined with "open space development design" (described in Chapters 14 and 15), effluent drains can help resolve current sewage disposal problems, promote traditional neighborhood design,

preserve open space, and lower costs (through less expensive facilities and expanded user populations, among whom costs would be shared).

Effluent treatment need not be restricted to conventional plants, but may occur though a variety of alternative facilities described in this chapter, including large soil absorption systems, contour systems, land treatment (or "spray irrigation"), and water reclamation/re-use systems. Some of these systems already utilize alternative wastewater collection technology, such as *low pressure sewers* (minimum 2-inch diameter, with grinder pumps) and *vacuum sewers* (minimum 3-inch diameter, with pneumatic valves at each connection). However, with virtually no mechanical components, effluent drains are simpler and less expensive, although they are limited to locations where very modest gravity flow is physically possible. Nevertheless, low-pressure and vacuum systems have generally performed well, and also represent a viable engineering alternative to conventional sewer construction (Kreissl, 1984).

WASTEWATER VOLUME REDUCTION

Treatment system size, cost, and land requirements can be reduced through a variety of simple techniques that lessen the volume of wastewater that is generated. This can be especially important in locations where the areal extent of soils suitable for subsurface disposal is rather limited, owing to generally unfavorable site conditions. Four broad approaches are described below: eliminating unnecessary water consumption, installing water-saving devices, recycling water for re-use, and employing waterless toilets.

Most households waste water on a daily basis, some much more than others. Examples of "nonfunctional water use" include flushing cigarette butts, running dishwashers half full, and allowing the taps to run while brushing teeth or shaving. Surprisingly, a steadily dripping faucet could double the water consumption of a typical family of four, wasting as much as several hundred gallons per day (Schmidt, Boyle et al., 1980). Leaking toilets and "sweeping" asphalt driveways with garden hoses are other common sources of waste.

Achievable reductions in water use range from 4 to 8 percent for "dams" or plastic bottles inserted into toilet tanks; 6 to 10 percent for low-flush toilets; and 6 to 15 percent for gadgets that convert conventional toilets into "dual-flush" toilets (making it possible for users to select a "low-flush" mode for liquid wastes). Flow restrictors and reduced-flow shower heads can cut normal 4 to 10 gallon per minute usage to 1.5 to 3-gallons per minute.

Wide variations exist in the water consumption of different clothes washers. Front-loading models can save 40 percent, and even greater reductions can be achieved in models that store and reuse the soapy wash-cycle water (fresh water is, of course, still used for rinsing). Water recycling has been taken much farther in home systems that reuse sink, bath, shower, and laundry water for toilet flushing, and sometimes for lawn irrigation, too. These systems typically involve storage tanks, filters, and chemicals.

In addition, unnecessary strains on wastewater treatment systems can be avoided by improved user habits, such as not flushing disposable diapers or sanitary napkins, not washing cooking fats or grease down the sink, and not using garbage disposals (which add significant quantities of BOD_5 and suspended solids, increasing sludge and scum accumulation (Schmidt et al., 1980).

Much has been written about "waterless" toilets (sometimes called "biological" or "composting" toilets). Originally designed for use in seasonal cabins in Scandinavia, these units have had to be extensively redesigned for year-round household usage there and elsewhere. Most modern units utilize ventilation fans, electric heating elements, and mechanical mixers to speed the evaporation of liquid wastes and to promote bacterial action and biological decomposition.

Because liquids account for 90 percent of total human body wastes, the importance of heaters and fans in evaporating this moisture cannot be underestimated. These heaters and fans add significantly to operating costs, as they typically consume about 6 kWh daily in households of five people (Kreissl, 1986). Because of their high operating costs, high capital costs (starting at $1,000), the need to empty humus residues every 3 to 4 months, and their limited capacity to deal with overload situations during social occasions, such units will probably not enjoy widespread popularity.

Another drawback is homeowners' continued need to treat their greywater adequately. Greywater typically comprises two-thirds of total household wastewater and contains pathogens (Kreissl, 1986). Field studies conducted for the USEPA indicate that standard septic tanks and soil absorption systems still offer the most reliable method of greywater treatment. Most of the alternative methods of dealing with greywater have "failed to perform their functions successfully" (Enferadi et al., 1986).

CHAPTER

14

Encouraging
Open Space Design

A number of different incentives can be offered to encourage developers to utilize progressive "open space design" techniques when laying out their subdivisions. While it is highly preferable that local planning jurisdictions adopt regulations requiring that developments adhere to the principles of open space development design (OSDD), in some instances such a course may not be politically feasible, at least not at the present. Although making open space development design a basic requirement is not an illegitimate extension of public authority, and although it does not in any way disturb a developer's constitutional right to a "reasonable and beneficial use" of his or her property, in some areas it may take more time (and further bad experience with conventional subdivision design) before this approach gains local acceptance. This chapter describes a variety of special incentives and other techniques intended to encourage developers to incorporate open space principles into their proposals.

CREATIVE SKETCHES AND
SPECIAL INCENTIVES

In such cases a less strict—but also less effective—policy is to require that developers simply prepare inexpensive conceptual sketch plans showing how their proposed subdivisions could be laid out under OSDD standards, as set forth in the zoning code. Just participating in such an exercise may help open a few minds to some of the possibilities for a more sensitive arrangement of roads and buildings. Special incentives to submit an OSDD layout, such as reduced street widths and center-

line radii, waiver of curb and catch basin requirements (where gross densities are less than four units per acre), and allowing for occasional gradients of 8 to 10 percent, could substantially reduce costs, while not jeopardizing public safety. (See Chapter 11 for a discussion of road standards appropriate for rural subdivisions.)

This approach is sometimes called "mandatory-voluntary" because the applicant is required to submit an open space sketch plan, which he or she is then free to pursue or reject. Occasionally the services of a local conservation organization (such as a land trust) can be enlisted to help with the "open space" design. In West Vincent Township in Chester County, Pennsylvania, the Brandywine Conservancy Environmental Management Center was hired to prepare alternative OSDDs, based on different objectives (i.e., preservation of land for informal recreation, and preservation of the agrarian landscape). Both of these alternatives are shown in Figure 14–1, along with the developer's "by right" large-lot proposal and the result obtainable using the township's currently weak "cluster" option (which provided no real design standards addressing the issues of farmland or rural landscape protection). After many months of further negotiation, the developer eventually agreed to follow a variation of the conservancy's "Alternative Open Space Plan." The result is a plan that contains 58 dwellings (40 rural lots, 10 village lots, and 8 attached units), while preserving 62 percent of the parcel as permanent open space, with an extensive trail system. Most importantly for the township, the rural landscape views

226

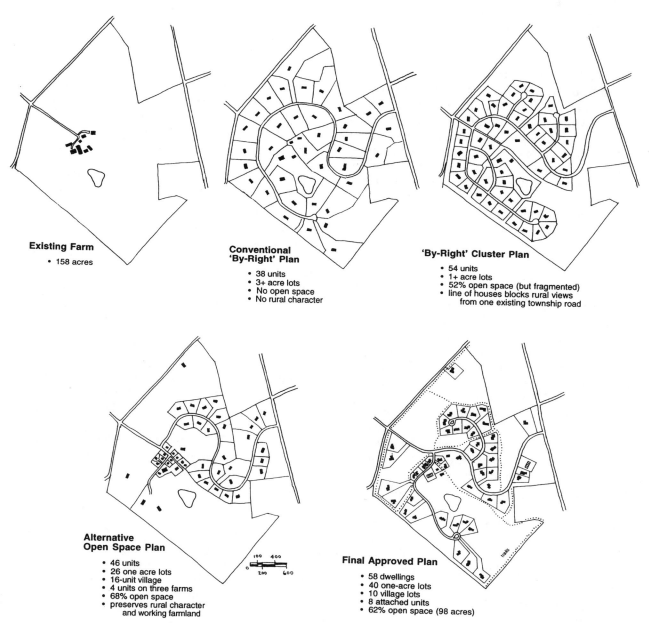

Figure 14–1. These sketches illustrate the preexisting situation at Larking Hill in West Vincent Township, Chester County, Pennsylvania, contrasted with the developer's "by-right" checkerboard plan for 38 three-acre lots; a simple cluster of 54 one-acre lots providing 52 percent open space; and a more sophisticated alternative cluster combining estate lots, large suburban lots, and village lots to permanently preserve 68 percent of the parcel as open space. The fifth sketch shows the final approved plan with 62 percent open space and an extensive trail system. *Source:* Brandywine Conservancy, 1992.

from existing public roads will be essentially protected. The open space, which will be jointly owned by a homeowners' association, will be rented to neighboring farmers.

Greater immediate success was achieved in Grafton, Massachusetts, when the planning board began to think creatively after losing a close vote on amending the town's ordinances to require two alternative layouts (conventional and OSDD) for all new subdivisions containing five or more lots. Even though applicants would be free to pursue conventional designs if they preferred to do so, after evaluating the open space alternative on their sites, certain influential landowners remained philosophically opposed to "cluster development." In a state where a two-thirds majority vote of residents at "town meeting" is required to adopt or revise zoning regulations, it is not difficult for objectors to raise a 34 percent minority vote to block progressive measures.

Shortly after its defeat at town meeting, the planning board invited leading opponents to attend a special meeting to discuss their objections to the amendment. At this meeting it became evident that the opposition had not understood the potential benefits possible by applying OSDD principles, and that they were fearful of the results of this "unknown" technique. At that point the idea arose to prepare an alternative, flexible subdivision design for a parcel owned by one of the principal objectors (for which he already had an approved conventional subdivision plan), purely for demonstration purposes. He readily agreed, and the board hired three graduate students from the Conway (Massachusetts) School of Landscape Design to suggest alternative layouts on that 70-acre property and also on another 20-acre rural site in town (Freed, Goodhue and Speth, 1991).

Care was taken to involve the two landowners in the design process, which proved to be highly successful in helping everyone to understand how the proposed amendment would work in real situations. The result exceeded the board's expectations, with former opponents becoming enthusiastic allies. The exercise also clearly showed how the bonus system operates, with 15 percent, 20 percent, and 25 percent density increases awarded if six, nine, or all of the twelve design guildelines contained in the ordinance were respected. These guidelines address issues such as maintaining open fields, preserving scenic vistas, protecting wildlife habitat, retaining natural vegetative buffers around water bodies or wetlands and along watercourses, preserving historic sites, creating adequate recreational areas, designing effective pedestrian circulation (including trail systems), and ensuring that the common land abuts protected open space on adjoining parcels, where such exists.

On one of the properties, 31 acres (43 percent of the site) was preserved as open space and road length was cut from 5,800 feet to 4,700 feet. This was achieved even while accommodating an increase in houselots, from 57 to 68, by using more compact houselots (16,650 versus 40,000 square feet, on average). The open space design included one mile of trails and protected three fields from development (parts of which are suitable for conversion to active recreational use, such as soccer fields).

A key aspect of the design process was that it was conducted by persons trained in landscape architecture (as required under Grafton's ordinance), who prepared multiple overlay maps of the site analyzing soils, slopes, wetlands/drainage, legal restrictions, vegetative cover, site assets, and most desirable house locations. Among the "site assets" identified were open fields, conifer stands, stone walls, outward views, and privacy afforded by wooded areas. The costs of such site analyses are modest when compared to total project costs, and the superior designs produced result in more salable real estate (see Chapter 16, "Greenways and Buffers"). Copies of this excellent report, which also contains the text of Grafton's "flexible development" zoning bylaw amendment (one of the better models), are available from the Conway School of Landscape Design, Conway, Massachusetts.

Local governments should consider requiring that subdivision plans be prepared by a team of professionals that must include landscape architects. Furthermore, site analysis of the type described above should also be required for most subdivisions. A modest density bonus (or modification of road standards) could easily offset any additional costs incurred. Subdivision regulations should also be amended to provide guidance to landowners, developers, and site designers, informing them of general principles basic to good design. Such a document has been published by the Vermont Council on the Arts (Babize and Cudnohufsky, 1991). Among its recommendations are:

- Avoid building in the center of a meadow
- Reduce visual prominence by building into woodland edges
- Maintain irregular field edges when they occur
- Avoid large setbacks from the road if the lot is small or near a village center
- Avoid building on north-facing slopes or on ridgelines
- Locate septic systems to the south to create a clearing allowing more winter sunshine into the home
- Open up views through pruning limbs and selective tree removal, as opposed to clear-cutting

Other site design criteria could address issues such as avoidance of critical wildlife habitat areas, preservation of significant site features (stone walls, large tree stands, etc.), and providing for road connections and trail linkages between current and future subdivisions.

Taking the idea of preparing creative sketches several steps further, the Natural Lands Trust, of Media, Pennsylvania, has for several years operated a "Community Land Stewardship Program." Key to this program's success has been its emphasis on building cooperative relationships between private landowners and local governments. Going beyond the scope of land-use regulation, the trust encourages rural property owners to consider a range of alternative methods that would achieve their financial objectives while also protecting natural resources, wildlife habitats, and working landscapes. These methods include land donations, dedication of conservation easements, limited development, and open space development design. What is somewhat different about the trust's approach is that it deals with entire rural neighborhoods comprising a number of adjacent landowners, so that the individual plans it pre-

pares will protect larger areas and avoid conflicting land-use patterns (Clarke, 1992). In these rural neighborhoods the trust's staff devises integrated strategies involving a variety of different techniques for land conservation, including both "limited" and "open space" development.

DENSITY BONUSES

Another type of incentive is to offer developers the opportunity to subdivide their land into a greater number of houselots. However, the difficulty here is that unless the financial incentive is substantial, most developers will not be willing to change from their conventional and familiar "cookie-cutter" approach (which is often the *only* form with which they have had any firsthand experience). And when incentives become too large it becomes difficult to preserve much buildable land as open space. In addition, there is often popular resistance to "giving" developers any extra units at all, even a modest percentage increase.

These opponents miss the point: that the resulting provision of open space is far more important to their community in the long run than the additional public costs associated with a marginal increase in the number of new residents living in the subdivision. Once land is checkerboarded into "wall-to-wall houselots," it is nearly impossible to retrofit greenways, trails, parks, and neighborhood playing fields into the established pattern. The approved plat, for better or worse, is essentially "chiseled in granite."

This opposition can be expected and must not be ignored. Experience in rural and suburban New England suggests that the vast majority of developers do not respond strongly to density incentives in the typical range of 10 percent to 15 percent. In Concord, Massachusetts, for example, only a small fraction have taken advantage of the voluntary cluster option that has been a local zoning option for nearly 20 years. In many other communities this option has never been exercised at all.

Large density incentives are more likely to be politically acceptable in areas where the legal development density is very low to begin with, because greater increases can be permitted without severely compromising the rural resource. A recently adopted zoning provision in the Bozeman area of Gallatin County, Montana, illustrates this approach. In rural areas where land may be split into 20-acre parcels without any governmental review or approval, the city-county planning board is encouraging more compact development by offering up to a four-fold increase in houselots. To qualify for this bonus, subdivided lots may not exceed one acre in size, and the balance of the development must be preserved for open space.

For example, as shown in Figure 14–2, 100 acres could yield five 20-acre parcels (much too small to farm or ranch in that climate) or twenty one-acre houselots (preserving 80 acres of open space for rangeland or crops). There is nothing special about any of the above numbers. Other areas with similar low-density zoning might prefer to allow a doubling of building parcels (from 5 to 10) while also allowing these lots to be up to two acres in size (if this is deemed necessary for sales purposes in the local real-estate market).

In addition to preserving certain percentages of the parent parcel as open space, density bonuses can be used in more sophisticated ways to encourage other related objectives. In the Conservation Point System devised by Judith Anderson for a small rural township in Charlevoix County, Michigan, extra credit is awarded according to a sliding scale that takes into account the length of shoreline, ridgelands, or public road frontage that clus-

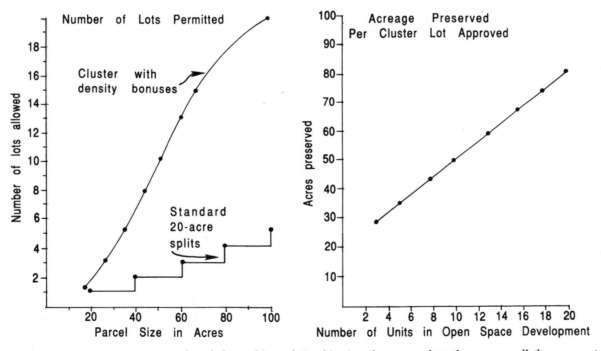

Figure 14–2. Density bonuses often fail to achieve their objectives because when they are small they are not used by many developers, and when they are large they typically defeat their purpose by leaving little opportunity for significant open space preservation. An exception to this rule is illustrated by these graphs, which show that when the base density is exceedingly low to begin with, density bonuses can be hefty (allowing a four-fold increase in units) while still protecting an impressive amount of acreage. In Gallatin County, Montana, 20-acre splits are not uncommon, dividing rangeland into "farmettes" too small to be useful in the semiarid climate around Bozeman. By allowing ranchers to build 20 houses (instead of only five) on a 100-acre parcel, but limiting maximum lot size to one acre, eighty acres of rangeland can be permanently preserved, in a manner that is economically attractive to the landowners.

tering would protect from development and visual intrusion. The greater the length of protected area, the larger the density credit. Similarly, points are increased when the preserved land is also opened for public access or for park purposes. To buffer existing conservation lands and to increase the amount of contiguous protected acreage, extra points are also given in proportion to the length of common boundary between the proposed open space and any adjoining parks, nature preserves, or properties under permanent conservation easement, a feature that should be of considerable interest to park professionals and local land trusts (Anderson, J., 1992).

An alternative to using density bonuses to provide incentives to create more compact development forms is to employ density *penalties* for squandering land in large-lot plats. On the Olympic peninsula in Washington, Clallam County officials have adopted an ordinance that would allow developers to build under current densities (one to five units per acre) only if they cluster. Those rejecting the cluster approach would not be allowed to develop at standard densities, but would be subject to new minimum parcel sizes of 30 acres (Bowers, 1991e). Unlike semiarid Gallatin County, where 20 or 30 acres is not a viable farming unit, climatic conditions in Clallam enable economic farming to occur on parcels of this size (underscoring the importance of drafting such area requirements carefully, based on local agricultural needs). (See also Chapter 18, "Retaining Farmland and Farmers.") A parallel restriction has been adopted for commercial forestland. Regulations incorporating a similar approach are on the books in another rural county at the opposite end of the Evergreen State. In Clark County, which borders Oregon, the basic 20-acre agricultural zoning contains an option allowing clustering to preserve approximately three-fourths of the farmland or forest resources on the development parcel. When the cluster option is chosen, densities are calculated more generously, on the basis of five acres per dwelling, plus two more houselots for every 20 acres of developable land. In other words, in these two Washington counties, the basic choice is between 20- or 30-acre divisions, and cluster-

ing a larger number of homes on approximately three-quarter-acre lots, with 75 percent open space preservation.

THE FOLLY OF LARGE LOTS

However, it is also equally necessary for rural planners to respond to developers' other reservations about downsizing their houselots to preserve open space. Frequently cited is the belief that buyers really want to own larger acreages around their homes. In fact, that is probably what many prospective buyers tell their agents, not considering the time and costs involved in maintaining that land, and not even beginning to think about the greater possibilities for enjoying open space if they were to buy into a development that pooled most of the land into a really large resource area for all the homeowners to enjoy.

For many people the dream of owning rural acreage turns into a nightmare as they discover their enslavement to maintaining large pieces of land. Even a two-acre houselot, if not wooded, is "too large to mow and too small to plow." Commuters with full-time jobs have little time to look after much more than a basic three-quarter-acre houselot. The oft-expressed desire "to look out my window and not see my neighbor's house" reflects a psychological need that is sometimes better satisfied with creative site design and smaller lots. The schematic layout in Figure 14–3 illustrates how all homeowners can have permanently protected views over 80 acres of pasture or cropland, while being screened from their neighbors on either side by plantings of fast-growing native species. (See Chapter 20, "case example" of Trims's Ridge, Block Island, Rhode Island, for detailed illustrations of landscape buffers between homes on an otherwise open site.) The critical factor, when trying to provide privacy on an unwooded parcel, is not distance but buffering. This may be effectively achieved through fencing, hedges, or massing of new evergreen plantings.

On many of the larger "houselots" (say, from 2 to 20 acres) created in agricultural or ranching areas, much of the land is now growing up into weeds. This is not only unsightly but is sometimes a major problem for adjacent farmers. In some

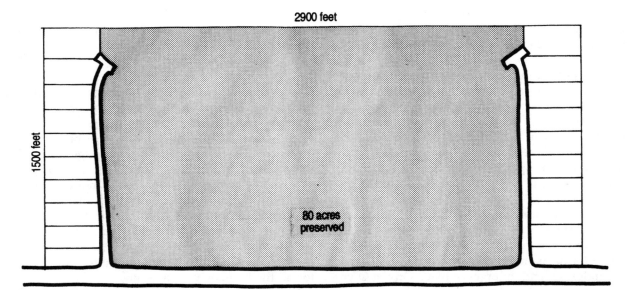

Figure 14–3. In this schematic diagram of a cluster plan for areas where base zoning density is vey low, 20 one-acre houselots with permanent views of the rangeland or farmland have been created, while preserving 80 percent of the 100-acre tract as open space. They are accessed from gravel surfaced "country lanes" or shared drives, constructed to official standards appropriate for their light traffic load (see Chapter 11). The alternative would be to divide this resource into large lots or farmettes, in sizes that would not be viable for commercial production (but which would succeed in cluttering the countryside, despoiling the view, and needlessly removing another 80 acres from its traditional rural use).

western states, hundreds of thousands of dollars are spent annually on weed control, where the principal culprit is large parcel residential development. If every realtor who showed such properties were to wear a large lapel pin proclaiming "Beware of what you set your heart upon: some day it may be yours," possibly fewer well-intentioned suburbanites would make the mistake of buying multiacreage sites to use simply as houselots.

For those who desire extra land for their horses (a frequently cited reason for purchasing such large lots), a far better solution is at hand. In areas where the residential base density is two acres per dwelling, instead of 10 two-acre houselots with no place to ride except around one's houselot and individual stable, 10 families could share a 10-acre pasture or woodland trail system abutting their 10 one-acre houselots. By locating the stables within easy walking distance (but farther than horseflies

are likely to roam), residents may enjoy convenience without nuisance.

REDUCING UNCERTAINTY

However important it is to inform developers, realtors, and the public about the greater advantages offered by open space development design, perhaps the most critical element in this process involves reducing the uncertainty associated with the plan approval process itself. In most jurisdictions, the cards are stacked plainly in favor of conventional cookie-cutter development, and strongly against creative open space alternatives. Standard checkerboard subdivisions are a relatively easy "by right" proposition where the hurdles are few in number and low in height. The most unimaginative conventional plan can readily clear those hurdles, partly because there is so little to review and partly because it is usually very easy to meet the basic requirements for such developments: lot frontage and area, enough dry soil for a foundation and a septic system, and an access road.

By contrast, zoning and subdivision regulations for open space development designs are often loaded with requirements that are vague, excessive, or even counterproductive. Approval is typically dependent upon a "special permit" process where arbitrary and discretionary decision-making is frequently the rule. Such procedures enable review boards to reject proposals on poorly defined grounds, such as "inconsistency with neighborhood character" (whatever that may mean). The fact is that board members in some localities are often more strongly influenced by popular sentiment expressed at hearings than by the degree to which a proposal satisfies all the provisions in their codes.

Some codes impose excessive requirements, such as *public* water and sewer connections, when centralized private facilities would otherwise be possible, or when individual systems could be designed to exceed normal standards. At other times, codes impose unreasonable and self-defeating design criteria, for example by mandating a 150-foot wide buffer around the perimeter of "cluster" subdivisions; much more than is typically required for trailer parks, gravel pits, or junkyards! And frequently the concept of open space development design is entirely prohibited by setting arbitrary limits on minimum parcel size (e.g., 20 acres), or maximum houselot number (20 dwellings, irrespective of acreage), as is done by an otherwise progressive Virginia county that sets no limits on the scale of conventional subdivisions.

Occasionally the restrictions placed on these developments have the effect of stultifying the creative design process, locking site designers into rigid patterns by limiting the number of houses in any single grouping to six or eight, or by requiring 60-foot deep front and side setbacks on 30,000 square foot lots. In other cases regulations call for each and every lot to abut the open space—which leads to some very strange and not particularly beneficial configurations. Other well-intentioned zoning provisions require houselots to be confined to one part of the parcel so that no portion of the

preservation area will "intrude between any development lots."

One basic difficulty in the regulatory world is that so few of the people who write the rules have ever designed (or built) the types of development that are being regulated. The key concepts to emphasize when regulating open space development are *flexibility* and *performance*. In other words, if the design works well from the standpoint of environmental protection, public safety, and rural resource conservation, "how it gets there" should matter little. To avoid such problems, planners without design experience (and most fall into this category) should always consult with creative landscape architects before drafting rules governing open space development design.

To address developers' legitimate concerns, and to correct existing abuses, local planning authorities should consider incorporating five regulatory reforms:

1. Revise the special permit procedure section of the ordinance to state that all applications that fully meet the requirements established for open space subdivisions will be approved.

2. Conduct a public meeting early in the process—at the sketch plan stage—and revise the code language to state that all comments must be directly related to the review criteria (thereby discouraging statements of general sentiment, or objections to the fact that current zoning permits certain uses at specific densities in particular districts, which abuttors may disagree with).

3. Replace vague criteria with clearer language, such as separate design standards for houselots and for the open space. Under the former, the concept of minimum and maximum dimensions for lot frontage and front setback are relevant to ensure a reasonably compact form, with allowances for both a maximum percentage of "flag lots" and/or common driveways. These dimensional standards should be based upon an understanding of traditional villages within the region, and they should be administered somewhat flexibly so that exceptions may be granted by the planning board without reference to strict variance criteria. Open space standards

should include requirements pertaining to the quantity of preserved land (minimum percentage of total site), its *quality* (maximum percentage of unbuildable land), and its *configuration*.
4. Grant irrevocable approval to the original sketch plan, subject of course to preliminary and final plans fully complying with all stated requirements in the relevant codes and ordinances.
5. Eliminate any arbitrary requirements that would inhibit creative designs that would otherwise satisfy the objectives of open space subdivisions, unless they are clearly needed to protect the public health and safety.

Replacing vague ordinance language with more detailed (but not inflexible) design criteria not only help developers and their designers, but also makes the task of review easier by reducing ambiguity. Additionally, it provides a benchmark by which a proposal's compliance may be more fairly measured. Finally, it helps neighboring property owners to understand the legal basis for objections, and goes a long way toward meeting constitutional tests that the zoning procedures guarantee "equal protection under the laws." With such explicit criteria, there is much less chance for discretionary action or special treatment, which may favor local applicants and work against outsiders.

ALTERING PUBLIC PERCEPTIONS

Education is essential to generate public support for OSDDs and to minimize local opposition to such developments when they are proposed. One of the first tasks that needs to be undertaken is to correct negative predispositions against this new approach to land development and conservation, which is often confused in the public mind with "cluster development." Whereas the principal emphasis in cluster housing (as frequently practiced) has often been on creating denser building areas to decrease the costs of site preparation and improvements (roads, utilities, etc.), with residual land leftover for snippets of green space here and there, the OSDD approach is essentially the opposite.

Under OSDD a significant percentage of otherwise buildable land is *designated* as open space from the beginning, in a location and configuration that relates to its ultimate purpose (farming,

outdoor recreation, landscape protection, etc.). Development areas are then designed *around* these natural features. It is this philosophical difference in approach that makes OSDD so suitable for use in rural areas, as well as in suburbanizing regions where residents wish to retain some of the present rural character.

People also need to understand that OSDD is not a devious tool to increase the overall number of houses being built on a parcel, by including wetlands and other unbuildable areas as part of the acreage upon which density is calculated. That OSDD is chiefly a technique to rearrange the pattern and distribution of the roads and structures on the site is a point that should be reemphasized time and again in public meetings.

Calculating density in open space developments must be done in a way that is fair to all parties. Whether or not density bonuses are also offered (and that is a quite separate issue), there must be a clear and equitable method for determining the number of dwellings that will be permitted on individual properties. When "cluster" developments were first being encouraged, during the 1960s, it was not uncommon for municipalities to adopt a simplistic approach to density determination based upon gross acreage, and this predictably produced some disastrous results.

For example, during that era a developer in Warren, Connecticut, calculated the number of dwellings by dividing his parcel size by the minimum lot area required in his district, as allowed under the zoning current at that time. Because half of his site was severely constrained by wetlands, the local planning commission realized that clustering had enabled the developer to effectively double the density he would ordinarily have been able to build had he located the homes on standard one-acre lots. Town officials disapproved his application, were immediately sued, lost in court, and promptly repealed the clustering provision, convinced that adopting flexible design techniques was the greatest mistake they had ever made. Rather than correcting the serious flaw in the way that density was calculated, they eliminated the only practical development design approach that would have allowed the town to preserve dry, buildable open space at no cost to anyone.

As word of similarly bad experiences with clustering filtered around New England, many towns either decided not to adopt cluster provisions at all, or wrote their regulations so that developers could claim no density credit whatsoever for any wetlands, floodplains, or steep slopes on their properties. It did not take the development community very long to figure out that they could easily build more homes in checkerboard subdivisions with standard one- or two-acre lots than they could build after "netting out" all their environmentally constrained lands and basing density on only the remaining portion. The reason, of course, is that zoning typically allows the rear portions of conventional houselots to include land that is wet, flood-prone, or steep. This is not a problem, as long as each houselot contains some minimum area (e.g., 30,000 square feet) that is dry, relatively flat, and suitable for homes, yards, wells, and septic systems.

The clearest, cleanest, and fairest method of determining density is through "yield plans," which are conceptual sketches of conventional layouts drawn realistically so that every lot meets the standard criteria for frontage, area, and minimum percentage of land suitable for homes and yards. In unsewered neighborhoods, applicants should be required to submit evidence that 10 percent of the lots could support septic systems (with local officials selecting the most dubious lots for testing). Lots that fail would be eliminated at once, with another 10 percent being tested until all those in the current sample pass muster. Proposed streets would also be examined to ensure that they would also meet local standards (particularly in terms of maximum gradient). The resultant "lot yield" would determine the number of units permissible in a cluster layout (subject to possible density bonuses, which might be offered as part of an agreement that a certain proportion of the dwellings would meet local affordability criteria).

Developers opting not to prepare conceptual sketch plans demonstrating the density potential of their sites could instead use a "netting-out" formula in the zoning ordinance, which should be carefully calibrated to ensure fairness. In West Bradford Township, Chester County, Pennsylvania, local planning commissioners have field-tested their proposed density formulas through numerous "reality checks," applying them to previously approved conventional subdivisions to make certain that the percentages they have selected for discounting various types of environmentally sensitive land would not have produced significantly more or significantly fewer units than were actually approved in those developments. The goal is to create a set of formulas that will generate new "open space developments" that are density-neutral, compared with conventional "cookie-cutter" layouts.

Another critical issue involves the question of whether *golf courses* may be counted as part of the minimum required open space. Because land for active recreation is a legitimate component of an open space system, a portion of such facilities could quite fairly be included as part of a development's open space requirements (whether they be for golfing, baseball, soccer, football, etc.). But it is strongly recommended that no more than half of the dry upland open space be developed for such uses. (If more land is needed for a course, developers can usually generate it by clustering their condominium units more closely together.)

It is important to retain a balance among the different types of open space, and under normal circumstances no less than one-quarter should remain as woodland or pasture, especially in suburban locations where such kinds of open space are rapidly disappearing under streets, buildings, and lawns. Developers can be expected to argue that golf courses do in fact constitute open space, but the truth is that they are the exclusive domain of a single kind of recreationist, and that this "open space" is unsafe for all other potential users if there is even a single golfer present. With respect to a recent development, cum golf course, proposal near Chapel Hill, North Carolina, the local Sierra Club observed that "considering golf courses as open space is like calling ketchup a vegetable."

Citizens must also be reassured that the open space thus reserved will be permanently protected, via conservation easements cosigned by local governmental bodies *and* by private non-profit organizations (such as land trusts). The two parties can easily prevent easement changes simply by declining any future requests to amend the document to allow further development.

Concerns about the effects on property-tax revenue also need to be squarely addressed. OSDD is tax-neutral, because it changes neither the number of houses nor the total acreage assessed, unless some of the open space is sold or given to local government for public park purposes—a situation that rarely arises.

Public uneasiness about septic system installation at perceived "higher densities" is also common. Fortunately, it can be fairly easily shown that the tremendous site design flexibility inherent in OSDD usually allows for *better* disposal solutions than usually can be achieved with rigid checkerboard lot layouts (see Chapter 13, "Sewage Disposal").

Maintenance and liability issues can also pose major obstacles to garnering public support, but again they can be dealt with to most people's satisfaction when certain safeguards and requirements pertaining to homeowners' associations (HOAs) are explained (see the "Maintenance and Liability Issues" section later in this chapter).

Finally, the public must begin to realise that the privacy enjoyed by new residents on smaller lots will not be appreciably less than they would experience on larger ones. Rural planners in Michigan produced the drawing in Figure 14–4 to show that there is only a 50-foot difference in house spacing between three-quarter-acre lots with a 1:3.3 width to depth ratio (100 feet × 330 feet), and two-acre lots with a similar ratio—1:4 (150 feet × 600 feet).

Proper landscaping and buffering produces greater privacy than an extra 50 feet of separation. The chief difference between these two lot sizes is in their backyard depth. However, since that depth is usually about 250 feet on the three-quarter-acre lot, few people would complain about its inadequacy. The 500-foot backyard depth on the two-acre lot is obviously excessive—nearly the length of two regulation-size football fields laid end to

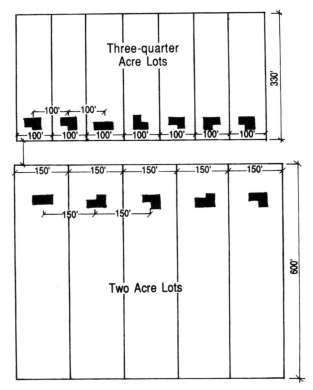

Figure 14–4. The fallacy that large lots are necessary to ensure privacy in one's home or backyard is widespread and deeply ingrained. Simple sketches such as this one, produced by the Livingston County (Michigan) Planning Department, can help dispel such myths by showing that two-acre lots often provide only 50 feet more distance from neighbors than three-quarter-acre lots. The truth is that visual screening (through hedges or fences) is necessary in both instances to create backyard privacy, and that the extra 50 feet of separation is of little value if a neighbor plays the radio or stereo system too loudly. Unfortunately, even a two-acre lot is not very helpful when neighbors are inconsiderate. The advantage of smaller lots is that, in the accompanying example, nearly nine acres of woods or farmland can be permanently preserved, at no extra cost to the developer or the municipality, while preserving the equity of the original rural landowner.

end, an analogy that is particularly useful to draw because it enables many people to visualize these enormous dimensions more concretely.

It is surprising how much difference terminology can make, but the public perception of OSDD was considerably improved in two New England towns when their sponsors coined first-name acronyms to describe this technique. In Granby, Connecticut, the advantages provided by the inherent flexibility of this design approach were underscored by the term "Flexible Residential Development" (or "FRED"). People began to focus upon the natural features that were able to be preserved on the site due to FRED, thereby helping to popularize the concept. Not to be outdone, planners in Marlborough, Connecticut, started referring to their new open space zoning provision as "OSCAR" (for "Open Space Conservation and Residential"). In addition to drawing attention to the positive aspects of these ordinance amendments, this creative terminology stimulated public interest and made discussions more colorful and enjoyable.

COMPARATIVE STUDIES OF REAL ESTATE VALUES IN OPEN SPACE SUBDIVISIONS VERSUS CONVENTIONAL DEVELOPMENT

Another way of building public support for OSDD is to document and publicize the positive economic impact of open space provision upon neighboring property values. While this influence is discussed elsewhere in this book (see Chapter 16, "Greenways and Buffers," and Chapter 17, "The Economics of Preserving Open Space"), it would be appropriate here to describe briefly the results of a research project conducted by the Center for Rural Massachusetts comparing the appreciation differences for homes in two subdivisions where the chief distinguishing difference was in their layout and open space provision (Lacy, 1990).

More than 800 property sales transactions were examined on 227 homes over a 21-year period, in two subdivisions that were built at nearly the same time in the same town at the same overall (gross) density, where the homes were very similar in size and original sales price. The study examined two subdivisions in Amherst, Massachusetts: Orchard Valley (a conventional approach) and Echo Hill (a creative design). Both were built

during the late 1960s and early 1970s at an overall residential density of two dwelling units per acre. Homes in both developments contained about 1,600 square feet of floor space, and sold for average prices of $26,300 and $26,900, respectively. In the former, houselots were about 24,000 square feet (one-half acre), while in the latter the lots were half that size (12,000 square feet, or one quarter acre).

The principal difference between the two subdivisions lay in their designs: Orchard Valley residents have very little open space (except for a relatively small amount of unbuilt land around a pond), while roughly half the acreage in Echo Hill has been designed as common open space, including a large 3.7-acre centrally located playing field (about 200 feet × 750 feet), an extensive woodland trail network, and two ponds, one of which was developed with a small swimming area and an adjacent tennis court and baseball diamond (with backstop). The tennis court also serves for basketball games, with hoops and nets installed along its perimeter fence.

After two decades, homes in each development have appreciated considerably, up to an average price of $134,200 in Orchard Valley and $151,300 in Echo Hill (see Figure 14–5). However the appreciation was 12.7 percent greater in the open space subdivision, where home values rose $17,100 more, on average, by the end of the 21-year study period. It seems clear that people are willing to pay more money for equivalent homes on smaller lots when other amenities are provided in the neighborhood.

TURNING THE TABLES IN PENNSYLVANIA

If sufficient steps are taken to encourage OSDD, such as by reducing an applicant's uncertainty and development costs (for example, through standards for less elaborate roads, as described in Chapter 11), it is possible that these more creative approaches to subdivision design will be proposed more frequently, even without density bonuses. A new approach to OSDD recently devised by the Montgomery County (Pennsylvania) Planning Commission shows how very large percent-

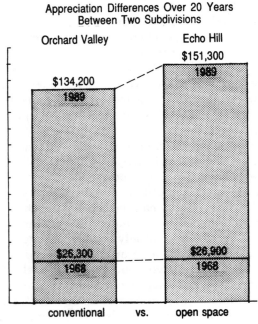

Figure 14–5. The value of neighborhood open space in subdivision design is illustrated in these two graphs of house price appreciation in two subdivisions in Amherst, Massachusetts, built at the same time and at the same overall density. Although homes in both developments were very similar in size and in original sales price, after 20 years the ones in the subdivision with smaller lots and 36 acres of common open space were selling for an average of $17,100 more than their counterparts on lots twice the size.

ages of open space (75 percent) can be preserved without offering any density bonuses or actually requiring such setasides.

Called the "Land Preservation District" (or "LPD"), the intent of this model ordinance is to preserve open space and natural lands on development parcels of 10 or more acres, while also permitting full-equity development in the form of compact residential areas carefully located and designed to reduce their perceived intensity (Montgomery County Planning Commission, 1991). A similar approach had already been implemented in Springfield Township in neighboring Bucks County, but the Montgomery planners took the basic idea several steps further. Although developers are not specifically required to follow this ap-

proach, the tables have been turned, so to speak, in favor of OSDD, chiefly through an ordinance provision allowing standard two-acre platting only as a conditional use. This course has also recently been advocated in Michigan (Livingston County Planning Department, 1991).

In addition to this new twist, LPD also differs from most previous "cluster" techniques in its hefty 75 percent open space requirement, which is achieved by reducing new houselots to 10,000 square feet, just one-eighth their normal two-acre size. Even more compact development can be achieved under this model through "zero lot-line" homes on lots as small as 6,000 square feet, and by setting design standards for traditional new neighborhoods with distinctive identities. Criteria for these neighborhoods limit their size to 25 dwellings, with each such housing group separated from others by buffer areas. Those with more than 10 dwellings are required to provide readily accessible recreational open space at the rate of 1,000 square feet per dwelling unit, typically in the form of a village common or green. Siting of these new neighborhoods is also controlled so that they will avoid sensitive natural areas (prime farmland, stream corridors, etc.), and be screened from nearby public roads, by being tucked behind topographic features or hidden by preexisting or newly planted native trees and shrubs set out in a naturalistic manner.

In addition to the compact neighborhoods, a limited number of estate lots are also allowed in LPDs. Comprising part of the protected open land, these lots must be at least 5, 10, or 15 acres in area, depending on whether the total tract is 10 to 19 acres, 20 to 29 acres, or over 30 acres in area. Standards restrict the building area, driveway, lawn, and gardens to a single acre of such estate lots, the remainder of which must be placed under permanent conservation easement to prevent further subdivision and domestic "improvements" (such as lawn/garden extensions). These lots are also subject to the same locational criteria as neighborhood groupings, that is, away from sensitive lands and concealed from public view to the maximum extent feasible). As explained by former county planner Suzanne Sutro Rhees, the purposes of these estate lots are to help retain working farms

COMMUNITY BUILDOUT
- Existing Conditions

COMMUNITY BUILDOUT
- Conventional 2 Acre Lotting

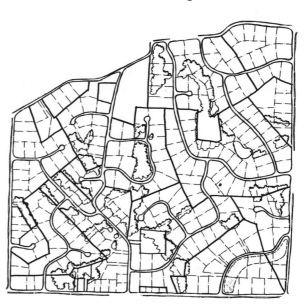

COMMUNITY BUILDOUT
- Land Preservation District

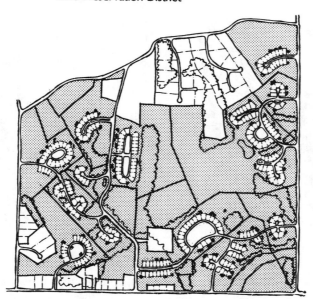

Figure 14–6. These three sketches, prepared by the Montgomery County (Pennsylvania) Planning Department, show a rural neighborhood and two alternative future scenarios. One is to become blanketed with wall-to-wall subdivisions, each consisting of a checkerboard of houselots and streets. Another is to preserve large blocks of land, with many open spaces adjoining one another, through cluster designs on each parcel. *Source:* Prepared by Montgomery County Planning Commission, October, 1990.

and to deal with local concerns about continued management of the preserved open space.

All dwellings in LPDs (except estate lots) are required to be served by a central water supply, either public or private. Septic waste disposal may be via individual septic systems, public sewer, or community systems, typically large absorption fields or "spray irrigation/land treatment" (described in Chapter 13). Despite the small size of neighborhood lots (10,000 square feet), individual septic systems are sometimes still feasible if soil conditions are favorable, because filter beds typically do not occupy more than 1,000 square feet of

land. Since the drinking water supply is centralized, lot size is not a critical concern. However, in most areas, filter beds are more likely to be located on the common or open land behind the downsized houselots (perhaps under neighborhood park facilities, such as playing fields), in locations specified for such facilities on the final plan, and protected for such use by easements.

The sketches in Figure 14–7 illustrate the contrast between conventional two-acre lots and more compact neighborhoods designed according to alternative LPD criteria to protect farmland or to preserve woodland.

DESIGN STUDY – LAND PRESERVATION DISTRICT
- Save Farmland

DESIGN STUDY – LAND PRESERVATION DISTRICT
- Save Woodland

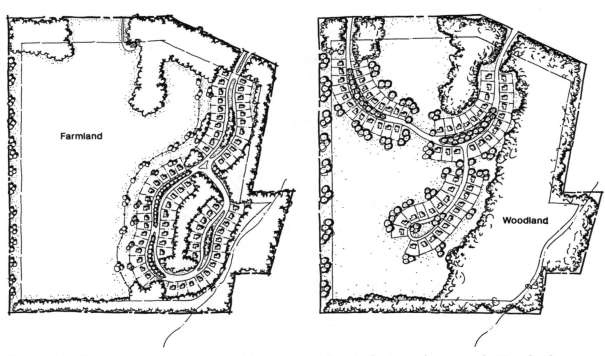

Figure 14–7. Open space preservation priorities vary according to the type of resource that is valued most highly. In wooded regions with relatively few fields and pastures, these open lands are often the areas community residents would most like to see preserved. In agricultural areas where woodland remnants and hedgerows are all that remain untilled, their value for wildlife habitat could alter priorities so that the preferred sites for new development would be on the least prime soil, at the far edge of fields as seen from the public roadway. *Source:* Prepared by Montgomery County Planning Commission, October, 1990.

Developers wishing to build large standard lots may file an application for a conditional use permit in which they must demonstrate to the municipality's satisfaction that all the following conditions are met: 1) the parcel is not suitable for compactly designed "neighborhood development" due to its location, size, shape, or natural features; 2) continued agricultural use (where applicable) is not feasible due to the size and shape of the remaining farmland, considering the efficient use of farm machinery; and 3) the proposed conventional large-lot development would be designed to minimize its visual impact, as seen from existing public roads (specifically discouraging "frontage lots" on such thoroughfares). Its layout and features must also be consistent with both the comprehensive plan and the township's open space plan, and the subdivision must not produce a disruptive effect upon existing topography, floodplains, wetlands, mature woodlands, or other natural features of the site.

Any application for development, either under the compact neighborhood approach or the conditional use standards, must include a complete environmental and visual inventory of the site. Also required for approval of the more compact neighborhood development, this inventory includes information on topography, soils (suitability for farming, septic systems, etc.), water bodies, watercourses, wetlands, floodplains, current land uses, historic/cultural resources (buildings and other structures), scenic views in to and out from the property, and the general context (outlines of buildings, water bodies, woodlands, pastures, etc. within 500 feet of the parcel, which may be traced from aerial photos).

In other areas where woodlands are more abundant and cleared fields are considerably rarer, or in a less suburban context where commercial farming is still a large industry, these model standards would probably take on a somewhat different cast. For example, criterion three above might include "disruptive effects on agricultural land," instead of those on mature woodland, unless the woodlands contained particularly special features, such as stands of rare or mature trees, or significant wildlife habitats. By the same token, the historic/cultural resources criterion might be expanded to include stone walls and abandoned cellar holes in places like New England.

Other variations might be to allow slightly larger houselots of up to 15,000 or 20,000 square feet. In districts where the base density is three or four acres per dwelling unit, such a change would not disturb the overall LPD goal of 75 percent open space protection. However, to maintain a traditional compact village character in the new development area, maximum frontages and front setbacks should be strongly considered (say, 80 to 100 feet and 15 to 20 feet, respectively). Otherwise, the slightly larger lot sizes could produce a decidedly suburban appearance. The LPD approach is outlined in a richly illustrated 21-page publication, *Land Preservation: Old Challenges, New Ideas,* published by the Montgomery County Planning Commission in Norristown, Pennsylvania.

MICHIGAN'S "PEARL"

"Table-turning" is also occurring in rural Michigan, where county planners have devised a model open space zoning amendment called "PEARL" (for "Protecting the Environment, Agriculture, and the Rural Landscape"). The PEARL report, which contains a comprehensive discussion of typical concerns involving open space zoning developments in a question-and-answer format, recommends that open space zoning be implemented by requiring OSDDs in various resource-related overlay districts, and includes a "safety valve" provision that would permit the local planning authority to approve standard large-lot layouts in truly exceptional cases: "only where it can be shown that PEARL is not feasible on the site" (Livingston County Planning Dept., 1991). Such criteria might include site size being too small, or the impossibility of providing open space in locations and amounts that are either usable or which contribute significantly to the preservation of the environment, agriculture, or the rural landscape. In the Michigan example, houselots are reduced from two acres to three-quarter acre to achieve open space preservation between 50 and 60 percent. These lots are not as compact as those provided for in the LPD approach from Pennsylvania because of the greater difficulty in obtaining approvals for alternative sewage disposal arrangements in Michigan and the expected sales resistance to such small lots in that particularly rural area. The PEARL approach is thoroughly described in a particularly well-written 70-page design manual published by the Livingston County Planning Department in Howell, Michigan.

"LANDOWNER COMPACTS"

Effective planning for conservation and development in rural communities can be accomplished on a neighborhood-wide scale through use of a cooperative technique known as the "landowner compact." This approach, a variation of one pioneered by professor Ann Strong three decades ago in *Plan for the Valleys* (Wallace and McHarg, 1963), enables owners of adjoining properties to plan their separate landholdings as a single entity in order to achieve broader conservation objectives, while also designing the total potential development in a more logical and intelligent manner than could be achieved on a parcel-by-parcel basis. Best of all, it does not require government involvement in purchasing development rights, transferring development rights, or land banking, and can usually be undertaken wherever simple "cluster" or OSDD regulations are in effect.

Briefly stated, this technique permits abutting landowners to plan their combined properties comprehensively, essentially allowing them to erase the boundary lines that had formerly separated them (Coughlin et al., 1991). Typically they would enter into a joint agreement describing the amount of developable land each party brings to the project, specifying that net proceeds be divided proportionately according to the *percentage* of the potential development contributed by each partner, regardless of the different land acreages involved.

For example, let us assume three landowners (A, B, and C) together control 200 acres, in parcels of 35, 65, and 100 acres, respectively. Conceptual sketch plans prepared for each property indicate potential development of 30 dwellings on A's land, 30 dwellings on B's, and 40 on C's, taking into account the township's one-acre and two-acre zoning and various site constraints (wetlands, floodplains, and steep slopes). These drawings and calculations determine each owner's "share" of the combined project's net proceeds, irrespective of where development and conservation areas are ultimately located. As shown in Table 14–1, the OSDD plan situates all the development on parcels A and B (where soil and slope conditions are the most favorable), leaving small parts of A and B and all of parcel C as permanent open space. (See also Figure 14–8.)

Parcel C, which includes some of the most scenic and visible features on the three properties, as well as containing the most fertile fields and a handsome stand of mature trees along a prime fishing stream, would have been compromised by any amount of development. High-intensity soil investigations identified large areas on parcel A as being suitable for septic systems, and several amply sized locations on parcel B for grouping

**Table 14–1. Distribution of Potential Development,
Planned Development and Conservation, and Net Proceeds, Utilizing
Three Parcels in a "Landowner Compact"**

	A	B	C	Total
Acreage	35 acres	65 acres	100 acres	200 acres
Minimum lot size	1 acre	2 acres	2 acres	—
Number of potential lots	30 lots	30 lots	40 lots	100 lots
Percent of potential lots	30%	30%	40%	100%
Planned number of lots	40 lots	60 lots	None	100 lots
Distribution of developed land	30 acres	50 acres	—	80 acres
Distribution of conserved land	5 acres	15 acres	100 acres	120 acres
Distribution of net proceeds	30%	30%	40%	100%

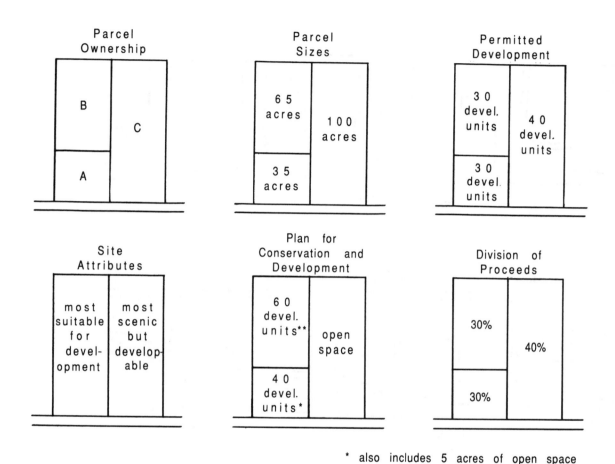

Parcel
Ownership

B

C

A

Parcel
Sizes

65
acres

100
acres

35
acres

Permitted
Development

30
devel.
units

40
devel.
units

30
devel.
units

Site
Attributes

most
suitable
for
devel-
opment

most
scenic
but
develop-
able

Plan for
Conservation and
Development

60
devel.
units**

open
space

40
devel.
units*

Division of
Proceeds

30%

40%

30%

* also includes 5 acres of open space
** also includes 15 acres of open space

Figure 14–8. Schematic drawings showing the potential for a "landowner compact" wherein three adjoining owners agree on a joint plan for the conservation and development of their properties. Each receives a share of the net proceeds in proportion to the number and value of units each could develop independently, irrespective of the total acreage owned by each participant (some of which might be severely constrained for housebuilding). In this voluntary arrangement, each partner must be satisfied with what he or she gives up and receives in return.

individual septic leaching fields (see Chapter 13 for further information on alternative designs for sewage systems). Creative site design utilizing the landowner compact approach and applying the principles of OSDD could therefore produce an optimum package of conservation and development for the three parcels.

This kind of cooperative approach should be actively encouraged by local governments and land trusts in situations where OSDD is not re-

quired and where significant resource areas (such as a stream corridor) cross individual parcel boundaries, as illustrated in Figure 14–9. In such situations, where planning boards lack the authority to mandate a cluster layout on each parcel to ensure protection of sensitive but otherwise developable lands (such as ridgelines, stream valleys, prime farming soils, special wildlife habitats, etc.), landowner compacts offer a nonregulatory opportunity that private land conservation groups could

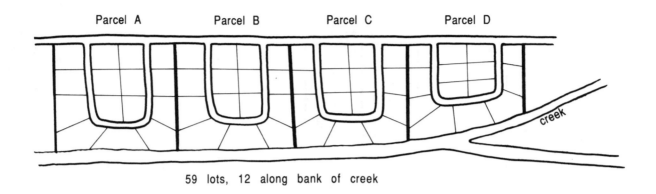

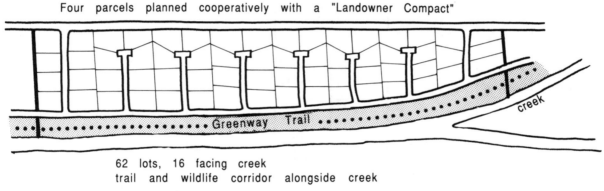

Figure 14–9. Practical advantages of encouraging cooperation among owners of adjacent parcels include interconnected street circulation systems and contiguous open space (allowing for longer greenways and footpath networks). In this example, incentives for forming a "landowner compact" include a small density bonus and a 33 percent increase in the number of lots with a direct view of the creek (plus the marketing advantage of a continuously protected natural area along the water, through which a neighborhood trail could be cut).

advocate. In addition to general advocacy, such organizations could initiate contacts with abutting property owners, offering their assistance in helping to identify appropriate locations for both conservation and development, structuring profit-sharing arrangements among the owners, and drafting easements for permanent open space protection.

Although useful in such situations, other circumstances exist where landowner compacts would be invaluable. Those involve areas where the sensitive but developable resource lies mostly

or wholly within a single ownership (as shown in Figure 14–10), where there is also little scope for internally rearranging the development pattern to avoid impacting the resource. In other words, there are situations where OSDD, performed on a site-by-site basis for separate parcels, can fail to accomplish neighborhood-wide conservation objectives, even in an incremental way. These are cases where planning techniques involving multiple ownerships become essential.

In such instances, it is preferable to remove potential development entirely to another parcel

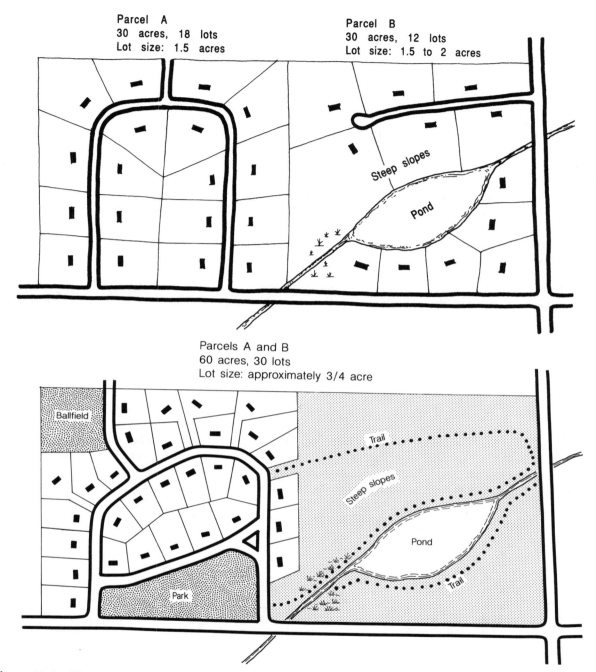

Figure 14–10. These sketches illustrate contrasting approaches to developing two adjoining parcels, each 30 acres in area. Parcel A contains very few site constraints and could easily be developed into the maximum number of lots permitted under local zoning: 18 lots. Parcel B contains some steep slopes, a pond, and a small wetland area, but could still be divided into 12 lots. However, much of parcel B is also covered with some rather special stands of trees, which would be completely unprotected under local regulations: mature hemlock groves around the pond, and numerous large beeches on the hillside. The landowner compact approach would allow the common boundary between the two parcels to be erased, so that an overall plan could be created for distributing houselots in a manner that would preserve all the important natural features on parcel B. The entire development of 30 homes could be located on parcel A, together with a natural park/buffer along the public road, and a ball field in one corner. Net proceeds would typically be divided in a proportional manner between the two owners, for example, 18/30ths (60 percent) for the owner of parcel A, and 12/30ths (40 percent) for the owner of parcel B.

or parcels (in the sketch in Figure 14–10 it has been transferred to an adjoining property, well away from the pond, wetlands, and steep slopes on parcel B). To the extent that such sites can be identified in the immediate neighborhood and that landowners are willing to cooperate, the "compact" method provides another tool to avoid conventional checkerboard layouts and to preserve significant resource areas.

When this approach was recommended in the early 1960s as a way of compensating valley-bottom landowners for the development they would "lose" if new subdivisions were restricted to higher elevations in two valleys northwest of Baltimore, it was an idea several decades ahead of its time (Wallace and McHarg, 1963).

Fortunately, times are beginning to change. An excellent example of cooperation among four adjoining landowners, which will create a major development and a new county park, is currently in the works on a 605-acre site located about five miles south of Reno, Nevada. (See Figure 14–11.) Through this creative approach to cooperative development, an 80-acre area straddling three of the four parcels is being dedicated to the county for a much needed regional recreational facility.

In this instance, the owner of one of the parcels approached three of his neighbors with the idea of working cooperatively on a master plan for all their properties. An important incentive—one that helped keep the plan on track but which was not a factor in the initial decision to jointly develop the land—was an arrangement with the county to allow the higher density development (for which only one of the parcels was zoned) to be shared by the other three properties. Although the total amount of higher density land-uses permitted under zoning was not increased, it was allowed to be more evenly distributed over the entire tract, in a manner reflecting sound planning principles and sensitivity to local site conditions. This was economically beneficial to all four landowners: three parcels could not otherwise have been developed with any high-density uses, and the developability of the fourth parcel (which the zoning had designated for such uses) was greatly limited by some of the most challenging physical constraints on the entire tract. The property owners have an agreement amongst themselves (the county is not a party) that identifies the value of the increased density they share, compared with the development value each would have pos-

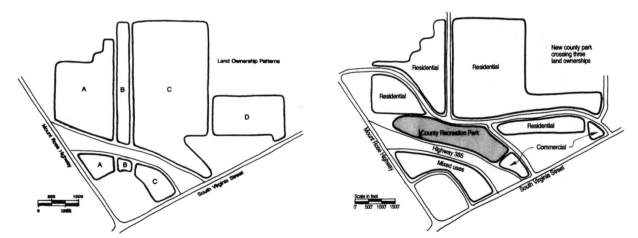

Figure 14–11. In this actual example of a landowner compact involving four parcels in Washoe County, Nevada (near Reno), three of the properties are bisected by a state highway and a creek that parallels it. These features not only fragment the properties, they also limit direct access to them. By joining together for cooperative planning, each owner stands to benefit more than if each one had proceeded independently. The county is a fifth beneficiary, proposed to receive 80 acres on which it will create a regional park.

sessed had the four properties been developed separately, without any comprehensive planning or cooperation. These values were based upon an analysis of comparable sales in the vicinity. The public will be a fifth major beneficiary of this cooperative action, with the new regional park and a comprehensive trail system becoming possible through the enlightened self-interest of all parties.

MAINTENANCE AND LIABILITY ISSUES

One of the greatest worries that has discouraged more open space developments from being proposed and approved is a concern shared by many landowners, developers, abutters, and local officials: how to ensure continued care and maintenance of the open space. When the open space is agricultural it may be retained and used by the original farmer, who may later sell it to an abutting farmer or to a young farmer who can afford only land with no further development potential. Or it might be sold to a nursery operation, an equestrian stable, or a gentleman farmer. In some cases the developer dedicates the agricultural open space to a homeowners' association (HOA), a not-for-profit automatic-membership organization of all the lot owners in the development. The HOA then manages the farm and forest land itself, or (preferably) leases the land on a long-term basis to a nearby farmer. (For further details, see Chapter 18, "Retaining Farmland and Farmers," and also several case examples in Part IV.)

For parkland and recreation facilities, public ownership is usually not a viable option because few local governments want to increase their responsibilities, and few developers trust the public sector to take proper care of these lands. However, when protected land fits well into the municipality's framework for open space provision, by extending or linking a greenway trail system for example (see Chapter 16), and when the associated maintenance costs would be moderate, a mutually agreeable arrangement might be possible.

In most cases, the protected land remains in private hands. While undeveloped open space on large "estate lots" in a subdivision would be managed by their individual owners, other parts of the protected landscape are apt to be jointly held by all residents of the HOA. (Another possibility is that it be given to a local land trust, but such nonprofit groups are increasingly reluctant to accept ownership responsibilities unless a property is accompanied by an endowment to cover administrative, maintenance, and insurance costs.)

SUCCESSFUL HOMEOWNERS' ASSOCIATIONS

Homeowners' Associations (HOAs) can easily be structured to achieve open space management objectives. Two cardinal rules for successful HOAs are automatic membership by all property owners and legal authority to place a lien on the property of any member who fails to pay his or her dues. Although rarely exercised, this authority is essential, should be required under the local zoning ordinance, and should be provided for through the "declaration" that is recorded by the developer before any lot is sold, permanently establishing the rights and obligations of the HOA and the lot owners.

Another feature of successful HOAs is a relatively low dues schedule, attainable when common facilities are kept simple and inexpensive to maintain (e.g., trails, playing fields, outdoor tennis courts, and ponds for swimming and skating, rather than chlorinated swimming pools, indoor tennis courts, and community recreation buildings). For example, at Echo Hill in Amherst, Massachusetts, where facilities include such low-maintenance items as woodland trails, a two-acre grassy common, a pond with a float or raft, two tennis courts, and a baseball diamond and backstop, annual dues rose from $20 to only $75 per family between 1969 and 1993. Being frugal Yankees, the residents have steered away from high-cost recreational features, and the results of that philosophy are reflected in the above figures.

Dues also cover premiums on the HOA's insurance policy, which shields them from liability suits. Liability is another perennial concern whenever open space is proposed, but insurance claims are paid only when there is a judgment against an HOA, and in order for such judgments to occur, gross negligence needs to be proved. When a hiker stumbles over an exposed root protruding from a woodland trail because he or she was looking at a warbler up in a red maple, the negligence is the hiker's, not the HOA's: unlike municipal sidewalks, trails are not expected to be perfectly flat and free of minor obstructions. However, if a swimmer cuts himself severely on a rusty nail protruding from a raft or dock, a case for negligence could be made fairly easily. (For further discussion on liability issues, see the section on "Comprehensive Greenway Planning" in Chapter 16.)

It is beyond the scope of this book to cover all the organizational and legal aspects that need to be understood to create and operate a successful HOA. Readers are referred to the definitive text on this subject: *The Homes Association Handbook*, by Byron Hanke et al., originally issued by the Urban Land Institute in 1964 as its Technical Bulletin No. 50. Last reprinted in 1970, it is available in major reference libraries across the country. Despite the passage of time, much of its material remains applicable today, and its 350 case studies of residential developments with common open space maintenance by HOAs constitute an invaluable resource. It also contains an extensive section on legal requirements, including covenants, forms of organization, bylaws, and model forms for articles of incorporation and the dedication of common areas. Technical assistance on establishing and running HOAs is also available from a national nonprofit group, the Community Associations Institute, 1630 Duke Street, Alexandria, VA 22314, which serves more than 5,000 HOAs across the country.

15

Requiring
Open Space Design

In addition to the various approaches for encouraging open space development design (OSDD) described in the previous chapter, other techniques are available to ensure that future patterns of development will be located and shaped in such a way as to conserve a large proportion of the natural lands and special features presently existing in a community.

In many communities where flexible design techniques such as cluster and OSDD are prohibited—the situation in the majority of rural New England towns—progressive planning board members and residents often feel that simply lifting the ban on more creative development techniques would represent a major leap forward. However, experience has shown that if a community does no more than make OSDD legal and remove some of the procedural obstacles, it will be lucky if 10 or 15 percent of the developers decide to opt for this approach. Therefore the "major leap" is likely to be little more than a tiny step, with the great majority of future developments following conventional "cookie-cutter" lines.

In situations such as this, an unusual degree of persuasion is often needed to convince the local legislative body that it must make some bold and fundamental changes in the way that land development is normally conducted. To help communities break out of the rut of unimaginative, land-consumptive checkerboard design, the Center for Rural Massachusetts has refined and employed a highly effective method of communicating just how much is at stake, over the medium- to long-term, as one parcel of land after another is converted from pastures, fields, and woods to a gradually coalescing mass of sprawling developments.

The end result of applying conventional zoning on every developable piece of land has been described as "wall-to-wall subdivisions" (interspersed with occasional shopping centers, office parks, and civic facilities). In rural areas this long-term prospect may not seem as threatening as it does to residents at the edges of metropolitan regions but, by the same token, rural people often relate very directly to the loss of individual fields or stream corridors that they have enjoyed and taken for granted all their lives. When shown alternative development patterns that can preserve many of these special features without reducing the landowner's equity, people's interest in improving current zoning regulations is often aroused.

"BUILD-OUT" MAPPING

One of the most understandable, inexpensive, and effective tools for showing local residents and officials the long-term result of implementing existing zoning and subdivision regulations is the "build-out map." Briefly stated, such maps plot the probable locations of new roads and houses that could legally be constructed on the vacant and buildable land remaining within a municipality. This technique may also be applied to particular sections of towns or even to large undeveloped parcels, but the most dramatic effect is produced when the unending pattern of contiguous subdivisions and road-front development is laid out across the full length and breadth of a municipality. Because so many people (both officials and residents) assume their town or township is adequately protected by existing zoning, it is often necessary to conduct a careful build-out analysis to reveal the likely future in a very graphic, understandable manner, before it actually occurs.

To preserve credibility, it is crucial that development not be projected into areas where natural or regulatory constraints would prevent it. Future build-out patterns must reflect reduced density, where features such as rough or steep terrain, damp or thin soils, or other factors would limit actual development. For example, in rural districts where one-acre houselots are allowed, but where developers normally find it impossible to lay out more than 10 lots on 20 typical acres, the build-out map should reflect the latter density. This is sometimes termed "natural zoning."

This build-out technique was probably first used by Ian McHarg and David Wallace in *The Plan for the Valleys* (Green Spring and Worthington Valleys, northwest of Baltimore) in the mid-1960s, where it was graphically described as the "Spectre of Uncontrolled Growth." A generation later it was revived and reapplied in New England during the first U.S.-U.K. "Countryside Stewardship Exchange," in which joint teams of British and North American land-use professionals worked intensively to help selected towns develop more effective strategies to retain their special character in the face of suburban development pressures. Working with local officials in the small farming community of Hadley, Massachusetts, the team of exchange participants created a large wall-map showing "net usable land area" (NULA) by deducting floodplains, wetlands, steep slopes, already developed areas, publicly owned lands, and parcels protected by permanent conservation easements.

In areas where soil types or infrastructure provision would allow maximum legal densities to be achieved, a hypothetical but realistic road network was plotted, the distance between parallel streets being estimated as twice the depth of a standard-sized houselot. Street locations were also laid out with general respect to the terrain (as shown on USGS topographical sheets) to stay within the

maximum gradients allowed under local regulations. Red dots representing new houses were spaced at distances corresponding to houselot area and frontage requirements. The surface of the resulting map, with its many hundreds of red dots, suggested that the town had contracted a terminal case of measles, hence the nickname "measles map." (See Figure 15–1.)

A detailed step-by-step description of this mapping process, entitled *A Manual of Build-Out Analysis* (Lacy, 1990), has been published by the Center for Rural Massachusetts to enable lay members of local planning boards and conservation commissions, citizen activists, and professional planners to conduct a similar "preview" of their town's future prospects under present regulations. A second product of this analysis is a projection of future dwelling-unit totals, together with estimates of future population and number of schoolchildren.

The build-out technique does not project future growth rates. They will vary for many reasons and are not as important, in the long run, as the ultimate *pattern* of development that will result through the continued application of current land-use policies. Typically the pattern is an unrelieved amalgamation of checkerboard subdivisions where the only open spaces left are likely to be wetlands, floodplains, and other remnant bits that are physically undevelopable.

Although creating an accurate "measles map" can be tedious and time-consuming, the tasks are not technically difficult to perform, and good results can be produced with readily available maps (medium-intensity soils from the USDA Soil Conservation Service, topography from USGS maps, floodplain information from the Federal Emergency Management Agency, wetlands from the Army Corps of Engineers, and parcel locations from local tax maps) and aerial photos showing existing developed areas. Typically drawn at a scale of 1 inch = 1,000 feet, townwide build-out maps created by the Center for Rural Massachusetts have cost about $3,000 each (utilizing graduate students and volunteer citizen labor).

Carefully executed, such a map is virtually impossible to argue against. It is an objective illumination of the facts of life under conventional

Current Situation   Future Build-out

Figure 15–1. These details from a "build-out" map prepared by graduate students at the Center for Rural Massachusetts (at the University of Massachusetts) show, in white, the developable land in one part of Deerfield, Massachusetts, as it appears today, and as it is projected to be subdivided when existing zoning regulations are fully implemented. This mapping technique is one of the most cost-effective tools to help residents and officials visualize the future. Without exaggerating the potential for growth, this technique blows the whistle on conventional zoning by revealing its ultimate inadequacy in protecting open space and community character.

zoning, and it suggests the worrisome question: what will it be like to live in this town when the conventional zoning is fully implemented? Its greatest contribution lies in helping people to identify current zoning regulations as a large part of the problem of suburban sprawl, and in getting their attention focused on *their* community's prospects unless the land-use rules are changed to reflect the type of future that most people seem to want (i.e., significant areas of farmland, woodland, stream corridors, ridgelines, etc., preserved intact).

Interest in the use of this technique is spreading westward from the northeastern states, and has recently been employed in an innovative fashion by the Livingston County Planning Department in Michigan. County planners there have prepared build-out maps and analyses for four contiguous townships surrounding the city of Brighton. In its report, the county raised a number of issues for discussion, as quoted below (Livingston County Planning Department, 1991):

1) Is the location of growth desirable?
2) Are infrastructure plans linked to the location and magnitude of development?

3) Once the community is built-out there will be few opportunities for additional growth. Will adequate revenues be available to pay for the services and infrastructure needed? (This is particularly important in townships where little land is zoned for future commercial or industrial uses.)
4) Are there adequate plans for public parks? The build-out pattern results in all areas that are developable being consumed into privately owned residential lots. Thirty years from now, where will the public swim, picnic, or play ball?
5) Does the build-out pattern in the community positively or negatively impact neighboring communities?

The report ends with this insightful observation: "On a *community-wide* basis, the build-out pattern should be assessed in terms of making it more rational and orderly, more supported (and supportable) by services and infrastructure, and more compatible between jurisdictions. On a *site-by-site* basis, thoughtful design of the growth allowed through local plans and zoning ordinances can permit increases in density while also maintaining pleasant, fiscally viable and environmentally sound communities." (ibid.).

It is sometimes sufficient to illustrate a partial build-out covering only a certain part of the municipality as a sample area, from which town-wide implications can be mentally extrapolated by residents. Occasionally it is enough to show the results of conventional subdivision techniques as applied to a particularly well-known and well-loved farm or woodland tract (possibly one containing a pond or abutting a lake). This approach was followed by the town of Wenham, Massachusetts, in conjunction with a community land-use conference held in 1989, where the alternative development layouts were prominently displayed and discussed (Kopkowski, 1989). The example chosen was hypothetical, and the landowner was happy to offer his property as a test site to show the results of applying the town's current two-acre zoning, contrasted with the open space that could be preserved via more creative development design (see Figure 15–2).

AREA-WIDE PLANNING FOR CONSERVATION AND DEVELOPMENT

Once a build-out map has been prepared and widely publicized (preferably with the active support of local officials), it is critically important to articulate a vision of a better and more promising future for the community. It is insufficient to merely illustrate the tremendous shortcomings of current methods of land regulation and develop-

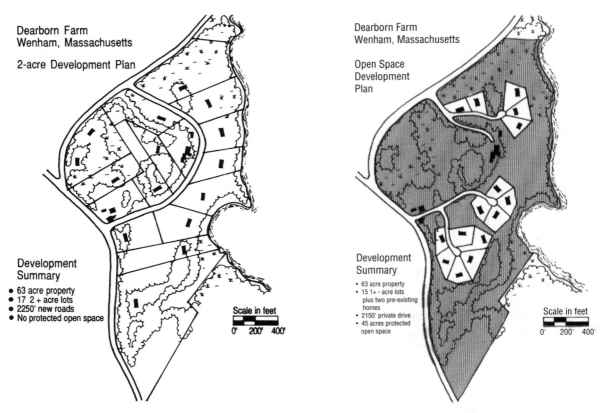

Figure 15–2. These two alternative designs for the Dearborn Farm in Wenham, Massachusetts, were prepared as part of an awareness raising project to help townspeople appreciate that, to a very considerable extent, the shape of their town's future lies largely within their own hands. Producing the same lot yield (15 new one-acre lots, plus the two preexisting homes on larger parcels), the creative design would also preserve two-thirds of the 63-acre site as open space. *Source:* Kopkowski, 1989.

ment. In addition to the negative impact produced by the build-out map, a positive image of the community's future must be projected so that the public does not become cynical or lose hope altogether. It also helps to generate support for zoning improvements to show people how much more of their valued rural surroundings could survive the development process if conventional approaches were to be replaced with more creative design techniques.

One of the best ways of doing this involves another highly visual device: a map identifying all areas that should remain permanently unbuilt, as well as those areas where all growth should be located. Known officially as a "Map of Conservation and Development" (and unofficially as "A Greener Vision"), this document should be included in a town's comprehensive plan and also incorporated as a regulatory feature of its zoning ordinance. (See Figure 15–3.) Landowners and intending developers would then be aware of both the constraints and the opportunities existing throughout the community. By referring to this map, people desiring to develop any particular parcel would be able to determine which parts of their land *will be required to be set aside for conservation purposes and which will be allowed to be more intensively developed.*

This was essentially the approach taken in the Washington Valley area of Bridgewater Township, New Jersey, where municipal officials prepared a large-scale map showing where development and open space should be designed to be located on every land parcel along the stream corridor (see Chapter 16, "Greenways and Buffers," for additional details about this project). In another central New Jersey township, consulting landscape architects and planners are hired on a regular basis to work with applicants at the sketch plan stage to ensure that an appropriate amount and type of open space is set aside in each new subdivision, and that these green areas are designed to connect with each other in adjoining developments. (This is further described in "The Alexandria Trilogy" case example in Chapter 20.)

The idea of an area-wide map for conservation and development was imaginatively refined in

1991 by officials of West Manchester Township in York County, Pennsylvania. After completing a "build-out" map illustrating the pattern of sprawl that would ultimately be produced by implementing existing zoning, township officials drew up a broad-brush map outlining growth areas and preservation areas, using tax-parcel maps for their base—which enabled them to avoid inadvertently coloring any parcels entirely green—for an important goal was to demonstrate that meaningful conservation could be accomplished without committing a "taking" of land without compensation (see Figure 15–4). Through this process, each parcel of vacant land was quickly evaluated for its conservation and development potential.

This level of guidance was provided by township officials to help landowners and developers visualize the general type of approach that would be needed on each property to ensure that an interconnected system of open space would result from application of the ordinance. Although many of the localities mentioned in this section are characterized by zoning densities of one to two acres per dwelling, standard lot sizes in West Manchester are in the 15,000 to 20,000 square foot range, reflecting the community's adjacency to the county seat of York and the availability of public water and sewerage. The goal of the ordinance is to protect 25 to 50 percent of each property as open space by limiting lot sizes to 10,000 square feet.

Areas to be shown for preservation on community-wide maps of conservation and development might typically include (in addition to wetlands and floodplains), farm fields, pastures, and stone walls; steep slopes, ridgelines, and hilltops; aquifers for public drinking water supplies; significant wildlife habitats; land alongside lakes, rivers, or the ocean; and locations comprising scenic views or scenic view corridors. To the maximum extent feasible, new development should be *required* to be located outside such areas and allowed to be clustered at higher net densities on other parts of an applicant's property. In essence this is simply an internal transfer of density involving the same number of dwellings.

However, when the features to be protected are particularly sensitive to encroachment, or when

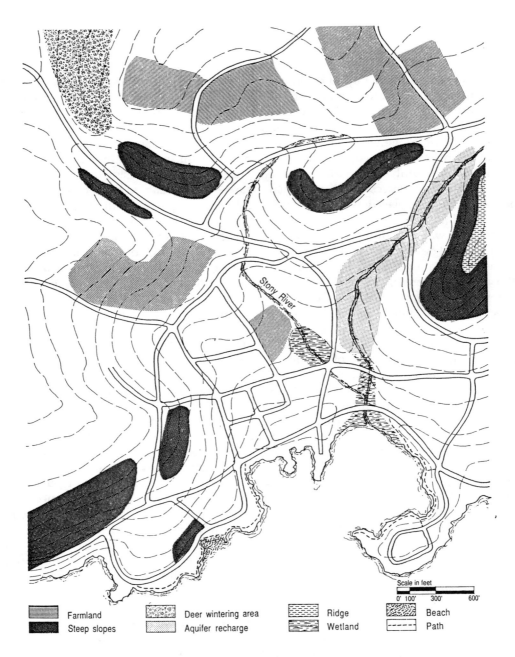

Farmland

Steep slopes

Deer wintering area

Aquifer recharge

Ridge

Wetland

Beach

Path

Scale in feet

0' 100'   300'   600'

Figure 15–3. Maximum effectiveness can be achieved through an area-wide "Map of Conservation and Development." Regulatory in nature, this map would identify all natural and cultural features worthy of preservation, plus all lands without any such features (where development would best be accommodated). Landowners wishing to develop their properties would be required, under local zoning, to utilize flexible "open space design" techniques to keep houselots away from those special areas, locating new homes and streets within those parts of their properties not shaded on this map. Building density would be calculated on the basis of the amount of developable land on any given parcel (or through a conceptual "yield plan" for such a parcel). This approach allows habitats that are fragmented into multiple ownerships to remain more intact, and for blocks of farmland or special woodlands to remain more whole. It is also a powerful tool for greenway planning, enabling a continuous ribbon of open space to be created along streams, for example, as each riparian parcel is subdivided.

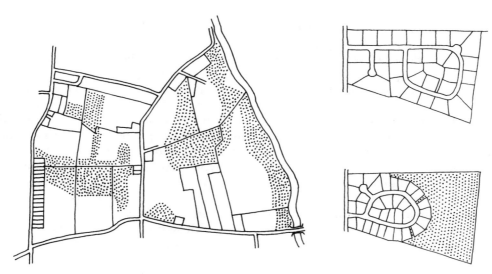

Figure 15–4. West Manchester Township, near York, Pennsylvania, has proceeded farther than any other small town in the country, in terms of giving guidance to landowners and developers about where open space should be located on their parcels when they are eventually subdivided. Township officials engaged a consultant to draw, on the official tax parcel maps, boundaries of the new open space system as it crossed various properties, showing how areas required to be preserved in each new development could be located so that they would eventually connect with each other. The two small sketches show how one developer worked within the township's greenspace system to design a subdivision where the preserved lands are located in accordance with West Manchester's new ordinance.

they cover all or most of an individual's land, mechanisms should be readily available to enable, and to encourage, inter-parcel density exchanges (such as the "landowner compacts" described in Chapter 14 and Howard County's "density exchange option" described in Chapter 18). In other words, a miniature version of "TDR" (transfer of development rights) should be facilitated by the creative zoning regulations. Other methods of protecting the land can and should be employed to supplement such regulatory measures, such as "PDR" (the selective purchase of development rights) and "limited development" (subdividing land for fewer, upscale properties).

In the past it has been traditional to include conservation "wish list" maps in municipal comprehensive plans and open space plans, but they have typically been no more than hopeful statements about what lands might be saved if landowners voluntarily restricted development on them, if public or private bodies had sufficient funds to purchase them for parkland, or if developers could be persuaded to utilize open space design techniques when laying out future subdivisions. It should no longer be necessary for planners to color maps green and cross their fingers. The critical difference in the type of map described here is that it would be an official regulatory document, like the map of zoning districts. In actuality, it would function as a map of overlay districts, in which the concept of open space development design would become *obligatory* for developers.

ORIGINS AND RATIONALE

The technique of *requiring* open space development design has been discussed for decades, but has begun to be implemented on a widespread basis only within the past several years—since it was popularized by the graphics and model ordinance provisions in *Dealing with Change in the Connecticut River Valley* (Yaro, Arendt, et al., 1988).

The origins of the concept are unclear, and probably even predate Ian McHarg and David Wallace's *Plan for the Valleys*, which in 1963 called for "mandatory clustering" of development on the wooded slopes of two beautiful river valleys outside Baltimore to save the bottomlands. In that highly regarded plan the authors argued that "[T]his zone should require as mandatory the provision of such open space, and the County should have design control over which part of each tract would be so dedicated to the owners in concert, or to the County" (Wallace and McHarg, 1963).

Although the local governments did not amend their zoning regulations to require clustering to create large areas of planned open space, the spirit of the report was implemented through other means (restricting new septic system installations in soils overlying the vulnerable Cockeysville marble limestone aquifer, and halting new sewer extensions into the flood-prone valleys). Because none of the principal authors of that plan claim to have originated the regulatory idea of *requiring* that new development be clustered, the genesis of this simple but powerful concept remains uncertain.

A decade later, Lane Kendig picked up on the idea of requiring clustering and included it in his seminal text *Performance Zoning* as an "open space ratio" (OSR). Under Kendig's system, an OSR of 0.5 indicates a 50 percent open space setaside, for example. Although there is little documentation on the first uses of this technique, it is possible that the record for the oldest ordinances mandating cluster development as a method of creating permanent open space (dating from the early 1970s) is held by a few Suffolk County towns on the rural, eastern end of Long Island, New York (where second-home development pressures have existed for decades).

The rationale behind this compelling idea is straightforward: the public has certain fundamental rights, exercised through general "police powers," to ensure that each community grows in a balanced manner. Property rights are not unconstitutionally abridged by regulations limiting a developer's ability to spread houselots and road systems out across his land. There is no inherent "right to sprawl" guaranteed by the Constitution,

the Bill of Rights, subsequent amendments, or relevant case law.

In most states, the right of local governments to require clustering is implicit in the state zoning enabling legislation. In New York, where this right was unclear to some conservative attorneys, the legislature removed any remaining doubt by enacting new provisions explicitly authorizing towns and incorporated villages to mandate cluster layouts. And in neighboring Connecticut, legislators moved in 1991 to encourage the greater use of cluster development as a means of preserving open space. Subdivision regulations may now require clustering, and each rural town must consider the use of cluster design as part of its Plan of Development (Tondro, 1992).

Another important reason for local planning jurisdictions to adopt regulations requiring more compact development with permanent open space setasides is that unless they do so, they will remain supplicants in the process, with no official authority to compel developers to follow OSDD principles. Many cases exist where towns and counties have literally begged developers to utilize OSDD or cluster concepts in their subdivisions, but to no avail. It is a bizarre situation when the public sector is reduced to a form of beggary, with developers free to embrace or reject progressive design standards that would produce a network of functional open space, while reducing both the initial private costs in constructing road and utility systems and the ultimate public costs involved in maintaining them.

This state of affairs, in which the public sector has forfeited its right to control the pattern of development, has been dubbed "The Vanna White School of Planning," because local planning officials essentially spin their "wheels of fortune," hoping and praying that the next developer to appear before them will be amenable to the open space development design approach.

But why should such a critically important ordinance provision be up to the developer to follow or not? Continuing the logic, perhaps we should consider allowing current requirements for street construction, parking, landscaping, drainage, buffering, and environmental performance standards to become optional as well, for developers to follow or ignore as they wish.

The simple fact is that whenever municipalities are serious about seeing that certain standards are respected, whether it be in the diameter of water mains or the diameter of shade trees provided in new subdivisions, minimum standards are set and adhered to. Surely the quantity, quality, and configuration of open space in new developments deserves equally serious attention from our public officials.

There is something to be said for letting certain nonessentials in life to remain voluntary, but few people would seriously consider allowing important features of our social and institutional framework, such as speed limits and income taxes, to be conducted on a strictly voluntary basis. Who, in fact, would be willing to serve on a planning board if zoning were not regulatory but only advisory? Yet, arguably, one of the most significant provisions in such ordinances is essentially voluntary: the part dealing with the pattern of development and the amount and location of functional open space preserved or consumed as part of the subdivision design process.

It is time that the public reassert its right to exercise meaningful control over development patterns and subdivision design. In response to the question "What is so wrong with the way we have always developed under conventional zoning?", some Midwestern planners have given this incisive reply: "Actually, nothing is wrong with conventional residential zoning if you are satisfied with the results, where every acre of land is designated for houselots, sidewalks, and streets. Communities following such a land-consumptive approach to development eventually end up with an endless web of subdivisions with no, or very little, land set aside as natural areas or open space" (Livingston County Planning Department, 1991).

The basic good sense of open space development design is beginning to be noticed at the federal level, where the National Park Service has expressed interest in adapting this technique to help preserve the presently rural character of private landholdings around some of its more vulnerable rural sites. After Congress voted $50 million to buy out developers who had every legal right to create a regional shopping mall next to the Manassas Battlefield, NPS officials were urged to consider preventive steps designed to avoid similar costly rescue missions in the future. Working with the Natural Lands Trust (based in Media, Pennsylvania), NPS staff have begun formulating an *adjacent lands strategy,* which will use a variant of this planning technique, in conjunction with other land conservation approaches, to preserve open space around these nationally significant sites in a cost-efficient manner that is also fair to private landowners.

Similar efforts could be undertaken at the state, county, and municipal levels, to protect open space around existing parks, forests, wildlife refuges, and conservation areas maintained by those governments. In fact, if planning officials do not initiate this type of approach on their own (being distracted by other issues), park and conservation supporters should begin promoting these ideas among their constituents, building the case for improved land-use regulations on the undeveloped lands around their sites. Use of this technique was among the recommendations in the *North Woods Study* conducted for the U.S. Forest Service, and in the "Land Use Element" prepared for the Blackstone River Valley National Heritage Corridor Commission, an arm of the National Park Service (Arendt, 1989).

One approach to mobilizing support for more progressive land-use planning has been refined by Calvert County, Maryland. In addition to inviting a nationally known speaker to give a slide presentation on open space development design, county planners ensured a large turnout by sending personal invitations to scores of elected and appointed county officials, plus a number of developers and large landowners. After the presentation a one-page survey containing thirteen questions was distributed, and the results were later tabulated and publicized. Lopsided majorities (commonly four-to-one and five-to-one) were recorded in favor of all the main points (except allowing gravel-surfaced "country lanes" in very small subdivisions). A copy of this survey form with the Calvert results is included in the Appendix to this book.

This gave an "instant mandate" for improved zoning and subdivision regulations to the county, which is presently considering many creative concepts that had been previously discussed but never implemented (see also the section on "Altering Public Perceptions" in Chapter 14).

DEGREES OF MANDATING OPEN SPACE DEVELOPMENT DESIGN (OSDD)

There is considerable variation in the way local governments have chosen to implement "compulsory open space development design." Some communities (particularly those in upstate New York) leave the determination up to their planning boards, who are authorized by their elected "town boards" to require OSDD in any situation where they feel it would be more appropriate, given the overall objectives of the comprehensive plan and the stated purposes of the zoning ordinance. This approach allows the planning board to apply this concept to create neighborhood parks in villages and hamlets where there is an established tradition of compact lots, in addition to applying it in more rural locations where wildlife habitat or farmland protection are the main goals.

In Honeoye Falls, New York, local officials recently enacted zoning provisions that combine an awareness of the village's traditional scale and compact development pattern with stringent requirements that up to 45 percent of the land area in subdivisions be designed as open space serving the new smaller lots. And in Lower Merion, Pennsylvania, which has adopted similar regulations, the potential for creating a *network* of greenways linking new subdivision open spaces with each other and with existing schools, municipal parks, trails, and Mill Creek is being studied by the Natural Lands Trust, at township request. Figure 15–5, showing some of the remaining subdividable properties in this maturing suburb, reveals the potential for such open space protection and interconnection. (Open spaces and greenway links that could be designated on each parcel, through the subdivision process, are shown in a dotted pattern.)

In Massachusetts, towns that have adopted "mandatory" OSDD regulations have generally

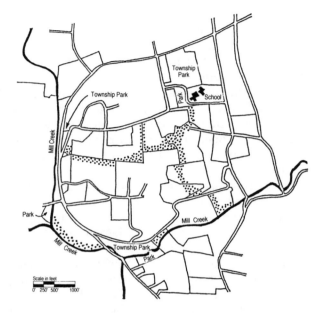

Figure 15–5. When Lower Merion, a leafy Philadelphia suburb, became the first township in Pennsylvania to adopt clustering *requirements* (for all parcels of five or more acres), local officials were given an effective tool to ensure that future subdivisions would not further interrupt the long-established but very informal (and previously unprotected) network of bridle trails connecting various neighborhoods. This sketch shows existing trail connections in the Mill Creek area of Lower Merion, linking schools and parks with each other and with the creek itself, in a continuous circuit.

been advised to allow landowners a certain number of essentially unregulated lot divisions before reaching the threshold for requiring OSDD. These exemptions have typically been in the order of three to five lots over a like number of years. The legal rationale to permit a small number of "by right" divisions is that it functions as a sort of "safety valve" to diminish the strength of any future legal challenge. This line of thinking appears to be similar to the rationale underlying the landowner exemptions typically embodied in state subdivision control laws, which permit one or two lots to be created in any five-year period before reaching the legal threshold for subdivision review.

In New England's first compulsory OSDD ordinance, South Berwick, Maine, officials limited this concept to subdivisions proposed on fields or pastures of more than 10 acres (as mapped from aerial photographs). Later amendments added criteria allowing the planning board to require OSDD whenever more than a certain percentage of particular resource areas (in addition to farmland) would be disturbed under conventional design approaches.

The current model OSDD ordinance prepared by the Center for Rural Massachusetts includes three overlay zones: for farmland, for land within 250 feet of certain water bodies and watercourses, and for steep slopes, ridgelines, and hilltops. Additional overlay districts could be specified for significant wildlife habitats and for aquifer recharge areas, especially those serving public drinking water supplies. Another application would be to use this approach in noncommercial zones along rural highways, where a deep buffer (several hundred feet in depth) could be created between the right-of-way and future housing developments. This would remove residents farther from traffic noise, while establishing an attractive green corridor along such highways (see Chapter 9, "Development in Town Centers and Along Highways," and Chapter 12, "Scenic Roads").

Several novel approaches should also be noted here. Hopkinton, Massachusetts, requires that subdivision plans submitted under its OSDD regulations be prepared by a landscape architect, working in conjunction with surveyors and engineers, on the basis that the former is better suited in his or her training to analyze a site's natural and scenic features and to prepare a layout that is sensitive to them.

The services of a professional landscape architect have been made available to rural landowners in the town of Calais, Vermont, through a grant from the state government under the "Act 200" program, which encourages municipalities to improve their local planning processes. This effort recognizes that large landowners are the key decision-makers with regard to how rural areas change, and that one of the most effective ways to improve planning for conservation and development is to enlighten the thinking of such individuals or families.

In another Vermont town, Braintree, the official subdivision regulations have been amended to require that all subdivision applicants first view the town's copy of a 60-minute video on creative rural development techniques (produced at the Center for Rural Massachusetts and available from the American Planning Association in Chicago) before submitting any drawings for planning board review. This may be the only instance in the country where a rural town is actively trying to expand the consciousness of developers by requiring them to watch an educational video.

Before closing this section, two examples from Chapter 14 should be mentioned again briefly. In both Clark and Clallam Counties in Washington State, clustering is very nearly required by low-density resource-based zoning that allows divisions of farmland and forests into minimum parcels of 20 and 30 acres, respectively. However, in both counties, an overall density of one dwelling per five acres is allowed if the development is clustered on individual lots of approximately three-quarter-acre. (In Clark County, an additional two dwelling units are also allowed for every 20 acres of developable land.) Faced with such large differences in the number of houselots available to them under the large-lot and the cluster alternatives, nearly every landowner and developer opts for the more compact form with more units. When such regulations replace conventional rural zoning that had previously allowed higher densities (typically on two- to five-acre lots), it does not constitute a "giveaway" to developers. Rather than an incentive bonus to encourage clustering, it functions more as a disincentive to discourage fragmentation of truly large parcels (100 acres or more) into small "farmettes."

COUNTY ZONING FOR OSDD IN VIRGINIA

Perhaps the first county-level zoning regulations requiring new subdivisions to be laid out according to OSDD principles were adopted by Isle of Wight County in southeastern Virginia, which has been subject to increasing development pressures from the Hampton Roads area. Similar in some ways to the new agricultural zoning currently being discussed as part of the comprehensive plan process in Howard County, Maryland (described in Chapter 18), the Virginia example described below involves ordinance requirements that will implement specific character protection standards in the county's comprehensive plan.

About 80 percent of the land area in Isle of Wight County has been designated as a Rural Preservation District, in which new subdivision development is prohibited from consuming more than 50 percent of any parcel. Operating from a base density of 10 acres per dwelling, open space is preserved by setting a maximum lot size of five acres, with the remaining land permanently restricted to farming or forestry use via conservation easements and subject to another provision barring further subdivision. Additional standards limit subdivision access to a single curb-cut along existing county roads and require a minimum 100 foot setback from such thoroughfares, half of which must be landscaped as a buffer to maintain or enhance rural character.

Beyond these regulations, greater open space set-asides are encouraged by a sliding-scale approach in the regulations, allowing the gross density to rise if the net area consumed by development is reduced. In other words, if open space rises from 50 percent to 60 percent, with a roadside buffer depth growing from 100 feet to 150 feet, landowners would be allowed a 20 percent increase in the number of houselots (e.g., 12 instead of 10, on a 100-acre tract). Maximum lot size would decline

from 5 acres to 3.3 acres each. These figures are shown in Table 15–1.

Preservation of 70 percent of the parcel would earn an additional eight lots, subject to a maximum area of 1.5 acres each. The only exemptions from the above standards are for parcels 20 acres or larger, intended for agricultural use and prohibited from further subdivision by covenants. Of course, many variations on this theme are possible. Planners who wish to increase the degree of open space protection might suggest that option C be revised to reflect the values shown in option C′ (the author's hybrid), which would consume only 16% of the buildable land, while allowing a 60% increase in dwelling units, compared with option A. Figure 15–6 includes sketch diagrams illustrating typical arrangements for houselots and open space in new developments following two of the three official approaches.

While this example utilizes densities and lot sizes that may or may not be applicable in other jurisdictions, it is laudable as a much more creative alternative to standard large-lot platting, which had been the nearly exclusive form of rural subdivision development in this county prior to the adoption of these ordinances. To understand the background behind some of these numbers, it is also useful to know that the previous base density in the county had been between one and two acres per dwelling unit. In short, Isle of Wight's approach resulted in density reductions to preserve rural character, while permitting small lot sizes to satisfy the interests of its farming community.

In Fauquier County in northern Virginia, which has also legislated a base rural residential density

Table 15–1. Sliding Scale for Open Space on a 100-acre Tract

Option	Open Space Preserved	Number of Lots	Maximum Lot Size (acres)	County Road Setback (feet)	Equivalent Gross Density (acres per dwelling unit)	On 100-acres	
						Land Saved (acres)	Land Developed (acres)
A	50%	10	5	100	10.0	50	50
B	60%	12	3.3	150	8.3	60	40
C	70%	20	1.5	200	5.0	70	30
C′	84%	16	1.0	250	6.3	84	16

Source: Redman-Johnston Associates

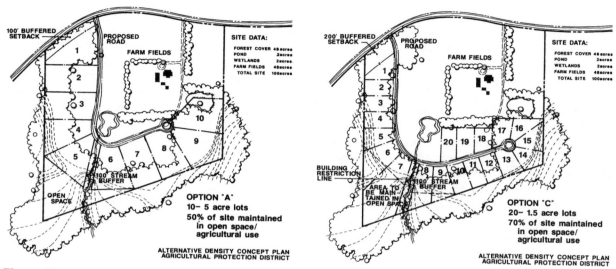

Figure 15–6. Two of the nation's first county-wide zoning regulations requiring developers to employ "open space design" techniques were adopted by Isle of Wight County, Virginia. These sketches illustrate two options under the new ordinance, where development density is limited to one dwelling per ten acres: preserving 50 percent of a 100-acre farm with 10 five-acre lots, or preserving 70 percent open space with 20 lots of 1.5 acres each. *Source:* Redman-Johnston Associates, Easton, Maryland.

of one dwelling per ten acres and a sliding scale to determine houselot yield, zoning requires that permitted development be designed to consume no more than 15 percent of the area of any given parcel in the rural district (which covers the vast majority of the county). In neighboring Clarke County, rural subdivision lots in the agricultural zone may not exceed two acres in area. The sliding-scale regulations there allow three dwellings on 50 acres and just 11 on 500 acres.

OSDD REQUIREMENTS IN CALIFORNIA

In certain parts of Marin County, north of the San Francisco Bay area, several rural districts are zoned for planned development, and cluster layouts are required in order to achieve the county ordinance's objectives of locating new homes in the most geologically stable and least visually prominent portions of the site (Corser, 1992). On grassy hillsides, home sites are required to be placed so that buildings "will be screened by existing vegetation, rock outcroppings, or depressions in topography." Ridgelines are protected by prohibiting

construction "within three hundred feet horizontally, or within one hundred feet vertically of ridgelines, whichever is more restrictive."

Compared with grassy hillsides, somewhat greater scattering is allowed on wooded slopes "to save trees and minimize visual impacts," but in farming areas tighter site design is required "to minimize disruption of existing or possible future agricultural uses." Anticipating potential conflicts between residents and farmers, the county also requires agricultural management plans for large-scale farm uses, addressing such issues as chemical and fertilizer application and runoff. Although farmlands that are preserved through cluster designs are not considered to be accessible for recreational uses, the county's policy is to accept fee title interest in cluster open space and easements on trails across private land, and to maintain such areas for public use, when such is offered by developers.

STATE-LEVEL REVIEW IN VERMONT

Although cluster requirements do not yet exist in the Green Mountain State, Criterion 8 in Vermont's Act 250 provides District Environmental Commission members with the legal basis to disapprove development proposals that are deemed to produce "an undue adverse effect on the scenic or natural beauty of the area, aesthetics, historic sites or rare or irreplaceable natural areas." In an exceptionally well-illustrated design manual, *Vermont's Scenic Landscapes: A Guide for Growth and Protection*, the state Agency of Natural Resource has provided both developers and lay members of the nine regional environmental commissions with a potentially very useful tool to help them understand the resources located on each parcel, appreciate the sensitive features, and make appropriate decisions (Courtney, 1992).

Six sites are examined with realistic perspective sketches illustrating the existing situation, contrasted with two postdevelopment views (conventional versus sensitive). All the recommended designs involve clustering. Depending on site characteristics, they use this approach to minimize tree clearing, hillside development and farmland consumption, and to protect shorelines and village "gateway" entrance roads. This handbook should help developers avoid site designs that would violate Act 250's aesthetic criterion, while strengthening the position of environmental commissioners who wish to see more emphasis placed on this aspect of the statute.

16

Greenways and Buffers

The term "greenway" was popularized during the 1950s and 1960s by William H. Whyte, as a combination of the words "greenbelt" and "parkway," to describe vegetated corridors used primarily for outdoor recreational pursuits such as walking, jogging, hiking, biking, and horseback-riding. Since that time it has attained fairly widespread currency among a variety of disciplines—planners, landscape architects, recreation specialists, wildlife managers, and so forth. It has also been popularized through the efforts of many small local groups that have recognized the greenway concept as a particularly cost-effective approach to open space protection, especially after the demise of federal grant programs for traditional parkland acquisition. In addition, a growing number of rural land management professionals and wildlife conservationists are beginning to use the greenway term more broadly to include lands protected for farming, forestry, and habitat, sometimes with no active or passive recreational component.

In his definitive book *Greenways for America,* Charles Little conceptualizes greenways as a sort of "linear commons" shared and used by a broad cross section of community residents (Little, 1990). Threading their way along natural features such as stream corridors and ridgelines, or alongside human-made elements such as abandoned railroad rights-of-way and canal towpaths, or gas pipelines and power-line easements, greenways offer opportunities for exercise, social interaction, and the quiet observation of nature and seasonal changes in the landscape. They can also provide buffers to help filter storm water flowing into lakes, ponds, rivers, and streams, and offer critical habitat for wildlife to dwell in and travel through.

Because of these attributes, and because they can often be located on existing rights-of-way or on otherwise unbuildable land, greenways are becoming increasingly popular, to the point where they are now being implemented in more than 200 different jurisdictions (Knack and Searns, 1990). According to the Rails-to-Trails Conservancy, over 435 rail-trails presently exist in 42 states, with a combined length exceeding 4,907 miles. Usage in 1990 was estimated at more than 30 million persons. In areas where the characteristics of typical greenway users have been studied (Raleigh and Charlotte, North Carolina), it was found that the largest group of users tend to be people living from two to five miles away, with only about 17 percent living within one mile. Although the largest proportion were college graduates, the most intensive users were the elderly (Furuseth and Altman, 1990).

GREEN EDGES AND LINKS

An articulate advocate, Little has emphasized two key features of greenways: edge and linkage. Due to their long, narrow nature, greenways possess a very high ratio of outer edge to total land area, which maximizes their ability to interface with surrounding development. Little cites the example of a roughly circular 100-acre tract having a total perimeter of just 7,400 feet, compared with a perimeter length of 41,800 feet for the same acreage arranged in a linear strip of land one-acre wide (208 feet). As a backdrop to development, as a separation between land uses, or as a protective buffer alongside watercourses, greenways provide between five and six times more "edge effect" than conventional parks of similar area. In other words, for every dollar spent on acquiring these "linear commons," it would cost $5.65 to purchase enough land in a standard park to produce an equal length of edge.

However, it is fair to point out that an edge maximization approach generally works against efforts to promote habitat biodiversity. This is especially true when the resource is of an elongated shape lacking any real depth. Sunlight penetration into the middle of such protected areas discourages the growth of flora and fauna favoring the more shaded conditions of forest interiors, while making it easier for invasive alien shrubs, vines, and trees (such as multiflora rose, Japanese honeysuckle, bittersweet, and Norway maple) to displace native species. Although such considerations do not diminish the recreational and aesthetic value of long, narrow greenways, or detract from their ability to serve as storm-water filters and wildlife corridors, they remind us of the continuing need to protect larger blocks of natural lands for other ecological reasons. In addition to lengthy edges, the second salient attribute of greenways is their ability to connect places, be they homes linked to schools, shops, and offices, neighborhoods linked to parks, or smaller parks linked to larger open areas.

This is another instance where the total is clearly greater than the sum of the constituent parts. Whereas a single park or open space area can offer only limited opportunities to humans and wildlife, several joined together via a path system can provide a longer trail experience and often a wider variety of park activities as well. Similar benefits accrue to wildlife, as greenways provide cover and naturally sheltered corridors to move through from their nests and burrows to their feeding places or hunting grounds, in addition to reducing habitat fragmentation. This and other important points are well-illustrated in an excellent publication by the National Park Service, *How Greenways Work: A Handbook on Ecology* (Labaree, 1992).

An increasing number of communities are beginning to recognize the synergistic effect of connecting previously separate parkland parcels. In Amherst, Massachusetts, for example, it has been official town policy for some years to acquire trail corridors or easements to link its existing and new conservation areas with one another and with two long-distance trails that cross through the town. When new conservation areas are acquired or new trails are constructed, the town conservation director enlists neighborhood volunteers to help trim branches or construct simple walkway platforms across shallow wetlands or seasonally soggy soils. (See Figure 16–1.) Experience has shown that people tend to use such trails more often, and to look

Figure 16–1. Residents of neighborhoods bordering town-owned conservation land in Amherst, Massachusetts, constitute a ready and willing source of volunteer labor to assist with routine trail maintenance activities. Organizing such events can help build community support for neighborhood trails and tends to increase usage by responsible adults, which in turn reduces inappropriate behavior on conservation land. *Source:* Photo by Pete Westover.

out for their care, when they have been involved in their creation or periodic maintenance. In fact, local interest in these paths has grown to the point where a voluntary organization (Amherst Ridgewalkers) has been formed to help town officials organize volunteer work parties and to conduct an ongoing but somewhat informal system of path monitoring throughout the community.

COMPREHENSIVE GREENWAY PLANNING

The most successful greenways will ultimately be those that were planned comprehensively. Although the idea of mapping out greenspace and greenway reservations before development occurs is not especially new, it is rarely practiced today (except in larger scale "planned communities"). In addition to Boston's famous "Emerald Necklace" of connected parks and greenways ringing much of the city, Cleveland, Cincinnati, Philadelphia and Washington, D.C. boast similarly foresighted park networks. In both Cleveland and Washington, ravines and creek corridors were reserved by visionary officials around the turn of the century, in areas that were then rather rural but that have long since been surrounded by suburban development.

In the late 1950s, Philadelphia planner Edmund Bacon mapped out a greenway network around which development would be required to fit, in a partially developed section of northwestern Philadelphia where such opportunities still existed at that time (Whyte, 1968). In Maryland, the recent Greenways Commission Report to the governor gave new impetus to this proactive approach, declaring that "A greenways system within a county can be preidentified as 'infrastructure' and zoned to prevent encroachments before it can be fully protected" (Maryland Greenways Commission, 1990).

Unless local planning authorities take such initiatives, however, they will be left with only the residual bits and pieces of unbuildable land that are not feasible for developers to use. Because environmental standards are generally much higher today than they were during Bacon's time, these difficult-to-use areas are seldom threatened by bulldozing and filling. However, their potential for greenway usage is often precluded by the standard practice of assigning every square foot of land in new developments to houselots or streets. Wetlands, stream corridors, and ridgelines may be protected from destruction, but they are also rendered inaccessible when lot lines are extended so that each building parcel adjoins other similar lots on all sides.

Because greenway networks typically take such a long time to be implemented, priority setting is very important. In Indianola, Washington, a small unincorporated town on Puget Sound, greenway planners have given highest priority to those areas most subject to change or development, and/or that represent critical linkages not easily replicated if taken for other uses (stream corridors, estuaries and beaches, landmark trees, etc.). Ranking at the next level are corridors that could be easily incorporated into the system at minimal cost or effort, thereby producing some instant and tangible results (publicly owned corridors, "paper streets," and properties belonging to supportive landowners). Lowest priority was assigned to areas where the development threat was lowest, or to areas that would require extensive negotiation with owners or abutters (Reckord, 1991). A unique feature of Indianola's greenway is its use of several long "paper streets," platted long ago but very unlikely ever to be needed for motorized traffic. Many older communities possess at least a few such rights-of-way—which are often eventually vacated and offered for sale to abutters (thereby foreclosing these special greenway opportunities) in the absence of any community footpath plan identifying them as key elements in creating a local trails network.

In Springvale, Maine, in a 1950s subdivision near Stump Pond where the street grid was platted but never entirely built, pedestrians walk along paths through these wooded 50-foot wide rights-of-way, connecting neighborhood areas in a manner that would have been impossible had town officials shortsightedly sold these paper streets to the adjoining landowners. In Indianola, the local land trust has developed a design approach for locating trails and bicycle paths within these undeveloped rights-of-way so that possible future needs (including gravel access lanes to adjoining properties) could be easily accommodated. By locating all nonmotorized uses, from the beginning, within one half of the rights-of-way, the other half could be reserved for potential low-level vehicular access, such as common drives or "village lanes" (Bentsen and Burrow, 1992).

Recognizing that it is far easier (and cheaper) to reserve greenway corridors in advance of development, rather than to acquire easements crossing numerous private property lines after land is subdivided and sold, a number of North Carolina municipalities have incorporated proposed greenway networks into their official master plan policies and maps. In Durham, for example, 93 miles of greenway trails and nature paths are indicated on the master plan map, in addition to another 25 miles of bicycle trails along railway and commuter routes. Although these numbers may seem high, they are in line with the National Parks and Recreation Association guideline of five miles of trail per 10,000 inhabitants. Durham's population is expected to rise to 276,000 by 2005, by which time it will need 135 miles of trails to keep pace with this standard. Other trail projects currently being planned include connections with two regional trails, one linking the three cities of the "Research Triangle," and another spanning the state from the mountains to the sea.

As ambitious as all these plans are, the state of North Carolina has adopted voluntary standards for trail provision that are even higher: one mile per 1,000 inhabitants. Because trails vary in function, this standard has been further refined: 0.4 miles per 1,000 people for hiking trails, and 0.2 miles per 1,000 people for walking, nature, or canoe trail types. No one expects these standards to be met in the near future, but they do constitute an important long-term planning objective that can be achieved gradually, with some tangible progress made every year. For example, Forsyth County is planning a county-wide system of greenways along 120 miles of major creeks. The first section, located along Salem Creek and connecting Peters Creek Parkway to Salem Lake, was opened in 1986. Another trail is currently under construction around Salem Lake itself.

Despite North Carolina's lead in greenway implementation, Maryland recently became the first state with an official policy calling for the creation of a statewide greenways network. Already off to an impressive start with 300 miles of protected stream corridors, Maryland officials have charted a course to supplement their new greenway system with trails along ridgelines, canals, railroads, barrier islands, and utility corridors. The principal obstacle to allowing public access on utility land appears to be the companies' concerns about their potential liability exposure. However, at least one public utility in that state is satisfied it is adequately protected by the Maryland recreation liability statute that changes the standard for private landowner liability from "negligence" to "gross negligence" (Maryland Greenways Commission, 1990).

Pennsylvania also provides broad statutory protection to landowners who permit public access and who do not charge a fee. Under the Pennsylvania Recreational Use of Land and Water Act of 1966, private landowners owe "no duty of care to keep the premises safe for entry and use by others for recreational purposes, or to give any warning of a dangerous condition, use, structure, or activity on such premises for persons entering for such purposes." Court decisions have upheld protection for landowners in situations involving injuries sustained when a hiker stepped into a hole on a trail, when a swimmer drowned in a creek, and when a snowmobiler struck a tree stump at the edge of a lake (Harper, 1991). Certain exceptions to this protection are included in the law, however, such as "willful or malicious failure to guard or warn against a dangerous condition, use, structure or activity." With the exception of North Carolina and Alaska, all states have enacted laws protecting landowners from lawsuits filed by non-fee paying visitors who use their property for recreational purposes. According to one researcher at the U.S. Forest Service, "in most states the claimant must prove at least gross negligence in order to establish a basis for suit under the Recreation Use Liability Statutes" (Hronek, 1989).

Although it has not yet adopted any statewide greenway policy, the New York State Legislature set a significant precedent in 1991 by creating the nation's largest greenway corridor, designating 3.5 million acres of land in 10 counties as the Hudson River Greenway. Stretching from Westchester and Rockland counties in the south to Albany and Rensselaer 160 miles to the north, this area has been targeted to receive special financial incentives to encourage participation by local governments.

Among the attractive features offered by the legislation are technical assistance, money to pay for the local greenway planning process, priority in obtaining state funds for land acquisition and infrastructure needs, and indemnification in the event of lawsuits brought pursuant to participation in the greenway. Annual revenues estimated at $700,000, generated by a hotel tax in the greenway area, provide a dedicated funding stream for participating counties and municipalities.

In addition to improving land-use controls (such as zoning ordinances and master plans) to help conserve farmland, protect scenic viewsheds, and preserve environmentally sensitive areas, a major goal of the Greenways Council is to create a Hudson River Trail on both sides of the river, connecting urban centers with natural areas and interpretively linking the many historic sites found in this remarkable valley. Planning attention is also being focused on certain roads in the river corridor as scenic routes, on the basis that aesthetic improvements along such thoroughfares will benefit a very large number of daily users, certainly many times more than the number of hikers on trails.

Plans to link seven existing parks between Philadelphia and Newtown, Pennsylvania, with a 15-mile greenway trail for bicycling and hiking are utilizing an approach known as "rail-banking," which allows the regional transit authority to resume train service in the future should it become feasible to do so. Running alongside the scenic Pennypack Creek, the trail will cross through undisturbed natural woodlands on a route that passes the ruins of more than 20 mills and several of the oldest stone bridges in southeastern Pennsylvania. Traversing a thickly settled area, the trail will connect many residential neighborhoods with two commuter rail stations, making it easier and more attractive for greater numbers of people to walk or bike to the train.

The notion of using the subdivision development process to create or extend greenways is an idea whose time is rapidly arriving, as residents and local officials begin to recognize two realities. The first is that without intervention, their townships will eventually become a quiltwork of "wall-to-wall subdivisions" with no new public spaces except for the streets and school playgrounds. (See the critique of conventional zoning and the description of "build-out" maps, in Chapters 2 and 15, respectively.) The second is that the extreme shortage of public money to finance significant open space acquisition and greenway creation is very likely to continue in the years ahead and that, even when such monies are appropriated, it is likely that they will be very small relative to the obvious need.

However, notable exceptions to this rule do exist. The Maryland General Assembly passed a bill in 1990 that would increase the state's annual appropriation for open space acquisition from $39 million to $100 million over a six-year period. (Unfortunately, due to the economic recession of 1991–92, all but $12 million of these funds were frozen by lawmakers, and it is likely that it will take much longer for the remaining appropriations to be made available.) Even with this substantial supplement, officials there recognize that the "buy-back" approach is inherently limited, and they are therefore encouraging local regulatory measures to complement future land purchases. One method of achieving this is to require local jurisdictions to adopt local greenway plans in accordance with minimum state guidelines, and to adopt more effective zoning provisions as a condition for receiving grants under the state's open space program.

Greenway advocates in all states will benefit from funding being made available under the 1991 federal Intermodal Surface Transportation Efficiency Act (ISTEA), which covers 80 percent of project costs for recreational trails, bicycle and pedestrian facilities, and certain unique demonstration projects. Also funded under ISTEA is a bicycle and pedestrian coordinator for each state (usually located in the state department of transportation), who can provide complete information on eligible projects.

GREENWAY ZONING AND
SUBDIVISION TECHNIQUES

Perhaps the most promising planning tool available to municipalities and counties today is the "open space zoning" technique, described in Chapter 15. While not providing a panacea, this approach restores the essential planning initiative to the public sector, which can then prepare area-wide maps showing lands where new development should be "clustered into," and other lands where it should be avoided. Designing one's development to conform to these maps should not be a matter of choice for developers: it should be a minimum requirement for plan approval. As one subdivision after another is developed, the greenway system can grow in length, eventually producing an interconnected network of trails along such linear features as stream corridors, lakefronts, or ridgelines, as well as alongside farmland blocks or across shallow or seasonal wetlands (on elevated planks). Such has been the approach of the Lake Forest Open Lands Association near Chicago. Due to its efforts, exactly half of the 32-acre McIlvaine estate has been preserved as common open space, adding 16 acres to a public greenway running across Lake County along the West Skokie River (Siewers, 1989). Significant gaps across properties not expected to be developed in the foreseeable future can be bridged through the purchase of conservation easements, or negotiated access agreements, on selected segments in the system. In Britain, the Countryside Commission has for several decades utilized access agreements to create footpath connections for "ramblers," as hikers are called there. Under this approach rural landowners are paid a nominal sum annually by the commission (an agency of central government), in addition to reimbursement for any property damages caused by the walkers (Johnson, 1971). A similar arrangement could be offered by municipal, county, or state governments in this country, where trail links would otherwise not exist.

The idea of *requiring* developers to utilize clustering concepts to create an interconnected system of open spaces within and between their subdivisions is gaining popularity in various locations around the country. Since 1989, Section 26–24(d) of the City Code in Fairfax, Virginia has required development proposals to provide for trail connections and bicycle paths where such systems exist or are being officially planned. Townships in the Ann Arbor area, for example, are being encouraged by planners at the University of Michigan "to require all development proposals that include creeks to be in the form of PUDs." The creek corridor could then be preserved as open space for use by residents of the developments. Minimum standards for PUDs could be established concerning the ratio of development to open space, the width of the creek corridor, and the placement of water retention ponds for maximum protection of the natural environment (Ann Arbor Area Creek Management Project, 1991). Similarly, as noted in Chapter 12, the New Castle County Planning Department in Delaware has recommended that zoning regulations be amended to include clustering *requirements* to preserve the scenic character and environmental integrity of the Red Clay Valley, a potential greenway combining an unspoiled creek and a scenic road (New Castle County Planning Dept., 1989).

In Cary, North Carolina, the town's existing trail network has recently been extended 8,600 feet by three planned unit developments. In fact, of the 32 miles of greenway currently in place there, all but 6.5 miles were contributed by developers. (See Figures 16–2 and 16–3.) According to the Cary greenway planner, the local development community has widely embraced greenway construction as an extremely inexpensive recreational amenity that offers strong marketing advantages. Town officials are currently negotiating with one homeowners' association to acquire access to a private 2.2-mile trail that would link two public greenways with schools and shopping centers.

Another municipality that has institutionalized trail creation as an integral part of the land development process is Pocopson Township in Chester County, Pennsylvania. When subdivisions are proposed in areas shown on the township's official trails master plan map, zoning and subdivision regulations specifically designed to help implement the community-wide trail network come into play.

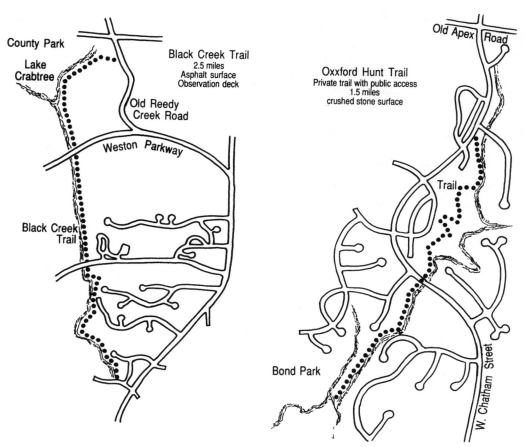

Figure 16–2. Of the 32 miles of trails in Cary, North Carolina, 25 miles were built by developers as part of the subdivision approval process. Recognizing the attraction these trails have for potential homebuyers, developers have begun including photos of adjacent greenway trails in their newspaper and magazine ads.

Although trail provision was initially resisted by some developers when the township first started requiring such dedications, the policy has been quite well-accepted since the adoption of the official trails map, which shows the larger picture and demonstrates that the requirements are not being selectively applied. This map has also allowed developers to see, from the beginning, the approximate location of the trail system, so that they may design around it (or suggest reasonable modifications to the alignment) when laying out their houselots and streets.

Another noteworthy aspect of Pocopson's approach is that the trail system is a public one,

whose use is not restricted to subdivision residents. In fact, the trail corridor itself is considered to be a public dedication, such as streets and neighborhood parks. Under the zoning enabling legislation in most states, including Pennsylvania, municipalities are allowed to "exact" a small percentage of land in each subdivision (typically about 5 percent) for public recreation. A narrow trail corridor, perhaps 15 or 20-feet wide, rarely consumes more than that.

In Delafield Township, Waukesha County, Wisconsin, a Milwaukee suburb, the Ice Age Park and Trail Foundation demonstrated the pivotal role that can be played by a private land conservation

Figure 16–3. Photograph of part of Cary, North Carolina's greenway trail system as it passes through one of many subdivisions connected by trails in that community.

group with a "ready fund" capable of buying and holding significant properties to prevent their total development. In this instance, the foundation purchased an old farm slated for development in order to establish several critical open space parameters and to find a buyer who shared the foundation's views about the importance of designing a creative subdivision around the Ice Age National Scenic Trail, which ran through the site. A perfect match was found with Siepmann Realty Corporation, which enthusiastically agreed to incorporate this regional trail into a new upscale subdivision, named "Hawksnest." Quickly recognizing the marketing tool offered by this amenity, Siepmann located the trail on land affording some of the best views available on the property (Holman, 1991). Homes are clustered on one-acre lots, with 80 of the 175 acres set aside as open space, containing several miles of interior neighborhood trails connecting with the regional trail at several points.

Because not all developers recognize the marketing value of designing new rural subdivisions around special features of the natural landscape preserved as permanent open space for the benefit of their residents, including trail networks, several townships along the route of the Ice Age Trail have begun to require subdivision applicants to

lay out their houselots and streets to respect and incorporate these elements into their plans. Such a foresighted approach could have avoided the protracted dispute between local officials in Delafield and another developer, Lewellyn Streff, who firmly insists upon his legal right to interrupt the trail with homes perched on the very crest of the ridgeline that the trail has traditionally traversed (Hayes, 1988).

Another point to be remembered is that even though greenway trail proposals generally enjoy broad community support, their public acceptance should never be taken for granted. In Westford, Massachusettts, a developer who suggested redesigning his conventional subdivision proposal to include open space and connecting trails, to link an existing conservation area on his eastern boundary with two existing trails on the western side of his property, encountered opposition from a few abutters whose lots his new trails would skirt. They complained about "strangers, dogs, and horses" passing through the woods along the rear edge of their one-acre lots. Fortunately this was not the preponderant opinion, and the "open space subdivision" was approved. Ironically the opponents lived in a conventional development whose creation had, years before, obliterated several well-established hiking trails that had crisscrossed this part of town, a fact not forgotten by a number of long-term residents who supported the new cluster proposal. Figure 16–4 shows a map of the new subdivision in its context of surrounding development and abutting conservation land and trails.

Although such trails are usually maintained by homeowners' associations or by the municipal parks staff, sometimes land trusts become involved. In Easttown Township, Pennsylvania, the Natural Lands Trust holds easements to and maintains a 4,400-foot-long trail system winding through "Sharp's Woods," a 34-acre conservation area of woodlands and wetlands in a subdivision containing 100 houses. Although most land trusts are private nonprofit organizations, a growing number are being created through partnership efforts between the public and private sectors. For example, Missoula, Montana's municipal open space plan is

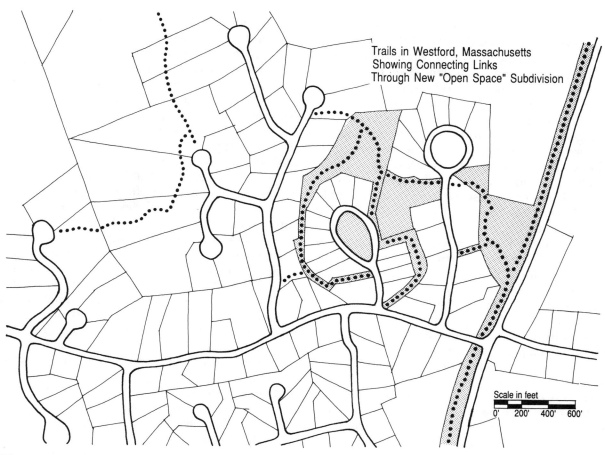

Trails in Westford, Massachusetts
Showing Connecting Links
Through New "Open Space" Subdivision

Scale in feet
0'   200'   400'   600'

Figure 16–4. Greenway trails do not consume much land, and can sometimes serve their primary connecting purpose with relatively narrow strips between larger blocks of open space. In this sketch, a trail network connects several adjoining subdivisions in Westford, Massachusetts. One of these trail proposals aroused opposition from a few abuttors, whose complaints were squelched by a native resident who reminded the audience that townspeople had formerly enjoyed free access through the abuttors' own subdivision, before it was built.

being implemented in part by the Five Valley Land Trust, which was initiated by the city planner and receives county funding. A similar approach is currently being explored on Mercer Island, Washington, where a land trust is proposed to maintain city-owned open space in this Seattle suburb (Kennedy, 1992).

When greenway trails are incorporated into subdivision plans it is essential that trail layout and construction be considered to be a "required improvement" for which the developer is responsible, with proper installation ensured by bonds or other performance guarantees (as is done with streets, sidewalks, drainage facilities, etc.). Trails are not expensive to create, but unless they are put in place as part of the original development, the homeowners' association will immediately inherit a large task that its members are unprepared to deal with. Such was the case at Radnor Chase, an upscale subdivision of single-family homes in Radnor Township, Pennsylvania, a "Main Line" suburb of Philadelphia. Twelve years after plan approval, the homeowners' association approached the Natural Lands Trust to help them plan a coherent trail system through 20 acres of woods and seasonal wetlands winding through their neighborhood, where the developer was never required to do more than convey the land deed to the association. The trust is also advising the association on installation and ongoing maintenance issues. A key element in the trust's approach is to actively engage the residents in the trail planning process and in annual spring cleanups, to increase their feelings of ownership and neighborhood pride, and to encourage them to use the open space on a regular basis for exercise, walking their dogs, or to simply enjoy observing seasonal changes in the natural landscape.

Trail development and natural area conservation objectives have also strongly influenced the site design for a new subdivision at Solomon's Landing in Calvert County, Maryland. At Sandy Oaks in Anne Arundel County, Maryland, local open space zoning requirements recently combined with state restrictions to protect wetlands and an endangered species in a new subdivision greenway along a stream corridor (Maryland Greenways Commission, 1990). And in Steamboat Springs, Colorado, after local officials convened a mini-conference on "open space zoning," a developer agreed to alter his subdivision proposal very substantially. The changes he made preserved much more of the preexisting trail system that traverses his property, which had been used informally for decades for hiking, biking, and cross-country skiing. As a result, he intends to capitalize on the extensive trails network as a one of his sales marketing tools. (See Chapter 20 for a site plan of this development, called "The Sanctuary.")

At Dunham Lake in Hartland, Michigan, and at Woodlake in Midlothian, Virginia, developers have challenged the conventional practice that houselots must extend down to the water wherever waterfront lots are possible. In both cases an extensive greenway buffer has been provided along the shoreline, creating a linear park through which trails and paths allow all community residents to walk, hike, or bike as they enjoy the natural beauty of these two lakes (see Chapter 20 for further details on Dunham Lake). As shown in Figure 16–5, greenways at Woodlake not only provide refresh-

ing lakeside walking experiences; they also link neighborhoods to playgrounds, shopping facilities, and to each other, in the classic fashion pioneered at Radburn, in Fairlawn, New Jersey, in 1928. It is not surprising that this development received the Urban Land Institute's 1990 award for being the best new community in the country (Churn, 1990). The fact that Woodlake contains a very wide range of housing types and prices, from about $75,000 to $500,000, is another point in its favor.

The strong sales records and high property values in these two subdivisions effectively counter arguments from conventional developers who maintain that routing trails along a lakeshore, between their houselots and the water, cannot be done without ruining marketability. Similarly, there is no evidence that the presence of a well-used pedestrian path ("Marginal Way") beside Maine's rocky coastline, along the seaward edge of hundreds of houselots in the villages of York Harbor and Ogunquit, has had any dampening effect on the enormously high prices of the abutting properties. In fact, as will be argued later in this chapter and in the following one, the presence of nearby trails and open space typically boosts real estate values, as evidenced in study after study.

Perhaps the longest network of greenway trails for walking, hiking, and biking in a single subdivision is currently being created at the Caughlin Ranch development in Reno, Nevada. Recipient of an award for its design excellence, given by the American Planning Association, Nevada Chapter, this development includes 20 miles of trails.

Not surprisingly, some developers are willing to incorporate greenway principles into their subdivisions, while others refuse to cooperate. Therefore, the only way to ensure that the system will operate effectively as an interconnected network is for the local planning authority to include greenway standards in its basic zoning requirements. When such ordinance amendments are proposed, certain landowners and developers will undoubtedly protest loudly, but as long as they are still allowed to build the same number of units (albeit in a somewhat more compact fashion), there should be no substantive constitutional basis for any threatened legal challenges.

Figure 16–5. At Woodlake, in Midlothian, Virginia, an extensive bikeway network not only connects neighborhoods with each other and with schools and shopping areas, it also winds through the wooded buffer paralleling the shoreline of the reservoir around which the development has been built. Although this trail passes between the community's most expensive residences and the shore, it has not dampened the enthusiasm of buyers for these lots, exploding another myth often voiced by developers who perceive trails negatively.

In fact, "down-zoning" to reduce overall density is legal, where a rational connection between the new zoning and well-supported health, safety, and welfare reasons have been documented in official plans. Although down-zoning may diminish raw land values for development, landowners are not constitutionally entitled to maximize their potential profits. The basic constitutional economic test in so-called "takings" cases is whether the regulations have substantially stripped the property of all reasonable and beneficial uses. In general, the federal courts have not been overly impressed by claims that zoning changes have simply lowered the market value of a plaintiff's land for development, provided, of course, that the governing authority can show good public interest reasons for its action (Humbach, 1989).

It should also be added that in some instances, where a ready market exists for upscale housing (in affluent commuter or resort areas), reducing the number of lots can actually increase total development value, a phenomenon proven many times through the "limited development" projects of mini-estates popular with many land trusts. Although these projects have generally not created any open space accessible to others (even other residents of the same subdivisions), they could very easily be designed to do so. This should be one of the major agenda items for land trusts in the 1990s.

One of the best examples in the country where a foresighted approach to subdivision design is producing a major local greenway is in Bridgewater Township, in New Jersey's Somerset County. Located at the crossroads of six major highways in a rapidly suburbanizing region, the township has experienced extremely heavy pressure for new development, typified by a residential building boom and the construction of a 900,000 square foot shopping mall. Surprisingly, a largely undeveloped area known as Washington Valley, comprising some 5,000 acres tucked between the two Watchung Mountains, still survives as a major open space corridor, partly because the area had been designated on official plans as a potential reservoir site for many years. After the dam proposal was defeated in a statewide referendum, the valley was earmarked for preservation by advisory local and county master plans and park plans, but no regulations were enacted to prevent its development.

Over the years both the township and the county acquired various parcels in the area, but these accounted for only 300 of the valley's 5,000 acres. Even after the adoption of the county land use master plan in 1970, which strongly stated the case for protecting Washington Valley, only 25 acres were purchased for public parkland over the following decade. When sanitary collector and trunk sewer lines were constructed through the valley in the early 1980s, it became abundantly clear to nearly everyone that urgent preservation action was needed, and that public funds to accomplish that task "the old fashioned way" (i.e., buying it back at development value) were totally inadequate.

Relying more on brainpower than on taxing power, township officials embraced the idea of using clustering principles in a coordinated manner to create an interconnected greenway system. This was one of the principal recommendations of a secondary impact study that Bridgewater was required to prepare as a condition of federal grant-in-aid sewer funding, and it incorporated many previous planning suggestions made by the township park board regarding the desirability of linking the existing public open spaces already located along the valley corridor (school sites, parks, water district management areas, etc.).

During the summer of 1984 a graduate student was hired to prepare inventory maps for the five-mile-long valley, showing slopes, soil types, vegetation patterns, floodplains, land ownership, existing land uses, and utilities. Joined together, her maps extended five feet in length, even at the scale of 400 feet to the inch. The following summer another intern was employed to prepare conceptual sketch plans showing "how each property in the valley could be developed under the current zoning ordinance in a way which used clustering to preserve as much of the critical environmental lands identified in the natural resource inventory as possible" (Madden and Thomas, 1987).

The resulting plan illustrated the township's approach to preserving a coordinated system of 1,100 acres of open space to create a continuous network of hiking trails and wildlife protection areas. Adopted in 1984, the Washington Valley Open Space Plan has been used by municipal officials as a way of showing developers, in advance, the township's overall strategic planning intentions for the area. (See Figure 16–6.) The approach has been to tell subdivision applicants that unless they can suggest a better way to achieve the plan's objectives, they should follow the clustering pattern shown on its maps. In fact, since its adoption, nearly every developer has not only joined in the plan's spirit—many have improved upon its generalized cluster arrangements and have dedicated even more open space than the average 40 percent shown on the plan's conceptual maps (Madden and Thomas, 1987). Other features of the plan include a continuous local street network to avoid overloading existing roads, no additional stream crossings, and a regional approach to storm-water management using new basins paid for by developers in lieu of providing detention ponds in each subdivision.

Bridgewater's visionary and proactive approach follows some of the bold, innovative ideas proposed in Wallace and McHarg's 1963 *Plan for the Valleys*, described in Chapter 15. It is also a recent echo of the wise advice given by William A. Harmon, a New York developer who, in an address to the American Civic Association in 1909, said: "Could we have seen ahead, as we can now look back, we would immediately have begun the segregation of lands for park purposes in all our subdivisions, and would not only have served the community better, but would have received a return in dollars and cents to repay amply for every foot of ground so utilized" (quoted in the 1932 Philadelphia Regional Plan). Some of the economic aspects of greenway creation are discussed in the next section of this chapter and in Chap-

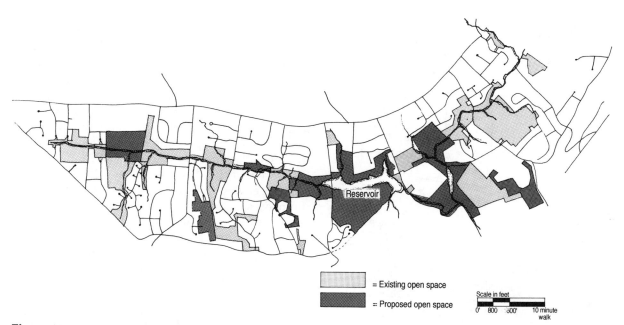

= Existing open space

= Proposed open space

Scale in feet
0' 800 600' 10 minute walk

Figure 16–6. An extensive greenway has been created along the Washington Valley in Bridgewater Township, Somerset County, New Jersey, by local planners who adopted a policy requiring developers to respect a broad, continuous natural corridor along both sides of the creek. Surprisingly, none of the developers objected, possibly because the arrangement was density-neutral (density credit was given for all buildable land within the greenway corridor, credit that could be utilized in other parts of an applicant's property).

ter 17. Harmon probably would have applauded local officials in Worcester Township, Montgomery County, Pennsylvania, who asked the Natural Lands Trust to redesign a proposed 21-lot subdivision along the Zacharias Creek. Noting that the development abutted public land at each end, trust staff sketched a new density-neutral concept plan with two-thirds of the property designated as a greenway connecting township land on the west with a state park to the east. This greenway buffers both banks of the creek, alongside which is planned an informal footpath or trail. (See Figure 16–7.)

GREENWAYS AND PROPERTY VALUES

There is a growing body of evidence to show that property values actually increase as a result of open space provision within and around developments where lot sizes have been trimmed to create that open space. The National Park Service annu-

ally publishes an updated and very detailed resource book on this subject, entitled *Economic Impacts of Protecting Rivers, Trails, and Greenway Corridors*. This report cites numerous studies on the measurable increase in real property value generated by proximity to traditional parks and to the newer greenways. Numerous examples of property value appreciation attributable to nearby open space, documented by the National Park Service, are cited in Chapter 17, "The Economics of Preserving Open Space." (See also the results of the case study comparing property values after 20 years in a conventional development and in an "open space" subdivision in Amherst, MA, reported in Chapter 14.)

Another very positive sign is that newspaper ads for real estate are beginning to mention proximity to greenways as a selling feature. For example, in the October 7, 1990, issue of the Sunday Raleigh *News and Observer*, no fewer than nine

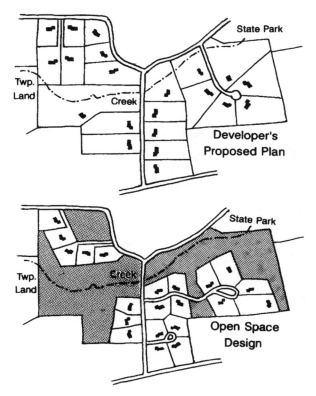

Figure 16–7. Although the developer's proposal for 21 three-acre lots and no open space was consistent with existing zoning (which in fact did not allow any design innovations), local officials in Worcester Township, north of Philadelphia, commissioned the Natural Lands Trust to sketch an alternative plan based upon the principles of open space development design. The Trust's concept plan contains 21 one-acre lots, most of which directly adjoin a 40-acre greenway that buffers a prolific trout stream and also connects two public open spaces. When the developer signaled his interest in the Trust's plan, township officials directed their solicitor to draft zoning amendments allowing for this greener approach.

classified ads noted that the homes and houselots for sale were adjacent to or near greenway corridors. (See Figure 16–8.) A recent full-page advertisement for a new subdivision in Cary, North Carolina, featured a large photograph of that town's Black Creek Greenway, with the caption "The Cary Greenway System is located immedi-

ately behind Harrison Place, and leads to Lake Crabtree." In fact, some realtors have started placing additional "for sale" signs in locations visible from the greenway paths. And in Front Royal, Virginia, a developer who advertised that his second-home subdivision abutted the Big Blue Trail (which was extended along the perimeter of his property, over an easement he donated to the Potomac Appalachian Club) sold all his houselots within four months (National Park Service, 1990).

In spite of the above evidence, some will argue that greenway trails create nuisances for abutting homeowners or farmers. In Hadley, Massachusetts, farmers whose fields adjoined a proposed rail-to-trail conversion claimed that cyclists would file nuisance suits against them for spraying crops with chemical pesticides, droplets of which could easily drift across field boundaries onto the bike path. When trail proponents asked these farmers why they had never expressed any previous concerns about the health of their neighbors, they dropped that line of attack and raised the issue of potential rapists attacking their wives and stealing away silently on their ten-speeds.

Sometimes a tragic incident occurs on a trail, providing ammunition for the local opposition. Such was the case in Downingtown, Pennsylvania, after a young woman was raped on the Horseshoe Trail, just outside town. Frequently mentioned in almost every public trail discussion in Chester County over the next several years, this solitary but loathsome crime was blown out of proportion until someone thought to inquire about how many rapes were committed in the area every year, and to point out that only one has ever occurred on a trail. Out of this discussion has arisen an understanding that young women should consider hiking with friends or with a protective dog to better ensure their personal safety, and that rapes are far more likely to occur in homes or on dates than on trails.

Unfortunately, vigorous opposition is not uncommon when greenways are proposed in areas where trails are a new phenomenon. However, in the Research Triangle region of North Carolina these corridors have become quite well accepted, as local experience grows and people begin to

WELL LOVED RANCH WITH FULL BASEMENT - backs up to city greenway, follow the path to Shelley Lake. 2 finished rms. in basement. Sandra 870-1550 (9739) $87,900

FARMINGTON WOODS Walk to school, perfect for growing family, greenway, 4 bedrooms, 3 baths (65451) 859-3300/4793 $144,900

UNIQUE CORNER cul-de-sac in Loch-mere, backs up to greenway, build your own dreamhome! (64075) 859-3300 $57,000

TRANSITIONAL RANCH Backs up to green-way, tongue-in-groove, cathedral ceiling, very open, (62617) 859-3358 $89,900

NEW LISTING 3 bedrm 2 1/2 bath home under construction in Planter's Walk. Fabulous 1st floor master with champagne bath. Lots of storage and 1 car garage. Deck. Great lot — adjacent to greenway. Only $106,475. Call Gina at 266-7612. Pulle homes.

VILLAGE ON GREEN Assume $6,000 town-home FHA 10.5%. End unit backs to greenway. Motivated! (59527) 876-7030

PREMO VIEW, privacy and access to greenway for exercise, affordable 2.5 bath townhome at $63,500. Nelson Bunn H563

SPACIOUS CARY TWNHSE, PI-rates Cove, 3 bedrms, 2.5 baths, living room, formal dining rm., large private deck overlooks greenway. exc. schools. $64,900. Owner pays closing costs. 467-4341

Figure 16–8. On any given Sunday in Raleigh and Durham, North Carolina, one can find numerous newspaper advertisements for homes and houselots, citing proximity to the greenway network. Shown here is a sampling from the October 7, 1990 issue of the Raleigh *News and Observer.*

understand how they are used. A recent study of the benefit of rail-trails, by researchers at Pennsylvania State University and the National Park Service, dispels many myths surrounding greenways. Interviews with residents whose houselots abut three very different rail-trails (in Iowa, Florida, and California) show that the overwhelming majority (76 to 99 percent) of neighboring homeowners use the trails and enjoy them on a frequent basis (47 to 141 times a year). In addition, respondents stated that they were pleased with their homes' proximity to the trails, and that they considered living near them to be a definite advantage (Moore, et al., 1992).

To nip negative arguments in the bud and to present a positive perspective, the Montour Trail Council in Pittsburgh has produced an eight-minute video including numerous interviews from a variety of individuals supportive of the Arrowhead Trail, an existing four-mile segment of the Montour Trail, which will eventually extend along 55 miles of former railbeds through rural, suburban, and urban areas in Allegheny and Washington

counties. Available for rental or sale, this video is an example of a simple but persuasive tool that could not only be shown more widely, but that could also be replicated by similar groups in other parts of the country to promote their own projects with interviews featuring local officials, realtors, and people who use and/or live next to trails in their own area.

Worries about crime, vandalism, and inappropriate activities (such as dirt-biking and beer parties) have made many municipalities less than eager to establish trail networks. Typical of affluent communities that have traditionally sought to preserve local open space solely for wildlife purposes is Redding, Connecticut, which has protected more than 1,250 acres of land since the late 1960s. When the original preservation leaders stepped aside to let a younger group of residents carry the torch, after about 10 years, they were astonished to learn that the new people in charge looked at their hard-won nature preserves as an ideal location to start a town-wide network of hiking trails. Fortunately, these older members kept their strong reservations mostly to themselves, thereby avoiding a potentially fractious squabble.

Sensing a degree of discontent with their proposal, trail advocates opened an experimental trail on one of the preserves, to see if it would be used much, by whom, and whether it would generate rowdy behavior, vandalism, or crime. An immediate success, the first trail was followed by another, and then another, until no fewer than 55 miles were completed by 1985. Today the community is immensely proud of its extensive public trail system, the use of which is encouraged by the publication of a 95-page trail guide published jointly by the municipal conservation commission and two local land trusts. Redding's current goal is to continue linking the shorter trails within each of the individual preserves into an interconnected network of longer "through-trails" (Ensor and Mitchell, 1985).

MINIMUM GREENWAY WIDTHS

The issue of appropriate minimum widths for buffers along streams and rivers or around ponds and lakes involves variables beyond those pertinent to greenway trails alone. When the only factor to be considered is the minimum physical width needed to accommodate a pathway, dimensional requirements can be quite modest. For instance, when space is at an absolute premium, as when trails are being retrofitted into an already developed area, they can function effectively even within relatively narrow corridors, less than 20 feet in width. Good examples of coastal paths where the walking experience is not diminished by such modest widths are the "Marginal Way" in Ogunquit and York Harbor, Maine, and the oceanside walkway in Newport, Rhode Island, which follows the cliff tops in front of New England's most famous row of mansions. At Woodlake, a large planned unit development outside Richmond in Midlothian, Virginia, paved cycling paths weave through a wooded greenway averaging 75 feet in width, between rear lot lines and the Swift Creek Reservoir. As long as interesting views remain on at least one side of a trail, users can still have very enjoyable experiences.

GREENWAY BUFFERS FOR WATER QUALITY

In other cases, however, variables other than trail construction are involved. In addition to providing access to walkers and cyclists, greenways can be designed to filter storm-water runoff from adjacent developments or from cultivated fields.

From the standpoint of water quality protection, greenways function as a trap for pollutants and excessive nutrients dissolved or suspended in storm runoff. Leaf litter and groundcover can also slow storm-water velocity, thereby reducing soil erosion and stream sedimentation. Reducing runoff velocity allows storm water to be absorbed into the soil and to be taken up by the vegetation. The minimum effective greenway width for water quality buffering therefore depends on factors such as the permeability of the soil, the steepness of the slopes, and the amount and type of plant material growing there, in addition to the volume and character of the pollutants likely to be found in the runoff. A study of fertilizer-rich agricultural runoff in the Chesapeake Bay area found that phosphorus and nitrogen were reduced by 80 percent and 89 percent respectively by a forested buffer 165-feet deep (Correll and Peterjohn, 1984). In eastern North Carolina, researchers have estimated that buffer widths of 256 feet would remove 90 percent of the nitrates from agricultural runoff (Phillips, 1989). To encourage farmers not to cultivate land immediately bordering rivers and lakes, the USDA Agricultural Conservation and Stabilization Service (ASCS) offers "rental payments" on untilled filter strips 66 to 99-feet wide.

GREENWAY CORRIDORS FOR WILDLIFE

When wildlife habitat needs are considered, even wider greenway corridors are recommended, usually in the range of 200 to 300 feet. To protect woodland bird species nesting and feeding along rivers in Maine, buffers of about 250 feet have been recommended by Small and Johnson (cited by Ganem, 1989), while 300 feet was the minimum distance estimated to be needed for breeding by a number of other water-dependent animal species in another study (Leedy, et al., 1978).

One of the more comprehensive recent investigations of habitat needs (which examined six different types of wetland landscape habitats in Florida) set 322-foot minimum widths for species associated with marshland ecosystems, and 550 and 732 feet for species associated with forested wetlands (Bowen, et al., 1990). The results of such studies have been incorporated into policy guidelines and standards in various states. For example, the Maine Department of Environmental Protection has recommended wildlife habitat and travel corridors 330-feet wide along rivers and around lakes. This is very similar to the 300-foot setback proposed in the model river conservation ordinance drafted by the New Jersey Department of Environment and Energy for communities bordering the Maurice River, which was recently nominated for national "wild and scenic" designation. The New Jersey model also requires five-acre building densities (which may be clustered to maximize blocks of undisturbed open space) and limits vegetative clearing to 20 percent of the land area. Although the protected riparian buffer strip is but 50-feet deep, the low densities, deep building setbacks, and stringent clearing standards combine effectively to protect much more than the 50-foot-deep strip listed in the ordinance. Footpaths 10-feet wide are also allowed to traverse the buffer strip to provide water access.

The value of greenways in protecting water quality and in providing wildlife habitat has been amply demonstrated in Hartland, Michigan, where a greenway buffer ranging in width from 100 feet to 400 feet has kept Dunham Lake water quality nearly pristine, despite the construction of thousands of feet of subdivision roads and hundreds of homes served by septic tanks on lots directly behind this green ring. Subdivided in the late 1940s by former Governor Murray Van Waggoner, the land was subject to a stipulation by the previous owners that such a buffer had to be created and maintained, to carry forward part of the proper-

ty's previous function as a waterfowl sanctuary. Other restrictions prohibit hunting and the operation of any type of motorized boats. Today the buffer area hosts a lakeside trail connecting various subdivision streets with the lake, a bathing beach, and a picnic/recreation area. (For further details, see the "case example" in Chapter 20.)

COMPOSITE GREENWAY STANDARDS

Width requirements for greenways should not be overly standardized or applied inflexibly. As seen from the above discussion, many variables exist and few situations are exactly alike. In Wake County, North Carolina, county planning staff members negotiate appropriate greenway widths with landowners, taking into consideration such factors as specific environmental conditions, stream size, and the nature of abutting land uses. Nevertheless, in order to establish some sort of baseline for these discussions, the county has published a table of "recommended" greenway widths, which can be increased or decreased according to the characteristics of each situation. Those widths, as measured back from each bank, are 150 feet along rivers and large creeks, 100 feet along other streams, and 50 feet along minor stream spurs (Wake County, 1987). Their inclusion in this section does not represent an endorsement, but is simply a description of the approach one Southern county adopted several years ago.

However, it should be noted that several inherent dangers arise from setting prescriptive minimum standards. First, they are almost never voluntarily exceeded by developers, or extended by local planning officials, even when site-specific conditions may warrant it. Second, they tend to become ossified over time, so that they are infrequently reexamined and updated. It is very important that such standards be reviewed periodically in the light of more recent studies and practical experience, and that they be applied more flexibily rather than in an across-the-board manner, to deal intelligently with different situations.

17

The Economics of Preserving Open Space

Elizabeth Brabec

OVERVIEW

Within the American economy, open land is commonly seen as an unused and wasted resource, one that will reach its full potential only if it is developed and put to a "productive" use. This attitude is often accompanied by strong opposition to open space preservation and clustering efforts. But, as communities become increasingly developed, as traffic grows heavier, and as open lands steadily dwindle away, the intrinsic values of such natural areas become more apparent to larger numbers of people.

This chapter cites a growing body of evidence that open space preservation and concurrent resource conservation are both economically and socially beneficial for many communities. For example, studies have shown that clustered developments with significant open space preservation areas tend to increase local property values.

Among the most common issues involving the value of open space are:

• requirements for clustering development and retaining a significant percentage of open space;

• requirements for public parkland setasides within PUDs and subdivision developments;

• municipal budgets for the acquisition of parkland and natural areas; and

• the acquisition, development, and protection of greenways through a community.

THE REAL COSTS OF SPRAWLING DEVELOPMENT

Across the country, when people are asked where they would prefer to live, work, shop, and recreate, they invariably select communities or neighborhoods that have an abundance of trees, open spaces, and uncluttered pedestrian ways. These preferences translate into clear economic terms: if a community is to succeed in attracting new residents and businesses, it must be concerned about its appearance, physical character, livability, and "feel."

Residents should be concerned not only about the number, type, and density of new subdivisions, but also about the effects those developments will produce on their townscape, the surrounding rural landscape, and their local "sense of place." Although new subdivisions can be designed to preserve a variety of open spaces, these advantages are generally not realized, and communities typically receive very conventional "cookie-cutter" layouts of just more houselots and more streets. After several decades of methodically reviewing and approving scores of such subdivisions, communities are able to see the negative effects and higher costs of sprawling development and the concomitant loss of open space. These costs may be grouped into two types, those felt by the community as a whole, and those accruing to the local government (often termed "fiscal impacts").

THE COSTS OF ENVIRONMENTAL DEGRADATION

The economic impacts of development, both positive and negative, extend much farther than is commonly appreciated. For many years researchers have been concerned about the land, air, and water pollution effects of low-density development. Our present land-consumptive system of development increases air and water pollution with both ecological and economic consequences. While it is difficult to quantify the total economic impact of the loss of open lands (because the effects form an interconnected network affecting industries as diverse as farming, fishing, and tourism), those losses can be substantial.

Land Consumption

Very few communities have escaped the effects of strip development and large-lot subdivisions. It sometimes seems to occur overnight: where there was a farm field yesterday, today stands a Burger King, a 7-Eleven, or a Wal-Mart. The pace has been sometimes fast and sometimes slow, but relentless, to the point where it is often accepted as inevitable.

Large-lot residential zoning, often enacted by communities that would like to preserve open space such as woodland and farmland, is to a large part responsible for the high levels of land consumption experienced by those communities. In Maryland, where half of the new construction occurs on agricultural parcels, 73,700 acres of farmland were converted to developed uses between 1985 and 1990 (Greer, 1991). A similar acreage of woodland was also taken for suburban expansion. By the year 2020, it is estimated that an additional 700,000 acres of open land in the state will be covered with development. What this means for local woodland wildlife habitats and for the local farming economy are that both are seriously threatened. In many suburbanizing areas agriculture has ceased to be viable because large, contiguous tracts of farmland are no longer available, and support services have become nonexistent (these issues are discussed in greater detail in Chapter 18).

Water Pollution

Conversion of land to development affects local water supplies through the pollution of rivers, streams, bays, and groundwater. As land is developed, the area of impervious surface increases, thereby reducing the volume of water infiltrating into the soil. Consequently, more water flows offsite and into rivers and streams. This runoff, commonly called non-point source pollution, carries with it sediment and such pollutants as fertilizers, pesticides, and motor oil.

Apart from the substances normally recognized as pollutants, soil erosion can cause serious water quality degradation. One study by the Maryland Department of Natural Resources in the Gunpowder Falls Basin, a watershed of the Chesapeake Bay, shows that forestland produces about 50 tons of sediment per square mile per year. In contrast, land stripped for construction contributes 25,000 to 50,000 tons per year. This sediment enters the tributaries of the Chesapeake carrying nutrients and pollutants that are slowly killing the bay (Ebenreck, 1988).

How is this pollution likely to affect the economy? The Chesapeake Bay is an excellent example of the network of economic impacts related to open space preservation. The Office of Research within the Maryland Department of Economic and Employment Development estimated the value of Chesapeake Bay to the economies of Maryland and Virginia at $678 billion (in 1989 dollars). Of this amount, $31.6 billion is generated annually from commercial fisheries, activities for the ports, ship and boat building, ship repair, and tourism specific to the bay. Water pollution is seriously harming the commercial fisheries upon which the regional economy depends, for both the fishing and tourism industries. The report states that:

> Should water quality decline, marine vegetation continue to die, wetlands be destroyed, and waterfowl and animal habitats vanish, then that portion of total land values around the Bay will decline as well.

> Likewise, some—though not all—major water-related commercial economic activities are threatened by further deterioration of the Chesapeake

Bay. . . . Tourism—which includes recreational fishing, boating, waterfowl hunting, as well as sightseeing—will also be adversely affected.

If we permit what can be generally described as the "quality factor" to decline, we can expect the real economic value of the Chesapeake Bay to decline as well. Conversely, if we improve the quality of the Chesapeake Bay, we can expect that its economic value will rise.

Air Pollution

The provision of greenways and greenbelts in communities function in two ways to reduce air pollution. Trees and other vegetation in greenspaces possess a large capacity for removing CO_2, particulates and other pollutants from the air. In addition, when nearby development is clustered (as a means of creating the greenspace), and when it is designed in a mixed-use manner, the resulting compact development form provides the base for a concentration of services, thereby reducing the number of vehicle trips per day.

Sprawling development negatively impacts air quality because it forces residents to drive to jobs, schools, and services. Because many existing zoning codes separate residential, commercial, and industrial uses, it is no longer possible to walk to a corner store in most new neighborhoods. Thus, we have become totally dependent upon the private automobile as our primary mode of transportation, even for our simplest everyday needs.

Studies have shown that each suburban household generates, on average, between 10 and 12 vehicle trips per day (Loudoun County Planning, 1990). Such numerous trips add substantially to air pollution, particularly in areas already experiencing air quality problems. Under the federal Clean Air Act, states are required to meet federally mandated air quality standards. While significant reductions in air pollution have been achieved, it is clear that many areas of the United States (California, for example) will be unable to meet air quality standards without curtailing the presently unrestricted use of cars in some metropolitan areas (Air Review, 1986).

Air pollution reduces property values. Two studies from Chicago indicate that high levels of particulate contamination depress real-estate values (Diamond, 1980; Smith, 1978). By looking at the premiums paid for homes in various locations, it was found that a reduction in air pollution particulates of 10 ug/m$_3$ was worth $3,000, and a premium of $5,000 was paid for properties in the areas of lowest air pollution.

FISCAL IMPACT ANALYSIS, OR HOW MUCH DOES SPRAWL COST THE TAXPAYER?

Apart from the effects of parkland and greenspaces on the value of surrounding property, a community can determine the effect of open space on the municipal coffers. This is done through a process called "fiscal impact analysis," which is a method of determining the costs of providing public services to a municipality. The public costs associated with development fall under five categories (The Nature Conservancy, The Hidden Costs of Development):

* educating children;
* constructing and maintaining public facilities, such as water and sewage facilities, solid waste disposal, and parks;
* providing public services, such as fire and police protection, and health and welfare services;
* constructing and maintaining roads and parking facilities; and
* administering local government.

A number of studies have been undertaken to determine the effects of various types of development upon a municipality's cost outlays. These studies have shown that the net public costs resulting from low-density or "sprawl" development are considerably greater than those resulting from higher density or "cluster" development for the same number of dwelling units. Put simply, it costs more to run school buses and emergency vehicles, to repair roads, and to collect garbage when homes are spread out over more miles of roads than when houses are located more closely together, as in a typical nineteenth-century town.

In a study of the fiscal impacts of major land uses in Culpeper County, Virginia, it was found that "for every dollar of revenue collected from residential land, $1.25 is spent on county services; for every dollar collected from industrial/commercial land, 19 cents is spent on services; similarly, for every dollar collected from farm/forest/open space, 19 cents is spent on services." Farm/forest/open space generates revenues of $1.9 million and expenditures of $350,000. Even with the deferral for current-use taxation, farm/forest/open space land provides a net tax benefit to the county (Vance and Larson, 1988).

In a study of development in DuPage County, Illinois, it was found that new growth, both residential and nonresidential, resulted in higher taxes. While most citizens and planners feel that nonresidential development will improve the tax base, when looking at the long-term and regional impacts, nonresidential development had more than three times the impact on raising taxes of residential development. The study showed that commercial and industrial development placed burdens on public infrastructure and services that were not being paid for by the increased value of the land (Bergman, 1991).

In its study of Loudoun County, Virginia, the American Farmland Trust (1986) found that net public costs were approximately three times higher ($2,200 per dwelling) where the density was one unit per five acres, than where the density was 4.5 units per acre ($700 per dwelling). The report states:

> Relatively low-density residential development (one to five or more acres per dwelling unit) generates higher net public costs primarily because it requires inefficient expenditures for public school operating, instructional, and transportation services, and also because it creates potentially higher public liabilities for road maintenance and future provision of public water and sewer services.
>
> . . . Low-density residential subdivisions, usually located in rural areas, remove relatively large amounts of land from agricultural uses while requiring public services (education, health and welfare, public safety, etc.), which are similar on a per dwelling or per capita basis to those required by high density subdivisions that convert far less land from existing agricultural or other economic uses.

The Costs of Sprawl, a study commissioned by the Council on Environmental Quality in the Department of Housing and Urban Development and the Environmental Protection Agency, found that "better planning and higher density result in lower economic, environmental, natural resource, and, to some extent, personal and social costs for a given number of dwelling units. Increased density is less expensive in terms of total costs and even more so in terms of that portion of total costs typically borne by the government" (Real Estate Research Corporation, 1974).

A recent review and evaluation of the literature conducted by the Urban Land Institute concluded that "development spread out at low densities increases the costs of public facilities" (Frank, 1989). The book looks at the range of costs induced by sprawling development and suggests that houses built in such sprawl may cost from 40 to 400 percent more to service than comparable homes in more compactly designed subdivisions.

THE VALUE OF OPEN SPACE

Open space preservation produces multiple economic benefits: those to the community as a whole, those to individual landowners, and those to developers. In terms of community benefits, open space preservation can produce far-reaching effects on the local economy in its effect on the local "quality of life." According to an annual survey of chief executive officers conducted by Cushman and Wakefield in 1989 (NPS, 1990), quality of life for employees was the third most important factor in locating a business. According to a 1988 report of the Governors' Committee on the Environment (NPS, 1990), the governors of five New England states officially recognized open space as a key element in the quality of life that brought rapid economic growth and a multi-billion dollar tourism industry to the region.

Through these studies we can see that "quality of life" has a tangible, economic value that can be "cashed in." One example of this phenomenon can be found in the relatively depressed economy of Colorado, where the city of Boulder has remained economically successful. Denis Nock, the president of the Chamber of Commerce, attributes Boulder's economic success to its quality of life, its trees, open spaces, and general livability. He states that businesses move to Boulder rather than locate elsewhere in the region, paying higher taxes and land costs, to take advantage of the amenities Boulder offers.

Increases in Property Values and Returns in Municipal Taxes

As long ago as the 1850s, Frederick Law Olmsted pointed out the economic benefits of creating a major open space in New York City. To justify the expense of creating Central Park (which would otherwise have been filled with more apartments, shops, and offices), Olmsted began tracking the value of real estate adjacent to the park while it was still under construction. He compared the higher tax revenues received from those adjacent properties with the interest the city was then paying for parkland acquisition and improvement. When it was only half complete, Central Park began to generate revenue. Olmsted documented a $55,880 net return in annual tax from the park in 1864 (Fox, 1990).

Olmsted used this economic justification for parkland in other areas of the country. An 1890 report, published under the authority of the Metropolitan Park Commissioners, stated that:

> The citizens of Boston had examples before them, in the parks of neighboring American cities, which assured them that, while the cost of necessary open space would be great, the returns in taxes from the enhanced value of real estate in the vicinity of the new parks, as well as the income from betterments, would ensure them a strong financial support. . . . The experience of other cities had proved that, aside from the benefits accruing from parks as attractions to travellers and as means for affording aesthetic delight in landscape, there was a tangible effect produced by them to improve the moral and physical welfare of communities (Fox, 1990).

Olmsted's analysis of tax receipts in New York City are still valid today, and provide a compelling reason for communities to preserve open space. Since one of a municipality's prime sources of funds is the real estate property tax, and because protected open space increases the value of the surrounding land (while creating little new demand for costly governmental services), it is in the public's best economic interest to preserve open space.

Since Olmsted's time, numerous other studies have been conducted to demonstrate similar effects elsewhere. For example, researchers evaluating the impacts of a greenbelt on neighborhood property values in Boulder, Colorado, found that the aggregate property value for one neighborhood increased $5.4 million with proximity to the greenbelt. Resulting in $500,000 of additional annual property tax, the increase in property tax alone could recover the initial costs of the $1.5 million purchase price in just three years (Correll, Lillydahl, and Singell, 1978).

California's secretary for the state resources agency anticipated that $100 million would be returned to local economies each year from an initial park bond investment of $330 million. The returns were to be in the form of increased value of properties and stimulated business (Gilliam, 1980).

In a study of Lake Merritt in Oakland, Lake Murray in San Diego, and La Mesa and the Santee Lakes in Santee, California, it was found that urban water parks had a marked effect on surrounding property values (Darling, 1973). Lake Merritt is an extensively developed urban water park located in the center of Oakland, California. The park contains the lake and a 3.18-mile greenbelt. Using a property value model, the park added an estimated $41 million in value to the surrounding property.

Lake Murray is a reserve reservoir for the central and eastern parts of San Diego. The park has a four-mile shoreline, but has only limited recreational use. The area is largely single-family residential. A property value model again showed an increase to surrounding property value attributable to the lake at over $1 million, with an additional $426,000 added to property value due to the view.

The Santee Lakes are five small ponds located in a lower-middle income, single-family housing area. The ponds have been developed for recreational use and include areas for swimming, fishing, and boating. The ponds added an estimated $227,000 to the surrounding property value. The lower figure here results from the smaller acreage of this area, and from the fact that the lakes are a recreational facility with virtually no urban beautification qualities.

In addition to the economic advantages, there are a number of other public benefits to open space that are just beginning to be quantified. Among these are improved public health, lower energy consumption, and increased tourism.

Increases in Tourism

By improving an area's image, open space helps to increase tourism. A poll commissioned by the President's Commission on Americans Outdoors found that natural beauty was the single most important criterion for tourists in selecting outdoor recreation sites. Greenways, rivers, and trails, which attract visitors from outside the local area, can stimulate the local economy by infusing it with "outside" dollars. A recent trend analysis shows that weekend trips to nearby areas are on the increase, while the traditional two-week summer vacation is on the decline for today's travelers (NPS, 1990), strengthening the market for local and regional recreational opportunities.

Observing, photographing, and feeding fish and wildlife provided enjoyment for 134.7 million Americans in 1985, no small figure when one starts to calculate what kinds of economic activity this generates. It is estimated that these 134.7 million participants spent over $14.3 billion for their activities in that year, an average of $221 per spender. The total spending included $4.4 billion for trip-related expenditures, nearly $9.4 billion for equipment, and $480 million for other expenditures (USFWS, 1985).

Wildlife viewing has been one of the fastest growing outdoor recreation activities in the 1980s. In 1987, spending by bird watchers contributed a total of $27 million in wages and business income to California's economy (Loomis and Unkel, 1988).

In a study of the St. Croix Waterway between Maine and New Brunswick, it was found that $776,000 (1986 dollars) were added to the local

economy. Although this amount represented only 1.8 percent of consumer retail sales in the area, the study found that there was significant opportunity for local business development and expansion of this figure. An important caveat to potential new development was found in the survey of users (Miles, 1987). Users indicated "a desire for little or no development" and "a wish to have the area left as it is. They come to the area because it is accessible, yet somewhat remote and undeveloped."

Recreation is one of Wisconsin's most important industries. An estimate of total purchases by recreationists on the Lower Wisconsin River in local economies was $401,000 per year. This generated an estimated $860,000 in sales by local businesses due to the business activities multiplier effect (Boyle, et al., 1984). When river users were asked what activities were extremely important to them while visiting the river, they rated viewing scenic beauty as second only to canoeing. On the average, people expressed a willingness to pay about $25 per year to maintain scenic beauty along the river. Combined with estimates of how many people use the river, this translates into about $311,000 per year.

In 1973, a study of the Elroy–Sparta bicycle trail in Wisconsin found that 72 businesses in 5 communities realized gross added sales of $295,100 as a result of trail use (Blank, 1987). In 1988, trail-user expenditures for the Elroy–Sparta Trail in Wisconsin were over $1.2 million. Data in this study were collected through on-site interviews with 1,125 trail users during the months of July and August (Schwecke et al., 1989).

A study of three recreational trails from across the United States found positive economic benefits for the local communities: the Heritage Trail, a 26-mile trail in eastern Iowa; the St. Mark's Trail, 16 miles from Tallahassee to the Gulf of Mexico; and the Lafayette/Moraga Trail, 7.6 miles east of Oakland. Through user surveys, the estimated total economic activity resulting from trail use was found to be $1,243,350 for the Heritage Trail; $1,873,400 for the St. Mark's Trail; and $1,588,000 for the Lafayette/Moraga Trail. In addition to these figures, trail users spent an additional $130 to $250 on durable goods, such as the equipment, clothing, and accessories that they used on the trail. These expenditures resulted in "new money" coming into the local trail counties annually by outside trail visitors of $630,000 for the Heritage, $400,000 for the St. Mark's, and $294,000 for the Lafayette/Moraga Trails (Moore et al., 1992).

Benefits to Landowners and Developers

Building on Olmsted's experience in Central Park, there is a growing body of evidence to show that property values actually tend to increase as a result of the provision of open space within and around developments. Protected open space in towns of all sizes benefits real-estate development because it increases the marketability of adjacent property. This can be an important factor both in sluggish markets and in terms of long-term resale value and appreciation. A few of the reported findings are summarized below.

Analysis of property sales in the vicinity of the 1,294-acre Pennypack Park in Philadelphia shows that nearby real estate is valued more highly than properties located elsewhere in the city. Using a multiple regression model to screen out influences other than access to the park, the location rent, or value of the property's location with respect to the park was found to be significant. At a distance of 40 feet, the park accounted for 33 percent of the land value; at 1,000 feet, 9 percent; and at 2,500 feet, 4.2 percent. A net increase of $3,391,000 in real estate value was directly attributed to the park (1974 dollars). Each acre of parkland generated about $2,600 in location rents, or increased value in the surrounding property (Hammer, Coughlin and Horn, 1974).

There is often a decrease in the value of property in proximity to heavily used, active recreation parks. A study of five parks in Columbus, Ohio, found the properties adjacent to the active park, which faced heavily used recreational facilities rather than scenery, sold for an average of 7 percent ($1,150) less than properties a block away. But the same study found that properties facing passive parks sold for 7 to 23 percent more than those a block away (Weicker and Zerbst, 1973).

A study of parcels surrounding four parks in Worcester, Massachusetts, found property values

increasing with greater proximity to the park, unless the properties were next to active recreation facilities. Houses within 20 feet of a park were worth approximately $2,675 more than a similar house 2,000 feet away from the park. For active recreation parks, property values increased one block away from the park. Overall, 219 acres of park generated $349,195 of economic benefit (Moore, Stevens and Allen, 1982).

In Dayton, Ohio, proximity to an arboretum added 5 percent to the average selling prices of homes, and proximity to the park and river added 7.35 percent (Kimmel, 1985).

In Boulder, Colorado, house prices declined by an average of $4.20 for each foot of distance away from a greenbelt, and the values of homes adjacent to the greenbelt were 32 percent higher than those for similar residences 3,000 feet away (Correll, Lillydahl and Singell, 1978).

In a study of land zoned as an urban greenbelt in Salem, Oregon, urban land adjoining farmland zoned exclusively for agriculture was worth $1,200 more per acre than similar land 1,000 feet away from the greenbelt (Nelson, 1986).

In Seattle, homes near the 12-mile Burke–Gilman trail sell for 6 percent more than other houses of like size, according to a survey of local realtors (National Park Service, 1990).

In a research project conducted by the Center for Rural Massachusetts, it was found that homes in a cluster subdivision appreciated 12.7 percent faster than similar homes in subdivisions without open space over a 21-year period. The cluster subdivision was distinguished by smaller lots (one-quarter acre), two ponds, a tennis court, a baseball diamond, a playing field/village common, and a nature trail with approximately 36 acres of open space. The conventional subdivision offered little more than larger lots (one-half acre) and a small amount of open space (Lacy, 1990).

THE ECONOMICS OF CLUSTERING AND OPEN SPACE PROVISIONS

It has often been politically difficult to enact open space preservation regulations. For this reason, many communities have adopted large-lot zoning in an ill-guided effort to preserve open space. The result of those measures has been to increase sprawl and to lose any of the economic or amenity advantages of preserved open space However, two commonly used programs, open space acquisition and cluster ordinances, are both economically viable methods of preserving open space.

Open Space Acquisition Programs

Acquisition programs for open space preservation range from land purchases (fee simple acquisition) to the purchase of certain specified rights in the land (through a variety of easements relating to different purposes, such as scenic protection, public footpath access, and limitation or prohibition of future development). "Purchase of development rights" programs, such as those in Massachusetts and Maryland, are often used at the state or county level to preserve farmland. These are permanent ways to prevent development, but they are extremely expensive and seldom preserve contiguous tracts.

Acquisition programs, particularly at the local level, are often viewed as frivolous. However, even without considering the related benefits of open space, it is often cheaper for a community to acquire open space than to see it developed. Following are a number of examples of this analysis.

In Closter, New Jersey, eighty acres of open space were acquired by this Bergen County township, which is located less than 15 miles from New York City. If the property had been developed according to Closter's zoning, 160 homes would have been built. To serve those homes would have required $144,000 in annual education spending for the children of the 160 families, and costs for police, garbage collection, and other services would have added $12,000 more. Property taxes, on the other hand, would have generated revenues of only $100,000 per year, creating an annual shortfall of $56,000. Based on an acquisition cost of $500,000, the annual tax deficit would equal the purchase price in 10 years (Little, 1968).

In Yarmouth, Maine, a public access and recreation committee analyzed the costs of providing municipal services to a specific parcel proposed for parks acquisition. The annual costs of those services, including fire and police protection, roads, and schools, would have exceeded property-tax revenues by $140,000. This was compared to an annual cost of $76,000 over 20 years to purchase the property (World Wildlife Fund, 1992).

In Alabama, the Huntsville Land Trust compared the public cost of development to the public cost of open space acquisition in its efforts to preserve acreage on Monte Sano, the city's scenic mountainous backdrop. Development of the area would cost $5 million in infrastructure costs and from $2,500 to $3,000 per acre annually for public services. Acquisition costs, on the other hand, would be $3.3 million, plus $75 per acre in annual maintenance costs for the open space (World Wildlife Fund, 1992).

This is not to say that all housing developments should be prevented in a community, nor that all vacant land should be bought and retained as open space. While open space acquisition may raise taxes, it will often times result in a smaller tax increase than that required by allowing the land to develop. For example, in Floyd Harbor, New York, planners estimated that acquisition would increase taxes by 18 percent, while development would increase taxes by 51 percent (Little, 1968).

Cluster Ordinances

When considering cluster ordinances, many communities have difficulty in determining appropriate lot-size reductions, and in deciding whether to offer density incentives. These and other issues are discussed in detail in Chapters 14 and 15, but in Howard County, Maryland, it was found that the local housing market would value one-acre houselots with adjacent open space equally with a typical 3- to 5-acre houselot (Legg Mason, 1990). Although size relationships will change with local market conditions, there will be a threshold in every community where clustering will produce an equal or greater return to the developer than a conventional subdivision.

Clustering lowers infrastructure costs for developers by reducing the lengths of roads and utilities. Assuming a gross density of one dwelling per five acres, and soil conditions suitable for individual on-lot septic disposal systems, approximately $3,500 in site development costs could be saved for each five-acre lot that is allowed to be down-sized to one acre (Maryland Office of Planning 1990). For example, if four additional dwellings were allowed on a five-acre parcel (producing a net density of one dwelling per acre), $14,000 could be saved in site costs, and 20 acres of open space could be permanently protected on the remaining land.

18

Retaining Farmland and Farmers

The national decline in both farmland acreage and the farming population during the past half-century, and particularly over the last several decades, is well documented. In the Northeast much of this land was literally abandoned and has gradually grown back into forest. But in many other regions of the country significant acreages have been bulldozed for suburban and exurban development, where the population has expanded into subdivisions of ever lower densities.

One of the primary reasons people have been able to move into these once rural areas is that construction of the interstate highway network has made it possible to drive much greater distances to urban jobs within tolerable commuting time (often as much as one hour in each direction). Superhighway extensions have frequently produced a "can-opener effect" upon the rural hinterland of metropolitan job centers. Eventually employers relocate to more suburban locations, thereby further extending the "commutershed" into adjacent rural counties.

This process has resulted in the creation of a "post-interstate landscape" of low-density exurban sprawl, which has multiplied problems for the indigenous farming community. A typical example is Washington State's Skagit Valley, whose 100,000 acres of rich bottomland is reputed to be among the most fertile in the country. Until the completion of Interstate 5 in the early 1970s, the valley was beyond reasonable commuting distance of Seattle (Nisbet, 1990). Slashing the driving time to 60 minutes, I-5 has exposed the Skagit Valley to increasing development pressures.

While farmers in the Skagit Valley have begun to organize themselves to protect their land resources, with assistance from the American Farmland Trust, there is evidence that commercial farming in other highly productive Seattle-area counties is succumbing to development. A recent survey of farmers in the fast-growing Puyallup Valley indicated that the present generation of farmers may be the last in that valley's history, despite annual revenues of $80 million from farm products (Nisbet, 1990).

This process of population growth and dispersal is typically characterized by an increasing frequency of conflicts between new residents and the established farmers. Complaints from newcomers often involve the issues of manure odor, noise from livestock or agricultural machinery, and environmental hazards posed by the regular application of pesticides, herbicides, and other chemicals. Complaints and legal actions brought by some of these new rural residents eventually resulted in greater protection given to the agricultural sector through new "right-to-farm" laws enacted by nearly every state legislature (Lapping and Leutwiler, 1989).

However, without the support of local police and planning authorities, and with poor communication between farmers and nonfarm residents, the truce is often an uneasy one. New residents continue to grumble and many farmers must continue to deal with the occasional vandalism and damage caused by neighborhood children and dogs. Since farming, as it is generally practiced today, is an essentially industrial process incompatible with immediately adjacent residential uses, it is entirely appropriate for planning authorities to insist that new subdivisions in rural areas provide substantial and effective buffers (assuming more effective ways cannot be found to separate these uses into entirely different districts). Urgently needed is further research on the most effective types of buffer plantings, in terms of dimensions and species.

METROPOLITAN AGRICULTURE

Due to such conditions, numerous observers have prophesied the ultimate demise of agriculture in metropolitan regions. If these predictions are accurate, then there is cause for widespread concern about the consequences, because metropolitan agriculture is not a minor phenomenon. Over 640,000 farms (one-third the national total) are located in Metropolitan Statistical Areas (MSAs), covering 159 million acres and accounting for 20 percent of the country's harvested cropland (Heimlich, 1989). In the Northeast half the farms are in MSAs, and in the Pacific Region the proportion is two-thirds (Heimlich, 1990). These percentages are large partly because some MSAs cover very extensive areas, extending many miles into the rural hinterland, as is the case in southern California, eastern Texas, and Florida. Nevertheless, without adequate regional growth controls, these hinterlands will continue to be extremely vulnerable to future waves of low-density sprawl development.

Nationwide, metro-farmers produce more than two-thirds of the country's fruit and vegetables, and generate over three-quarters of all nursery and greenhouse crop sales. These farms also account for 40 percent of all dairy production and half of the national total for specialty livestock sales, including domestic pets (Heimlich and Brooks, 1989). Continued heavy losses of metro-area farmland would undoubtedly cause further escalation in the price of fresh foods for large numbers of people.

CHARACTERISTICS OF METRO-FARMS

Although less than half the size of their nonmetropolitan counterparts (247 vs. 518 acres, on average), metro-farms are more intensively cultivated.

Their profiles show higher proportions of irrigated and harvested cropland (47 percent, versus 36 percent for non-metros), which allows metro-farmers to double the value of their product per acre ($243 versus $113) (Heimlich, 1988). In the older metro areas (i.e., those designated by the U.S. Census before 1970) the differences are even greater, with 49 percent of the acreage intensively used and a per-acre product of $260. This is achieved by a greater focus on high-value crops, such as fruit, vegetables, nursery stock, flowers, turf grass, specialty livestock (horses, furbearing animals, bees, lab animals), categories that account for only 16 percent of sales by non-metro farmers, who generally raise more traditional field crops (corn, wheat, cotton, soybeans, etc.).

Historically, such approaches are far from new. On Long Island, adaptive farmers in the 1820s "appeared to be prospering by concentrating their energies on less land and new crops," growing high cash-value crops, such as spinach, lettuce, cauliflower, and broccoli, to feed New York City's nearby growing population (Stilgoe, 1988). The demise of most of those farms during the present century owes more to the absence or ineffectiveness of resource-based land-use planning in an area with skyrocketing land values than it does to other factors, as evidenced by continued successful agriculture in other metropolitan regions where land-use controls have been much stricter for decades (as in Oregon and the democracies of Western Europe).

However, these higher value crops are often produced only with the addition of greater inputs of capital, labor, and chemicals. Measured in terms of dollars per acre of harvested cropland, metro-farmers spend 50 percent more on fertilizer, twice as much on other agrochemicals, and three and one-half times as much on hired labor (Heimlich, 1988). Although 60 percent of metro-farmers depend on off-farm income to supplement their earnings from the land (compared with half the non-metro farmers), more than one-third of them have no other employment. From that one might assume they are very committed and are able to survive economically on their own.

CHARACTERISTICS OF METRO-FARMERS

Efforts to protect the agricultural base in metropolitan counties should be founded upon an understanding of the dynamics of metro-agriculture as a land use, a business, and as a way of life. Fundamental to that understanding is an awareness of the varied and heterogeneous nature of farming in these areas. Among those who continue to farm "in the shadow of the city," there are significant subgroups whose different characteristics are important for land-use policy planners to be aware of. In the Northeast, where metro-farmers have been studied in some detail by researchers at the U.S. Dept. of Agriculture's Economic Research Service, three subgroups have been identified: "traditional" (48 percent), "recreational" (35 percent, earning less than $2,500 per year from their farms), and "adaptive" (17 percent).

ADAPTIVE METRO-FARMERS

Farmers who derive at least one-third of their farm income from sales of high-value crops and activities occupy the "adaptive" subgroup. The value of their products, expressed on a per-acre basis, is 44 percent higher than that of their traditional counterparts in the same metro areas, who typically farm much larger acreages in a more conventional manner. They also earn more off-farm income, possibly because they also tend to be younger and to have had more formal education.

Observers of these subgroups emphasize the importance of nurturing the adaptive farmers in particular, because they may constitute the last best hope for continuing agricultural operations in metro regions. In the Massachusetts Agricultural Viability Study, researchers noted that the greatest decline in farms between 1959 and 1978 occurred among the more traditional enterprises, such as dairy and poultry. During that same period, those farmers concentrating on fruits, vegetables, and specialty livestock all increased their share of total agricultural output (Bailey et al., 1982).

The fact that the adaptive subgroup appears to be doing better financially, with less land, bodes well for the future, as aging traditional farmers sell off their less productive land for housing in order to obtain financial security in their retirement years. To the extent that their best land can be protected from development pressures (through agricultural protection zoning, the purchase of development rights, "limited development," and/or "open space development design"), the possibility remains for it to be acquired by a new generation of more innovative farmers, who are proving that it is still possible to succeed as tillers of the soil even when surrounded by new development.

In an effort to create conditions favorable to the continuation of agriculture, officials in Cumberland County, New Jersey, have recommended the creation of "Agricultural Enterprise Districts" (AEDs). Modeled after Urban Enterprise Zones, where private investment is encouraged by reducing state sales taxes and conferring benefits to employers who hire unemployed people, AEDs would operate on similar principles of voluntary participation and incentives. Benefits to participating farmers would include current-use taxation, marketing support, job training, reduced sales taxes, regulatory relief (exemptions from certain environmental requirements), "grandfathering" under existing zoning (to protect land equity), and access to capital as an alternative to selling off lots. According to proponents, costs of the program would be offset by reduced residential development, which typically generates less property-tax revenue than needed to provide public services (Heinrich et al., 1991). However, other observers criticize this approach as conferring too many benefits on farmers without requiring any corresponding restrictions on their ability to convert their land into sprawling low-density residential developments.

As has been noted in a recent report on the viability of farming in Maryland's metropolitan-fringe, "Traditional farming is relocating to areas more conducive to its practice, and is being replaced by 'contemporary agriculture,' which is emerging as a lucrative way of life with its own unique benefits to the general public" (Scarfo,

1990). That same author summed up the situation best with these words: "Farming is not dying—it is changing." It is also fair to note that these changes are often very painful for those "traditional" farmers who are essentially being driven out of their home areas because local officials have not acted soon enough to protect the farmland base on a large scale, through agricultural zoning and programs where development rights could be purchased (PDR) or transferred to more suitable locations (TDR). In addition, it should be admitted that continued farming within the context of a developing area is not without its share of difficulties but, as the next section shows, there are ways to turn adversity to advantage for those who are able and willing to adapt their methods.

PROBLEMS AND OPPORTUNITIES

The difficulties of surviving as a working farmer in expanding metropolitan regions should not be minimized, however. In addition to nuisance complaints and vandalism, the realities include higher taxes, higher land costs to buy additional cropland, greater difficulty in obtaining long-term land leases, increased wage scales (often due to higher housing and living costs), labor shortages (because of alternative employment opportunities), crop damage, and traffic congestion (making it difficult to use local roads to move agricultural machinery from field to field). As neighboring farmers sell out, an "impermanence syndrome" affects those remaining on the land, who tend to reinvest less in their buildings and machinery, feeling they might be the last generation of farmers in their district. Once the agricultural base declines below a certain threshold, equipment dealers and large-animal veterinaries begin to relocate their businesses, adding to the cost and inconvenience of continuing to farm in that locality.

On the positive side of the ledger, a number of countervailing factors give some observers cause for guarded optimism about metro-farming's future. Among those most often cited are:

• the ready market for fresh, high-value produce in suburban supermarkets and restaurants, including a higher demand for more naturally produced meat, fruit, and vegetables;

• the greater viability of "U-pick" fruit and berry operations;

• increased local demand for nursery stock, horse stabling services, and aquaculture products from farm ponds and lakes (fresh fish sales and, possibly, also recreational fishing enterprises);

• lesser dependence on types of crops most affected by changing export policies (e.g., grain) or by fluctuating federal subsidy programs; and

• higher land values, which make it easier to borrow larger sums against equity to help finance long-term capital improvements and to replace or upgrade machinery. (This factor may explain why the percentage of financially vulnerable farmers in MSAs is half that found in non-metro areas.)

However, regarding the last item above, Robert Coughlin of the University of Pennsylvania has pointed out that although commercial banks do lend against the market value of a farmer's land for potential development, farm lending institutions (such as Farm Credit and the Farmer's Home Administration) base loans on farm business plans and the ability of farming operations to support such loans. In other words, when a farm is profitable, it is not really necessary for the owner to get a commercial bank loan, because funds are available through normal farm lending institutions (Coughlin, 1984).

In addition, there appears to be a growing number of metropolitan-fringe residents who support farmland retention programs, from the purchase of development rights to creative development techniques protecting open space through designs for more compact residential areas. They are also inclined to support the creation of farmers' markets, and tend to patronize them regularly. Many of these new residents are somewhat more politically sophisticated and affluent (Heimlich, 1989). However, in these same areas it is not uncommon to encounter many long-established farming families strongly opposed to stringent new land-use regulations, which they see as penalizing them after neighboring farmers "cashed in" on land deals to developers when laws were more lax.

The term "caring conserver" has been coined by one farm researcher to describe people who bring more acute awareness of environmental and land-use concerns to growing rural areas. To the extent that the above factors can be encouraged and nurtured, the future of metro-area farming may hold fair promise. However, such farming will always be, in Mark Lapping's phrase, "the agriculture of compromise." The following sections deal with the issue of reducing the conflicts that typically arise when nonrural people move into farming areas.

MINIMIZING CONFLICTS WITH FARMERS: URBAN GROWTH AREAS, EXISTING USE ZONING, AGRICULTURAL PROTECTION ZONING, AND BUFFERS

If the best way to minimize conflicts between new residents and the farming community is to keep them physically separated, there is probably no better model in this country than Oregon's statewide Land Use Act. Since 1975, nonagricultural development has been largely confined to designated urban growth areas, which surround each of the state's towns and cities. Property rights elsewhere are essentially limited to agriculture, silviculture, horticulture, viniculture, ranching, and commercial recreation.

Unsuccessfully challenged several times through referenda, this remarkable legislation exemplifies the concept of "existing use zoning" in a state where farming and forestry comprise between 40 and 45 percent of the total state economy. This law's initial passage and subsequent support has been due to a widely held belief by the state's voters and political leaders that "strong protection of this resource base is vital for Oregon's future economic health and prosperity" (Oregon Department of Land Conservation and Development, 1991).

However, some adjustments to the Land Use Act are currently under consideration, including stricter rules governing permissions to build "farm dwellings" (in light of recent studies showing that a majority of "farm dwellings" built since the act was passed are not being lived in by farmers or agricultural workers, but rather are hobby farms and upscale "martini ranches"). Most of these abuses have occurred on smaller farms (less than 40 acres), where the owner typically works only part-time on the land and earns less than $10,000 per year from that source (ibid., 1991).

However large the percentage of illegal "farm dwellings" may be in certain rural areas, their numbers have been relatively small, as Table 18–1 shows. For example, in the Bend study area, a resort community attractive to retirees, more development occurred outside the Urban Growth Boundary (UGB) than inside it, but only 2,705 dwellings were involved, compared with close to 50,000 new homes built in the four study areas taken as a whole. Although there have been other incursions into the fringe areas outside the designated UGBs, the fact remains that over a recent five-year period 89 percent of the new houses built in four large study areas (around Portland, Medford, Bend, and Brookings) were located within the official UGBs (ibid., 1991).

Oregon planners have responded to some of these rural incursions by increasing minimum lot size requirements for land outside UGBs. In the Brookings area, for example, the amount of fringe development decreased substantially when the lot size minimum was more than doubled to 10 acres. At the same time, trends seem to be improving in terms of efficient land utilization inside UGBs: average houselot size dropped from about 13,000

Table 18–1. Residential Development in Oregon, 1985 to 1989

Location	Portland SA	Medford SA	Bend SA	Brookings SA
Inside UGB	41,104	1,694	2,023	443
Outside UGB	2,051	529	2,705	256
Total	43,155	2,223	4,728	699

Note: SA refers to study area; UGB refers to Urban Growth Boundary.
Source: Oregon Department of Land Conservation and Development

square feet in the early 1980s to 8,800 square feet at the end of the decade. Over the same period, other corroborative data show that the percentage of smaller lots (under 10,000 square feet) increased to 66 percent, up from 28 percent in the early 1980s.

Jurisdictions that wish to create a similar shift could adopt *"maximum* lot sizes" as well, to prevent land-consumptive low-density sprawl developments. This point is emphasized in Gail Easley's comprehensive and well-researched report on UGBs, where she concludes that "to a large degree, the success of an urban growth area depends upon achieving the minimum densities targeted in planning for the area" (Easley, 1992). In the communities she studied, those minimum densities ranged from no fewer than six units per acre to an average of 12 or 14 in many jurisdictions. Conversely, in the rural zones UGB regulations should not allow land to be divided into units smaller than would be viable for continued resource management (such as farming or forestry operations), or should be zoned for "exclusive agricultural uses."

There exists a pervasive notion in many parts of the country that landowners possess a constitutionally protected right to develop their land. However, this notion is factually baseless. To repeat an old analogy, property rights may be visualized as a bundle of sticks, each stick representing a particular type of right (to sell, to lease, to harvest timber, to farm, to fence, to mine, to fill, to build on, to bequeath, etc.). Hardly anyone today could seriously argue that all these rights are unlimited, for the authority of the government to limit floodplain construction or to prohibit wetlands alteration is well-established and generally accepted (Piedmont Environmental Council, 1981).

The right to develop land that is neither wet nor flood prone has also been limited, chiefly through zoning that establishes permitted uses and allowable building densities in various districts. For example, industrial, commercial, and high-density residential uses may be allowed on serviced land, while agriculture, forestry, and very low-density residential uses are allowed on unsewered land that is environmentally sensitive (e.g., overlying aquifers or possessing severe limitations for septic systems).

The land right that is constitutionally protected is the right to not have it "taken" without compensation (guaranteed by the Fifth Amendment in the Bill of Rights). The issue of what level of governmental action constitutes a "taking" has been argued before the bar and adjudicated in numerous court cases. Although no universal standard clearly emerges from this body of case law, various legal scholars (and some prominent practicing attorneys) contend that land-use regulations may be extremely restrictive provided that: 1) they are supported by well-researched master plans documenting an overriding public interest directly served by those development limitations, and 2) they allow the landowner a "reasonable and beneficial use" of his property (Humbach, 1989).

It is well-settled legal doctrine that the opportunity to maximize one's potential monetary gain is not a constitutionally protected right. In fact, in its very first zoning case—*Euclid* v. *Ambler Realty*, in 1928—the U.S. Supreme Court upheld zoning that restricted the plaintiff's land to uses of far less real-estate value than would have been possible without the ordinance.

In a detailed legal analysis, *Law and a New Land Ethic*, professor John Humbach argues eloquently for the concept of "existing use zoning" (Humbach, 1989). Under this approach, landowners are entitled, by right, to continue the current uses of their land, but are generally not permitted to change such uses to more intensive ones. In other words, a farm may continue to be farmed or converted to an orchard, ranch, or timber operation. However, conversion to a housing development or a shopping or office complex would be prohibited.

It is doubtful that this idea will ultimately enjoy widespread acceptance in the United States (as it has been accepted in Western Europe) because of deeply ingrained beliefs concerning one's "right to develop" land. Many rural landowners who do not subscribe to the extreme philosophy of the so-called "wise use" movement (a misnomer if there ever was one) would nevertheless argue that ownership of real property carries with it the right to convert it from agricultural to residential, commercial, or industrial uses.

In a briefer article prepared for the APA's *Zoning News* (which also contains a one-page model existing use ordinance for rural townships), Humbach advocates managing growth under what he calls "truly comprehensive plans," ones that designate some areas for development within the foreseeable future; other areas as a reserve to accommodate development over the longer term; and still other areas, "perhaps most of the zoned community's tax base, for no foreseeable developed uses whatsoever" (Humbach, 1992).

Humbach cautions that each political jurisdiction must zone an adequate amount of land as growth areas to accommodate a reasonable amount of new development. Another imperative is that variance criteria must allow for cases of extreme hardship where a *total* taking of value would result. However, if boundaries of "existing use zones" were drawn to include only that land that is potentially productive for agriculture, horticulture, silviculture, or commercial recreation, Humbach argues that constitutional rights would not be abridged. Quoting the 1992 *Lucas* case, he reminds readers of the majority opinion that held that "government may . . . affect property values by regulation without incurring an obligation to compensate."

Land-use regulations incorporating this basic concept have been adopted for many years in a number of rural municipalities and counties (chiefly in the Midwest, but in the Northwest as well) under the heading "agricultural protection zoning" (Toner, 1984). In order to be successfully implemented, however, such zoning needs strong support and continued commitment from the local farming community. This approach to zoning has been implemented even in the country's most densely settled state, New Jersey, where a 1991 State Supreme Court decision upheld 40-acre agricultural zoning, which also required that residential development on 40-acre parcels be limited to one-acre "building envelopes," with the remaining 39 acres permanently dedicated to agriculture (*Gardner* v. *New Jersey Pinelands Commission*).

However, it is important to recognize that only a very small proportion of "agricultural protection zoning" ordinances limit land uses to farming

activities exclusively. Most of these ordinances permit a small amount of nonfarm development, either on extremely large "lots" (from 10 to 640 acres), or on smaller houselots located on a minor fraction of the property. (These two approaches are discussed in the next section of this chapter.)

Not surprisingly, support for highly restrictive agricultural zoning is most forthcoming in rural areas beyond the reach of heavy development pressures. Farmers in those types of areas view their land more as a resource to pass along to their sons and daughters rather than as a commodity to be sold off to provide financial security to themselves and their families. In many of these areas farming is still reasonably profitable, and encroaching suburbia has not yet created either significantly higher land values (for development purposes) or a large, diverse range of alternative employment opportunities (to lure the grown children of farmers off the farms). In some other areas where suburban pressures and opportunities are clearly present, as in the "Amish" regions of southeastern Pennsylvania, strong cultural commitments to the independent way of life offered by farming provides the local political base for adopting very restrictive agricultural zoning of one building lot per 25 acres, in most cases.

In Lancaster County, more than 270,000 acres of farmland are located in agricultural protection zoning districts in 35 different townships. The percentage of land so zoned in these townships varies widely: in two-fifths of them, 75 percent or more of the total land area is zoned at farming densities, while in one-quarter of these townships less than 30 percent of the land is zoned in this manner. In contrast to neighboring York County, where agricultural zoning reached a plateau in 1977, the number of townships in Lancaster County that have adopted this approach has steadily increased each year. Researchers cite strong leadership from many quarters: both township and county officials, the county planning commission, the county chamber of commerce, the county newspaper, the county agricultural preserve board, a county land trust, and prominent solicitors (Coughlin, 1993).

In a survey of several hundred local governments that have adopted some form of agricultural protection zoning, researchers at the American Planning Association found that agriculture was considered to be "the highest and best use" for those districts in 94 percent of the communities surveyed (Toner, 1984). An even higher percentage said that the purpose of this restrictive zoning was "to preserve the agricultural economic base." Other objectives cited by respondents included: curtailing farmland loss (90 percent); reducing conflicts between farms and subdivisions (79 percent); protecting natural resources, including water quality, woodlands, groundwater recharge areas, and wetlands (65 percent); and keeping a lid on public service costs associated with sprawl (61 percent).

In areas where existing-use zoning and agricultural protection zoning districts are not politically feasible, planners have tried to minimize housing/ farming conflicts by requiring buffer zones around new developments. These range in width from 50 feet in Delaware (where it applies only in agricultural districts formed under the new PDR program) to 100 feet in Maine (to protect farms enrolled under the state's Farm and Open Space Tax Law). The trend, however, is toward wider buffers: proposals in Harford County, Maryland, would raise the minimum width to 200 feet, while new legislation in Sacramento County, California, would require buffers of 300 to 500 feet (Bowers, 1991d). To the extent that these jurisdictions allow flexible "open space development design" (as described in Chapters 14 and 15), these buffers can be created without negatively impacting the development value of adjoining land, and they can also serve open space functions ranging from active and passive recreation to wildlife habitat purposes.

In areas where agricultural protection zoning has been adopted, more stringent buffers are sometimes adopted. In several townships in Lancaster County, Pennsylvania, for example, local ordinances prohibit homeowners from planting trees within 30 feet of any lot line that abuts a farm field, on the basis that trees create shadows that diminish crop yield—an extreme regulation proposed by the farmers. Not reported in the literature is whether farmers in such areas eradicate all hedgerows, tree lines, stream-bank woodlands and other sunlight obstructions on their *own* prop-

erties, removing valuable wildlife habitat and creating featureless prairie landscapes in the process, in their quest for full sun.

LOW-DENSITY AGRICULTURAL ZONING, SLIDING SCALE, PDR, TDR, AND "OPEN SPACE DEVELOPMENT"

Less restrictive than agricultural protection zoning is the idea of very low density standards for new development. "Quarter-quarter zoning" (meaning one-quarter of one-quarter of a square mile, or 40 acres) is popular in some parts of the rural Midwest, and 20- to 25-acre zoning has been implemented in many other states, including several mid-Atlantic ones (Maryland and Pennsylvania). In some areas, such zoning prevents farmland from being divided into parcels below a certain threshold size, which is sometimes related to the minimum tract area considered to be farmable. In a 1984 study of "farm core areas" in three townships in York County, Pennsylvania, where it was found that three-quarters of the farms were larger than 100 acres (the three-town average), "a general standard of 100 acres was chosen as the limit beneath which division should not be permitted outside the subdivision process" (Coughlin, 1988).

Another approach to agricultural zoning is to require that new homes be located on much smaller parcels, to avoid fragmentation of the resource base into "farmettes" of 5 to 40 acres. In planning jargon, this approach is known as "Area Based Allocation Zoning" (or ABAZ). Under ABAZ the number of houselots allowed is directly proportional to the farmer's total acreage (e.g., one lot for every 20 acres), but these lots are subject to *maximum* size restrictions (often one acre), and are sometimes further required to be located on the parts of a property that are least suitable for farming.

A useful variation on this theme introduces a "sliding scale," wherein the number of potential dwellings increases at a slower rate as the farm tract increases in acreage. This approach is illustrated by the following example: one dwelling for the first five acres, another for the next 10 acres, a third for the next 20 acres, and a fourth for the next 30 acres, with each additional dwelling requiring

40 more acres. Thus, a 34-acre farm would yield three dwellings (required to be located on 3 acres, leaving 31 acres in agriculture), while 110 acres would yield 6 houses (on 6 acres), and 235 acres would produce 9 homes. Results of applying sliding-scale zoning to various land tracts are shown in Table 18–2. Tract size at the time these regulations are adopted governs density.

The primary rationale for the "sliding scale" variation is that smaller farms are often less suited for long-term agriculture and are frequently held with the expectation of future conversion. Another reason is that it is easier to build local political support by allowing small farmers the opportunity to create several houselots (for retirement income, or to give to family members), which they would not be able to do under rigid 30-acre zoning.

The above example is very similar to one adopted by the Township of Mt. Joy, Lancaster County, Pennsylvania, in 1978. In Mt. Joy, however, the land increment per additional dwelling jumped to 50 acres after the second division, allowing six units on 200 acres—compared with eight units in the Table 18–2. If the political situation in an area is such that it would be difficult to secure adoption of 50-acre increments, designating 30-acre increments would not produce a significant increase in the number of new dwellings on farmland—which is a key issue with strict farmland preservationists. These densities correspond generally with research results from neighboring York County, where farmers in two rural townships

Table 18–2. Dwelling Yield and Acreage Protected Under Sliding-Scale Zoning

Size of Tract (acres)	Dwellings Permitted by Ordinance	Analysis of Resulting Acres per Dwelling Unit
1 but less than 5	1	1.0 – 5.0
5 but less than 15	2	2.5 – 7.5
15 but less than 35	3	3.0 – 10.1
35 but less than 65	4	3.9 – 16.1
65 but less than 105	5	12.5 – 21.0
105 but less than 145	6	17.5 – 22.2
145 but less than 185	7	20.7 – 26.5
185 but less than 225	8	23.2 – 28.1

identified a range of 2.5 to 5 nonfarm dwellings per 100 acres as the upper density limit beyond which they thought it would be too difficult for them to continue farming (Coughlin, 1991). Obviously these were not "adaptive metro-farmers," as described by Heimlich.

More important than dwelling number, however, is the *location* of new development with respect to farming operations and to the areas of most productive soil. Soil quality considerations were incorporated into sliding scale ordinances in several York County, Pennsylvania, townships in the late 1970s, when the construction of I-83 posed the threat of exurban development for long-range commuters from Baltimore.

"Covering 12,700 acres or 70 percent of the township, the Peach Bottom Agricultural District Ordinance allows dwelling units as a conditional use if located on poorer soil classifications, or on land which cannot be farmed because of physical features. . . . If location on Soils IIIe-3 through VIIs-2 is not feasible, dwellings can be located on better soils, but on the least agriculturally productive land" (Chester County Planning Commission, 1986). In addition, small-density bonuses are awarded if all dwellings are situated on soils IVe-5 through VIIs-2. These ordinances typically also include *maximum* lot size restrictions, to limit the acreage consumed by new development.

Sliding scale ordinances such as Peach Bottom's have been upheld by the Supreme Court of Pennsylvania when they form an "integral part of a larger comprehensive zoning scheme substantially related to the Township's goal of farmland preservation" (*Boundary Drive Associates* v. *Shrewsbury*, 1985).

Besides helping to minimize the impact of new subdivisions on adjacent agricultural uses, another virtue of low-density zoning is the opportunity it creates for other land protection techniques to be applied. Purchasing development rights is an expensive undertaking under any circumstances, but it becomes more feasible to accomplish significant protection where the smallest unit of land division for development purposes is 20, 30, or 40 acres. The success of the PDR program in Carroll County, Maryland, for example, is attributable in large part to the fact that the county was able to place a permanent conservation easement on 20 acres each time it bought a single development right. In other words, a 300-acre farm could be completely protected by purchasing the rights to develop just 15 houselots. The object of purchasing development rights in such situations is to reduce potential conflict between rural housing clusters and commercial agriculture, and to eliminate any possibility that sewer lines and other urban infrastructure would have to be extended into these farming areas in the future.

In areas such as New England, New York, New Jersey, and Pennsylvania, where zoning typically allows building lots of one to two acres each, PDR monies achieve only one-tenth to one-twentieth the effect they have accomplished in areas where the "minimum lot size" actually approximates the minimum acreage needed to sustain a small independent farming unit. Commenting on the new PDR program in Delaware, where much farmland is zoned for one-acre houselots, Jim Riggle of the American Farmland Trust said "Zoning which allows residential uses at such densities will assure any purchase of development rights program will be too expensive to be effective" (Bowers, 1991b).

Nevertheless, this technique could be helpful as long as the public is aware that in densely zoned areas with metropolitan pressures it is essentially a tool to preserve particular farms. Such is the case, for example, in Montgomery County, Pennsylvania, just outside Philadelphia. In rapidly suburbanizing counties such as this, PDR is usually not a cost-effective approach for protecting a significant portion of the agricultural land base (where conversion of farmland to development will almost certainly outpace land protection via PDR by a lopsided margin, sometimes as much as ten-to-one, as it does in Massachusetts).

However, this technique could play a very worthwhile role to the extent that it is coordinated with and supplemented by other methods of land protection (such as TDR, agricultural zoning, and open space zoning). Although it is enormously expensive to operate PDR programs in states where rural zoning typically allows houses on one- or two-acre lots, long-term program funding can be assured by dedicating a state tax for farmland preservation purposes. So far, only four states have followed this route: Maryland, Maine, Vermont, and Pennsylvania. In Maryland it is a real-estate transfer tax on farmland, while in neighboring Pennsylvania the program has been funded by a two-cent tax on cigarette packs since 1993 (Bowers, 1991c).

Zoning for low densities (such as 20 to 40 acres per dwelling) also helps with the implementation of other progressive land use techniques, such as TDR and open space development design ("rural cluster"). The reason is simple: it allows a fairly large amount of land to be preserved for each new dwelling unit that is constructed through these techniques. As with PDR, these approaches can be followed at almost any scale or density, but the acreage protected diminishes as the legally permitted housing density rises. For example, as Figure 18–1 shows, for every 10 dwellings in an open space design with one-acre lots, the amount of land protected via clustering would be 188 acres at 20 acres per dwelling unit, 138 acres at 15 ac./d.u., 87 acres at 10 ac./d.u., 37.5 acres at 5 ac./d.u., and 7.6 acres at 2 ac./d.u.

Even in areas where very low development densities are the rule, and where generous density

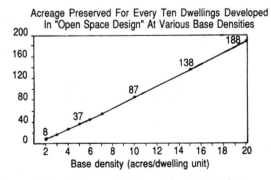

Figure 18–1. This graph shows the diminishing amount of open space that can typically be preserved by clustering ten homes, as one moves down the scale from agricultural zoning of one dwelling per 20 acres (188 acres saved), to suburban zoning of one dwelling per two aces (eight acres saved). *Source:* Howard County, Maryland, Office of Planning and Zoning.

bonuses are offered for more creative layouts, it can be difficult to encourage innovative design. Typical of such areas is Kent County, Maryland, which incorporated open space preservation techniques into its zoning in 1989 through an "enclave" option under which developers in agricultural zones have been strongly encouraged to cluster their new homes on lots of one-half to two acres each. The incentives come in the form of generous density bonuses, so that landowners can double or treble their building density (from one unit per 20 or 30 acres to one unit per 10 acres) if they follow the county's standards for compact "enclaves." These housing enclaves may not exceed 10 dwellings and are also required to be designed and sited to resemble groups of farm buildings, as seen from public roadways (Bowers, 1991a). Because the enclave option has not attracted many applicants in several years, Kent County planners are proposing that the conventional large-lot subdivision option be eliminated in rural districts, so that developers' choices would be narrowed to 30-acre farmettes or compact enclaves (or larger "villages," where permitted), restricting cluster lots there to one acre or less.

So much has already been written about the TDR technique that this chapter will mention it only briefly. The best known example of successful TDRs is in Montgomery County, Maryland, where 15,000 acres of farmland have been protected over a 10-year period at the cost of one administrative worker's salary. However, Maryland's TDR experience did not begin in Montgomery but rather in Calvert County, which since 1977 has employed this technique to preserve nearly as much land (on a proportional basis) as has Montgomery.

A recent TDR transaction in Calvert County illustrates the ability of this technique to be used creatively with other land planning methods. Briefly stated, the residents of an established "open space subdivision" (Scientists' Cliffs, which is further described in Chapter 20) spearheaded the effort to form American Chestnut Land Trust (ACLT) to acquire and protect 436 acres of land adjacent to their development. In addition to raising funds through private donations, ACLT negotiated for the development rights to be sold to developers through the county's TDR ordinance. These rights were transferred to another rural parcel, enabling the owner to develop at a more efficient density there. Not only were a variety of techniques used, but open space was preserved on one property and the ultimate subdivision tract was developed in a more efficient and less land-consumptive manner.

In areas where very low development densities are not politically feasible, additional steps need to be taken if farmland preservation efforts are to succeed. The following section describes another innovative and multifaceted program in Maryland whose framers recognized the need to supplement moderate, typically three-acre zoning with additional techniques to help protect the remaining farmland base.

COMBINATIONS FOR SUCCESS: HOWARD COUNTY, MARYLAND

Lying midway between Baltimore and Washington, D.C., Howard County is nearly surrounded by other counties with relatively low density agricultural zoning (requiring 10 or more acres per dwelling). By contrast, the rural parts of Howard County have for many years been zoned at the more growth-inducing density of three acres per dwelling. One of the political realities of planning in Howard County is that the time when rural landowners would be willing to accept serious down-zoning to truly agricultural densities has long since passed, and this is no longer an option. Development pressures have been quite substantial for many years and land values are consequently very high.

Still, much of the western part of the county has remained agricultural, with a relative abundance of soils considered to be either prime or suitable for intensive cropping. In response to economic realities and geographical opportunities, farmers there have gradually been shifting from traditional crops (corn, oats, barley, wheat, beef, and dairy) to crops with higher value per acre, such as nursery stock, fruits, vegetables, horses, aquaculture, and viniculture, which find ready markets in the nearby cities and suburbs. Although half the farmland in the western part of the county is protected from development, the other half (nearly 25,000 acres) is not. County officials project that this remaining unprotected acreage could easily be subdivided within 10 years, if recent development trends continue (Howard County, 1990).

In response to this situation, and recognizing the limitations inherent in their previous conventional PDR program, the county Department of Planning and Zoning updated its general plan, introducing an imaginative three-tier approach to "nurturing agriculture in transition." The resulting proposal (which received a national award from the American Planning Association in 1991) will, if adopted, integrate state-of-the-art techniques for PDR, clustering, and TDR.

Having learned from experience that PDR is an expensive proposition even when legal building densities are moderate, because of the vast acreages that must be bought to maintain a critical mass of agricultural activity ($13 million spent during eight years to preserve 7,700 acres, or $1,700 per acre), the county has completely restructured its approach to leverage its comparatively meager resources for maximum purchasing power. The old "cash purchase" approach to PDR was simply no longer viable, due to the limited dollars available to fund that program.

The new spin on this familiar technique is to buy permanent conservation easements through long-term installment agreements that offer tax-exempt income streams to farmers (consisting of interest paid semiannually on the outstanding principal, at above-market rates), with the principal being paid in a large "balloon" installment at the end of the purchase period (Howard County, 1991). The county's ability to make such balloon payments 30 years hence is guaranteed by "zero coupon bonds," which the county buys for about 9 percent of face value.

Three other features of these installment agreements are:

1. the landowner's ability to defer capital gains tax until he or she receives the principal;

2. the landowner's ability to sell the agreement (which is a negotiable document) on the open market at a premium (if other prevailing rates fall), and

3. the possibility of a charitable deduction, over a five-year period, on the difference between the appraised value of the development rights and the amount for which they were purchased. Due to the structure of the federal tax laws, landowners can sometimes net more by selling property at a discounted price, paying lower taxes on that sales income and receiving a charitable deduction for the transaction as well. This means the county also spends less, per acre, under the installment approach than it would through an outright purchase.

Because of these special features, this program has been able to compete very well with private purchase offers from intending developers. The success of Howard County's PDR installment technique is evidenced by the fact that nearly 4,500 acres of farmland were voluntarily committed into this program during 1990, its first full year of operation. This was as much land as had been protected during the previous five years under the old PDR program.

Officials at the Agricultural Preserve Board in Lancaster County, Pennsylvania, have obtained a "private letter ruling" from the U.S. Internal Revenue Service for an alternative method of payment for farmland development rights. The innovative idea of using a "like-kind" exchange, wherein cooperating farmers would receive another piece of land in lieu of cash, exempts such participants from heavy capital gains taxes they would otherwise be subject to if they received a standard cash payment for their development rights. The rationale is that the farmland protection easements they sell are essentially just another form of real estate, and should be considered to be similar to the real estate these farmers would receive in such "like-kind exchanges."

The second major feature of Howard County's innovative rural planning proposal is the simple but effective requirement that all new subdivisions in the "Rural Conservation Districts" will be designed according to the principles of "open space development design" (clustering). Gross densities are proposed at one dwelling per five acres, excluding floodplains and steep slopes (compared with current three-acre zoning in rural Howard

County). The rationale for this 1:5 density, in a county where lower densities are not politically feasible, is illustrated in Figure 18–2. It shows that the increase in the percentage of land protected under large-lot zoning begins to reach a point of diminishing returns above the five-acre size. (This does not conflict with Figure 18–1, which deals with the *acreage* protected, rather than the *percentage* of land protected.) Lot sizes of one acre for new homes with individual wells and septic systems (or 33,000 square feet with shared septic systems) ensure that 75 percent of the buildable and farmable land will be permanently preserved.

Following adoption of the Howard County General Plan in 1990, parallel zoning revisions drafted by county staff were formally approved in September 1992, containing performance standards to incorporate the general plan's creative ideas into actual regulations. The county has also published illustrated design guidelines to show landowners and developers how roads, lots, and open space may be laid out to protect farmland, other natural resource areas, and/or to create a neighborhood atmosphere and a distinctive "sense of place." To

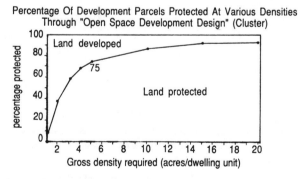

Percentage Of Development Parcels Protected At Various Densities Through "Open Space Development Design" (Cluster)

Assumes one-acre cluster lots with an additional 25% development factor

Figure 18–2. Planners in Howard County, Maryland, produced this graph to show how the percentage of protected land reaches a threshold plateau at a base density of five units per acre (where 75 percent of the parcel can be saved). From this they concluded that the greatest advantage, regarding percentage of land protected, can be achieved at that five-acre density. (This assumes one-acre cluster lots, with an additional 25 percent development factor.) *Source:* Howard County, Maryland, Office of Planning and Zoning.

help keep residential areas separate from farming operations, standards could require the provision of a wooded (or thickly planted) buffer strip along the interface between these two different types of land use. This buffer could be provided very easily as part of the 75 percent required open space. Figure 18–3, reproduced from the general plan, illustrates several design possibilities for new rural clusters in Howard County.

Ownership and management of the agricultural open space created by clustering development may be allowed to remain in the hands of the original farmer. In this way he or she could continue farming the land under permanent conservation restrictions (as the "development rights" to that part of the property were sold to the developer at the time of subdivision approval). In such cases the developer would use those rights to increase the buildable density on other parts of the farm parcel. Alternatively, the protected farmland could be owned and managed by a land trust or a homeowners' association (HOA). Many examples exist of the first approach. The second is less common, but is sometimes the most feasible. One of the "case examples" in Chapter 20 describes a situation where a HOA owns the fields and leases them on a long-term basis to a local farmer ("Farmcolony" in Stannardsville, Virginia).

A similar situation exists at South Meadow Ridge in Concord, Massachusetts, with almost 40 acres of productive fields in this Boston suburb protected through a cluster design (where a local farmer is delighted to be able to lease them from the HOA, whose members are very pleased to have someone work the land that forms their view). Another example involves a subdivision in Bucks County, Pennsylvania ("Farmview"), where half the land is owned and leased out to local farmers by a land preservation trust (also described in Chapter 20). A fourth example is a ranch in Colorado where 300 acres of rangeland are jointly owned by the residents of a second-home development located in an adjacent wooded area (Whyte, 1968).

A final example involves a 126-acre coastal farm in Sedgewick, Maine, where conservation easements held by the Blue Hill Heritage Trust allow the original farmer to continue harvesting blue-

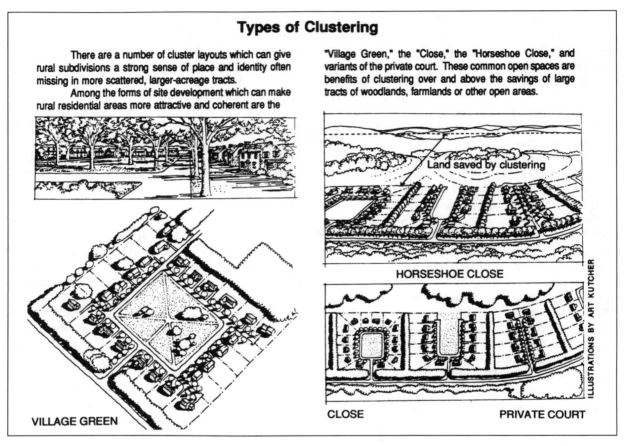

Figure 18–3. In order to help residents and officials visualize some of the design possibilities offered by open space design, the planning staff of Howard County, Maryland, produced these illustrations.

berries and timber on the majority of land covered by the 10 large houselots he created, which range from 10 to 19 acres in area. Each lot is restricted to one single-family home, which must be located within one-acre "building envelopes" designated on the approved subdivision plan (Carter, 1992). Although these residences are not clustered, the low density of this "limited development," coupled with the fact that agricultural rights have been reserved by the farmer on the 115 acres not within the actual building sites, make this unconventional arrangement noteworthy. This example has applicability in similar areas where proximity of homes to the farmland does not pose problems because of the types of crops involved (in this case, native blueberries and trees, which require few chemical imputs and little machinery, and which are not particularly vulnerable to trespass, trampling, or vandalism).

When farmland in any "open space development" is not retained by a farmer, staff at the American Farmland Trust strongly recommend that it be transferred to a land trust rather than to a HOA, as an added safeguard to ensure that active farming operations will be encouraged to continue long into the future. Communities that have adopted clustering *requirements* for subdivisions proposed to be located on farmland are Arundel and South Berwick, Maine; Amherst and West Tisbury, Massachusetts, Cromwell, Connecticut; Easthampton, New York; and Readington Township, New Jersey. These cluster requirements are sometimes limited to specific parts of the municipality. In Arundel, for example, clustering is required for subdivisions proposed on land registered under the state law providing property-tax reductions for farmland in active production. In Readington Township, the cluster requirement applies to tracts of 30 acres or more located in the Hunterdon County "Agricultural Development Area." In other parts of Arundel and Readington, rural clustering is encouraged but not required. Counties that have adopted zoning provisions requiring cluster design specifically to help save farmland include Clallam County, Washington, and Marin County, California. Further details on clustering are provided in Chapters 14 and 15.

The third principal component, called the "density exchange option" (DEO), provides substantial incentives to encourage landowners and developers to work together to preserve larger blocks of farmland while also benefiting from reduced infrastructure costs. This option would be available in certain overlay zones where the permitted development density would be one dwelling per two net acres (instead of one per five).

Essentially a variation on TDR, this option would reward cooperation resulting in the relocation of potential subdivisions away from areas where they would otherwise interrupt or separate adjoining farm parcels. This approach offers more advantages than clustering alone can produce. Yet these benefits can be achieved without requiring the new development to be transferred into special "receiving districts," which tend to be large and politically difficult to designate. This should help the "density exchange option" avoid some of the problems typically associated with implementing TDRs. It should also be noted that this option does not involve the county government in complex land-banking schemes (as often happens with TDR), because the arrangements are solely between private buyers and sellers.

The incentive for the farmer owning the parcel to be protected is that he or she is entitled to receive value based on a density upgrade (one dwelling per three acres, rather than one dwelling per five acres). Thus, if the farmer participates in such an exchange, on a completely developable parcel that would theoretically yield 20 dwellings, he or she would receive value for 33, a bonus of 13 units or 65 percent. Incentives to the owner of the "receiving" parcel are provided by allowing him or her to develop up to the density of one unit per two acres. If the owner's parcel is 200 acres in size, the 1:5 base density would yield 40 units. Added to that the 33 units from the sending parcel produces 73 units, which allows the owner to add another 27 units before reaching the maximum density of 100 units on 200 acres. The extra 27 units (above the 40 the owner would otherwise be entitled to build) equates to a bonus of 67 percent. By allowing 100 dwellings to be built instead of 60 (300 acres at 1:5 density), there is an increased possibility of units becoming more affordable to a greater proportion of county residents.

At the same time, critics argue, this technique would inject a larger population into the countryside, exacerbating traffic congestion on rural roads and increasing demands for urban services. While this is undeniable, and while planners can agree that the best solution would be to contain new development within "urban growth areas" around existing centers, such ideal solutions are rarely practicable in the real world of local politics where such decisions are made. The primary advantage of the "density exchange option," from a farmland preservation viewpoint, is that 100 acres would be preserved in a strategic location, helping to create a protected "critical mass" of contiguous cropland (see Figure 18–4).

The particular aspects of the "density exchange option" were tailored to conditions in Howard County. In most cases they would need to be adapted for application in other areas. Nevertheless, to provide a starting point for ordinances elsewhere, it is helpful to know some of the details. Among the criteria that "sending parcels" are required to meet are:

• minimum area of 50 acres in the Resource Conservation Zoning District

• minimum "LESA" score of 200 ("Land Evaluation and Site Assessment," a USDA rating technique)

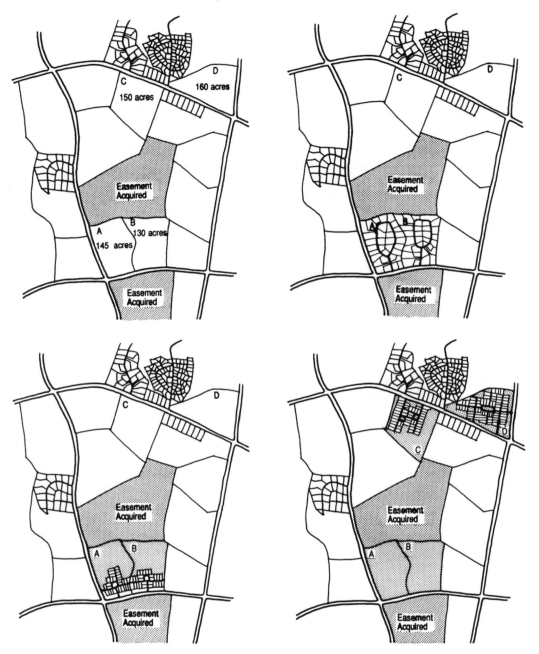

Figure 18–4. These four sketches illustrate the advantages of the "density exchange option," as advocated by planners in Howard County, Maryland. The first sketch shows a typical situation involving two large, separate, noncontiguous farm tracts that are permanently protected, and several conventional subdivisions located a small distance away. In the second sketch, unprotected farmland lying between the two protected farms is subdivided conventionally, preventing those two farms from becoming part of a larger "critical mass" of farmland, and increasing potential for conflicts between new residents and the farmers on either side. In the third sketch, the intervening land is instead developed according to the county's "basic cluster" standards, with a gross density of 1:5 and 75 percent open space protection. Though reducing farmland loss and potential conflicts, the "critical mass" possibility is foreclosed. In the fourth sketch, farmland protection is maximized by creating a protected "critical mass" consisting of all three farms in one large block, with less direct interface with suburban development. Density is exchanged (or transferred) to another parcel in a more developed area, where the new subdivision will fit into the prevailing pattern of land use.

• located within one mile of a block of protected farmland at least 200 acres in area

The "receiving parcels" must also meet certain standards:

• located in an area at least partly surrounded by existing or planned development

• able to absorb extra density without environmental degradation

• must cluster units to preserve 20 percent open space within new subdivisions (e.g., for neighborhood parks), and must follow other county design guidelines for clustering

• may receive density from more than one parcel

Although it is true that the "density exchange option" does not produce perfect results, from the strict viewpoint of farmland preservation, it may be the only politically feasible approach to keep development from consuming the remainder of Howard County's agricultural land base. To the extent that some of the protected blocks of farmland may abut suburban housing clusters, effective buffering will be necessary. No one is claiming that these creative planning approaches provide a panacea for the problem of suburban sprawl. They do, however, perhaps represent some of the best ideas to be advanced so far in the rural land-use debate, where ultimate implementation is governed by political considerations. "Planning," as one of my university professors liked to say, "is the art of the possible."

Figure 18–4 illustrates the advantages of the "density exchange option" in four sketches. Sketch A shows a typical situation involving two large separate, noncontiguous farm tracts that are permanently protected, and several conventional subdivisions located a small distance away. Sketch B illustrates how the unprotected farmland lying between the two protected farms is subdivided conventionally, preventing those two farms from becoming part of a larger "critical mass" of farmland, and increasing potential for conflicts between new residents and the farmers on either side. In sketch C, the intervening land is instead developed according to the county's "basic cluster" standards, with a gross density of 1:5 and 75 percent open space protection. Though reducing

farmland loss and reducing potential conflicts, the "critical mass" possibility is foreclosed. Finally, in sketch D, farmland protection is maximized by creating a protected "critical mass" consisting of all three farms in one large block, with less direct interface with suburban development. Density is exchanged (or transferred) to another parcel in a more developed area, where the new subdivision will fit into the prevailing pattern of land use.

LESA: ADAPTABLE TOOL FROM SCS

One need facing users of all the planning techniques described above involves rating farmland parcels with respect to their future agricultural viability. Nationwide, some 150 local governments utilize a system originally developed by the U.S. Department of Agriculture in 1981 to measure impacts of federally funded actions on farmland. Congressionally mandated for use by all federal agencies by the Farmland Protection Act of 1981, this rating system is being used voluntarily by a growing number of local governments, which are free to weight some of the criteria to reflect local issues or values. Called LESA (for "Land Evaluation and Site Assessment"), this approach combines traditional soil suitability data with information concerning social and economic variables, such as the compatability of neighboring land uses. Among the uses to which LESA is put by local governments in rural and suburbanizing areas around the country are the following (Steiner et al., 1991):

• zoning permit decisions   57%
• environmental impact assessments   41%
• designation of zoning districts   37%
• purchase of development rights   34%
• designation of agricultural districts   28%
• transfer of development rights   14%
• property tax assessments   10%

(Note: Most governmental units use LESA for more than one purpose.)

This tool is seen by most of the local officials who use it as being fair, consistent, and reliable. Once established—typically by a community committee with input from the county Soil Conservation Service agent—it is relatively easy to apply. LESA's perceived objectivity and flexibility are evidenced by the fact that it is being used by 60 jurisdictions as part of state and local environmental impact reports, and that it has been adapted by 33 others to help protect forest land (Steiner et al., 1991). In all but five cases the LESA system is used in an advisory manner, typically as one of a number of complementary techniques employed in the decision-making process. Among the states with a large or high proportion of local governments using LESA are Vermont, Illinois, New Jersey, Pennsylvania, West Virginia, and Georgia.

One criticism voiced about LESA, and particularly relevant to those involved in land-use regulation, is that many jurisdictions weight farmland viability relatively low when neighboring parcels are zoned or developed for residential use. While some conflicts are probably inevitable, such weighting creates a self-fulfilling prophecy, for land so situated will tend to be ranked low and will be assigned low priority for protection. As hope is abandoned for that parcel by the LESA system, it is more likely to be offered for development, bringing new houses that much closer to the next farm, whose LESA rating will also decline as a result. This could help accelerate a downward spiral of thinking concerning the continued viability of these farms, hastening their demise (especially if the parcels become ineligible for inclusion in an agricultural district, a development rights purchase, or for special property tax abatements, because of their low LESA ratings). Although LESA committees often tend to exhibit such attitudes, the system itself is sufficiently flexible to give higher ratings to farmland near or abutting new subdivisions.

CONTINUING CONCERNS

Many staunch farmland preservationists look askance at creative development techniques, such as those described in this chapter, as an effective way to protect the agricultural base. They may be correct that rural regions could still lose the "critical mass" of farmers needed to retain equipment dealers, large-animal vets, feed stores, and so forth, as farms become smaller in size and fewer in number. (Because such "critical masses" are fairly local in nature—based upon convenient driving distances—they are particularly vulnerable to in-

trusive, nonagricultural development.) And the doubters may also be correct about the conflicts between new residents and farmers being irreconcilable, given certain necessities of producing crops competitively with their "traditional" counterparts who have many fewer nonfarming neighbors.

It has not been the purpose of this chapter to suggest that creative development techniques be introduced into rural areas with strong farming economies and/or successful agricultural zoning regulations. However, in many metropolitan fringe areas across the country, agricultural protection zoning and 40-acre parcel minima are not politically feasible. Of course, where there is political will, almost anything is possible. But without strong, broad-based support from rural landowners and the general population, it is not likely that political leaders will enact highly restrictive land-use ordinances of the kind that are needed to protect "traditional agriculture."

In such areas it is probable that agriculture will both contract and undergo a major transition, adapting to new conditions. Farmers in eastern Washington laugh at their counterparts around Seattle, but the fact remains that much smaller farming units are economically viable in the metropolitan Puget Sound region, where producers are able to market their crops directly in a large and popular farmers' market located in the heart of Seattle. In the words of King County planner LeRoy Jones, "Pike Market farms, which are full-income farms for a family, averaged four to seven acres in size. These were full-income units, very intensively operated and marketed through Pike Place Market or a roadside stand" (quoted in Scarfo, 1990).

It is inevitable that much of this nation's farming will continue "in the shadow of the city," because there will always be a great deal of interface land around the edges of towns and other developed areas. The "adjacency problem" must be resolved, and not evaded. Even with adequate funds to purchase development rights on millions of acres of farmland, and the political will to enact strict 40-acre zoning and to implement complex TDR programs in other areas, many farmers will continue to have many nonfarming neighbors.

The challenge lies in fashioning land-use approaches that are appropriate for each type of political area. "Second-best" techniques, such as rural clustering, should generally be used only when superior methods of farmland preservation have proved impossible to enact. But in many areas without a vibrant agricultural sector, where today's generation of traditional farmers look forward to the sale of their land as their "last crop," more creative designs for the resulting development must at least be considered, and in many cases should be mandated through open space development design standards.

In some cases this approach may help innovative, adaptive metro-farmers to continue productive agricultural activities. In other cases, it may result in hobby farms and gentlemen's farms, or in outdoor recreational land uses. Essentially "open space development design" is just that: a development layout that preserves significant chunks of land, which may then serve a variety of open space uses, including certain forms of agriculture. In areas where serious agricultural or open space preservation is not politically or economically feasible, the only alternative is to allow low-density suburban sprawl to ooze over the countryside, submerging traditional rural landscapes under a continuous covering of subdivisions, shopping centers, office complexes, and industrial parks.

It will also be necessary to nurture and encourage the emerging "adaptive metro-farmers," for they have an important role to play in the supply of fresh produce and landscaping materials for the surrounding suburban and urban regions. The establishment of more farmers' markets, and the encouragement of small industries utilizing locally produced crops, should become part of the economic development program offered by town and county governments in rural areas.

The success of the next generation of farmers will depend, in large part, upon the support they receive from their own communities. That must not be forgotten. The next time people in your town complain about the aroma of freshly spread manure, gently inform them that they have just discovered one of the best things about living in the country. And ask them to think about the alternatives—usually more houses, higher taxes, and higher food prices.

Regional Contexts for Growth Management

ROBERT D. YARO

OVERVIEW

The focus of most of this book is on ways that new patterns of growth can be achieved at the local level or in individual developments. To preserve the character of whole regions, however, it will be necessary to utilize new area-wide planning systems that can make improved plans and design standards the norm rather than the exception throughout rural or metropolitan regions.

Effective regional planning will be especially important in those parts of the country where municipal planning is strong and county planning is weak or absent altogether; in particular, New England and the mid-Atlantic states. Because of continuing rapid decentralization of metropolitan regions, these areas are increasingly likely to encompass dozens, and frequently, hundreds of municipalities, multiple counties, and often more than one state. Vast rural areas at the fringe of these regions face proposals for speculative subdivisions, highway strips, office parks, and other physical manifestations of metropolitan development. Resort regions in the nation's mountain, seacoast, and rural amenity regions face similar pressures that are difficult to control in rural communities lacking the resources or planning expertise (and often the will) to control this development juggernaut.

A case in point: the New York metropolitan region, which encompasses three states, 31 counties, and more than 750 municipalities with land-use regulatory powers, including several million acres in rural communities that are part of metropolitan housing and employment markets. In complex regions such as this one, implementing improved plans and regulations on a voluntary, community-by-community basis simply will not succeed in maintaining the character of these areas. By the time they all adopt new land-use planning and regulatory systems, most of the significant natural and cultural features contributing to regional character will already be lost. Equally important, local officials in each community are facing metropolitan development pressures that are difficult to control at the receiving end. A more effective approach would be one in which larger scale metropolitan or regional planning systems were instituted, capable of shaping regional patterns of growth affecting municipal governments.

Even formerly isolated rural regions now face metropolitan development pressures, and the lines between metropolitan and rural places is becoming increasingly blurred. In the Indianapolis region, for example, a metropolitan government, "Unigov" was established in the 1970s to encompass the entire metropolitan region, then consisting entirely of Marion County. Today the metropolitan area consists not only of Marion County, but of several adjacent fast-growing suburban counties beyond the reach of Unigov and its planning controls. The Twin City Council in the Minneapolis–St. Paul region is experiencing comparable trends, with suburban development overspilling its boundaries.

Resort regions face similar pressures. Mountains, seacoasts, and other amenity areas hundreds of miles from the nearest metropolitan region—in places as diverse as Cape Cod, the Outer Banks, the Florida Keys, the Wisconsin Dells, and Ozarks, the range and mountains of Wyoming and Montana, and the Cascade Range outside Seattle—all face a subdivision, resort, and second-home development threat difficult to control with volunteer planners working at the local level. As a result, many of the nation's most special resort areas and scenic regions are developing the same garish commercial strips, townhouse complexes, and large-lot subdivisions from which metropolitan residents believed they were escaping. Instead, they have just brought the accoutrements of metropolitan life with them. In response to these challenges, a number of promising new prototypes for more effective state, regional, and metropolitan planning are being implemented across the country, from which other places with similar concerns could learn.

STATE PLANNING INITIATIVES

In a movement that has been termed "the quiet revolution in land-use control" (Bosselman, 1971), nine states (Hawaii, Oregon, Washington, Florida, Georgia, New Jersey, Maine, Vermont, and Rhode Island) have adopted new land-use planning and regulatory systems that depart from the traditional "State Zoning Enabling Act" (SZEA) model first promulgated by U.S. Commerce Department Secretary Herbert Hoover in 1924. The SZEA model (still largely in place in the remaining 41 states) delegates all land-use regulatory responsibilities to municipalities, generally without any policy guidance—and commonly without any planning requirement at all.

The new state planning systems provide a state policy framework for local planning and zoning, in which municipalities and counties are required—or provided with strong incentives—to adopt regulations consistent with local plans. These plans must also be consistent with state policies or goals, which generally include the protection of natural and historic resources and community character, provision of a range of housing types, and so forth.

States also provide grants for preparing and administering improved municipal plans and regulations and, in some cases, they also provide funds for infrastructure in accordance with those plans. Florida's system, enacted in 1985, also includes a "concurrency" provision, requiring that infrastructure needed to support new development be in place concurrent with that development.

One of the most important features of some of these systems is the requirement, particularly in Maine and Oregon, for more compact patterns of growth. Oregon's pioneering 1972 state planning program, for example, requires the designation of urban growth boundaries (UGBs) in each county and municipality in the state, clearly demarking the outer limit of urban development. Beyond the UGBs, farms and woodlands are zoned for exclusive agriculture or forestry use, effectively limiting any new residential or commercial development in rural areas outside designated centers.

One shortcoming of Oregon's program, however, is that it does not require improved standards for design and site planning within the UGBS, so that although development is more compact, it is typically not any more sympathetic to traditional community character than conventional suburban forms. Much of the recent suburban development within the Portland metropolitan urban growth boundary, for example, is indistinguishable from its counterparts in other states. It does, however, have finite limits, and cannot spread beyond the UGB into adjoining areas of farm and forest zoned under state law for exclusive agricultural or forestry use.

The difference that these programs will ultimately make, as evidenced in higher quality development, will depend on how they are administered at all levels of government. In the hands of distracted state officials and unimaginative community planners, the result could be just an additional layer of regulatory process. In New Jersey, for example, the jury is still out after more than seven years of planning activity. The Garden State's 1985 state planning act culminated in adoption of the state "Development and Redevelopment Plan" in June 1992, after an arduous process of negotiations between state, county, and municipal governments, through which the content of plans at each level of government have been "cross-accepted." Consistency between municipal plans and state goals remains at the discretion of each local government, however, and it is still too soon to say whether the resulting form and appearance of metropolitan development will be improved by this procedure and its counterparts in other states, although the potential exists for this improvement.

Constant vigilance will be required to ensure that the potential of these programs is realized. With this goal in mind, statewide nonprofit organizations, such as the "1000 Friends" groups in Oregon, Florida, and Georgia, and New Jersey Futures, have been established in most of these states to provide independent monitoring of the performance of state and local officials in achieving state planning goals.

REGIONAL PLANNING INITIATIVES

While county planning and zoning is found in most areas of the United States, another feature of the "quiet revolution" since the 1970s has been the creation of more than a score of new regional planning and land-use regulatory districts, most commonly in threatened resort or natural resource areas. While most have been established by state action, a growing number have been created with federal assistance, or through congressional action.

The content and process contained in these programs varies widely. Most, but not all, include some kind of policy framework or area-wide natural resource plan. Some exist to protect natural resource corridors (such as the Columbia River Gorge National Scenic Area, or the California Coastal Commission), while others, such as the Cape Cod and Lake Tahoe commissions control development for entire bio-regions. And the degree of regional control also varies widely, ranging from simple advisory powers, as in the Illinois and Michigan National Heritage Corridor (in Illinois), to the strict regulatory control of New Jersey's Pinelands Commission. Some, such as the Martha's Vineyard Commission, have regulatory responsibility in designated critical areas, or for control of "developments of regional impact," but have little influence over the content of municipal

plans or incremental patterns of growth. Other regional commissions, including the Pinelands Commission and the Adirondack Park Agency, have authority to impose zoning and subdivision regulations on municipalities that fail to prepare local plans and regulations meeting regional standards.

One of the newest regional land-use regulatory initiatives is Massachusetts' Cape Cod Commission (CCC), established in 1990 as a result of a citizen initiative. In 1991 the CCC completed a "regional policy plan" that identified proposed "districts of critical planning concern," and set standards for municipal planning by the region's 15 towns. The commission will finance improved town plans and regulations that must become consistent with the regional policy plan. Under its state enabling act, future state and federal policies and investment and regulatory actions (through the state's coastal plan and federal CZM consistency provisions) on Cape Cod must also be consistent with the CCC's plans and policies. Much of the remaining 40 percent of Cape Cod that is still undeveloped will be designated by the CCC as districts of critical planning concern, requiring high standards of development in those areas.

Another new initiative is a growing national system of "national heritage corridors" (NHCs), three of which—the Illinois and Michigan (in Illinois), the Blackstone Valley (in Massachusetts and Rhode Island), and the Delaware and Lehigh (in Pennsylvania)—have already been designated by Congress.

Designation of other potential NHCs await congressional action. Under the NHC model, the National Park Service provides technical support and funding to regional corridor commissions to prepare plans for recreation, land conservation, historic preservation, and economic development in these historic river and canal corridors. Federal, state, and local funds are then provided to carry out plans, although they have no regulatory responsibilities. Corridor commissions do, however possess the ability to marshall public support for improved development standards, and to encourage state and local actions to preserve important open spaces and regulate development in the corridors.

The federal government has also been a partner in other regional planning and land-use regulatory initiatives, including the New Jersey Pinelands Commission (intended by the Carter administration to become the first in a system of national reserves) and the Columbia Gorge National Scenic Area (in Washington and Oregon). Recently, the U.S. Forest Service has been directed by Congress to lead studies of regional planning options for protection of the 25 million acre Northern Forest Lands region of New York, Vermont, New Hampshire, and Maine, and the urbanizing Highlands region straddling the New York–New Jersey border.

METROPOLITAN PLANNING INITIATIVES

Most U.S. metropolitan areas have advisory, and largely ineffectual, regional planning bodies created as a result of federal planning requirements in the 1960s and 1970s. Over the past two decades, however, several metropolitan regions, including Minneapolis–St. Paul, Jacksonville, Indianapolis, and Portland, Oregon, have created new regional institutions to put teeth into efforts to manage growth and coordinate infrastructure expansion. These groups generally have the power to control patterns of development by approving or disapproving proposals to extend the regional infrastructure (typically sewers). Although they have had some success in shaping metropolitan form, they have generally not achieved better quality design in new development.

Most are now experiencing another problem: development that is leapfrogging beyond their jurisdictions into the surrounding countryside, so that the perverse result of improved metropolitan planning has been to increase suburban sprawl. Portland's Metropolitan Service District (known as "Metro")—the only elected regional body in the country—is having more success in this regard because its powers are nestled in an effective state planning program.

Several West Coast regions, including Seattle, Sacramento, and San Diego, are preparing new metropolitan plans, organizing new growth in compact centers built around planned rail systems. These initiatives are, in part, a product from the 1990 federal Clean Air Act Amendments (CAAA) and the 1991 Surface Transportation Efficiency Act ("ISTEA"), which encourage land-use elements designed to attain clean air standards.

In some large metropolitan areas, independent planning organizations are developing metropolitan plans that will be implemented through state legislation. The oldest of these, the Regional Plan Association (RPA), established in 1922 to prepare a regional plan for the New York–New Jersey–Connecticut region, is now developing its third regional plan. A central goal of this plan is to focus new development in "transit friendly" communities organized around its 1,600-mile commuter rail system. RPA is also proposing the creation of a "metropolitan greensward," a network of protected open lands, working landscapes, and traditional parks that would contain the outward movement of suburban development in the region. State plans in each state would be created or modified to achieve this goal, promoting the use of "existing use zoning" in areas beyond a designated metropolitan growth boundary (Regional Plan Association, 1991).

San Francisco's Greenbelt Alliance is pursuing similar goals for the seven-county Bay Area region. In conjunction with the Bay Area Council, in 1989 the Alliance established the BayVisions 2020 Commission, which has recommended that urban growth be channeled into more compact patterns and contained by a permanent greenbelt. The Philadelphia based Pennsylvania Environmental Council and Chicago's Open Lands Trust are developing similar plans for their regions and, in cooperation with RPA and the Greenbelt Alliance, have established the National Greenspace Alliance to promote new initiatives of this kind in other metropolitan areas.

CONCLUSION

Across the country, a number of states and metropolitan and rural regions are taking steps to reverse the destructive, decentralized development trends of the post–World War II era. Whether these will become the norm or just the exception remains to be seen, although growing federal incentives and mandates under the Clean Air and

Surface Transportation Assistance acts could encourage or require widespread adoption of these models in metropolitan regions.

Whether they will produce more livable regions and communities also remains to be seen. There are now good templates in many places that can be emulated across the country, but in most cases they are still "blunt instruments" in need of refinement. As with any innovation, the effectiveness of these programs must be closely monitored and continuously refined to ensure that they meet both region-wide goals of encouraging more compact and sustainable patterns of growth, and the fundamental goal of encouraging more humanly scaled, attractive communities. New flexible land-use and design regulatory systems that respond to the landscape and physical and social structure of each region and community will be needed if we are to avoid merely replacing conventional zoning and subdivision provisions with another kind of regulatory straightjacket. And, a new generation of creative planners, designers, and developers will be needed if the potential of these systems to build better places is to be realized.

PART

IV

Case Examples

Part IV provides brief descriptions of several dozen developments that illustrate, to one degree or another, some of the creative design principles discussed elsewhere in this book. These descriptions are not intended to be definitive; their purpose is to show a variety of examples where innovative developers and site designers have collaborated to produce residential and commercial developments that are exemplary in one or more aspects. In addition to a summary of project highlights, each case example includes a schematic site plan showing the location of buildings, vehicular access, open space and other landscape areas, and several photographs. All of these designs could benefit from refinements and improvements based upon hindsight and subsequent experience. Despite their imperfections, they all exhibit certain noteworthy features, placing them several cuts above the standard fare that has represented the medicore norm in development design over the past four or five decades.

Going beyond the hypothetical examples contained in Part II, these developments represent actual residential and commercial projects that have been conceived, proposed, reviewed, approved, financed, sold, and lived in (or rented, in the case of shops or offices). They demonstrate the viability of creative thinking in development layout and design, and challenge the conventional wisdom of less progressive souls who propose, regulate, review, approve, or market homes in checkerboard subdivisions or rental spaces in strip malls across the country.

Unless we, as a society, begin to set our sights a good deal higher, we will continue to be plagued by poorly designed development. As long as our land-use and planning standards remain so low that developers can gain legal approval for "cookie-cutter" subdivisions without providing any significant open space, and for commercial development that either disrupts the traditional fabric of small town centers with inappropriate setbacks and inharmonious building designs, or that disfigures our arterial roads with "a thousand points of blight," we are the ones to blame. After all, developers simply follow the rules we set and administer. It is perhaps painful to recall Mark Twain's observation that "in a democracy people generally get what they deserve." But, on the other hand, it is difficult to argue with that logic.

Hopefully the examples presented in the following pages will inspire at least a few landowners, developers, site designers, professional planners, and lay members of planning boards and commissions in various parts of the country to take a second look at alternative approaches to providing homes, shops, and offices in their communities. After examining such alternative patterns, perhaps they, too, will no longer be satisfied with the sad results that many people have mistakenly come to regard as inevitable. To paraphrase Russell Baker: "Many terrible things which have been proposed with the justification that they were necessary for progress have been found, upon closer examination, to have been neither necessary nor progressive, but simply terrible things."

Much of the responsibility for the present state of affairs, and for changing it, lies with planners, both professionals and volunteers who sit on planning boards and commissions. In the final analysis, these are the people who are best positioned to elevate the expectations of the local governments they serve, and to begin requiring developers to provide more than "houselots and streets" as a substitute for livable neighborhoods, and boxy nondescript buildings set at the far edge of large expanses of asphalt as a poor excuse for shopping districts.

The words of one of the country's most progressive planning spirits, Clarence Stein (designer of the internationally recognized "Radburn" subdivision in northern New Jersey) still ring true today. When asked why he and Henry Wright chose to locate their innovative project in Fairlawn, New Jersey, in 1928, he replied that they did so because sufficient land was available and because the township had not yet adopted any rigid zoning regulations that would have made their creation impossible (Stein, 1957). That is an observation worth pondering today, when so many small rural communities are saddled with inappropriate suburban-based land use regulations that will produce new development reflecting neither their traditional character nor the type of future most residents desire.

It comes down to this: we can continue to accept mediocrity, or we can work to make a positive difference. The choice is ours.

Residential Cases

This chapter features 22 examples of developments where the overall designs have preserved open space. The protected lands include natural areas such as woodlands and meadows, farmed areas such as cropland and pastures, semiformal community greens and commons, and recreational facilities such as playing fields, in addition to unbuildable, environmentally sensitive areas (such as wetlands, floodplains, and steep slopes).

A second characteristic of many of these developments is that their houselots are more compact, more like those found in a traditional village than those in ordinary suburban subdivisions. Due to the combination of their somewhat more compact pattern and the presence of attractive and conveniently located common lands, residents of many of these developments inform us that they experience a greater sense of community, with a stronger neighborhood feeling.

Most of the examples contain only single-family homes, although a number include semidetached and multifamily residences (Radburn, Merriam's Close, Long Hill Farm, Dragon Hill, Winslow Co-housing, Battle Road Farm and Chatham Village). The units themselves span a broad price range from starter homes (at Radburn and Martin Meadow) to large expensive residences (Strathmore Farms and Farmview), to "empty-nester" houses (such as at Deerfield Knoll and Long Hill Farm).

The developments are located in a wide variety of locations, from within or at the edge of established settlements (Narbrook Park, Shipcarpenter Square, Merriam's Close, and Winslow Co-housing), semirural suburban areas (Long Hill Farm and Strathmore Farms), to freestanding rural locations out in the countryside (Farmcolony, Dragon Hill, and "The Alexandria Trilogy").

Related to the type of location is the presence or absence or public sewerage. Most of the developments in this chapter are served by individual septic systems or by private community systems. In the unsewered subdivisions where lots are the most compact, individual septic disposal fields are located within the common open space (as at Trim's Ridge and Strathmore Farms). In other developments the disposal fields are shared by more than one house (as at Long Hill Farm and Merriam's Close). In larger developments central sewage treatment systems can be economically viable, such as at Deerfield Knoll (where a small, conventional, mechanical plant serves 120 homes), or at the Fields at Long Grove (where an innovative but well-established technology is used to aerate the wastewater, after which it is sprayed onto part of the open land).

Another common theme of open space developments is the network of footpaths and trails that often run through them. Although some of these are short neighborhood loops (Merriam's Close, Echo Hill, and Chatham Village), others are fairly extensive (Woodfield Village, Dunham Lake Estates, Farmcolony, and Scientists' Cliffs), while others link with larger public trail systems (Battle Road Farm and The Sanctuary).

Regardless of the house type, price range, sophistication of sewage disposal facilities, or length of trails, all these developments have preserved open space and are fostering a stronger neighborhood atmosphere. Although all could probably be improved upon, with hindsight, they stand as remarkable examples demonstrating that when people are truly interested in creating better places to live, they can often translate their visions into reality, despite the shortsightedness of those who say "nice idea, but it can't be done here."

Narbrook Park

Location: Borough of Narberth, Montgomery
County, Pennsylvania
Date: 1914–1915
Site Designer: Robert Anderson Pope, Forest Hills,
New York

The idea of designing a residential development
in a park-like setting in this "Main Line" suburb of
Philadelphia was the brainchild of George M.
Henry, newly elected Burgess of the Borough of
Narberth in 1914. Planned as a cooperative undertaking by a progressive group of borough residents known as the Narberth Civic Association,
the 14-acre parcel today occupied by Narbrook
Park was assembled by purchasing small pieces of
various properties in the neighborhood. Retained
as project designer was Robert Anderson Pope, a
city planner and landscape architect who studied
at Harvard under Frederick Law Olmsted, Jr., and
who is believed to have worked with Olmsted in
the design of Forest Hills Gardens in Queens
beginning in 1908. Building plots were not sold on
a first-come basis; instead, ownership was determined in March 1915 through the drawing of lots
by association members and other interested citizens from Narberth and Wynnewood (in nearby
Lower Merion Township). Another early example
of the participatory approach that has given this
community its special quality of life was the
contest to select a new permanent name to replace
its first "working title" as Narberth Gardens.

An elegant but relaxed and informal expression
of the "Garden City" movement that began in
England shortly after the turn of the century,
Narbrook Park contains 35 single-family homes
designed by various local architects. These residences, which vary in size and appearance, share
a broad "family resemblance," possibly denoting
the influence of the park's supervising architect,
D. Knickerbacker Boyd, who also was associated
with the Russell Sage Foundation and its Forest
Hills development.

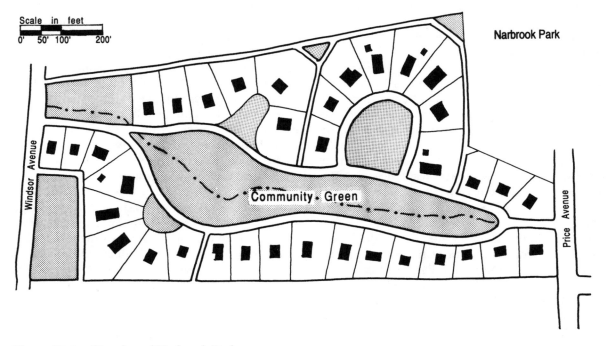

Figure 20–1a. Site plan of Narbrook Park.

Figure 20–1b. Stone cottage facing onto the western end of the green.

Figure 20–1d. Sidewalks help create a pedestrian-friendly atmosphere.

Figure 20–1c. The brook is bordered by clumps of wild iris as it flows through the green.

Figure 20–1e. Nearly all the homes face onto the main green or secondary open space areas.

Landscaping in the park has deviated from the original Olmsted vision of trees planted beside the loop road, bordering a long, open interior area. Much of this original openness has been altered by more recent plantings, especially along the stream meandering through the park. Many of the older Japanese cherry trees were planted by a Danish-born landscape architect named Anton Emil Wolhert, who resided at No. 26, and who became a national advocate for such trees in urban beautification projects.

Ownership turnover in the park is very low, as residents tend to remain there for decades. Even today, residents who would prefer to have larger houses for their growing families frequently choose to stay on in Narbrook, because no other area offers such pleasant parklike surroundings. Community spirit in the park is also quite special, with a neighborhood picnic every May after residents participate in traditional Spring clean-up activities. Less frequent are the public pageants, which have taken place on several occasions in the small "outdoor amphitheatre" formed by the horseshoe loop access road to the north of the long "community green."

Radburn

Location: Fairlawn Avenue and Plaza Road North, Fairlawn, New Jersey
Date: 1927–1931
Site Designers/Architects: Clarence Stein and Henry Wright

Well-known to students of town planning in the United States, Canada, and Britain, Radburn and its lessons are not widely appreciated by the majority of developers and planning board members in small towns across the country, who have never received any formal training in the history of subdivision design.

Originally conceived as a way of providing safe, attractive, and enjoyable neighborhoods for families of very modest means, Radburn was based upon the principle of separating vehicular traffic and pedestrians. Accordingly, through traffic is routed around the residential area on collector roads that surround a "superblock" of quiet access

F = Athletic field
P = Pool and playground
S = Elementary School

Entire development as originally planned.

Figure 20–2a. Entire development as originally planned.

Figure 20–2b. Section built before the Great Depression.

streets. An extensive network of sidewalks and footpaths connects each house with several long, serpentine parks (covering 23 acres), which lead to the neighborhood school, playing fields and com-munity pool at one end of the development, and to shops and offices at the other. Other recreational facilities include two tot lots, two playgrounds, three ballfields and four tennis courts.

Figure 20–2c. Homes face onto paved footpaths leading to the two large parkland areas.

Figure 20–2e. The footpath network connects homes with active recreation areas and local shops. Here a young man is helping his grandfather bring the family groceries back home.

Figure 20–2d. The "Long Green," one of the two principal open spaces in Radburn.

Figure 20–2f. Modest homes grouped around a small cul-de-sac.

Where paths cross major thoroughfares, pedestrian underpasses allow children to run or bike safely. Although the site was no more than a cornfield in 1928, extensive shade-tree plantings have made it a veritable forest today.

Radburn includes a mixture of 638 detached, 50 semidetached ("duplex") and 100 multifamily homes. The single-family models are sited on lots typically measuring just 50 feet × 100 feet (a net density of eight units per acre), but this is balanced by the large amount of high-quality open space within a short walking distance of every home. Overall, the gross density of the entire subdivision is approximately five units per acre. According to an Urban Land Institute study, Radburn's "walk layout, the orientation of homesites toward cul-de-sacs and the internal parks increase personal acquaintance within the development. The result is a cohesive community with a high level of participation in association affairs" (Hanke, 1973).

Radburn's lifestyle is so appealing that it is able to boast a number of second-generation residents, who grew up there and moved back as adults so their children could enjoy the same pleasures and benefits. The essential secret of Radburn is that it is truly "a subdivision within a park." Its attractiveness, however, has had the unfortunate effect of elevating property values to levels higher than the moderate-income families, which the development was originally intended to serve, can afford to pay. Despite their small lots, Radburn homes are much in demand by young professional couples, who enjoy living in a remarkable parklike setting.

Echo Hill

Location: Belchertown Road, Amherst, Massachusetts
Date: c. 1966–1978
Designer: Per Nylen, ASLA, Duxbury, Massachusetts
Developer: William Aubin

This project contains a beneficial mixture of larger homes on standard one-half-acre lots, 102 smaller

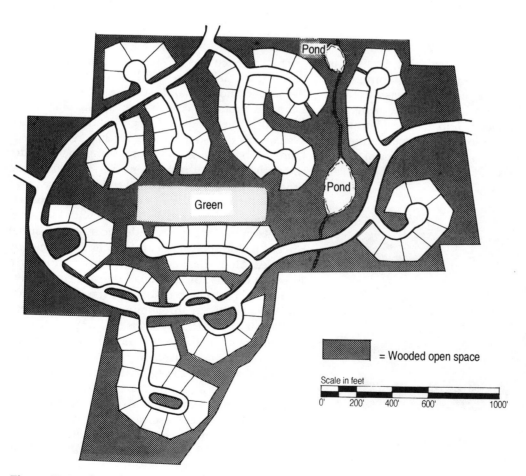

= Wooded open space

Scale in feet

0'   200'   400'   600'   1000'

Figure 20–3a. Site plan of Echo Hill (Section with ¼-acre lots).

Figure 20–3b. The 3.7-acre common in the middle of Echo Hill is about twice the size of a traditional New England town green.

Figure 20–3d. Homes in Echo Hill are surrounded by woodlands, very little of which was cleared during the course of development, keeping lots cool and shady in summer.

homes on one-quarter-acre lots all adjoining an open space network, townhouse condominiums, and a small commercial area. This case example focuses upon the second of these elements (the smaller lots with associated open space) because it is probably the most relevant and replicative feature of Echo Hill, in the context of typical development possibilities in small towns.

Figure 20–3c. The formal recreation area consists of a small pond with sandy beach and wooded picnic area, a tennis court that doubles as an informal basketball facility, and (out of the camera's range) a baseball diamond and backstop.

The presence of a 3.7-acre meadow in the middle of this thickly wooded site inspired both the developer and his landscape architect to design Echo Hill around a core of open space. This "common" or "green" lies at the heart of the open space system, which also includes over 30 acres of woodlands with walking trails connecting each cul-de-sac with two small ponds (one for swimming, the other for skating) and a formal recreation area provided with a tennis court (also fitted with basketball hoops) and a baseball diamond with backstop. With its many fingered cul-de-sac system leading toward major open space areas, Echo Hill is clearly modeled after the Radburn design tradition. To improve circulation, these cul-de-sacs could have been paired into loop roads, or even interconnecting loops, without threatening pedestrian safety. But, for its time, the layout is still impressive.

The "green" is the venue for Echo Hill's annual spring picnic, and is used on a daily basis throughout the year by residents of all ages. Possibly because of this focal point, and the variety of recreational amenities available in the neighborhood, residents tend to feel a sense of community pride. Despite its amenities, homeowners' dues in Echo Hill are only $75 per year, because the facilities have deliberately been designed to be basic and easy to maintain.

This section of Echo Hill maintains the ambience of a park, which explains a large part of its charm. In fact, some visitors comment that the modest, one-story contemporary homes, set on their compact one-quarter-acre lots (half the size normally required in this zoning district) under the dense canopy of white pines, almost remind them of tents in a campground. One of Echo Hill's lessons is that good neighborhoods make for successful real estate, and that thoughtful open space provision contributes significantly to neighborhood quality of life. (For details on property value appreciation in Echo Hill, compared with conventional developments, see Chapter 14, "Encouraging Open Space Design".)

Martin Meadow

Location: Martin Meadow Road, Plainfield, Vermont
Date: 1946
Site Designers/Developers: David Johnson and Noyle Johnson, Plainfield, Vermont

Located at a comfortable walking distance from the village center in Plainfield, Vermont, Martin Meadow is a small, 17-acre development of 21 single-family homes, half of which look out over a lovely two-acre green that is roughly trapezoidal in shape. In both its area and its irregular shape, the green is similar to many of the commons that punctuate New England townscapes. Unlike others, however, the commons at Martin Meadow is less than 50 years old, and it is not publicly owned or maintained.

The Meadow, as residents refer to it, was the creation of two local men, David and Noyle Johnson, descendants of one Willard Martin, the owner of a large estate known as Greatwood Farm (which now houses Goddard College). The Meadow is one of Martin's old pastures, where he raised prize-winning Merino sheep from 1912 to 1930. Sensitive to the beauty of the meadow, the Johnson brothers refrained from doing as almost every

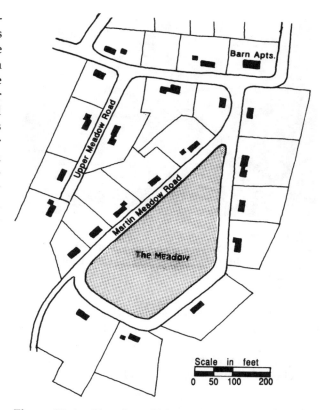

Figure 20–4a. Site plan of Martin Meadow.

Figure 20–4b. Entering Martin Meadow, looking down a gentle slope into the central open space.

Figure 20–4c. Nearly all homes face the meadow, which is mowed weekly during the summer by the adjoining families (each of whom is responsible for that part of the meadow nearest their front yard).

very smoothly, and is a further example of the community spirit and cooperation that the layout fosters.

Although no sociological surveys have been conducted by graduate students to prove (or disprove) the thesis, residents feel that the people in their neighborhood know each other better and interact more than people in standard subdivisions, where there is no focal point, no common ground for afternoon games or evening strolls (or annual picnics!). Life at Martin Meadow is apparently so agreeable that at least one person who grew up there bought a house and moved back as an adult, to raise a family in her own childhood neighborhood. Apart from Radburn, New Jersey, there are probably very few subdivisions where similar examples can be cited.

other postwar developer did; they left a large grassy open area in the center, and arranged half their houselots around it. The homes are typical of the period in both style and floorspace (Capes and ranches of about 1,200 to 1,500 square feet), and fall within the middle range of local housing prices. Lots range from 12,000 square feet to 28,000 square feet in area, and are served by town water and sewer. A barn from the old Martin estate occupies one of the lots, and has been converted into three apartment units.

The central green is owned by an organization known as the Meadow Association, a group composed of the homeowners of the surrounding lots. A yearly dues of $5 per family pays for insurance and a neighborhood picnic at the end of the summer (a similar tradition is also enjoyed by residents of Echo Hill in Amherst, Massachusetts, described earlier in this chapter). Maintenance consists of mowing the grass, and each homeowner whose house fronts on the green is responsible for cutting a section of the common in front of his or her house. Residents generally know which "patch" is theirs to mow, and if anyone is not feeling well enough to cut his or her section on a given weekend, a neighbor usually takes care of it and the favor is returned the following Saturday. According to long-time residents, this all runs

Shipcarpenter Square

Location: Lewes, Delaware
Date: 1983–1992
Site Designers: David Dunbar and Jack Vessels, Lewes, Delaware

This infill subdivision in the attractive and historic coastal town of Lewes, Delaware, was designed by two individuals with no prior experience in development, which may account for its unconventional, nonsuburban layout (no curvilinear streets or cul-de-sacs). Instead of following standard practices, Dunbar and Vessels applied their common sense and instincts to their 11-acre site, deciding to complement the surrounding rectilinear street pattern with a subtle variation involving a loop road with three straight segments and two tight 90-degree turns. Fortunately, a plan for a strip shopping plaza and 88 cookie-cutter houselots, drawn up for the site in the 1970s by another developer, was never implemented.

Lots at Shipcarpenter Square (named for an old nearby street) range in size from 7,500 to 12,000 square feet, somewhat larger than, but still in

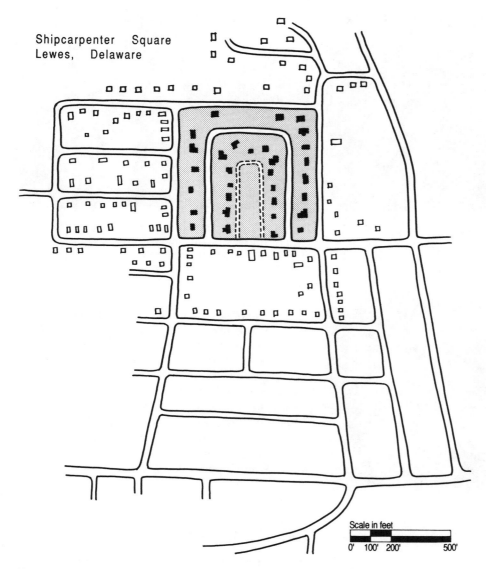

Figure 20–5a. Site plan of Shipcarpenter Square, within its surrounding context.

keeping with, those in the general neighborhood. Thirty-six lots were arranged along the U-shaped access road, enclosing a two-acre interior "common," whose upkeep (largely mowing) is provided by a homeowners' association with "automatic membership." Opening out onto one of the town's major streets, the common faces an historic church, which serves as a visual focal point of the open space. Residents of Shipcarpenter Square use the common for a wide variety of activities, including walking, playing soccer, and flying kites. Three annual neighborhood events are also held there: Easter Egg Hunts, Labor Day Picnics, and Christmas tree decoration in December. This shared central area has provided an opportunity for such community activities to occur, and has also fos-

Figure 20–5b. Looking down the green, toward a nineteenth-century church that faces Shipcarpenter Square.

Figure 20–5d. Homes are arranged formally, lining the green in a straight row, with relatively modest side yards, as is traditional in the older parts of Lewes.

Figure 20–5c. The footpaths circling the green are paved with local clamshells.

usual aspect is that homes abutting the common face inward, away from the street, in the style of Radburn, New Jersey (described in an earlier case example in this chapter). The design objective was to present a more formal line of facades bordering the common. In effect, these homes have two "front sides," the less formal one facing the street. Although there was no conscious effort to replicate a New England town green, familiarity with that concept may have influenced at least one of the site developers, who is a native of that region.

Deerfield Knoll

tered the growth of a neighborhood spirit and camaraderie all but absent in conventional subdivisions consisting of only houselots and streets.

This subdivision is unusual in two other respects. The first is that all the houses are historic homes rescued from demolition or fire-fighting exercises by Dunbar and Vessels, who moved them onto the site for restoration. The homes date from 1730 to 1880, and all but two are from within a 40-mile radius in Delaware (the other two originated in Maryland and Virginia). The second un-

Location: Dutton Mill Road, Willistown Township, Pennsylvania
Date: 1986–1991
Site Designer/Developer: Blair and Son, Bryn Mawr, Pennsylvania

Nestled into the contours of this 42-acre site, Deerfield Knoll's 119 homes are clustered into groups of four and six houses. Dwellings are two-story, single-family detached townhouses de-

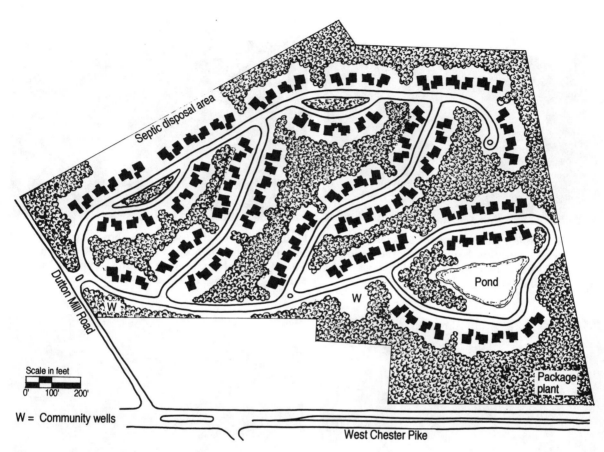

Scale in feet

0'   100'   200'

W = Community wells

Figure 20–6a. Site plan of Deerfield Knoll.

signed in a richly detailed Williamsburg style, all approximately 2,100 square feet in area (plus a full basement), with attached garages for one or two cars. The visual dominance of some of these garages has been lessened by facing their overhead doors to one side (rather than to the street). Although the garages could have been detached and accessed through back lanes or alleys, such siting would have been difficult for topographical reasons. Also, it is questionable, in this rural-suburban context, whether such an urban form would have been acceptable to buyers.

Front setbacks are modest and lateral spacing between homes within each cluster is minimal, often about 15 feet between exterior walls. Backyard privacy is assured by solid wooden fences

and serpentine brick walls enclosing patios and sitting areas covering about 1,500 square feet of land behind each home. The homes are popular with young professional couples and empty-nesters, who desire the convenience of a townhouse but who also prefer living in a freestanding residence with well-defined private outdoor spaces that serve as an extension of the living room during the warmer months. The market success of Deerfield Knoll is partly due to the substantial amount of townhouse development in the general area, from which a sizable number of dissatisfied people have moved. Its detached townhomes fill a previously unmet housing need, providing a neat compromise between condominiums and suburban houses.

Figure 20–6b. Building arrangements are varied at Deerfield Knoll, with three homes facing the pond and two facing each other across a small green space, perhaps just 60 feet wide.

Figure 20–6d. Of the five homes shown here, four are in pairs where one house backs up to the windowless side of its neighbor, keeping the development pattern fairly tight without sacrificing livability.

Figure 20–6c. Little land is wasted on side yards, and privacy between units is assured by eliminating most side windows.

Figure 20–6e. The four homes in the background consume an average 55 feet of street frontage each.

Beyond the private back gardens are a mixture of grassy and wooded common lands covering more than 30 acres (including a large pond). Every May, residents enjoy a "garden tour day" during which many homeowners open their small but intensively landscaped rear gardens for their neighbors to visit and share ideas.

Drinking water is supplied from two wells in the southern part of the property. Tanks under one of the wellhouses hold a 60,000 gallon reserve for peak demand and emergency uses. Sewage is conducted via gravity mains to a central facility in the southeast corner, where the wastes receive aerobic treatment and are denitrified. From there the processed effluent is pumped to drainage fields located along the site's northern boundary, where it receives further natural treatment as it percolates down through the soil, eventually recharging local groundwater supplies.

Merriam's Close

Location: Edmond's Road, off Lexington Road,
Concord, Massachusetts
Date: 1979–1981
Site Designer: Per Nylen, ASLA, Duxbury,
Massachusetts

The wooded sandhill that originally occupied the
site of Merriam's Close, located off the Lexington
Road in Concord, Massachusetts, had been cleared
and mined away to provide fill for the expansion
of Boston's Logan Airport, some 20 miles distant,
when landscape architect Per Nylen visited the
property in the late 1970s to consider its reclamation possibilities for his developer client. Although
the back half of the 24-acre parcel was relatively
undisturbed, its woods were rather wet and clearly

off-limits to development under municipal and
state regulations. According to town lore, it contained the "quaking bog" mentioned in Henry
David Thoreau's journals.

In order to achieve an economic rate of return
on investment in this affluent community where
land prices are above the regional median, places
for 20 dwellings had to be found. The design solution was based on local historic building traditions: village-scale lots with modest front setbacks
(sometimes referred to in New England as "dooryard gardens"). Within the small flat area left by
the sand extraction operation, 20 houselots were
created on 3.42 acres, averaging 7,500 square feet
each. (All homes are served by town water and a
community septic system.)

By arranging fourteen units in seven "semidetached" pairs using zero-lotline techniques, and by
setting foundations 18 feet back from street curbs,
space was borrowed from unproductive front and

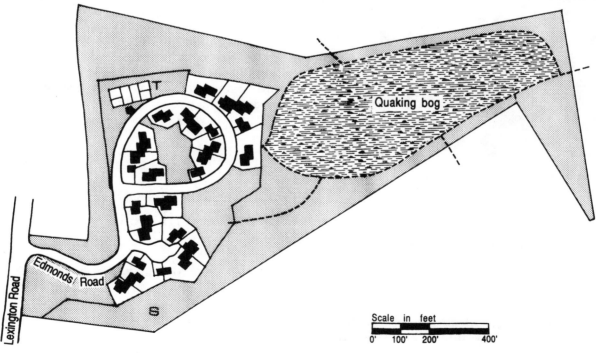

S = Community septic disposal area
T = Tennis courts

Figure 20–7a. Site plan of Merriam's Close.

Figure 20–7b. Homes are located in villagelike arrangements, each residence facing the road, with just 55 feet between opposing house fronts.

Figure 20–7d. Streets measure 18 feet across, from edge to edge, adequate for the light traffic flow they receive and for emergency vehicles.

Figure 20–7c. Front yards are a modest 18 feet between foundation and curb, quite enough along the quiet residential access streets that serve them.

side yards and allocated to backyards instead (which affords more privacy for outdoor activities). Because the street system serves less than two-dozen homes, it was allowed to be built 18 feet wide. The result is that door-to-door distances between homes facing each other across the street is 55 to 60 feet, precisely at the scale of eighteenth and early nineteenth-century streetscapes in the villages and small towns in this part of the country.

Designed to resemble large single-family residences, the "paired" homes easily blend with the

six detached dwellings that are interspersed among them. All of the units, whether two-family or single-family, have about 2,100 square feet of floorspace, plus a full basement and a garage. According to residents, homes in The Close are rarely vacant: demand for such units is very strong, because of their design and amenities, including 17 acres of open space with tennis courts and woodland trails around the quaking bog (where Louisa May Alcott, author of *Little Women,* is reputed to have skated as a child).

Woodfield and South Woodfield Villages

Location: Town of Merton, Waukesha County, Wisconsin
Date: 1972–1980
Site Designer: William Nelson Associates, Milwaukee, Wisconsin

These two adjoining subdivisions were both developed by Siepmann Realty Corporation and were planned to complement one another. Alto-

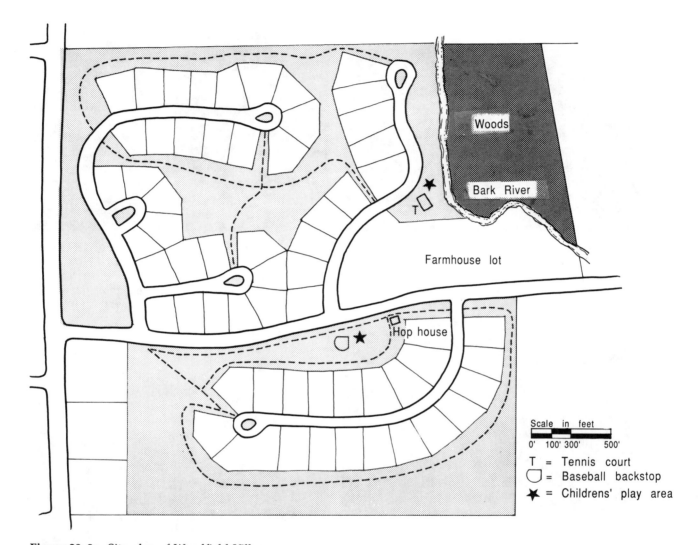

Figure 20–8a. Site plan of Woodfield Village.

gether they contain 65 lots on 160 acres, 75 of which are designated as common open space. A single homeowners' association maintains recreation facilities comprising two tennis courts, a baseball diamond, two childrens' play areas, and a riding ring. An informal network of walking trails traversing the open space provides convenient access to these amenities from all corners of the subdivision. Houselots vary in size between one-half and one acre, except for three 3-acre lots in the southern section, and one 14-acre lot with the

original farmhouse and three barns. Homes in this upscale subdivision range in size from 2,200 to 4,000 square feet. The open space consists of field, successional woodland, and mature forest. A formal orchardlike planting of crabapples in the open space in and around a U-shaped access court provides an attractive focal point and amenity, which is also visible from the county road bounding the western edge of the subdivision. The homeowners' association also maintains a small historic hop-house, one of the very few remaining

Figure 20–8b. Looking down across tennis courts and horse pastures to the Bark River, whose banks remain undeveloped as it flows through Woodfield Village.

Figure 20–8d. Ron Siepmann, the developer, listens as one of the subdivision residents explains why she moved to her landlocked lot from her former lakeside home (she cited the 75 acres of open space, several miles of trails, the active recreation facilities for both children and adults, and the beautiful parklike surroundings).

Figure 20–8c. Many houselots adjoin open space, such as this former meadow, now planted with different tree species to produce a more varied habitat.

Figure 20–8e. Flowering ornamental trees planted in a formal orchardlike pattern in a small open area surrounded by a neighborhood grouping of five homes. *Source:* Photo by Ron Siepmann.

examples of this unusual building form (with its second-story drying room), dating from the mid-nineteenth century when this area produced hops for nearby breweries in Milwaukee.

The open space also contains a segment of the Bark River, a wading creek of moderate depth where neighborhood children catch tadpoles and turtles, and anglers fish for panfish and an occasional northern pike. In retrospect it is unfortunate that the trail system was not originally extended to parallel this river, because recent proposals by the Ice Age Park and Trail Foundation to create a greenway trail along the Bark, as it flows through the Town of Merton, have met with predictable opposition from residents of the two Woodfield subdivisions.

Although there is substantial evidence that greenway trails increase the value of neighboring properties and enhance quality of life by making it possible to take longer walks and to experience a variety of habitats and natural features, existing subdivision residents often resist new trail proposals in their neighborhood, expressing unrealistic fears of crime and vandalism. Studies published by the National Park Service (described in Chapter 16, "Greenways and Buffers") document the very positive feelings expressed by people whose properties abut preexisting trail systems. Apparently, fear of future trails is based largely on the unknown; people living near established trails know from personal experience that such features provide an enjoyable amenity, and are not the "conduits of crime" imagined in the abstract by others who are unfamiliar with the real situation. Evidence that this is true is provided by another Siepmann Realty subdivision in the nearby Town of Delafield, where the new Hawksnest development is being successfully marketed as having an extensive neigh-

borhood trail network connecting with the 500-mile Ice Age Trail that winds through the uplands woods portion of Hawknest's open space. The lesson for site designers and local officials is that trail provision along linear features offering the possibility of future interconnections should always be part of the original plan, wherever possible.

Long Hill Farm

Location: Long Hill Road, Guilford, Connecticut
Date: 1987–1991
Developer/Architect/Site Planner: Lauren E. Meyers, Jr., AIA

Set on a 50-acre site in rural Guilford, Long Hill Farm includes a patchwork of former pastures and deciduous woodland in a rolling terrain where

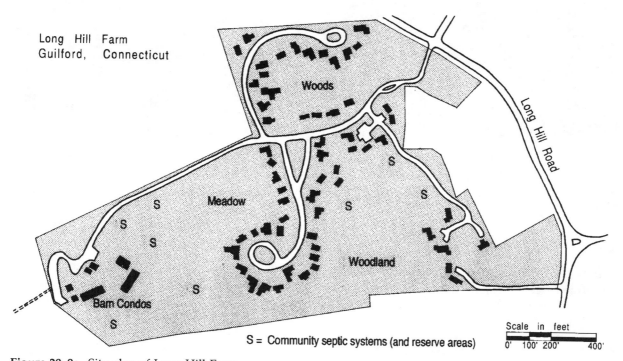

Figure 20–9a. Site plan of Long Hill Farm.

Figure 20–9b. One of the nicest new subdivision roads anywhere, this street follows the lay of the land and curves deliberately around large trees in a respectful, countrylike manner.

Figure 20–9d. Some of the garages are detached and sit close to the road, creating more privacy for residents.

Figure 20–9c. Nearly all the homes in Long Hill Farm look out onto permanently preserved open space, such as this meadow. Note that rear lot lines follow the old stone wall, a feature that the site designer took care to preserve.

Figure 20–9e. About 40 percent of the dwellings are in multiple-unit residences, designed in harmony with the scale and massing of traditional New England barns.

granite bedrock outcroppings are fairly common. Fifty-five single-family residences have been sited with an exceptionally skillful eye to take advantage of optimal locations in the uneven forest topography. So much care was taken to preserve large trees near the houses that most homes appear, at first glance, to have been there for generations.

Lot sizes in this upmarket development typically range between 4,500 square feet and 5,000 square feet (comparable to those at Radburn) with modest clearings for dooryard gardens and landscaped patio areas. Privacy issues have been addressed by the orientation of each house and the wooded buffers between their yardspaces. Setbacks follow no fixed pattern, as buildings sit where they will be the least intrusive upon the natural features. In some cases garages are located close to the roadway, with homes tucked behind them on higher ground. The roads themselves wind through the woods with more regard paid to minimizing site disturbance than to conforming to a highway engineer's manual (which is the basis for most subdivision road design standards). All utilities have been installed underground, and just enough woodland has been cleared to accommodate the 18-foot-wide access road network (with minimal shoulders).

The location, shape, and size of the preserved open space were some of the major design determinants for the development layout. The reason was not primarily aesthetic or recreational, but pragmatic: septic systems had to be placed on the best soils available on the site. This meant siting subsurface drainage areas in the meadows, while occasionally building homes on solid ledge. Many of them have been oriented to take full advantage of long views across the protected open fields, a feature typically not possible in conventional "checkerboard" subdivisions.

In addition, 35 multifamily condominium units have been created in several barnlike buildings at the western end of the site. Garages and storage lofts are contained in smaller barn-type structures within the "compound." Designed to blend in with vernacular building patterns, the barns have

received an award from the Guilford Preservation Alliance, which has recognized them as a "much-needed demonstration that multi-unit developments can be designed to harmonize with older neighborhoods and the rural countryside."

The Fields at Long Grove

Location: Village of Long Grove, Illinois
Date: 1989–present
Planner: Lane Kendig, Inc., Mundelein, Illinois

Located in an area where the midwestern prairie gives way to eastern woodlands, The Fields at Long Grove has received awards for its outstanding design and innovative features. Through the use of clustering techniques, three-quarters of this 160-acre tract has been preserved as permanent open space. The open space consists of 50 acres of former farmland restored to native Illinois prairie; a mature 10-acre oak forest; 3.5 miles of walking trails; a lake with a sandy beach for swimming, boating, and fishing; and several ponds for wild-

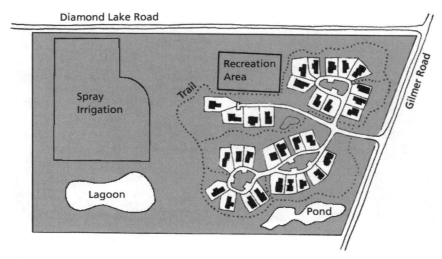

Figure 20–10a. Site plan of The Fields (western section).

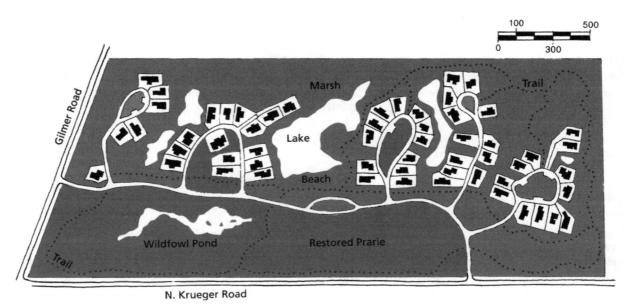

Figure 20–10b. Site plan of The Fields (eastern section).

life. The homeowners' association operates a community satellite dish, and holds a three-acre site reserved for future recreation facilities (tennis courts, ball fields, and possibly a pool).

The project's 87 homesites are arranged around these features to take full advantage of attractive views and to provide easy access to these amenities. Instead of offering houselots of one to one and one-half acres, as is typical in this area, developer James McHugh decided to reduce site disturbance and to maximize environmental benefits by limiting lot size to roughly one-quarter acre. With many homes in the 2,500 to 3,500 square foot range, the smaller yards permit homes to be positioned to maximize views of wetlands, ponds, prairie, and forest. Privacy between homes is pro-

Figure 20–10c. View along entry road, looking toward the wildfowl pond and part of the restored prairie.

Figure 20–10d. Homes grouped around one of the smaller ponds, which are landscaped with native species such as red osier dogwood.

vided with landscape plantings, and by designing units with a windowless wall located against one of the side lot lines. Clustering permits a rural atmosphere to be preserved for both the village residents and the surrounding community. Generous open space areas (some 400 feet deep) have been preserved alongside the public ways bordering this subdivision, so that views from the road are largely ones of prairie and hedgerows, rather than ones of conventional one-acre houselots lining the perimeter.

Figure 20–10e. Hedgerows are wide enough to accommodate part of the neighborhood trail system.

Figure 20–10f. Large expensive homes located relatively close to the aeration lagoon (where community sewage is odorlessly treated, prior to being sprayed onto adjoining fields).

Reversing a century of ecological damage to the property caused by modern agriculture practices, McHugh has sown a variety of native grasses and wildflowers in a 60-acre prairie restoration area (where controlled burning is conducted to kill alien species and with the intention of providing the heat required for native seeds to germinate). He has also removed extensive areas of drainage tiles to allow wetland habitats to reemerge. Herons are frequent visitors to the ponds, which are now ringed with native wetland species (such as sawgrass) planted by the developer. The prairie, which took five years to become well established, offers valuable upland habitat for birds and small mammals.

Another innovative feature is a state-of-the-art wastewater treatment system, consisting of an aeration lagoon and spray irrigation apparatus over cultivated farmland. Rather than piping wastewater to a distant sewage plant that empties into a major river or lake, the groundwater table underlying the area is continually recharged through this on-site facility. Stormwater runoff is also reduced by limiting street pavement width to 18–20 feet, eliminating curbs, and allowing drainage to seep into broad grassy swales.

The Sanctuary

Location: Steamboat Springs, Colorado
Date: 1991–present
Site Designer: Eric Smith Associates, Boulder, Colorado

Although the original plans for developing this site were designed with typical real-estate considerations in mind, they did take some of the existing trail network into consideration. However, local residents who had informally used these trails for hiking, biking, and cross-country skiing for decades had expected a fuller recognition of the importance of the trails in the developer's plans. In this outdoors-oriented community on the western slopes of the Rockies, recreational

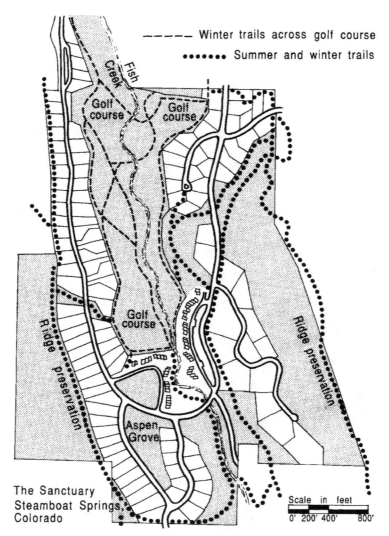

Figure 20–11a. Site plan of The Sanctuary.

amenities are a high priority for many citizens, who value their quality of life and rank accessibility to trails as one of their area's greatest assets.

After attending a local conference on open space preservation (organized by opponents of the subdivision), the developer agreed to recast his proposal, and engaged an award-winning design firm from Boulder to reconfigure his original plans (which had been drawn by engineers). The new team of designers made trail preservation one of their primary objectives, and worked the lots into a pattern that avoided affecting the majority of

existing trails. Where it was not feasible to save an entire trail, segments were generally moved to other acceptable locations, maintaining their continuity and integrity. Another goal of the design process was to minimize intrusive development and road construction in three environmentally sensitive areas: a stream corridor, an aspen grove, and the highly visible steeper slopes and ridges surrounding the core site.

Altogether 49 percent of the 232-acre site is being preserved as permanent open space, in addition to the preexisting golf course that the subdi-

Figure 20–11b. Year-round trails meander through woodlands and traverse the ridges, while the golf course is used for cross-country ski trails during the long Colorado winter.

Figure 20–11d. Most of the surrounding slopes have been set aside as permanent preservation areas, with summer-and-winter trails for hiking, biking, and alpine skiing.

Figure 20–11c. Slow-growing aspen stands are protected on the hillsides and in a large grove within the development, which was designed around such natural features.

vision abuts on three sides. Most of the lots average one-half acre or slightly larger in size, more modestly proportioned than the developer was initially comfortable with (even for those adjoining the golf course), due to perceived demand for larger yards in this rural area. However, he ultimately agreed that the extensive trail network, and the large acreage of protected land adjacent to the vast majority of lots, could be used as positive marketing tools. In other words, the sales strategy can be based, in part, upon the development's recreational amenities, protected views, and accessible open space, features that competing subdivisions cannot match.

Strathmore Farms

Location: River Road, Madison, Connecticut
Date: 1986–1992
Site Designer: Eric Anderson Associates, Guilford, Connecticut
Developer: Robert Dowler, Madison, Connecticut

Six acres of horse pasture separate Strathmore Farms' 25 single-family homes from River Road, helping to preserve the rural character of this country road and providing a visual and recre-

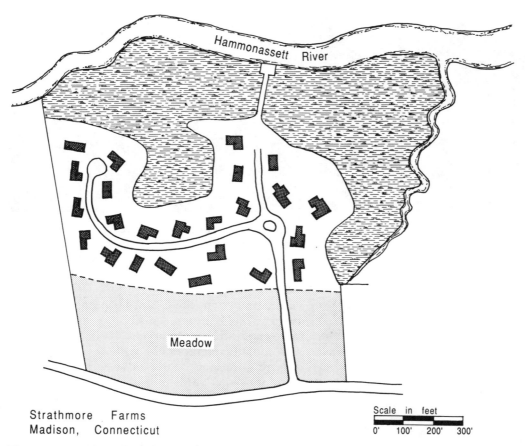

Strathmore Farms
Madison, Connecticut

Scale in feet
0'   100'   200'   300'

Figure 20–12a. Site plan of Strathmore Farms.

ational amenity that would not have been possible had the developer chosen to subdivide his 29-acre parcel into a conventional checkerboard pattern of houselots and streets.

Most of the homes also enjoy attractive views toward a tidal marsh along the Hammonassett River, bordering the property to the east. A short boardwalk (175-feet long) leads to a gazebo built at the river's edge, affording views up and down the meandering estuary. A small private dock at this location provides access to the river and to Long Island Sound, one mile downstream. Located 45 minutes from Hartford, Madison is also a two-hour drive from both New York City and Boston.

Within the site, homes are generally located 40 to 45 feet apart (from side to side) and typically sit

Figure 20–12b. View from the town road, across an enclosed six-acre horse pasture, toward eight homes overlooking this protected open space.

Figure 20–12c. Homes at Strathmore Farms are generally 40 to 50 feet apart, but all enjoy views of either the pasture or the tidal marshes.

Figure 20–12d. Two-thirds of the homes are orientated toward the wetlands along the Hammonassett River, which provide nesting and feeding habitat for many varieties of waterfowl.

about 20 feet from the edge of the roadway, which itself has a paved width of 18 feet, helping to create the feeling of an informal rural neighborhood. All the land is commonly owned in this condominium development, but if individual lot lines existed, each home would sit on a lot of about 10,000 to 12,000 square feet. Half the homeowners are "empty-nesters," and half have children ranging in age from one to eighteen. Al-

though this village-scale arrangement was very unusual for new large-home developments in rural New England in this price range (about $430,000 to $640,000), units sold quickly and turnover has been very low. Homes come in four traditional architectural styles and range in size from 2,700 square feet to 4,900 square feet.

Homes are served by town water and by individual septic systems maintained by a homeowners' association.

Farmview

Location: Lower Makefield Township, Pennsylvania
Date: 1987–present
Site Designer: Bob Heuser, Sullivan Associates, Philadelphia, Pennsylvania
Developer: Realen Homes, Berwyn, Pennsylvania

Set on a 431-acre site in Bucks County, 30 minutes north of Philadelphia, Farmview's 310 houselots cover just half the property. Located in a zone where the lot size minimum is one acre, the developers were permitted lots averaging 22,000 square feet (one-half acre), with 110 feet of street frontage (instead of 160 feet), under a special cluster zoning amendment adopted to encourage the conservation of 51 percent or more of a subdivision tract as permanent farmland. Overall density was determined by a concept plan (or "yield" plan) showing the number of lots achievable under a conventional layout.

The lot size reduction enabled 137 acres of highly productive farmland to be saved, in addition to more than 100 acres of woods and wetlands. Other design criteria required that resulting farm parcels contain at least 12 acres and be reasonably proportioned. Ownership of the cropland (which includes some of the best soils in the county) was transferred to the Farmland Preservation Corporation, a quasi-independent munici-

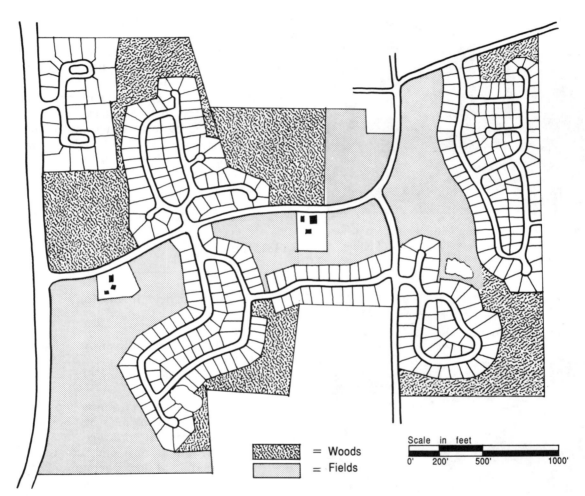

= Woods

= Fields

Scale in feet

0'   200'   500'   1000'

Figure 20–13a. Site plan of Farmview.

pal body that leases its holdings to two local farmers. Planted with sweet corn, alfalfa, rye, and soybeans, the farmland is separated from backyards by a vegetated buffer, required under the ordinance. Another design goal was to locate most of the houselots away from existing town roads, to maintain unblocked rural views.

Buyer response has been highly favorable, with sales outpacing those in all other subdivisions within its price range around the county, even during the sluggish 1991 market. Farmview's sales strategy, advertising "a community that will be forever surrounded by acres of preserved farm-

land, open fields and woodlands," has not gone unnoticed by competing developers: two more subdivisions with very similar land preservation arrangements have also been proposed and approved under Lower Makefield's new farmland cluster ordinance. Reductions in developed land area and lot width have also produced a shorter street system, saving on both construction and long-term public maintenance costs. All lots are served by public water and sewers.

Winner of an award from the Pennsylvania Planning Association, Farmview has begun to set an example in its area. Although the enabling

Figure 20–13b. Erected beside the public roadway running past Farmview, this is perhaps the only historic marker in the nation commemorating land that has been conserved by a developer. (This 31-acre tract is the first of five such preserves that is being created within this subdivision.)

Figure 20–13d. Many of the houses contain about 3,000 square feet of floorspace, and fit comfortably on their one-half-acre lots. They have outsold similar houses on lots twice the size in nearby conventional subdivisions, where the only views are of other people's picture windows or back yards.

Figure 20–13c. View from the township road, across the protected farm fields, toward a number of new homes built by Realen.

ordinance is commendable, refinements to those regulations have been encouraged by both developers and professional planners, who support reducing minimum road widths from 30 feet and front setback distances from 40 feet. More appropriate dimensions for both these elements would be in the order of 20 feet each (see Chapter 11, "Street Design for Rural Subdivisions").

"The Alexandria Trilogy"

Location: Alexandria Township, Pittstown, New Jersey
Date: 1987–present
Site Planners: Madden/Kummer, Inc., Flemington, New Jersey, and West Chester, Pennsylvania

Alexandria Township, Hunterdon County, located in the still rural western part of central New Jersey, strongly encourages developers to reduce lot sizes from the three-acre minimum by offering clustering "by right" in its performance-based zoning ordinance. The township retains the firm of Madden/Kummer, Inc. to provide planning and landscape architecture services to assist developers in the layout of their proposals, thereby facilitating the review process and improving the design quality of the results. Subdivision review fees are set at levels that enable the township to recover its costs for such services.

During the late 1980s, three adjacent parcels covering 363 acres of farmland and wooded areas

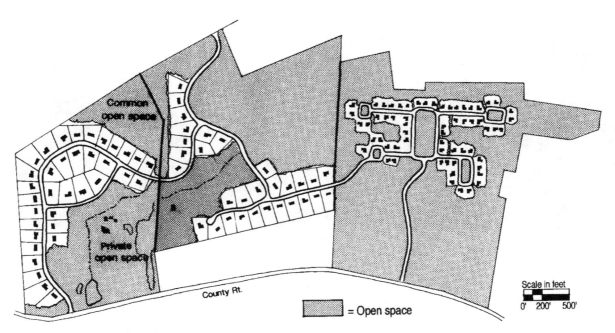

Figure 20–14a. Site plan of the three adjoining subdivisions.

paralleling County Route 513 were all proposed for subdivision approval by three separate developers. Working with each applicant individually, but very cognizant of the opportunities for designing an integrated open space system encompassing all three properties, the township's consultants produced distinctive residential layouts while permanently protecting 249.7 acres of open space on four farms (69 percent of the combined total subdivision acreage).

The first of the three subdivisions, "Shy Creek," involved redesigning plans originally submitted by the developer that were technically in compliance with the township's clustering provisions. However, no one was pleased with the applicant's unimaginative design featuring a row of houselots rigidly arranged around the parcel perimeter, enclosing the preserved farmland on three sides. Beside being uninspiring, the first plan virtually eliminated a mature stand of trees at the northern end of the property, provided no linkage with the adjoining parcel, and involved a difficult and expensive stream crossing. Madden/Kummer's alternative layout avoided all these problems,

retained the developer's lot count (35 homes on 99 acres), and advanced the township's overall open space objectives, saving 53 percent (53 acres) of the tract.

The second subdivision, "Woodside," also utilized one-acre lots as a tool to preserve land. This time 82 acres were protected, comprising 69 percent of the 119-acre property. The preexisting farm was retained and a new one was also created. Lots on both these developments are served by individual wells and septic systems. An even higher percentage of land preservation (80 percent) is being achieved with the third development, "The Hamlet at Alexandria," in spite of the fact that its gross density is substantially higher than that of the other two subdivisions in this group (approximately two acres per dwelling, instead of the standard three-acre density in this part of the township). These results are possible because it uses village-scale lots of 10,000 square feet, served by a central sewage collection and treatment facility involving community disposal fields in part of the open space. The design of this development is much more formal, with a large three-acre com-

Figure 20–14b. Nearly 40 acres of open space frame the foreground view of Shy Creek Estates (the subdivision on the far left of the site plan), as seen from the county road. Except for a few acres of common land around the pond, most of this foreground open space has remained with the preexisting farmhouse. This land has, however, been permanently protected through a conservation easement preventing further development.

Figure 20–14d. This farm pond also functions as a stormwater detention facility for the new development.

Figure 20–14c. Care was taken in the detailed site planning to preserve original hedgerows and other tree groups, which provide "instant mature landscaping" with a rural flavor in front of these new homes.

mon and four smaller satellite greens (ranging in size from three-eighths to three-quarters of an acre). A substantial portion of the property will be retained as deed-restricted farmland. Altogether

the three subdivisions have just two entrances onto the county road, and a third entrance onto Sky Manor Road behind "Woodside."

Farmcolony

Location: Parker's Mountain, near Stanardsville, Virginia
Date: 1974–1976
Site Designer: Michael Redd

Located on 289 acres of rolling pastureland and woods in the Blue Ridge foothills, Farmcolony was the concept of Gilbert Edwards, chairman of the Farm Development Corp. Two-thirds of this site, some 190 acres, are permanently preserved and owned by a homeowners' association, in which buyers are automatically enrolled at the time of their purchase. Day-to-day operations on the 120-acre working farm are overseen by a farm manager, but the pastures and cropland could as easily be leased to a local farmer. The foods produced (meat, eggs, fruit, and vegetables) are made available to all owners at prices set by the association. To minimize labor needs, the farm is run

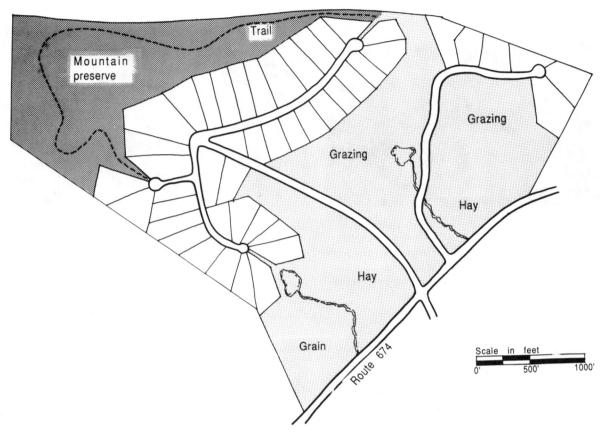

Figure 20–15a. Site plan of Farmcolony.

primarily as a cow/calf grazing operation, with some sheep to graze pastures not appropriate for cows. In addition, Farmcolony possesses 70 acres of sloping woodland, a forest preserve, and bird sanctuary with trails for hiking and riding.

Homesites are situated on the ridges and wooded hillsides surrounding the farm, on land of little productive use. Of the 48 lots, most are in the 1.5 to 2.5 acre size range, with individual wells and septic systems. Nearly all homes enjoy commanding views of the fields and pastures, the barn, and the nineteenth-century farmhouse (which is now a community center and meeting place with several furnished bedrooms for guests, plus a kitchen, library, and an activity room). Facilities are also available for stabling and pasturing horses.

Figure 20–15b. As one enters Farmcolony, the view to the left is of pastures and woodlands, and several homes located where these two areas meet.

Figure 20–15c. Looking across pastures grazed by sheep and cattle, the original farmhouse and related buildings occupy the middle distance, with new homes overlooking all this protected land from the distant hillside.

Figure 20–15d. View from the veranda of one of the homes shown in Figure 20–15c, with Farmcolony open space sweeping downhill as far as the eye can see.

The view into this subdivision from the public road is one of cattle and farm buildings. Almost all the homes are tucked into the woods for privacy and seclusion. Building design is not rigorously regulated, although all designs are subject to the association's Architectural Review Committee (which is mostly interested in avoiding conspicuous colors, heights, and building locations). Other

regulations prohibit discharging firearms, for reasons of public safety.

Some county officials who were originally skeptical about Farmcolony's approach to protecting open space and preserving rural character have reconsidered their positions, in light of this development's success. Although it does not represent a panacea for preventing farmland loss, Farmcolony does demonstrate that sensitive site design can minimize the conflicts that often arise when homes are built near agricultural operations, and that there is a practical alternative to conventional large-lot development. Winner of the Culpepper Soil and Water District's Conservation Award and Virginia's Clean Water Award, Farmcolony is also the recipient of the Governor's Environmental Excellence Award for 1991.

Dunham Lake Estates

Location: Hartland Township and Highland Township, Michigan
Date: circa 1950–1970

The land presently comprising Dunham Lake Estates was owned during the 1920s by Hartland resident Henry Wallace, who assembled various parcels contiguous to his farmhouse to create a nature sanctuary. Wallace planted the old farmland with countless trees and berry-producing shrubs, and sowed wild rice in the shallow waters around the edge of the 110-acre glacial lake to attract Canada Geese. After Wallace's death in 1949 the property was sold, with restrictions prohibiting hunting, to a development consortium headed by former Michigan Governor Murray VanWaggoner. Other stipulations of the sale required the developers to design a plan preserving the lake's beauty and purity. VanWaggoner's response was to create a greenbelt park along the lakeshore, ranging in width from 100 to almost 400 feet. Today this greenbelt contains extensive trails near the shoreline and up on the wooded ridges, plus two sandy

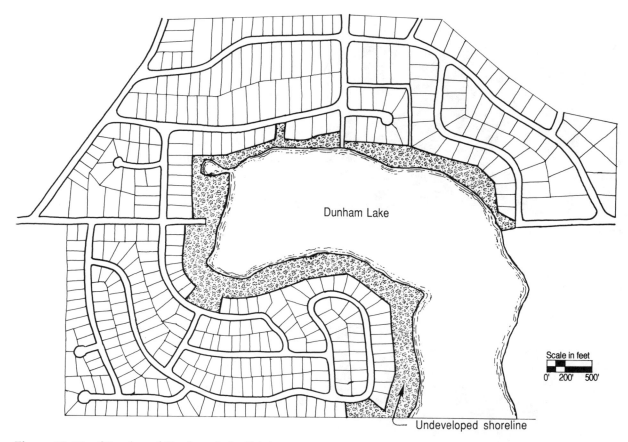

Dunham Lake

Scale in feet

0'   200'   500'

Undeveloped shoreline

Figure 20–16a. Site plan of Dunham Lake Estates.

beaches and a lakeside park with playground equipment and picnic tables (Convery, 1987). Because facilities are simple and relatively inexpensive to maintain, annual dues are very reasonable: $75 per lot, in 1991. In appreciation for his vision, homeowners at Dunham Lake dedicated their greenbelt park to VanWaggoner in 1984.

Although other aspects of the subdivision layout are quite conventional, this development is very significant for the location and size of its open space provision. That it has been a successful real estate venture without a single waterfront lot provides ample evidence of the fallacy that "lake frontage is essential for sales and marketing." The existing arrangement of houselots allows all residents to enjoy the amenities of a natural lake. The

Figure 20–16b. The heart of this community is its lake and surrounding greenbelt.

Figure 20–16c. The neighborhoods are thickly wooded, and have been maintained that way to afford greater privacy on fairly modest-sized lots.

Figure 20–16d. Early morning joggers take a refreshing run on greenbelt trails around the frozen lake.

alternative would have given exclusive lakefront rights to less than one-fifth of the houses, eliminating the scenic, recreational, and wildlife benefits that the greenbelt provides to the entire neighborhood. Additional dividends of the design are exceedingly high water quality and an excellent fishery in the lake (both of which are well documented). The fact that all homes utilize septic systems on permeable sandy soils makes this all the more remarkable, and underscores the importance of such buffers as filter areas where nutrients are taken up by the deep-rooted vegetation.

Trim's Ridge

Location: West Side Road, New Harbor, New Shoreham, Rhode Island
Date: 1980
Site Designer/Architect/Developer: The Manitou Co., Boston, Massachusetts

When architects Edward Dusek and Paul Kelly bought this 10-acre site on Block Island, the property was zoned for a standard layout of ten one-acre lots, five on each side of a straight cul-de-sac. That unimaginative design reflected the conventional approach to subdivision regulations that the island's regulations encouraged by allowing clustering only as a cumbersome option, subject to very general standards allowing local officials considerable discretion to deny innovative proposals unpopular with neighboring property owners (a practice that is both legal and widespread in New England).

Knowing they could design a much more attractive development and confident they could persuade local officials and the neighbors of the advantages that a more creative approach could produce, Dusek and Kelly purchased the land and submitted a cluster concept drawing to the planning board. Although officials are extremely pleased with the results at Trim's Ridge (which received a regional design award in 1991), the town's cluster option provision remains unwieldy and inflexible in some basic respects (such as requiring all houselots to possess 100 feet of street frontage). This underscores the difficulties involved in proposing unconventional, site-sensitive designs to planning boards in rural areas, where there is generally little experience in reviewing such applications, and often no professional help to assist layperson officials.

The cluster layout approved at Trim's Ridge preserves most of the original network of fieldstone walls crisscrossing the site, and allows all units to take advantage of water views to the north and south, while also reserving the broad flat ridge

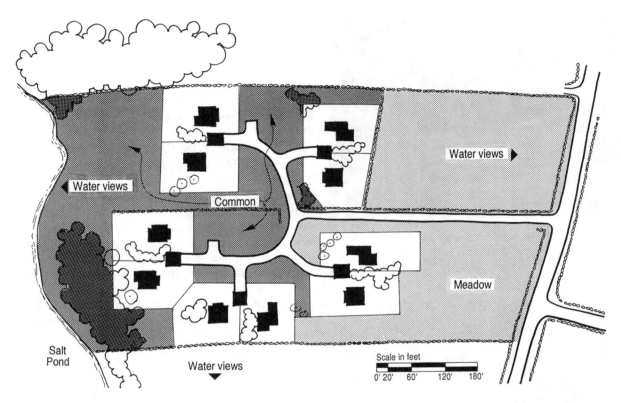

Figure 20–17a. Site plan of Trim's Ridge.

Figure 20–17b. Ancient stone walls enclose two protected pastures separating this ten-lot development from the town road.

Figure 20–17c. A gravel access road serves this small rural development extremely well. Septic systems are located off lot in the common grassy areas, and homes are buffered from each other by evergreen plantings.

Figure 20–17d. Houses are situated on the knoll to capture water views in two directions. Most of the land between the community dock and this house lies within the common area.

Scientists' Cliffs

Location: Calvert Cliffs, near Prince Frederick, Maryland
Date: 1937–1970s
Site Designer/Developer: George Flippo Gravatt

Located on a 250-acre site atop Calvert Cliffs, a series of fossil-rich marl bluffs some 100-feet high along the western shore of the Chesapeake, Scientists' Cliffs began as a simple and inexpensive summer colony of campsites and cabins for Washingtonians, "where people of comparable means and similar tastes might relax by the Bay," according to its fiftieth anniversary history.

After the first summer during which cabins were rented, community founder Flippo Gravatt (a forest pathologist with the U.S. Department of Agriculture) established an automatic-membership homeowners' association and began to sell lots. The community presently contains 229 homes, 40 percent of which are lived in on a year-round basis. In addition, there are 64 unimproved housesites. Lot dimensions are modest (many are 80 feet × 120 feet) but the thick woodland vegetation provides considerable screening and privacy. The layout is divided into eight major groups of houselots, each group occupying its own headland area. Headlands are separated by deep glenlike ravines, which are owned by the association and connected to each other and to the shared beach below by rustic footpaths.

Over the years common facilities and amenities have grown to include a ball field, tennis courts, a pool, a pond for fishing and ice skating, a meetinghouse, a beach, a fossil museum, a community garden, a skating pond, an historic tobacco barn, and several miles of woodland trails. The Scientists' Cliffs Association now owns and maintains these facilities, in addition to the road network and the water wells and distribution system. More than two-thirds of the community area is in common open space owned and maintained by the

(the highest point on the property) as a central open space. Other significant open space exists along the town road, which is bordered by old stone walls and a three-acre pasture between the road and the nearest housing clusters. On the opposite side of the development two more acres of open space form a broad buffer along the shores of Trim's Pond, where a small community dock is available for residents. Altogether three-quarters of the site is open space, which operates as a visual extension of the individual lots. The ten single-family detached homes are arranged in pairs, each on a one-quarter-acre lot sharing a double-bay garage straddling their common boundary.

Each dwelling has impressive water views, but remains visually private through sensitive siting and orientation. Buffering between lots is accomplished by dense plantings of native species such as white pine, northern bayberry, and wild sea rose, by the shared garages, and by the property's natural contours. A central well on the ridge supplies all units, which have separate septic systems located in the common areas adjacent to their lots.

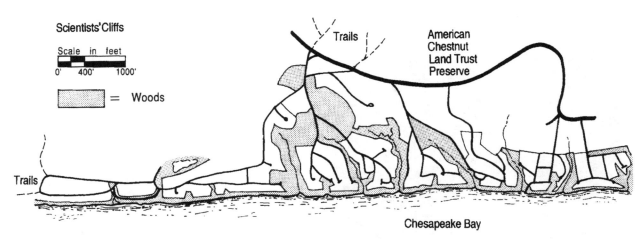

Figure 20–18a. Site plan of Scientists' Cliffs.

homeowners' association, including 150 acres purchased by the association in 1985 from the developer's widow.

Scientists' Cliffs may be the only subdivision where residents have dedicated a memorial garden to honor the memory of its developer, a man who lived among them for more than 30 years, who recognized the value of open space and shared amenities in enriching community life.

In recent years, Cliff residents formed the American Chestnut Land Trust to purchase the remaining undeveloped 436 acres from the Gravatt estate, employing a variety of creative land preservation techniques described in Chapter 18, "Retaining Farmland and Farmers."

Figure 20–18c. Active recreation facilities inlcude a tennis court, ball field, and swimming pool.

Figure 20–18b. Although the streets are extremely narrow, they function adequately for the low levels of traffic involved.

Figure 20–18d. Neighborhoods are connected to each other and to the beach below through a network of footpaths.

Dragon Hill

Location: Mohawk Trail, Shelburne, Massachusetts
Date: 1988–present
Site Designer: Dodson Associates, Ashfield, Massachusetts

Nearly half of this 74-acre site has been conserved through a cluster design that maximizes outward views and privacy between units. Over 6,000 feet of trails for walking, hiking, and cross-country skiing are threaded throughout the 41-acre commonly owned conservation area, which includes a mixture of open fields, wooded hillsides, and a small wetland fed by a perennial stream.

Set 1,200 feet back from the Mohawk Trail, a major two-lane rural highway (Massachusetts Route 2), all building sites are accessed by a curving entrance road (22-feet wide) that winds across open meadowland, gradually ascending the low

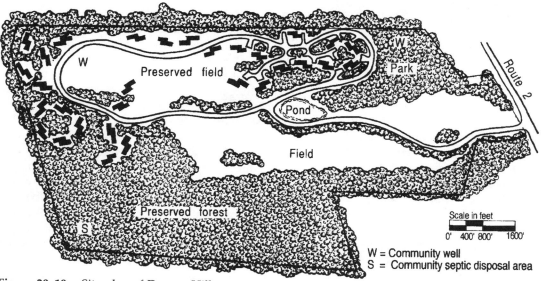

Figure 20–19a. Site plan of Dragon Hill.

Figure 20–19b. Entry road curves through the open space as it ascends the hill, in this view from the Berkshire Trail (Route 2).

Figure 20–19c. Homes are semidetached in Dragon Hill, each unit containing 1,500 square feet of floorspace.

Figure 20–19d. Most of the homes have entrance porches facing in different directions, which makes them look more like large single-family residences.

hill, atop which 64 semidetached dwelling units are located in 32 different (duplex) structures designed in a traditional New England manner. Each residence contains 1,500 square feet of floorspace, plus a porch, a one-car garage, and an outdoor parking space. Many of the units are arranged in a creative "side-to-back" manner, an orientation that helps to produce the visual effect of a large farmhouse and to differentiate outdoor yard spaces. Target markets for these two-family designs are young couples and "empty-nesters."

All homes are served by a central well and water distribution network, and a community septic disposal system (whose filter beds occupy a five-acre portion of the property).

Winslow Co-housing

Location: Bainbridge Island, Washington
Date: 1989–1992
Site Designer: Edward Weinstein, Architect, Seattle, Washington

Within 38 months of a slide show on the co-housing concept being shown in Winslow (the main center on Bainbridge Island), this 30-unit neighborhood was conceived, funded, designed, reviewed, approved, built, and fully occupied. Based closely upon similar endeavors in Denmark, where more than 120 co-housing projects have been built since 1972, this Winslow development comprises 30 dwellings and a 5,000 square foot common house located on 4.85 acres. Organized as a cooperative, members purchase shares and receive a proprietary lease for their own individual units, which range in size from studios (570 square feet) to units with four bedrooms (1,391 square feet). The project is not subsidized and units sell for prevailing market prices, comparable to those of other similarly sized dwellings on the island (Giese, 1990).

Although designed at the density of six dwellings to the acre, the site contains a surprising amount of open space, including a trail winding through a small woodland park and an allotment garden where residents may cultivate their own vegetables, in addition to modest yard space behind most of the units. Two-thirds of the dwellings are attached in pairs that, together with a four- and a six-unit building, are arranged in a compact fashion not unlike a European village. In one area the distance between opposing housefronts is about 40 feet, an area that is landscaped with small lawns and dooryard gardens, through which runs an eight-foot-wide paved pedestrian path (that also provides necessary access for moving vans and fire engines).

Building styles reflect nineteenth century vernacular farmhouse architecture on the island, with clapboard siding, front porches, and multiple roof gables facing forward. Parking spaces are provided at the northwest corner of the site.

At the project's center stands the common house, with a large kitchen and dining room, laundry, child-care facilities, and a "teen room." Residents are encouraged but are not required to share in preparing and enjoying dinners together with their neighbors several times a week. The mix of ages and family sizes is good, among the 48 adults and 30 children who lived there during the first neighborhood census, taken in August 1992. Residents include singles, married couples with and without children, and retirees.

Only the second such project in the U.S., it was the first to be designed and developed by the

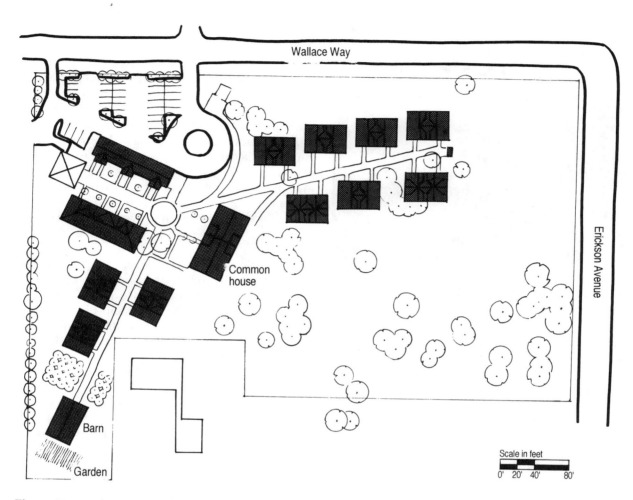

Figure 20–20a. Site plan of Winslow Co-housing.

Figure 20–20b. Homes face each other just 25 to 35 feet apart, separated by dooryard gardens and an eight-foot-wide paved access lane.

Figure 20–20c. Back yards are also modest, and look onto a central open space.

Figure 20–20d. Most of the homes are arranged in pairs such as these, whose designs are reminiscent of European semidetached bungalows of the 1920s.

owner/residents. Funding was provided by the Kitsap Federal Credit Union, which is itself a cooperative. Future plans include another jointly owned building with multiple purposes (barn, bicycle shed, and guest accommodation).

Note: Co-housing is a term applied to pedestrian-oriented residential developments characterized by strong resident participation in planning and design, usage of extensive common facilities that supplement private living areas, and management of their neighborhood through community meetings. Their physical design intentionally fosters a deep sense of community (McCamant and Durrett, 1988).

Battle Road Farm

Location: Old Bedford Road, Lincoln, Massachusetts
Date: 1987–1991
Architect: William Rawn Associates, Boston, Massachusetts
Landscape Architect: Michael Van Valkenberg Associates, Cambridge, Massachusetts

Bounded on the south by Minuteman National Park, this 24-acre rolling, wooded site was acquired for affordable housing in 1986 by the town of Lincoln (which simultaneously designated another 23 acres from the original parcel to remain as permanent open space). Over the previous 15 years the town had seen four development proposals for the property, none of which had obtained zoning approval. Deciding that the best way to see good planning realized on the site was to buy it, Town Meeting approved the purchase, with assurances that much of the public investment could be recouped while preserving seven acres as conservation land to serve as a buffer to the National Park.

After discussions with several teams of developers, architects, and landscape architects, Lincoln selected the Cottonwood Company and Keen Development Corp. to prepare a site plan meeting the town's general criteria that the layout reflect traditional New England principles and that the buildings harmonize with the community. Of the 120 dwelling units, 72 were designated as affordable units with below-market mortgage interest rates, reserved for first-time homebuyers. In March 1991, the town authorized the percentage of subsidized units to market-rate units to be somewhat lower, in the 40 to 50 percent range.

Because no one in town wanted the units to look like they were subsidized, unusual care was taken to ensure that "both the dwellings and the site design possess so much character they manage to camouflage their tight budgets" (Langdon, 1991). As noted in Chapter 10 "Affordable Housing," the connected New England farmhouse was chosen as a model for economically massing four units into an historically familiar structure, with shrubs and trees typical of nineteenth-century farms (lilac, bridal wreath, crabapple) planted around them. Two other designs, called the Carriage House and the Meadow House, provide variety of form, interior layout, and price. All units are designed to the same high standards of design and workmanship, whether subsidized or market rate.

In addition, modest front setbacks were adopted (22 feet from columned porches to the street) not only to reflect traditional patterns but also to create conditions favorable to casual conversation between residents and neighbors walking by. Seven of these "farmhouses" also face onto a grassy

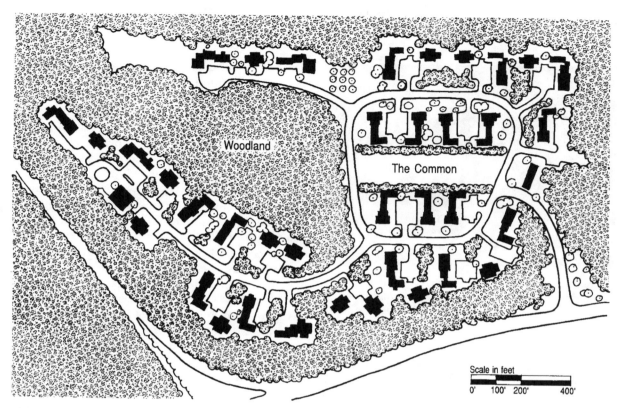

Figure 20–21a. Site plan of Battle Road Farm.

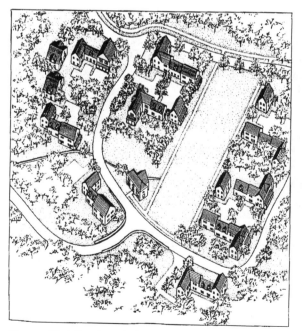

Figure 20–21b. Aerial sketch showing relationship of buildings to each other, the street, and the central open space.

Figure 20–21c. Gable-ends and front porches face the street in this traditional streetscape.

Figure 20–21d. Classical Greek Revival columns and strong cornices harmonize with the vernacular building tradition in eastern Massachusetts, and dispel the negative image of subsidized multifamily accommodation.

meadow or "common," located behind them, which functions as an informal outdoor space for neighborhood activities and recreation. Parking is accommodated in numerous small areas to avoid visual blight and long walking distances. Accessible by public transportation, the site will also be connected to the town's extensive trail system.

Chatham Village

Location: Mount Washington, Pittsburgh, Pennsylvania
Date: 1930–1935
Site Designers/Architects: Henry Wright and Clarence Stein

Chatham Village is quite possibly one of the most attractive multifamily developments in the United States, designed specifically for moderate-income families (in this case, clerical workers). Although it has been featured in planning and landscape architecture textbooks for decades, it is probably all but unknown to volunteer planning board members and local advocates in small towns around the country. This is highly regrettable because the site planning lessons it offers careful observers are still relevant today.

When Stein and Wright were hired to draw up conceptual plans for this 45-acre wooded hillside, the Buhl Foundation had already decided it wanted to use this property to create a state-of-the-art community housing project for people of limited means, and to demonstrate that investing in large scale, well-designed, socially responsible efforts such as this could be a secure financial investment. Applying innovative principles they had pioneered at Radburn (dwellings facing interior greens, with traffic separated from pedestrians and routed around the perimeter of "superblocks"), Stein and Wright arranged short rows of two-story townhouse rental units around five small but nicely proportioned and superbly landscaped parks planted with shade trees, grass, and thousands of flowering shrubs.

A four-acre recreation area with playground equipment, a baseball diamond, three tennis courts, and 25 acres of wooded greenbelt threaded with two miles of walking trails provide further amenities. Many of the 197 townhouses are built into the hillside, so that nearly half have garage space in their basements. Houses whose basement level leads out onto one of the interior greens have sunrooms facing these parks; they also each have reserved spaces in one of the three nearby "garage compounds."

During its fifty years of leasing (the foundation began selling the individual units several years ago), tenant turnover was always exceptionally low, indicating that residents were very pleased with their homes and neighborhood. Chatham Village's traditionally long waiting lists were another indication of the project's popularity.

Chatham Village

Virginia Avenue

Tennis courts

Woodlands

Playing field

Green

Green

Green

Green

Green

Community house

Scale in feet

0' 50' 100'   200'   300'

▦ = Residences

■ = Garages

•••••••• = Trail

– – – – – = Path

Figure 20–22a. Site plan of Chatham Village.

Figure 20–22b. Residences are horizontally attached and are located to form courtyards and enclosed greens throughout the site.

Figure 20–22d. Frontyards face onto a continuous sidewalk system connecting all units, the greens, the active recreation areas, and the informal trails that wind through the wooded greenbelt.

Figure 20–22c. The greens are well shaded by a large number of native specie deciduous trees.

Figure 20–22e. Vehicles and pedestrians are as well-separated in Chatham Village as they are in Stein and Wright's Radburn plan, executed six years prior.

21

Town Center Commercial Cases

Because the historical or traditional fabric of town centers is so easily and frequently disrupted by insensitive new development, it is particularly important to illustrate more harmonious ways to expand or redevelop in such areas. The half-dozen examples included in this chapter show a variety of successful approaches taken by developers in various parts of the country in recent years.

In all of these examples buildings have been sited in a traditional manner along the "street line" with parking behind, except at Winslow Green where a very attractive three-quarter acre community common has been established in front. This development also demonstrates the viability of combining residential uses on upper floors with retail space at the ground level. Another mixed-use example in this chapter is the Village Galleria, where residential units have been built in the air space above the rear parking lot.

Architectural styles in these projects range from historically faithful (Kent Town Center), to contemporary interpretations of traditional vernacular building conventions (Heritage Square), to thoroughly contemporary expressions (Winslow Green and the Village Galleria). Although architecture is sometimes very important, it really occupies a secondary level of significance in comparison with more fundamental parameters, such as the front setback, parking location, building height, volume and massing, and roof shape.

Because of the opportunity to provide affordable housing in central locations, using the same land (and often the same foundations and roofs) more efficiently, it is unfortunate that more recent

small-town examples of mixed use projects could not be found for this chapter. As pointed out in Chapters 9 and 10, this is fertile ground for such developments, notwithstanding the obstacles posed by local zoning and fire codes.

Carriage Shops

Location: South Pleasant Street, Amherst, Massachusetts
Date: 1972
Site Designer: Jerald Gates and Richard Johnson
Architect: Thomas Kirley, Shutesbury, Massachusetts

Consisting of three buildings facing Amherst's principal shopping street, the Carriage Shops contain approximately 20,000 square feet of floor space, on two levels. Typical tenants include a sports equipment store, a pet shop, a bookseller, a travel agent, a law firm, an antique dealer, a pizza parlor, an orthodontist, a beautician, and various offices. Each of the three structures maintains a close relationship to the sidewalk, with 45 parking spaces located in a well-landscaped central courtyard area screened from the street.

The original Victorian residence occupying this 35,400 square foot site was replaced by an L-shaped motel in 1962, which was built along two sides of the property. When the motel was converted to shops and offices a decade later, two new

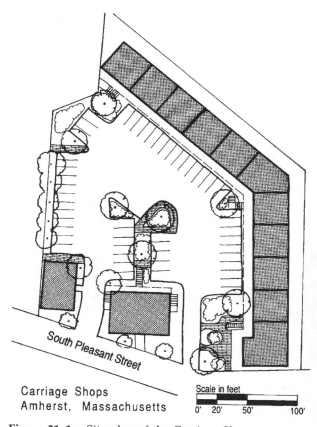

Figure 21–1a. Site plan of the Carriage Shops.

traditionally designed brick structures were located at the front of the large open parking lot, creating a more formal edge in keeping with established streetscape principles. (A similar approach could be taken with conventional shopping centers: arranging a row of new buildings along the roadway would help to screen the wide expanses of asphalt parking that usually dominate the appearance of such centers, while allowing the owner/investor added floor space to sell, lease, or rent. As parking provision in most shopping centers is excessive, the loss of a small number of spaces is usually not even noticed.)

Figure 21–1c. The rear parking lot and the original motel building, now converted into two levels of shops and offices.

Figure 21–1b. The left and central buildings as they face the street, with sidewalks and shade trees in front, and parking, flowering ornamental trees, and another range of shops behind.

Figure 21–1d. View down into the parking lot and back toward the main street, from a second floor balcony.

Kent Town Center

Location: Main Street, Kent, Connecticut
Date: 1990–1991
Site Designer: Johnson & Richter, Amherst, Massachusetts
Architect: Richard Donohoe, Sherman, Connecticut

This infill project is located on a 1.5 acre parcel in the heart of the small historic village of Kent, Connecticut. Previously used as a lumberyard, the site had constituted a gap in the otherwise continuous line of Victorian homes and commercial buildings along Main Street.

Due to extremely high land values in this picturesque New England town (which has become a summer haven for affluent Manhattanites), the developer was obliged to construct a building with five times as much floor space as nearby residences and commercial premises. The challenge to the architect was to design the development to harmonize with the traditional scale and character of Main Street, while maximizing the rentable floor area, providing adequate off-street parking, and creating inviting public spaces to attract pedestrians into the shops.

The design solution involved dividing the project into two buildings, each located along the established "street line," with a brick-paved courtyard connecting the sidewalk with shop doors and the rear parking lot. Entrance to the courtyard is through a shallow plaza, used as a sidewalk cafe. Beyond that is a more spacious interior courtyard lined with shopfronts and planted with two linden trees. A line of lindens was also planted along the edge of the sidewalk, continuing the town's shade tree pattern.

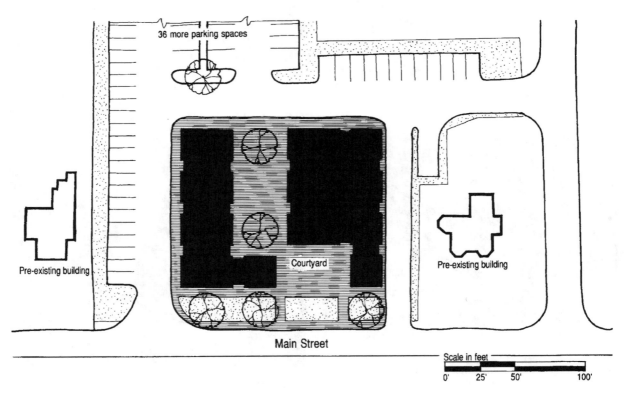

Figure 21–2a. Site plan of Kent Town Center.

Figure 21–2b. Streetscape showing how the new buildings (at far right) harmonize with the older ones, in terms of front setback, height, massing, roof pitch, and gable orientation.

Figure 21–2c. Street elevation maintains the village's traditional character of nineteenth-century vernacular architecture.

Figure 21–2d. View between the two buildings, through the pedestrian court, to the rear parking area.

The structures themselves were carefully designed to blend in with the nineteenth-century Greek Revival vernacular architecture common throughout the village, with steep roofs, gable-ends facing the street, clapboard siding, wide flat trimboards, overhanging eaves, and small-paned windows. As shown in Figure 21–2a, the configuration and placement of the two buildings effectively conceal their true size and bulk from the eye of casual passersby, looking at the project from across the street.

Originally intended for entirely commercial occupancy, the buildings were designed for a combination of ground-floor shops with offices above. However, the project's timing coincided with both the national recession of 1991 (which severely affected the New England real-estate market) and with a significant oversupply of office space in the region. Because the second-floor space had not been built with sprinklers or with respect to certain other fire code requirements for residential units in commercial premises (which are costly to retrofit), they could not be easily converted to apartments, and are consequently underutilized at the time of this writing, according to the town's code officer.

Winslow Green

Location: Winslow, Bainbridge Island, Washington
Date: 1981
Site Designer/Architect: Robert J. Peterson, Poulsbo, Washington

This highly successful mixed-use development on a 2.5 acre site combines 20,000 square feet of retail commercial space on the ground level with 34 two-bedroom residential condominiums on the second two floors. Dwellings contain approximately 1,100 square feet and many include attached garages at the rear, which are at the second floor level (as seen from the front) because the site slopes upward. Other advantages of stepping the site include reducing the number of flights of stairs necessary to reach the top level, and avoiding the need for continuous corridors and fire stairs (as would have been required for three-story buildings).

Situated at a prominent corner at the western end of Winslow Way, the main commercial street in downtown Winslow, this project was deliberately designed to provide a formal, landscaped open space in the heart of the island's principal settlement. This area, nearly three-quarter acre in extent, now serves as Winslow's unofficial town square or common, and is the site of the community's Christmas tree, plus numerous sales, bazaars, and other activities throughout the year.

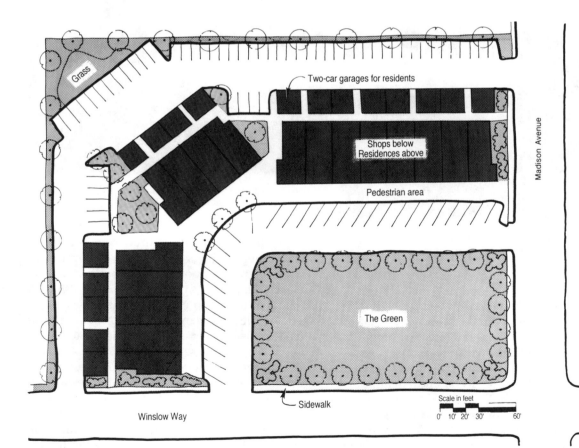

Figure 21–3a. Site plan of Winslow Green.

Figure 21–3b. The green as seen from the corner of Winslow Way and Madison Avenue, one of the principal downtown intersections.

Figure 21–3c. Alfresco dining area in front of the local bakery. Shops occupy ground level spaces, with two floors of residential uses above.

Figure 21–3d. Drivers' view into Winslow Green, entering from Winslow Way. Although customer parking is provided directly in front of the shops, its visual impact is greatly reduced by the three-quarter-acre green.

Combining three previously recorded parcels and utilizing regulations allowing Planned Unit Developments, the site designers enjoyed more flexibility in laying out the buildings and parking areas. Because parking needs for commercial and residential uses peak at different times of the day and week, parking requirements were able to be reduced to a certain extent.

Located close to other shops and restaurants downtown, the commercial premises at Winslow Green operate as a natural extension of the central business area. This proximity helps the new retailers to attract customers, and makes it convenient for upper floor residents to patronize downtown shops and even to walk to the Seattle ferry terminal at the eastern end of Winslow Way.

Heritage Square

Location: Main Street, Belchertown, Massachusetts
Date: 1980
Site Designer/Architect: Studio One, Springfield, Massachusetts
Developer: Ludlow Savings Bank

This downtown infill project is located on a seven-acre site opposite the central green in the middle of a small rural town. Rows of nineteenth-century vernacular buildings facing the common create a strong visual character. The project site itself lies between a church and a residence that are each 100 to 150 years old. Despite the absence of any municipal guidelines or regulations governing the design of new buildings in this historic streetscape, the project architect and developer agreed from the outset that their proposal should relate very closely to its traditional surroundings.

Even though the three new buildings were designed in a contemporary manner, front setbacks, massing, roof shapes and pitches, and exterior materials and colors were all selected to harmonize with the neighborhood. Of these, the importance of the front setback, holding the "street line" by locating parking to the rear, can hardly be overemphasized, especially in infill situations. All 77

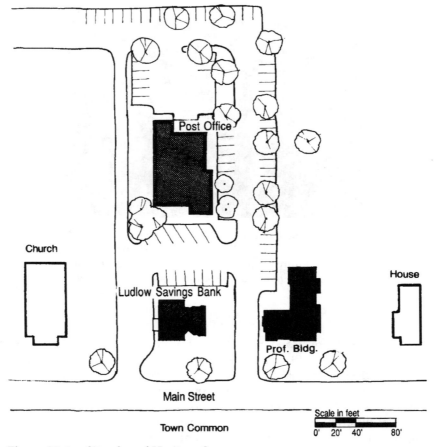

Figure 21–4a. Site plan of Heritage Square.

Figure 21–4b. The two new buildings in the center and at the right maintain the town center's traditional setback and scale, and have siding, window proportions, and roof pitches in keeping with the regional vernacular.

Figure 21–4d. To the right of the old church is the new post office, located immediately behind the new bank. Although it can be seen from the street, prominent visibility is not a key requirement for such facilities.

Figure 21–4c. Parking behind the bank is also convenient for the new post office, a vital establishment that communities must sometimes work hard to keep in their center.

parking spaces on this site are visually screened from the street.

Situated in the middle of the rear parking area, the new post office forms a small inner courtyard behind the savings bank and professional building. Total floor space is 11,460 square feet (2,280 in the bank, 4,390 at the post office, and 4,790 for the professional office building).

Village Galleria

Location: Corner of Pearl Avenue and Fay Avenue, La Jolla, California
Date: 1985
Architect: Delawie Bretton Wilkes Associates, San Diego, California

Within this group of four buildings, the two that face major shopping streets provide 10,000 square feet of retail and banking floor space. A pedestrian walkway cuts diagonally across the 28,000 square foot site, between the two principal buildings, connecting the busy corner of Pearl and Fay Avenues in downtown La Jolla with the rear parking area, where there is a landscaped planter, benches, and 32 spaces for cars and small trucks. The two principal facades maintain a traditional "street line" by their location at the edge of the sidewalk, thereby also screening parking and preventing it from intruding into the townscape.

Above nine of the parking stalls are two additional buildings (a one-story and a two-story) containing five dwelling units (one single-bedroom

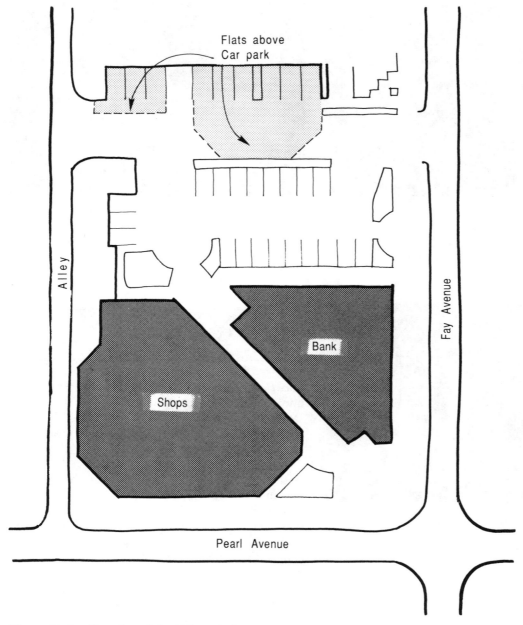

Figure 21–5a. Site plan of the Village Galleria.

unit with approximately 600 square feet of floor space, and 4 two-bedroom units each having approximately 1,000 square feet). In jurisdictions where building or fire codes make it difficult and expensive to design dwellings above retail and office space, the "Village Galleria" offers a creative approach to realizing mixed-use objectives in central locations.

Figure 21–5b. Main shopping facade, as seen from Pearl Avenue.

Figure 21–5d. Looking from rear parking lot down the pedestrian alley toward the intersection of Pearl and Fay.

Figure 21–5c. Residential units built over rear parking spaces provide in-town dwellings opportunities, and are buffered from street noise by the shop buildings.

This in-town housing provision was created partly in response to a proactive municipal planning policy encouraging such use mixtures, and partly because the Village Galleria displaced a preexisting house on the site. During periods of economic recession when some commercial floor space may become vacant, regular income from residential rental units can help project developers maintain positive cash flows. Downtown apartments and condominiums also help boost evening business activity for neighborhood merchants and restauranteurs.

The Village Commons

Location: College Street (Route 116), South Hadley, Massachusetts
Date: 1986–1991
Site Designer/Architect: Graham Gund Architects, Inc., Cambridge, Massachusetts

Situated in the heart of South Hadley, opposite the campus of Mt. Holyoke College and the town green, The Village Commons occupies the site of an old inn and a commercial block of stores, which were destroyed by a series of fires in 1985 and 1986. In order to make room for the 11 new structures comprising The Village Commons, two other nonhistoric buildings had to be removed, including a 1960s modern single-story bank that was highly incongruous to South Hadley's nineteenth-century townscape. It is located on a seven-acre site owned by the college, which created the Center Redevelopment Corporation to revitalize this core area.

The project contains approximately 100,000 square feet of leasable floor space, including a mixture of shops, offices, a restaurant, a pub, two 140-seat theatres, a deli, several specialty shops, a

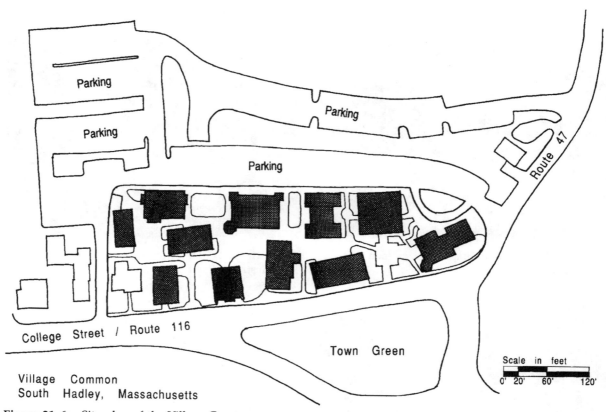

Village Common
South Hadley, Massachusetts

Figure 21–6a. Site plan of the Village Commons.

Figure 21–6b. Aerial perspective sketch of the development, with the South Hadley Town Green shown at the lower right.

branch bank with a drive-through window, and 19 residential units. Unlike most single-use shopping areas, the inclusion of residential units brings life to The Village Commons 24 hours a day—people are always there. (From a financial viewpoint, such units also augment a project's economic return, as there is often strong demand for in-town living opportunities.) The buildings facing College Street vary slightly in setback and in orientation, but all maintain a fairly close traditional relationship

Figure 21–6c. Front elevations as seen from Main Street.

Figure 21–6d. New shopfronts and painted picket fence maintain the traditional "street line." (The older Greek Revival building on the left was originally built as a residence, and is now part of Mt. Holyoke College.)

Figure 21–6e. Interior courtyards are scaled perfectly as comfortable "people-places."

with the sidewalk. As the site slopes downward away from the street, the second row of buildings are at lower elevation, and are accessed either by landscaped staircases (from College Street) or at grade level (from several parking areas—offering 292 spaces—located behind the complex, at several levels).

The grounds between the buildings are landscaped as pedestrian-friendly courtyards and passageways, inviting shoppers to stroll into and around the various stores. This walking experience is similar to that which one might feel perambulating around an old European town, where outdoor spaces are irregular, connected, visually stimulating, and typically well-used. Architectural design at The Village Commons is quite varied and eclectic, blending decorative forms popular

during various nineteenth-century Revival eras with more modern technology. (Gund presumably drew some of his inspiration from architectural features found on many of the college's Victorian Gothic buildings.)

Apart from its highly creative building designs (about which opinions may differ), this mixed-use infill project is exceptional in several other ways. It has maintained the traditional "street line," it accommodates parking in an inconspicuous way (as seen from the street), and it provides for deliveries and waste removal from service entrances and loading docks connected to the buildings by underground tunnels from one of the lower rear parking lots (which allows pedestrians to approach each building from all four sides without seeing a "back door," dumpster, or service area). Last but not least, the design connects everything in a visually appealing and functional manner.

Roadside
Commercial Cases

This is, quite frankly, a chapter I wish that I did not have to write, because building commercial developments alongside major traffic corridors is generally not an advisable policy. Where I was trained, in Great Britain, this is simply not an issue, because all major commercial and residential development there is contained within established settlements, or added incrementally at the edges. This sensible policy works well in almost every way, including keeping the trunk arterial road system free of congestion caused by vehicles turning into roadside businesses.

However, in order to be relevant to the needs of communities across this country, where there is little political will to down-zone highways for truly rural uses, ten examples of "improved American models" are included here.

All but one of these examples has been built within the past twenty years or so. The Queen's Buyway is interesting because it was among the first car-oriented "shopping strips" to be built, during the boom of the 1920s, but it remains notable because it continued the traditional "streetline" of shopfronts and accommodated all parking in the rear or at the curbside. (Although Mill Pond Shops occupy older buildings, they were not used as retail stores until fairly recently.)

None of the examples is huge, but most are of a size not uncommon near small towns or in rural areas. Several have tastefully incorporated older traditional buildings (Mad River Green, Freeport McDonald's, and 13 Dartmouth College Highway); several others have adopted vernacular building styles (Sycamore Square, Mashpee Commons,

and River Village); while only two are decidedly modern in appearance (Village Square and Market Square).

A few of the examples contain dwelling units (Mad River Green, Village Square, Mashpee Commons, and 13 Dartmouth College Highway), the latter being partly converted to residential use as an afterthought because of sinking demand for commercial space during the 1991 recession. Luckily, the developer had designed this project so well that this shift in use was easily accomplished.

Greens and open space have been incorporated into the designs of many of the examples (Mill Pond Shops, Mad River Green, Market Square, River Village, and 13 Dartmouth College Highway). In some instances, these greens also serve a more practical function as areas for subsurface septic disposal beds. Roadside open space buffers have been particularly well designed at Mad River Green, Sycamore Square, and Lincoln Center. In general, all parking is located to the side or rear of the main buildings. Exceptions to this are Mashpee Commons and River Village, where highly visible parking detracts significantly from the otherwise very high standard of design.

It would be wonderful if the art and practice of land-use planning in this country rose to such a level as to make this chapter irrelevant. Until such time as that may happen, these examples should demonstrate the invalidity of arguments that it is absolutely necessary to locate parking in front of shopping centers, and that it is simply not possible to mix residential uses with new retail projects. Dinosaurs who propound such primitive viewpoints should be marginalized from the scene by new development standards based upon sounder planning principles. The alternative is to allow such people the latitude they need, under conventional zoning, to continue creating what James Kunstler calls so appropriately "the geography of nowhere" (Kunstler, 1993).

Queen's Buyway

Location: Main Street and Palmer Avenue, Falmouth, Massachusetts
Date: 1926
Architects: Whitten & Gore, Boston, Massachusetts

Situated at a corner location along Falmouth's main shopping street, this retail center contains 13 stores. Designed to harmonize with the local vernacular architecture on Cape Cod, the buildings are of weathered wood shingle with white painted trim boards.

When the Queen's Buyway was built during the mid-1920s, it was conceived as an extension to the original central business district. Although it was located "on the main highway from Boston," it kept the traditional "street line" character of the town center, a short distance away, by arranging its parking to the rear. Several small freestanding signs and a large awning sign still remind summer visitors that ample parking can be found behind the stores.

Originally that rear area was to have accommodated 18 additional shops, but parking needs (for

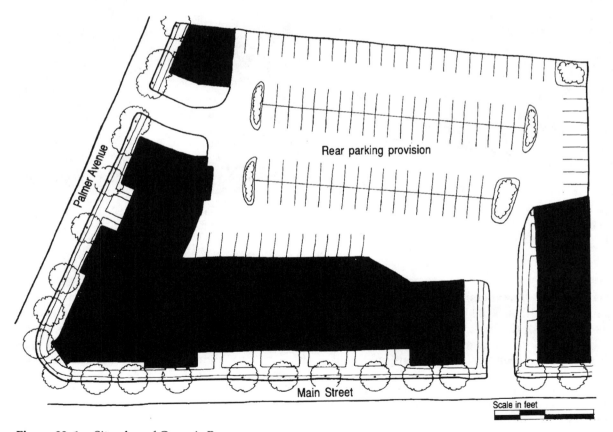

Figure 22–1a. Site plan of Queen's Buyway.

Figure 22–1b. Perspective sketch on the original real estate offering brochure, circa 1926.

Figure 22–1c. Shops line the streets in a traditional manner and screen the rear parking from public view, without apparent detriment to anyone's business.

Figure 22–1d. Looking back toward Main Street from the rear parking area.

merchants and customers) prevented them from being built on this 30,000 square foot site. The units planned for the back portion of the site were eventually built on another parcel on the opposite side of Palmer Avenue, in an extension to the complex.

Discussions with the present owners revealed that the Queen's Buyway has never experienced business problems, despite the fact that its parking is not visible from the main thoroughfare (thereby violating a basic tenet of the contemporary shopping center developers' faith). It is said that these shops remained rented even throughout the Great Depression. When interviewed, tenants expressed little concern about the parking arrangements. Typical remarks were: "There's sufficient parking here" "Local customers know where the parking is, and tourists see directional signs to the rear parking" and "If business were poor in this shopping area, I'd move out."

Mill Pond Shops

Location: Main Road, Tiverton Four Corners, Rhode Island
Date: 1981–1984
Developer: T.L. Holland Real Estate Consulting
Architect: Sakonnet Housesmiths, Newport, Rhode Island

A group of four historic buildings, including a former grist mill, grange, and barn, were con-

verted to retail commercial premises in the early 1980s by Terry Holland, a local realtor, and her husband Jim. Their location along the edge of the main road leading into the hamlet of Tiverton Four Corners left no room for highly visible parking in front of the buildings. Two gravel-surfaced parking lots to the side and rear of the complex serve the businesses conveniently and well. This arrangement allows the buildings themselves, with their strong, simple nineteenth-century lines, to be seen to best advantage.

Forming a traditional "hard edge" along the village's southern approach, this grouping also

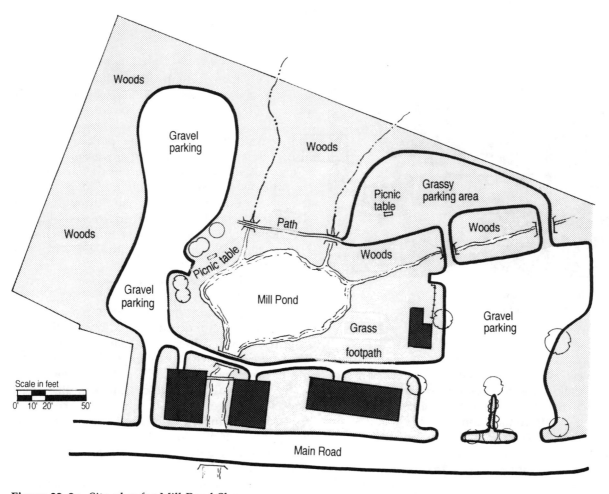

Figure 22–2a. Site plan for Mill Pond Shops.

Figure 22–2b. The shops are located hard by the road, in old buildings renovated for modern retail use.

Figure 22–2d. The footpaths pass by attractive park-like areas and link with a short trail that circles around the original mill pond.

Figure 22–2c. All shops are accessed at the rear, via gravel footpaths leading from the various parking lots.

screens most of the parked cars, a few of which can usually be seen over the drystone wall and between the shade trees that separate the side parking area from the main road. Mill Pond Shops is possibly the only shopping center in New England where the developer has, of her own accord, planted two Copper Beech trees, an extremely special and beautiful species normally seen only around older homes in historic neighborhoods.

All the shops are entered by doors facing the parking areas or the mill pond. A brick footpath runs behind the three major buildings, crossing the millrace via a short, wooden truss-bridge; it connects all the shops with the parking lots and also with an informal picnic grove and a small sitting-out area in a shady part of the lawn down near the pond. A short walking trail loops around the back end of the millpond, through some deciduous woodland and a grassy area that is occasionally used for overflow parking when special events are scheduled, before rejoining the complex.

The developer feels that her efforts to incorporate elements not typically found in retail centers has made Mill Pond Shops into an attraction itself, where customers return time and again with visiting relatives and friends, to share with them the pleasant experience of strolling through the park-like surroundings that link the stores together.

The four buildings, which range in size from 1,700 square feet to 5,400 square feet, comprise about 12,700 square feet in all. Present and recent occupants include two clothing stores (for women and children), a garden ornaments and herb shop, a toy store, a gift shop, a bookseller, an antiques dealer, and a real-estate agency. The parcel size is just over 60,000 square feet.

Mad River Green and Village Square

Location: Route 100, Waitsfield, Vermont
Mad River Green
Date: 1984
Site Designer: Patrick Thompson, Brothers Building Inc., Waitsfield, Vermont
Architect: John Baborouic, Scarsdale, New York
Village Square
Date: 1984
Site Designer/Architect: Beaudin Associates, Waitsfield, Vermont

These two small shopping centers are situated on opposite sides of Route 100, one of Vermont's principal scenic highways. Located just north of the Route 17 intersection in the Irasville District (planned as the town's modern automobile-oriented commercial area), they lie about one mile south of Waitsfield's historic village center. They

Figure 22–3b. View of Mad River Green from Route 100, with the original farmhouse at right, and an attractive green in the left foreground (which also serves as a septic disposal area).

both share the unusual design feature of internal parking lots, which are essentially not visible from the highway, being screened behind a row of shops in each case.

The local "anchor," a 15,000 square foot Grand Union food store, has parking immediately in front, but both the grocery and its parking are located behind a preexisting line of nineteenth-century buildings (formerly residences) now containing shops, so they are effectively buffered

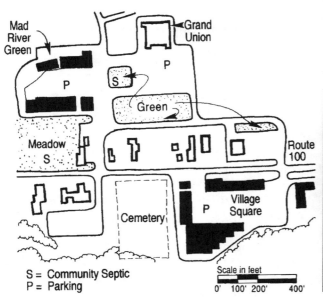

S = Community Septic
P = Parking

Scale in feet
0'   100' 200'   400'

Figure 22–3a. Site plan of Mad River Green and Village Square.

Figure 22–3c. Rear parking area behind Mad River Green, with a second row of shops on the far right.

Figure 22–3d. Village Square as seen from Route 100, with signs and shop windows facing the roadway, across a modest, landscaped buffer strip.

Figure 22–3e. Parking located behind Village Square, with a second set of display windows and signs facing the parking court. Some of the buildings contain second-floor residential units, providing a few affordable housing opportunities for local people.

from roadside view as well. Access to the Grand Union, the shops in front of it along the highway, and a new Mobil station and convenience store, are by way of the "Slow Road," a small parallel service road about 200 feet west of Route 100. Curb cuts along the highway are limited to the shopping center entrances and exits, and to individual businesses that predate Waitsfield's progressive planning regulations.

The architectural design of Mad River Green is more traditional than that of Village Square, and includes a new wooden silo and large barnlike structures recalling the area's agricultural past. Its shops and parking are set back some 250 feet from Route 100, at the far edge of a small grassy meadow (where the common septic system is located). The shops at Mad River Green contain approximately 27,000 square feet of floor space. Typical tenants include a branch bank, the post office, a hardware store, photo center, children's store, pub/restaurant, and gift shop. Office space is also provided on the second floor of the main building.

Village Square is more contemporary and sits much closer to the highway, with signs and display windows facing both Route 100 and the 212-space parking area behind. Its 37,500 square feet of floor space are occupied by a pharmacy, Mehuron's Market (the valley's other grocery), video store, bookseller, state liquor store, restaurant, realtor, and travel agency, with six residential apartments above one group of shops.

The idea for arranging these retail facilities in this manner occurred to Waitsfield officials after the town built a parking area behind the shops along Main Street to relieve parking problems there. The success of that effort set a precedent that shopping developers were required to follow.

Market Square

Location: Route 360 and Old Hundred Road, Midlothian, Virginia
Date: circa 1978–1983
Site Designer: The Brandermill Group, Midlothian, Virginia

This shopping center was built as part of the 2,500-acre Brandermill planned unit development, located 12 miles southwest of Richmond, Virginia. Brandermill itself was recognized by the National Association of Home Builders and *Better Homes and Gardens* magazine as the best planned com-

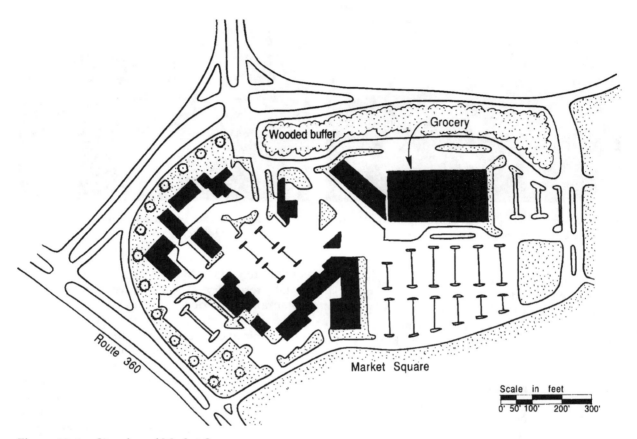

Figure 22–4a. Site plan of Market Square.

munity in the country in 1978, and its shopping center has won a design award for its signage system. Despite initial problems becoming recognized by area residents outside Brandermill as a place they, too, could shop, Market Square enjoyed 98 percent occupancy in late 1991. However, its anchor tenant, a 42,000 square foot Safeway grocery, does not provide a particularly large "draw," being a relatively weak competitor in the Richmond area (with only 15 percent of the regional market share, compared with 30 percent for the locally based Ukrop's chain, which incidentally operates a very successful competing store in nearby Sycamore Square, another "case example" illustrated in this chapter).

Like Sycamore Square, another creatively designed shopping center lying six miles to the

Figure 22–4b. A large sign identifies the location of Market Square along Route 360, from which the shopping center is almost impossible to see, as it nestles in a hollow.

Figure 22–4c. Looking across the rear parking lot toward the buildings that parallel the highway.

Figure 22–4e. Market Square's entrance from the Old Hundred Road is tasteful and low key.

north, none of the shops and parking at Market Square are visible from the state highway. Set back from the road behind a partially wooded buffer, most of the buildings and parking spaces are situated about 15 feet below the highway, at the base of a gentle slope. The main entrance road from Route 360 passes a small group of offices that are set into the hillside; their lower level contains a line of shops facing onto a large parking area, the supermarket, post office, and other stores. Another entrance off Old Hundred Road brings shoppers into the center, past a branch bank.

Figure 22–4d. Because of its special site design, Market Square looks more like a residential development or office park, as seen from the Old Hundred Road, near its junction with Route 360.

Other tenants at Market Square include a video rental store, dry cleaner, office supply, French restaurant, film developer, gift shop, pet store, photo studio, pizza carryout, bicycle sales/service, comic and greeting card store, floor covering specialist, interior decorator, barber, beautician, insurance agent, title and escrow service, family counselor, three dentists, a physician, an accountant, and a financial planner. These shops, services, and offices are located in about a dozen buildings arranged around one of two large parking areas (the other is in front of the Safeway). Altogether Market Square contains 120,000 square feet of gross leasable area, of which approximately 6,000 square feet are offices.

Sycamore Square

Location: Midlothian Turnpike (Route 60) and Crowder Drive, Midlothian, Virginia
Date: circa 1970
Site Designer and Developer: Douglass Woolfolk
Architect: Charles Schifflett

Located on a 9.5 acre suburban site alongside a busy arterial road six miles west of the Richmond city line (and 10 miles from the city center), Sycamore Square possesses 85,000 square feet of gross

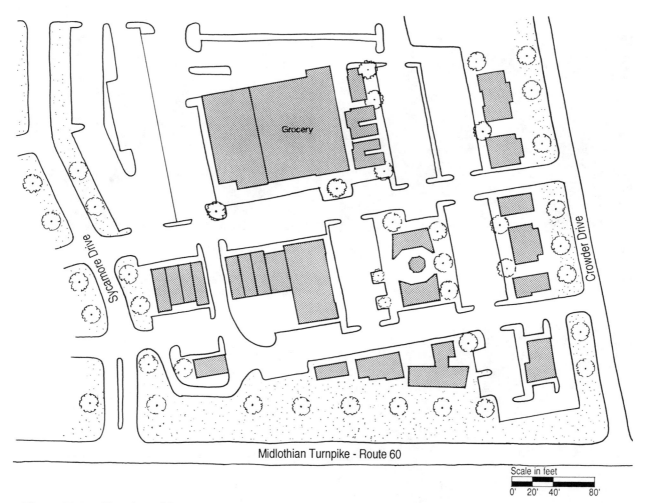

Figure 22–5a. Site plan of Sycamore Square.

leasable retail space and about 10,000 square feet of second-floor office space. Anchor tenants account for 36,000 square feet of the total, including a grocery store from a local chain (Ukrop's) which remains very popular (and profitable) despite the fact that it does not sell beer or wine, does not offer coupon promotions, and closes on Sundays.

Even more remarkable, from the standpoint of conventional wisdom dispensed by nearly every North American shopping center developer, is the fact that this retail complex faces inward and sits behind a landscaped buffer that graces its entire highway frontage (except for the principal entrance/exit). With neither shop fronts nor parking

visible from the highway, Sycamore Square competes extremely favorably with its closest competition, a standard strip mall facing it from the opposite side of the road.

In the absence of any other obvious reasons, it is likely that simple things such as attractive landscaping, traditional architectural design, quality merchandise, competitive prices, and freely available parking (in its 606-space lot) make the critical difference between business success and failure. Having visible parking is clearly not necessary when the clientele are familiar with the shopping district, or when they can read prominent signs informing them that ample parking is located

Figure 22–5b. Sycamore Square presents itself to the Midlothian Turnpike (Route 60) as a row of large traditional homes or inns, separated from the highway by a narrow lawn landscaped with mature trees.

Figure 22–5d. All the buildings have traditional pitched roofs, including the supermarket, which is located at the far edge of the commercial area, and is completely invisible from the highway.

Figure 22–5c. Circulation and parking at Sycamore Square are designed somewhat in the manner of town streets, creating an urbane and familiar atmosphere.

within or behind the complex. With its pleasant ambience and Williamsburg-style shops and offices, Sycamore Square enjoys full occupancy and a wide range of shops and restaurants, including a pharmacy, sports equipment dealer, toy store, plant shop, bookseller, dry cleaner, hairdresser, gift shop, travel agent, two branch banks, three insurance agencies, and three physicians.

Mashpee Commons

Location: Junction of Route 28 and Route 151, Mashpee, Massachusetts
Date: 1985–present
Site Designers: Fields Point Land Planning, Mashpee, Massachusetts; Duany Plater-Zyberk, Miami, Florida; and The Cavendish Partnership, Cavendish, Vermont

A dramatic facelift to six undistinguished 1960s era retail buildings in the former "New Seabury Shopping Center," together with the construction of seven new buildings designed in the "neotraditional" style (executed by different architects), have transformed a conventional 82,000 square foot strip mall on Cape Cod into an exciting 150,000 square foot mixed-use project with much potential.

The principal organizing concept operating in this plan involved the introduction of two new streets running at right angles through the old parking lot, with new and existing buildings facing the streets to create a traditional "Main Street" ambience, complete with granite curbs, parallel curbside parking, shade trees, sidewalks, lamp

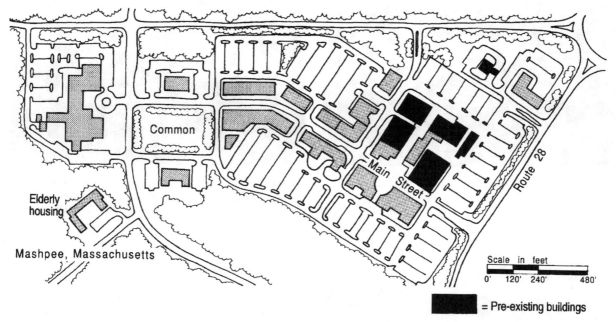

Figure 22–6a. Site plan of Mashpee Commons.

posts, street signs, benches, and shop fronts with awnings, at the sidewalk's edge.

Attention to details of facade design and street furniture was supplemented with an understanding of scale relationships in traditional street-scapes. For example, distances between opposing shop fronts along "Market Street" and "Steeple Street" measure 60 feet, forming a width/height ratio of about 3:1, which compares closely with cross-sectional distances and ratios along Main Street in Wellfleet, one of Cape Cod's more traditional village centers (as discussed in Chapter 9, "Development in Town Centers and Along Highways"). Additional parking is provided behind the new shops, which are arranged alongside the two new streets. The need for a variance from the town's deep 40-foot front setback requirement (which would have prevented building in the style of a traditional town) was avoided by keeping the internal street system under private ownership and maintenance.

This project is also notable for its negotiations and "horse trading." After extensive discussions

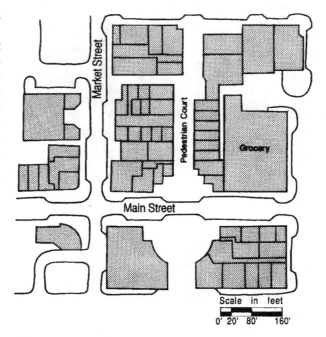

Figure 22–6b. Detail of the core area, showing the location of the grocery store and pedestrian court.

Figure 22–6c. Looking down Market Street from its intersection with Main Street, one sees a traditional downtown arrangement of buildings, shop fronts, sidewalks, parallel parking spaces, street trees, street lamps, and street furniture.

Figure 22–6e. Shops face directly onto sidewalks, which are separated from the parallel parking spaces by shade trees and granite curbs, in a deliberate manner based closely upon relationships common in traditional shopping streets.

Figure 22–6d. Civic spaces and second-floor offices and apartments add to the traditional townscape of Mashpee Commons.

between the developer, town planner, and the selectmen, land on the north side of Route 151 was dedicated to the town for open space in front of the fire and police stations, and a two-acre site was set aside south of Route 151 within the development so that the new public library could become part of this emerging town center (historically Mashpee never had a proper commercial center, although it has had a small concentration of civic buildings around another intersection). Located at right angles to a new Roman Catholic church, the library faces onto a landscaped common. Adjacent

to the church are 24 units of subsidized elderly housing (built on a 3-acre parcel given by the developer to the local housing authority, as part of an agreement for the town's rezoning 16 acres of his land on the north side of Route 151 from residential to commercial use). In addition, permission to create 100 residential units above the shops was granted by the town.

In addition to the existing supermarket, drugstore, six-theatre cinema, post office, restaurants, and over 50 retail shops, future plans include several compact, high-density residential neighborhoods, 150,000 more square feet of shops and offices, and mixed-use areas (including a site offered to the community for a new Town Hall).

Like River Village in Bonsall, California, the design of the commercial component of Mashpee Commons is presently flawed by the large amount of parking still visible from the highways. A real opportunity to introduce a row of smaller, traditionally designed retail or office buildings along these main routes, to screen these expanses of asphalt from roadside view, has been overlooked. At the very least these unattractive outside edges should be buffered with naturalistic plantings of native-specie plant material, or formal allees of specimen shade trees. In three other projects described in this chapter, preexisting woodland areas serve this purpose (Market Square, Sycamore Square, and 13 Dartmouth College Highway).

River Village

Location: Mission Road and Highway 76, Bonsall, California
Date: 1988–1991
Site Designer: Andrew J. Herbruck, San Diego, California
Developer: CentrumInvent, Stockholm, Sweden

Inspiration for River Village came from three sources: the compact central areas of Santa Barbara, Rancho Santa Fe, and Mission San Luis Rey. Located on the site of a former quarry at the junction of two well-traveled roads in the San Luis Rey River Valley, this 155,000 square foot commercial node was built in an expanding rural community 40 miles north of San Diego, which had never before had any central activity point or core area. Site planning for this project reflected the developer's wish to incorporate the spatial relationships and building design features of traditional towns in Southern California, with an interconnecting net-

River Village
San Luis Rey, California

Scale in feet
0'   50'   100'   250'

Figure 22–7a. Site Plan of River Village.

Figure 22–7b. Model of River Village.

Figure 22–7c. Aerial sketch of Main Street.

Figure 22–7d. Townscape elements carefully designed and arranged to create a traditional downtown atmosphere, complete with streets, sidewalks, two-story buildings, and small civic areas.

work of streets, sidewalks, arcades, and pedestrian alleys and a variety of outdoor spaces for benches, fountains, and alfresco dining.

Because most of the parking is provided along the streets in "head-on" stalls to maximize the number of spaces, curb-to-curb distances are unusually wide (about 60 feet) compared with a 40-foot width in towns where parking spaces are parallel to the curb. Although this arrangement tends to broaden the streetscape, a more traditional feeling will eventually emerge as tree plantings grow and mature. Originally, local fire officials had wanted the two-lane travel corridors to be six to eight feet wider, but they dropped that request when the developer opted to provide all buildings with sprinklers.

Planned by an investment firm that has developed over 200 shopping centers, River Village was conceived as an alternative to conventional malls, a one-stop destination for food, merchandise, entertainment, and services. From the beginning, it was also intended to provide a sense of place with a distinct identity—a local gathering point and meeting spot, a place for civic and cultural activities such as parades, art shows, festivals, and other events.

Among its mix of retail and service uses are a specialty grocery store (17,000 square feet), a six-screen cinema (1,350 seats), a bank, pharmacy, photo/camera shop, dry cleaner, liquor store, restaurants, cafes, and medical and professional offices. A community arts center and open air theater is also being planned by the local community.

Figure 22–7e. Arcaded sidewalks, street trees, plantings and benches create an inviting sense of place.

Figure 22–7f. Pedestrian alleys lead to small court-yards with fountains, offering refreshing oases to pass through or to linger and relax in.

Although the site design contains many excellent features, it is flawed by its lack of any strong or compelling visual presence as viewed from the highway. This could have been avoided by eliminating perimeter parking, relocating the grocery so that its unappealing rear and side walls would not face the highway, and positioning a principal building at the major property corner (where Bonsall Road meets Highway 76).

Freeport McDonald's

Location: Main Street and Mallett Drive, Freeport, Maine
Date: 1983
Site Designer/Architect: Steven Moore, Moore/ Weinrich & Woodward, Brunswick, Maine

When McDonald's representatives appeared before town officials with plans to demolish a vernacular mid-nineteenth-century farmhouse on Main Street, along with its connecting buildings and

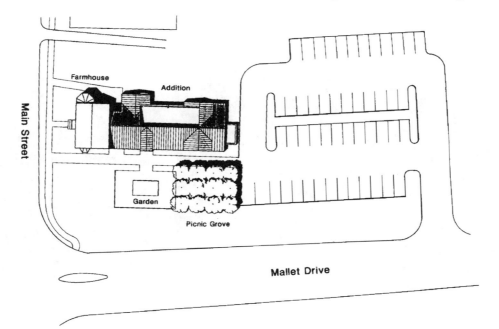

Figure 22–8a. Site plan of Freeport McDonald's.

Figure 22–8b. Perspective sketch of the original farmhouse with its contemporary but harmonious addition.

barn, to make way for a new burger restaurant designed in one of the modern corporate styles, they were cooly received. Under the zoning then in effect, restaurants required a special permit from the Board of Appeals. At the public hearing an enormous outcry was expressed by residents (including many recent arrivals), who saw the proposal as a symbol of the loss of their community to fast food, plastic, and commercialism.

Sensing they would not receive approval for the project as proposed, McDonald's sought to meet the principal aesthetic objections by hiring a local architect who understood "Maine forms of architecture." Because the house itself was in sound condition it was retained and restored, but the barn, connecting "ell" and old "summer kitchen" (which were in worse shape and very difficult to adapt to new uses) were sacrificed. They were replaced, however, by a 3,000 square foot addition whose footprint, massing, roof shape and pitch, and exterior materials closely followed the lines and textures of the original structures (wooden clapboards, standing-seam metal roof, etc.). The general appearance of other key features was also

Figure 22–8c. From Main Street the view is of the old house, whose preservation maintains Freeport's traditional streetscape, while providing a unique opportunity to demonstrate how corporate needs can be reconciled with community goals.

Figure 22–8d. The full extent of the new addition can be appreciated in this view from Mallett Drive. Parking is screened from Main Street by the building itself and by landscaping.

Figure 22–8e. This close-up photo shows how the architect worked with the original building lines and exterior materials, while satisfying his client's commercial objectives.

to worship fast food. But the architect deserves special commendation for taking a second look at the classic shape of the farmhouse gables and repeating this pattern to create the only Greek Revival McDonald's sign in the United States.

During the course of the McDonald's episode Freeport amended its zoning to include design standards for new commercial construction, so the burger chain's proposal became the first project to be reviewed under these new rules. A later amendment specifically prohibited "drive-thru" serving windows, a ban unsuccessfully challenged by McDonald's in the state court.

Perhaps the most important lesson of the Freeport experience is that major corporations often have alternative "fall-back" plans that they are willing to use when necessary to obtain approvals. Local officials who recognize this fact may then feel more comfortable drafting, adopting, and applying design standards that require franchises and other businesses to reflect regional architectural traditions when proposing new construction in highly visible locations in the townscape. However, great care must be taken to avoid results that trivialize the dignity of historically significant building styles, results which Maine architect Steven Moore describes as "the commodification of the traditional vocabulary."

respected on the new addition, though they were simplified: cornerboards and eave overhangs became narrower, and traditionally proportioned double-hung sash windows had fewer panes (one-over-ones instead of six-over-sixes). A community meeting room was also provided upstairs.

McDonald's eventually became enthusiastic about the project and installed cherry wainscotting in the front parlor of the old house (now a dining room), an expensive touch the original farmhouse certainly never had. The architect won extra points by designing a clerestory "window" above the side entry, with golden arches as tracery between the "panes." One interpretation of this imagery is that McDonald's had created a cathedral to the hamburger, where hungry tourists go

Lincoln Center Office Building

Location: Old River Road and Route 116, Lincoln, Rhode Island
Date: 1988
Architects: Cornelis J. deBoer, AIA, Irving Haynes & Associates, Providence, Rhode Island, and John Christie, AIA, Weygand, Oricuch & Christie
Landscape Architect: Gates, Leighton and Associates, East Providence, Rhode Island
Developer: Lincoln Center Properties, Inc., Lincoln, Rhode Island

Developers Clayton Field and Paul Foster traveled across New England viewing different attempts to

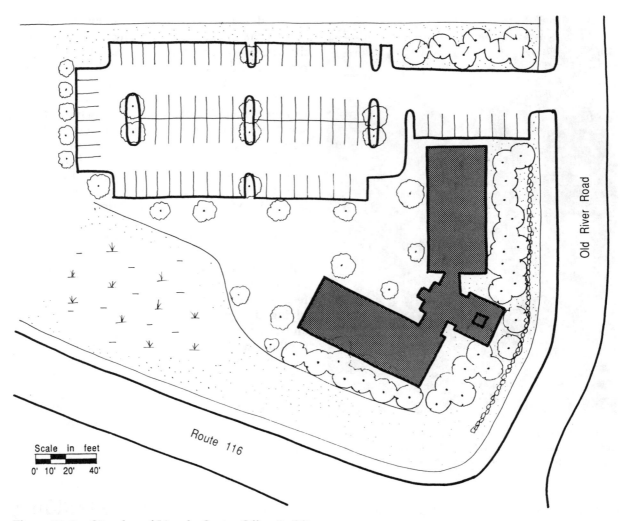

Figure 22–9a. Site plan of Lincoln Center Office Building.

design new office space that captured the spirit of historic buildings. After examining numerous examples that fell short of their expectations, they returned to the mill-oriented history of their own area—the Blackstone River Valley. Field and Foster were both struck by the architectural form and massing of the historic Slater Mill in nearby Pawtucket, whose overall shape and proportions seemed to lend themselves readily to a contemporary adaptation. That famous mill plus several others in Lincoln were used as historical architec-

tural references to develop an appropriate vocabulary for the new offices. Given its strategic location at the crossroads of two principal roads, a clock tower was introduced as a landmark feature, and to serve as a fulcrum for the two office wings, recalling the central role of mill buildings in the growth of many New England villages. Wood clapboards were chosen to reflect the appearance of the earliest mills in the valley and to render a more domestic scale to the offices, appropriate for its rural setting.

Figure 22–9b. Lincoln Center as seen from the intersection of Route 116 and Old River Road. Note the building's relatively close relationship with the street, the preserved tree line and stone wall, and the architect's use of traditional nineteenth-century industrial building forms as a vehicle for a contemporary office complex.

Figure 22–9c. Rear parking is screened from Old River Road by the buildings, and from Route 116 by native-specie landscaping along the edge of a small wetland.

In addition to erecting a structure that is very sensitive to regional building traditions, unusual care was taken to preserve the old stone walls along the front edge of the property, and to retain a stand of tall hardwoods just behind that low wall of weathered fieldstone. The large 90-stall parking area is visually unobtrusive, located behind the office block and landscaping features.

Due in part to the building's aesthetic qualities, the property reported full occupancy prior to 1991 while many other new speculatively built offices in the area were half full at best. This 20,000 square foot professional building contains 18 office suites ranging in size from 600 square feet to 1,025 square feet. As a result of the design process, the building can be easily modified to offer suites up to 4,500 square feet.

The Lincoln Center Office Building has become the professional center of this small town, with a tenant mix primarily of doctors and lawyers. Its comfortable two-story lobby also functions as a popular location for informal gatherings and local seminars.

Working cooperatively with municipal officials, the developers later created a public ice-skating and recreational facility on an adjoining parcel, for the enjoyment of Lincoln residents.

13 Dartmouth College Highway

Location: Route 10, Lyme, New Hampshire
Date: 1979–1986
Developer: Bayne Stevenson, The Bayson Co., Hanover, New Hampshire
Architect: Randall Mudge
Landscape Architect: James Kennedy, AIA

To create this unique office park the Bayson Company moved and reassembled a dozen eighteenth-century houses from locations across New England, where they had been threatened by demolition and impending redevelopment. The buildings occupy a 30-acre site along a two-lane rural highway just south of Lyme's village center. Of its 52,800 square feet of floor space, 47,700 is net rentable. In 1991, tenants included architects, attorneys, data processing firms, a publisher, a research group, an insurance agency, a French restaurant (with 60 seats), a caterer, a foundation, and a secretarial

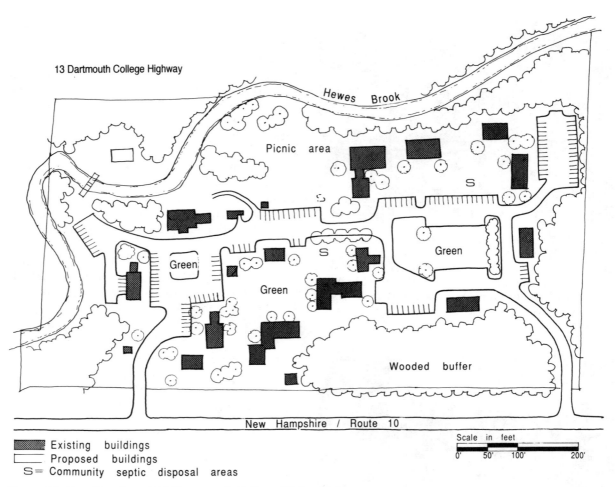

13 Dartmouth College Highway

Hewes Brook

Picnic area

S

S

Green

S

Green

Green

Wooded buffer

New Hampshire / Route 10

▨ Existing buildings
▢ Proposed buildings
S= Community septic disposal areas

Scale in feet
0'   50'   100'   200'

Figure 22–10a. Site plan of 13 Dartmouth College Highway.

service. In addition, there are twelve apartments ranging in size from 650 to 1,250 square feet, in five of the buildings. The residents enjoy living there because of the setting, and tend to be away most of the time that the offices are occupied, enabling much of the parking to be shared.

The buildings are arranged informally and asymmetrically around three village greens or commons, which also provide space for several of the subsurface leaching fields (part of the common septic system serving the complex). Most of the property is screened from Route 10 by a low wooded hill paralleling the highway. Site amenities include a picnic area in an old orchard alongside Hewes

Brook (a tributary of the Connecticut River), and a 20-acre wooded nature area across the brook (accessed by a wooden footbridge). Parking includes 150 spaces located in front of some buildings, to the sides of others, and behind still others. Access roads and parking spaces are all gravel surfaced, to maintain rural character and to minimize storm water runoff into the brook.

Because of the quality of the site design and the buildings themselves, these office units are capable of being easily readapted to residential use, which is a distinct advantage in the event of a decline in demand for commercial space in this small rural town.

Figure 22–10b. Perspective sketch of the building group seen as one first enters the site.

Figure 22–10c. Looking past a dooryard garden in front of an office building and restaurant, down a gravel-surfaced lane, lined with granite bollards and rail fences.

Figure 22–10e. The unique villagelike design of 13 Dartmouth College Highway enabled its owner to convert it to a mixed-use office and residential development when the New England office market softened in the late 1980s.

Figure 22–10d. Buildings are arranged informally but according to traditional village principles, while grassy areas double as lawns and subsurface septic disposal areas.

Figure 22–10f. Residentially scaled buildings are located around informal courtyards resembling front lawns in a small town setting. The beauty of this commercial project is that it does not look like one.

Appendix A

Rural Hamlets and Villages:

A Traditional Planning Approach to Managing Rural Growth in Loudoun County, Virginia

Richard Calderon

INTRODUCTION

The rural hamlet and village ordinances form part of the Loudoun County Board of Supervisors' Rural VISION initiative of June 1988. This policy landmark was occasioned by the very intense public debate which invariably accompanied attempts to subdivide rural Loudoun land under existing A-3 agricultural-residential zoning rules. Public hearings became forums about "equity preservation" versus "farmland conversion, groundwater protection, and rural traffic safety" issues. By 1988 some 50,000 acres or one-third of rural Loudoun had been divided, although only a small fraction of this land was actually converted from farming to residential use.

Following a six month staff study, a special five-day retreat by the County Board of Supervisors determined that while the weakness within the agricultural sector was a product of many social, economic, and organizational forces outside the control of local government, the county could manage the consequent farmland conversion in a better way than the prevailing pattern of sprawl. Exurban residential development on three to five-acre lots divides farmland into parcels too small for economic agricultural use, compromises rural views, and makes the delivery of public services very expensive. Should groundwater become polluted—a major concern of the Health Department—the cost of providing public water would be prohibitive.

During the retreat the board reviewed various development options, including: severe regulatory restriction of rural development (e.g., down-zoning); massive purchase and/or transfer of development programs; and the clustering of growth in new towns, villages, and hamlets. The board decided that a combination of mixed-use rural villages and small residential hamlets were the preferred development options. Grid A-3 subdivision would remain an option, if possibly a less and less used one, as the flexibility and marketing popularity of the alternatives became apparent.

The key idea of rural villages and hamlets is the concentration and ordered arrangement of new dwellings allowed by existing A-3 zoning into compact new settlements modeled on Loudoun's many historic towns and villages, which attract a strong housing market and provide the focus of a vibrant tourism industry. The new settlements would differ from their models, however, by occupying no more than 20 percent of a tract and would be surrounded by permanently preserved farms and open space. Rural landowners developing these small lots would match conventional A-3 lot prices because village and hamlet lot purchasers would buy, in addition to their lot, an open space conservation easement on the farmland surrounding the settlement—an exchange of real estate for secured rural views.

Given western Loudoun's Piedmont topography of rolling hills, hedgerow screens, forested mountain tops, and stream valleys, extensive deployment of the rural village and hamlet options would preserve rural views similar to those of today.

Community meetings in September and October 1988 confirmed public support of the board's VISION initiative and the supervisors directed the staff to proceed rapidly with necessary research, comprehensive planning, and zoning ordinance amendments.

OVERVIEW OF THE RURAL HAMLET ORDINANCE

The Loudoun County Rural Hamlet Zoning Ordinance Amendment was adopted by the Board of Supervisors on June 19, 1990, and was intended "to conserve agricultural, forestal, and open space land, historic and natural features at the same time that such land realizes the development potential allowed in the A-3 zoning district." The ordinance continues in Section 601.7.3.1 by noting that "Such clustered development is intended to place no greater burden on the natural environment, the rural road network, public services and facilities than would be generated by sprawl A-3 and is intended to permit the compact grouping of homes located so as to blend with the existing landscape—such as the rise and fall of the topography, hedgerows, and wooded areas—and to preserve to a greater extent the agricultural, forestal, and visual character of the landscape." With this statement of intent and purpose the county established the overall objective of the hamlet development option and thereby the standard by which to evaluate hamlet proposals.

Section 601.7.3.2 establishes that the new hamlet subdivision provisions will apply throughout rural Loudoun in the A-3 zoning districts, while Section 601.7.3.3 introduces and defines four categories of lots which constitute the hamlet.

Hamlet Lots

The first category of lots are those of the hamlet itself, which the section defines as 5 to 25 "smaller residential lots located in a contiguous group, with adjacent and fronting lots oriented towards each other in some ordered geometric way—as on a street, a green, or a paved square—and forming a distinct boundary with the surrounding countryside." Notice the careful, while flexible, way the text seeks to relate the 5 to 25 lots to each other and to the surrounding landscape.

The text continues by creating two categories of hamlet lot land, that which is designated for development and that which is called the "building area," and an optional category which is to be maintained in an open space conservation easement. (See Figures A1–1, A1–2, and A1–3.) The reasons for this feature are to:

a. Limit the location of buildings on hamlet lots and thus assure hamlet lot owners of certain views regardless of adjacent lot development.

b. Draw hamlet buildings into proximity with each other in order to generate the impression of enclosure and community.

Common Open Space

The second category of lots is that of the optional common open space. Defined by the text as lots on the outer periphery of the rural hamlet, owned in common by the hamlet and subject to an open space conservation easement, common open space is required only if wastewater disposal cannot be accomplished on the hamlet lots themselves. (See Figure A1–4.)

Hamlet Green/Square

The third category of land is that of the optional hamlet green/square. Defined as land owned in common by the hamlet community, the hamlet green/square is located in the interior of the settlement and is subject to a permanent open space conservation easement. (See Figure A1–4.)

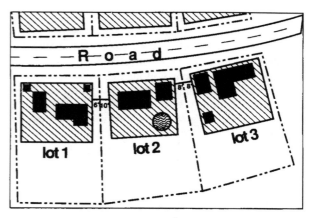

Figure A1–1. Illustration of Hamlet Lot and Building Area.

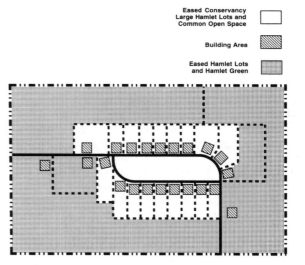

Figure A1–2. Example of Hamlet Calculations and Ratios: Illustration of Eased Land and Building Areas in Hamlet.

Assume an 88 acre tract of land with 22 drain fields and that the developer opts for a mix of cluster lot sizes but a maximum sized building area of $\frac{1}{3}$ acre.

Table 1. Lot Calculations

Lot Type	#	Total Area	Building Area	Eased Area
Hamlet 3½ ac.	2	7 ac.	⅔ ac.	6 ⅓ ac.*
Hamlet 2 ac.	1	2 ac.	⅓ ac.	1 ⅔ ac.+
Hamlet 1⅓ ac.	3	4 ac.	1 ac.	3 ac.+
Hamlet 1 ac.	8	8 ac.	2 ⅔ ac.	5 ⅓ ac.+
Hamlet ⅔ ac.	6	4 ac.	2 ac.	2 ac.+
Hamlet Green	1	3 ac.	-	3 ac.+
Conservancy 20 ac.	2	40 ac.	⅔ ac.	39 ⅓ ac.*
Common Open	1	17 ac.	-	17 ac.*
Road R-O-W	1	3 ac.	-	-

Eased open space land surrounding Hamlet (6⅓+39⅓+17) = **62⅔ ac.**

Total eased open space land (62⅔+1⅔+3+5⅓+2+3) = **77⅔ ac.**

Percentage of eased land surrounding Hamlet (62⅔÷88x100) = **71.2%**

Percentage of total eased land (77⅔÷88x100) = **88.3%**

* Eased land surrounding the Hamlet

\+ Eased land within the Hamlet

Figure A1–3. Example of Hamlet Calculations and Ratios: Lot Calculations (table).

88 ac. / 20 Hamlet and 2 Conservancy lots

71% eased perimeter land

88% all eased land

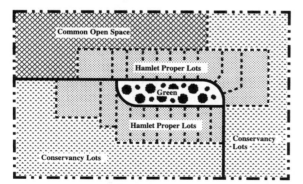

Figure A1–4. Example of Hamlet Calculations and Ratios: Hamlet Example Summary.

Conservancy Lots

The fourth category of land is that of the required conservancy lots. Defined as the residual portion of the tract, the conservancy lots would be owned in fee simple, like the hamlet lots, and like them also would contain a "building area" for development purposes but would otherwise be subject to an open space conservation easement. (See Figure A1–4.)

Section 601.7.3.4 lists the various uses permitted on different types of hamlet land. Residential and accessory uses such as garages and guest houses are limited to the "building areas" of hamlet and conservancy lots. Agricultural, forestry, and fishery uses would take place on the balance of these lots. Hamlet common open space and green/square areas would accommodate either rural or recreational uses "accessory, incidental, and subordinate" to the hamlet. The section thus locates buildings and structures within the hamlet and limits their intrusion into the surrounding land which is primarily intended to continue in traditional rural uses.

Section 601.7.3.5 specifies that the minimum tract size needed to create a rural hamlet is 40 acres. This number is generated by the sum of minimum hamlet lot sizes, supporting roads, and the minimum perimeter large lot open space requirements mandated in 601.7.3.8.

Section 601.7.3.6 establishes minimum lot requirements. Key elements of this requirement are:

Hamlet Lots

Hamlet lots are permitted to be a very narrow 64 feet and side yards may be as small as 6 feet, as long as the side yards of adjacent lots total 16 feet. While narrow lot dimensions permit significant site development cost savings, the major reason for the provision is that of spatial containment and enclosure. To ease a concern of the Fire Department, the section specifies a building restriction line generated by the fire ladder geometry. Firemen place ladders against walls at an angle of four vertical feet per one horizontal foot. The 3:1 building restriction line established in the text is designed to allow firemen ladder access to the side of a building. (See Figure A1–5.)

Common Open Space and Conservancy Lots

Loudoun's agriculture historically took place on fields which were 30 acres (plus or minus) in size. This was an acreage that a farmer could cultivate seasonally with horse-drawn ploughs and was a good size for cattle grazing as well. The rural ordinance seeks to surround

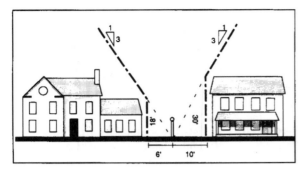

Figure A1–5. Illustration of Side Yard and Building Restriction Line.

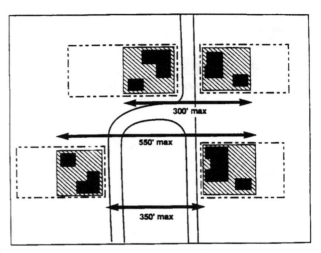

Figure A1–6. Illustration of Maximum Widths in Rural Hamlets.

the rural hamlet with open spaces of comparable size and appearance and the original text actually required a minimum lot size of 30 acres. However, many farmers and developers, although articulating general agreement with the goal, nevertheless suggested that greater lot size flexibility would be needed. The text was accordingly modified to permit one house per 30 acres of open space land surrounding the hamlet but also to permit such acreage to be subdivided into lots as small as 7 acres in size, so long as three or fewer conservancy and common open space lots totaled a minimum of thirty acres in size. (For example; an 80-acre hamlet might have two common open space lots of 11 acres each, two conservancy lots with a house of 14 acres each, and one conservancy lot without a house of 10 acres.)

Hamlet Green/Square

The text permits buildings facing across a hamlet green/square to be a maximum of 350 feet apart, and this number represents a compromise. (See Figure A1–6.) Generally, green/square widths should be no more than three or four times the height of facing buildings. People in wider spaces tend to lose the feeling of enclosure and will tend to avoid such spaces. Bigger is not necessarily better. (Planting of very tall trees within the green, or a very tall tower, can mitigate loss of enclosure. The famous St. Mark's Square Bell Tower in Venice is just such a device to mitigate the proud, but unfortunate, decision to enlarge that space in the late Middle Ages. In our time, Boston is attempting to enclose the vast, unused spaces surrounding City Hall—spaces which measure four times the area of St. Mark's Square!)

Section 601.7.3.7 establishes three methods of determining the development potential on a tract of land. This section has considerable interest for A-3 district

landowners since geometrical road requirements and soils with variable septic field potential make the determination of a tract's development potential a costly and ambiguous exercise.

The first method sets a density floor for rural Loudoun of one dwelling per 10 acres of land minus flood plains and steep slopes. The first method may be advantageous on a site with very poor soils. In the second method, the County Department of Natural Resources prepares an estimate based on soils and A-3 zoning district regulations. In the third method, the rural hamlet applicant prepares a schematic conventional A-3 design, submits the proposal initially to Natural Resources for verification of accuracy and then to the Loudoun County Health Department for approval. Thus, the hamlet ordinance honors development potential established under the prior A-3 district regulations.

Section 601.7.3.8 on Open Space Requirements is without a doubt the most important part of the ordinance. This section is the pivot upon which all of the design flexibility contained elsewhere is based. The text establishes four open space rules:

First Rule. Large lots in open space conservation easement surrounding the hamlet must total 70 percent of the tract.

Second Rule. All hamlet lands in open space conservation easement must total 80 percent of the tract.

Neither of these open space rules is difficult to meet so long as the applicant accepts hamlet lots averaging one acre or less. If there is a tendency by developers to press for larger average hamlet lot sizes, recall the philosophy of exchanging real estate for quality views—the conceptual foundation of the hamlet ordinance.

Third Rule. There shall generally be a minimum of 400 feet between the building area of hamlet lots and the tract boundary, and a minimum of 800 feet between the building areas of hamlet lots of adjoining hamlets on the same tract.

The third rule requiring a 400 foot setback from the tract boundary may be termed the "modified neighbor provision," as it is intended to buffer the hamlet from adjoining farmers and rural residents. The provision may be waived by the Board of Supervisors, pursuant to section 601.7.3.12, upon a finding that topographic, forestal screening, or other causes render the provision unnecessary.

Fourth Rule. The outside boundaries of the building areas of hamlet lots facing one another across a street shall not exceed 300 feet. The outside boundaries of building areas of hamlet lots facing one another across a hamlet green/square shall not exceed 550 feet.

The fourth rule is intended to generate a compact hamlet appearance both from within the settlement and from without. Note that the fourth rule, like the third, refers to the rear boundary of hamlet lot building areas. Theoretically, the eased portion of hamlet lots could extend right up to the boundary line. (See Figure A1–6.)

Section 601.7.3.9 deals with the various utilities needed to serve the hamlet. The text has a large number of utility provisions: hamlet lots may be served by individual wells on lot or by a communal water system; hamlet lots may be served by individual wastewater septic fields located within the lot or within the common open space; every hamlet shall have all-weather access for a pump truck to an adequate pond, or a water tank sufficient for fire protection; seven hamlet lots or less may be served by a private, 18-foot-wide gravel road; 25 or fewer lots may be served by a tertiary VDOT road—which permits greater curvature and slope in design, lower depth of roadbase and road topping; every hamlet lot shall include off-street parking for at least four cars.

It would be well to review the reasons associated with a number of these provisions. Regarding individual septic systems, many planning commissioners considered that a community sewage system approach was the better way to proceed in terms of agricultural preservation and the environment, but hesitated to require communal systems. Such systems would require a discretionary special exception permit. The county had noted considerable criticism about discretionary special excep-

tion requirements in an earlier draft of the code and the planning commission was determined to write a hamlet ordinance which would be ministerial in character. Moreover, the planning commission judged that it might take months to arrange necessary conferences and agreements between state and local authorities concerning innovative, small-scale, low-cost package sewer treatment plants, while a hamlet ordinance was needed immediately.

Regarding the private access easements, the commission did not distinguish between conservancy and hamlet lots served. Since the county had deemed seven lots as an appropriate number to be served by easements elsewhere in the zoning ordinance, and since seven had been noted in professional literature as a good number for decision making, seven lots would be the number chosen in the proposed hamlet text.

Regarding off-street parking provisions, the planning commission was aware that the Virginia Department of Highways and Transportation would be more comfortable about approving soft shoulder roads if residents and visitors had somewhere else to park their cars.

Section 601.7.3.10 concerning Home Owner Association requirements needs little explanation, while 601.7.3.11, a "Right-to-Farm" clause, reflects the board's decision to alert hamlet lot purchasers that farming with all its aesthetic and practical aspects (e.g., disking at four in the morning, top dressing with manure in the spring) will remain an important use in rural Loudoun.

Section 601.7.3.12 concerns modification of land use regulations. The section distinguishes between modifications which are automatic in character and others which will require a special exception decision by the board of supervisors.

Both the planning commission and the board were aware that general zoning, subdivision, and site development rules, originally created, perhaps, to cope with an urban development or A-3 zoning district concern, might be inappropriate in a rural hamlet settlement. Thus, subsection *a* automatically overrides inappropriate provisions which conflict with those explicitly contained in the hamlet ordinance itself.

Subsection *b* establishes a special exception modification provision for two other situations upon showing of cause:

i. Reduction of the 400 and 800 feet setback rules.

ii. Modification of general zoning, subdivision, or site plan requirements which conflict with the general intention and philosophy of the rural hamlet ordinance.

The ordinance specifies that in order to grant the modification, the board of supervisors must reach a finding that:

i. The general regulations serve public purposes to a lesser degree than the rural hamlet.

ii. The design proposed by the applicant satisfies public purposes to a greater degree.

iii. Strict implementation of general regulations would prevent well-designed rural hamlet development.

Requests to modify general regulations are thus not a light matter and need to be fully documented.

OVERVIEW OF RURAL VILLAGE ORDINANCE

Section I of the proposed rural village ordinance opens with a brief description of the County Rural VISION policy concerning clustered and sprawled development. The text continues with an affirmation of traditional mixed-use village and hamlet settlements surrounded by farmland and open space and expresses the county's intention to allow public water and wastewater treatment systems in the rural areas to render village settlements possible. The section closes with a list of the design features associated with new rural villages:

1. A distinct physical settlement surrounded by a protected rural landscape of generally open land used for agricultural, forestal, recreational, and environmental protection purposes;

2. A strong sense of community identity based on a shared, coherent, functionally efficient physical environment and a shared economic, political, social, and cultural environment;

3. Dwellings, shops, and workplaces generally located in close proximity to each other;

4. Modestly sized buildings fronting on and aligned with streets in a disciplined manner, uninterrupted by parking lots;

5. A generally rectilinear pattern of streets and blocks arranged to provide comprehensible and interesting routes of travel;

6. A hierarchy of streets, some narrow and convenient for a balanced mix of both pedestrians and automobiles while others are wider to carry greater traffic.

7. Well-configured squares, greens, landscaped streets, and parks woven into street and block patterns and dedicated to collective social activity, recreation, and visual enjoyment;

8. Civic buildings for assembly, or for other civic purposes, that act as visual landmarks and symbols of identity within the community;

9. A recognizable, functionally diverse, visually unified village center, focused on a village green or square; and

10. A development size and scale which accommodates and promotes pedestrian travel rather than motor vehicle use for trips within the village.

Section II provides a set of definitions. The section is needed since the proposed ordinance operates within a design paradigm different from that of conventional Planned Unit Development and uses previously undefined words such as "enfront–vista termination–workplace" and gives new definition and precision to others such as "accessory" and "ancillary" dwellings.

Section III establishes both the procedural mechanisms and the general requirements associated with rural villages development. The number of single-family detached dwellings permitted under A-3 zoning would be clustered in a Rural Village Subdivision (RVS). This clustered subdivision development would surround and be the prerequisite for the rezoning of two mixed-use districts, the Rural Village Core (RVC) and Rural Village Workplace (RVW) districts. (See Figure A1–7.) The concentration of such uses on 60–160 acres of land necessitates the creation of a water and wastewater utility district and will require the developer's acquisition of a Rural Village Utility-Special Exception (RVU-SE).

Section III concludes with an overview of the factors which the county will review through the means of a Concept Development Plan in the granting of special

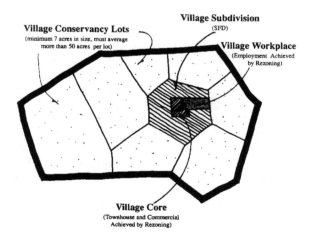

Village Conservancy-Minimum 80% of Tract

Village Proper-Maximum 20% of Tract

Figure A1–7. Major Village Areas.

exception, subdivision, and rezoning applications. (See Figure A1–8.) These factors include:

1. Accordance with the County Comprehensive Plan.
2. Sufficient land to generate the requisite single-family detached houses and to permit an appropriately designed village.
3. Adequate protection of conservancy land from uses not consistent with open space and from further subdivision.
4. Properly funded utility systems compatible with the environment.
5. Adequate roads within the settlement and connecting with the rural network.
6. Village arrangement and design compatible with the intent of the ordinance.
7. Appropriate maintenance and ownership of public and community lands and structures.

A number of very significant policy decisions are codified by Section III. Much debate surrounded the question of whether rural villages should be reviewed by means of a discretionary rezoning or a ministerial subdivision process. The development community—mindful of a "Not in My Backyard" reaction—would definitely prefer a ministerial subdivision procedure, to the point of choosing grid A-3 or rural hamlets over a village, while many community residents appreciate the decretion afforded the county of a rezoning.

The ordinance adopts the position that since villages are a preferred option, the procedure for the single-family detached house portion of the village should match that of A-3 or hamlets, hence the Rural Village Subdivision (RVS). However, to obtain the prerequisite and discretionary Rural Village Utility-Special Exception (RVU-SE) and the latter Village Core and Workplace District rezoning a developer would need to produce a binding Concept Development Plan acceptable to the county.

Section IV, for sequential reasons, is devoted to identifying key components of the Concept Development Plan. Section IV is designed to provide all parties involved in the review with a checklist of the matters which will be reviewed during the utility special exception, subdivision, and rezoning process. The detail required by Section IV is intentional and is designed to prevent ambiguous "blob-plan/hide-and-seek" sequences which the community has been subject to in past years. Section IV is divided into seven parts, Subsections A through E.

First, the Concept Development Plan will establish where the village itself, called the "village proper," is located and precisely how it will be surrounded by the land placed under open space conservancy easement, called the "village conservancy." Subsection IV.A further establishes overall size, shape, density, and a village proper to conservancy ratio of 1:4.

Next, the Concept Development Plan will demonstrate that the number of single-family detached dwellings proposed for village proper does not exceed the number of units which could have been developed on the tract under conventional A-3 subdivision regulations. Subsection IV.B establishes three methods for determining a tract's density, which are identical to those of the rural hamlet. Subsection B also establishes the residential bonuses associated with the Rural Village Core (RVC) district. These bonuses, which would accrue to the Rural Village Core (RVC) district upon rezoning, would be based on the A-3 development potential established earlier and would include a 20 percent townhouse bonus, a 20 percent affordable apartment bonus, and a 20 percent market apartment bonus.

Subsection IV.C provides more detailed requirements concerning the location of the village proper in the Concept Development Plan. The subsection identifies certain critical and sensitive environmental areas—flood plains, limestone outcrop belts and regional water impoundment areas—as unsuitable for a village proper.

Subsection IV.E establishes transportation requirements. A village proper should have at least two access points to a paved collector road while access to primary

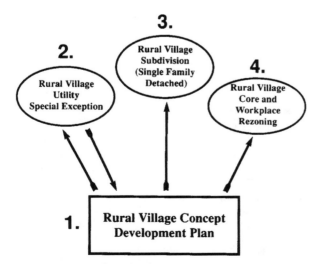

Figure A1–8. Rural Village Review Process.

roads is discouraged. Inter- and intracounty collector roads should not serve as internal streets within the village proper unless a new bypass road with a similar function is provided.

Subsection IV.F references village design requirements noted implicitly in Section I.G and specified explicitly in Section VI. Since the design requirements are very detailed, they were placed in a separate section.

Subsection IV.G outlines the utility requirements in the Rural Village Concept Development Plan, such as adequacy and potability of water supply, environmental compatibility of wastewater treatment systems, and a financing plan for system construction and operations. The concern about financing, particularly operational costs, is a product of the county's recent experiences with very small package treatment plants. These installations require considerable monitoring and may cost $580,000 to $100,000 a year to operate.

Section V involves permitted and permissible uses associated with Village Conservancy (VC), Rural Village Subdivision (RVS), Rural Village Core (RVC) and Rural Village Workplace (RVW) districts. Section V.A establishes general use regulations dated with the settlement, while subsections B through F distinguish particular regulations governing the several areas. Compared with conventional A-3 zoning, the village settlement does expand the range of permitted and permissible uses, with the Rural Village Core (RVC) and Rural Village Workplace (RVW) districts having the widest range of all.

Section V differs somewhat from the conventional by distinguishing scale of uses and by allowing a wide mixture of appropriately scaled uses within districts. The policy to expand potential mixtures of uses while controlling scale is consistent with the intent of the County Rural VISION Initiative and with the ideas of neotraditional thinkers such as Leon Krier and Andres Duany.

With Section VI, "Land Use Arrangement and Design," the Rural Village Ordinance opens a new chapter in Loudoun County zoning and reflects the neotraditionalist insight that community harmony is not merely a function of compatible uses but also a function of form, arrangement, and design. The section establishes general design "etiquette" in VI.B.1–4, while more specific rules appropriate to the Village Conservancy (VC), Rural Village Subdivision (RVS), Rural Village Core (RVC), and Rural Village Workplace (RVW) districts are contained in VI.C through F.

Section VI.B.1, "Overall Form," describes the major defining features of the settlement:

a. The rural village proper will be distinguished from the village conservancy by a well-defined "hard edge"

of closely spaced buildings, in contrast with the open, largely unbuilt farm, forestal, and open space character of the conservancy.

b. The rural village proper will be built in a generally rectilinear pattern of blocks and interconnecting streets, well defined by buildings, street furniture, and landscaping, as distinct public places to be shared equally by pedestrians and cars.

c. A hierarchy of parks and squares will be distributed strategically for maximum benefit and convenience throughout the village proper and culminate in a central civic park, called the main village green.

d. At a minimum, each rural village proper will consist of a Rural Village Subdivision (RVS) and may also contain a Rural Village (mixed-use) Core (RVC) and Rural Village Workplace (RVW) district. While a variety of uses are allowed in each of these parts, the special character of each should be expressed in the physical design of the streetscapes, landscaping, lighting, and buildings.

Section VI.B.2, "Land Use Mix," institutes a set of very significant ratios based on the overall tract size. Note the open space conservancy and the 2–2.4 percent minimum set aside for parks and civic uses within the village proper.

Section VI.B.3, "Locational Relationships," identifies key spatial relationships among the components of the rural village:

a. The Village Conservancy (VC) shall surround the Rural Village Subdivision (RVS) unless explicitly exempted by the board upon a finding that unique topographical or other natural features or preexisting boundary constraints require an alternative arrangement. (See Section VIII.B.)

Table A1–1. Land Use Table

Land Use Area	Percent of Tract Land Area
Rural Village Subdivision	
Village conservancy	Minimum 80%
Single-family detached uses	Maximum 18%
Civic uses	Minimum .6%
Greens, parks, and squares	Minimum 1.4%
Rural Village Core	
Townhouse uses	.4–.8%
Storefront uses	.4–.8%
Civic uses	Minimum .2%
Greens, parks, and squares	Minimum .2%
Single family detached uses	None Required
Rural Village Workplace	Maximum 1.6%

b. The Rural Village Core (RVC) district should be surrounded either by a Rural Village Subdivision (RVS) or by a Rural Village Workplace (RVW) district.

c. The townhouse area of a Rural Village Core (RVC) should generally be located between the storefront area of the district and the Rural Village Subdivision (RVS), thereby providing a transition between the largely residential and business uses associated with the two areas.

d. The Rural Village Workplace (RVW) district should abut the Rural Village Core (RVC) district storefront area, should be located on the periphery of the village proper, and should be designed to have the least impact on residential areas within the village proper or on adjacent properties from which the workplace district will be well buffered.

e. Every Rural Village Subdivision (RVS) shall be provided with a centrally located main village green. The main village green should furthermore abut any Rural Village Core (RVC) district associated with the settlement.

f. Similar land uses shall generally enfront one another, while dissimilar land uses shall generally abut along alleys or rear property lines.

Thus, paragraph *a* establishes that the conservancy should surround the village proper. Paragraphs *b, c,* and *d* describe relationships between the single-family detached, the commercial core, and townhouse areas within the village proper. Paragraph *f* above contains an important design device used by Duany to further mixed-use design. Single-family detached houses should front other single-family detached houses; likewise townhouses, apartments, and shops. The different uses may share alleys along rear property lines and this is the preferred boundary. Of course, in these circumstances garages and parking spaces enfront one another and the policy of matching uses is consistently maintained.

Section VI.B.4, "Design," codifies design requirements of the major "structural" elements of the settlement—blocks, lots, streets, parking, landscaping, and utilities. Section VI.B.4 is copied in its entirety below. Note that the text seeks to explain the reason underlying a requirement, especially if modern design conventions have departed significantly from historic approaches.

4. DESIGN

a. Blocks

Blocks of a generally rectangular shape should be the main organizing feature of rural village propers. While topography, existing vegetation, hydrology, and design intentions should determine block shape and size, the perimeter of rural village subdivision blocks should range from 1,000 to 1,800 feet in length as measured from lot frontage lines.

b. Lots

i. The boundaries of Village Conservancy (VC) lots, which may be as small as 7 acres in size while averaging at least 50 acres, should be designed to follow natural boundaries whenever possible and provide for an agriculturally economic use of the land.

ii. The blocks of rural village propers may be subdivided into lots, having frontage on a street, whose generally rectangular shape should respond to the environmental factors, proposed use and design intentions of the proposed rural village. The intent of this ordinance is best served by designing village proper lots to include a variety of sizes.

iii. Since pedestrian movement is stimulated by travel routes associated with a succession of varied housing forms and architectural details and declines with boring routes, village proper lots should minimize both front and side yards, garage aprons and doors, and blank garden walls, and should generally have as narrow a width as is practical.

iv. In order to ensure that lot purchasers in rural villages will continue to enjoy designed views, village proper lots shall distinguish those portions of land, called the building area, which may be developed with dwellings, garages, and other such structures, from those portions of land, called the eased area, which may be developed with structures presenting little significant above grade intrusion on the landscape, such as swimming pools, tennis courts, and small, generally open, ornamented garden structures with a footprint of 250 square feet or less.

c. Roads and Streets

i. Road and street patterns should be designed in a hierarchial, generally rectilinear pattern with geometrical variation as required by traffic safety, environmental reasons, and design intentions. The hierarchy of village roads may include, as appropriate, arterial and major collector roads, secondary collector and local access streets and alleys. Village proper streets should furthermore terminate on other roads and streets.

ii. Streets shall furthermore be designed to:
- Parallel and preserve existing fence lines, tree lines, hedgerows and stone walls;
- Minimize alteration of natural site features;
- Secure the view to prominent natural vistas;
- Minimize the area devoted to motor vehicle travel;

- Promote pedestrian movement so that it is generally more convenient and pleasant to walk short distances than to drive; and
- Promote the creation of vista terminations.

iii. While every effort should be made to render all rights-of-way attractive, rural village proper secondary collector roads and local access streets are to be designed as the main "public rooms" of the settlement and should be designed to accommodate pedestrian, bicycle, and vehicular movement and parking; foreground and entryway into private residences, civic and commercial buildings; and social space. Consequently, these roads and streets should be designed as a set of parallel zones:

- A zone of moving vehicles.
- A buffer area of street trees, parked cars, and planting.
- A pedestrian movement and meeting zone.
- A privacy zone adjacent to residential buildings, and an "eddy" area adjacent to commercial buildings.

iv. To define the road and street space, buildings facing each other across the right-of-way should generally be placed no more than three or four times their height apart, and should usually be placed much closer, while spatial definition should be reinforced with the regular planting of street trees chosen to develop an overhead leaf canopy.

v. Further street definition should be sought by emphasizing block corners and by designing the streets to terminate on a significant feature, such as a centrally placed building facade, view of a church spire or clock tower, or some significant view.

d. Parking

i. Parking for residential, civic, commercial, workplace and recreational uses in rural village propers should generally be located at the rear of lots and no off-street parking shall be permitted in front yards. Adjacent off-street parking lots shall have off-street vehicular and pedestrian connections. Continuous parallel parking for additional cars and visitors should be provided on the streets in front of such lots.

ii. Curb cuts and driveways off streets fronting single-family detached house lots in rural village propers may be designed as the primary form of rear lot parking access if curb cuts are spaced to allow parallel parking for at least two cars per lot but otherwise access for off-street parking shall be achieved by means of alleys, off-street vehicular connections between adjacent parking lots and side streets.

iii. Off-street parking areas and garages in rural village propers shall not be located at the vista termination of roads and streets, shall not be the principal use

of corner lots and should be designed to have a low visibility. To this end, garages and carports should be located a minimum of six feet behind the principal building facade and the visual dominance of large garage doors should be minimized by offset from direct view and/or architectural means whenever possible. Any off-street parking space or parking lot which abuts a street shall be buffered by a landscaped area no less than four feet wide, in which is located a continuous row of shrubs no less than three and one-half feet high, or by a wall no less than three and one-half feet and no more than six feet high.

iv. All off-street parking shall conform to the requirements of Section 525 of the Zoning Ordinance and Chapter 7.000 of the Facilities Standards Manual.

v. The board may reduce requirements for off-street parking serving a particular lot to the extent that the applicant can demonstrate that adequate parking is provided on-street and/or within a distance of 200 feet from the lot.

e. Landscaping

i. The applicant shall submit a comprehensive landscape master plan at the time of Preliminary Subdivision Plan and/or Rural Village Core (RVC) and Rural Village Workplace (RVW) rezoning application, identifying the location and size of both existing vegetation to be retained and proposed new vegetation, typical planting materials, the phasing of landscape installation, and planting methods.

ii. Streets in Rural Village Subdivisions (RVS) and the townhouse areas of Rural Village Core (RVC) districts shall be planted on both sides with street trees no more than 35 feet apart. Streets in the storefront areas of Rural Village Core (RVC) and Rural Village Workplace (RVW) areas shall be planted with trees no more than 35 feet apart on at least one side.

iii. Parking lots larger than 19 spaces and/or 6,000 square feet in size shall have internal landscaping as well as buffering landscaping on the edge of the lot.

iv. The village Home Owner Association documents shall provide for maintenance of street trees, and other community landscaping, such as in village greens, parks, and squares.

f. Utilities

i. Utilities should generally be located underground within street and alley rights-of-way; but not actually under street pavement unless a means of service access is provided which allows maintenance without disturbing the pavement.

ii. All above ground utility boxes and other facilities should be clustered and screened from street view.

iii. Potable and emergency water supply and treatment facilities and distribution lines, wastewater treatment and collection lines shall be designed, sized, and installed in accordance with specific uses and all applicable state, county, and LCSA standards.

Section VII requires the creation of a Homeowner Association (HOA) for each village, and references Addendum 2 concerning county preferences in this matter. This nonbinding addendum seeks to promote a "civic" model of homeowner association with a balance of responsibilities and authorities—mayor, council, board of code compliance—in contrast with the "corporate" board of directors model of centralized rule characteristic of conventional homeowner documents. The concepts advanced in Addendum 2 first came to the county's attention when Duany designed an urban community in eastern Loudoun in 1988–89. His analysis of "corporate" HOA shortcomings, primarily a consequence of poorly checked, centralized power, touched a responsive chord within many in county government. Unfortunately, the Commonwealth of Virginia Supreme Court commitment to the so-called "Dillon Rule" of narrow interpretation precludes a more direct county promotion of civic self-rule at this time.

Section VIII, the final portion of the Rural Village Ordinance, provides an override of ordinances through a special exception modification by the board of supervisors on reviewing a Concept Development Plan, the reasons for the waiver and upon a finding that:

1. These other regulations serve public purposes to a lesser degree than the requirements of the rural village ordinance, and

2. The designs and solutions proposed by the applicant, although not literally in accord with these other regulations, satisfy public purposes to a greater degree, and

The strict implementation of these other regulations would prevent well-designed rural village development

Addendum 1 was added to the text when community meetings revealed that many developers and citizens were not familiar with the county's methods of determining development potential. Addendum 1 provides a detailed explanation of the geometrical technique used by the Department of Natural Resources to determine development potential. Soils on a particular tract of land are first classified according to percolation potential. A plat of the tract is then overlaid with grids representing rectangles of three and one-half acres in size. Those rectangles containing a correct proportion of suitable soil are deemed to support a dwelling unit. Rect-

angles which individually do not quality for "perk," but which do so in combination, are also deemed to support a dwelling unit.

The geometrical technique, created by the Loudoun County Department of Natural Resources, appears to duplicate the results of expensive field testing with considerable success and at a fraction of the time, manpower, and cost.

A LOCAL TEST

In early 1988 the staff was invited to a meeting in Waterford concerning a subdivision proposal of two cul-de-sac streets serving large-lot homes with deep frontyards and wide sideyards. The southern cul-de-sac would have destroyed an important group of trees that served as an entry feature, while the northern cul-de-sac would have dominated a ridge above the community. Moreover, the loose and random layout of new houses would have compromised the distinct order and edge of the historic village. (See Figure A1–9.)

Figure A1–9. Waterford Case Study: Developer's Proposal for Huntley Farm. Suburban-style cul-de-sacs break the traditional village street pattern, and lot locations block distant views out of the village and dominate higher elevations. Virtually all of the preserved open space is hidden behind new houses.

At the request of community leaders, the developer, county planning commissioners, and supervisors, the planning staff agreed to prepare an alternative design. In the staff proposal, the southern group of trees and the northern ridge are left untouched. Existing Janney Street is extended eastward and rises from a subordinate and restricted situation, accentuated by retaining walls and overhanging trees, to an elevated position commanding a new and unexpected view of the Catoctin Mountains seen across a village green. To emphasize the urban-rural dichotomy, houses on three sides of the green are closely spaced. Turning northward on a new Huntley Street, which runs parallel to Second and High Streets in the classic urban tradition, a slight jog in the road focuses the pedestrian or driver on the large simple dignity of the Huntley Farm barns and then funnels the view into a very urbane environment of regularly planted street trees and homes with shallow frontyards. Huntley Street terminates at a renovated Fairfax Street, just across from the Old Waterford School, an early twentieth-century Greek Revival building of composure and grace, long hidden from prominence. (See Figure A1–10.)

Another way to explore the staff proposal would be to imagine a journey up High Street, noting the view of the historic Huntley Farmhouse across a lawn preserved by an open space easement; take a right onto Fairfax Street and right again onto Huntley Street. The generally linear road is initially aligned to focus attention and terminate the view on the Huntley barns, then turns slightly to suddenly reveal the spectacular Catoctin Mountain view across the green. A functional aspect of this design is the way school children would be able to walk to school without risking their lives on High Street, an intracounty collector.

When viewed within the overall context of the village, the staff subdivision proposal shares the essential character of the earlier development and can be distinguished only with difficulty from the existing settlement.

While the staff proposal certainly does not exhaust the possibilities inherent in the Huntley Tract, it demonstrates the attractive practicality of traditional design principles in a contemporary situation.

CONCLUSION

Such then is the Loudoun approach to rural farmland open space preservation. Recall that the agricultural crisis in America is the product of many factors and will need to be managed on many fronts. On some fronts, such as zoning and subdivision, planners move in

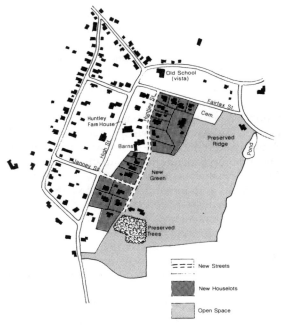

Figure A1–10. Waterford Case Study: Staff's Design Proposal. Homes are located along interconnected streets extending the historic pattern. For part of its length the new street borders a new village green, offering views eastward toward the Catoctin Mountains. The new street also terminates with a view of the old school at its northern end. Finally, tree groups and ridge areas are kept free from intrusive development.

familiar territory, while on others, such as probate, planners may need to acquire altogether new road maps and guides.

While farming's fundamental difficulties were not generated by land use controls, nevertheless, clustering of development permits farm families to distinguish between their land's agricultural and real estate values. If farm families can realize 80 percent of their equity while selling no more than 20 percent of their land, they may save their overall operation while meeting both inheritance taxes and the equity requirements of heirs no longer associated with the farm.

Growth tends to generate well-founded concerns regarding loss of community character. Traditional settlements within or near your jurisdiction may provide excellent models on which to pattern new ordinances that will preserve and strengthen community character as you grow.

Appendix B

Village Design Standards,

Kent County, Maryland

The purpose of these guidelines and objectives is to give a sense of the physical aspect of the village environment to those contemplating new development in the community. Pertinent to this physical appearance is the design of the site, buildings, and structures, planting, signs, street hardware, and miscellaneous other objects that are observed by the public. These standards are not intended to restrict imagination, innovation, or variety, but rather to assist in focusing on design principles which can produce creative solutions that will develop a satisfactory visual appearance within the County, preserve taxable values, and promote the public health, safety, and welfare.

A. Village District General Design Standards

1. The landscape shall be preserved in its natural state, insofar as practicable, by minimizing tree and soil removal. Any grade changes shall be in keeping with the general appearance of neighboring developed areas. The orientation of individual building sites shall be such as to maintain maximum natural topography and cover. Topography, tree cover, and natural drainageways shall be treated as fixed determinants of road and lot configuration rather than as malleable elements that can be changed to follow a preferred development scheme.

2. Streets shall be designed and located in such a manner as to maintain and preserve natural topography, cover, significant landmarks, and trees; to minimize cut and fill; and to preserve and enhance views and vistas on or off the subject parcel.

3. Proposed development shall be related harmoniously to the terrain and to the use, scale, and architecture of existing buildings in the vicinity that have functional or visual relationship to the proposed buildings. Proposed buildings shall be related to their surroundings.

4. All open space (landscaped and usable) shall be designed to add to the visual amenities of the area by maximizing its visibility for persons passing the site or overlooking it from nearby properties.

5. The color, size, height, lighting, and landscaping of appurtenant signs and structures shall be evaluated for compatibility with the local architectural motif

and the maintenance of views and vistas of natural landscapes, recognized historic landmarks, parks, and landscaping.

6. The removal or disruption of historic, traditional or significant uses, structures, or architectural elements shall be minimized insofar as practicable, whether these exist on the site or on adjacent properties.

B. Village District Design Elements

1. New developments should be an extension of the overall village development pattern rather than stand in contrast to it.

2. New designs should consist of small, understandable neighborhood segments rather than a single, large suburban theme.

3. New developments should reflect the unordered, historical growth of the village and avoid the cookie-cutter sameness of many new residential subdivisions.

4. Any opportunities for a strong, central focus should be studied and developed. These central places are usually a key to establishing community identity.

5. The types of open space provided should be a reflection of how passive and active open spaces are now used in the village, whether they are adequate, and how they may be complemented.

6. Strong provision should be made for walking as opposed to vehicular connections both within and without the new community.

7. Street widths and alignments should be carefully scaled to neighborhood size and be patterned after the character of existing residential streets.

8. The streetscape of new developments should be designed in detail to avoid repetitious setbacks, driveways, elevations, and landscaping.

9. New developments should carefully study and reflect the physical diversity of the existing village in regard to the mixture of housing types; a mixture of housing styles; and a mixture of lot sizes and shapes.

10. It is particularly important that new construction meet minimum design criteria in order that it may blend with the surroundings. New construction throughout the village should be compatible with surrounding properties, in terms of formal charac-

teristics such as height, massing, roof shapes and window proportions. When new construction is surrounded by existing historic buildings, building height and exterior materials shall be harmonious with those of adjacent properties.

C. Village District Cluster Development Standards

1. The Planning Commission, in accordance with the provisions of this section, is authorized to alter dimensional requirements for building spacing, front, side or rear yards, lot widths, building size or height, parking requirements, number of units in a structure, and other design standards.

2. The burden of proof shall be upon the builder or developer wishing to have the standards varied. The builder or developer shall submit drawings, models or plans, including alternatives, as specified by the Planning Commission. The builder may be required to post bond to insure compliance with the decision and any conditions imposed by the Planning Commission.

3. Standards

   a. *Building Spacing.* The requirement for building spacing, or side yards as they are often defined, is based on several related factors:

   (1) *Privacy.* The minimum building spacing requirement is intended to provide privacy within the dwelling unit. Where windows are placed in only one of two facing walls or there are no windows, or where the builder provides adequate screening for windows, or where the windows are at such a height or location to provide adequate privacy, the building spacing may be reduced.

   (2) *Light and Air.* The building spacing provides one method of insuring that each room has adequate light and air. Building spacing may be reduced where there are no windows or very small window areas, and where rooms have adequate provision for light and air from another direction, or where building orientation, layout and shapes are such that adequate light and air are available.

   (3) *Use.* Areas between buildings are often used as service yards for storage of trash, clothes lines, or other utilitarian purposes. Where this is similar for both houses, a reduction of building space permitting effective design of a utility space shall be permitted. Kitchens and garages are suitable uses for rooms abutting such utility yards.

   b. *Front Yards.* The minimum front yard is intended to provide privacy and usable yard area for residents. In practice, however, front yards are rarely used, so that the privacy factor is important. Where the developer provides privacy by reducing traffic flow through street layout such as cul-de-sacs, or by screening or planting, or by facing the structure toward open space or a pedestrian way, or through the arrangement of rooms and design of the front of the building, it is possible to reduce the front yard requirement. Where garages are placed on the lot, these need not meet the minimum setback, although adequate visibility must be provided for safe backing onto the street.

   c. *Lot Width.* A minimum lot width is intended to prevent the construction of long, narrow buildings with inadequate privacy, light and air. There are situations as in cul-de-sacs, steep slopes or off-set lots, where because of lot configuration or topography, narrow or irregular lots provide the best possible design. Where the design is such that adequate light, air, and privacy can be provided, especially for living spaces and bedrooms, a narrow lot width may be permitted.

   d. *Building Size or Number of Units in Structure.* These requirements are intended to prevent monotony in developments. In fact, these requirements often prevent the land planner from using interesting types of layout and working with unique site conditions; or they lead to a dull repetition of similar units. Where it can be demonstrated by presenting alternative site plans that a superior and less monotonous plan will result by granting relief from these standards, this may be done.

   e. *Height.* Limitations on height are often used to regulate the light available in limited yard areas and to prevent fire losses where inadequate equipment is available. Where unique site conditions and design permit height standards to be relaxed without adverse effects on light and air or privacy, then this may be done.

   f. *Parking.* Parking requirements are set for typical family situations. Where housing for the elderly is being built these standards shall be relaxed. In no case shall there be less than one parking space per two dwelling units. Where these standards are relaxed, the County shall insure that adequate parking is provided at the owner's expense if the building's use is changed. A notation to the effect shall be required on the recorded plan.

g. *Roads.* Standards for roads expressed in this Ordinance are intended to provide for the safe and intelligent layout of streets that may easily be maintained. There are several aspects which may lead to varying the size or design of specific streets.

(1) *Road Width.* The width of roads has been established to ensure adequate movement of traffic in times of greatest parking loads. Where a road is designed so that all units face onto secondary streets, and where overflow parking of three-tenths (.3) spaces per dwelling unit is provided, the road width may be reduced. The overflow parking is a requirement to ensure adequate parking space since the street normally provides this function. All proposed road widths must be approved by the Kent County Roads Department.

(2) *Right-of-Way Width.* Right-of-way width is intended to provide enough land for roads, sidewalks, or utilities. Secondly, it is intended to provide an additional buffer between home and street where sidewalks are not run along the street. Widths may be reduced where utilities are located outside of the right-of-way or where houses do not front on the street. A reduction in the width of the right-of-way may be permitted, if approved by the Kent County Roads Department.

(3) *Curbs.* Curbs are used to channel water to stormwater systems and to keep cars off grass. In low-intensity development, natural drainage shall be encouraged. The soils and topography must be considered.

h. *Sidewalks.* Sidewalks are intended to provide a separate means of movement for pedestrians. Modern design practice encourages moving sidewalks away from streets. In doing so, the function of sidewalks must be kept in mind. First, the walks must be all-weather and easily cleared of snow. Second, they must be convenient for the most frequent trips. Where deemed appropriate, one or both sidewalks within street rights-of-way may be eliminated.

D. Village District Specific Design Standards

For Residential Development in the Village District:

1. Site access shall be subject to the following regulations to help ensure traffic safety and alleviate traffic congestion.

a. Where property abuts a primary, secondary, or collector road, access to the property shall be by way of the secondary or collector road. Exceptions to this rule shall be instances where the Planning Commission determines that direct access onto the primary road would promote traffic safety.

b. Where one or more contiguous parcels abutting a primary road are under single ownership and any one of the parcels abuts a secondary or collector road, access to all of the parcels under single ownership shall be by way of the secondary or collector road.

c. No more than one direct access approach onto a primary road shall be provided to any individual parcel of record as of the date of this Ordinance.

(1) *Exceptions*

(a) The Planning Commission may, with approval by the State or County Highway Commission, approve additional access if the additional access is deemed to be significantly beneficial to the safety and operation of the highway or if allowing only one access approach would be a safety hazard or increase traffic congestion.

(b) The Planning Commission may approve additional access when the parcel is bisected by steep slopes or other topographic features in such a manner as to render some portion of the property inaccessible without additional road access.

d. Where a future roadway is designed on an approved County map, site plans for development adjacent to the designated roadway shall include provisions for future access to the roadway.

e. Access shall be consolidated where ever possible.

2. Building Arrangement and Site Design

The purpose of imposing regulations governing building arrangement and site design is to help protect significant environmental and historic features, promote a sense of neighborhood and community identity, and reduce the visual impact of high density residential developments on the surrounding area.

a. Where existing buildings express a traditionally modest (pre-zoning) front setback, creating a characteristically close relationship with the street (as in village and town centers and along their approach roads), it is highly desirable to continue this pattern in order to retain the area's character. Therefore, the maximum setback of new construction should harmonize with the average setbacks of existing adjacent buildings. Outside of the areas of generally uniform building setback (where existing structures are located at various distances from the roadway), front setbacks may vary to a greater degree, and principal buildings shall generally be located within 40 feet of the front lot line unless there are substantial counter-balancing considerations (such as irregular topography, wetlands, or the preservation of natural rural features, including pastures, cropland, meadows, or timber stands). In all instances, parking shall be excluded from such areas, between the principal building and the roadways.

b. Where significant trees, groves, waterways, historic, archaeological, or prehistoric sites or unique habitats are located within the property boundaries of a proposed Village District project, every possible means shall be provided to preserve those features. In addition to identifying existing natural features as per Article VI, Section 5, of this Ordinance, an inventory of existing on-site historic and archaeological features may be required.

c. *Size, Scale, and Building Mass*
   (1) To avoid monotonous linear development, multifamily development shall be in small clusters designed as neighborhood units. A cluster shall not include more than 30 units.
   (2) The number of units in a row is to be limited to a maximum of eight.
   (3) Offsets at party walls and/or front and rear facades or similar devices are required to visually reduce building mass and create individualized spaces (courtyards, seating areas, etc.) for all multifamily projects. Drawing of the building elevations will be required.

d. *Vehicular Circulation.* The purpose of these requirements is to promote road safety, assure adequate access for fire and rescue vehicles, and promote adequate vehicular circulation.
   (1) Roads shall be designed to minimize the visual size and scale of the development and help discourage excessive speeds.
   (2) Street widths and alignments should be carefully scaled to neighborhood size and be patterned after the character of existing residential streets.
   (3) The amount of road pavement should be minimized through efficient layout and design.

(4) The use of one-way roads is encouraged where practical, to reduce the ratio of pavement to buildings and open space.
(5) The applicant must demonstrate that access from a primary road to the site is adequate, has the capacity to handle traffic generated by the proposed project, and will not endanger the safety of the general public.
(6) Direct automobile links should be made to the existing village to emphasize the connections between existing and new development.

e. *On-Site Pedestrian and Bicycle Circulation*
   (1) Walkways and bicycle paths shall be provided to link residences with parking lots, recreation facilities (including parkland and open space), school and church sites, and commercial developments.
   (2) The design and construction of walkways will be evaluated on the basis of safety, accessibility, suitability for use by motor-impaired individuals, and surface suitability in terms of anticipated use and maintenance requirements. The applicant may be required to install hard surface walkways adjacent to units and along pedestrian circulation routes connecting units with each other and with recreation or commercial areas. In less intensive areas, other pervious and non-erodible surface materials may be approved.
   (3) Outdoor lighting is encouraged along all major pedestrian walkways and required between parking lots and residences. Lighting is to be limited to residential scale lighting fixtures.

f. *Parking and Parking Lots.* The purpose of this section is to provide for adequate parking for multifamily residential developments. All parking areas shall be designed for pedestrian safety.
   (1) A minimum of one parking space for one bedroom units and two parking spaces for two or more bedroom units is required. A minimum of an additional 15 percent of the total number of spaces provided for residents within a building cluster shall be provided for guests and overflow parking.
   (2) At least 10 percent of all parking lot areas where more than ten parking spaces are provided shall be landscaped. This may be waived by the Planning Commission.
   (3) To avoid large expanses of paved parking area, the following provisions, which may be

waived by the Planning Commission, shall apply:

(*a*) No more than 12 parking spaces will be permitted in a continuous row and the break between rows (the island) must be landscaped.

(*b*) The ends of parking rows and land-scaped islands shall be a minimum of 6 feet wide and shall be adequately land-scaped with shade trees, ground cover, and shrubs.

(*c*) Double rows of parking shall be separated by a minimum 6 foot planting strip adequately landscaped with shade trees and shrubs.

(4) Parking area design shall include provision for the physically handicapped as required under state standards.

(5) All lighting in parking areas shall be arranged to prevent direct glare of illumination onto adjacent properties.

(6) Off-street parking areas and driveways, exclusive of required landscaping, shall be surfaced with materials approved by the Planning Commission.

(7) Required residential off-street parking facilities shall be located on the premises they are intended to serve, and shall not extend into a required front yard or any other required yard abutting a street.

g. *Outdoor Storage*

(1) Outdoor trash receptacles for individual residences are to be screened from neighboring residences.

(2) Large outdoor trash receptacles, such as dumpster boxes, shall be adequately screened and located so as to provide easy truck access and not conflict with parking or through traffic. Trash receptacles may not be located in residential parking spaces and must be on concrete or asphalt pods large enough to accommodate trash pick-up trucks.

(3) A storage area for boats, recreational vehicles, trailers of all kinds, unlicensed vehicles, and inoperative vehicles shall be provided. The area shall be a minimum of 200 square feet for every 5 units and shall be screened from the road and adjoining properties. If covenants prohibit these types of vehicles, this requirement may be waived.

h. *Landscaping.* Landscaping is required to promote attractive development, to protect and preserve the appearance and character of the surrounding area, and to delineate and define vehicular and pedestrian passageways and open space within the development. This may be waived by the Planning Commission.

(1) *General Requirements*

(*a*) All plant material installed shall be healthy and of the best quality.

(*b*) All plant material installed shall be balled and burlapped or container grown.

(*c*) All trees shall be a minimum 1½ inch caliper at breast height at installation.

(*d*) A maintenance agreement for the plant material shall be included in the property covenant.

(*e*) Plant material shall be bonded for one year. A planting schedule shall be included in the bond and shall be based on seasonal considerations.

Appendix C

Notes on Architectural and Site Design Principles

for Use with Density and Intensity Bonuses

1. Overview

The following commentary offers thoughts on possible design criteria to be used when evaluating requests to increase the density of a proposed residential development, or to increase the intensity of a proposed commercial or mixed-use development. This approach to standard setting addresses aesthetic concerns and exceeds the type of controls that are normally permissible outside local historic zoning districts.

While such standards might ordinarily be considered impermissible as general requirements, their legality in these situations rests largely on the basis that they would apply only when applicants ask the local government for additional density or use-intensity. In exchange for agreeing to increase the value of individual properties for development purposes, local governments may legitimately require a *quid pro quo* in terms of the extra effort demanded of applicants to harmonize their new developments into the community's traditional streetscape or townscape.

Such standards are particularly useful in improving the appearance of low- and moderate-income housing, where construction budgets are typically much too tight to allow architects to provide certain exterior elements and features needed for the buildings to more closely resemble market-rate dwellings (such as porches, overhanging eaves, steeper roof pitches, breaks in rooflines or facades, wider corner boards, casing boards and lintels around doors and windows, and windows that are larger and more traditionally spaced). The density bonuses related to exterior design would, of course, be in addition to those given to reduce the per-unit land cost—which are often essential to ensure an affordable product. An excellent example where architectural design was significantly improved as a result of a substantial density increase is the Battle Road Farm project in Lincoln, Massachusetts, described at the end of Chapter 20.

Such an approach can also help to improve the appearance of new commercial buildings in town centers or along highways. In order for this to work, however, the zoning in those areas must not already allow density to be maximized to the point where the entire lot may be covered with buildings, parking, circulation, and stormwater management facilities, or with high-volume uses. The most effective kind of situation is one in which land is zoned for small businesses with low to moderate traffic generation, or where maximum floor space is limited to 2,500 square feet per building, for example, but where the intensity of use may be increased. In such cases, lesser uses such as convenience stores could be allowed to expand into grocery superstores or be replaced by discount department stores, provided that extra measures are taken to accomplish certain aesthetic or social goals as identified in the ordinance. For example, rather than constructing a plain, boxy one-story building, a commercial developer seeking a use-intensity could be required to build a two-story mixed-use facility, with dwellings located above the retail or office premises, in exchange for permission to develop a larger, more lucrative use.

This kind of mixed use occurs infrequently in new construction, but is illustrated in the Winslow Green and Village Galleria projects described in Chapter 21. It has been said that one of the major reasons why this country is currently experiencing such a huge housing affordability problem is that since the 1940s there have been so few dwelling units constructed above new commercial premises—a building pattern that historically provided considerable low-rent housing in locations within walking distance of many employment and shopping opportunities. Whether or not the new dwellings in mixed-use developments are affordable to people with low or moderate incomes—and the two examples in Chapter 21 are not—they do add to the vitality of an area by increasing the number of people who are likely to be there and use it both day and night.

The following standards reflect traditional architectural values expressed in the vernacular buildings found in many small towns in the northeastern part of the United States, as interpreted by the author. If proposed to be used in other sections of the country, these standards should be reviewed for applicability, and modified to reflect local building traditions.

2. Standards for Residential Developments

This section contains criteria that address issues pertaining mostly to new housing, particularly those proposed to be provided below market rates. Ironically, these standards represent a step backward in time to those set more than 70 years ago by architects for the first federal housing projects in this country, which were funded by Congress to increase the number of shipbuilders living near shipyards during World War I. In those new communities great efforts were taken to harmonize the new housing with local architectural traditions. For example, row houses in Yorkship Village in Haddon Township, New Jersey (later renamed "Fairview" and annexed by Camden), were deliberately designed to closely resemble the two-and-one-half story brick townhouses found in the Delaware River Valley in locations such as Society Hill in Philadelphia and New Castle, Delaware.

The importance of improving current design standards for affordable housing is underscored by the fact that places such as Yorkship Village and its sister project, Dundalk, at Sparrow Point just outside Baltimore, have always been well regarded by their residents, who demonstrate their pride in these handsomely designed communities by taking good care of their homes, yards, and common areas. These early projects are briefly described in Chapter 10. Unfortunately, the lessons learned in 1917 had been forgotten or ignored by 1943, when the second generation of shipbuilders' housing was constructed, and visitors to the newer sections of Dundalk today see an enormous difference in the way that residents of the two sections regard their respective neighborhoods. The World War II housing units were constructed more monolithically in larger flat-roofed structures resembling barracks, with far less attention paid to aesthetics, site planning, street tree planting, and landscaping. Tellingly, these bleak World War II era neighborhoods exhibit much lower levels of maintenance and higher levels of vandalism, and pedestrian activity is far less, compared with what visitors see in the sections built in 1917.

The following standards are organized according to those exterior design features that collectively influence the overall appearance of residential buildings.

a. Roof Shape, Materials, and Eaves

The visual significance of roofs is often not fully appreciated, but their shape it is one of the most important determinants of how well a building fits into its surroundings. Traditional buildings generally have pitched roofs, the degree of pitch typically reflecting the era when they were constructed. Except for the brief Federal period when flatter hipped roofs were common, these pitches usually range from 8/12 to 12/12. Attempts to introduce mansard roofs in new construction should be soundly rejected unless the relatively rare Second Empire style is well-represented in the community, and unless other aspects of the building design are in accordance with this tradition (such as very tall windows and doorways with archlike tops, and projecting eaves decorated with brackets). Neo-mansard roofs generally represent very poor attempts to disguise otherwise flat roofs, and are one of the cheapest ploys available to low-end builders. The type, color, and texture of roof materials should be in keeping with roofs in the immediate neighborhood. White or tan asphalt shingles should generally be prohibited. Roof eaves should project outward over all exterior walls to the extent that is typical of local construction in the early years of this century or before.

b. Building Height

The height of new residential buildings, as measured from the average grade along the front facade, should not vary more than 10 percent above or below the average height of other residential buildings in the immediate neighborhood (a distance of three buildings in each direction up and down the street, for example). Additional stories should not be introduced by starting the first floor one-half story below grade, as seen from the front (which is the case with "raised ranches," an ungainly style that confuses observers who sometimes cannot decide whether the building has been elevated by a rising water table or has sunk into soggy soil). If an extra half-story is desired, it should be located on the top floor, preferably with small dormers for extra light and ventilation (larger shed-type dormers are permissible on the rear side).

c. Window Size, Proportions and "Rhythm"

The vertical height of windows should relate comfortably to those on older homes in the neighborhood. There is an unfortunate tendency for windows in new buildings to be squat, with higher sills, and to be placed in pairs to reduce the number of openings in the exterior walls. The height:width ratio of windows should generally not be less than 1.8:1 (which is the proportion of a 56 inch by 30 inch window). This design standard favors double-hung and casement windows over "sliders" or "awning types" that are hinged at the top. They should be framed on the outside with casing boards, typically 4 inches wide, and should be rationally ordered both vertically and horizontally so that the building facades will be visually well-balanced. In most cases, windows should be located singly rather than in groups of two or three (unless that tradition is common in the community among buildings more than 50 years old).

d. Exterior Materials

A relatively wide latitude is appropriate with regard to siding materials, particularly because there is such a broad range of vernacular materials, from wooden clapboards to brick and stone. It is easier to identify those materials that would probably *not* be appropriate in traditional streetscapes. When wooden clapboards are used and are proposed to be stained, they should never be reversed to expose the rough-sawed side. Artificial clapboards made of vinyl may be allowed, provided the clapboards are narrow (3 inches to 4 inches wide) and have a non-reflective, matte-type finish. Textured siding with fake wood grain should never be permitted. Plywood siding such as "T-lll" should also be prohibited, as should rough-sawed board-and-batten (unless this is characteristic of the area). Wooden shakes as siding material should always be straight cut and not randomly cut. Brick should be of a color, size, and texture that is typical of older buildings, and should never be "used" or spray-painted to resemble used brick. Joints should be as thin as possible, neatly finished with ivory-colored mortar (rather than grey, brown, or black). Artificial brick (sometimes actually colored cement or stucco, incised to resemble brickwork) should be prohibited because of its unrealistic appearance and short life-span. Artificial stone should be allowed only in areas where stonework is an historic tradition, and only when its visual appearance is highly realistic.

e. Parking

In larger projects involving new streets, the need for parking lots should be minimized by requiring site designers to provide *parallel* curbside parking spaces along both sides of the streets. These spaces should be landscaped with deciduous shade trees planted at 40 foot intervals between sidewalks and curbs, along both sides of the street. Appropriate species include oak, maple, sweet gum, sycamore, ash, and little-leaf linden. Streets should interconnect wherever physically feasible, and cul-de-sacs should be avoided. When that is not possible, cul-de-sacs should be designed as large, heavily-landscaped "parking courts" with a variety of shade trees and native specie shrubs and perennials. Off-street

parking should be minimized and should be provided, when necessary, through garages that are internal to the residential building or that are grouped together (both of which are done at Chatham Village, illustrated in Chapter 20). Non-garage off-street parking that is unavoidable should be inconspicuously sited in a number of small areas located in side yards between units, and landscaped with shade trees, as has been done at the Battle Road Farm, mentioned above.

3. Standards for Commercial and Mixed Use Developments

The design of new commercial and mixed use facilities should be guided by timeless principles as expressed in the pattern of traditional downtown business districts and by the centers of new communities planned between 1865 and 1935, such as Riverside and Lake Forest, Illinois; Mariemont, Ohio; Winter Park, Florida; and Radburn, New Jersey (in addition to Yorkship Village and Dundalk, Maryland, described above). This is not to suggest that the architecture of new development should mimic older styles, but rather that the buildings be two to three stories in height, and that they be located at the edge of the sidewalk, with curbside parking spaces and additional parking in the rear. The use of upper stories should be encouraged to be mixed, with offices and residential units on various floors.

a. Building Height

When commercial developers seek variances or rezoning in order to expand or replace an existing operation with a larger facility, or to construct new premises that require rezoning, local governments should require that at least part of the new building be two or three stories in height. This not only improves the scale but also makes better use of land and infrastructure, and helps promote greater use of the development during evening hours. The appearance of additional vertical height can also be achieved through the use of parapet walls. Mixed office and residential uses should be encouraged on the upper floors.

b. Location of Building(s) and Parking

Buildings should be constructed at the edge of the sidewalk in town center locations, or around courtyards or other pedestrian facilities. Parking provision along the street should be maximized, supplemented with screened auxiliary parking lots to the side and rear of the new commercial buildings (never in front). In other areas, such as along arterial roads and highways, landscaped buffer yards are generally appropriate between buildings and the thoroughfare, and they should be planted with deciduous shade trees and native specie shrubs. A similar prohibition against front parking lots applies here as well. Shared parking arrangements between generally non-competing uses (such as residential and retail) should be devised according to formulas such as those published by the Urban Land Institute, and parking lots on adjacent premises should be connected by internal driveway links. Consideration should be given to utilizing the airspace above parking stalls, as has been done at the Village Galleria project in La Jolla, California (see Chapter 21). Curbside parking should be landscaped with deciduous shade trees planted at 40 foot intervals.

c. Building Design

New buildings should generally follow contemporary design approaches, but should also respect and reflect the traditional scale, proportions, rhythms, and mood of traditional commercial structures. These traditional architectural values should be interpreted into contemporary building design, but the use of imitation historic building details and ornaments should be discouraged. Building design must also be internally consistent, and amalgamations of historically unrelated stylistic elements should generally be prohibited. Exterior materials should reflect local building traditions (typically red brick and wooden clapboards). Shop front windows should generally be rather tall with low sills and high lintels, as is traditional, but they may be detailed in a contemporary fashion. Transom windows should be encouraged above doors and display windows. Blank walls facing the street or highway should generally be disallowed. Flat-roofed buildings should have decorative parapets, and mansard roofs should be prohibited. Other standards from Section 2 above, and from Chapter 8, "Commercial Infill Development Along a Major Street," may also be applied to new commercial buildings, as deemed appropriate by the Planning Board or the Design Review Board.

Appendix D

Architectural Drawings of

Compact Single-Family Homes

Figure A4–1. Perspective sketch of houses facing one of the greens. Squire Green, Pawling, NY.

Figure A4–2. Perspective sketch of streetscape with traditional proportions between opposing housefronts.

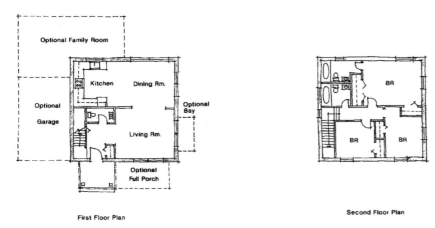

Figure A4–3. Floor plans of homes, showing optional expansion areas (family room, garage, front porch, and living room bay). An expandable house is an affordable house, and homes for moderate-income families should be predesigned for such additions.

Figure A4–4. House Type "A" (Basic Model), front and side elevations. Measuring about 25 feet on each side, this two-story home contains approximately 1,250 square feet.

Figure A4–5. House Type "A" with full porch, garage, and family room, front and side elevations. The family room adds about 300 square feet to the house. With the garage and family room added, house width increases from 25 feet to 36 feet. (The living room bay would add another four feet.)

Figure A4–6. House Type "B" (Basic Model), front and side elevations. This is essentially the same house as Type "A," except that its gable-end faces the street.

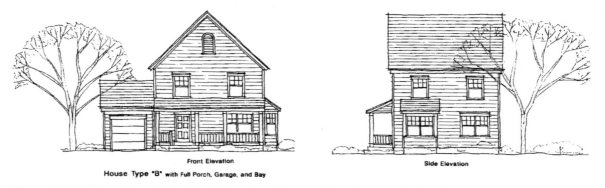

Figure A4–7. House Type "B" with full porch, garage and bay, front and side elevations.

Figure A4–8. House Type "B" with garage, fireplace, and family room, front and side elevations.

Appendix E

Questionnaire Results After Slide Presentation

on Creative Rural Planning in Calvert County, Maryland

Several ideas were presented in the slide show. Which of these ideas do you think should be pursued for possible use in Calvert County?

	Pursue	Don't Pursue	Can't Decide	Total % Pursue
If farm or forest land in a rural area is to be subdivided:				
1. retain at least 50% of the site as open space	66	3	8	86
2. retain existing open fields and use as community owned farmland, pasture, recreation, etc.	67	4	6	87
3. place houses at forest edges and away from sensitive areas and wildlife habitat	78	1	0	99
4. incorporate existing historic and cultural features (houses, barns, farm roads, orchards) into the site design	72	2	5	91
5. maintain existing rural landscapes through careful placement of houses	73	0	2	97
6. retain existing vegetation near waterways while providing for filtered views	76	0	3	96
7. use traditional rural villages as models for new rural subdivisions	60	2	12	81
8. use the following traditional features in rural subdivision design:				
a. village green	59	5	10	80
b. narrow, tree-lined streets	62	3	6	87
c. small front yards; large back yards	60	3	9	83
d. compact placement of houses	62	5	6	85
e. community surrounded by open space	72	2	0	97
f. gravel roads in small subs	48	15	10	66
9. permit duplexes (triplex, quadriplex) in rural subdivisions	38	13	22	52
a. require attached houses to look like single-family detached houses	67	2	7	88
If town centers are located along roadways:				
1. require parking lots to be located to the rear of buildings	68	6	5	86
2. plant trees along roadways	76	1	2	96
3. use wooden signs instead of plastic signs	72	1	6	91
4. screen parking areas	76	1	2	96

Bibliography

Alexander, Christopher et al. 1977. *A Pattern Language: Towns, Buildings, Construction.* New York: Oxford University Press.

American Farmland Trust. 1986. *Density-Related Public Costs.* Washington, DC: American Farmland Trust.

American Society of Civil Engineers, National Association of Home Builders, and Urban Land Institute. 1990. *Residential Streets,* 2nd ed. Washington, DC: American Society of Civil Engineers, National Association of Home Builders, and Urban Land Institute.

Anderson, Damaan L. et al. 1984. *Technology Assessment of Intermittent Sand Filters.* Cincinnati: U.S. Environmental Protection Agency Municipal Environmental Research Laboratory, Office of Research and Development.

Anderson, Judith. 1992. *A Conservation Point System: A Method to Encourage the Balance Between Growth and the Preservation of Rural Character.* Ann Arbor: University of Michigan.

Anderson, Judith. 1992. "A Conservation Point System to Protect Open Space." *Planning & Zoning News,* Vol. 10, No. 6, April. Lansing, MI: The Planning and Zoning Center.

Ann Arbor Area Creek Management Project. 1991. *Protecting Creeks in a Changing Landscape.* Ann Arbor: University of Michigan School of Natural Resources.

Arendt, Randall. 1989. "Commercial Kudzu and the Townless Highway: Theory and Practice of New England Roadside Planning." *Journal of the New England Landscape,* Vol. I. Amherst, MA: Center for Rural Massachusetts, University of Massachusetts.

Arendt, Randall. 1989. "Patterns in the Rural Landscape." *Orion Nature Quarterly,* Vol. 8, No. 4, Autumn, pp. 22–27.

Arendt, Randall et al. 1989. *Land Use Management Report for the Blackstone River Valley National Heritage Corridor.* Uxbridge, MA: BRVNHC Commission.

Arendt, Randall. 1987. "Retaining Natural Landscapes Along the River's Edge." In Conference Proceedings for *Planning for the Changing Rural Landscape of New England: Blending Theory and Practice.* Durham, NH: New England Center, University of New Hampshire.

Arendt, Randall. 1982. "Manufactured Housing: An Innovative Approach to Municipal Siting Standards." *Maine Townsman,* Vol. 44, No. 7, July.

Arnold, Henry. 1992. "Planning for Trees: Viewing Trees as an Integral Part of the Infrastructure." *Planning Commissioners' Journal,* Vol. 1, No. 1, January–February, pp. 1–8.

Avin, Uri et al. 1991. *Develop or Preserve? An Integrated Approach to Agricultural Protection in a Metropolitan County.* Ellicott City, MD: Howard County Planning Department.

Babize, Molly, and Walter Cudnohufsky. 1991. *Designing Your Corner of Vermont: Protecting Your Property Investment Through Good Site Design.* Montpelier, VT: Vermont Council on the Arts.

Baker, Jeffrey, and Bruno Funaro. 1952. *Shopping Centers: Design and Operation.* New York: Reinhold.

Barnard, Ellsworth. 1988. *A Land Ethic for Massachusetts.* Amherst, MA: published by the author.

Barylski, Michael. 1989. "Scenic Roads: Getting There Can be Half the Fun." *The Conservationist,* September–October. Albany, NY: New York Department of Environmental Conservation.

Bentsen, Lief, and Charles Burrow. 1992. *The Village Lane: A New Concept in Kitsap County Road Design.* Indianola, WA: Indianola Land Trust Greenway.

Bergman, David. 1991. "Does Development Really Pay for Itself?" *Newsreporter,* September–October. Warrenton, VA: Piedmont Environmental Council.

Bobrowski, Mark. 1990. "Acton: TDR As a Tool in Commercial Planning." *Land Use Forum,* August–September.

Bookout, Lloyd W., Jr. et al. 1990. *Residential Development Handbook,* 2nd ed. Washington, DC: Urban Land Institute.

Bosselman, Fred et al. 1973. *The Taking Issue.* Washington, DC: Council on Environmental Quality.

Bosselman, Fred, and David Callies. 1971. *The Quiet Revolution in Land Use Control.* Washington, DC: U.S. Council on Environmental Quality, U.S. Government Printing Office.

Bowers, Deborah. 1991a. "Agricultural Zoning in Maryland Offers Developer Options." *Farmland Preservation Report,* May, pp. 1–3.

Bowers, Deborah. 1991b. "Local Zoning Could Jeopardize Delaware's Fledgling PDR." *Farmland Preservation Report,* September, pp. 1–4.

Bowers, Deborah. 1991c. "Cigarette Tax Hike to Support Farmland Preservation in PA." *Farmland Preservation Report*, September, p. 8.

Bowers, Deborah. 1991d. "Prescribed Buffers in Ag Elements." *Farmland Preservation Report*, September, p. 2.

Boyle, K., and Bishop, R. 1984. "Economic Benefits Associated with Boating and Canoeing on the Lower Wisconsin River." *Economic Issues*, No. 84. Madison, WI: University of Wisconsin.

Bozeman and Gallatin County City-County Planning Board. 1990. *1990 Bozeman Area Master Plan Update.* Bozeman, MT: Bozeman and Gallatin County City-County Planning Board.

Brandywine Conservancy Environmental Management Center. 1990. *The Lexington-Frankfort Scenic Corridor: Protecting a World Class Landscape.* Lexington, KY: Lexington-Frankfort Scenic Corridor, Inc.

Breckenfeld, Gurney. 1971. *Columbia and the New Cities.* New York: Ives Washburn.

Brown, M. T. et al. 1990. *Buffer Zones for Water, Wetlands and Wildlife in East Central Florida.* Gainesville, FL: Center for Wetlands, University of Florida, CFW Publication 89–07.

Bucks County Planning Commission. 1989. *Village Planning Handbook.* Doylestown, PA: Bucks County Planning Commission.

Bucks County Planning Commission. 1980. *Performance Streets: A Concept and Model Standards for Residential Streets.* Doylestown, PA: Bucks County Planning Commission.

Bunker Stimson Solien Jacob. 1988. *Site Planning for Affordable Housing: Four Case Studies in Falmouth, MA.* Falmouth, MA: Bunker Stimson Solien Jacob.

Burchell, R. W., and David Listokin. 1980. *Practitioner's Guide to Fiscal Impact Analysis.* New Brunswick, NJ: Rutgers University Center for Urban Policy Research.

Burlington Community Land Trust. 1990. *A Citizens' Guide to Conserving Land and Creating Affordable Housing.* Burlington, VT: Burlington Community Land Trust and the Vermont Land Trust.

Cahners. 1991. "Affordable Plans." *Professional Builder and Remodeler.* Des Plaines, IL: Cahners Publishing Co.

Calderon, Richard. 1989. *Planning Approaches for Growth in Rural Areas.* Leesburg, VA: Loudoun County Planning Dept.

Caputo, Darryl F. 1979. *Open Space Pays: The Socioenvironomics of Open Preservation.* Morristown, NJ: New Jersey Conservation Foundation.

Carroll County Commissioners and Westminster Common Council. 1985. *Comprehensive Plan of Westminster and Environs.* Westminster, MD: Carroll County Commissioners and Westminster Common Council.

Carter, Jennifer. 1992. *Productive Uses for Conserved Land: A Case Study of the Economic Benefits of Land Conservation.* Stonington, ME: Island Heritage Institute.

Center for Governmental Studies. 1979. *A Guidebook for Fiscal Impact Analysis of Residential Developments Proposed for Unincorporated Areas of DeKalb County.* DeKalb, IL: Northern Illinois University.

Center for Public Interest Polling. 1987. *Housing Preferences of New Jerseyans.* New Brunswick, NJ: Rutgers University Eagleton Institute of Politics.

Chellman, Chester E. 1989. *A Discussion of Street Geometry and Design Criteria for "Traditional Neighborhood Development."* Ossipee, NH: White Mountain Survey.

Chester County Planning Commission. 1986. *Sliding Scale Zoning.* West Chester, PA: Planning Bulletin No. 29.

Chester County Planning Commission. 1984. *Scenic Roads Handbook.* West Chester, PA: Local Government Handbook No. 3.

Chester County Planning Department. 1990. *Utilization of Irrigation in Wastewater Treatment.* West Chester, PA: Planning Bulletin No. 40.

Churn, Virginia. 1990. "Urban Land Institute Names Woodlake Best U.S. Community." Richmond *Times-Dispatch*, November 3.

Clarke, Michael G. 1992. *The Community Land Stewardship Program.* Media, PA: Natural Lands Trust.

Clarke, Michael G. 1992. "Community Land Stewardship: A Future Direction for Land Trusts." *Land Trust Exchange*, Vol. 11, No. 2, pp. 1–9.

Clarke, Michael G. et al. 1985. *A Growth Management Plan for the Borough of West Chester.* West Chester, PA: West Chester Borough Planning Commission.

Community Vision Inc. and Center for Rural Massachusetts. 1992. *A Design Guideline Manual for Sustainable Development on Cape Cod.* Barnstable, MA: Cape Cod Commission.

Convery, Patricia. 1987. "Dunham Lake: Not Spoiled by Shoreline Development." *The Michigan Riparian*, November.

Cooper-Marcus, Clare. 1986. "Design As If People Mattered." In Peter Calthorpe and Sim Van der Ryn (eds) *Sustainable Communities: A New Design Synthesis for Cities, Suburbs, and Towns.* San Francisco: Sierra Club.

Corbett, Michael N. 1981. *A Better Place to Live: New Designs for Tomorrow's Communities.* Emmaus, PA: The Rodale Press.

Correll, D. L., and W. T. Peterjohn. 1984. "Nutrient Dynamics in an Agricultural Watershed: Observations on the Role of a Riparian Forest." *Ecology,* Vol. 65, pp. 1466–1475.

Correll, Mark R., Jane H. Lillydahl, and Larry D. Singell. 1978. "The Effects of Greenbelts on Residential Property Values: Some Findings on the Political Economy of Open Space." *Land Economics,* Vol. 54, No. 2.

Corser, Susan Ernst, and Willis and Ratliff Bucher. 1992. *Preserving Rural Character Through Cluster Housing.* Steamboat Springs, CO: unpublished paper.

Coughlin, Robert E. 1993. *The Adoption and Stability of Agricultural Zoning in Lancaster County, Pennsylvania.* Philadelphia: University of Pennsylvania Department of City and Regional Planning, Research Report Series No. 15.

Coughlin, Robert E. 1991. "Formulating and Evaluating Agricultural Zoning Programs." *Journal of the American Planning Association,* pp. 183–192.

Coughlin, Robert E. 1988. "Information Needs for Formulating and Evaluating Agricultural Zoning Programs." *Land Use in Urbanizing Areas.* USDA Economic Research Service, pp. 183–194.

Coughlin, Robert E. 1984. *The Effects of Agricultural Zoning on the Ability of Farmers to Borrow Money.* Philadelphia: University of Pennsylvania Department of City and Regional Planning, Research Report Series No. 8.

Coughlin, Robert E., Joanne R. Denworth, John C. Keene, and John W. Rogers. 1991. *Guiding Growth: Building Better Communities and Protecting Our Countryside.* Philadelphia: Pennsylvania Environmental Council, Inc.

Courtney, Elizabeth. 1992. *Vermont's Scenic Landscapes: A Guide for Growth and Protection.* Waterbury, VT: Vermont Agency of Natural Resources.

Craighead, Paula M. 1991. *The Hidden Design in Land Use Ordinances: Assessing the Visual Impact of Dimensions Used for Town Planning in Maine Landscapes.* Portland, ME: University of Southern Maine New England Studies Program.

Cudnohufsky, Walter, and Molly Babize. 1990. *Town of Wendell: Community Vision of the Future.* Conway, MA: Conway Design Associates.

Cullen, Gordon. 1964. *Townscape.* New York: Reinhold.

Daniels, Thomas L., and Arthur C. Nelson. 1986. "Is Oregon's Farmland Preservation Program Working?" *Journal of the American Planning Association,* Vol. 52, No. 1, pp. 22–32.

Darling, Arthur H. 1973. "Measuring Benefits Generated by Urban Water Parks." *Land Economics,* Vol. 49, pp. 22–34.

Davidson-Schuster, Mark et al. 1988. *Housing Design and Regional Character: A Primer for New England Towns.* Cambridge, MA: MIT Department of Urban Studies and Planning.

Davis, Hugh C. 1988. "The Challenge of Scenic Roads." In *Planning for the Changing Rural Landscape of New England: Blending Theory and Practice,* pp. 126–134. Durham, NH: New England Center, University of New Hampshire.

Davis, Norah Deakins. 1991. "Developers Can Wear White Hats" *American Forests,* May/June.

Diamond, Douglas B., Jr. 1980. "The Relationship Between Amenities and Urban Land Prices." *Land Economics,* Vol. 56, pp. 21–32.

Doble, Cheryl et al. 1992. *Managing Change: A Pilot Study in Rural Design and Planning.* Watertown, NY: Tug Hill Commission.

Dodson, Harry et al. 1989. *Combining Land Conservation With Affordable Housing.* Amherst, MA: Center for Rural Massachusetts, University of Massachusetts.

Doucette, Robert, Sterling Dow III, and Janet Milne. 1977. *The Comparative Economics of Residential Development and Open Space Conservation: A Manual for Municipal Officials and Other Townspeople.* Portland, ME: University of Maine, Center for Research and Advanced Study.

Dover, Victor et al. 1990. *Davie Settlement.* Coral Gables, FL: Urban Design Inc. (Report to the Davie, Florida, Redevelopment Agency).

Downey, Kirstin. 1991. "Study Finds Fewer Can Buy Homes." *Washington Post,* June 14.

Duany, Andres, and Elizabeth Plater-Zyberk. 1992. "Zoning for Traditional Neighborhoods." *Land Development* (National Association of Home Builders, Washington, DC), Vol. 5, No. 2, Fall, pp. 20–26.

Duany, Andres, and Elizabeth Plater-Zyberk. 1990. *Sandy Spring: A Village for Montgomery County, MD.* Miami, FL: DPZ Architects and Town Planners.

Duerksen, Christopher J. 1986. *Aesthetics and Land Use Controls: Beyond Ecology and Economics.* Chicago: American Planning Association, Planning Advisory Service Report No. 399.

Dunham-Jones, Ellen. 1989. *Of Time and Place: Regionalism and Critical Regionalism.* Paper presented at Landscape Architecture Symposium on Regionalism, School of Architecture, University of Virginia, Charlottesville.

Dunlop, Beth. 1991. "Plan Would Reshape Davie's Center." *Miami Herald,* March 17.

duPont, Elizabeth N. 1978. *Landscaping with Native Plants in the Middle-Atlantic Region.* Chadds Ford, PA: Brandywine Conservancy.

Easley, V. Gail. 1992. *Staying Inside the Lines: Urban Growth Boundaries.* Chicago: American Planning Association, Planning Advisory Service Report No. 440.

Ebenreck, Sara. 1988. "Measuring the Value of Trees." *American Forests*, Vol. 94, No. 7 & 8, p. 31.

Emergency Fleet Corporation. 1920. *Housing the Shipbuilders*. Philadelphia: U.S. Shipping Board.

Enferadi, K. M. et al. 1986. *Field Investigation of Biological Toilet Systems and Grey Water Treatment*. Cincinnati: USEPA Water Engineering Research Laboratory, EPA/600/S2-86/069.

Ensor, Joan and John Mitchell. 1985. *The Book of Trails, II*. Redding, CT: Redding Conservation Commission, Redding Land Trust and Redding Open Lands, Inc.

Fabel, John. 1989. "Guidelines for Design in Keeping with the Character of Wellfleet Village." In *Eastham/Wellfleet Rt. 6 Corridor Study*. Amherst, MA: Department of Landscape Architecture and Regional Planning and the Center for Rural Massachusetts, University of Massachusetts.

Federal Highway Administration. 1988. *Scenic Byways*. Washington, DC: U.S. Department of Transportation, Publication No. FHWA-DF-88-004.

Fluornoy, William L., Jr. 1972. *Capital City Greenway: A Report to the Council on the Benefits, Potential and Methodology of Establishing a Greenway System in Raleigh*. Raleigh, NC: University of North Carolina, unpublished master's thesis.

Foruseth, Owen J., and Robert E. Altman. 1990. "Greenway Use and Users: An Examination of Raleigh and Charlotte Greenways." *Carolina Planning*, Vol. 16, No. 2, Fall, pp. 37–43.

Fox, Tom. 1990. *Urban Open Space: An Investment That Pays*. New York: Neighborhood Open Space Coalition.

Frank, James E. 1989. *The Costs of Alternative Development Patterns: A Review of the Literature*. Washington, DC: Urban Land Institute.

Franklin County Planning Department et al. 1989. *Affordable Limited Development: A Model for Housing in Rural Communities*. Greenfield, MA: Franklin County Planning Department.

Freed, Kent, Nat Goodhue, and Robert Speth. 1991. *The Flexible Development Amendment to Grafton's Zoning Bylaw: A Comparative Study of Conventional and Flexible Subdivision Zoning Applied to Two Sites for the Town of Grafton*. Conway, MA: The Conway School of Landscape Design.

Gaadt, John. 1989. "The Red Clay Valley Scenic River and Highway Study." *Environmental Currents*, Vol. 14, No. 3, Winter Issue. Chadds Ford, PA: Brandywine Conservancy Environmental Management Center.

Ganem, Barbara. 1989. *Greenways: How Wide?* Unpublished paper. Fitchburg, MA: Nashua River Watershed Association.

Gellen, Martin. 1985. *Accessory Apartments in Single-Family Housing*. New Brunswick, NJ: Center for Urban Policy Research, Rutgers University.

Gerdom, Joseph L. 1988. *Image Processing in Planning and Design*. Chicago: American Planning Association, Planning Advisory Service Memo.

Gerhold, Henry D. et al. 1989. *Street Tree Factsheets*. University Park, PA: Pennsylvania State University School of Forest Resources.

Giese, Jo. 1990. "A Communal Type of Life, and Dinner's for Everyone." *New York Times*, September 27.

Glassford, Peggy. 1983. *Appearance Codes for Small Communities*. APA PAS Report No. 379.

Gloucester County Planning Commission. 1989. *Gloucester County Comprehensive Plan*. Gloucester, VA: Gloucester County Planning Commission and Redman-Johnston Associates.

Greenbie, Barrie. 1981. *Spaces: Dimensions of the Human Landscape*. New Haven, CT: Yale University Press.

Greer, Jack. 1991. "Shaping the Watershed: How Should We Manage Growth?" *Watershed*, Vol. 1, No. 1.

Hammer, T. R., R. E. Coughlin, and E. T. Horn. 1974. "The Effect of a Large Urban Park on Real Estate Values." *Journal of the American Planning Association*, Vol. 40, pp. 274–277.

Hanke, Byron R. 1973. *Planned Unit Development With a Homes Association*. Washington, DC: U.S. Department of Housing and Urban Development, Federal Housing Administration Land Planning Bulletin 6.

Hanke, Byron R. et al. 1974. *The Homes Association Handbook*. Washington, DC: Urban Land Institute, Technical Bulletin No. 50.

Hare, Patrick H. 1991. *Accessory Apartments: The State of the Art*. Washington, DC: Patrick Hare Planning and Design.

Hare, Patrick and Caroline Honig. 1989. *Bicycle Commuting and Better Housing, or Financing a Home With a Bike*. Washington, DC: Patrick Hare Planning and Design.

Harper, Catherine M. 1991. *Legal Issues Affecting Space*. Unpublished paper presented at the Open Space Planning and Management Seminar, Ambler, PA: Temple University Department of Horticulture and Landscape Architecture.

Hayes, Paul G. 1988. "Scorning a Glacial Gift." *Wisconsin Magazine*, August 21, pp. 10–19.

Heimlich, Ralph E. 1989. "Metropolitan Agriculture: Farming in the City's Shadow." *Journal of the American Planning Association*, Autumn.

Heimlich, Ralph E., and Charles H. Barnard. 1990. *Agricultural Adaptation to Urbanization: Farm Types in Northeast Metropolitan Areas.* Truro, Nova Scotia: Northeast Agricultural and Resource Economics Association.

Heimlich, Ralph, and Douglas H. Brooks. 1989. *Metropolitan Growth and Agriculture; Farming in the City's Shadow.* Rockville, MD: U.S. Department of Agriculture, Economic Research Service, Agricultural Economic Report 619.

Heinrich, Helen et al. 1991. *The Agricultural Enterprise District: Incentives for Open Space and Farming Viability for Cumberland County.* Bridgeton, NJ: Cumberland County Agricultural Development Board.

Herr, Philip B. 1991. *Saving Place: A Guide and Report Card for Protecting Community Character.* Boston: National Trust for Historic Preservation.

Hinshaw, Mark L. 1992. *Design Objectives Plan: Entryway Corridors.* Bozeman, MT: City-County Planning Board.

H.R.H. The Prince of Wales. 1989. *A Vision of Britain: A Personal View of Architecture.* London: Doubleday.

Hiss, Tony. 1990. *The Experience of Place.* New York: Alfred M. Knopf.

Holman, Jean. 1991. "Ice Age Trail Runs Beside Hawksnest Homes." *Waukesha County Freeman,* July 3, p. 4D.

Houstoun, Lawrence, Jr. 1988. "Living Villages: Thoughts on the Future of the Village Form." *Small Town,* November–December, pp. 14–25.

Howard County Department of Planning and Zoning. 1991. *Develop or Preserve? An Integrated Approach to Agricultural Protection in a Metropolitan County.* Ellicott City, MD: Howard County Department of Planning and Zoning.

Howard County Department of Planning and Zoning. 1990. *General Plan for the County.* Ellicott City, MD: Howard County Department of Planning and Zoning.

Hoxie, Donald, and Albert Frick. 1984. *Sub-Surface Wastewater Disposal Systems Designed in Maine, The Site Evaluation Method: System Design, Land Use Trends, and Failure Rates.* Augusta, ME: Maine Department of Human Services, Division of Health Engineering.

Hronek, Bruce. 1989. *Managing Risk on the Ranger District: Understanding and Reducing Legal Liability.* Bloomington, IN: Indiana University Department of Recreation and Park Administration.

Hubka, Thomas. 1984. *Big House, Little House, Back House, Barn.* Hanover, NH: University Press of New England.

Humbach, John R. 1992. "Existing-Use Zoning." *Zoning News,* American Planning Association, December.

Humbach, John R. 1989. "Law and a New Land Ethic." *Minnesota Law Review,* Vol. 74, No. 2, December, pp. 339–370.

Humstone, Beth. 1992. "Turning Planners Into Designers." *Monadnock Perspectives,* Vol. 13, No. 4, pp. 1–3.

Hylton, Thomas. 1991. "Six Ways Trees Enrich Our Lives and Protect Our Earth." Pottstown (PA) *Mercury,* April 26.

Image Network. 1991. *Davie Settlement.* Coral Gables, FL: Image Network.

Isle of Wight County Planning Commission. 1991. *Isle of Wight Comprehensive Plan.* Isle of Wight, VA: Isle of Wight Planning Commission and Redman-Johnston Associates.

Johnson, Warren A. 1971. *Public Parks on Private Land in England and Wales.* Baltimore: Johns Hopkins Press.

Kendig, Lane et al. 1980. *Performance Zoning.* Chicago: Planners' Press.

Kendig, Lane, and Hammer Siler George Associates. 1990. *Economic Development Potential: An Analysis of the Boston Post Road Rt. 1 Corridor in Guilford, CT.* Mundelein, IL: Lane Kendig Associates.

Kennedy, Carolyn. 1992. "Accessory Units: The Back-Door Approach to Affordable Housing." *Zoning News,* American Planning Association, April.

Kennedy, Carolyn. 1992. "New Tack on Land Trusts." *Environment and Development,* American Planning Association, Vol. 1., No. 2, February.

Kenyon, James B. 1989. "From Central Business District to Central Social District: The Revitalization of the Small Georgia City." *Small Town,* Vol. 19, No. 5, pp. 4–17.

Kimmel, Margaret M. 1985. *Parks and Property Values: An Empirical Study in Dayton and Columbus, Ohio.* Thesis. Oxford, OH: Miami University, Institute of Environmental Studies.

Knack, Ruth. 1988. "Rules Made To Be Broken." *Planning,* November, pp. 16–21.

Knack, Ruth, and R. Searns. 1990. "The Paths Less Travelled." *Planning,* Vol. 56, pp. 6–10.

Kopkowski, Claudia. 1989. *Wenham's Landscape: Guiding Growth for Tomorrow.* Wenham, MA: Wenham Open Space and Housing Study Committee.

Kreager, William H. 1992. "Building Small-Lot Homes in Your Community." *Land Development,* Vol. 4, No. 3, pp. 22–26.

Kreissl, James F. 1986. "North American and European Experience with Biological Toilets." *Water Science Technology,* Vol. 18, pp. 95–102.

Kreissl, James F. 1984. *Alternative Sewer Systems in the United States.* Cincinnati: USEPA Municipal Environmental Research Laboratory.

Krohn, Alison. 1992. *Madison County Development Primer.* Watkinsville, GA: Oconee River Resource Conservation and Development Council.

Kunstler, James Howard. 1993. *The Geography of Nowhere: The Rise and Decline of America's Man-Made Landscape*. New York: Simon and Schuster.

Labaree, Jonathan M. 1992. *How Greenways Work: A Handbook on Ecology*. Ipswich, MA: National Park Service and the Atlantic Center for the Environment.

Lacy, Jeff. 1991. *Manual of Build-Out Analysis*. Amherst, MA: Center for Rural Massachusetts, University of Massachusetts.

Lacy, Jeff. 1990. *An Examination of Market Appreciation for Clustered Housing with Permanently Protected Open Space*. Amherst, MA: Center for Rural Massachusetts, University of Massachusetts.

Lamb, Linda. 1992. *Greenways: The Natural Connection*. Chicago: American Planning Association, Planning Advisory Service Memo, May.

Lamb, Richard F. 1989. *Subdividing the Catskills: The Environmental and Fiscal Impacts*. Arkville, NY: The Catskill Center for Conservation and Development, Inc.

Lancaster County Planning Department. 1990. *Livable Communities Forum: Community Design Guidelines*. Lancaster, PA: Lancaster County Planning Department.

Lancaster County Planning Department. 1990a. *Comprehensive Plan-Policy Plan*. Revised draft. Lancaster, PA: Lancaster County Planning Department.

Langdon, Philip. 1991. "In Pursuit of Affordability." *Landscape Architecture*, April, pp. 42–47.

Lapping, Mark, and N. Leutwiler. 1989. "Agriculture in Conflict: Right-to-Farm Laws and the Peri-Urban Milieu for Farming." In W. Lockeretz, ed., *Sustaining Agriculture Near Cities*. Cantley, IA: Soil Conservation Society of America.

Leccese, Michael. 1990. "Front Porch Society." *Architecture*, July.

Leedy, D. L. et al. 1978. *Planning for Wildlife in Cities and Suburbs*. Ellicott City, MD: Urban Wildlife Research Center.

Legg, Mason. No date. *Real Estate Report on Cluster Developments in Howard County, MD*. Unpublished.

Lehrer, Phyllis. 1991. "Ren's Mobil to Stay Full-Service Station." *Amherst Bulletin*, October 18, p. 1.

Lessinger, Jack. 1991. *Penturbia; Where Real Estate Will Boom After the Crash of Suburbia*. Seattle: Socio-Economics, Inc.

Lewes Long Range Planning Committee. 1988. *Proposed Long Range Plan for Lewes*. Lewes, DE: Lewes Long Range Planning Committee.

Libby, Steve, and Sam Wear. 1988. "Preserving a Vermont Viewshed: A Strategy for Local Action." In *Planning for the Changing Rural Landscape of New England: Blending Theory and Practice*. Durhan, NH:

New England Center, University of New Hampshire.

Liberman, Ellen. 1991. "Westerly Consultant Welcomes Role as Promoter of Downtown Interests." *The Day*, September 15.

Liebs, Chester. 1989. *What Might Your Community Look Like?* Burlington, VT: University of Vermont Historic Preservation Program Visual Laboratory.

Listokin, David, and Carole Walker. 1989. *The Subdivision and Site Plan Handbook*. New Brunswick, NJ; Rutgers University Center for Urban Policy Research.

Little, Charles E. 1992. *Hope for the Land*. New Brunswick, NJ: Rutgers University Press.

Little, Charles E. 1990. *Greenways for America*. Baltimore: Johns Hopkins Press.

Little, Charles E. 1968. *Challenge of the Land*. Open Space Action Institute, Inc.

Livingston County Planning Department. 1991. *PEARL: Protecting the Environment, Agriculture, and the Rural Landscape: An Open Space Zoning Technique*. Howell, MI: Livingston County Planning Department.

Livingston County Planning Department. 1990. *Brighton Area Population and Household Projections Using Build-out and Small Area Forecast Methodologies*. Howell, MI: Livingston County Planning Department.

Longfield, Robert F., Jr. 1978. *The Vermont Backroad: A Guide for the Protection, Conservation, and Enhancement of Its Scenic Quality*. Woodstock, VT: Ottauquechee Regional Planning and Development Commission.

Loomis, J., and C. Unke. 1988. "Economic Contribution of Wildlife Viewers." *Outdoor California*, p. 84.

Loudoun County Board of Supervisors. 1988. *A Vision for Rural Loudoun*. Leesburg, VA: Loudoun County Government.

Lynch, Kevin. 1971. *Site Planning*. Cambridge, MA: MIT Press.

MacKaye, Benton. 1930. *Cornerstones of the Townless Highway*. Unpublished typescript. Hanover, NH: Dartmouth College Library, File No. ML5-184-46.

MacKaye, Benton. 1930. "The Townless Highway." *The New Republic*, Vol. 62, pp. 93–95.

MacKaye, Benton. 1928. *Zone the State Highways: The Lesson of the Mohawk Trail*. Boston: Massachusetts Forestry Association.

McCamant, Kathryn, and Charles Durrett. 1988. *Cohousing: A Contemporary Approach to Housing Ourselves*. Berkeley, CA: Ten Speed Press.

McHarg, Ian. 1971. *Design With Nature*. Reissued 1992. Garden City, NY: Doubleday/Natural History Press.

McKenzie, Ricki et al. 1980. *The Pinelands Scenic Study*. Philadelphia: U.S. Department of the Interior, Heritage Conservation and Recreation Service.

McMahon, Edward T. 1991. "Saving Our Sense of Place." *Historic Preservation Forum,* January–February.

Madden, John, and John Thomas. 1987. *Washington Valley Space Park Plan.* Bridgewater Township, NJ.

Mariemont Company. 1925. *Mariemont: The New Town— "A National Examplar."* Cincinnati: The Mariemont Company.

Maryland Department of Economic and Employment Development. 1989. *Economic Importance of the Chesapeake Bay.* Baltimore: Office of Research, Maryland Department of Economic and Employment Development.

Maryland Greenways Commission. 1990. *Maryland Greenways: A Naturally Better Idea.* Annapolis, MD: Maryland Greenways Commission.

Massachusetts Housing Partnership. 1989. *Opening Doors: Housing Innovations in Massachusetts.* Boston: Massachusetts Executive Office of Communities and Development.

Massachusetts Office of Executive Affairs et al. 1990. *Final Generic Environmental Impact Report on Privately Owned Sewage Treatment Facilities.* Boston: Massachusetts Office of Executive Affairs.

Mastran, Shelley S. 1992. *The Protection of America's Scenic Byways.* Washington, DC: National Trust for Historic Preservation, Information Series No. 68.

Metzger, John. 1990. "Visual Solutions Through System Integration." *Landscape Architecture,* April.

Miles, L. B. 1987. *The Economic Impact of Recreational Use of the St. Croix Waterway.* Thesis. Orono, ME: University of Maine.

Montgomery County Planning Commission. 1991. *The Land Preservation District: Model Zoning Provisions.* Norristown, PA: Montgomery County Planning Commission.

Montgomery County Planning Commission. 1990. *The Land Preservation District: The "New" Cluster.* Norristown, PA: Montgomery County Planning Commission.

Moore, Albert C., and John P. Sullivan. 1988. "Putting the Old Neighborhood in the New." *New York Times,* June 26.

Moore, Roger L. et al. 1992. *Benefits of Rail Trails: A Study of the Users and Nearby Property Owners from Three Trails.* Washington, DC: National Park Service.

More, Thomea, T. Stevens, and P. Allen. 1982, "The Economics of Urban Parks: A Benefit-Cost Analysis." *Parks and Recreation,* August, pp. 31–33.

Mullin, John R. et al. 1990. *The Mall.* Unpublished research paper. Amherst, MA: Department of Landscape Architecture and Regional Planning, University of Massachusetts.

National Association of Home Builders. 1986. *Cost Effective Site Planning: Single Family Development.* Washington, DC: NAHB.

National Park Service. 1990. *The Economic Impacts of Protecting Rivers, Trails, and Greenway Corridors: A Resource Book.* Washington, DC: Rivers and Trails Conservation Assistance Division, National Park Service.

Nelessen, Anton. 1990. *Community Image Preferences: A Guide to Future Development in Chesterfield Township, NJ.* Princeton, NJ: Anton Nelessen Associates.

Nelessen, Anton. 1989. *Village and Hamlet Development.* Princeton, NJ: Anton Nelessen Associates.

Nelson, Arthur C. 1986. "Using Land Markets to Evaluate Urban Containment Programs." *Journal of the American Planning Association,* Vol. 55, No. 2, pp. 156–171.

Nelson, Arthur C. 1985. "A Unifying View of Greenbelt Influences on Regional Land Values and Implications for Regional Planning." *Policy, Growth and Change,* Vol. 16, No. 2, pp. 43–48.

New Castle County Planning Department. 1989. *The Red Valley Scenic River and Highway Study.* New Castle, DE: New Castle County Planning Department and Brandywine Conservancy Environmental Management Center.

New York State Department of Environmental Conservation. No date. *Preserving New York State Scenic Roads.* Albany, NY: New York State Department of Environmental Conservation.

Nigrelli, Gale E. 1990. *Design in the Commercial Corridor: Route 6 in Eastham and Wellfleet, MA.* Master's project. Amherst, MA: Department of Landscape Architecture and Regional Planning, University of Massachusetts.

Nisbet, Briggs. 1990. "Of Flowers, Floods, and Farmland." *American Farmland,* Winter 1990–91, pp. 8–10.

Oldenburg, Ray. 1989. *The Great Good Place.* New York: Paragon House.

Oregon Department of Land Conservation and Development. *Analysis and Recommendations of the Results and Conclusions of the Farm and Forest Research Project.* Salem, OR: Oregon Department of Land Conservation and Development.

Otis, Richard J. 1983. *Small Diameter Gravity Sewers: An Alternative Wastewater Collection System for Unsewered Communities.* Cincinnati: USEPA Center for Environmental Research Information.

Parsekian, Penny. 1992. "Shelter Politics: Who Needs Affordable Housing?" Westerly *Sun,* October 9, p. S1.

Pask, David. 1989. *On-Site Sewage Disposal in Nova Scotia: The Contour Disposal Field and Related Techniques.* Halifax: Nova Scotia Department of Health and Fitness.

Peterson, Pat, and Roger Sternberg. 1990. *A Citizens' Guide to Conserving Land and Creating Affordable Housing*. Burlington, VT: Burlington Community Land Trust.

Pivo, Gary, and Russell Lidman. 1990. *Growth in Washington: A Chartbook*. Olympia, WA: Washington State Institute for Public Policy.

President's Commission of Americans Outdoors. 1987. *Americans Outdoors: The Legacy, The Challenge*. Washington, DC: Island Press.

Ragan, Francis, J. 1979. *Homeowner Associations: Issues in Their Operation and Formation*. West Chester, PA: Chester County Planning Commission, Planning Bulletin No. 3.

Reagan, Judith H. 1991. *Governance of Planned Communities*. Boca Raton, FL: Community Consultants, Inc.

Real Estate Research Corporation. 1974. *The Costs of Sprawl: Executive Summary and Detailed Cost Analysis*. Washington, DC: U.S. Government Printing Office.

Reckord, Terrence. 1991. *Indianola Greenway*. Indianola, WA: Indianola Land Trust.

Regional Plan Association. 1991. *Where We Stand: Principles for the Regional Plan*. New York: Regional Plan Association.

Regional Planning Federation. 1932. *The Regional Plan of the Philadelphia Tri-State District*. Philadelphia: Regional Planning Federation.

Reps, John W. 1965. *The Making of Urban America*. Princeton, NJ: Princeton University Press.

Robinson, Charles Mulford. 1901. *The Improvement of Towns and Cities, or the Practical Basis of Civic Aesthetics*. Detroit: Bay View Reading Club.

Roddewig, Richard and Christopher Duerksen. 1989. *Takings: Responding to the Takings Challenge*. Chicago: American Planning Association, Planning Advisory Service Report No. 416.

Rodrigues, Carlos Macedo. 1992. "Warren Town Center Plan: Retrofitting the Suburbs." In *AICP Planners' Casebook*. Chicago: American Planning Association, Spring.

Rohling, Jane. 1988. "Corridors of Green." *Wildlife in North Carolina*, May, pp. 22–27.

Rourke, Bryan. 1991. "The Malling of a Small Town." *Mondanock Perspectives*, Vol. 12, No. 1.

Rubenstein, Lynn, ed. 1989. *Affordable Limited Development: A Model for Housing in Rural Communities*. Greenfield, MA: Franklin County Planning Department.

Sanders, Welford et al. 1984. *Affordable Single-Family Housing: A Review of Development Standards*. Chicago: American Planning Association, Planning Advisory Service Report No. 385.

Scarfo, Robert A. 1990. *Cultivating Agriculture: A Report of Current Trends and Future Viability of Farming in Maryland's Metropolitan Fringe*. Baltimore: Maryland Office of Planning.

Schaefer, William et al. 1989. *Eastham/Wellfleet Route 6 Corridor Management Study*. Amherst, MA: Department of Landscape Architecture and Regional Planning, University of Massachusetts.

Schmidt, Curtis J., William C. Boyle et al. 1980. *Design Manual: Onsite Wastewater Treatment and Disposal Systems*. Cincinnati: USEPA Municipal Environmental Research Laboratory, EPA 625/1-80-012.

Schutz, Franklin R. 1992. "TVA's New Design Guidelines for Constructed Wetlands Alter Size, Shape Design Process." *Small Flows*, Vol. 6, No. 1, January.

Schwecke, T., D. Sprnen, S. Hamilton, and J. Gray. 1989. *A Look at Visitors on Wisconsin's Elroy-Sparta Bike Trail*. Madison, WI: University of Wisconsin-Extension, Recreation Research Center.

Sharp, Thomas. 1946. *The Anatomy of a Village*. Harmondsworth, Middlesex, England: Penguin Books.

Sheaffer, John R. 1987. *Land Treatment: An Opportunity in Illinois*. Paper presented to the Illinois Pollution Control Board, October 7.

Sheaffer, John R. 1979. "Land Application of Waste: An Important Alternative." *Ground Water*, January–February, pp. 62–68.

Sheaffer, John R., and William Sellers. 1994. *Wastewater Reclamation and Reuse Systems*. Unpublished draft. Chadds Ford, PA: Brandywine Conservancy.

Siewers, Alf. 1989. "Preservationists Land a Big One: Lake Forest Preserves Open Space." *Chicago Sun-Times*, December 31, p. 4.

Smart, Eric et al. 1985. *Making Infill Projects Work*. Washington, DC: Urban Land Institute and Lincoln Institute of Land Policy.

Smith, Barton A. 1978, "Measuring the Value of Urban Amenities." *Journal of Urban Economics*, Vol. 5, p. 370–387.

Smith, Kathleen, and Karl Kehde. 1991. *The Land Use Forum Guide*. Mendham, NJ: Association of New Jersey Environmental Commissions.

Stein, Clarence S. 1957. *Toward New Towns for America*. Cambridge, MA: MIT Press.

Steiner, Frederick et al. 1991. *Agricultural Land Evaluation and Site Assessment: Status of State and Local Programs*. Washington, DC: USDA Soil Conservation Service.

Sterling Forest Corporation. 1991. *Comprehensive Plan for the Preservation and Development of the Sterling Forest Community*. Tuxedo, NY: Sedway Cooke Associates.

Stern, Robert A., and John M. Massengale. 1981. *The Anglo-American Suburb*. London: Architectural Design.

Stilgoe, John R. 1988. *Borderland*. New Haven, CT: Yale University Press.

Sussman, Carl, ed. 1976. *Planning the Fourth Migration: The Neglected Vision of the Regional Planning Association of America*. Cambridge, MA: MIT Press.

Sutro, Susanne. 1991. *Re-Inventing the Village: Planning Zoning and Design Strategies*. Chicago: American Planning Association, Planning Advisory Report No. 430.

Tate, Anne, Chester E. Chellman, and Joel S. Russell. 1992. *Proposed Rural Siting Guidelines for the Town of Hillsdale*. Columbia County, NY.

Tatman and Lee Engineers. 1992. *Facts About Spray Irrigation*. New Castle: New Castle County Department of Public Works.

Thomas, Holly. 1991. *The Economic Benefits of Land Conservation*. Poughkeepsie, NY: Dutchess County Planning Department.

Thomas, Richard E. 1984. *Overland Flow: A Decade of Progress*. Washington, DC: U.S. Environmental Protection Agency, Municipal Technology Branch.

Tondro, Terry L. 1992. *Connecticut Land Use Regulation*. Wethersfield, CT: Atlantic Law Book Company.

Toner, William. 1984. "Ag Zoning Gets Serious." *Planning*, December, pp. 19–24.

Tunnard, Christopher and Boris Pushkarev. 1963. *Man-Made America: Chaos or Control?* New Haven, CT: Yale University Press.

UDA Architects. 1991. *Route 208 Corridor Study for Spotsylvania County*. Spotsylvania Courthouse, VA: Spotsylvania County Planning Department.

U.S. Environmental Protection Agency. 1986. *Large Soil Absorption Systems: Design Suggestions for Success*. Washington, DC: USEPA.

U.S. Environmental Protection Agency. 1984. *Management of Small Waste Flows*. Cincinnati: Municipal Environmental Research Laboratory, EPA-600-2/78-173.

U.S. Environmental Protection Agency et al. 1981. *Process Design Manual: Land Treatment of Municipal Wastewater*. Cincinnati: USEPA Center for Environmental Research Information, EPA 625/1-81-013.

U.S. Fish and Wildlife Service. 1985. *1985 National Survey of Fishing, Hunting and Wildlife Associated Recreation*.

Unwin, Raymond. 1909. *Town Planning in Practice: An Introduction to the Art of Designing Cities and Suburbs*. London: T. Fisher Unwin Publishers.

Valley 2000. 1988. *Valley Futures*. Amherst, MA: University of Massachusetts, Department of Landscape Architecture and Regional Planning, Valley 2000 Interim Report.

Vance, Tamara A., and Arthur B. Larson. 1988. *Fiscal Impact of Land Uses in Culpeper County, VA*. Warrenton, VA: Piedmont Environmental Council.

Vermont Housing and Conservation Board. 1990. *Report to the General Assembly*. Montpelier, VT: Vermont Housing and Conservation Board.

Vermont Local Roads Program. 1987. *When to Pave a Gravel Road*. Fact Sheet T-110. Winooski, VT: St. Michael's College.

Vermont Scenery Preservation Council and the Vermont Transportation Board. 1979. *Designating Scenic Roads: A Vermont Field Guide*. Montpelier, VT: Vermont Scenery Preservation Council and the Vermont Transportation Board.

Wake County Parks and Recreation Commission. 1987. *Status of the Wake County Greenway Program*. Raleigh, NC: Wake County Parks and Recreation Commission.

Wallace-McHarg Associates. 1963. *Plan for the Valleys*. Green Spring and Worthington Planning Council, Inc.

Weicker, John C. and Robert H. Zerbst. 1973. "The Externalities of Neighborhood Parks: An Empirical Investigation." *Land Economics*, Vol. 49, pp. 99–105.

White, S. Mark. 1993. *Affordable Housing: Proactive and Reactive Planning Strategies*. Chicago: American Planning Association, Planning Advisory Service Report No. 441.

Whyte, William H. 1968. *The Last Landscape*. Garden City, NY: Doubleday and Company.

Williams, Harold S. 1991. "Of Settlements and Subdivisions . . ." *Small Town*, March–April.

Williams, Norman, Jr., Edmund H. Kellogg, and Peter M. Lavigne. 1987. *The Vermont Townscape*. New Brunswick, NJ: Center for Urban and Policy Research, Rutgers University.

World Wildlife Fund. 1992. *Local Land Acquisition for Conservation*.

Yaro, Robert, Randall Arendt, Harry Dodson, and Elizabeth Brabec. 1988. *Dealing With Change in the Connecticut River Valley: A Design Manual for Conservation and Development*. Cambridge, MA: Lincoln Institute of Land Policy.

Zenick, Mark. 1988. "Limited Development and Affordable Housing: Complements of Farmland Preservation." *Exchange: The Journal of the Land Trust Alliance*, Fall, pp. 9–10.

Index

9374